D1536229

www.wadsworth.com

wadsworth.com is the World Wide Web site for Wadsworth and is your direct source to dozens of online resources.

At *wadsworth.com* you can find out about supplements, demonstration software, and student resources. You can also send email to many of our authors and preview new publications and exciting new technologies.

wadsworth.com
Changing the way the world learns®

Community-Based Corrections

Fourth Edition

Belinda Rodgers McCarthy
University of Central Florida

Bernard J. McCarthy, Jr.
University of Central Florida

Matthew C. Leone
University of Nevada, Reno

WADSWORTH

THOMSON LEARNING Australia • Canada • Mexico • Singapore • Spain • United Kingdom • United States

Executive Editor, Criminal Justice: Sabra Horne
Development Editor: Terri Edwards
Editorial Assistant: Cortney Bruggink
Marketing Manager: Jennifer Somerville
Marketing Assistant: Karyl Davis
Project Editor: Jennie Redwitz
Print Buyer: Karen Hunt
Permissions Editor: Joohee Lee
Production Service: Vicki Moran, Publishing Support Services

Text Designer: Harry Voigt
Copy Editor: Colleen McGuiness
Cover Designer: Yvo Riezebos
Cover Image: Digital Vision Photography
Compositor: Thompson Type
Cover and Text Printer: Von Hoffmann Press, Inc.,
Custom Printing Company

COPYRIGHT © 2001 Wadsworth Group. Wadsworth is an imprint of the Wadsworth Group, a division of Thomson Learning, Inc. Thomson Learning™ is a trademark used herein under license.

ALL RIGHTS RESERVED. No part of this work covered by the copyright hereon may be reproduced or used in any form or by any means—graphic, electronic, or mechanical, including photocopying, recording, taping, Web distribution, or information storage and retrieval systems—without the written permission of the publisher.

Printed in the United States of America
1 2 3 4 5 6 7 04 03 02 01 00

For permission to use material from this text, contact us by
Web: http://www.thomsonrights.com
Fax: 1-800-730-2215
Phone: 1-800-730-2214

ISBN: 0-534-516734
Library of Congress: 00-053444

Wadsworth/Thomson Learning
10 Davis Drive
Belmont, CA 94002-3098
USA

For more information about our products, contact us:
Thomson Learning Academic Resource Center
1-800-423-0563
http://www.wadsworth.com

International Headquarters
Thomson Learning
International Division
290 Harbor Drive, 2nd Floor
Stamford, CT 06902-7477
USA

UK/Europe/Middle East/South Africa
Thomson Learning
Berkshire House
168-173 High Holborn
London WC1V 7AA
United Kingdom

Asia
Thomson Learning
60 Albert Street, #15-01
Albert Complex
Singapore 189969

Canada
Nelson Thomson Learning
1120 Birchmount Road
Toronto, Ontario M1K 5G4
Canada

Dedication

This text is dedicated to the ladies in my life—my wife, Deborah Lynn and our daughter, Angela Christine. Without their love and support a work of this magnitude would have been impossible.

M.C.L.

Brief Contents

Chapter 1   Introduction to Community-Based Corrections / 1

PART ONE   The Community Corrections Continuum / 37

Chapter 2   Diversion, Pretrial Release, and Community Courts / 39

Chapter 3   Probation / 79

Chapter 4   Probation Supervision / 102

Chapter 5   Parole and Other Prison Release Programs / 120

PART TWO   Case Management and Supervision / 159

Chapter 6   Offender Supervision: Control and Public Safety Issues / 161

Chapter 7   Economic Sanctions: Fines, Fees, Restitution, and
Community Service / 210

Chapter 8   Community Residential Centers (Halfway Houses) / 240

Chapter 9   Problems and Needs of Drug- and
Alcohol-Abusing Offenders / 273

Chapter 10   Special Problem Offenders: Mentally Ill and Sex Offenders in
Community Corrections / 310

Chapter 11   Problems and Needs of Female Offenders / 329

Chapter 12   Programs for Juveniles / 354

Contents

Preface / xiii

Chapter 1
Introduction to Community-Based
Corrections / 1
Objectives of Community-Based
    Corrections / 1
Community Protection / 1
Proportionality / 2
Rehabilitation and Reintegration / 3
Restorative and Community Justice / 5
Cost-Effectiveness / 8
Objectives in Conflict / 9
Development of Community-Based
    Corrections / 9
"Broken Windows" Probation: The Next
    Step in Fighting Crime / 10
The Emergence of Community-Based
    Corrections / 12
The Reexamination of Community-Based
    Corrections / 14
Contemporary Community-Based
    Corrections / 17
Oklahoma Struggling with Truth-In-
    Sentencing Law / 20
The Future of Community-Based
    Corrections / 23
Perspectives on the Study of Community-
    Based Corrections / 31
Systems Analysis / 31
The Correctional Continuum / 32
Correctional Case Management / 33

Summary / 34
Key Words and Concepts / 35
Questions for Discussion / 35
For Further Reading / 36

Part One
The Community Corrections
Continuum / 37

Chapter 2
Diversion, Pretrial Release,
and Community Courts / 39
The Concept of Diversion / 40
Avoidance of Unnecessary Prosecution / 41
The Concept of Pretrial Release / 41
Avoidance of Unnecessary Jailing
    of Offenders / 42
Avoidance of Bail and Commercial
    Bondsmen / 43
Development of Contemporary Diversion
    and Pretrial Release Programs / 43
Diversion Programs / 43
Pretrial Release Programs / 44
Objectives of Diversion and Pretrial
    Release Programs / 46
Contemporary Diversion Programs / 46
Programs for Drug-Abusing Offenders / 46
The Drug Court Experience Compared
    with Traditional Adjudication / 50
Drug Center Experiences / 52
Dispute Resolution Programs / 54

*A Court-Referred Mediation Case
    Involving Juveniles* / 56
Contemporary Pretrial Release
    Programs / 59
    Program Models / 59
    Basic Services of Pretrial Release
        Programs / 60
    The Milwaukee Court Intervention Unit / 64
Research on Pretrial Release
    Programs / 65
    Electronic Monitoring / 66
    Research on Drug Testing and Urine
        Monitoring / 67
Pretrial Release Options Proposed / 68
Alternatives to Diversion and Pretrial
    Release / 70
    Differentiated Case Processing / 70
    Community Courts / 74
*In New York City, a "Community Court"
    and a New Legal Culture* / 74
    Manhattan's Midtown Community Court / 76
Adjudication Partnerships / 76
Summary / 77
Key Words and Concepts / 78
Questions for Discussion / 78
For Further Reading / 78

Chapter 3
Probation / 79
Defining Probation / 79
Objectives of Probation / 80
Court Use of Probation / 81
Historical Perspective / 82
    The English Tradition / 82
    Early U.S. Practices / 83
*John Augustus and the Beginnings
    of Probation* / 84
Trends and Issues in Probation / 85
    Administrative Issues / 85
    Types of Offenders Served by Probation
        Services / 87
Probation Today / 88
Federal Probation / 90
Research on Probation / 93
    Outcome Measures / 93
    Defining Recidivism / 93

*ROBO-PO: The Life and Times of a
    Federal Probation Officer* / 94
    Studies on Recidivism / 96
    Evaluations of Specific Treatment
        Strategies / 98
    The RAND Study / 99
Summary / 100
Key Words and Concepts / 100
Questions for Discussion / 100
For Further Reading / 100

Chapter 4
Probation Supervision / 102
Granting Probation / 102
    Sentencing Guidelines / 102
    Standardized Sentencing Instruments / 104
    Presentence Investigation Report / 104
Probation Supervision / 107
    Supervisory Styles / 107
    Service Delivery Strategies / 109
    Caseload Management / 110
    Conditions of Probation / 111
    Revocation / 113
Innovations in Probation / 114
    Probation Classification Systems / 114
    Domestic Violence / 114
The Future of Probation / 115
Summary / 118
Key Words and Concepts / 119
Questions for Discussion / 119
For Further Reading / 119

Chapter 5
**Parole and Other Prison Release
Programs** / 120
What Is Parole? / 121
*Molester Seeks Castration;
    Texas Agrees* / 122
Justice Objectives / 123
Societal Objectives / 124
Historical Development / 125
Contemporary Parole / 127
    Administrative Structure / 130
    Essential Elements of Parole / 130
    Sentencing Flexibility / 130
    Changes in Parole Powers / 131

Sentencing Models / 132
The Truth About Polly Klaas / 133
   Qualified Parole Board / 134
   Qualified Parole Staff / 134
   Freedom from Influence / 135
   Effective Parole Administration / 135
   Proper Parole Procedures / 135
The Iowa Parole Board / 136
   Promising Parole Strategies / 140
The Future of Parole / 147
Summary of Parole / 147
Temporary Release Programs / 148
   Types of Contemporary Programs / 149
   Objectives / 152
   Problems and Issues / 153
   New Directions / 154
*Willie Horton and the 1988 Presidential
   Election* / 155
Summary of Temporary Release
   Programs / 156
Key Words and Concepts / 156
Questions for Discussion / 157
For Further Reading / 157

Part Two
Case Management
and Supervision / 159

Chapter 6
Offender Supervision: Control and
Public Safety Issues / 161
Objectives of Intermediate Sanctions / 161
   Community Protection / 162
   Enhancement of the Correctional
      Continuum / 162
   Economic Objectives / 163
Scaling Correctional Options and the
   Correctional Continuum / 165
Intensive Supervision Programs / 166
   Program Development / 167
   ISP Goals / 168
*Georgia's Intensive Supervision
   Program* / 170
*New Jersey's Intensive Supervision
   Program* / 172

*Massachusetts's Intensive Supervision
   Program* / 174
   Research on ISPs / 174
*The Experience of the BJA/NIJ Prison
   Diversion Programs* / 177
   The Future of ISPs / 178
Boot Camps / 179
   Definition / 179
   Program Objectives / 179
*Inmate Preferences for Incarceration
   over Intermediate Sanctions* / 180
   Program Development / 182
   Boot Camps Today / 182
   Research on Boot Camps / 183
*Program Variation Within the NIJ
   Study: The Examples of Georgia
   and New York* / 186
   The Future of Boot Camps / 188
Home Confinement and Electronic
   Monitoring / 188
   Objectives / 189
   Program Development / 190
   Implementation Issues / 191
   Program Effectiveness / 193
   The Future / 193
Day Reporting Centers / 194
   Objectives / 194
   Development of Day Reporting Centers / 194
A Composite Day Reporting Center / 195
   Program Characteristics / 196
   Program Illustrations / 198
*Local Jurisdiction Boot Camp:
   Harris County (Houston), Texas* / 200
   Future of Day Reporting Centers / 204
Residential Programs / 205
   Objectives / 205
   Program Characteristics / 205
   Participant Characteristics / 206
Summary / 206
*Prison Without Walls: A Typical Day
   Reporting Experience* / 207
Key Words and Concepts / 208
Questions for Discussion / 209
For Further Reading / 209

Chapter 7
Economic Sanctions: Fines,
Fees, Restitution, and Community
Service / 210
Fines / 211
   Impediments to the Use of Fines / 211
Day Fines / 213
   How Day Fines Are Calculated / 216
   The Staten Island Experiment / 216
   The Milwaukee Municipal Court
      Experiment / 219
   Structured Fines Research / 220
Fees and Surcharges / 220
   Revenue Generation / 221
   Fee Schedules / 221
Debt Collection / 223
   Problems of Enforcement / 223
   New Jersey's Model Collection Process / 223
   The Privatization of Collection Activities / 225
Restitution and Community Service / 225
   Contemporary Applications / 226
   Extent of Use / 227
   Historical Perspective / 227
   Contemporary Support for Growth in
      Restitution and Community Service / 228
   A Closer Look at Correctional Objectives / 229
   The Restitution and Community Service
      Process / 230
   Community Supervision and Residential
      Alternatives / 233
   Victim Compensation Programs / 234
   Costs and Benefits / 235
Summary / 237
Key Words and Concepts / 238
Questions for Discussion / 238
For Further Reading / 238

Chapter 8
Community Residential Centers
(Halfway Houses) / 240
Agency-Operated or -Funded Halfway
   Houses / 242
Objectives / 242
   Benefits to the Offender / 243
   Benefits to the Community / 244
   Benefits to the Justice System / 244

Historical Perspective / 244
   Program Models / 246
Montgomery County, Maryland,
   Prerelease Agreement / 248
   Program Illustrations / 250
Program Planning and Operations / 252
   Target Population Selection / 252
   Location and Site Selection / 253
   Personnel and Training / 254
   Treatment Services / 255
   Resident Security and Community
      Protection / 256
Problems and Issues in Halfway
   Houses / 257
   The Dilemma of Being Half-In and
      Half-Out / 257
Freedom: Halfway House Style / 258
The Mariana, Florida, Community
   Center / 259
The Inmate Code in a Halfway House:
   A Source of Resistance to
   Constructive Reintegration / 260
   Halfway House/Community Relations / 262
Program Evaluation / 263
   National Evaluation Program / 263
   NEP Recommendations / 265
   GAO Survey / 266
   Minnesota Evaluation / 266
The Future of Halfway Houses / 267
   Management by Objectives / 267
   Management Information System / 268
   Mutual Agreement Programming / 268
Summary / 269
Key Words and Concepts / 269
Questions for Discussion / 270
For Further Reading / 270

Part Three
Supervising Special
Populations / 271

Chapter 9
Problems and Needs of Drug-
and Alcohol-Abusing Offenders / 273
Special Problems of Drug Abusers / 273
   Drug Abuse and Crime / 273

Fact Sheet: Methamphetamine / 275
Emerging Drugs / 276
  The Narcotics User: A Portrait in
    Diversity / 276
  Characteristics of Narcotics Addicts / 278
  The Addict Personality / 278
  Causes and Purposes of Drug Addiction / 278
I Did Drugs Until They Wore Me Out,
  Then I Stopped / 280
  Postaddiction Syndrome / 280
Treatment of Drug Abusers / 282
  Methadone Maintenance / 282
  Therapeutic Communities / 283
Prison: A Self-Contained Treatment
  Community / 284
Learning Life Skills Through Delancey
  Street / 285
  Community-Based Correctional Programs
    for Narcotics Addicts / 286
Bureau of Justice Assistance Fact Sheet:
  Treatment Accountability for Safer
  Communities / 286
Probation Work with Drug
  Offenders / 288
Narcotics Addicts on Parole / 290
Special Problems of Alcohol Abusers / 293
  Alcohol and Crime / 293
  Research on Arrested Persons / 293
  Studies of Prisoners / 293
  Effects of Alcohol / 295
Heavy Drinking: Long-term Effects / 295
  The Alcoholic and the Problem Drinker / 296
  Causes of Alcoholism / 296
The Stages of Alcoholism / 297
  Diagnosing the Problem / 298
Treatment of Alcoholics and Problem
  Drinkers / 298
  Goals / 298
  Treatment Modalities / 299
Community-Based Correctional Programs
  for Alcoholic Offenders / 300
Alcoholics Anonymous:
  The Twelve Steps / 301
The Effectiveness of Alcohol
  Treatment / 303
  Alcohol Consumption / 303
  Behavioral Impairment and Adjustment / 303

  Patient and Treatment Characteristics / 303
  Treatment Prerequisites and the Criminal
    Justice System / 303
The Hazelden Rehabilitation Program,
  Center City, Minnesota / 304
Summary / 306
Goals of the 1995 National Drug Control
  Strategy / 307
Key Words and Concepts / 308
Questions for Discussion / 308
For Further Reading / 309

Chapter 10
Special Problem Offenders: Mentally
Ill and Sex Offenders in Community
Corrections / 310
Mentally Ill Offenders / 310
Prevalence of the Problem / 311
History of the Problem / 315
Special Problems / 317
Mentally Ill Offenders Summary / 318
Sex Offenders / 318
Extent of the Problem / 319
System Responses / 319
Sexually Violent Predators Acts / 320
Principal Features of Sex Offender
  Registration Laws / 326
Sex Offenders Summary / 326
Containing the Sex Offender in the
  Supervision Triangle / 327
Key Words and Concepts / 327
Questions for Discussion / 327
For Further Reading / 328

Chapter 11
Problems and Needs of Female
Offenders / 329
Special Problems of Female
  Offenders / 330
  Women and Crime / 330
Women Doing Crime, Women Doing
  Time / 331
  The Female Offender and the Criminal Justice
    System / 334
  Social Roles and the Needs of the Female
    Offender / 336

Services / 338
   Economic Assistance / 338
   Programs for Parents / 339
   Survival Training / 340
Community-Based Correctional
   Programs / 341
   Major Issues in Programming / 341
   National Council on Crime and Delinquency
      Survey / 342
Girl Scouts Beyond Bars: Florida's
   Programs / 344
   NCCD Program Illustrations / 347
   Program Effectiveness / 349
   Drug Treatment Programs / 350
   Intermediate Sanctions / 351
Issues in the Treatment of Female
   Offenders / 351
Summary / 352
Key Words and Concepts / 353
Questions for Discussion / 353
For Further Reading / 353

Chapter 12
Programs for Juveniles / 354
Criminal Justice and Juvenile Justice / 354
Overview of the Juvenile Justice
   System / 355
   The Offenders / 357
   Processing Juvenile Offenders / 359
A Closer Look at Intake / 362
Community-Based Programs
   for Juveniles / 363
Programs for Runaways / 365
Juvenile Diversion Programs / 366
   Outreach Programs / 366
   Programs Targeting Minority Youth / 367
Mentoring Men of Distinction / 368
   Mentoring Programs / 368
   Youth Service Bureaus / 369
   Youth Courts / 369
   Specialized Programs / 371
   Diversion and the Juvenile Justice System / 371
Teens Face Jury of Their Peers / 372
Community Alternatives to Secure
   Detention / 372
   Home Detention Programs / 373
   Detention Aftercare / 374

Juvenile Probation Programs / 374
Detention Aftercare in New York / 375
   Programs for Youths with School-Related
      Problems / 376
   Drug Treatment Programs / 378
   Restitution and Community Service
      Programs / 379
Making a Difference / 380
   Day Treatment Programs / 381
   Wilderness Experience Programs / 382
   Specialized Programs / 382
Marine Institute Graduates Celebrate
   Love, Life Skills / 384
Community-Based Residential Programs
   for Juveniles / 385
   Foster Care / 385
   Group Homes / 386
   Independent Living Programs / 387
Juvenile Aftercare / 388
Research and Program Models for
   Serious Chronic Delinquents / 390
   Research on Urban Delinquency and Substance
      Abuse / 390
   The OJJDP Plan / 390
Problems and Issues in Community-
   Based Correctional Programs
   for Youths / 395
   Treatment Versus Control / 395
   Deinstitutionalization of Juvenile
      Corrections / 397
The Future of Community-Based
   Correctional Programs
   for Juveniles / 398
   Crime Control Moderated by a Continuing
      Concern for Rehabilitation / 398
   Continued Efforts to Develop Alternatives
      to Confinement / 399
Summary / 400
Key Words and Concepts / 401
Questions for Discussion / 402
For Further Reading / 402

Notes / 403

Index / 413

Preface

In the 1980s, when the first edition of *Community-Based Corrections* was prepared, the focus of community-based corrections was offender rehabilitation and reintegration. The goal of many community-based programs was to create and provide opportunities for convicted criminals to develop the skills necessary to fully function in the community. When the second edition was published in 1991, the community corrections field was in a state of transition. Intermediate sanctions were starting to be viewed as both valuable and necessary and the criminal justice system became more dependent on them to help relieve prison and jail overcrowding. Reintegration remained an important correctional objective, but the operational costs of prisons had become an equally important part of the public debate. Any program with the ability to decrease institutional costs would be considered. The third edition, published in 1997, reflected the renewed emphasis on community safety and offender control. Community corrections had helped to divert some offenders from traditional corrections, but some of these offenders had re-offended while in the community, and the public wanted some assurances that the criminal justice system was not sacrificing public safety to cut costs. The public and the corrections practitioner drew a line between those offenders who were in need of programming and treatment, and those who posed a threat to the public safety and consequently needed supervision and

control. Intermediate sanctions again received the support of the public, largely because this method of corrections could better match the level of community control and offender punishment to the person and the act. Cost-effectiveness remained an important issue, but the savings associated with community-based corrections became more difficult to assess. The increasing numbers of offenders in both traditional and community-based corrections began to indicate that the long-standing fear of including offenders into the correctional system who did not require such supervision had become a reality. The third edition also featured descriptions of several correctional programs commonly referred to as community-based corrections and described the specific offender groups appropriate for these programs.

Since the third edition, the process of increasing acceptance and conservative utilization of community corrections has continued. Programs have expanded, and many successful programs have been duplicated in different jurisdictions. Community-based correctional programs are preferable to incarceration for many offenders, but many offenders prefer incarceration to intensive supervision. Furthermore, some residential programs work best with intensive follow-up counseling and absent that counseling, these programs have a success rate that is negligible. Much of what has transpired since the third edition has been positive, but the success of community-based programs carries a cost. Criminal justice practitioners must be more aware than ever of these expanding programs. Those who work in the community corrections field are faced with increasing caseloads and often with more serious offenders than in years past. This fourth edition will provide the reader with comprehensive information about the changing nature of community corrections and will guide the reader toward a critical understanding of the politics and practices that exist in the field of criminal justice. The reader is encouraged to approach this text as a sourcebook on community-based corrections, a guide to how these various programs developed, why they grew in popularity, which type of offender works best in them, and how they can be used most effectively.

The text is divided into three parts. The first part deals with the history and development of community-based corrections from the perspective of community corrections as a continuum of restrictive sanctions. This section begins with diversion and pretrial release procedures, and it covers the history and problems associated with these practices. Several program examples are offered, and the effectiveness of these programs is discussed. Then, probation and parole are examined from both practical and historical perspectives. In addition, officer issues and styles of operation are reviewed in the context of current intermediate sanctions and operations.

The second part of the text gets into more detail regarding the practice of community-based corrections. Levels of supervision and different methods of offender monitoring are examined, and programs that utilize many of these methods are presented and their relative effectiveness is discussed. Following this, the focus shifts to typical offender problems and challenges, including issues such as alcohol and other drug addiction, the long-term effects of incarceration, and employment issues and opportunities. Programs that address these needs, as well as promising strategies and treatment modalities, are discussed.

The third part of the book is devoted to the special problem offender—the sex offender, the mentally ill client, the female offender, and the juvenile offender. This area of inquiry has been long ignored by community corrections researchers and programs specifically designed to address the needs of these special clients are examined.

As is the case with any text that is undergoing constant revision and updating, space and time do not permit inclusion of all pertinent programs and studies. Furthermore, while valuation of community-based programs is an important part of each chapter in this book, many programs have not yet been subjected to intense and comprehensive study. Consequently, many programs that may over time prove to have merit are not included here.

We are indebted to the reviewers of this edition: Mark Jones, East Carolina University; Shadd Maruna, University at Albany; Robert T. Sigler, University of Alabama; and Thomas Sullenberger, Southeastern Louisiana University. Their suggestions and direction were essential in the creation of this new edition, and their willing donation of their expertise has made this edition far more comprehensive than it would have been if left to the devices of the authors. In addition, we are grateful for the diligent editing of Colleen McGuiness and Vicki Moran, and the research assistance of Brad Windfeldt and Amie Butters. We would also like to thank Sabra Horne and her staff for smoothing the rough publishing path and helping to speed this manuscript to completion. Without their tireless effort and dedication, this edition would have never made it to press.

Belinda Rodgers McCarthy
Bernard J. McCarthy, Jr.
Matthew C. Leone

In Memorium

Michael Sean Sullivan
Student and Friend
1967–2000

Chapter 1

Introduction to Community-Based Corrections

Objectives of Community-Based Corrections

Development of Community-Based Corrections

Perspectives on the Study of Community-Based Corrections

Summary

Community-based corrections is the general term used to refer to a variety of sanctions and noninstitutional correctional programs for criminal offenders. These include:

1. Efforts designed to divert accused offenders from the criminal justice system or jail prior to prosecution,

2. Sentences and programs that impose restrictions on convicted offenders while maintaining them in the community, and

3. Efforts designed to smooth the transition of inmates from prison to freedom.

Diversion, pretrial release, fines, restitution and community service, probation, intensive supervision, house arrest, electronic monitoring, day reporting, boot camps, residential centers, temporary release, and parole and other forms of prison release create a continuum of options for dealing with offenders in the community. Although these sanctions and programs differ in the restrictions they impose and the types of offenders they serve, their similarities outweigh their differences.

Objectives of Community-Based Corrections

Community Protection

All community-based correctional programs must first deal with the issue of **community protection** by determining offender **eligibility.**

1

A determination is made of what broad classes of offenders could participate in a particular form of sentence or program. A **selection process** then takes place; that is, a case-by-case review of individuals who meet program eligibility requirements. Programs deal with eligibility criteria and the process of selection in a variety of ways. Diversion and pretrial release programs usually specify which offenders are eligible or ineligible for their programs, and then staff examine each offender's personal characteristics to determine his or her suitability for their programs. Legislatures and sentencing commissions give careful consideration to the types of offenders they wish to make eligible for nonincarcerative sentences. Their judgments appear in penal codes and sentencing guidelines. Judges then work within the framework of the sentencing structure in their jurisdiction to determine the level of risk posed by each offender they must sentence. Correctional and parole authorities review inmates for temporary release and parole, first according to statutory and program guidelines, and then at an individual review or hearing.

In addition to carefully devising eligibility criteria and selection processes, community correctional programs make judgments about the type of **restrictions** or **level of control** an offender will require upon release to the community. Control may be accomplished, for example, through the use of prescriptive and proscriptive restrictions on offender behavior. Conditions may specify the level of supervision the offender will receive, determine a curfew, or require that the offender attend school or get a job. Other conditions may restrict the use of alcohol and prohibit drug use and any contact with persons engaged in illegitimate activities. Sometimes offenders are required to live in a supervised environment, such as a halfway house or a diversion center that provides daily structure.

Enforcing these conditions can be difficult, often requiring frequent telephone calls and personal visits to the offender at work and at home and contacts with family members, employers, and other associates. Rules and rule enforcement are used both to deter the offender from inappropriate conduct and to identify, before crime occurs, those persons who cannot be maintained in the community.

Although they cannot achieve the level of control that prisons do, community-based programs attempt to provide offender monitoring sufficient for the degree of risk posed by each program participant. **Risk assessment** (the process of identifying and classifying offender risk) and **risk management** (the development of levels of structure and supervision sufficient for each level of risk) are among the greatest challenges confronting community-based corrections.

Proportionality

American society generally agrees that the punishment should fit the crime. That is, more severe offenses should be met with more punitive responses. While much debate occurs over how aggravating and mitigating factors should influence this equation, and how other objectives such as rehabilitation and deterrence should be accounted for, the desire to see offenders receive the right amount of just deserts is a strong one. This principle of proportionality seems to be at the heart of much of the U.S. system of justice: Punishment should be neither too light nor too harsh in response to the harm done by a criminal act.

The range of behavior included within criminal conduct is extremely broad and diverse. Prohibited conduct ranges from the virtually harmless to the dangerous and destructive. Offenses range from those that attack persons or property to those that harm virtually no one but the lawbreaker. And offenders themselves are a diverse group, including naive first offenders as well as chronic predators and everything in between. Any effort to properly fit punishments to such diverse behavior requires a finely tuned continuum of penalties available for sanctioning.

Incarceration is, however, a very difficult penalty to fine tune. One can increase or decrease the number of months or years of confinement, and one can vary to some degree the conditions of imprisonment. But the vast majority of jails and prisons in the United States are similar in virtually all respects. They function solely to confine, and their variations in security level or treatment programs are minimal when it comes to significantly modifying the impact of incarceration. A consideration of confinement is essentially an "in-or-out" decision. Once that judgment is made, evaluations of the length of imprisonment become less critical on every dimension. If meaningful differentiations are to be made among penalties, the focus must turn to community corrections.

Community-based corrections provide a **continuum of sanctions** and a **continuum of programs** that makes it possible to fit the punishment not only to the crime, but also to the criminal. Although much of the original focus on community-based corrections addressed the issues of reintegration and cost-effectiveness, greater attention is now being placed on how to make sanctions such as probation suitable for more serious offenders. The objective is to refine community alternatives to better meet the community's need for protection and to reduce the costs of confinement.

Today's efforts to establish a true correctional continuum address the diversity of offenders and explore new uses for traditional sanctions and innovative sentences. Research on day fines has examined the extent to which offenders who pose no risk to the community might be dealt with solely through economic penalties based on their ability to pay. Conditions such as house arrest and the use of electronic monitoring to enforce home confinement are attempts to provide more control than traditional probation. Intensive supervision programs combine restrictions and enhanced levels of offender contacts with probation staff to increase community protection.

Many community-based correctional programs thus serve as **intermediate punishments;** that is, alternatives to traditional probation or incarceration. In the continuum of sanctions, which range from fines or probation to incarceration, selected community-based programs such as intensive supervision, house arrest, electronic monitoring, and boot camps provide mid-range dispositions that better reflect the severity of the offense than prison or probation alone. While many offenders require reintegrative efforts to facilitate a law-abiding way of life, and many persons cannot be safely released to the community without supervision, many offenders deserve a punishment that is less harsh than prison but more severe than a fine or minimum supervision probation.

Consider, for example, the second- or third-time property offender who is placed on probation for prior offenses. How should he or she be handled? At some point more must be done than was done the last time, both as a means of discouraging further criminal conduct and in recognition of the failure of prior dispositions. It is important to demonstrate a desire to accomplish something with each sanction, something other than "more of the same."

Intermediate punishments are also frequently employed as **alternatives to revocation** for probationers and parolees who run into difficulty in the community. Although putting a probation or parole violator in prison is legally possible, it is often not desirable to do so. An individual who is obeying the law and holding down a job but who continues to have problems with the use of drugs probably should not be sent to prison, because so many aspects of his or her life may be working out. A clear need exists to respond to probation and parole violations, even those that involve new crimes, with efforts that recognize the positive steps that the offender may have achieved.

Rehabilitation and Reintegration

All correctional programs attempt in some way to protect the community and provide the right amount of punishment. Community-based correctional programs today are distinct in that many of them also attempt to have a positive impact on the offenders. Although virtually all correctional programs and policies make reference to **rehabilitation,** community correctional programs are structured and operated to have meaningful impact.

Sometimes the benefits to offenders occur almost by default. Programs designed to increase the supervision of offenders require the probation staff to have more contacts with offenders. House arrest programs require criminals to spend more time at home and less time on the street. They also require families to adjust their patterns of living given the offender's restrictions. Urine-testing programs may provide incentives to participate in drug treatment if the drug user is serious about maintaining freedom even though he or she has little motivation to stop using drugs. These community protection strategies are expected to make it more difficult to engage in criminal activity and may thus propel the offender toward a number of desirable lifestyle changes.

But the rehabilitative benefits of community-based corrections are more than the accidental impact of control strategies. These community-based correctional strategies permit the offender to maintain existing ties to the community and can assist in the development of new and more positive linkages. This latter objective is known as **reintegration.** Reintegration was a major thrust of correctional programming in the 1960s and 1970s. The 1967 President's Commission on Law Enforcement and Administration of Justice wrote:

The task of corrections therefore includes building or rebuilding solid ties between offender and community, integrating or reintegrating the offender into community life, restoring family ties, obtaining employment and education, securing in the larger sense a place for the offender in the routine functioning of society. This requires not only efforts directed toward changing the individual offender, which has been almost the exclusive focus of reha-

bilitation, but also mobilization and change of the community and its institutions.[1]

Reintegration is based on the premise that crime and delinquency are as much symptoms of community disorganization as they are evidence of the psychological and behavioral problems of individual offenders. The community's failures are seen as "depriving offenders of contact with the institutions that are basically responsible for assuring development of law-abiding contact: sound family life, good schools, employment, recreational opportunities, and desirable companions."[2]

Reintegration strategies try to improve the positive fit between the offender and the community in terms of work, family, and social connections. These efforts may be directed at offenders who are sentenced to community-based programs or to those who have been incarcerated and are preparing for release or postconfinement supervision in the community, often referred to as parole. These latter programs of **graduated release** are designed to reduce the severity of impact of an abrupt transition between prison and freedom.

To achieve the objectives of reintegration, community-based correctional programs must meet the following requirements:

1. A location within and interaction with a meaningful community. (A meaningful community may be defined as an environment that offers opportunities that fit the offender's needs. Generally, the offender's home community or an environment similar to the one in which the offender will eventually live will be appropriate.)

2. A nonsecure environment—a setting with a minimum of physical restrictions; for example, the offender's home, a surrogate home, or a communal residence in which the offender lives as a responsible person with minimal supervision

3. Community-based education, training, counseling, and support services. (These are

provided by noncorrectional public and private agencies as well as by correctional staff and are organized into a comprehensive service-delivery network.)

4. Opportunities to assume the normal social roles of citizen, family member, student, or employee.

5. Opportunities for personal growth and change. (Such opportunities are made possible by experiences that serve to educate and empower and that test a person's ability to function independently. Such testing should occur in an environment that responds to failure with tolerance, encouragement, and guidance and rewards success by increasing responsibility.)

Enthusiasm for rehabilitation and reintegration as correctional objectives has diminished considerably since the 1970s. At that time, a body of research began appearing that asserted that "nothing works" in the area of correctional programming.[3] However, these early studies misstated the issues. In reality, "nothing works with all offenders equally well." Subsequent research has indicated that various elements of correctional programs have been found to reduce recidivism in some groups of offenders, but problems of implementation make categorical statements in this regard hard to support. Much of the focus on rehabilitation and reintegration programs today is on efforts to determine which particular elements of specific types of programs work best with which offenders. At the same time, newer correctional objectives (and terminology) have been added to the mix of goals for community corrections.

Restorative and Community Justice

Restorative justice in some ways builds on the objective of reintegration, but with an enhanced role for the crime's victim in the process of reparation (Table 1-1). The concept of restorative justice is an ancient one, with roots in early tribal efforts at restitution, but its modern origins can be traced from the 1970s and 1980s victims' rights movement and from experiences with programs involving mediation and dispute resolution.[4] Restorative justice often incorporates a strong emphasis on community protection and offender accountability, making it somewhat of a "re-integrative model for the 90's, appealing equally to liberal and conservative thinkers alike."[5] When the emphasis on community safety supersedes the role of the victim in the process of restoration, the term **community justice** is often employed.

Much of the interest in restorative justice is focused on juvenile crime, because the willingness of victims to participate in the process and the community's interest in restoration seem especially high when youthful offenders are involved. The concepts, however, are equally applicable to the criminal justice system. Examples of restorative justice programs include victim impact statements, in which victims express their concerns to the court and prosecutors; victim impact panels, which give victims an opportunity to confront groups of offenders (not necessarily those who attacked them personally) and express the anger and rage they feel as a result of the offenses against them; and citizen reparation boards, where trained volunteers provide offenders with an understanding of the impact of their crimes on the community and an appropriate assignment to repair the damage.[6]

In an attempt to develop model systems for the supervision of juvenile offenders, the Office of Juvenile Justice and Delinquency Prevention funded the Balanced and Restorative Justice Project. The goal was to build on national juvenile restitution training, incorporating restorative sanctions and processes into a truly community-based model with an emphasis on offender accountability; in effect, to integrate victim and community restoration.

Table 1-1   Retributive and Restorative Assumptions

Retributive Justice	Restorative Justice
Crime is an act against the state, a violation of a law, an abstract idea.	Crime is an act against another person or the community.
The criminal justice system controls crime.	Crime control lies primarily in the community.
Offender accountability defined as taking punishment.	Accountability defined as assuming responsibility and taking action to repair harm.
Crime is an individual act with individual responsibility.	Crime has both individual and social dimension of responsibility.
Punishment is effective. a. Threat of punishment deters crime. b. Punishment changes behavior.	Punishment alone is not effective in changing behavior and is disruptive to community harmony and good relationships.
Victims are peripheral to the process.	Victims are central to the process of resolving a crime.
The offender is defined by deficits.	The offender is defined by capacity to make reparation.
Focus on establishing blame, on guilt, on past (did he/she do it?).	Focus on problem solving, on liabilities/obligations, on future (what should be done?).
Emphasis on adversarial relationship.	Emphasis on dialog and negotiation.
Imposition of pain to punish and deter/prevent.	Restitution as a means of restoring both parties; goal of reconciliation/restoration.
Community on sideline, represented abstractly by state.	Community as facilitator in restorative process.
Response focused on offender's past behavior.	Response focused on harmful consequences of offender's behavior; emphasis on the future.
Dependence upon proxy professionals.	Direct involvement by participants.

Source: Balanced & Restorative Justice, Program Summary (Washington, D.C.:
Office of Juvenile Justice and Delinquency Prevention, 1994), p. 7.

That research articulated new roles to be carried out by justice professionals, offenders, and the community (Figure 1-1).

The model for juvenile offender supervision emphasizes collaborative efforts at crime control, integrating the efforts of police, prosecutors, and community corrections officials. Extending the conceptualization of community policing, community justice in some ways blurs the boundaries between corrections and law enforcement, with officials from all organizations joining in efforts to promote public safety. In some ways, community justice strategies look more like crime control than a humanistic approach to reduce deviance, but the role of community corrections is changing as the definition of community and place evolves.

Clear has identified five "crime and place" challenges for community corrections—mis-

sion, geography, crime prevention, involvement, and coordination. They evolved from the place movement in criminology, which has focused on the routine activities of potential offenders and the community problem-solving approach of contemporary law enforcement.[7] The "routine activities" approach to explaining crime considers not just the offenders' motivation for crime, but also the availability of potential targets and the absence of capable guardians. The offender is no longer the center of explanations of crime; he or she is part of a triad. The community, and all of its citizens, becomes the focus.

Mission Community safety becomes the goal of correctional efforts, opening up a broad range of intervention targets, which might

Figure 1-1 Juvenile Justice System, Offender, and Community Roles in Accountability, Competency Development, and Community Protection

Accountability—When a crime occurs, a debt incurs. Justice requires that every effort be made by offenders to restore losses suffered by victims.

Juvenile justice system role: Direct juvenile justice resources to ensure that offenders repay victims and complete other relevant restorative requirements as a top system priority. *Intended outcome:* Efficient, fair, and meaningful restorative justice practices; increased responsiveness to victims' needs.	**Offender role:** Actively work to restore victims' losses and participate in activities that increase empathy with the victim and victims generally. *Intended outcome:* Understanding of consequences of offense behavior; increased empathy; feeling of fairness in justice process.	**Community role:** Assist in the process by providing paid work opportunities for offenders, helping to develop community service work projects, and supporting victim awareness education. *Intended outcome:* More participation in and support for the juvenile justice system; message that victims receive priority.

Competency development—Offenders should leave the juvenile justice system more capable of productive participation in conventional society than when they entered.

Juvenile justice system role: Assess youths' strengths and interests and identify community resources to build on those strengths in a way that demonstrates competency. Engage youth in these activities and provide necessary supports for successful completion. Build prevention capacity through productivity partnerships with employers, educators, and other community agencies. *Intended outcome:* More opportunities for youth competency development; improved image of juvenile justice; increased competency.	**Offender role:** Become actively involved in activities that make a positive contribution to the community while building life skills; make continuous progress in improving educational skills while using existing skills to help others. *Intended outcome:* Increased sense of competency and self-esteem; exposure to and interaction with positive adult role models; improved public image of youth.	**Community role:** Become partner with juvenile justice system in developing opportunities for youth to make productive contributions to the community while learning positive civic and other values. *Intended outcome:* Increased community involvement in and ownership of delinquency problem; new attitudes toward youth; completion of positive work in communities. Improved quality of life.

Community protection—The public has a right to a safe and secure community; juvenile justice should develop a progressive response system to ensure offender control in the community and develop new ways to ensure public safety and respond to community concerns.

Juvenile justice system role: Ensure that offenders are carefully supervised by staff and a range of community guardians and that offenders' time is structured in productive activities; develop a range of supervision restrictiveness options and alternative responses to violations and incentives for progress. *Intended outcome:* Increased public support for community supervision.	**Offender role:** Become involved in competency building and restorative activities; avoid situations that may lead to further offenses. *Intended outcome:* No offenses while on supervision; reduced recidivism when the period of supervision is over.	**Community role:** Provide input to juvenile justice system regarding public safety concerns; share responsibility for offender control and reintegration. *Intended outcome:* Increased feelings of safety in the community; increased confidence in juvenile community supervision.

Source: Balanced & Restorative Justice, Program Summary (Washington, D.C.: Office of Juvenile Justice and Delinquency Prevention, 1994), p. 4.

include working with victims, organizing community groups, and developing crime-prevention strategies.

Geography The vast majority of offenders in most states come from a few geographic areas. These communities, in which large numbers of offenders live and work, can be the target of correctional efforts and resources. In this way of thinking, places as well as people can be seen as posing a risk. Just as law enforcement has worked on changing the risk generation potential of localities by targeting "quality of life" crimes, so can corrections work to reduce neighborhood crime generation characteristics, such as abandoned buildings and an absence of appropriate jobs.[8]

Crime Prevention Here the focus may include increasing the availability of capable guardians, through enlisting the aid of family members and employers in the monitoring of offenders who may show signs of re-offending, or addressing the design of physical structures in ways that may modify criminal activity. The challenge is to shift the attention away from intervening solely in offenders' lives to a broader effort to reduce crime.

Involvement Restorative justice approaches can empower victims, ex-offenders may provide meaningful inputs that facilitate program development, and community involvement may make citizens feel less estranged from correctional objectives. The focus here is on locating community corrections staff in the community they serve, transcending traditional objectives related only to the offenders.

Coordination Coordination requires that probation, parole, and other community corrections officials work alongside police, neighborhood prosecutors, and school officials to develop integrated public services.

Restorative and community justice shift the focus from the individual offender to the victims of crime and to the larger community. These approaches open up a wide range of additional interventions and provide some real opportunities to redress criminal wrongs. Community justice also provides for the pooling of extensive human resources, as law enforcement and community correctional staff join forces to prevent crime. The danger in these strategies is that the objective of offender change can easily get lost, eroded by public safety objectives that are more easily served by removing problem individuals from the community than integrating them.

Cost-Effectiveness

The cost of maintaining and expanding punishment systems is an expensive endeavor—more than $25 billion annually. In addition to ensuring the protection of the community while providing the appropriate level of punishment and rehabilitation, community-based corrections programs and sanctions attempt to provide punishment at a low cost. For many supporters of such programs, the most possible punishment (or community protection or rehabilitation) at the least possible cost is the most appropriate objective of nonincarcerative correctional efforts.

While this might seem the simplest of the objectives of community-based programs, it is not. **Cost-effectiveness** cannot be determined in isolation but must rely on a comparison of alternative approaches to determine which of two or more options is least costly. Often community-based programs are compared with the cost of confinement, and usually such examinations reveal that imprisonment is more expensive. The matter becomes more complicated, however, when one begins considering cost-effectiveness criteria such as normative sanctions and programs, external costs and savings, and marginal costs of incarceration.

The first criterion, normative sanctions and programs, considers the dispositions normally employed for offenders being placed in community programs. Determining whether a new program might provide a cost savings is impossible until what is currently being done is examined critically. If a new program for first-time property offenders includes house arrest with electronic monitoring and twice-weekly personal contacts with a supervisor, and presently such criminals receive only a single monthly phone contact, the odds are that the house arrest program will be more expensive. All things being equal, the house arrest program will not be cost-effective.

But all things may not be equal. The second criterion, **external costs and savings,** addresses the need to consider all the related costs of programming and not just the limited expenses of program operations. An inexpensive program that greatly increases the level of crime in a community may save money in program operations only to increase the overall costs of criminal justice system operations. A program that provides employment services may be more expensive than simple probation, but the increased taxes paid by employed offenders may offset such expenses. Community-based programs that maintain mothers in the community may avoid the costs of child care, and so on.

Comparisons of community-based programs' costs to those of confinement often presume that the placement of an individual in a community program somehow "saves the cost of confinement." Unless such a placement produces an empty bed in a prison or jail, thereby reducing operating costs, there is no savings. Often the movement of a group of offenders to a community-based program only frees up prison or jail space for other criminals. While this may be socially desirable, it does not yield any savings.

When a prison bed space is vacated, the dollar value of savings usually equals not a reduction in prison staff or a percentage of the cost of new construction, as some comparisons report, but the marginal costs of incarceration, the actual dollars not expended for sustenance of the inmate occupant of that space. This is not to say that community-based programs cannot be cost-effective. Some punishments cost more than others and those that do not utilize confinement tend to be less costly to operate. The difficulty lies in the inability to achieve real savings. Given the rapidly increasing use of incarceration, few prison or jail beds stay empty for long.

Objectives in Conflict

Potential conflicts exist among the goals of community-based correctional programs. Intermediate punishments will cost more than current practice, if current practice is traditional probation or a willingness to ignore probation or parole violations. Reintegration requires efforts to assist offenders, a carefully calculated strategy that involves much more than control of offenders. Electronic monitoring may temporarily accomplish this goal, but alone it will do little to assist the offender in developing a crime-free lifestyle.

The conflicts are ever-present in community-based corrections, often making it difficult to determine which program components are accomplishing which objectives and how new programs fit into and alter the current scheme of correctional dispositions. Much of this conflict can be better understood by examining the chronological sequence in which each objective was identified, promoted, and then "tacked on" to existing program purposes. Each new objective was promoted to address a newly identified problem. Assembled in pell-mell fashion, community-based correctional programs seemed at one time to offer something for everyone.

Development of Community-Based Corrections

The community has not always been viewed as holding the answers to offender problems.

Program Focus

"Broken Windows" Probation:
The Next Step in Fighting Crime

The Manhattan Institute in 1999 issued a report recommending a radical rethinking of probation. Prepared by veteran practitioners, including several present or former leaders of the National Association of Probation Executives and American Probation and Parole Association, it emphasized a community justice approach to probation. Its recommendations are summarized below.

Successful Probation Programs

1. Put public safety first.

2. Supervise probationers in the neighborhood, not the office.

3. Require probation officers to spend more time supervising those offenders who are most at risk.

4. Enforce violations of probation conditions quickly and strongly.

5. Develop partners in the community.
   - Creating a system that has meaningful participation from victims and the community.

- Developing partnerships with neighborhood groups, schools, businesses and the faith communities to bring offenders into an environment that has pro-social supports.
- Establishing cooperative partnerships between probation, law enforcement and other criminal justice agencies that focus on public safety.
- Partnering with human service, treatment and non-profit agencies to provide enhanced services to assess, diagnose, treat and supervise offenders.
- Creating a comprehensive education campaign to make citizens aware of the crime problem, the steps being taken to address it, and communicating the message that their involvement is desired.

6. Establish performance-based initiatives using information-based decision making.

7. Require leadership from the top.
   - In the final analysis, leadership is the most important ingredient for success . . . . [I]t flows from individuals who are risk takers, willing to enthusiastically

In fact, for many years, the community was viewed only as harboring the causes of crime. The evil influences of drink and bad companions were seen as the principal sources of criminal behavior. Not surprisingly, correctional institutions seemed to offer a respite from temptation. Removed from a corrupting environment and placed in solitary confine-

ment, an offender could repent and change his or her ways. Many early community-based correctional efforts were criticized because they were contrary to the "reform-through-isolation" approach. It was believed that bringing ex-offenders together in halfway houses or group therapy would be asking for trouble because behavior would inevitably

embrace a new narrative for their field and the practice of probation.

Structural Issues in Rethinking Probation

1. Case assignments and job responsibilities.
   - Case assignments must reflect geographical specialization.
   - Practitioners must necessarily work the hours during which they can be most effective in their assigned area.
   - Supervisors become resource persons for their field officers.

2. Hiring, job description and training.
   - The job description must reflect the new and expanded responsibilities associated with working in the community. Probation officers will require such skills as community organizing and advocacy, creative problem solving, and a capacity to work as much with adults and local stakeholders as with offenders on their caseload.
   - The hiring decision will likewise need to be tailored to the community.

   - Training methods will incorporate mentoring of new officers with reduced caseloads.

3. Caseload, resources and technical support.
   - The paradigm shift that is proposed and the new and redefined role of the probation officer as captured in the job description can be achieved only if caseloads become much smaller than they are now.
   - If the base of operation moves out of the probation office, then laptop computers, palm corders, cellular phones and flashlights will become the new tools of the trade.
   - Sophisticated yet user-friendly management information systems are essential for communication and information retrieval on a daily basis.

4. Community involvement and support.
   - It is essential that partnerships be built and sustained with local neighborhood organizations.

Source: Manhattan Institute, *"Broken Windows" Probation: The Next Step in Fighting Crime*, Civic Report 7, August 1999.

---

sink to that of the lowest common (criminal) denominator. Overcoming this view of crime, criminals, and the community took many years.

Each type of community-based correctional program has its own unique history. Some programs, such as halfway houses and restitution, have been in existence for centuries. Others,

such as alcohol detoxification programs and mediation programs, are relatively new developments, although the desirability of such efforts has long been recognized. In the late 1950s and 1960s, however, the general concept of community-based corrections began to gain recognition and support. Gradually, the diverse programs now known under the umbrella term community-based corrections began to be viewed as distinct and essential components of the correctional policy. Several social currents were responsible for the emergence of community-based corrections.

The Emergence of Community-Based Corrections

Transition from Soldier to Civilian   Community-based corrections can be traced back to the years following World War II, when returning veterans encountered adjustment problems as they attempted to reenter civilian life. People soon realized that many persons required assistance in making the transition from soldier to civilian.[9] This assistance ranged from informal outpatient counseling, to education and job preparation, to intensive therapy offered in residential settings. One concern was overriding—to prepare veterans for civilian life as quickly and effectively as possible. These men had to be exposed to civilian life while assistance was being provided. Trying to help persons in isolation was found to be less than useless; it only encouraged institutionalization and dependence. Reintegration, the replacement of the individual in the community and the reestablishment of community ties, required a community-based effort.

A parallel development was occurring in the field of mental health. Careful observation of persons confined for years in mental hospitals revealed a general pattern of learned dependency—an inability to function outside the institution. Although treatment in confinement might cure some aspects of mental illness, mental health required an ability to interact with one's environment positively and effectively. One could not learn the symbiosis required to achieve mental health in an authoritarian environment where independence and personal responsibility were lacking. At best, the mental hospital could provide only a way station through which some individuals

might have to pass on the road to mental health. It was gradually recognized that the environment most conducive to mental health was the environment in which healthy individuals lived—the free community.

Labeling Theory   At the same time, a relatively new sociological theory was receiving considerable attention from criminologists. **Labeling theory,** which focuses not on the criminal's behavior but on society's reaction to crime, eventually influenced how deviance and crime control strategies were perceived. According to labeling theory, societal reactions to crime that stigmatize offenders and emphasize their differences from others, not their similarities, serve to excommunicate them (in the secular sense of the word) and encourage subsequent criminal behavior. Removed from society, having no stake in obeying its laws and mores, offenders have no reason to refrain from crime. Such individuals can only seek out persons like themselves, who have nothing left to lose. Together, they establish new reference groups that reward deviant instead of conforming behavior.

The labeling theorists viewed formal processing through the criminal justice system and incarceration in prisons and jails as the most serious forms of excommunication. Cut loose from law-abiding society and forced into schools of crime, the offenders understandably left the system more antisocial in attitude and behavior than when they entered.

Labeling theory showed how the criminal justice system could encourage crime by stigmatizing offenders and removing them from the larger community, thus encouraging the development of criminal reference groups. Labeling theory also provided a series of answers to the correctional dilemma of how to respond to crime in a deviance-reducing manner. Correctional programs that avoided stigmatizing offenders and enabled them to maintain ties to the larger community could be expected to encourage responsible, law-abiding behavior.

Dissatisfaction with the Criminal Justice System Labeling theory focused attention on the impact of the criminal justice system, and most observers did not like what they saw. Research produced evidence that the criminal justice system unfairly discriminated against poor and disadvantaged members of society. Pretrial confinement, too often the fate of only poor defendants, was found to increase the likelihood of conviction and a prison term in situations where a person able to buy freedom prior to trial often received only probation. Observers saw a slowly working system that allowed offenders to languish in jail and to bargain for justice, a system that penalized persons who exercised their right to trial.

Studies of incarceration revealed that little resembling rehabilitation was occurring in U.S. prisons, which were generally warehouses that were barely able to control their captives and keep their residents busy. Although the myth of the "hotel prison" gained some popular acceptance, few such facilities could be found. "Luxuries" such as nourishing food, adequate health care, and the education and training necessary to achieve functional literacy and self-sufficiency were unavailable to all but a few prisoners.

The Great Society All these developments reached culmination during the 1960s, when the words *country* and *community* took on a new meaning. The **Great Society** was envisioned as a nation whose greatest resource was its people, a nation that was enriched by every effort to enhance the status and position of disadvantaged persons and to integrate them into the community. The goal was to make economic opportunity and self-sufficiency available to all persons without regard to color, creed, or gender. Numerous federally funded programs were established throughout the United States, especially in urban areas, where the problems of disenfranchisement and disaffection were the greatest. Many of these community-based programs permitted or encouraged offender and ex-offender participation.

Criminal Justice: A System and an Academic Discipline The 1960s witnessed changes in how many societal institutions, including the agencies devoted to crime control, justice, and corrections, were viewed. Before the late 1960s, law enforcement agencies, the courts, jails, and prisons were basically seen as independent organizations with separate administrative problems and objectives. Sparked by the President's Task Force Reports on Law Enforcement and Administration of Justice, this perception began to change.

The achievement of an effective and efficient system of justice required more than independent, isolated efforts to change police officers, judges and district attorneys, guards and wardens. Reform required a comprehensive examination of the interrelationships among the agencies. An offender's eye view of the system slowly developed. It focused on the process of justice and how the agencies affected each other, as well as on the problem of crime. This increasingly sophisticated view of the justice process led to the current conceptualization of the criminal justice system.

The conceptualization of criminal justice as a system required the development and expansion of academic criminal justice studies. An intensive study of the problem of crime and the policies and practices of the agencies of justice was essential to design and implement legislation, administrative policy, and programming effectively. Efforts to professionalize criminal justice agency employees, from law enforcement officers to prison guards, took on new meaning as college-level criminal justice studies expanded. Growing research capabilities and an increasingly complex view of their responsibilities prompted many criminal justice professionals to search for more effective and efficient strategies to reduce crime and rehabilitate offenders. Community-based correctional programs provided many of the answers for which they were looking.

The Reexamination of Community-Based Corrections

Community-based correctional programs originally seemed almost too good to be true. They appeared to offer the solution to so many problems that they were too often represented as solving them all. Just as the Great Society came to be seen as a dream that was never fully realized, community-based corrections was revealed to be a strategy with many strengths, but also some limitations.

Rapid Expansion and Replication   During the 1970s, community-based correctional programs sprang up across the country. The federal government funded many through such agencies as the Law Enforcement Assistance Administration (LEAA), the Office of Juvenile Justice and Delinquency Prevention (OJJDP), the Department of Labor, and the Department of Health, Education, and Welfare.

Some of these new programs were carefully planned to fit the needs, resources, and objectives of the communities in which they were established. Others, encouraged by the availability of federal funds, were only vaguely conceptualized and poorly implemented. Some early efforts that had been identified as model projects were subsequently tried in new areas without adequate attention to important differences between the originating community and the new sites. Community-based programs were often tacked on to the criminal justice system with too little consideration of the role of eligibility criteria and the impact of the new program on existing programs and other components of the criminal justice system. Because of these factors, many communities found themselves paying more for corrections than before because they were supervising and servicing offenders who previously would have received little or no assistance.

Research Findings   In the mid-1970s, research results of studies evaluating the effectiveness of community-based corrections began to appear. In general, the findings of these studies, many of which were federally funded, were less positive than expected. Such results only exacerbated growing cynicism regarding the effectiveness of correctional treatment. Although the studies demonstrated that community-based correctional programs could operate at a lower cost than such traditional practices as incarceration, they found that many programs were relatively costly when compared with the alternative of doing nothing. Because little documented proof was available that community-based programs significantly reduced criminal recidivism, some observers began asking, "Why community-based corrections?"

This question echoed across the nation. Crime continued to increase; the economic recession deepened; and concern for criminal offenders' futures declined. As a result, many communities allowed federally funded programs to die rather than to assume their funding. There was growing support for increased prison construction and growing belief on the part of the states that the federal government should provide economic assistance for it.

Political and Economic Realities During the Reagan-Bush Era   By the time the Reagan administration came into office in the early 1980s, the impetus for growth in community-based corrections had significantly declined. The Carter administration had virtually eliminated LEAA and its massive funding program. The Reagan policy supported budget cuts in all branches of federal government, including the Bureau of Prisons; the National Institute of Corrections; the Office of Justice Assistance, Research, and Statistics (a significantly scaled-down version of LEAA); the U.S. Parole Commission; and OJJDP.

At the same time, however, the Reagan administration took steps that were to eventually lead to dramatic increases in the size of the Federal Bureau of Prisons and ultimate costs of the federal justice system. The Sentencing

Table 1-2 Trends in State Spending, 1980 and 1988

Spending Category	1980	1988	Percent Change
Corrections	$.22	$.35	+59
Medicaid	.45	.60	+33
Health and hospitals	.60	.62	+3
Elementary-secondary education	2.37	2.32	−2
Higher education	.94	.91	−3
Highways	.74	.66	−11
Welfare (non-Medicare)	.51	.37	−27

Note: Spending figures reflect state spending per $100 of personal income.
Source: John Irwin and James Austin, *It's About Time: America's Imprisonment Binge* (Belmont, Calif.: Wadsworth, 1994), p. 17.

Reform Act of 1984 created a commission that specified sentencing guidelines and required offenders to serve 85 percent of their sentences. This requirement for **"truth in sentencing"** produced a dramatic effect on the federal prison population. After the bill took effect in 1987, the average sentence for violent crime actually decreased, while time served increased by 60 percent. The sentencing guidelines also increased the likelihood of incarceration for all federal offenders—the percentage of convicted federal offenders sent to prison increased from 46 percent to 75 percent between 1980 and 1992. The combined effects of these reforms produced massive increases in the number of federal inmates.[10] President Ronald Reagan's leadership in costly efforts to "get tough on crime" strongly influenced state policies. Many state legislatures enacted their own strict crime control policies and their correctional costs rapidly escalated. The impact of these policies is shown in Table 1-2. Spending for corrections increased by almost 60 percent during this period, about twice the rate of growth for any other category of government spending.

Throughout the 1980s, it became increasingly clear that there would never be enough money for all the new prisons the states desired. While the courts were increasingly requiring state correctional systems to meet minimum standards in regard to the space allotted each inmate, increased conservatism fostered a growing willingness to rely on prisons as a correctional sanction. **Collective incapacitation** (the policy of locking up any offender who is considered to be a crime risk) as opposed to **selective incapacitation** (targeting the most serious offenders for incarceration) became the principal objective of corrections. Prison populations skyrocketed (Figure 1-2). Laws that mandated minimum sentences for habitual offenders (often defined as those who committed more than two offenses of any type) and determinate-sentencing statutes that limited judicial **discretion** to punish all offenders also had the effect of increasing prison populations.

The War on Drugs During this same period, drug use—especially that of crack cocaine—became the major focus of the war on crime, and that war escalated throughout the decade. While increasing drug arrests, convictions, and sentences to prison was possible, the end product by the time Reagan left office in 1989 was not a reduction in crime but a system in chaos.

An examination of Washington, D.C.'s effort to contain drug crime provides a vivid illustration of the problem. A 1988 study by the RAND Corporation indicated that drug arrests

Figure 1-2   Sentenced Prisoners in U.S. State and Federal Institutions, 1925–1997

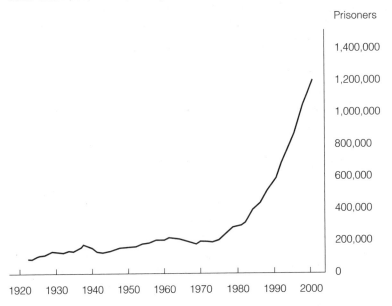

Note: Prison population data were compiled by a year-end census of prisoners held in custody in state and federal institutions. Data for 1925 through 1939 include sentenced prisoners in state and federal prisons and reformatories whether committed for felonies or misdemeanors. Data for 1940 through 1970 include all adult felons serving sentences in state and federal institutions. Since 1971, the census has included all adults or youthful offenders sentenced to a state or federal correctional institution with maximum sentences of over one year.

Beginning on December 31, 1978, a distinction was made between prisoners "in custody" and prisoners "under jurisdiction." As defined in a 1978 report (U.S. Department of Justice, Bureau of Justice Statistics, *Prisoners in State and Federal Institutions on December 31, 1978,* NPS Bulletin SD-NPS-PSF-6 (Washington, D.C.: U.S. Government Printing Office, 1980)), "in custody" refers to the direct physical control and responsibility for the body of a confined person. "Under jurisdiction" is defined as follows: A state or federal prison system has jurisdiction over a person if it retains the legal power to incarcerate the person in one of its own prisons. Jurisdiction is not determined by the inmate's physical location; jurisdiction is determined by the legal authority to hold the inmate. Examples of prisoners under the jurisdiction of a given system, but not in its custody, are those housed in local jails, in other states, or in hospitals (including mental health facilities) outside the correctional system; inmates on work release, furlough, or bail; and state prisoners held in federal prisons or vice versa.

Data for 1997 are preliminary and subject to revision.

Source: Sourcebook of Criminal Justice Statistics (Washington, D.C.: Bureau of Justice Statistics, 1997).

increased from 11,478 to 19,502 between 1981 and 1986; arrests for drug sales rose from 408 to 5,274 during that same period (Table 1-3). Prosecutions and convictions similarly increased, so that by 1986 more than half of all prosecutions and convictions were drug offenses. Increased arrests, prosecutions, and convictions were followed by increases in prison commitments and sentences. The average length of stay increased 83 percent during the five-year period; the minimum sentence length increased more than 450 percent.

What was the effect of this crackdown? Despite the massive increase in law enforcement,

Table 1-3 Drug-Related Enforcement Statistics
for Washington, D.C., Criminal Justice System, 1981 and 1986

Activity	1981	1986
Sale and manufacture arrests	408	5,274
Felony drug prosecutions	734	5,101
(% of all felony prosecutions)	(13.1)	(52.6)
Felony drug convictions	273	3,309
(% of all felony convictions)	(9.6)	(52.6)
Drug commitments to correctional facilities	1,025	4,333
(% of all commitments)	(12.5)	(36.5)
Average minimum sentence (months)	5.5	25.6
Total minimum prison years for drug commitments	469.8	9,243.7

Source: Peter Reuter, John Haaga, Patrick Murphy, and Amy Praskac, *Drug Use
and Drug Programs in the Washington Metropolitan Area* (Santa Monica, Calif.:
RAND Corporation, 1988). Reprinted by permission.

prosecution, and correctional efforts, indications are that drug enforcement had little impact on either the level of drug use or the crime rate.[11] By the end of the Bush administration in the early 1990s, prisons all across the country were flooded with drug offenders. Inmates charged with drug crimes as their most serious offense came to represent an increasingly large portion of the prison population, limiting the space available for violent criminals and property offenders (Table 1-4). That pattern continues to this day.

Without sufficient resources, states struggled to find ways to manage their growing prison populations. For example, Griset describes the strategies employed in New York state, which found that mandatory sentencing statutes and the war on drugs combined to dramatically increase the rate of prison admissions with no corollary increase in custodial space.[12] To deal with the crisis, the New York Department of Corrections diverted inmates to boot camps, temporary release, and day reporting programs, and it created a system of earned eligibility, which shortened the period of time until release. All of these measures occurred while the legislature continued to talk tough about crime without funding the correc-

tional space necessary to implement the laws it enacted.

Contemporary Community-Based Corrections

Despite the enormous costs of a decade of rapid growth in incarceration rates and considerable evidence that lesser offenders were the source of much of the growth in prison populations, public demand for greater crime control continued into the 1990s. The political response was to further toughen sentencing requirements. Although data on the anticipated costs of incarceration under restrictive sentencing policies were produced in a number of states, the public ignored these fiscal projections, amidst numerous anecdotal reports of atrocities committed by inmates who served a fraction of their sentences. Many states considered the Federal Sentencing Reform Act of 1984 as a model. By the time President George Bush left office, **"three strikes and you're out"** bills and other tough provisions for repeat offenders were being introduced in most state legislatures. Truth-in-sentencing provisions were also increasingly

Table 1-4   Percent of Sentenced State Inmates, by Category of Crime

Category of Crime	1986	1990	1997
Violent	55%	46%	47%
Property	31	25	22
Drug	9	22	21
Public-order	5	7	10

Source: Allen J. Beck and Christopher J. Mumola, *Prisoners in 1998* (Washington, D.C.: Bureau of Justice Statistics, August 1999), p. 11.

popular as states took steps to ensure that time served more closely resembled the actual sentence received. Not surprisingly, correctional costs continued to lead the way as the fastest growing item on state budgets, with states frequently posting growth in correctional costs as high as 20 to 30 percent in a single year.

The Violent Crime Control and Law Enforcement Act of 1994   In 1994, a bipartisan federal crime control bill provided further impetus to the continuation of stricter sentencing and greater use of incarceration. The **Violent Crime Control and Law Enforcement Act of 1994** was a massive piece of legislation with more than thirty-three separate titles. In many ways the bill reflected a more complex and sophisticated view of crime control than other recent initiatives. The bill reflected the public's continuing fear of crime in its provision of more than $8 billion in "incentive grants" for the construction of prisons or boot camps that could be used to free conventional prison space for violent offenders. The legislation required states to demonstrate their efforts to increase the sentences of violent offenders prior to receiving the funds. Truth in sentencing was also a critical element of the bill, emphasizing the need for states to demonstrate that violent offenders were serving 85 percent of their sentences.

But for the first time in more than a decade, there were indications of an awareness of the need to incorporate humane treatment into prisons and community-based approaches into the spectrum of corrections. In addition to

the requirement that states prove their punitiveness toward violent offenders before they could receive prison construction funds, they were required to show that they had adopted an "integrated approach" to corrections. This included rehabilitation; treatment, education, and employment programs for inmates; diversion; community corrections projects; and post-release assistance aimed at reducing recidivism. One hundred and fifty million dollars was included in the bill to support community-based programs for young offenders. This included restitution, community-based residential programs, weekend confinement, electronic monitoring, community service, and substance abuse treatment. The bill provided $1 billion to support drug courts, designed to speed the processing of drug offenders and to provide treatment and aftercare services.

Finally, the bill reflected an interest in more selective incapacitation. Prison space was an increasingly scarce and costly resource that needed to be reserved for serious and dangerous offenders. The act incorporated new sentencing guidelines that permitted an avoidance of federal mandatory minimum sentences for most minor drug offenders.[13] To ensure that any prison space freed up by the removal of minor drug offenders would not go unutilized, the act also incorporated a "three strikes and you're out" provision. This established a mandatory sentence of life in prison for anyone convicted in federal court of a serious violent felony if the person had two or more convictions in a state or federal court for serious violent felonies, or one for a serious violent crime and one or more for serious drug charges.

A 1995 Bureau of Justice Statistics study found that despite the efforts of state legislators throughout the country to get tough on crime, most states were ill prepared to meet the requirements of the prison construction incentive grants. Violent offenders released from state prison served on average about half of their sentences in prison; actual time served averaged about forty-three months on a sentence of eighty-nine months. Percentage of time served was on the increase, but this resulted as much from a slight decrease in total sentence as an increase in time served in prison.[14] States had been extremely effective in increasing the number of arrests and the likelihood of incarceration, especially for serious crimes. But the major growth in prison populations achieved during the last decade was a result of an increasing volume of offenders entering the system, rather than longer terms. The new Republican majority in Congress turned to this issue after its victory at the polls in November 1994.

The Contract with America Crime Bill   As part of their Contract with America, Republicans voted to rescind or reduce funding of a number of elements of the Violent Crime Control Act aimed at the prevention of crime or the treatment of offenders. They also altered provisions of the prison incentive grants to toughen requirements for truth in sentencing. States would be required not only to demonstrate that they were moving toward 85 percent time served for violent offenders, but they would also have to further show that they were increasing the rate of incarceration for violent offenders and sentencing them to longer terms as well. This move was to avoid the possibility that states might achieve the 85 percent time served by reducing the length of sentences instead of increasing time in prison. And to forestall the intervention of federal courts should these moves lead to increases in

overcrowding, their bill contained provisions limiting the federal court's authority to require remedies for state prison overcrowding. Many states moved quickly to bring their systems into compliance with the legislation of 1994 and 1995. More than a dozen states had passed truth-in-sentencing provisions by the end of 1995.

Some states followed the federal model in attempting to remove minor drug offenders from the prison system. New York state proposed to reduce mandatory sentences for such offenders, sending them to treatment and community service programs, offering electronic monitoring, and providing job training, while increasing time served for violent offenders to bring sentences in line with federal requirements for prison grants. Because sufficient prison capacity would not be freed up by the removal of drug offenders to meet truth-in-sentencing provisions, recommendations were also made to permit double bunking of inmates in maximum security institutions.[15] Other states looked toward the privatization of corrections for savings as they worked toward compliance. Illinois approved truth in sentencing that would require convicted murderers to serve the entire sentence and violent offenders at least 85 percent. Because no additional funding was approved to support the prison construction needed to house the inmates serving more lengthy sentences, the state considered a variety of strategies to privatize prison construction and operation.[16] None of the above strategies was in any way expected to cover the costs of increased confinement. Instances in which legislatures reviewed the fiscal impact of legislation and then revised it to selectively focus only on those offenders they could afford to incarcerate were rare, but they did happen.[17] Most states and most voters supported strategies designed to maximize incarceration in the broadest possible terms, despite the incredible fiscal impact and despite the best efforts of those working both within and outside the criminal justice

Issues in Community Corrections

Oklahoma Struggling with Truth-In-Sentencing Law

Implementing truth-in-sentencing proved difficult in Oklahoma, as this 1998 report illustrates: At issue are complaints from prosecutors, sheriffs, and others that the current reform plan, contrary to the claims of its supporters, would actually reduce the chances that violent offenders would serve any time behind bars. County and city officials also are worried that the measure would shift some of the costs of the criminal justice system from the state onto local governments.

Oklahoma has a sentencing system in which prisoners on average serve about 40 percent of their sentences. The 1997 Truth-in-Sentencing Act was designed to force violent and habitual criminals to serve at least 85 percent of their sentences. One advantage of that figure is that it would make Oklahoma eligible for federal truth-in-sentencing grants. The law also repealed controversial early-release laws that had allowed thousands of offenders to be released from prison after having served small fractions of their sentences.

In approving the Truth-in-Sentencing Act, the legislature anticipated that overhauling the entire sentencing system would be difficult, and provided more than a year for bugs to be worked out. By late last year, critics had begun to say the law had bigger problems, and some legislators urged that it be scrapped entirely.

"Contrary to what we were told when the legislature passed this bill, evidently it doesn't do what it's supposed to do," said state Rep. Leonard Sullivan. "Despite what the lawyers told us, I've heard nothing but complaints from sheriffs, judges, and prosecutors ever since we passed truth-in-sentencing. I think we should repeal it lock, stock, and barrel and start all over again."

Prosecutors said the law's basic problem is that it was written to deal with "the reality of limited resources"; the length of individual sentences would be based on the number of available bed spaces, not on the severity of the crime or public safety considerations. And the matrix of sentences would be recalculated annually, which could mean that the same crime could result in different sentences in different years. That could leave the state vulnerable to

system to better inform legislatures and the public.

The Impact of Truth in Sentencing   By the end of the 1990s, twenty-seven states and the District of Columbia had received incentive grants for meeting the eligibility criteria of the truth-in-sentencing program.[18] Another thirteen states had adopted laws that required selected offenders to serve a specific percentage of their sentence. To qualify, states had to ensure that offenders convicted of serious violent crime would not serve less than 85 percent of their prison sentences. Some states developed somewhat less restrictive standards, requiring 50 to 75 percent of the sentence to be served. Fourteen states abolished discretionary parole board release for all offenders; other states abol-

equal protection lawsuits by offenders, prosecutors said.

Prosecutors also said that many serious crimes generally would be treated far too leniently under the truth-in-sentencing law, and that many offenders who would have received prison terms under the old system would be given community-based sentences under the new law.

Supporters of the law disagreed. A survey of 65 randomly selected prison inmates convicted of violent crimes found that 62—or 95 percent—would have served longer prison terms under the truth-in-sentencing law, according to state Sen. Cal Hobson, a sponsor of the 1997 law. For example, a Tulsa County man convicted of committing a drive-by shooting served less than 19 months under the old system, but would have served 140 to 165 months under the Truth-in-Sentencing Act, Senator Hobson said.

"When you get past all the scare stories and misleading statistics, the fact is truth-in-sentencing is a lot tougher on violent criminals," Hobson said. "I can't understand why the district attorneys have spent so much time defending the status quo. The sentences today don't mean anything. That's an indefensible system that has to change."

As the Oklahoma legislature ended its week-long special session last month dealing primarily with the sentencing issue, Rep. Dwayne Steidley, a sponsor of the 1997 law, won approval of a measure calling for the collection of additional information on the subject to help legislators next year. That includes studies of sentencing practices in each of the state's 77 counties, prisoner assessment tools, and updated projections of inmate populations.

"It is very difficult to try to negotiate when everyone comes in with preconceived ideas, and I believe it compounds the process when we are in an election year and everyone involved is afraid of how new legislation will be perceived," Representative Steidley said. "No one wants to be perceived as being soft on crime."

Source: Criminal Justice Newsletter, 29 (13), July 1, 1998, pp. 3–4. (rev. 11/2/99)

ished such release only for the most serious offenders.

The unintended consequences of all this legislation may have been to reduce both the lengths of sentences meted out to felony offenders and the percentage of felons sentenced to prison. A 1998 Bureau of Justice Statistics report shows that states are meeting their targets, but while the percentage of time served has increased, the length of sentences imposed by the courts has decreased. The increase in time served has been no more than a few months per offender (Table 1-5). At the same time, total prison commitments had decreased from 44 percent to 38 percent between 1992 and 1996, and jail sentences rose from 25 percent to 31 percent.[19] It can be argued that truth in sentencing has been purchased in large part by reducing prison sentences and sending more convicted felons

Table 1-5   New Court Commitments to State Prison, 1990 and
1996: Maximum Sentence Length and Minimum Time to Be Served

Most serious offense	Mean maximum sentence length[a]		Mean minimum time to be served [b]	
	1990	1996	1990	1996
All offenses	72 months	68 months	40 months	42 months
Violent offenses	107	104	67	70
Murder/non-negligent manslaughter	233	253	176	215
Negligent manslaughter	106	117	63	61
Rape	153	140	90	72
Other sexual assault	97	107	62	64
Robbery	101	101	53	60
Assault	74	72	49	46
Other violent	96	82	70	54
Property offenses	62	54	31	30
Burglary	75	67	37	37
Larceny/theft	50	43	24	25
Motor vehicle theft	51	41	27	29
Fraud	54	47	23	22
Drug offenses	63	57	30	32
Possession	62	51	24	30
Trafficking	66	62	33	34
Public-order offenses	41	44	26	25
(Number of admissions)	(278,417)	(256,705)	(129,489)	(128,863)

Note: Includes only offenders with a sentence of more than one year. Excludes
sentences of life without parole, life plus additional years, life, and death.
[a] Maximum sentence length an offender may be required to serve for the most serious offense.
[b] Minimum time to be served is the jurisdiction's estimate of the shortest time each admitted
prisoner must serve before becoming eligible for release.

Source: Jodie M. Brown, Patrick Langan, and David Levin, "Felony Sentences in
State Courts, 1996." *Bureau of Justice Statistics Bulletin,* May 1999.

to jail, which are ill equipped to do more than warehouse pretrial detainees.

The California Lesson: The Costs of Collective Incapacitation

Research by the RAND Corporation on the potential impact of California's "three strikes and you're out" bill illustrates the costs and benefits of various strategies to target violent offenders.[20] The research was conducted after the law went into effect but before it went to a public vote for ratification. The California law, which was an especially sweeping piece of legislation, provided that after two serious felony convictions, any felony would trigger a sentence of twenty-five years to life. In addition, the law doubled sentences on the second offense, required that the sentence be served in prison and not with community alternatives, and limited good time to 20 percent of the sentence.

When RAND assessed the potential impact of the law, they determined that its desired effect clearly would be achieved. Serious felonies committed by adults could be expected to drop by between 22 and 34 percent as a result of this legislation. The costs, however, would be enormous—an extra $4.5 billion to $6.5 billion each year. To assess the benefits that might be achieved by more selective laws, RAND compared their impacts in both crime control and cost. The comparisons consisted of an examination of four alternatives: (1) implementing only the second strike provision of the law, (2) implementing the law only for three-time violent offenders, (3) implementing a comparison bill that in its entirety would have been harsher on violent offenders and less severe on other criminals, and (4) implementing only a guaranteed full-term sentence for all serious offenders on each and every offense.

While all the alternatives were less costly than the proposed three strikes law, the guaranteed full-term law was projected to be the most effective in reducing violent crime. This was true for the simple reason that it would increase all sentences for serious offenders (even the first offense) and pay for it by not imprisoning many minor offenders. Citizens nevertheless approved the original legislation when it came to a vote. By 1998, forty thousand offenders had been sentenced under California's three strikes legislation.

Today, three strikes laws are widely available throughout the nation, but again unintended consequences resulted. Except for California and Georgia, where several thousand offenders have struck out, most state laws have had minimal impact.[21] Most states wisely chose to draft their laws much more narrowly than did California and had few people sentenced under their laws.

Even in California, questions arose as to the impact of the law—crime has been reduced, but whether preexisting patterns of decreasing crime or the three strikes law was responsible is unclear.[22] The California law also seems to be especially harsh on African Americans, who make up a disproportionate number of the offenders sentenced. Prosecutorial discretion has resulted in much disparity, and many of those sentenced under the three strikes laws were punished for nonviolent offenses.

The Future of Community-Based Corrections

The past decades have witnessed massive increases in the prison population, far outpacing the rates of criminal activity or arrest. National surveys of victimization indicate that rates of personal victimization have decreased significantly over the past five years. Violent crimes have declined more than 27 percent, while property crimes have decreased about 32 percent.[23] An examination of arrest rates, including arrests for violent crime, indicates that while those numbers had been increasing steadily into the 1990s, they have now begun to stabilize and have declined since 1995 (Figure 1-3). It appears that, by all measures, criminal activity is decreasing.

While the use of incarceration has decreased for convicted felons, an apparent increased willingness to revoke parole is continuing to swell prison populations.[24] The number of parole violators admitted to prison increased ten times faster than the rate of new commitments between 1990 and 1997 (Table 1-6). Increases in the total rate of incarceration, the number of sentenced prisoners per 100,000 persons in the population, have thus far been enormous. Since 1990, the rate of incarceration has increased by another 55 percent and the prison population has almost doubled again.[25] Although the growth in community corrections during this period has received much less attention, its increases have been equally large. Today, almost six million people are under correctional supervision (Table 1-7). What has been achieved is not a focused crackdown on serious offenders, but a system that is increasingly willing to deliver

Figure 1-3   Four Measures of Serious Violent Crime

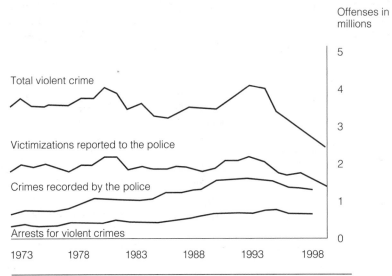

Source: "Serious Violent Crime Levels Continued to Decline in 1998," Bureau of Justice Statistics website, www.ojp.usdoj.gov/bjs/glance/cv2.htm.

punishment and supervision to all types of offenders at every point along the correctional continuum. The results are staggering.

It is tempting to think that the decrease in crime has been purchased by the increase in incarceration. While undoubtedly many factors are underlying these decreases in crime witnessed during the 1990s—including the declining impact of crack cocaine usage, changing demographics, innovations in law enforcement strategy, and increased incarceration—the rate of increase in incarceration has been so dramatic, and the decrease in crime so much less so, that the data actually argue against the position that incarceration reduces crime. Over decades, crime rates have fluctuated about a relatively stable mean, while incarceration rates have escalated dramatically. If collective incapacitation were such an effective strategy, the decreases in crime would have been far greater than what has thus far been experienced.

Blumstein argues that society continues to cling to the myth of the benefits of massive incarceration despite a number of facts.[26] Most serious offenders are already being incarcerated, so increasing the rate of incarceration only serves to lock up less serious offenders, whose rate of offending has less impact on crime patterns when they are imprisoned. Making sentences longer also serves to incarcerate offenders after their criminal careers may have terminated, so more incarceration is wasted than ever before. Drug offenders imprisoned for entrepreneurial activity may be more likely to emerge from prison with more generalized patterns of criminal activity.[27] Finally, the assumption is that if the average middle-class citizen would be deterred by the prospects of being convicted, sentenced, and incarcerated, so would any potential offender. The challenge thus becomes determining how much incarceration will deter the most individuals. For many offenders without middle-class opportunities, that form of calculus is irrelevant. Ironically, increasing the level of incarceration in such circumstances reduces the stigma achieved by imprisonment and consequently lessens the deterrent effect.

Table 1-6   Number of Sentenced Inmates Admitted
to State Prisons, by Type of Admission, 1990–1997

Year	All admissions	New court commitments	Parole violators
1990	460,739	323,069	133,870
1991	466,286	317,237	142,100
1992	480,676	334,301	141,961
1993	475,100	318,069	146,366
1994	498,919	322,141	168,383
1995	521,970	337,492	175,726
1996	512,618	326,547	172,633
1997	538,375	334,525	186,659
Percent change			
1990–1997 16.9		3.5	39.4

Note: Sentenced inmates are those with a sentence of more
than one year. Admissions exclude returned escapees, those
absent without leave, and transfers from other jurisdictions.
Admissions for Alaska were estimated for 1994.

Source: Allen J. Beck and Christopher J. Mumola, *Prisoners in 1998* (Washington,
D.C.: Bureau of Justice Statistics, August 1999), p. 12.

The International Perspective   Many observers have questioned why the United States has chosen such a costly and punitive approach, when European countries appear increasingly willing to adopt more moderate and more humane correctional strategies than imprisonment. Intermediate sanctions such as day fines, conditional releases know as prosecutorial fines, and community service sentences have spread throughout Europe, but there has been no parallel European trend toward three strikes sentences, boot camps, or efforts to achieve truth in sentencing. Tonry writes that this disparity may be the result of several factors.[28] Crime control rhetoric and policies in the United States are highly partisan and ideological. The politician's immediate need to appear tough on crime often supersedes the importance of establishing a more complex and balanced public policy that addresses economic, educational, and health needs as well as public safety.

Even though the basic tenets of the criminal justice systems are similar in the United States and western European countries, parochialism and cultural variations serve to limit the spread of innovations across national boundaries. This is especially true in regard to the value placed on punitiveness as a goal of criminal justice policy. Western European countries seem to be more concerned with the instrumental qualities of a correctional measure (what it accomplishes) than its severity vis à vis the crime committed. Furthermore, judges and prosecutors are removed from partisan politics in most western European counties, where they are civil servants or selected by merit schemes. Career professionals may be less likely to look at short-term solutions or judge innovations based on their appeal to the electorate or the political party responsible for the judicial appointment. The absence of a strong appeal to public opinion from the rhetoric of western European criminal justice debates may facilitate a more instrumental approach to the development of crime control policy in those countries, but one which has little impact on efforts in the United States.

Table 1-7 Adults Under Community
Supervision or in Jail or Prison, 1990–1998

Year	Total estimated correctional population[a]	Community supervision		Incarceration	
		Probation	Parole	Jail	Prison
1990	4,348,000	2,670,234	531,407	403,019	743,382
1995	5,335,100	3,077,861	679,421	499,300	1,078,542
1996	5,482,700	3,164,996	679,733	510,400	1,127,528
1997	5,726,500	3,296,768	694,787	557,974	1,176,922
1998[b]	5,890,300	3,417,613	704,964	584,372	1,232,900
Percent change					
1997–1998	2.9	3.7	1.5	4.7	4.8
1990–1998	35.5	28.0	32.7	45.0	65.9
Average annual percent change					
1990–1998	3.9	3.1	3.6	4.8	6.5

Note: The probation and parole counts may vary from previously reported estimates.
Counts are for December 31, except for jail counts for June 30. All jail and prison counts
are for inmates in custody.
[a] A small number of individuals had multiple correctional statuses; consequently,
the total is an overestimate. The total for 1998 excludes 36,527 probationers in jail
and 13,012 probationers in prison.
[b] The 1998 prison count is an estimate.

Source: Thomas P. Bonczar and Lauren E. Glaze, "Probation and Parole in the
United States, 1998," *Bureau of Justice Statistics Bulletin,* August 1999.

The United States certainly has a problem with ever-increasing prison populations. In the coming years, the alternatives available to support this strategy will be to either raise taxes or reduce funding in virtually all other areas of government and reallocate existing funds. But, as history teaches, there is an ebb and flow to government policy. The current emphasis on collective incapacitation by legislative action is a response to the years of indeterminacy and reliance on correctional strategies with undemonstrated success and too many promises. It also reflects a dissatisfaction with the experts—the judges, corrections authorities, and parole boards whose errors of judgment were frequent enough to sustain outrage at the system.

Issues today are both more simple and more complex. In some ways it all boils down to dollars and cents. The future likely will bring a greater willingness to examine the costs of government services, such as corrections and the benefits they provide. Such research has begun in many areas. Its impact can be anticipated when other vital government services begin to suffer to support high rates of incarceration. Calls for reform can be expected that focus on a search for a better way, a means of achieving crime control at lower costs and perhaps with equally effective results. Such initiatives will no doubt include two elements: a reintroduction of indeterminacy at the judicial level and a focus on alternatives to incarceration. Such proposals will blend fiscal and policy objectives and focus on removing lesser offenders from prison, especially drug offenders. Signs in this direction can already be seen, both among the states and in criminal justice studies.

Structured Sentencing The North Carolina General Assembly and the state's Sentencing and Policy Advisory Commission worked to create a sentencing structure that would increase the certainty and length of imprisonment for serious offenders, while using community and intermediate sanctions for lesser offenses.[29] The goal of controlling correctional costs would be achieved through the use of **structured sentencing,** an alternative to mandatory minimums, which creates a set of sentencing rules (usually called guidelines) that consider both the offense committed and the personal characteristics of the offender, such as prior record. These rules make sentencing more uniform, while still providing an opportunity for judges to impose different sentences as long as a rationale is provided. Structured sentencing also allows for the consideration of the available correctional resources, before crowding becomes a problem. Almost all states now have developed some form of sentencing guidelines. Permanent commissions are often established to review the guidelines and continue to assess their impact on correctional resources.

North Carolina's effort was especially worthy of note because it is a large state with a sizable prison population, because it has continued to receive bipartisan legislative support, because it is in the mainstream of political thought on issues of crime and punishment, and because it successfully integrated intermediate sanctions into the guidelines. The sentences to be meted out to felons charged with crimes ranging from murder to cocaine possession, depending on the severity of the offenders' prior record, are shown in Figure 1-4 and Figure 1-5. A similar set of guidelines was established for misdemeanor offenses. Community punishments consisted of outpatient drug treatment and unsupervised probation; intermediate punishments included nonprison sanctions requiring more intensive supervision, such as boot camp or day reporting centers.[30] Judges could impose the presumptive sentence or one within the aggravated or mitigated range.

Establishing these ranges was one of the most difficult tasks of the commission. Its original assessments of what would be an appropriate sentence had to be reduced to avoid the price tag that the original decisions would have cost—more than $1 billion in new prison construction. The North Carolina legislature repeatedly asked the commission to reduce anticipated prison construction costs, reversing the role played by commissions and politicians in most states. The legislature also strongly supported the funding of community corrections, providing local communities the opportunity to determine which approaches would be utilized in each jurisdiction. The submission of a unified community corrections budget, under the auspices of the commission, greatly facilitated this objective.

The North Carolina guidelines proposed sending fewer persons to prison for lengthier terms by increasing the use of community corrections and intermediate sanctions. In the past, few correctional options were available for offenders not sent to prison. This proposal created two levels of option, with such sanctions as residential treatment and electronic monitoring filling the gap between unsupervised probation and prison. Although the next few years brought many pressures for stiffer penalties and mandatory approaches such as three strikes laws, the requirement that any proposal be accompanied by an impact statement detailing the correctional costs of new measures assisted efforts to maintain the guidelines approach. Although three strikes legislation was adopted, as were enhanced penalties for gun crimes and rape, the penalties were reduced from those originally proposed as a result of impact statements. The effect of changes in habitual felon law, just recently introduced, will be more difficult to assess.

The North Carolina prison system continues to grow, but each year the use of impact statements and the united input of criminal justice professionals have served to moderate proposed legislation to reduce growth. Perhaps the most dramatic illustration of the

Figure 1-4 Felony Punishment Chart in Months
(Effective for Offenses Committed On or After 12/1/95)

Felony Type	Prior Record Level					
	I 0 Pts.	II 1–4 Pts.	III 5–8 Pts.	IV 9–14 Pts.	V 15–18 Pts.	VI 19+ Pts.
Murder 1	D/LWP	D/LWP	D/LWP	D/LWP	D/LWP	D/LWP
Rape	P	P	P	P	P	P
	240–300	288–360	336–420	384–480	LWP	LWP
	192–240	230–288	269–336	307–384	346–433	384–480
	144–192	173–230	202–269	230–307	260–346	288–384
Murder 2	P	P	P	P	P	P
	157–196	189–237	220–276	251–313	282–353	313–392
	125–157	151–189	176–220	201–251	225–282	251–313
	94–125	114–151	132–176	151–201	169–225	188–251
Kidnaping	P	P	P	P	P	P
	73–92	100–125	116–145	133–167	151–188	168–210
	58–73	80–100	93–116	107–133	121–151	135–168
	44–58	60–80	70–93	80–107	90–121	101–135
Armed robbery	P	P	P	P	P	P
	64–80	77–95	103–129	117–146	133–167	146–183
	51–64	61–77	82–103	94–117	107–133	117–146
	38–51	46–61	61–82	71–94	80–107	88–117
Voluntary manslaughter	I/P	I/P	P	P	P	P
	25–31	29–36	34–42	46–58	53–66	59–74
	20–25	23–29	27–34	37–46	42–53	47–59
	15–20	17–23	20–27	28–37	32–42	35–47
Involuntary manslaughter	I/P	I/P	I/P	P	P	P
	16–20	19–24	21–26	25–31	34–42	39–49
	13–16	15–19	17–21	20–25	27–34	31–39
	10–13	11–15	13–17	15–20	20–27	23–31
Burglary second degree	I/P	I/P	I/P	I/P	P	P
	13–16	15–19	16–20	20–25	21–26	29–36
	10–13	12–15	13–16	16–20	17–21	23–29
	8–10	9–12	10–13	12–16	13–17	17–23
Breaking and entering	C/I/P	I/P	I/P	I/P	I/P	P
	6–8	8–10	10–12	11–14	15–19	20–25
	5–6	6–8	8–10	9–11	12–15	16–20
	4–6	4–6	6–8	7–9	9–12	12–16
Possession of cocaine	C	C/I	I	I/P	I/P	I/P
	6–8	6–8	6–8	8–10	9–11	10–12
	4–6	4–6	5–6	6–8	7–9	8–10
	3–4	3–4	4–5	4–6	5–7	6–8

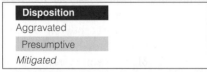

Disposition
Aggravated
Presumptive
Mitigated

Dispositions:
D = Death
LWP = Life without parole
P = Prison
I = Intermediate sanction
C = Community corrections

Notes: • Slash in dispositions means the judge can choose among the disposition options.
• Numbers shown are in months and represent the range of minimum sentences.

Source: Ronald Weight, *Managing Prison Growth in North Carolina through Structured Sentencing,* National Institute of Justice Program Focus (Washington, D.C.: U.S. Department of Justice, February 1998), p. 5.

Figure 1-5   Form for Scoring Prior Record for Felony Sentencing

Number of Occurrences	Prior Conviction	Calculation	Total Points
	Murder 1	x 10	
	Rape	x 9	
	Murder 2, Kidnaping, or Armed Robbery	x 6	
	Voluntary Manslaughter, Involuntary Manslaughter, or Burglary Second Degree	x 4	
	Breaking and Entering or Possession of Cocaine	x 2	
	Prior Misdemeanor Class A1 or 1*	x 1	
		Subtotal	
If all the elements of the present offense are included in the prior offense:		+1	
If the offense was committed while on probation, parole, or postrelease supervision; or while serving a prison sentence; or while escaping:		+1	
		Total	
*Misdemeanors are categorized as Class 1, 2, and 3 based on the length of punishment assigned to them before the guidelines were implemented. Recently, a fourth class, Class A1, was created to categorize violent assaults and a few other serious misdemeanors.			

Source: Ronald Weight, *Managing Prison Growth in North Carolina through Structured Sentencing*, National Institute of Justice Program Focus (Washington, D.C.: U.S. Department of Justice, February 1998), p. 6.

effectiveness of the approach can be found in Figure 1-6, which demonstrates the increases in punishment severity after the guidelines were implemented for serious offenders. In many ways, the strategic use of community corrections, supported by the sentencing commission and criminal justice professionals, purchased this achievement.

The Advantages of Selective Incapacitation

Recent programmatic research evaluating the costs and benefits of collective incapacitation has strongly supported the growth and development of intermediate sanctions, as part of a strategy to more selectively incapacitate. Research from a different perspective has reached the same conclusion. Recognizing both the need to punish offenders and the varied limitations of all available penal sanctions, an extensive econometric analysis of the utilization of prison, traditional probation, and newer intermediate punishments concluded that intensive supervision, day reporting centers, or electronic monitoring may be only slightly better than regular probation (or doing nothing), but this difference may be enough to justify a fairly dramatic shift in prison construction policies. And because they involve few fixed costs, intermediate sanctions are likely to prove more flexible should conditions change. Thus if further research reveals that some intermediate sanctions are even slightly effective at reducing crime, further development of these sanctions is probably the least-cost alternative.[31]

Although these views imply new problems and challenges, community-based programs will continue to play a critical role in any attempt to fit the punishment to the crime in a manner that is economically viable. The

Figure 1-6   Percentage of Offenders Receiving Prison Sentences Before and After Implementation of Structured Sentencing

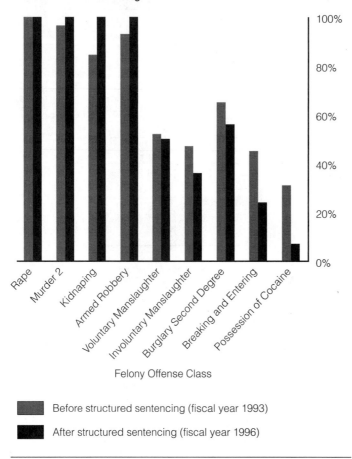

Felony Offense Class

■ Before structured sentencing (fiscal year 1993)

■ After structured sentencing (fiscal year 1996)

Note: Offenders convicted of Murder 1 are not included in this exhibit. All received prison sentences.
Source: Ronald Weight, *Managing Prison Growth in North Carolina through Structured Sentencing,* National Institute of Justice Program Focus (Washington, D.C.: U.S. Department of Justice, February 1998), p. 14.

primacy of community protection as a public and political concern mandates a system that provides a continuum of options and restrictions on offender behavior. Economic reality demands that this matter be approached in the most cost-effective manner possible.

No interest exists in returning to the days when community-based correctional programs were touted as the solution to every correctional problem. The need is to improve and

enhance the community-based strategies currently employed, to identify less costly alternatives to current practice, and to protect the public from the crimes of convicted offenders released to the community. In many ways, the struggle is to achieve a more mature approach to corrections. Community-based programs can provide community protection, but enforcing restrictions can be costly. Offenders can and do respond to some program services, but finding the right match of offender to program is not easy. Saving money requires a firm commitment to pursue the least costly alternative, and the use of intermediate sanctions requires a clear understanding of alternative parameters. The goal of all these efforts is to achieve a continuum of cost-effective sanctions that protect the community while benefiting the offender.

Perspectives on the Study of Community-Based Corrections

An understanding of community-based corrections requires an understanding of systems analysis, the correctional continuum, and offender **case management.** The examination of the factors that influence programs (inputs) and the manner in which they exert influence (outputs) is referred to as systems analysis. This approach recognizes the fundamental reality that correctional programs do not operate in a vacuum but are part of the larger context of criminal justice system operations and the community. The correctional continuum provides an organizing frame of reference for this study of community-based programs, beginning with those that deal with offenders who have not yet been convicted and ending with those programs designed for released prisoners. Correctional case management refers to the process of assessing offender risk and needs; developing a program of counseling, behavior monitoring, and services; and implementing that program. It also involves evaluating outcomes in terms of renewed involvement in crime and behavior change. This approach to the study of community-based corrections requires an examination of the risk posed by various types of offenders, the strategies available to control that risk, and the various needs of specific offender groups—drug abusers, juveniles, sex offenders, and so on.

Systems Analysis

Systems analysis is a two-way examination of inputs (influences on programs) and outputs (influences from programs). A closed system approach examines only the program's internal characteristics (such as personnel requirements and administration). An open system analysis considers both the internal and external factors.

A key concept in systems analysis is interdependence. Each component or subsystem influences other components and affects the functioning of the entire system. Change in one component can be expected to require change in others. The criminal justice system is an open system, reacting to outside influences and presenting influences to the outside. The police, courts, institutional corrections, and community-based programs are interdependent. All the organizations are influenced by the nature of crime and criminals; each organization influences the functioning of the others.

To illustrate the interdependence of criminal justice agencies, suppose the police noted a significant increase in the number of arrests of drug offenders. This action could produce any of the following results:

1. Jail overcrowding
    a. Increase in use of pretrial release programs
    b. Relaxation of bail requirements

2. Increase in number of prosecutions
    a. Increase in court backlog and delay
    b. Increase in use of plea bargaining to reduce the number of trials

3. Increase in number of persons sentenced to prison
    a. Prison overcrowding
    b. Relaxation of parole requirements and increase in number of early releases from prison granted
    c. Backlog of state prisoners in local jails (when state prisons are under court order restricting overcrowding)

4. Increase in use of probation
   a. Less supervision of probationers as size of caseloads swells

A different picture of the influences affecting community-based corrections would be obtained if they were viewed as a subsystem of local government or of a community's social welfare network. For example, community-based correctional programs for juveniles may be just one component of a community's child welfare system. The efforts of juvenile probation officers and residential and nonresidential correctional programs would then be seen as part of a larger network of programs and services for troubled families and physically, emotionally, and socially disadvantaged youth. Any significant change in practice by one component of the child welfare system would necessarily alter the activities of the remaining components. If status offenses were decriminalized, then the problems of truants, runaways, and incorrigible youths would fall much more heavily on the remaining social programs because juvenile court staff and correctional programs would no longer be working with these children.

All assessments of community-based corrections within the context of systems analysis, regardless of the type of system under study, provide a greater understanding of how and why community-based correctional programs function as they do. No system conceptualization is right or wrong; its usefulness can be judged only by assessing the information and insight it provides.

Community-based corrections in this volume is considered a subsystem of local government or social welfare, but the primary focus on community-based correctional programs is within the criminal justice system. The interdependence of criminal justice agencies and the function of community-based programs within the criminal justice system are the predominant themes of this book.

The Correctional Continuum

Many issues must be addressed if an understanding of the function and impact of community-based correctional programs is to be reached. Two issues, which affect every aspect of programming, from legislative intent to budget matters, seem especially critical: the alternatives and eligibility questions. These factors define the context—the parameters of the correctional continuum—in which particular programs operate.

Program Alternatives   Community-based correctional programs are sometimes viewed as an alternative to formal criminal justice processing, pretrial detention, or a commitment to jail or prison. This view is, in part, correct. Many persons are diverted from the criminal justice system because arrest or prosecution is considered unnecessary and unwarranted. Pretrial release is an alternative to pretrial confinement for persons who are unlikely to abscond prior to trial. Probation and parole are alternatives to imprisonment or continued incarceration for persons who can benefit from community supervision and assistance and who pose no threat to the community.

However, viewing community-based corrections as an alternative misrepresents the current operation of the criminal justice system. Without the involvement of a single organized diversion program, many offenders (especially juveniles) are diverted from the justice system because police, prosecutors, or juvenile intake staff do not believe that arrest, prosecution, or filing a petition is necessary or desirable. Many persons are currently released prior to trial because they have the money to make bail; pretrial release programs do not so much keep criminals out of jail as equalize the opportunities for freedom between poor and not-so-poor offenders.

If an alternative is considered as something other than the norm, then incarceration and release after completion of the maximum sentence are alternatives to probation and parole. Today, even with the massive increases in incarceration over the last decade, almost four persons are on probation or parole for every one inmate in a state or federal prison. Although the use of probation, prison, and parole varies from crime to crime and from jurisdiction to jurisdiction, most of the offenders processed through the criminal justice system commit crimes for which probation is part of the standard disposition. The remaining offenders enter institutions from which parole is still the typical method of release.

In evaluating a new community-based correctional program, it is important to consider what would have happened to the offender in the absence of the new alternative. If there were no diversion program, no supervised pretrial release program, no special counseling program or halfway house for probationers or parolees, what type of treatment would the offender have received?

In some communities, offenders have been placed in new community-based correctional programs when little or no correctional intervention was needed. This practice often occurs when a program appears to offer so much benefit that "it couldn't hurt" to provide the offender with counseling or supervision, even though it is really not essential. Such practices may be well intended, but they invariably change the objectives of these programs. If the clients of community-based corrections are offenders who do not need help, instead of persons who would otherwise be formally processed or institutionalized, then community-based corrections can become a costly luxury rather than a low-cost reform. These offenders might include first offenders, petty criminals, or perhaps juvenile offenders who demonstrate the wrong attitude but show no real proclivity toward crime. In the end, social control, instead of reintegration, will become the program's function.

Eligibility Requirements   The issue of how community-based programs are used—as an alternative to what?—is directly related to the issue of program eligibility requirements. Whom the system chooses to divert, to release prior to trial, or to supervise in the community directly affects both the offenders and the role of community-based corrections in the correctional system. Programs that accept only first-time and other low-risk offenders (those whose crimes are not real threats to the community—e.g., petty theft without personal contact) who need little assistance can easily demonstrate high success rates, but they are not very useful correctional efforts. Such programs offer a helping hand to those who do not need it, and the criminal justice system is left substantially unchanged.

Correctional Case Management

If systems analysis provides a macro-level view of community corrections and the correctional continuum provides an offender's eye view of correctional programs, then case management provides a micro-level analysis focusing on the individual offender's threat to the community and the need for services and accountability to the victim and the community. The vast majority of individuals working in community-based corrections, whether they are in diversion, probation, community service, or parole organizations, experience community-based corrections through this lens. Their challenge is to assess the offender, design a plan to achieve various objectives, and work to oversee the implementation of that plan. Generally the final phase of case management occurs when the offender is released from supervision, because of either program completion, or fulfillment of sentence, or release conditions.

Much case management occurs under far less than ideal conditions. Large caseloads make it impossible to give every offender as much attention as is best, so the goal becomes to establish ways of assessing offender risk and need so that more time and resources can be devoted to those offenders who need them most. The assessment process itself is not a simple one. While offense severity and offender history provide an important indication of public safety risk, patterns of substance abuse, work history, and other factors may also be important. Complicating matters is the reality that offender problems and needs are not necessarily correlated with risk; that is, low-risk offenders may have a great many problems and needs. In such circumstances, the prudent **community supervision officer** (CSO, a term that applies to any correctional employee who supervises offenders) will direct the greatest attention to the highest risk offender. Public safety concerns rightfully dominate correctional planning. The difficulty occurs when public safety objectives become the only focus, because the resolution of offender problems and needs may be the best long-term solution to public safety problems and crime prevention.

In some situations, offender case management is governed less by offender risk and need and more by sentence requirements and release conditions. In other settings, limitations in the number of staff and services make it impossible to offer more than rudimentary counseling and supervision to any offender. In environments where real choices can be made, assessment instruments can help CSOs objectify the decision-making process and determine appropriate levels of supervision and services. Supervision levels might vary in terms of frequency of regular and unannounced contacts with the offender, use of electric monitoring, and so on. Services might include employment assistance, education or training, substance abuse programming, child care assistance, and other social services.

Most people who work in community-based correctional programs do so because they want to have a positive impact on the world around them, by enhancing public safety, aiding offenders in need, or increasing offender accountability for their actions. Accountability may be achieved through accepting responsibility for one's actions, providing restitution to the victim or community, or paying fines or fees. Increasingly, expectations of the community justice model, including some form of reparation, are being introduced into the philosophy and substance of case management.

Summary

Community-based correctional programs have many rationales, but first and foremost they must protect the community. Community-based programs also make it possible to create a continuum of sanctions and programs to fit the punishment to the crime and the criminal. Rehabilitation and reintegration and the development of cost-effective sanctions are also objectives of community-based corrections.

Community-based corrections developed as a result of dissatisfaction with institutional confinement and in recognition of the problems encountered by inmates reentering society after prolonged incarceration. Criminological theories that emphasized the stigmatizing effects of criminal justice processing encouraged the search for less debilitating alternatives. The adoption of a systems approach to the analysis of the criminal justice process and the professionalization of criminal justice employees also stimulated a willingness to explore new directions.

The 1970s witnessed phenomenal growth in community-based corrections, but often this growth was poorly planned or implemented. When research began to demonstrate that community-based correctional strategies were valuable but not invariably effective, program growth slowed. The political conservatism and economic recession of the 1980s also contributed to the decline in program growth. Yet even as new program development slowed, the need to find less costly alternatives to incarceration prompted continued interest in community-based corrections. Offenders continued to be sentenced to probation and released on parole in increasing numbers, at rates reflecting growth comparable to that observed within the prison populations.

Truth-in-sentencing and "three strikes" bills swept the country during the 1990s. Prison construction projects continued, with no indication that building efforts would ever be able to meet demand. As correctional budgets appeared ready to sap the strength and resources of a nation, interest again began to build for more selectivity in correctional efforts—focusing limited resources on serious offenders, while providing alternatives for more minor criminals. Proposals were also made to inject greater discretion into judicial decisions regarding lesser offenders, again, with the objective of providing alternatives for those who do not require lengthy periods of confinement.

Today the challenge is to develop, implement, and evaluate appropriate alternatives for the diversity of criminal offenders. By using a systems perspective, and focusing on the function of programs within the correctional continuum, students of community corrections can best evaluate their potential impact and assess the types of offenders each program can best serve. By utilizing the case management perspective, one can determine the best way to serve community needs for safety and accountability, as well as offender needs for change and reintegration.

Key Words and Concepts

alternatives to revocation

case management

collective incapacitation

community justice

community protection

community supervision officer

continuum of programs

continuum of sanctions

cost-effectiveness

discretion

eligibility

external costs and savings

graduated release

Great Society

intermediate punishments

labeling theory

level of control

rehabilitation

reintegration

restrictions

risk assessment

risk management

selection process

selective incapacitation

structured sentencing

systems analysis

"three strikes and you're out"

"truth in sentencing"

Violent Crime Control and Law Enforcement Act of 1994

Questions for Discussion

1. Discuss a certain type of offender. What is the typical criminal justice response to this offender in your community? What problems are there with these responses? What might the criminal justice system do to make the sanctions more effective?

2. What are the goals of reintegration? Why did the criminal justice system of the 1960s and 1970s consider reintegration so important? How has the process of reintegration changed from the ideas of the 1970s to the practices of the twenty-first century?

3. What historical and legal changes made the practice of criminal justice more interested in the idea of restoration? What crimes

and criminals are best suited for a restorative response? What crimes are more difficult for restoration?

4. How can community-based corrections alter the impact of "time and place" to control crime and reduce offender risk?

5. Discuss how the crackdown on drugs and drug-related crime has created problems in the criminal justice system, and how these problems may have contributed to increases in certain types of crimes.

6. How has the use of structured sentences reduced the potential for treatment and diminished the role of community-based corrections in the rehabilitation of low-level offenders?

For Further Reading

Dunlap, Karen, *Community Justice: Concepts and Strategies* (Lexington, Ky.: American Probation and Parole Association, 1998).

Irwin, John, and James Austin, *It's About Time: America's Imprisonment Binge,* 2nd ed. (Belmont, Calif.: Wadsworth, 1996).

Walker, Samuel, *Sense and Nonsense About Crime and Drugs,* 4th ed. (Belmont, Calif.: Wadsworth, 1997).

Walsh, Anthony, *Correctional Assessment, Casework, and Counseling* (Lanham, Md.: American Correctional Association, 1997).

Part One

The Community Corrections Continuum

Chapter 2   Diversion, Pretrial Release,
             and Community Courts

Chapter 3   Probation

Chapter 4   Probation Supervision

Chapter 5   Parole and Other Prison Release Programs

Chapter 2

Diversion, Pretrial Release, and Community Courts

The Concept of Diversion

The Concept of Pretrial Release

Development of Contemporary Diversion and Pretrial Release Programs

Objectives of Diversion and Pretrial Release Programs

Contemporary Diversion Programming

Contemporary Pretrial Release Programs

Research on Pretrial Release Programs

Alternatives to Diversion and Pretrial Release

Adjudication Partnerships

Summary

Diversion and pretrial release programs provide alternatives to traditional criminal justice processing. **Diversion programs** may be offered in lieu of arrest or prosecution, giving offenders an opportunity to obtain assistance in the form of medical services, counseling, education, and vocational training. Other diversion programs direct victims and offenders into nontraditional forms of complaint management such as dispute resolution. Some diversion programs screen offenders into innovative courts, which provide expedited case processing, efforts to enhance offender accountability, and referrals to treatment and other services. These programs include drug courts and quasi-diversion programs such as community courts and other specialized court programs.

Diversion programs provide important ways to reduce the workload of the criminal justice system by weeding out less serious offenders who do not require traditional processes of conviction and sentencing. These offenders may be processed more speedily and often in a manner more suited to the nature of their offense and community needs. The disposition and offender monitoring provided in diversion programs may be similar to or even more rigorous than that provided in regular probation programs.

Pretrial release programs serve a different but related objective. These programs are alternatives to the pretrial detention of arrestees and the release of such offenders on commercial bonds. Although these offenders remain within the jurisdiction of the criminal justice system, pretrial releasees are permitted to stay in the community while they await adjudication.

Although neither diversion nor pretrial release programs are designed for convicted offenders, they are considered correctional programs because they serve persons accused of crimes, providing them with supervision and various forms of community assistance. Diversion programs represent the community's first and often best chance for intervention—a chance to provide appropriate defendants with individualized attention, in an attempt to resolve the problems that led to the alleged criminal behavior or provide swift lessons in accountability. Pretrial release programs lessen the unnecessary pains of incarceration while reducing jail populations and reliance on financial forms of release.

Both diversion and pretrial release programs can be controversial and both have changed significantly in recent years. During the 1970s and 1980s, many diversion programs acted to swiftly direct offenders into treatment and educational programs "for their own good." Observers who viewed the criminal justice system as too intrusive and not sufficiently tolerant of minor deviance believed that such programs coerced minor offenders into supervision and treatment who normally would not have been prosecuted. These critics viewed diversion programs as "widening the net" of social control through the unwarranted and often costly expansion and formalization of discretion. More recently, public safety-minded observers viewed these treatment-oriented programs as promoting an avoidance of offender responsibility. Consequently, quasi-diversion programs developed in the era of community justice are more likely to require some form of accountability than in the past and to be designed to also achieve community and criminal justice system objectives.

In the 1980s, pretrial release programs emerged as a major strategy to reduce jail crowding. Their goal was to decrease the number of offenders detained in jail awaiting trial, while providing a more equitable form of release than commercial bail. Today, pretrial release programs provide a firmly established means of avoiding detention for many offenders, but their impact on jail populations and commercial bail is questionable. Pretrial detention populations have continued to soar and cash bail is still the principal form of release in most jurisdictions. The problems of jail overcrowding and the need for new ways to divert offenders from unnecessary (and ineffective) criminal justice system involvement continue to be major topics of concern in community corrections.

In recent years, a variety of **adjudication partnerships** have been formed that bring together community and court officials, and sometimes law enforcement and correctional partners, to provide enhanced problem solving and collaboration. These partnerships may unite diversion and pretrial release services, as well as other programs. The objective of these comprehensive programs is to benefit both offenders and the community and to reduce operational costs.

The Concept of Diversion

The concept of diversion is as old as the system of criminal justice. Although it is a well-established principle that American society should be ruled by written law instead of the arbitrary actions of public officials, it is acknowledged that the administration of law needs to be flexible enough to meet the complex problems of contemporary life. In general, criminal statutes are broadly formulated to cover a wide range of behaviors that may be considered offensive to social norms. Criminal justice system officials are authorized to use considerable **discretion** or subjective judgment in their efforts to enforce the law. The criminal statutes may be interpreted in terms of the problems and needs of the individual offender, the impact of his or her offense, or the expectations of the community in which the crime occurs. Officials may evaluate the advantages and disadvantages of various courses of action prior to deciding which course of action to take.

Neither police officers nor prosecutors are required to invoke the criminal justice process every time a crime is committed. Police officers may arrest an alleged criminal or they may choose to dismiss with a reprimand, refer to a social service agency, or ignore the offense entirely if it is not a serious one. Prosecutors may file criminal charges against an alleged offender, pursue an alternate course of legal action (such as initiating civil commitment proceedings against a defendant who is believed to be mentally ill), or seek some informal remedy to the problem (such as permitting a defendant to make restitution to avoid prosecution for shoplifting). Whenever a criminal justice system official chooses not to invoke the criminal justice process, he or she is diverting that individual from the criminal justice system.

Contemporary diversion programs resulted from attempts to expand and formalize traditional diversion—in effect, to take a good idea and make it better. Their goal was to increase opportunities to avoid unnecessary arrest and prosecution.

Avoidance of Unnecessary Prosecution

The criminal justice system is increasingly overwhelmed by the challenge of managing the growing pool of offenders that society wishes to arrest and prosecute. The problem is particularly acute in major cities. One of the main concerns is the lack of resources. The funds and personnel needed to effectively prosecute, convict, and sanction have failed to keep pace with the ever-expanding volume of offenders. Efforts to get tough on crime through new laws and harsher penalties have meant that more offenders are coming into the system, but relatively fewer programs, staff, and facilities are available to respond to them. Efforts to divert offenders who pose little risk to the community make good economic sense, because they permit the focus of scarce resources on more serious criminals.

But even if resources were plentiful, reasons would exist to avoid unnecessary arrest and prosecution. The criminal justice system is widely perceived to have a poor track record of effectively dealing with the problems of crime. Its rehabilitative efforts are not widely successful, frequently failing to put many offenders back on the right path. The system is often viewed as steering many of its clients in the wrong direction by classifying them with more serious criminals.

The Concept of Pretrial Release

Contemporary pretrial release programs developed from efforts to formalize and organize practices that had been ongoing in the criminal justice system for hundreds of years. The history of pretrial release programs can be traced back to medieval England, when those accused of crimes were detained in local jails until a traveling magistrate arrived in their jurisdiction. These individuals were often detained for months at a time in unsanitary and disease-ridden dungeons. Because these early jails were not designed to hold offenders securely for long periods of time, many escaped. Local sheriffs, who did not enjoy the role of jailer, were anxious to see these individuals removed from their custody. To accomplish this, they frequently turned a defendant over to a willing friend, relative, or employer. This third party would offer himself or money as surety, a person who is legally liable for the conduct of another, for the accused person's appearance before the magistrate.[1] If the defendant failed to appear in court, the surety could be imprisoned or forced to pay a sum of money to the sheriff. A modern corollary to this practice is used by most citizens on a daily basis. It involves the payment of a premium to an agent who agrees to cover damage to persons or property made by the client. Based on the client's past record, these premiums may increase or decrease. This exercise, known as insurance, is similar in both practice and name to the old form of surety.

The practice of releasing a defendant prior to trial with a personal or financial guarantee of court appearance became known as release on bail. Although the origin of the term is uncertain, it appears to come from the French word *bailer,* which means "to hand over or deliver."[2] The practice of **bail** was abused and misused almost from its inception. Many sheriffs simply released anyone who could provide surety and jailed the rest. To remedy this problem, in 1275 specific offenses were established as "bailable" (persons accused of these acts could be released on bail) and other crimes were designated "not bailable." Eventually, the authority to set bail was removed from the sheriff and vested in justices of the peace.

In an attempt to discourage the setting of unreasonably high bails, the English Bill of Rights in 1689 stated that excessive bail should not be required, a stipulation later incorporated into the U.S. Constitution, which states in the Eighth Amendment (ratified in 1791) that excessive bail may not be required. Questions remained about how to set appropriate levels of bail. Originally, the setting of bail amounts was not much of a problem, because so many capital crimes were unbailable. But gradually the number of offenses punishable by death was reduced by legislation, and judges assumed considerable discretion in the setting of bail amounts. Bail amounts tended to be high because judges were as concerned about the likelihood of additional crime as court appearance.

As the population grew and became more mobile, the posting of bond became commercialized. The function once served by friends or relatives of the defendant could now be purchased for a fee. Although they did not offer the supervision of defendants that friends and employers might offer, bondsmen were willing to post the required amount of bond and assume financial liability if the defendant fled. The importance of personal ties within the community through friendship and employment diminished, if they did not disappear.

The practice of **commercial bonding** soon created as many difficulties as it solved. During the 1920s, numerous studies of criminal justice systems across the country documented the problems: [3]

1. The conditions in local jails were appalling. Legally innocent persons were frequently held for unreasonably long periods of time alongside convicted criminals in decaying, unsanitary, and overcrowded facilities. Persons without funds were given virtually no opportunity to obtain pretrial release.

2. No standards were utilized in setting bail and discriminatory treatment was common.

3. Generally less than 5 percent of the defendants who were released failed to appear for their scheduled court proceeding(s).

4. One-third of all defendants jailed prior to trial were never convicted. Pretrial detainees were more likely to be indicted and convicted and to receive prison sentences after conviction than defendants freed prior to trial.

5. Bail bondsmen were found to pose significant problems for the administration of justice. In addition to the discriminatory treatment of potential clients, many of them were unreliable and posted bond when they had insufficient funds.

Through the years, additional research continued to support these findings, but no significant improvements were made until the 1960s.

Avoidance of Unnecessary Jailing of Offenders

If an offender does require arrest and prosecution, many reasons exist to avoid jailing him or her prior to prosecution. As a constitutional matter, the purpose of pretrial detention is to ensure appearance at trial; as a practical matter, many criminal justice system officials and much of the general public want jails to protect the community from the potential crimes of defendants. But many offenders pose no flight risk and no threat to the community, and they would suffer needlessly as a result of incarceration. Jails are universally regarded as the worst of all correctional facilities. Many suffer from limited funding, inadequate facilities and staff, routine violence, and a near absence of medical care. Most facilities do not have sufficient work opportunities to keep offenders occupied, and very few have anything to offer in the way of educational or therapeutic programs. Jail time is regarded by many offenders as dead time, because little happens to shorten one's sentence or improve one's life on the outside. Pretrial detention also interrupts the fulfillment of offender responsibilities such as work and child rearing, thus imposing costs on family members as well as the defendant. From the criminal justice system perspective, pretrial detention is a scarce resource, which needs to be reserved for individuals likely to flee the jurisdiction and for serious repetitive offenders.

Avoidance of Bail and Commercial Bondsmen

Requiring defendants to purchase their freedom has always been a questionable approach to protecting the public and ensuring the offender's presence at trial. While creating an incentive for court appearance is logical, the reliance on economic means to secure the defendant's presence is discriminatory and generally unrelated to the likelihood of flight risk. That is, there is no reason to suppose that individuals with the means to secure commercial bond pose less of a flight risk than persons of more limited resources. Decades of research have shown that factors unrelated to wealth are better predictors of flight risk than financial means. In addition, because bondsmen provide no supervision to defendants, their efforts are of no benefit to public safety. The only real ad-

vantage of commercial bail is that it achieves the release of some offenders without cost to the taxpayer-supported criminal justice system.

Development of Contemporary Diversion and Pretrial Release Programs

Diversion Programs

Consistent with society's general interest in social welfare and rehabilitation in the 1960s and 1970s, the perceived need for formal diversion programs was met with action from many government agencies. These early programs focused on opportunities to divert offenders in need of employment assistance, substance abuse treatment, and conflict resolution services.

The Department of Labor began funding pretrial intervention programs for vocationally disadvantaged offenders in 1967 and funded additional projects in the early 1970s. Programs such as the Manhattan Court Employment Project became models for programs in more than thirty cities. In 1971, the White House Special Action Office for Drug Abuse Prevention developed a diversion model for drug abusers known as Treatment Alternatives to Street Crime (TASC). Several states quickly followed this effort with the development of special legislation for the diversion of drug abusers from the criminal justice system.

Other police-based diversion programs developed during this period focused on removing alcoholics from the revolving door of local jails and on family crisis intervention as a response to domestic violence. While these programs never gained nationwide acceptance, other efforts were more successful. A dispute settlement mechanism for more general categories of interpersonal conflicts was established in Columbus, Ohio, in 1971. A few years later, the Department of Justice funded Neighborhood Justice Centers (NJCs), which became models for **dispute resolution programs** across the country.

These diversion programs received considerable support from professionals in the field of criminal justice and from commissions established to study the problems and needs of the criminal justice system. The President's Commission on Law Enforcement and Administration of Justice reported that "it is more fruitful to discuss not who can be tried as a matter of law, but how the officers of the administration of criminal justice should deal with people who present special needs and problems."[4] This commission recommended the early identification and diversion of offenders who needed treatment but did not require criminal dispositions.

Further support for diversion was provided by the President's Task Force on Prisoner Rehabilitation, the American Bar Association, and the American Correctional Association. Criteria and procedures for diversion were outlined in the 1973 report of the National Advisory Commission on Criminal Justice Standards and Goals. National and state organizations were established to promote the expansion of pretrial intervention programs. The number and types of diversion programs grew throughout the 1970s. During that time, the Law Enforcement Assistance Administration alone funded more than twelve hundred diversion programs for adults and juveniles at a cost of more than $112 million.

In the 1980s, much of the federal aid for diversion programs was withdrawn. Legislative and public attention focused on get-tough policies such as mandatory sentencing, not on efforts to remove minor offenders from the criminal justice system. However, the value of some diversion programs, particularly those linked to courts or utilizing alternative means of conflict resolution, was well established within the criminal justice system, and many programs were firmly entrenched in their communities. In such instances, state and local governments acted to assume the costs of diversion programs. TASC and dispute resolution programs were among those most likely to be maintained and even expanded in recent years.

In 1989, community concerns about the drug-crime nexus led to the creation of the first drug court. Since that time, the drug court movement has expanded rapidly, serving the needs of a crowded criminal justice system and offenders whose principle problem is a function of drug use.

Pretrial Release Programs

While diversion programs were being developed in the 1960s, similar initiatives were beginning in the area of pretrial release. Like the Manhattan Court Employment Project, these efforts also originated in New York City.

In 1960, Louis Schweitzer, a wealthy retired chemical engineer, visited the Brooklyn House of Detention at the suggestion of a friend. Schweitzer, as an immigrant Russian boy, had once lived a few blocks from where the jail stood. Schweitzer reported:

I'd never been in a criminal court and hardly knew anybody who had. . . . I visited the prison and was appalled. The youngsters were treated like already convicted criminals, despite our treasured principle that people are presumed innocent until proven guilty. The only crime we knew they committed was the crime of being too poor for bail. I found out later that most of them were eventually given suspended sentences or acquitted after an average wait in jail of more than a month each.[5]

After discussions with a variety of criminal justice professionals, Schweitzer established and funded the Vera Foundation (which he named for his mother) and its Manhattan Bail Project. The original purpose of the Vera Foundation (now known as the Vera Institute of Justice) was to assist judges in their efforts to identify individuals who could be released on their own recognizance, or promise to appear, prior to trial. New York judges, like magistrates in most jurisdictions, already had the authority to release persons accused of crimes without bail when they gave their word that they would appear at trial. What judges needed, however, was a method of gathering and verifying information about defendants—their family, employment, and community ties—to determine when **release on recognizance** was appropriate. Without this information, judges were understandably reluctant to release defendants only on the basis of their promise to appear.

The staff of the Manhattan Bail Project solved this problem. They interviewed defendants and contacted their references to verify the interview statements. They provided the judges with this information and with recommendations regarding the accused person's suitability for an on recognizance (OR) release.

The Manhattan Bail Project was originally designed as an experimental program. Because its impact on the criminal justice system was potentially far-reaching, every effort was made to monitor program operations closely so that its effectiveness could be measured.[6] After careful evaluation, it was judged an unqualified success.

The results of the Manhattan Bail Project encouraged jurisdictions across the country to replicate the Vera Foundation's effort. These new projects showed similar positive results. And additional benefits accrued: In many areas judges became more willing to independently exercise their discretion to release defendants on their own recognizance even without the special services of a pretrial release agency.

By the 1980s, more than two hundred cities had developed pretrial release programs. Ironically, judicial willingness to release defendants without the input of formal pretrial release organizations reduced the pressure to establish new pretrial release programs, or sometimes to maintain existing ones. Supervised pretrial release (SPTR) was subsequently developed to enable individuals considered to be poor risks for release on recognizance to be released under community supervision prior to trial. This development provided a way to increase the number of individuals who could avoid pretrial detention, as well as to provide renewed justification for pretrial release program services.

In the 1980s, SPTR projects began to serve a second purpose. They provided a means to respond to growing public safety concerns by monitoring pretrial releasees in the community. Community protection concerns began to dominate program objectives, and many pretrial release programs experienced reductions in the number of individuals who could be released without supervision. In some jurisdictions, most defendants released were required to accept some form of supervision to achieve a nonfinancial form of release.

The growing agenda of pretrial release programs stimulated the development of multipurpose pretrial service agencies. These agencies provide comprehensive pretrial services, including supervision of persons released by the court; provision of recommendations for specific conditions for release; development and monitoring of support; rehabilitative and crisis intervention services for defendants; and coordination of relations between the courts and law enforcement agencies related to the identification and apprehension of persons who fail to appear.

The 1980s witnessed a major shift in the public's views of crime and justice—an escalation of public fear and heightened concern about community protection. This concern influenced pretrial release programs in a couple of ways. First, it led to the supervision of increasingly large numbers of offenders as a condition of release. Second, it changed the basic presumptions under which release decisions were made.

During the 1960s, federal legislation created a presumption in favor of release and the imposition of the least restrictive form of pretrial release that would ensure appearance at trial. The 1984 Federal Bail Reform Act expanded the criteria to be used for the release decision to include protection of the community. This act permitted judicial officials, following a hearing, to detain individuals on the basis of the perceived threat they posed to the community. The pretrial detention provisions of the act made special reference to particular categories of offenses and offenders, authorizing pretrial detention for defendants charged with crimes of violence, offenses with possible life (or death) penalties, major drug offenses, and felonies in which the defendant has a specified serious criminal record.

In addition, the act created a rebuttable presumption that no conditions of release would assure the defendant's court appearance or community safety under the following circumstances: the defendant committed a drug felony with a ten-year maximum sentence; the defendant used a firearm during the commission of a violent or drug-trafficking offense; or the defendant was convicted of specified serious crimes within the preceding five years while on pretrial release.[7]

Although the constitutionality of preventive detention was later questioned in *U.S. vs. Salerno* (1987), the Supreme Court upheld the ability of a magistrate to confine an offender presumed to be dangerous. Numerous legislative actions expanded this rationale for pretrial detention to the state courts.

Today almost 600,000 inmates are in local jails, over half of whom are pretrial detainees.[8] The most recent jail census indicated that the number of adult inmates of local jails had approximately doubled in the decade since 1984. During that same time period, jail construction added nearly one-quarter of a million beds to existing inventories. Of special concern is that rates of incarceration have risen significantly more rapidly for blacks than whites. Blacks are now confined at a rate more than five times that of whites.

Communities are looking for new ways to reduce jail populations. Once again, community and court partnerships seem to be providing much of the new direction in this area.

Objectives of Diversion and Pretrial Release Programs

Diversion and pretrial release programs serve many similar objectives. They both work to benefit the offender and to reduce justice system costs, while ensuring public safety. Diversion programs have broader and more comprehensive objectives: They attempt to individualize and simplify defendant processing; provide appropriate treatment, services, and offender monitoring; and enhance accountability to both victim and the community. Diversion programs provide an alternative to traditional prosecution and sentencing.

Pretrial release programs have a much narrower focus. Their objective is the short-term goal of providing a nonfinancial form of release from pretrial detention. For most offenders, pretrial release is a procedural alternative to bail. The supervision they receive, if any, is generally for the purpose of securing court appearance and community safety, not providing rehabilitation or ensuring accountability to the victim or the community. Most pretrial releasees ultimately are processed through the criminal justice system and receive routine dispositions.

Contemporary Diversion Programs

Programs for Drug-Abusing Offenders

Two major approaches to the diversion of drug-abusing offenders are in use today: **Treatment Alternatives to Street Crime** diversion model and specialized **drug courts**. Both these approaches provide for the deferred prosecution of drug users, but they do so in different and complementary ways. The TASC model provides for the establishment of liaison services between the criminal justice system and drug treatment programs to encourage diversion. The specialized drug court, as the name implies, provides expedited processing and court-monitored treatment to reduce the defendant's drug-using behavior.

Treatment Alternatives to Street Crime   TASC programs identify drug abusers from the population of arrestees, diagnose their drug problems, refer them to appropriate community drug treatment programs, monitor their progress in the programs, and report this information back to criminal justice system officials. The first TASC program was established in 1972 in Wilmington, Delaware. It provided pretrial diversion for opiate addicts with nonviolent criminal charges who were identified in jail by urine tests and interviews. After assessment of their suitability for treatment and treatment needs, arrestees who volunteered for TASC were referred and escorted to appropriate community-based treatment. While in the program, the addicts were monitored for continued compliance with treatment requirements. Successful completion usually resulted in dismissed charges.

The Law Enforcement Assistance Administration (LEAA) began funding TASC projects the following year, expanding the focus to sentencing alternatives as well as pretrial diversion. Over the next ten years, the number of federally sponsored TASC projects grew to 130. When LEAA funding was eliminated, state and local governments picked up more than 80 percent of the projects.[9]

Federal funding was reestablished in 1986, in the form of support from the Bureau of Justice Assistance. Block grants provided to the states as part of the Federal Anti-Drug Abuse Initiative provided funds to TASC programs for technical assistance and basic operations. The National Consortium of TASC programs provides coordination and guidance for further program development. Hundreds of TASC programs are now operating at numerous sites in more than half of the states.

The Evolving Focus of TASC Programs   Criminal justice officials in many communities have proved reluctant to permit the TASC diversion of any but the most youthful and situational user of so-called soft drugs. TASC programs had the option of serving only this small group of minor offenders or expanding their efforts to include programs for convicted drug abusers. Most programs chose the latter option. Today relatively few of TASC's clients are pretrial divertees.[10]

Polydrug and alcohol abusers, juveniles, and in some places both victims of domestic violence and offenders with mental health problems are eligible for program participation. Even services to traffic offenders have been added in a number of jurisdictions.[11] Because these offenders reflect a diverse group of substance abusers with many problems and deficits, today's TASC program resembles a network more than a bridge (Figure 2-1). The TASC challenge is to coordinate the range of programs and services that clients require for assistance.

TASC programs are confronted not only by more severely troubled offenders than in the past but also by an overwhelming growth in the number of offenders. Pretreatment waiting periods may extend for up to six months, during which time many offenders lose interest in and motivation for treatment. The maintenance of treatment readiness requires continued contact with referred defendants, as well as education and counseling to maintain offenders in the pipeline, by confronting denial, providing information on the human immunodeficiency virus (HIV), and so on. Additional challenges include the need to better match clients to treatment type and level of services and to improve staff training.[12]

Research on TASC Programs   LEAA required TASC programs to conduct independent evaluations of their efforts. More than forty studies were completed during the period of LEAA oversight. Results generally indicated that the programs were successfully able to identify previously untreated drug-dependent offenders, provide an intervention, and link the criminal justice and treatment systems.

Subsequent research by the Lazar Institute concluded that legally sanctioned referrals such as those provided by TASC were more effective than informal referrals into drug treatment.[13] Research indicated that the most successful programs were those that had the support of the treatment system and the broad-based support of the justice system. The most effective programs also included a monitoring function that held the offender accountable for his or her behavior. Continued problems in TASC

Figure 2-1 The Evolving Focus of Treatment Alternatives to Street Crime (TASC) Programs

The Current Model: The TASC Bridge

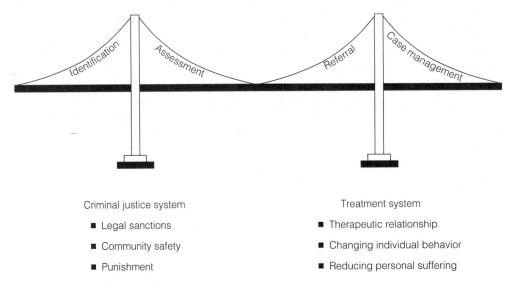

Criminal justice system

- Legal sanctions
- Community safety
- Punishment

Treatment system

- Therapeutic relationship
- Changing individual behavior
- Reducing personal suffering

Source: TASC Programs, *Program Brief,* Bureau of Justice Assistance, 1988, p. 1.

The Current Model: The TASC Network

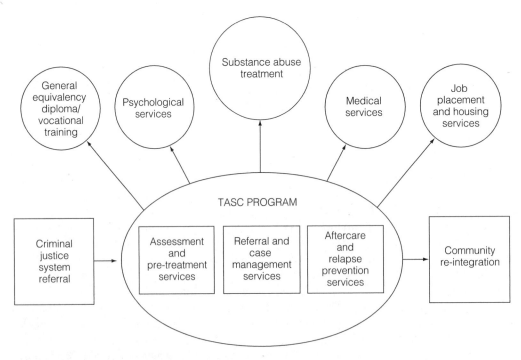

Source: James Swartz, "TASC—The Next 20 Years: Extending, Refining, and Assessing the Model," in *Drug Treatment and Criminal Justice,* James Inciardi (ed.) (Newbury Park, Calif.: Sage, 1993).

data collection, however, made it impossible to conduct long-term evaluations of many critical elements of the programs, such as assessing the program's impact on drug-related crime or case processing in the justice system.

The results of a study of five TASC programs outcomes were reported in 1999. The rigorous research design examined the impact of TASC case management procedures (as opposed to other procedural models) in two of the jurisdictions and the impact of TASC management on service delivery, drug use, and recidivism in all sites. The results indicated that while TASC programs were effective in enhancing service delivery and reducing drug use, the results on recidivism impact were mixed.[14] While TASC programs delivered more treatment services to offenders, typically including drug counseling, urinalysis to detect drug use, and acquired immune deficiency syndrome (AIDS) education, there was no clear evidence of reductions in either new arrests or technical violations because of TASC involvement. The most positive results were achieved with the most hard-core offenders, indicating the importance of utilizing TASC programs for offenders who can most benefit from the services, instead of for those who pose the least threat or seem the easiest to treat.

Drug Courts   Drug courts are established to selectively process felony drug cases, thus reducing crowded felony dockets and case processing time, and providing a mechanism for more creative and effective dispositions.[15] While some drug courts' primary goal is to speed the disposition of drug cases through the use of differentiated case management, others are treatment-oriented. These latter projects use court-monitored drug treatment under a diversion, deferred prosecution, or deferred sentencing arrangement to achieve changes in defendants' drug-use behavior.

The first diversion-oriented court was established in Miami in 1989. By 1993, fifteen drug court projects were in operation across the country. The next year, the Crime Act of 1994 authorized funding to expand the drug court movement and established the Drug Courts Program within the Department of Justice. Forty-five million dollars were awarded to 270 jurisdictions over the next three years to plan, implement, or enhance drug courts. In December 1998, the Department of Justice and the Office of National Drug Control Policy jointly funded the National Drug Court Institute to provide training, education, and other support for drug courts around the nation. By 1999, more than four hundred drug courts had been implemented or were planned.[16] In 1999 alone, 150 jurisdictions received grants of more than $27 million to plan, implement, enhance, and track the progress of drug courts.

In 1997, the Department of Justice identified ten key components of drug courts:

1. Drug courts integrate alcohol and other drug treatment services with justice system case processing.

2. Using a nonadversarial approach, prosecution and defense counsel promote public safety while protecting participants' due process rights.

3. Eligible participants are identified early and promptly placed in the drug court program.

4. Drug courts provide access to a continuum of alcohol, drug, and related treatment and rehabilitation services.

5. Abstinence is monitored by frequent alcohol and other drug testing.

6. A coordinated strategy governs drug court responses to participants' compliance.

7. Ongoing judicial interaction with each drug court participant is essential.

8. Monitoring and evaluation are used to measure the achievement of program goals and gauge effectiveness.

9. Continuing interdisciplinary education promotes effective drug court planning, implementation, and operations.

10. Forging partnerships among drug courts, public agencies, and community-based organizations generates local support and enhances drug court effectiveness.[17]

Issues in Community Corrections

The Drug Court Experience Compared with Traditional Adjudication

Intensive Supervision Provided Where Little Existed Before Traditional Adjudication Process

Under the traditional adjudication process, supervision of defendants released pretrial usually consists of a weekly call-in and periodic reporting to a pretrial service agency during the pretrial period (usually 60–120 or more days following arrest); after conviction, supervision usually consists of monthly reporting to a probation officer. Urinalysis is generally conducted only periodically, and treatment services provided only if available. The court's involvement occurs only when probation violations are reported—generally when new crimes are committed. Bench warrants may be issued for defendants who fail to appear for court hearings, but their actual execution (e.g., the defendant's arrest) may not occur for months and often is triggered only by a new arrest.

Drug Court Process

Defendant supervision and monitoring—as well as treatment services—in all of the drug court programs are significantly more immediate and intensive than would have been provided to the typical drug court defendant prior to the program. Drug court defendants come under the court's supervision very shortly after arrest, and throughout a typical 12–15

month period, are required to attend treatment sessions, undergo frequent and random urinalysis, and appear before the drug court judge on a regular and frequent basis. Almost all of the drug courts have instituted procedures for immediate execution of bench warrants (often within hours) for defendants who fail to appear at any court hearing.

Capacity to Promptly Deal with Relapse and Its Consequences

Traditional Adjudication Process

It is particularly common for defendants on probation for drug offenses to fail to comply with probation conditions entailing attendance at treatment programs or abstaining from drug use. Frequently, their failure to comply is evidenced by a new arrest for a drug or drug-related offense, generally becoming known to the justice system months after the defendant's drug use has resumed, if it ever ceased in the first place. This violation hearing, which generally results in imposition of the original sentence suspended when (1) the defendant was placed on probation, and (2) conviction for the new offense, often resulting in an additional sentence of incarceration. It is common for this cycle to continue indefinitely once the defendant is released, with an enhanced

In addition, while many drug courts focusing on treatment handle only drug possession cases, some accept low-level drug sale cases and others process any drug felony. Generally, treatment-oriented courts tend to exclude defendants charged with the sale, delivery, or trafficking of drugs unless their role in the offense was relatively minor or their drug addiction is clearly driving their participation in drug selling.

incarceration sentence imposed each time to reflect the defendant's lengthening criminal history.

Drug Court Experience

Recognizing that substance addiction is a chronic and recurring disorder, the drug court program maintains continuous supervision over the recovery process of each participant, through frequent court status hearings, urinalysis, and reports from the treatment providers to the supervising judge. Drug usage or failures to comply with other conditions of the drug court program are detected and responded to promptly. Immediate responses—ranging from enhanced treatment services, more frequent urinalysis (daily, if necessary), imposition of community service requirements, and "shock" incarceration—are some of the options drug court judges use to respond to program noncompliance.

Capability to Integrate Drug Treatment with Other Rehabilitation Services to Promote Long-term Recovery

Traditional Adjudication Process

Although there are strong correlations between drug abuse and other attributes of so-

cial dysfunction exhibited by drug users, such as poor reading skills, dysfunctional family relationships, low self-esteem, etc., most courts do not address these problems when sentencing drug-using offenders. At best, they refer them to a treatment program and/or a special skills class, with no regular monitoring of their participation or its results, absent a violation of probation filed by the probation officer.

Drug Court Experience

In contrast, a fundamental premise of the drug court approach is that cessation of drug abuse requires not only well-structured treatment services but coordinated and comprehensive programs of other rehabilitation services to address the underlying personal problems of the drug user, and promote his or her long-term re-entry into society.

Source: Looking at a Decade of Drug Courts (Washington, D.C.: U.S. Department of Justice, Drug Court Clearinghouse and Technical Assistance Programs, June 1998).

Research on Drug Courts   An early study of treatment-oriented courts in Broward and Dade counties, Florida, Oakland, California, and Portland, Oregon, indicated that these programs are reducing recidivism and drug

use, have high completion rates, and have lowered jail and prison costs. The Miami study reported that maintaining a defendant in treatment for a year cost only $700 because large caseloads (up to twelve hundred clients)

Program Focus

Drug Center Experiences

In **Pensacola,** for example, the first two graduates of the family (dependency) drug court established in early 1996 illustrate the impact of the drug court on the families of these women: one of the women had four minor children, the other had five minor children. Both had a long history of drug usage; one had been in state prison for 3 years, having been sent to prison by the drug court judge when he presided over her previous case. She was a long-term crack addict; the other was primarily alcohol- and marijuana-addicted. Neither had any permanent residence or work history. Their cumulative total of 9 children was living in foster care. Both now have a home (one rents; one owns); one is working; both families are reunited; nether mother currently uses drugs, and both have been clean for at least 7 months.

In **Portland,** almost all of the more than 100 female participants who lost custody of their minor children due to their substance abuse regained custody of their children at the conclusion of their participation in the drug court.

In **Kalamazoo,** at least 15–20 percent of the women in the female drug court program at any one time are also involved with probate court proceedings regarding loss of custody of their children; almost all of them regain custody of their children following completion of the drug court. Participants in the newly established male drug court, while not as extensively involved with the loss of *custody* of their children, have brought in letters from their children and wives expressing their gratitude at having their fathers and husbands "back" from drugs.

In **Las Vegas,** at least 40 women who have lost custody of their children have regained them after completing the drug court program.

Source: Looking at a Decade of Drug Courts (Washington, D.C.: U.S. Department of Justice, Drug Court Clearinghouse and Technical Assistance Programs, June 1998).

have been successfully managed.[18] Recidivism rates after eighteen months of drug court supervision were about half the rates for a comparable group of offenders from a period before the court opened. Drug court defendants also had a longer time before re-arrest and were re-arrested for less serious offenses.

The Drug Court Resource Center at American University conducted a study of twenty drug court programs in operation for at least one year.[19] This study also reported positive results in terms of both recidivism and substance abuse reduction for drug court participants and a number of positive side effects of program operations, including the birth of a significant number of drug-free babies to women enrolled in the program. The programs also appeared to be cost-effective, with expenses running between $900 and $1,600 per participant.

In 1997, the U.S. General Accounting Office surveyed more than 130 drug court programs and issued a report, which documented the tremendous growth in drug courts, the diversity of their characteristics, and their completion and retention rates.[20] Almost half of the programs (44 percent) deferred the prosecution of offenders who entered the program, while others (38 percent) allowed offenders to enter the program postadjudication. Still others allowed offenders to enter the program on a trial basis, after they had entered a plea. While all programs provided some form of treatment, the specific types of treatment varied widely, as did the intensity of treatment. The type of offenders participating also varied considerably, but most clients were adult nonviolent offenders with a substance abuse problem. About 16 percent of the programs accepted juveniles. More than sixty-five thousand persons had been admitted to drug court programs since 1989.[21]

One year later, the National Drug Court Institute Review published the National Center on Addiction and Substance Abuse's assessment of thirty drug court evaluations involving twenty-four courts. The study found that "Drug courts provide closer, more comprehensive supervision and much more frequent drug testing and monitoring during the program, than other forms of community supervision. More importantly, drug use and criminal behavior are substantially reduced while offenders are participating in drug courts."[22] At present, drug courts are enjoying a high level of support from all criminal justice professionals, because they appear to be efficiently and effectively increasing the supervision, monitoring, and treatment of drug offenders, while they free up criminal justice system personnel and other resources for more serious criminals.

Breaking the Cycle   Given the similarity of focus, it makes sense for communities to draw from the strengths of both TASC and drug court models in their efforts to manage drug offenders. In 1998, Birmingham, Alabama's TASC program received funding to undertake a systemwide initiative to curb drug abuse, called **Break the Cycle (BTC)**, which encompassed all drug-involved offenders under community supervision.[23] The ambitious goal was to identify all drug users early, assess them for treatment needs, make referrals to appropriate treatments, monitor their drug use through

regular testing, and provide immediate sanctions for any drug use. Birmingham already had twenty-five years' experience with TASC programming, which included a deferred prosecution program (charges against defendants were dropped upon successful completion of treatment), a drug court and pretrial release program, and a program for probationers. Birmingham also had a jail built for 750 offenders that in 1996 housed 1,200. Addressing that problem was a stipulation of BTC funding.

BTC integrated drug testing, referral to treatment, judicial supervision of treatment, and graduated sanctions. Specific elements of the program plan reported in 1998 include:

Close Collaboration Between Criminal Justice and Drug Treatment Every drug-using defendant is to be assessed by a neutral organization serving neither prosecution nor defense. An individualized treatment plan will be developed, and the offender's progress in treatment will be supervised by the court, with drug testing at each appearance.

Early Intervention The goal is to intervene immediately after arrest, requiring pre-arraignment drug testing before the first court appearance. A clinical assessment then places the abuser in the appropriate treatment modality.

Judicial Oversight Building on the lessons learned from drug courts, judicial oversight accompanies all treatment program participation. Judges have broad authority to impose and enforce pretrial release conditions. Compliance information will be presented at each court appearance.

Use of Graduated Sanctions and Incentives Risk is managed through the immediate application of sanctions and incentives by the court.[24]

To achieve these objectives, Birmingham developed a multipronged strategy to (1) upgrade existing probation facilities, (2) enhance drug testing, (3) develop better case management techniques, and (4) manage information more effectively by adopting a state-of-the-art information management system developed in New York's Brooklyn drug court. These efforts included collaborative planning across all relevant agencies to facilitate system operation, the development of new policies and procedures for early case identification and intervention, the establishment of a case management and tracking system, and the expansion of treatment options. New treatment options included the development of a day reporting program, expansion of electronic monitoring, establishment of a cognitive behavioral training program, arrangement of contracts for additional drug treatment beds through community providers, and expansion of intensive outpatient drug treatment.

Birmingham's BTC is now being evaluated by the Urban Institute. Preliminary indications are that the program has doubled the number of individuals receiving treatment. Impact evaluation will include an assessment of the incidence of drug use and criminal behavior among the subject population, indicators of social functioning, and use of detention facilities.

Dispute Resolution Programs

Dispute resolution programs differ from other types of diversion programs in that they focus on resolution of the interpersonal conflicts that lead to criminal charges, instead of the treatment of defendants. These programs have grown dramatically since their origins in the late 1960s. Encouraged by Department of Justice funding as well as the American Bar Association, the American Arbitration Association, and the Institute for Mediation and Conflict Resolution, dispute resolution programs grew to number almost two hundred by the mid-1980s. At present hundreds of programs are in operation.

Dispute settlement programs attempt to informally resolve (that is, without court action) the hassles that arise from everyday life.[25]

Using techniques such as conciliation, arbitration, mediation, and fact finding, they serve to speed up the justice process. These low-cost alternatives to formal proceedings are generally within the reach of most citizens.

The underlying assumption of these programs is that many interpersonal conflicts can be resolved informally and that informal resolutions can be achieved more effectively and efficiently than resolutions reached through a formal court process. Citizen dispute resolution programs attempt to avoid the problems often associated with the judicial system: long delays, high costs, and citizen dissatisfaction.

Most dispute resolution programs focus on problems between people with ongoing relationships; such programs frequently handle disputes among neighbors. Quarrels between strangers are difficult to mediate because little incentive exists to work out some sort of mutually satisfactory agreement. Dispute resolution programs usually focus on relatively nonserious crimes, although some programs mediate felonies.

Complainants are referred to these programs from a variety of sources, such as friends, co-workers, police, prosecutors, and judges. Some dispute resolution programs engage in active case management and attempt to maintain participation in the program after the initial complaint has been made. Others view attrition as a sign that the dispute may have been informally resolved and even encourage the dropping of complaints by requiring a cooling-off period prior to a hearing.

Some programs request both complainants and respondents to sign agreements to participate in the hearings. Although the agreements are voluntary, they may encourage disputants to recognize the seriousness of the proceedings. A few threaten respondents with prosecution if they fail to appear for hearings. However, programs cannot force respondents to agree to an informal dispute settlement, and no program that deals with criminal matters attempts to utilize compulsory arbitration.

Voluntary mediation is the principal method of resolving disputes involving criminal matters.

It begins with the provision of an opportunity for each disputant to air his or her grievance; in some cases, solutions can be negotiated at this time. If no agreement is reached, the mediator then assumes the role of a neutral third party and questions the participants to clarify the issues and identify areas of agreement and disagreement. The mediator may introduce potential solutions, either in individual sessions or with all participants present. Sometimes private sessions are effective. Concessions are often more easily made out of the presence of other disputants, where face-saving requirements might inhibit any action that has the appearance of giving in.

Dispute resolution programs use a variety of personnel, including lay citizens with special training in mediation, law students, lawyers, and professional mediators. Each type of employee or volunteer had advantages and disadvantages. Citizens may be difficult to recruit and train, but they can be expected to know and understand their communities. Law students may be plentiful and can be trained within the academic setting, but they may lack the maturity to handle difficult negotiations and may be available for only a short time. Lawyers and professional mediators may be highly skilled and experienced, but they are also costly.

Neighborhood Justice Centers   In 1980, the Institute for Social Analysis reported the results of a lengthy study of three experimental programs known as **Neighborhood Justice Centers.** The evaluation of these programs, which were established in Atlanta, Georgia, Los Angeles, California, and Kansas City, Missouri, was designed to answer several critical questions concerning community dispute settlement programs. Researchers wanted to know if they resolved problems better, quicker, or more inexpensively than the court system.

The study reported that the programs handled almost four thousand cases during their first fifteen months of operation.[26] Almost half the complaints were not resolved by the NJCs because respondents refused to participate,

could not be contacted, or one or both of the disputants failed to appear for hearings. About one-third of the cases were resolved through mediation. The remaining cases were settled by the disputants prior to a hearing. The resolution rate was comparable to that achieved by courts handling similar cases.[27]

Disputants whose complaints were resolved by the NJCs were overwhelmingly satisfied with their experiences and reported that the agreements reached through mediation were still in force six months after the hearings. NJCs also appeared to resolve complaints more quickly than the courts. In Kansas City, for example, dispute settlement typically was accomplished in less than one-fourth the time required for court settlement.

Although judges in all three cities supported the NJCs, they reported no significant decline in their caseloads. At an average cost of $150 per case, the NJCs were competitive with current court costs. The research team recommended increased public awareness and use of NJCs as a means of lowering case management costs.

Twenty years later, all of the NJCs are still in operation, but many in altered forms, which mirror changes in the community mediation field. Atlanta's center is now known as the Justice Center of Atlanta and has handled more than forty thousand cases since its founding. Its mission has expanded to include binding and nonbinding arbitration services, group facilitation, school-based peer mediation, conflict resolution training, technical assistance, and related services. The Los Angeles center is now part of Dispute Resolution Services Inc., and its services include community mediation, court programs, school mediation, attorney-client services (focusing on the resolution of fee disputes), and training and consultant services. The Kansas City program continues to operate much as originally established and has resolved more than fifteen thousand disputes since its founding.[28]

Modifications of the original NJCs reflect changes that have occurred throughout the

Program Focus

A Court-Referred Mediation Case Involving Juveniles

A clear lesson learned by many mediation centers is that relatively minor incidents can escalate into lethal conflicts. One center case involving high school students illustrates the value of mediation in preventing serious violence among disputing parties. The case involved escalating conflict that arose from a name-calling incident between two students. The student who delivered the initial verbal insult was subsequently beaten by friends of the student who was insulted. The friends of the beaten student, in turn, retaliated. Soon a series of fights escalated to the point that some of the students in one of the groups engaged in a drive-by shooting of a pedestrian.

Individuals on both sides of the argument swore out warrants, and the district attorney's office prepared to charge the individuals involved in the drive-by with attempted murder. However, the police were unable to identify the gunman in the drive-by shooting, and the prosecutor feared that the case would have to be dropped for lack of evidence. As a result, the prosecutor and the court decided to refer the case to mediation to resolve the growing conflict.

Fifteen students and 30 parents agreed to participate in mediation. Student peer mediators ensured that everyone involved attended the hearing. Backgrounds of the students involved varied widely; some were from upper-middle-class families; others were from economically disadvantaged families in public housing. The two groups of students were able to air their concerns in the mediation session, which was held at a local church. After 1 hour, members of the two groups apologized to one another. Apparently, neither group had wanted the dispute to escalate to the extent that it did, but the students were unable to resolve the matter in a way that ended the conflict, while still allowing the students to maintain their reputations and self-respect. In light of the student apologies and the expressed interest of the youths to move past the conflict, the parents of 11 of the 13 students who had sworn out warrants agreed to have the cases dismissed. The parties signed forms requesting dismissals, and the court subsequently dismissed the 11 cases at the prosecutor's recommendation. The parents of the other two students who had sworn out warrants were not ready to settle the dispute at mediation and decided to proceed to court. When they reached court, however, the two cases were dismissed by the judge because the two groups had reconciled at the mediation session.

Source: Daniel McGillis, "Resolving Community Conflict: The Dispute Settlement Center of Durham, North Carolina," National Institute of Justice Program Focus (Washington, D.C.: U.S. Department of Justice, 1998), p. 3.

dispute resolution field in the last decade. Growth has been the result of continuing concerns with limits on access to justice from court backlog, delay, and costs; the reduced role of traditional dispute resolvers (extended families); acceptance of the appropriateness of alternative dispute resolution procedures; increased interest in community members in resolving disputes; external funding; and the role of national, state, and local organizations.

The growth of community policing provides many increased opportunities for dispute resolution. Some indications exist that calls for police diminish when mediation services are available. Some established dispute resolution programs are developing innovating relationships with community policing to enhance referrals and resolve conflicts. Also, more than four thousand schools offer dispute resolution programs. Many specialized materials have been developed and catalogs of available coursework have been distributed to fifty-five thousand schools by the Safe and Drug Free Schools program, to encourage use of its funds for peer mediation and conflict resolution.[29]

In many ways, dispute resolution programs have exceeded expectations. They have markedly diversified their range of services, created impressive state-level support systems, and increased nonprofit community mediation. Momentum is growing for internationalizing the dispute resolution movement. Comparative research results continue to be impressive, especially regarding participant satisfaction and speed of resolution, but results regarding the impact on court caseloads are less positive. Meanwhile, public awareness and funding remain low, caseloads continue at relatively low levels, and most programs are concentrated in small number of states, especially California, New York, and North Carolina.[30]

North Carolina Mediation Programs   Some of the best research on dispute resolution was conducted by the Institute of Government at the University of North Carolina at Chapel Hill.[31] North Carolina currently operates numerous **mediation programs**. Mediation is conducted by trained volunteers, and efforts are coordinated statewide by the Mediation Network of North Carolina, which works to secure funding and provides technical assistance. The programs accept criminal cases— primarily misdemeanors, such as simple assault, simple larceny, and criminal trespass, which almost always involve complainants and defendants with ongoing interpersonal relationships. Minor civil cases, divorce and family mediation, public policy problem solving, workplace dispute resolution, and school mediation are also accepted.

The North Carolina study compared the resolution of disputes in three counties with mediation programs with the handling of disputes in comparable counties without such programs. The research found that most cases eligible for mediation were not mediated, because disputants were unaware of the programs. In a few cases complainants were reluctant to participate, but the most significant factor seems to be the intake strategy of the mediation program. The most effective program (in Henderson) used personal contact with disputants in court sessions, a review of recently served arrest warrants, and a review of court dockets to obtain referrals. Once cases did enter mediation, the success of all programs was similar; about 90 percent of cases were successfully mediated.[32]

The study addressed the difficult question of whether the mediation programs diverted eligible cases from trial and conviction, thus reducing costs to courts and disputants. Because of its effective intake system, only the Henderson program appeared to have diverted a significant number of cases and reduced the number of trials. Two of the programs appeared to have slowed the processing of cases by about one month.

Disputes in counties without mediation programs resulted in informal arrangements with defendants to dismiss charges in about 25 percent of the cases. These agreements were similar to those of mediated settlements but were achieved without the formal skills of a mediator or the emphasis on placing disputants on an equal footing. Four months after court disposition, records showed that the filing of new charges was less than 5 percent for both mediated and nonmediated cases. Mediation did appear to significantly increase the procedural satisfaction of disputants, over and above the gains achieved by case outcome.

Based upon this research, many of the programs in North Carolina have now implemented more aggressive intake procedures. The Durham center, for example, conducts a daily review of new warrants issued at the court clerk's office.[33] Incoming complaints at the district attorney's office are also reviewed. Presentations have been made to new police officers and line personnel to encourage police referral. The dispute center handles many routine interpersonal disputes, as well as a large number of worthless check cases. These cases involve making arrangements for payments by the check writers to the recipient of the worthless check. The program has been so successful (handling more than two thousand cases annually) that the chief superior court judge and chief district court judge have ordered all worthless check cases to be referred to mediation before a warrant is issued, thus drastically reducing the number of case filings.

These findings illustrate one of the truisms of diversion programs. Good diversion programs can achieve their objectives. But without careful monitoring, diversion programs can provide a more costly (and sometimes a more bureaucratic) alternative to the informal, yet effective, unprogrammed discretion generally present in the criminal justice system.

Victim-Offender Mediation Programs Victim-Offender Mediation Programs (VOMP) generally focus as alternatives to juvenile court processing. Today, more than one hundred Victim-Offender Mediation Programs are in operation in the United States; twenty-six, in Canada.[34] Mediation consists of a four-step program:

1. Case intake from referral.

2. Individual meetings in preparation for mediation.

3. Mediation—a discussion of the incident(s), what occurred, how people feel, a negotiation of restitution, and so on.

4. Follow-up—monitoring restitution and completion of terms of the agreement.

A four-state study of VOMPs in Albuquerque, New Mexico, Minneapolis, Minnesota, Oakland, California, and Austin, Texas, provides some insight into the experiences of victims and defendants. Three of the programs were privately supported, while the fourth (Austin) was operated by the local juvenile court. All such programs worked closely with the local juvenile courts and offered a variety of services, including parent-child mediation, school mediation, and mediation for youth in correctional facilities.

Interviews with subjects indicated that victims and offenders had different expectations entering into mediation. Victims were most likely to describe an interest in recovering their losses and helping the offender, followed by an interest in being able to explain to the offender the effect of their crime. Offenders were interested in making things right and having the opportunity to apologize.

Following mediation, victims expressed positive feelings about what had occurred, reflected by such statements as:

It gave us a chance to see each other face to face and to resolve what happened.

It reduced my fear as a victim because I was able to see that they were young people.

Offenders' remarks were similar:

After meeting the victim I now realize that I hurt them a lot. . . . [T]o understand how the victim feels makes me feel different.

I realized that the victim really got hurt and that made me feel really bad.[35]

Although the small number of cases studied in each jurisdiction made it impossible to determine if re-offending was reduced by the mediation process, mediated agreements did produce a higher degree of completed restitution agreements than other forms of court-ordered restitution.

Contemporary Pretrial Release Programs

Program Models

The two primary alternatives to the traditional practices of jail or bail are on recognizance releases and conditional, supervised releases.

Recognizance Releases   On recognizance releases are known as personal recognizance, promise to appear (PTA), and release on recognizance (ROR). All these measures provide for the release of a defendant prior to trial based on his or her signed promise to appear for all scheduled court proceedings. No restrictions are placed on the defendant's pretrial conduct and no financial payments are required.

Judges are responsible for the final ROR decision. Pretrial release program staff provide information and recommendations to the court regarding individual defendants' eligibility and their appropriateness for release. Suitable defendants are usually released at their initial appearance. In some jurisdictions, however, the pretrial release agency is authorized to release persons charged with minor offenses without judicial involvement, and defendants can be released prior to initial appearance.

In the federal judicial system and a number of state programs, OR releases are accompanied by the execution of an unsecured appearance bond. This form of bond, also known as a personal recognizance bond, requires defendants to pay the full amount of the bond only if they fail to appear in court. The unsecured appearance bond therefore serves as a fine to be paid if the defendant fails to appear.

Conditional and Supervised Pretrial Release
These nonfinancial forms of release impose restrictions on a defendant's conduct as a prerequisite for his or her release. Such conditions may require him or her to report regularly to the pretrial release agency, to restrict travel out of the jurisdiction, or to obtain counseling or vocational training. Some method of monitoring the defendant's compliance with pretrial release conditions is usually authorized. **Conditional release** generally refers to release under minimal or moderately restrictive conditions with little monitoring of compliance. **Supervised pretrial release** refers to a release that imposes more restrictive conditions, often including the defendant's participation in therapeutic or rehabilitative programs, and that entails considerable supervision.

Third-party release is a form of supervised pretrial release under which an appropriate third party assumes responsibility for the defendant's court appearance. The third party may be the accused's friend, relative, employer, attorney, or clergyman; a volunteer; or a social services agency. The third party may arrange for or provide specialized therapeutic or helping services in addition to supervisory ones.

Supervised pretrial work release is in reality a form of pretrial detention. Defendants are, however, freed during working hours so they may continue employment during incarceration.

Conditional and supervised pretrial releases are usually obtained at the defendant's initial appearance. In some jurisdictions, however, supervised pretrial release is seen as a means of providing release for individuals who fail to obtain ROR and who are jailed following initial appearance. Conditions imposed on release usually are nonfinancial, although in some jurisdictions deposit bail is occasionally used as a condition of release.

A sequential illustration of pretrial release alternatives to detention as they might be available to prospective defendants is presented in Figure 2-2. The earliest and least restrictive form of release is the summons; pretrial work

Figure 2-2   Pretrial Alternatives to Detention

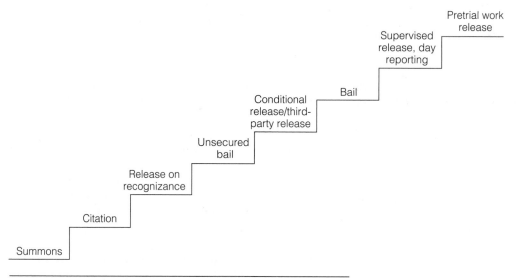

Source: Adapted from *Instead of Jail: Pre- and Post-Trial Alternatives to Jail Incarceration: Volume I* (Washington, D.C.: U.S. Government Printing Office, 1977), p. 8.

release is normally the defendant's last hope of release. Although all alternatives are generally not available in every community, a combination of approaches is normally employed. The most frequently utilized forms of release for felony defendants in the largest counties are described in Table 2-1.

Basic Services of Pretrial Release Programs

In determining the appropriate form of release, judges frequently rely upon the services of pretrial release programs and their staff. These agencies provide five basic services: interviewing, verification, screening for release eligibility, release recommendations, and follow-up procedures. The Enhanced Pretrial Services Project, undertaken by the National Association of Pretrial Service Agencies, studied more than two hundred programs to determine how federal, state, and local pretrial release programs conduct their operations.[36]

Interviewing   Pretrial release programs interview defendants to obtain information about their backgrounds and community ties. Defendants may be interviewed prior to being booked, after booking but before their initial appearance, or following initial appearance. The time at which an individual is interviewed determines the time at which he or she can be released and how much detention time must be served. Individuals interviewed prior to or immediately following booking may be released after spending less than a few hours in custody; individuals interviewed after initial appearance may spend a number of days in jail.

Most offenders are interviewed prior to initial appearance but after booking. This means that some offenders spend unnecessary time in detention, but it also allows programs to focus their efforts on offenders most likely to be detained.

The selection of defendants for pretrial release interviews varies from program to program. Today about two-thirds of pretrial release

Table 2-1   Percent of Felony Defendants in the Seventy-five Largest Counties

| Most Serious Arrest Charge | Released before Case Disposition | | | | | | | | | | Detained until Case Disposition | |
| | Financial Release | | | | | Nonfinancial Release | | | | | | |
	Total Financial	Surety Bond	Deposit Bond	Full Cash Bond	Property Bond	Total Non-financial	Recog-nizance	Con-ditional	Un-secured	Emer-gency Release	Held on Bail	Denied Bail
All offenses	29%	18%	7%	2%	2%	34%	24%	6%	4%	1%	30%	6%
Violent offenses	29	19	6	2	2	26	19	5	1	—	35	10
Murder	16	7	4	0	5	5	0	4	1	0	23	61
Rape	31	13	9	4	4	22	14	7	1	0	37	12
Robbery	18	11	4	1	2	25	21	3	1	—	48	13
Assault	37	25	8	2	2	28	22	5	2	—	29	5
Other violent	28	20	5	2	2	28	18	9	2	0	33	4
Property offenses	28	17	7	2	2	36	24	7	5	1	30	5
Burglary	22	14	5	2	2	24	15	6	3	1	47	6
Theft	31	20	6	3	2	36	22	10	5	1	29	5
Other property	28	16	8	2	2	45	34	5	7	1	19	4
Drug offenses	28	18	7	1	2	37	25	5	6	1	29	5
Trafficking	30	21	7	1	1	31	23	5	2	1	32	6
Other drug	26	15	7	2	2	42	27	5	9	1	25	4
Public-order offenses	31	18	9	3	1	40	29	6	5	—	22	7
Weapons	32	14	13	3	2	32	18	4	10	—	26	5
Driving-related	30	20	5	3	2	41	31	7	2	0	16	5
Other public-order	21	14	6	1	—	34	28	5	1	0	23	12

Note: Data on type of pretrial release or detention were available for 90% of all cases. Detail may not add to total because of rounding.

— = Less than 0.5%

Source: Timothy C. Hart and Brian A. Reaves, *Felony Defendants in Large Urban Counties* (Washington, D.C.: U.S. Department of Justice, Bureau of Justice Statistics, October 1999), p. 17.

programs exclude defendants based on the nature of their charges. Persons charged with violent crimes, sex crimes, or drug sales are most likely to be excluded from program consideration. Those being held on a warrant or detained from another jurisdiction are usually not eligible for program participation. Persons who have a record of prior failures to appear in court,

who have no local address, or who are arrested while on probation or parole are also frequently excluded from consideration.

Verification   One of the most important functions of pretrial release programs is verification of the information received from a defendant. Although judges can interview defendants at the bail hearing about their backgrounds, employment histories, and community ties, they cannot reliably determine the accuracy of the defendant's statements. Pretrial release agencies check the accuracy of defendants' statements by contacting persons named as references and asking them for information about the defendant. They also review the defendant's criminal history.

Screening for Release Eligibility   All pretrial release programs use some criteria for determining if an interviewed defendant is a good candidate for release. Most programs use the same standards for release originally developed by the Manhattan Bail Project. These criteria focus on the defendant's community ties (measured by employment status, length of residence, and family contacts), prior record, and current charge (Table 2-2). The defendant's appropriateness for release is then measured against these criteria on a predetermined point scale or may be considered subjectively and individually by program staff. Some programs employ a combination of these approaches.

The most pronounced change in pretrial release programs in the last decade has been the greater focus on offender dangerousness in the screening process. More programs are now setting restrictions on which offenders can be interviewed and placing greater weight on the significance of the offense charged and prior record in release decision making. However, little research has been done on the effectiveness of pretrial release program assessment schemes since they were first implemented. Few programs have attempted to validate their interview methods or schedules.

Release Recommendations   About three-quarters of pretrial release programs make recommendations to the court instead of simply supplying the judge with the information that has been gathered. About 20 percent make recommendations when requested. About 40 percent have the authority to release offenders, who are usually misdemeanants but are often felons as well.

The early pretrial release programs generally made recommendations only on the appropriateness of OR releases. Now more than three-quarters of all programs have available both supervised and financial releases (Table 2-3). Deposit bail is available as an option in more than half of all state and local programs and virtually all federal jurisdictions.

The most frequently utilized recommendations are for nonfinancial conditional releases. Four out of five state and local programs and almost all federal agencies use them. Financial releases are still widely employed, with deposit bail options utilized less frequently than other forms. The explanation for this finding, given the long-stated interest of pretrial programs in reducing financial inequities in release, is said to be simple expediency, coupled with the increased costs of supervised forms of release.

The conditions most frequently imposed automatically on releasees are presented in Table 2-4. About half of all state and local programs make referrals for mental health counseling, and more than one-third impose time and travel restrictions. Both drug testing and substance abuse monitoring are imposed by about 25 percent of programs, as is the requirement that defendants report regularly to the program. Electronic monitoring is imposed by only about 5 percent of programs. The average length of pretrial supervision across all state and local programs is 112 days; for federal programs, 150 days.

Follow-up Procedures   Most pretrial release programs take steps to ensure that persons re-

Table 2-2   Criteria Used in Pretrial Release
and Detention Eligibility Background Investigation

	Number of Programs		Percent of Programs	
Criteria[a]	State/Local	Federal	State/Local	Federal
Local address	189	55	94.0	87.3
Employment/education or training status	187	62	93.0	98.4
Length of time in community	186	62	92.5	98.4
Prior convictions (any type)	183	62	91.0	98.4
Currently on probation, parole, or has another open case	179	63	89.1	100.0
Prior court appearance history	176	62	87.6	98.4
Length of time, current address	169	58	84.1	92.1
Living arrangements	165	60	82.1	95.2
Prior arrests	159	57	79.1	90.5
Use of drugs and/or alcohol (self-report)	137	62	68.2	98.4
Length of time at prior local address	134	51	66.7	81.0
Identification of references who could verify and assist defendant in complying with conditions of release	132	51	65.7	81.0
Physical/mental impairment	131	53	65.2	84.1
Parental status and/or support children	126	51	62.7	81.0
Ownership of property	120	61	59.7	96.8
Visible signs of symptoms of drug or alcohol use (interviewer observation)	117	60	58.2	95.2
Comments from arresting officer	113	48	56.2	76.2
Income level or public assistance status	97	44	48.3	69.8
Comments from victim	96	26	47.8	41.3
Possession of telephone	68	21	33.8	33.3
Someone expected to accompany defendant to arraignment	32	12	15.9	19.0
Drug test (urinalysis) results	21	44	10.4	69.8
Miscellaneous	34	5	16.9	7.9

[a] Question answered by 196 state/local and 63 federal programs, which is the
basis for the percentages. Programs consider multiple variables simultaneously.
Source: National Association of Pretrial Services Agencies, *Pretrial Services and
Practices in the 1990's: Findings from the Enhanced Pretrial Services Project*
(Washington, D.C.: Bureau of Justice Assistance, 1991).

leased prior to trial appear at their scheduled court proceeding. Generally, the defendant receives a notice during a regular supervision contact. The defendant may also be mailed a reminder of the date, time, and place of his or her court proceeding; some programs contact the defendant by phone.

Pretrial release programs usually attempt to locate defendants who fail to appear and attempt to persuade them to return voluntarily. The variety of approaches used when defendants fail to appear is described in Table 2-5. Slightly over half the programs provide information to the police on such occasions. Although the

Table 2-3   Release Options Available in Jurisdictions

	Number of Programs		Percent of Programs	
Type of Release[a]	State/Local	Federal	State/Local	Federal
Personal recognizance[b]	190	61	94.5	95.3
Cash bond	155	64	77.1	95.3
Supervised release	151	63	75.1	100.0
Surety bond	140	60	69.6	98.4
Deposit bail	115	62	57.2	96.9
Personal bond	93	59	46.3	92.2
Third-party surety	79	60	39.3	93.8
Other	37	9	18.4	14.1

[a] Multiple responses were permitted. Percentages are based on 64 federal programs and 201 state and local programs.

[b] Category also included own recognizance (OR) as well as release on recognizance (ROR).

Source: National Association of Pretrial Services Agencies, *Pretrial Services and Practices in the 1990's: Findings from the Enhanced Pretrial Services Project* (Washington, D.C.: Bureau of Justice Assistance, 1991).

authority is rarely utilized, the staff of about 13 percent of the pretrial release programs are empowered to arrest defendants who fail to appear.

The Milwaukee Court Intervention Unit

The Court Intervention Unit (CIU) in Milwaukee, Wisconsin, serves a community with significant jail overcrowding problems and illustrates the variety of programs that may be found in a contemporary pretrial services agency. The local jail that was built for 459 housed 650 in the 1980s. Although a hospital was renovated to give additional jail space, it provided insufficient relief to overcrowding. A special master, appointed when the jail was found to be unconstitutionally overcrowded, released more than five hundred persons in one month to reduce overcrowding.[37]

The pretrial services unit, referred to as the Court Intervention Unit, consists of twenty-nine staff organized into teams, including:

Bail Evaluation Unit This unit interviews virtually every adult misdemeanant and felon. Interview questions elicit information about employment, family, and ties to the community. Information on the defendant's past and present criminal charges is available on computer. The unit calculates a risk score for each defendant and provides that information plus a release plan to the court. Options include release on bail; nonfinancial release with no supervision, medium supervision, or restrictive supervision; or no release. The team also reviews the cases of persons who have failed to make bail and brings appropriate cases back for a new bail hearing.

Court Notification This unit maintains contact with defendants by mail and phone. Defendants are encouraged to appear in court and cajoled to appear immediately if a date has been missed.

Pretrial and Intense Supervision This unit requires visits to the team's offices by the defendant; frequent, sometimes daily, phone contacts; and, in some cases, electronic surveillance. The team makes referrals to drug and alcohol programs, monitors attendance at such programs, and reports to the court before every pretrial

Table 2-4 Automatic Conditions Placed on Defendants

	Number of Programs		Percent of Programs	
Automatic Conditions[a]	State/Local	Federal	State/Local	Federal
Return to court as scheduled	132	37	71.3	57.8
Obey all laws/refrain from criminal activity	109	64	58.9	100.0
Abstain from illicit drugs and alcohol	43	17	23.2	26.6
Routine reporting to pretrial program/probation officer	59	13	31.9	20.3
Change of address notification	50	16	27.0	25.0
Travel restrictions	55	13	29.7	20.3
No contact with victim	32	11	17.3	17.2
Other[b]	49	6	26.5	9.4
Seek/maintain employment	20	3	10.8	4.7
None	12[c]	0	6.5	0.0

[a] Multiple responses were permitted. Percentages based on 64 federal and 185 state and local programs.

[b] Four primary conditions at the state and local level: retain/keep in contact with attorney; waiver of extradition; notify program of rearrest; and obey court orders.

[c] Includes one program that places no automatic condition on its prerelease defendants but does on other classes of defendants.

Source: National Association of Pretrial Services Agencies, *Pretrial Services and Practices in the 1990's: Findings from the Enhanced Pretrial Services Project* (Washington, D.C.: Bureau of Justice Assistance, 1991).

appearance of the defendant. This team also monitors defendants released by the special master.

Drug Testing This unit initially tested the urine of most felony arrestees during a federally funded project. Loss of funds eventually curtailed program tests.

Mental Health This unit identifies mentally ill arrestees entering the system and those already in custody to determine if they can be moved to mental health treatment options. Chronically mentally ill individuals are often involved in minor property offenses or public or private disorderly conduct. The unit also does follow-up to ensure that appropriate services are secured for the offenders.

Operating While Intoxicated Unit This program assists in getting offenders into alcohol treatment during the nine-month period that normally occurs between arrest and trial.

Other units of the Wisconsin Correctional Service that are not specifically dedicated to pretrial defendants coordinate with other pretrial service programs. These include efforts to provide substance abuse treatment, community support for the mentally ill, and community service.

Research on Pretrial Release Programs

The most recent comprehensive research on pretrial release programs found that two-thirds of state and local agencies and three-quarters of federal programs track the failure-to-appear rates of releasees.[38] Forty-two percent of state and local programs and 60 percent of federal projects also track re-arrest rates. Of those programs that monitor such data, 75 percent reported failure-to-appear rates of 10 percent

Table 2-5 Steps Taken to Contact
Defendant If the Defendant Fails to Appear in Court

Steps Taken by Program[a]	Number of Programs		Percent of Programs	
	State/Local	Federal	State/Local	Federal
Phones defendant urging return to court	99	40	63.9	74.1
Assists police in locating defendant	80	38	51.6	70.4
Sends letter to defendant urging voluntary return to court	66	17	42.6	31.5
Tries to locate defendant who has apparently left the jurisdiction	51	18	32.9	33.3
Places defendant back on the court calendar	42	4	27.0	7.4
Locates defendant and quashes the warrant	34	1	21.9	1.9
Makes home visit to defendant urging return to court	26	30	16.8	55.6
Program staff may arrest	20	2	12.9	3.7
Request court to issue bench warrant/file with court[b]	17	3	11.0	9.3
Miscellaneous[c]	26	11	16.8	20.3

[a] Multiple steps may be undertaken and total exceeds the 54 federal programs and 155 state and local programs that responded to this question and form the basis for the percentage.

[b] Not included in the original list of responses in the questionnaire. Therefore, this response, in all likelihood, under-reports the number of programs that may take such steps.

[c] Included in this category are the following: contact family, friend, or references (collateral contacts); notify defense or prosecuting attorney; act at court direction; and no steps taken.

Source: National Association of Pretrial Services Agencies, Pretrial Services and Practices in the 1990's: Findings from the Enhanced Pretrial Services Project (Washington, D.C.: Bureau of Justice Assistance, 1991).

or less, with federal rates being even lower. This compares favorably with the national average rate for reappearance of 85 percent. No difference was reported regarding the failure-to-appear rates achieved by different forms of pretrial release.

Re-arrest rates were reported by sixty-six of the programs. One-half reported re-arrest rates of 5 percent or less. One out of four programs reported rates of 10 percent or above. These reported rates of pretrial crime are higher than those reported in previous program surveys but are within the same range reported in today's national statistics, which vary from a low of 3 percent to a high of about 20 percent.

All of the effectiveness data described here are self-reported. Definitions of outcome may vary, so caution should be exercised in interpreting these findings. On the whole, however, these reports are not inconsistent with other research findings.

The project's most significant finding pertaining to pretrial release program evaluation is the overall lack of any comprehensive research effort. Two-thirds of programs have conducted no research in the last five years. This is twice the number of "research inactive" programs identified by a study conducted a decade ago. The one in five programs that did conduct some form of research was as likely to focus on program cost as program effectiveness.

Electronic Monitoring

Electronically monitored supervision (EMS) is used in only a small number of pretrial release programs; a brief illustration of one such program may show why that is the case. Over a four-year period between 1986 and 1990, Lake County, a suburb north of Chicago, electronically monitored one-third of all defendants released.[39] Sex offenders and other serious offenders were the most likely to receive this form of supervision. The number and type of defendant who received EMS were primarily a function of the amount of equipment the jurisdiction owned.

Research indicated that EMS had a higher violation rate than other forms of release— 19 versus 14 percent. This difference resulted primarily from the higher technical violation rate of EMS offenders, not a difference in rates of pretrial crime. This finding raised questions about the utility of a device that primarily detected technical violations, misconduct that pretrial release program staff may prefer to ignore, given the limited alternatives available for sanctioning technical violators. Meanwhile, EMS releasees were much less likely to fail to appear, but this finding probably stemmed from the fact that the more serious offenders (who usually have high reappearance rates) had been selected for EMS.

These findings indicate that jurisdictions should consider carefully the results they wish to achieve before implementing electronic monitoring.

Research on Drug Testing and Urine Monitoring

Drug testing was first utilized in the criminal justice system in the mid-1960s as a means of identifying individuals in need of treatment.[40] In later years, public concern about the linkage between drug use and crime led to the introduction of urine monitoring as a means of ensuring compliance with the requirements of community supervision. This expansion was also spurred by the development of on-site drug testing programs, which allowed criminal justice agencies to do their own testing. Urine monitoring was specifically identified as a condition of pretrial release in the 1984 Federal Bail Act. Drug use among pretrial releasees had been a focus of concern almost since program inception. Offender drug use was routinely assessed in most programs through the use of self-reports, observation, and reference to past arrests and convictions for drug use. During the 1980s, the use of drug testing to monitor offender behavior gained increased acceptance, in recognition of the unreliability of self-reports of drug use and the nation's growing concern with drug crime. Funded by the National Institute of Justice, the District of Columbia Pretrial Services Agency (DCPSA) was the first pretrial program to implement its own on-site testing program. Drug testing was utilized both to inform the release decision and to ensure compliance with release conditions. Five more sites were funded as a result of the program's success.

A National Institute of Justice study of the six sites attempted to determine the value of drug testing as a means of forecasting pretrial misconduct. Results were mixed—in some jurisdictions testing positive for cocaine was related to a higher failure to appear; in others, testing positive for opiates was related to a higher probability of re-arrest. No finding was observed in all of the sites. One of the biggest problems appeared to be the test's inability to distinguish between casual and heavy drug users.[41]

This multisite study was useful as much for its identification of the nature of implementation problems as for the light it shed on the effectiveness of urine monitoring. Implementation problems were numerous, including the difficulty of integrating urine monitoring within an existing program structure, creating a computerized tracking system, locating a convenient testing facility, informing new and rotating personnel about the program, and scheduling court hearings for those who did not comply. Meanwhile, the effectiveness of urine monitoring in predicting failures to appear and deterring drug

Issues in Community Corrections

Pretrial Release Options Proposed

Deland—Get thrown in jail in Volusia County and one of two things generally happens.

You pay a bail bond company to cover the cost of getting out, or you are diverted to a pretrial release program run by the county, which lets you out for free, but with stringent controls.

Some people would like to see that equation whittled down to the point that the release program, which costs taxpayers about $1.2 million per year, is used only by those who can't come up with the money to bail out.

The issue has set up a showdown between the bail bond industry and the court system, including many lawyers, and caught the ear of Volusia County Council members.

"I'm interested in some alternatives," said Councilwoman Ann McFall. "The cost of the pretrial release program is more and more each year. It's getting out of hand."

On the other side, judges and lawyers say the program serves a valuable function in the judicial system, ensuring accused criminals are monitored pending their trials and upholding the innocent-until-guilty legal principle.

"This isn't some bleeding-heart liberal, get-out-of-jail-free card as some people are portraying it," said Richard Orfinger, outgoing chief judge of the 7th Judicial Circuit. "This is how we meet our statutory obligation."

The debate in Volusia County follows a trend in the state. Hillsborough County changed to a largely scaled-back program several years ago, which now serves as a prototype to reform advocates.

It left a pretrial release program in place, but stipulated that no one arrested could be enrolled in the program, and thereby released for free, until 72 hours passed.

The intent is for as many people as possible to get antsy and pay their bail, making themselves and the bail bond companies—rather than the county government—responsible financially until the trial.

The county issue is separate from a proposed state law that Gov. Jeb Bush vetoed two weeks ago. That proposal, an amendment to a bill that would allow those accused of DUI [driving under the influence] manslaughter to be held without bond, would have barred any public money from being used on pretrial release programs.

Bush issued the veto, citing the same issues brought up by Orfinger: that pretrial release

use is still uncertain. Urine testing may be useful in selecting defendants for release, but tests may not be equally predictive of re-arrest and failure to appear in all jurisdictions. Similarly, regular drug testing may not decrease pretrial misconduct for all defendants, but some may benefit.[42]

Although many pretrial programs have the authority to test for drugs, most do not. Problems that restrict the use of drug testing include:

- The expense of testing.

- Inconclusive findings on the value of testing.

- Objections to intruding in a defendant's privacy.

- Objections to imposing sanctions on defendants who continue to test positive.

- The belief among some programs that testing, with its strict requirements for chain of custody, is too difficult to implement.

programs include monitoring, drug testing and other controls that much better supervise accused criminals. The Volusia County Council asked Bush to veto the measure.

Advocates cite statistics that say as many as 80 percent of those arrested bond out before 72 hours pass, and a large number of cases are actually disposed of by guilty pleas.

Bail bond companies have pressed the issue around the state, including Volusia County. They say their industry is set up to take the financial risk of the accused not showing up for court, and government should not bear that burden.

"It's gotten to where it's hurting the bail industry for sure," said Bob Barry, who owns a bail bond company in Daytona Beach. "You've got . . . people being paid for the job we should do. Bondsmen do this at no cost, except for the user fee."

Barry, who has lobbied County Council members on the issue, said he does not want to get rid of the pretrial release program, but scale it back to the point it is only used for those who cannot afford to bail out in 72 hours.

There are serious flaws with that program, Orfinger said.

First is a legal issue. State law requires everyone accused of a crime to be released pending trial, and bail is supposed to be used only when it is absolutely necessary to ensure the person returns for trial, Orfinger said.

Forcing everyone to spend three days in jail unless they bail out may violate the intent of the law, Orfinger said.

The controls on released defendants are not even debatable, Orfinger said. They are carefully watched through pretrial release, and they're not monitored at all when bailed out.

Orfinger said there is a place in the system for bondsmen, but their motivation in this case is obviously for financial gain.

Barry acknowledged he and others stand to make more money, but said it benefits everyone.

"If I'm driving a bigger car next year, it's because I saved the county money," Barry said.

County staff members are researching the issue and will report their findings to the council in about two months.

Source: Matt Grimson, "Pretrial Release Options Proposed," Daytona Beach, Florida, *News-Journal*, June 21, 1999, pp. 1–2A. Reprinted with permission.

In 1995, President Bill Clinton directed the implementation of drug testing for all federal arrestees before the decision is made for pretrial release and the development of a policy to encourage states to adopt and implement the policy. In 1996, drug testing was implemented in twenty-four of the ninety-four federal districts. Congress provided $25 million in increased funding to the states in 1997 to support the use of effective drug testing in all stages of the criminal justice system, beginning with pretrial release.[43]

Today, the options for drug testing include:

1. Setting up an in-house analyzer-based testing facility.

2. Contracting with a private laboratory.

3. Sending specimens to a private laboratory.

4. Testing with the sweat patch.

5. Hair analysis.

Each of the methods has strengths and weaknesses. On-site programs may serve many criminal justice agencies. Hand-held devices, which include credit card-size instruments that allow drops of urine to be deposited into a sample well, provide results in a few minutes, usually through the use of a color change. Tamper-proof sweat patches can detect drug use within forty-eight to seventy-two hours and are usually worn by the subject for a week. Forty federal agencies are currently using the sweat patch, which, like hair analysis, has the advantage of reducing the intrusiveness of testing but with less cost and more reliability (Table 2-6).

A review of current federal and state pretrial drug testing programs indicates a variety of program components (Table 2-7). The federal projects and the DCPSA are the only programs to test subjects prior to release. The remaining projects use drug testing to ensure compliance with release conditions. Most of the federal programs use the hand-held devices, while local programs use on-site facilities. Most programs test defendants on a regular basis, although some utilize irregular scheduling to minimize the likelihood of a false negative. All programs make referrals to treatment if the defendant continues to test positive.

Alternatives to Diversion and Pretrial Release

One of the principal arguments against the diversion programs is that offenders are not held accountable by the criminal justice system. Because of this concern, diversion programs are limited to a relatively small proportion of offenders. A preferable alternative might provide some measure of accountability, while still diverting the offender from the more harmful effects of criminal justice processing.

Arguments against pretrial release programs have similarly reduced their impact. Concerns about failure to appear and the potential for pretrial crime keep many offenders unnecessarily in jail. An alternative to the potential risk of pretrial release would be to provide expedited processing of offenders through the criminal justice system.

For many observers, a perfect solution to the limitations of both programs would involve the speedy processing of offenders through a justice system that provided accountability, but a concern for both diversion and pretrial release offender and community welfare. Many drug courts began experimenting with such efforts, focusing less on treatment and diversion and more on differentiated case processing of offenders.

Differentiated Case Processing

Differentiated case processing utilizes specialized courts to expedite the processing of their cases so as to minimize both the costs of confinement and the problems that incarceration visits on offenders and their families.[44] Drug courts developed to reduce disposition time are today found in Chicago, Milwaukee, New York, and Philadelphia. Others in Michigan and Minnesota combine both treatment and expedited case management programs.

Drug courts designed to achieve more speedy trials aim to:

- Concentrate drug case expertise in one courtroom.

- Reduce the time to disposition, without compromising due process or public safety considerations.

- Reduce the pending drug felony caseload.

- Reduce pressures on nondrug caseloads by diverting drug felonies out of mixed-calendar courtrooms.

- Increase overall trial capacity.

To achieve these goals, expedited drug case management programs have to establish clear guidelines for consistent and reasonable plea

Table 2-6   Drug Testing Cost Comparison

Testing Approach	Average Cost Per Screen[a]	Included in the Cost	Not Included in the Cost
In-house analyzer-based instrument	$5–$10	Chemicals to conduct test.	Equipment purchase or lease. Facility renovation. Maintenance contract for analyzer. Specimen collection supplies. Staff time to collect specimen, calibrate and maintain analyzers, mix chemicals, and run test. Confirmation of positive result.
In-house, hand-held device	$12.50–$22.50	Testing device.	Specimen collection supplies. Staff time to collect specimen and run test. Confirmation of positive result.
Private, local certified laboratory	$80–$120	Conducting test. Confirmation of positive result.	Specimen collection supplies. Staff time to collect specimen. Costs to transport specimen to laboratory.
Private, nonlocal certified laboratory	$10–$15	Conducting test.	Specimen collection supplies. Staff time to collect specimen and prepare it for shipment. Shipping expenses. Confirmation of positive results.
Sweat patch	$23	Price of the patch. Shipment to the laboratory. Conducting the test.	Confirmation of positive results.

[a]These costs vary depending on a number of factors. For example, many programs that use analyzer-based in-house testing find that testing costs average $1 per test, or $5 for a five-drug screen. Other programs with a low volume of testing might pay higher costs for reagents. Volume may also affect the prices of testing at an outside laboratory.

Source: D. Alan Henry and John Clark, *Pretrial Drug Testing: An Overview of Issues and Practices* (Washington, D.C.: U.S. Department of Justice, Bureau of Justice Assistance, July 1999).

offers aimed at the early resolution of cases. Firm and consistent dates for plea negotiations, trials, and the filing of motions are also important. And efforts are made to bypass the grand jury process wherever possible.

Results to date indicate that processing time for felony drug cases and detention time can be greatly reduced, producing significant cost savings. The Milwaukee drug court was able to increase the rate of drug trials, because of increased trial capacity and reduced disposition times in the general felony courts. Other courts have found that expedited processes reduced the percentage of drug cases going to trial.

Maximizing the utility of drug courts requires the cooperation of the defense attor-

neys, who may resist the pressure placed on their defendants to accept pleas and the reduced time they are permitted to prepare motions, assess the state's case, and prepare detention, disposition, or sentencing alternatives. New York City's drug courts were found to be underutilized, because the majority of defendants refused to waive grand jury rights, rejected early plea offers, and sought trials through regular adjudication. Nevertheless, cases processed through the New York drug courts had significantly faster processing times—less than one-half those of similar cases processed through regular courts.

The success of both forms of drug courts, those that focus on treatment and expedited case processing, has led to the development of

Table 2-7   Drug Testing Program and Policies by Site

Site	Test to Identify Users	Drug Panel	Testing Approach
		Federal[a]	
Arkansas (Eastern)[b]	Before initial appearance.	Amphetamines, cocaine, opiates, PCP, and marijuana.	Analyzer-based in-house facility.
Minnesota[c]	Before initial appearance.	Amphetamine, benzodiazepine, cocaine, marijuana, and opiates.	Analyzer-based in-house facility.
Nebraska	Before initial appearance.	Amphetamines, cocaine, marijuana, opiates, and PCP.	Hand-held in-house testing for initial test, supervision tests sent to private laboratory.
New Hampshire	Before initial appearance.	Amphetamine, cocaine, marijuana, and opiates.	Hand-held in-house testing.
New Jersey	After initial appearance.	Amphetamines, cocaine, marijuana, opiates, and PCP.	Hand-held in-house testing plus sweat patch.
North Carolina (Middle)	After initial appearance.	Amphetamines, cocaine, marijuana, and opiates.	Hand-held in-house testing.
		Local	
District of Columbia	Before initial appearance.	Amphetamines, cocaine, methadone, opiates, and PCP.	Analyzer-based in-house facility.
Maricopa County, Arizona	N/A	Wide range of drugs.	Contract with TASC program, analyzer-based facility.
Milwaukee County, Wisconsin	N/A	Cocaine, marijuana, and opiates.	Analyzer-based in-house facility.
Pima County, Arizona	N/A	Amphetamines, cocaine, and opiates.	Analyzer-based facility operated by probation.
Prince George's County, Maryland	N/A	Cocaine, opiates, and PCP.	Analyzer-based in-house facility.

[a]Represents a sample of federal programs currently conducting pretrial testing.
[b]One of the original federal pilot drug testing sites; it is now participating in Operation Drug Test.
[c]One of the original federal pilot drug testing sites.
N/A = Not applicable; TASC = Treatment Alternatives to Street Crime.

Confirmation Policies	Supervision Testing Practices	Program Responses to Continued Positives
	Federal[a]	
Retest all positives. Positives sent to private laboratory if defendant does not admit use.	Defendants tested once a week on a regularly scheduled basis; tested randomly once every other week.	Refer to treatment. Court action requested after second positive.
Positives sent to private laboratory if defendant does not admit use. When defendant admits use, sample is saved for one month.	Defendants tested twice a week at outset. Frequency gradually reduced to twice a month, then once a month if results are negative.	Testing frequency increased and treatment offered. Court action may be requested if continued positive.
Positives sent to private laboratory if defendant does not admit use. Exception: All amphetamine positives sent to private laboratory.	Three testing phases: defendants tested four to six times a month in Phase 1 and one to two times in Phase 3. Defendants call hotline every day to see if they must report for test.	Response depends on defendant's history and cooperation with treatment. Responses range from reprimand to requesting court action.
Positives sent to private laboratory if defendant does not admit use.	Defendants tested randomly, at officers' discretion, but at least once a month.	First positive, address with defendant. If continued positive, testing frequency increased, refer to treatment.
Positives sent to private laboratory for confirmation.	Testing frequency determined on case-by-case basis; can be regularly scheduled appointments or random.	Refer to treatment at first positive. Court action requested only if defendant does not cooperate with treatment.
Positives sent to private laboratory for confirmation.	Defendants randomly tested once a week for at least four weeks. If results are negative, frequency reduced to twice a month.	Second positive, refer to treatment. If continued positive, court hearing requested, but no recommendation made at hearing.
	Local	
Retest all positives. Positive specimens frozen. If result challenged, specimen sent to local laboratory for confirmation.	Defendants tested once a week on a scheduled basis.	Increase frequency of testing or refer to treatment. Court action requested if defendant misses treatment or testing appointments.
Confirm if defendant does not admit use and results may lead to revocation.	Defendants tested twice a week on a scheduled basis. Frequency reduced if results are negative.	Notify court, request revocation if continued positive.
Retest all positives. Positive specimens sent to private laboratory if defendant does not admit use.	Assigned to one of three supervision levels depending on overall risk. Testing frequency determined by level placement.	Second consecutive positive result after the initial supervision test reported to court along with treatment plan.
Retest all positives. Defendant can request and arrange for independent confirmation.	Defendants tested at least twice a week on a scheduled basis; occasionally called in or field visit made for a random test.	First positive refer to treatment and notify court of action taken. Schedule court hearing if continued positive.
First positive during supervision period sent to private laboratory for confirmation if defendant does not admit use.	Defendants tested once a week on a scheduled basis if in treatment; twice a week if not in treatment.	Continue to work with defendant if in treatment. Court action requested if defendant refuses treatment or misses testing appointments.

Source: D. Alan Henry and John Clark, *Pretrial Drug Testing: An Overview of Issues and Practices* (Washington, D.C.: U.S. Department of Justice, Bureau of Justice Assistance, July 1999).

Program Focus

In New York City, a "Community Court" and a New Legal Culture

At 10 A.M., John Megaw's cubicle on the sixth floor is crowded with luggage—tote bags, a plastic sack of kid's clothes, and a black canvas duffel bag the size of a small refrigerator. These are the worldly possessions of Carol, whose daughter Tamika, an energetic 3-year-old, is running around the office as if it were her personal playground.

Megaw shoves his way past the luggage to his desk. If all goes as planned today, Carol and Tamika should be going home. Several days ago, the 20-year-old was again arrested for prostitution, sentenced to 4 days of community service, and put to work in the mail shop down in the basement. There she met Willie Figueroa, the ex-con who runs the shop and doubles as informal counselor to his workers.

Carol trusted Figueroa and confided to him that she was in over her head. She and Tamika had hooked up with some friends and come to New York from Kansas 10 months ago, high on dreams of a fast life and easy money on the streets of Manhattan. Now she had crashed: A pimp took her money, abused her when she complained, then took Tamika and held her hostage when Carol tried to leave. She had finally managed to get Tamika away from him and moved in with a girlfriend. But now she wanted out. The quieter streets of Kansas City

and a room at her mother's house never looked better.

Figueroa spoke to Megaw, head of social services for the court, who mobilized his team. They discovered that Carol had an outstanding warrant on a previous arrest, which would have to be pled out. But they believed they could get everything resolved if she promised to leave town. They called her mother and made sure she would be willing to take her daughter back. They then got the Traveler's Aid Society to pay for one-way bus tickets to Kansas City. Today they would take the whole matter before the judge.

The Sentencing Process

By 12 noon, Carol and Tamika have settled in the acupuncture room. "I was down to 100 Centre Street three times" on arrests for prostitution, she says. "The first time they gave me 2 days community service."

Did she do it? "No," she giggles. She just ignored the order, and nothing more happened. "I never received a warrant or anything."

At her second appearance downtown, "They let me go because they kept me in there so long" before arraignment—a sentence New York judges call "time served."

specialized courts with an even broader focus—that of addressing communitywide issues in the expedited disposition of minor offenders. These courts aim to remove offenders from the mainstream of criminal justice processing, thus providing a more targeted use of criminal justice resources as well as a means to provide a more

individualized and community-based form of justice.

Community Courts

Community courts provide the newest form of community corrections. They incorporate the

After the third appearance, she again ignored her community service assignment. The judge issued a warrant, but the police never followed up.

And how does the community court compare with that?

"Every time that I came in here and had to do community service, I did it. There was only one time that I didn't finish up the 2 days, and they gave me a warrant, like, the next day."

The Court's Impact

At 4:30 P.M., Megaw huddles in the courtroom with Carol's attorney and the assistant district attorney at the bench while Carol stands at the defense table, Tamika squirming in her arms. Megaw and Carol's lawyer explain the deal: She will plead guilty to the outstanding warrant from downtown if the judge will sentence her to the 4 days of community service she has just completed. Then Megaw will make sure she goes home. The prosecutor agrees, the judge nods, and all return to their places.

Asked how she pleads to the charge of loitering for purposes of prostitution, Carol answers "guilty" in a barely audible voice.

"I understand you have plans to go a different route in life," Judge Kluger says, looking down at her from the bench. "I wish you luck."

The court appearance went well enough, but Megaw still is not free to relax. Carol now has to get herself, her daughter, and all that luggage down to the Port Authority terminal, pick up her money from Traveler's Aid, purchase tickets, and board a bus.

He assigns two of his more muscular caseworkers to accompany her, partly to help tote the bags and partly because he fears her pimp might show up and try to abduct her back into the life. "Prostitution is a rough business," Feinblatt observes as he watches the crew assemble in the corridor. Carol makes a last phone call to Willie Figueroa, thanking him for everything and bidding him goodbye, before she hauls Tamika onto the elevator loaded with all her stuff.

Megaw's phone does not ring until 8:45. His men report that they were unable to make the 6 o'clock bus and had to wait for the next one, which did not leave until 8:30. The choice of escorts turns out to have been prudent: As they waited for the bus, Carol had indeed spotted her pimp, who often spends his evenings in the terminal. He had seen her, too, but after sizing up her companions, he decided to keep his distance.

Source: David C. Anderson, *In New York City, a "Community Court" and a New Legal Culture,* National Institute of Justice Program Focus (Washington, D.C.: U.S. Department of Justice, February 1996), pp. 2–12.

goal of expedited case processing with the objectives of community justice. Along with community policing, this model of criminal justice system operations encourages the development of collaborative, problem-solving relationships with the community and partnering with other criminal justice system components. Specialized courts provide immediate intervention, nonadversarial adjudication, hands-on judicial involvement, treatment programs with clear rules and structured goals, and a team approach that brings together the judge, prosecutor, defense counsel, treatment provider, and correctional staff.[45] Drug courts are clearly the best example of this approach, but an increasing number of courts have begun to serve more diverse offenders.

Manhattan's Midtown Community Court

The recently initiated Midtown Community Court, whose jurisdiction sprawls across more than 350 blocks of Manhattan, contains everything it needs inside one building: a courtroom, a social services center, a community service program, and innovative computer support.[46]

The court, housed in the old Magistrate's Court building next to the Midtown North police station, follows a philosophy that differs from most traditional courts in its handling of misdemeanor arraignments. Focusing on low-level offenses that can bring down a community's morale, it holds defendants immediately accountable for their crimes. But the court also addresses issues underlying the problems that led to the offenses by providing social services such as drug treatment. The building itself presents an atypical image: It has clean, light-filled rooms that are secured with glass panels, not steel bars.

In its first fourteen months, from October 1993 to December 1994, the Midtown Community Court arraigned 11,959 defendants. Today the court hears about fifty-five to sixty new cases per day. Court administrators are proud of the 75 percent completion rate for sanctions for community service, which, they say, exceeds that of other busy urban courts. Another indicator of effectiveness is that about 16 percent of offenders sentenced to community or social services have voluntarily continued with such programs as drug treatment, HIV testing, and employment counseling after completing their sentences.

Community service projects are assigned in conjunction with police officers and with the Times Square Business Improvement District. The police consider the court a new resource for their community policing activities, and the business association provides work for ten to twenty offenders per week. Many projects involve painting and cleanup tasks to improve the neighborhood and deter crime.

For those who draw a short community service sentence of one day's work, it is possible to be arrested, to be arraigned, and to complete six hours of community service in less than twenty-four hours. The court aims to make accountability swift because delays between conviction and assignments to fulfill community service sentences have allowed many to avoid their obligations. This efficiency wins the praise of police as well as court administrators, defendants, and residents.

The custom-designed computer software, the high community service compliance rates, and the positive response of defendants to the social service programs may indicate promising strategies. A National Institute of Justice-sponsored evaluation of the court is being conducted.

Adjudication Partnerships

Much of the innovative programming being developed today focuses on court and community-based partnerships. Growing interest in collaboration and problem solving has prompted the Bureau of Justice Assistance to identify Key Elements of Successful Adjudication Partnerships.[47] These partnerships involve prosecutors, public defenders, and judges working together (often alongside police and corrections officials) to identify problems, develop goals and strategies for addressing the problems, and oversee implementation of the plans. Such partnerships may work to enhance the development and use of intermediate sanctions, expedite case management, create a specialized court or program, or to set up a coordinating committee to establish better communication and interagency and community problem solving.

For example, a Detroit, Michigan, judge established a handgun intervention program, working with volunteers that included probation officers, police, members of the clergy, and community leaders. The program requires adults charged with felony firearm offenses to attend a four-hour presentation on the dangers of gun violence and its consequences before they are eligible for bail. Other participants attend voluntarily. The program, which is held each Saturday morning, involves police officers, probation officers, and a judge who present a message aimed at raising awareness, reinforcing the need to make positive life choices and take responsibility for one's own life.[48]

In Los Angeles, for example, LA Fast was established to reduce the backlog of superior court trials by expediting the disposition of less serious, nonviolent, first-time felony offenders. Initially the program served only first-time drug possession cases, but it was later expanded to include welfare fraud and escape cases. The district attorney, public defender, and probation officers worked to establish procedures that resulted in adjudication of such cases within three days. Since the establishment of the program, between three hundred and five hundred felony cases per month have been removed from the Los Angeles County court system.

The Jail Utilization Systems Team in Monroe County, New York, meets monthly to discuss local criminal justice issues and jail population levels. The program regularly collects data to monitor and evaluate its performance on numerous measures of jail population and implementation of release and sentencing alternatives for nonviolent offenders.

It employs a three-pronged strategy: early screening process for first-time, nonviolent offenders by a senior district attorney who recommends cases for early disposition; a multifaceted effort to develop and enhance an array of graduated sanctions for pretrial releasees and convicted misdemeanants; and the development and implementation of an integrated justice information system. Accomplishments include significant reduction in case processing time and average length of jail time for nonviolent offenders.[49]

In Oregon, the Willamette Criminal Justice Council was established to facilitate the efficiency and effectiveness of interagency communication among criminal justice services. The council initiated a strategic planning process, which developed mission and vision statements, short- and long-term goals, and a plan to implement high-priority projects. As a result of its success, the Oregon legislature requires all counties to appoint a local public safety coordinating council. Its successes include the creation of a citizens committee appointed to work with government officials on community issues, the development of a child abuse investigation protocol, the creation of a data systems integration project, the development of a victimization and juvenile justice crime prevention plan, and the demonstrated growth in minority outreach efforts. Working with twenty-six other counties, the group also led the development of a case management system for use by all of the counties, thus saving costs from duplication of development efforts.[50]

Summary

Diversion and pretrial release programs work to remove offenders from traditional criminal justice system processing. While pretrial release programs serve the limited objective of removing arrested persons from jail prior to trial, diversion programs work to direct offenders into treatment of dispute resolution or to expedite case processing.

For both of these programs, the determination of eligibility criteria and the selection of appropriate participants are key issues. While few would question the need for all offenders to be prosecuted or jailed prior to trial, the issues of public safety and accountability must also be addressed. Because of concern about these matters, diversion and pretrial release programs have changed considerably since their initial development and expansion in the 1960s and 1970s.

Pretrial release programs provide an equitable means of releasing offenders who pose no threat of flight or danger to the community. Bail systems put the burden of decision making regarding release and bonding onto the private sector. Although the commercial bail process has many problems, it is unlikely to disappear any time soon.

Today, diversion programs also serve offenders in need of drug treatment or those engaged in interpersonal conflict. Community courts have developed as a means of providing expedited case processing while ensuring community involvement in efforts to provide accountability. Creative adjudication partnerships are developing in some jurisdictions as a way to combine the authority of the courts with the assets of the community.

Key Words and Concepts

adjudication partnerships

bail

Break the Cycle (BTC)

commercial bonding

community courts

conditional release

differentiated case processing

discretion

dispute resolution programs

diversion programs

drug courts

mediation programs

Neighborhood Justice Centers

pretrial release programs

release on recognizance

supervised pretrial release

Treatment Alternatives to Street Crime

Questions for Discussion

1. What are the goal and the reasoning behind the idea of diversion? How has this idea been used throughout history, and how has it changed in recent years?

2. What is the overall goal of bail programs, and how does the use of bail bonding agencies create punishment in the absence of legal guilt?

3. What is the goal of a drug court? How do drug courts differ from traditional courts, and how effective are these courts in reducing the caseloads of the other courts in the system?

4. What factors would be important in the release on recognizance decision? Why would you consider these important given the goals of the release process?

5. How do courts that offer expedited case reviews and faster trials enhance the process of criminal justice? What are some of the negatives that could be associated with this form of processing?

For Further Reading

Alexander, Rudolph, Jr., *Counseling, Treatment, and Intervention Methods with Juvenile and Adult Offenders* (Belmont, Calif.: Wadsworth/Thompson, 2000).

Dillingham, Steven D., Reid H. Montgomery Jr., and Richard W. Tabor, *Probation and Parole in Practice*, 2nd ed. (Cincinnati, Ohio: Anderson Publishing, 1990).

Simon, Jonathon, *Parole and Control of the Underclass 1980–1990* (Chicago, Ill.: University of Chicago Press, 1993).

Chapter 3

Probation

Defining Probation

Objectives of Probation

Court Use of Probation

Historical Perspective

Trends and Issues in Probation

Probation Today

Federal Probation

Research on Probation

Summary

Probation has long been one of the most popular forms of correctional disposition, and it remains the most widely used sentence handed down by the court. Between 1997 and 1998, the number of persons on probation increased from 3,296,513 to 3,417,613, an increase of 3.7 percent. Regionally, the largest increase was in the western United States (6.6 percent in a single year). Today, as in the past, almost two-thirds of all convicted offenders serve their sentences on probation. As a sentencing option, probation is designed to keep the offenders in their home community while carrying out the sanctions imposed by a court. These sanctions include controlling the offenders in the community by utilizing both deterrence and supervision and by providing treatment resources drawn from their immediate community environment to assist in law-abiding behavior. As with other forms of corrections, probation has grown enormously in the last decade and its clientele have changed from primarily misdemeanor offenders to both misdemeanants and low-level felons (Table 3-1).

Defining Probation

Probation is a multifaceted concept and may be defined in several different ways. First, probation is a sentencing option or sanction. Second, probation refers to a process. Third, probation has been called an organizational structure (that is, a subsystem of corrections).

Table 3-1   Change in the Number of Adults on Probation, 1990–1998

Year	Annual Increase	
	Number	Percent Change
1991	58,238	2.2
1992	83,139	3.0
1993	91,450	3.3
1994	77,961	2.7
1995	96,839	3.2
1996	87,135	2.8
1997	131,517	4.2
1998	121,100	3.7
Total increase 1990–1998	747,379	28.0
Average annual increase 1990–1998	93,422	3.1

Source: Thomas P. Bonczar and Lauren E. Glaze, *Probation and Parole in the United States, 1998* (Washington, D.C.: U.S. Department of Justice, Bureau of Justice Statistics, 1999).

Fourth, probation refers to the special legal status of offenders.

In considering probation as a sentencing option or sanction, the American Bar Association Model Adult Community Corrections Act of 1984 provides a useful definition of typical (as opposed to intensive) probation supervision. Probation is a judicially imposed criminal sanction permitting court supervision of the offender within the community.[1] Probation as a sentence consists of four essential elements. First, probation is now viewed as a stand-alone sanction imposed by a judge, instead of a deferred or suspended form of punishment. Second, the offenders remain in the community while serving their sentence. Third, while the offenders remain in the community, their freedom is conditional, subject to court-imposed restrictions on their behavior. Fourth, these offenders are supervised by a representative of a probation organization who serves as an agent of the court. The probation agency's responsibility is to ensure that the probationer follows the conditions set forth by the judge. If the offender violates those conditions, the probation organization is responsible for initiating the revocation of probation and returning the offender to custody.

Probation as a process has two main functions—the preparation of **presentence investigation (PSI) reports,** which are ordered by the court or prescribed by law, and the handling and management of persons placed on probation. The PSI screens offenders for suitability for community placement (based on a risks and needs assessment) and the case management process ensures that the offender carries out the sanction imposed by the court and does not pose a risk to the public.

Probation is considered a major subsystem of corrections and is by far the largest component of the correctional process. This perspective views probation as a bureaucratic structure and employs a systems analysis in understanding the impact and role of probation within the criminal justice system.

Viewing probation as the offenders' legal status focuses attention on the restricted nature of the offenders' liberty. Although offenders remain free in the community, the conditions placed on their freedom, the specialized supervision provided by a probation officer, and the ever-present threat of revocation and subsequent incarceration distinguish them from the average free citizen. For example, they may be required to obtain employment, attend drug counseling programs, and pay restitution. Offenders may also have certain constitutional liberties restricted or suspended, based on the nature of their offense. Probationers may also be subject to unannounced searches and drug testing.

Objectives of Probation

The major objectives of probation have changed over the past decade. They include:

- To protect the community.

- To carry out the court-ordered sanctions imposed by the court.

- To assist offenders to change.

- To support crime victims.

- To coordinate and promote the use of community resources in an efficient and effective manner.[2]

In the 1960s and 1970s, one of the principal objectives of probation was the reintegration of the offender into the community. This focus led to the release of some offenders who later proved dangerous to the community and, which engendered a loss of faith in the probation screening process. Today, while reintegration is still considered an objective, it is not considered more important than **community protection.** Community protection is an objective that probation shares with all other forms of correctional programs. One of the basic purposes of corrections is to provide public protection by aiding in the prevention of crime. Probation addresses this goal by preparing the PSI report to assist judges in sentencing and supervising offenders. The PSI permits the probation agency to screen offenders according to the risk or danger they may pose to the community. Those viewed as posing a threat to the community can be identified and referred to more secure placements, usually involving incarceration. The supervision functions of probation also protect the community by monitoring probationers' behavior and removing them from the community when they violate the conditions of their probation. In assisting offenders to change, probation also serves two important functions. First, it attempts to determine the offenders' special needs through an assessment process. Second, it tries to meet those needs through the use of community resources. In many jurisdictions, the probation officer serves as an advocate and facilitator for the offender to receive specialized treatment resources available in the community. The probation agency then monitors the offender receiving the service as well as the agency providing the service. Private community agencies play a major role in the delivery of correctional services, such as drug and alcohol treatment, job training, and vocational education, for probationers.

In addressing the objective of enforcing court-ordered sanctions, the probation organization is responsible for informing and educating the offender regarding the orders of the court and expectations regarding the offender's compliance with the rules and regulations of probation. Probation officers typically are required to enforce restitution requirements as well as to do drug testing. They also make sure offenders find and retain jobs, respect restraining orders, and so on.

The probation agency also plays an important role in supporting crime victims. As part of the PSI function, probation officers in many states collect information regarding the impact the criminal offense had on the victim. This information, referred to as a victim impact statement, is presented to the sentencing court and is considered when the court sentences an offender. It is particularly valuable when the court issues a restitution order. Probation officers also play a key role in ensuring that restitution is paid by the offender to the victim. The probation agency is usually responsible for collecting the debt.

Court Use of Probation

Understanding the probation process first requires knowledge of how offenders are placed on probation. Judges can sentence individuals to terms of probation in several ways, depending upon state legislative provisions.

First, judges may sentence an offender directly to a term of probation as a sentence. Second, under certain statutory provisions, a judge can impose a prison sentence on an offender and then suspend it and place the offender under probation supervision. Under both procedures, the offender's continued presence in the community is contingent upon his or her good behavior. If probation is revoked under the first procedure, the court must set a prison sentence if incarceration is required. Under the second procedure, the probationer whose probation is revoked serves the previously imposed but suspended prison sentence. Depending upon the jurisdiction, time spent in the community may or may not be subtracted from the length of sentence.

Third, the judge defers formal sentencing and places the offender on probation. This choice is usually used with minor or young offenders. If the offender remains law abiding during the prescribed term, the original charges are usually dropped. This procedure is comparable to postconviction diversion. Fourth, in some jurisdictions, the judge sentences the offender to a short jail or prison term or placement in a boot camp prior to commencing a term of probation. This practice is often referred to as a split sentence or shock incarceration. Increasingly this form of sentence is used to toughen up the sanctions of probation.

Historical Perspective

The English Tradition

Probation, like many other major correctional reforms (such as the penitentiary, the indeterminate sentence, and parole), took form in the United States, but it was essentially an outgrowth of several practices found in English common law. Probation developed as a variation of the English practice of the conditional suspension of punishment pending the offender's good behavior. Probation was not the result of a deliberate legislative or judicial act; instead, it was the result of the gradual growth and modification of existing legal practices.[3] These practices were designed to lessen or avoid the imposition of severe penalties on certain offenders. The widespread use of se-

vere punishments in the past, including executions for relatively minor crimes, led judges and prosecutors to search for ways to soften the harshness of legal penalties.[4]

The early procedures used to circumvent the mechanical application of the criminal justice process included the benefit of clergy, judicial reprieve and pardon, and release on recognizance (with and without surety).[5] Each of these practices enabled judicial officials to consider the individual factors of each case, thus avoiding the automatic application of prescribed punishments.

The **benefit of clergy** permitted religious officials to have the privilege of avoiding secular forms of punishment (usually execution) by having their cases transferred to a religious or ecclesiastical court. The prescribed penalties were generally less severe in these nonsecular courts. To receive benefit of clergy, a defendant was required to prove his or her literacy, generally by reading a passage from the Bible. The benefit of clergy proved to be so popular that it was later extended to all persons who could demonstrate literacy. Not surprisingly, abuses set in when illiterates began memorizing the required biblical passage. The practice continued in England until the mid-1800s but was never formally adopted in the United States.

The judicial reprieve was another legal technique that judges used. It involved the temporary suspension of either the sentencing decision or the execution of sentence. During the period of suspension, the defendant could appeal the conviction by seeking a pardon. In some cases, the temporary suspension of punishment was followed by the dropping of criminal proceedings against the individual. In other cases, judges used the reprieve when they were not satisfied with the end result of the criminal proceeding and decided to take independent and contrary action.

The recognizance, with and without surety, provided for the release of an individual from custody during the criminal proceeding. Initially, this release took place prior to trial, but, in some cases, it was extended to other stages, including the postconviction period. The recognizance was used to ensure that the offender would show up for his or her trial and also as a type of sentence for certain offenders. During the 1800s, the recognizance was used in the United States with juvenile offenders when the court felt that imprisonment was inappropriate. In 1836, Massachusetts passed a law that officially provided for the release of minor offenders on recognizance with sureties at any stage of the criminal proceeding. In the United States, the court's power to suspend sentences became a source of controversy. The issue was essentially an argument over the separation of powers. Those supporting the judiciary's position maintained that the precedent of judicial reprieve permitted the courts to suspend sentences indefinitely. Persons supporting the legislative position argued that the courts had the authority to suspend sentences only temporarily, not indefinitely. This view held that, by indefinitely suspending sentences, the courts were usurping legislative prerogative.

This controversy reached a conclusion in 1916, when the U.S. Supreme Court decided in *United States* vs. *Killets* that the federal courts could not indefinitely suspend the imprisonment or execution of a sentence; this was a legislative right. The Court did suggest, however, that Congress had the legislative authority to provide the courts with the discretion to suspend sentences temporarily or indefinitely. Congress enacted legislation authorizing the suspension of prison sentences, and probation was eventually adopted as a formal sentencing option.

Early U.S. Practices

The evolution of probation practices in the United States can be traced to the lower courts of Boston, Massachusetts. In 1841, **John Augustus,** a shoemaker by trade, became interested in helping minor offenders. With judicial approval, Augustus was permitted to stand bail for petty offenders, usually drunkards, and to receive them into his custody. Action against these offenders was deferred until after a specified period of time, when offenders would be ordered to reappear before the presiding judge and account for themselves. Augustus appeared alongside the defendants and gave testimony regarding their conduct in the community. If the defendants had been law abiding, sober, and industrious, the charges were dropped; if they had failed to rehabilitate themselves, prosecution continued. During Augustus's time of service, he was credited with helping more than two thousand persons, few of whom returned to the courts as failures. Augustus was credited with devising rudimentary forms of investigative and screening procedures, supervision practices, and the delivery of social services to offenders.[6] These early accomplishments provided the foundation for modern probation.

Two points regarding Augustus's activities must be emphasized if his work is to be put into proper perspective. First, John Augustus was unpaid and, as such, was probably the first volunteer in probation. His involvement with the offender was a result of a deeply felt personal commitment, and he was free of the bureaucratic trappings of modern probation. Second, his efforts were not universally hailed. He encountered considerable resistance from local criminal justice officials, particularly those who received fees based on the conviction and sentencing of offenders.[7] These officials had a vested interest in processing and convicting as many offenders as possible, and Augustus's activities threatened their source of income. Fortunately, Augustus had enough supporters among the lower court judges to permit his experiment to continue.

After Augustus, the practice of having volunteers work with the courts to divert and assist certain minor offenders continued. In 1878, Massachusetts authorized the first formal probation statute, which provided the mayor of

Issues in Community Corrections

John Augustus and the Beginnings of Probation

"In the month of August, 1841, I was in court one morning, when the door communicating with the lock-room was opened and an officer entered, followed by a ragged and wretched looking man, who took his seat upon the bench allotted to prisoners. I imagined from the man's appearance, that his offense was that of yielding to his appetite for intoxicating drinks, and in a few moments I found that my suspicions were correct, for the clerk read the complaint, in which the man was charged with being a common drunkard. The case was clearly made out, but before sentence had been passed, I conversed with him for a few moments, and found that he was not yet past all hope for reformation. . . . He told me that if he could be saved from the House of Correction, he never again would taste intoxicating liquors, there was such an earnestness in that tone, and a look of firm resolve, that I determined to aid him, I bailed him, by permission of the Court. He was ordered to appear for sentence in three weeks from that time. He signed the pledge and became a sober man; at the expiration of this period of probation, I accompanied him into the court room. . . . The Judge expressed himself much pleased with the account we gave of the man, and instead of the usual penalty-imprisonment in the House of Correction—he fined him one cent and costs amounting in all to $3.76, which was immediately paid. The man continued industrious and sober, and without doubt has been by his treatment, saved from a drunkard's grave."

Source: John Augustus, *A Report of the Labors of John Augustus, for the Last Ten Years, in Aid of the Unfortunate* (Boston: Wright & Hasty, 1852). Reprinted as *John Augustus, First Probation Officer* (New York: Probation Association, 1939), pp. 4–5.

Boston with the authority to appoint a probation officer who would report to the chief of police. Subsequently, several other states adopted similar programs.

The probation movement did not gain real momentum as a social reform and become widely accepted until the early 1900s. In 1900, only six states provided for probation. By 1920, every state permitted juvenile probation, and thirty-three states permitted adult probation.[8]

The rapid growth of probation in the early 1900s has been attributed by some to the *Killits* case, which laid the groundwork for probation legislation. Other observers link probation's growth to its association with the juvenile court movement, which began in 1899 and spread rapidly in the early 1900s. A third explanation attributes the rapid growth of probation to the efforts of the Progressives, a social reform movement of the era.[9] As a social movement, the Progressives were essentially anti-institutional and were in favor of less restrictive forms of social control. They also supported an individualized, case-by-case approach to justice that stressed the informal and flexible rehabilitation of the offender.[10] Probation appeared to be a reform that fit the bill. By 1954, every state had adopted it as a form of correctional disposition.

Trends and Issues in Probation

Administrative Issues

The administrative structure of U.S. probation services reflects the decentralized and fragmented character of contemporary corrections. As with other forms of corrections, no single model or standard has been established for organizing or operating a probation agency. Two issues appear to underlie the variegated structure of probation services.[11] The first concerns the level of government—city, county, or state—responsible for administering the probation agency. The second addresses the appropriate location of probation agencies in the governmental structure. Should they be a part of the judiciary or the executive branch?

Regarding the first issue, studies of governmental responsibility for probation services have identified three basic administrative models: the state-administered, locally administered, and mixed models. In the state-administered model, a state-level agency is responsible for coordinating staffing and funding of probation services statewide. The locally administered model places the responsibility for probation services in the hands of a city or county government. The mixed model involves the state and local forms of government sharing the responsibility for providing probation services. In the mixed model, the state agency is generally responsible for setting standards and monitoring the provision of services to probationers, and localities (usually counties) are given responsibility for day-to-day system operation. Table 3-2 presents a state-by-state breakdown of probation administration by level of government. In thirty-four states, the responsibility for probation services rests with the executive branch; in nineteen states probation is a function of the judiciary either at the state or local level.

More than twenty years ago, after a considered review, the National Advisory Commission on Criminal Justice Standards and Goals in Corrections concluded that the state-administered probation system is superior to the locally controlled model.[12] The principal advantages of this approach are that it ensures uniformity in the quality and delivery of services provided throughout the state and maximizes the efficient use of increasingly scarce resources. Proponents of the alternative models argue that the benefits of local control outweigh the disadvantages resulting from limited resources. Despite this criticism, the trend toward state control of probation has continued.[13]

A national survey commissioned by the National Institute of Corrections found that states chose one of four basic patterns of probation.

1. Probation was a state function and the agency responsible for probation supervision was a state-level agency. Twenty-five states reported this model.

2. Probation was primarily a state function but some local jurisdictions chose to provide their own supervision of probationers. Eleven states use this model.

3. Probation was primarily a local function. Six states reported this model.

4. Probation supervision is a function of local community agencies with a state-level agency providing training, standards, and so on. Eight states were employing this model.[14]

The second major issue focuses on the branch of government that is best suited to administer probation services. Arguments in favor of placing probation under the authority of the courts include the following:

- The organization, structure, and delivery of probation services would be more responsive to judicial concerns.

- Judges would become more knowledgeable regarding the outcome of their decisions and whether the offender complied with the condition imposed by the court.

- Judges would become more aware of the need for resources and, by virtue of their status in the justice system, would be able

Table 3-2 Probation Administration, by Government Level

| State-Level Probation Only | Local Probation Only | State and Local Probation | | |
	County Only	State and Local	State and County	State and City
Alabama	Arizona	Arkansas	Florida	Alabama
Alaska	California	Colorado	Georgia	Kansas
Connecticut	Hawaii	Michigan	Mississippi	Kentucky
Delaware	Illinois	Minnesota	Oregon	New Hampshire
District of Columbia	Indiana	Missouri	Pennsylvania	Oklahoma
Florida	Iowa	Nebraska		
Idaho	Massachusetts	New York		
Kentucky	New Jersey	Ohio		
Maine	Texas	Wyoming		
Mississippi				
Maryland				
Montana				
Nevada				
New Hampshire				
New Mexico				
North Carolina				
North Dakota				
Oklahoma				
Rhode Island				
South Carolina				
Utah				
Vermont				
Virginia				
Wisconsin				
Wyoming				

Source: A Survey of State and Local Probation Systems in the United States: A Survey of Current Practice (Washington, D.C.: U.S. Department of Justice, National Institute of Corrections, 1993).

to effectively argue for increased resources and services.

- Pretrial diversion would be used more if judges were more knowledgeable about probation services.[15]

Making courts responsible for probation services has been criticized because of the lack of judicial expertise in the area of administration and management and because it is feared that court administration could lead to a reordering of probation priorities in such a way that more emphasis would be given to services to the court than to probationers. Probation staff could easily be misused and be required to perform nonprobation tasks such as those performed by bailiffs or law clerks.

Several arguments exist for locating probation services in the executive branch of government.

- It would provide coordination and integration with other forms of corrections. All other subsystems for carrying out court disposition of offenders are in the executive branch. Closer coordination and functional integration with other corrections personnel could be achieved by a common organizational placement, particularly as community-based correction programs increase. Furthermore, job mobility would be enhanced if related functions are administratively tied.

- It would achieve coordination and integration with other forms of human service agencies. The executive branch contains the allied human services agencies, including social and rehabilitation services, medical services, employment services, education, and housing. Where probation also is in the executive branch, opportunities are increased for coordination, cooperative endeavors, and comprehensive planning.

- The executive branch makes decisions involving resource allocations and establishment of priorities. The chief executive initiates requests to the legislature for the appropriation of funds and, by doing so, sets priorities for allocating limited tax dollars. When probation is included in the total corrections system, more rational decisions about the best distribution of resources can be made.

- Probation administrators are in a position to negotiate and present their case more strongly if they are in the executive branch as opposed to the judicial branch where the priorities of the court and judges would in all likelihood come first.[16]

In general, evaluations of the desirability of executive versus judicial administration of probation services conclude that the executive branch is better suited for administrative tasks, while judicially controlled agencies may place more emphasis on the rehabilitative aspects of probation. In many jurisdictions, however, state and local levels of government share this function whether the authority for probation rests in the executive or judicial branch of government. Irrespective of the administrative control issue, agencies and probation agents seem to recognize the dual goals of supervision and rehabilitation, and they work to achieve these goals. [17]

Types of Offenders Served by Probation Services

Probation agencies are responsible for managing offenders other than probationers. A national survey conducted by the National Institute of Corrections reported that in only seven states were probation agencies responsible for supervising only probationers. In most states, probation agencies also supervise parolees.[18] In thirteen states, probation agencies are responsible for supervising both adult and juvenile caseloads. In addition to adults and juveniles on probation as well as parolees, probation agencies are responsible for providing services to felons and misdemeanants' pretrial services and the supervision of interstate compact cases.

Probation is clearly the most frequently used form of correctional disposition. However, in examining the use of probation by the individual states, a great deal of variation seems to exist among the states. Table 3-3 provides a state-by-state breakdown of the total number of persons on probation as of December 31, 1998, the percent change in the probation population during 1998, and the rate of probation per 100,000 adults in the population.

Texas continues to lead the country in the number of offenders on probation with 443,758 and California is second with 324,427. When population variations and probation entries are taken into account, the distribution among the states changes. Washington has the highest probation rate, with 3,619 offenders per 100,000 serving on probation; Kentucky the lowest with

Table 3-3 Adults on Probation, 1998

Region and Jurisdiction	Probation Population, 1/1/98	1998 Entries	1998 Exits	Probation Population, 12/31/98	Percent Change in Probation Population during 1998	Number on Probation per 100,000 Adult Residents, 12/31/98
U.S. total	3,296,513	1,672,910	1,555,762	3,417,613	3.7	1,705
Federal[a]	33,532	14,871	14,861	33,254	–0.8	17
State	3,262,981	1,658,039	1,540,901	3,384,359	3.7	1,688
Northeast	561,707	238,520	209,318	590,684	5.2	1,509
Connecticut	55,989	32,318	30,797	57,510	2.7	2,316
Maine[a]	7,178	:	:	6,953	–3.1	730
Massachusetts	46,430	40,165	40,028	46,567	0.3	993
New Hampshire	4,876	3,760	3,461	5,175	6.1	584
New Jersey[b]	130,565	58,200	55,538	133,227	2.0	2,175
New York	181,105	48,384	38,971	190,518	5.2	1,393
Pennsylvania[b]	108,230	43,091	30,227	121,094	11.9	1,325
Rhode Island[b]	19,648	7,099	6,404	20,343	3.5	2,710
Vermont	7,686	5,503	3,892	9,297	21.0	2,068
Midwest	746,286	441,239	416,898	774,455	3.8	1,664
Illinois	119,481	68,232	55,863	131,850	10.4	1,488
Indiana	96,752	84,946	79,798	101,900	5.3	2,326
Iowa	16,834	17,184	15,571	18,447	9.6	862
Kansas[c,d]	16,339	19,306	19,482	16,163	–1.1	837
Michigan[a,b,e]	165,449	61,755	58,729	172,147	4.0	2,369
Minnesota	94,920	54,671	58,618	90,973	–4.2	2,625
Missouri[b,e]	46,301	17,815	16,110	48,006	3.7	1,191
Nebraska	16,439	12,560	13,062	15,937	–3.1	1,309
North Dakota	2,700	1,622	1,664	2,658	–1.6	559
Ohio[a,b,e]	113,493	74,298	70,719	117,618	3.6	1,406
South Dakota[a,b,f]	3,730	4,098	3,958	3,480	–6.7	648
Wisconsin	53,848	24,752	23,324	55,276	2.7	1,427
South	1,306,375	658,788	638,146	1,327,705	1.6	1,874
Alabama[a,b,e]	38,720	17,279	15,626	44,047	13.8	1,348
Arkansas[g]	28,294	13,668	8,379	33,583	18.7	1,782
Delaware[b]	18,837	11,013	9,820	20,030	6.3	3,548
District of Columbia	10,043	9,840	9,278	10,605	5.6	2,524
Florida[a,b,e]	239,694	144,384	142,007	239,021	–0.3	2,101
Georgia[e]	149,963	60,206	58,304	151,865	1.3	2,702
Kentucky	12,093	6,554	5,755	12,892	6.6	437
Louisiana	35,453	16,136	18,561	33,028	–6.8	1,039
Maryland	74,612	40,179	36,740	78,051	4.6	2,029
Mississippi[c,d,h]	10,997	6,461	5,928	11,530	4.8	578

385 per 100,000 (Table 3-4). These variations may be attributed to a number of factors, but two that are certainly important are differences in sentencing philosophies and the availability of probation resources within the states.

Probation Today

Probation is one of the most widely utilized correctional dispositions. Approximately one-third of all convicted felons in state courts received a sentence of probation. Overall, of the 5.9 million offenders under correctional supervision in 1998, 3.4 million were under some form of probation supervision, as opposed to 1,232,900 in prison. As with other forms of corrections, probation services experienced explosive growth in the past decade. During the 1980s, the number of probationers increased by more than 125 percent. In the 1990s, while the rate of growth was not as extreme, probation still grew 36 percent between 1990 and 1998. Unfortu-

Table 3-3   *(continued)*

Region and Jurisdiction	Probation Population, 1/1/98	1998		Probation Population, 12/31/98	Percent Change in Probation Population during 1998	Number on Probation per 100,000 Adult Residents, 12/31/98
		Entries	Exits			
North Carolina	105,416	59,436	60,154	104,698	–0.7	1,861
Oklahoma[b,e]	28,790	13,912	13,760	28,942	0.5	1,173
South Carolina	43,095	15,280	17,066	41,309	–4.1	1,436
Tennessee[b,e]	35,836	23,368	21,796	37,408	4.4	913
Texas	438,232	196,385	190,859	443,758	1.3	3,140
Virginia	30,002	24,687	24,113	30,576	1.9	594
West Virginia[a,g]	6,298	:	:	6,362	1.0	452
West	648,613	319,492	276,539	691,515	6.6	1,576
Alaska[c,g]	4,212	1,745	1,501	4,456	5.8	1,057
Arizona[b,e]	44,813	28,944	21,177	52,580	17.3	1,544
California[g]	304,531	167,106	147,210	324,427	6.5	1,366
Colorado[a,b,e]	45,499	26,477	21,337	47,792	5.0	1,631
Hawaii	15,401	7,443	7,133	15,711	2.0	1,756
Idaho	6,367	3,138	1,828	7,677	20.6	875
Montana[a,g]	4,683	:	:	5,133	9.6	782
Nevada[b]	11,670	5,794	4,903	12,561	7.6	981
New Mexico[b,e]	8,905	8,926	7,371	10,460	17.5	849
Oregon	43,980	16,876	16,047	44,809	1.9	1,824
Utah	9,519	4,130	4,174	9,475	–0.6	678
Washington[a,b,e]	145,547	45,839	41,123	152,609	4.9	3,619
Wyoming	3,486	3,074	2,735	3,825	9.7	1,088

: = Not known.

[a]Because of incomplete data, the population on December 31, 1998, does not equal the population on January 1, 1998, plus entries, minus exits.

[b]Some data are estimated.

[c]Data do not include absconders.

[d]Data do not include out-of-state cases.

[e]Multiple agencies reporting.

[f]Data are for year beginning July 1, 1997, and ending June 30, 1998.

[g]All data are estimated.

[h]Data do not include inactive cases.

Source: Thomas P. Bonczar and Lauren F. Glaze, *Probation and Parole in the United States, 1998* (Washington, D.C.: U.S. Department of Justice, Bureau of Justice Statistics, 1999).

nately, the number of probation officers hired to supervise these probationers did not keep up with the number of offenders. As a result, caseloads increased dramatically, leading to a probation crowding problem that rivals institutional crowding. More than 3.4 million adult offenders were on probation in 1998 (Table 3-5). States used four different methods of sentencing offenders to probation. The largest single category was a direct imposition of a probation term (51 percent). Ten percent of these offenders received a term of probation with incarceration. In terms of the status of supervision, 77 percent were under active supervision and 9 percent were designated as inactive; an inactive case means that the offender is not being supervised by a probation agency. Ten percent of offenders were considered absconders; absconders are offenders who have failed to report and are in an escape status.

Other highlights of the survey are that 79 percent of offenders on probation were male, 64 percent were white, 35 percent were black,

Table 3-4 Community Corrections Among the States, Yearend 1998

Ten States with the Largest 1998 Community Corrections Populations	Number Supervised	Ten States with the Largest Percent Increase	Percent Increase	Ten States with the Highest Rates of Supervision, 1998	Persons Supervised per 100,000 Adult U.S. Residents[a]	Ten States with the Lowest Rates of Supervision, 1998	Persons Supervised per 100,000 Adult U.S. Residents[a]
Texas	443,758	Vermont	21.0	Washington	3,619	Kentucky	437
California	324,427	Idaho	20.6	Delaware	3,548	West Virginia	452
Florida	239,021	Arkansas	18.7	Texas	3,140	North Dakota	559
New York	190,518	New Mexico	17.5	Rhode Island	2,710	Mississippi	578
Michigan	172,147	Arizona	17.3	Georgia	2,702	New Hampshire	584
Washington	152,609	Alabama	13.8	Minnesota	2,625	Virginia	594
Georgia	151,865	Pennsylvania	11.9	Michigan	2,369	South Dakota	648
New Jersey	133,227	Illinois	10.4	Indiana	2,326	Utah	678
Illinois	131,850	Montana	9.6	Connecticut	2,316	Maine	730
Pennsylvania	121,094	Iowa	9.6	New Jersey	2,175	Montana	782

Note: The District of Columbia as a wholly urban jurisdiction is excluded.

[a]Rates are computed using the U.S. adult resident population on July 1, 1998.

Source: Thomas P. Bonczar and Lauren E. Glaze, *Probation and Parole in the United States, 1998* (Washington, D.C.: U.S. Department of Justice, Bureau of Justice Statistics, 1999).

and 15 percent considered themselves as Hispanic. Almost 60 percent of the offenders were felony offenders. Finally, of the offenders leaving probation in 1998, 59 percent were defined as successful completions and of the failures 9 percent were returned to incarceration with new offenses (Table 3-6).

Federal Probation

The release of offenders from state-level prisons is accomplished using parole boards and legislated release practices. Nearly all states maintain a parole board, which hears cases and makes decisions based on the specific legal guidelines of the state; the opinions of victims, friends, and family members; the other players in the justice system; and the personal progress of the offender. This practice is more difficult in states where the geographic area is large and the population is small, which requires either the inmates or the board to move great distances to attend release hearings. While such a situation is manageable at the state level, when the area of supervision is large and the number of facilities is proportionately greater as well, the problems of management become much more challenging. This was the situation within the federal parole system until the 1970s.

In 1929, the Federal Bureau of Prisons was established, which called for the creation of three facilities and the establishment of a full-time parole board at the federal level. At the time, with three new facilities to supervise (McNeill Island, Washington; Atlanta, Georgia; and Ft. Leavenworth, Kansas), these parole board members were able to review the cases and decide release with minimal difficulties. As the federal system of prisons grew, and the number of facilities and inmates increased, it became more difficult to have a single board review each case and provide release hearings where the inmate was allowed to face the board and present his or her case.

Table 3-5   Adults Under Community Supervision or in Jail or Prison, 1990–1998

Year	Total Estimated Correctional Population[a]	Community Supervision		Incarceration	
		Probation	Parole	Jail	Prison
1990	4,348,000	2,670,234	531,407	403,019	743,382
1995	5,335,100	3,077,861	679,421	499,300	1,078,542
1996	5,482,700	3,164,996	679,733	510,400	1,127,528
1997	5,726,200	3,296,513	694,787	557,974	1,176,922
1998[b]	5,890,300	3,417,613	704,964	584,372	1,232,900
Percent change					
1997–1998	2.9	3.7	1.5	4.7	4.8
1990–1998	35.5	28.0	32.7	45.0	65.9
Average annual percent change					
1990–1998	3.9	3.1	3.6	4.8	6.5

Note: Counts are for December 31, except for jail counts for June 30. All jail and prison counts are for inmates in custody.

[a]A small number of individuals had multiple correctional statuses; consequently, the total is an overestimate. The total for 1998 excludes 36,527 probationers in jail and 13,012 probationers in prison.

[b]The 1998 prison count is an estimate.

Source: Thomas P. Bonczar and Lauren E. Glaze, *Probation and Parole in the United States, 1998* (Washington, D.C.: U.S. Department of Justice, Bureau of Justice Statistics, 1999).

Having parole board members move across states to visit the many federal camps, correctional institutions, and prisons, to decide who had qualified for release, proved both difficult and time consuming. This problem reached a critical point in the 1970s, when the public's appetite for releasing prisoners was low, but federal prison populations were continuing to increase. The federal prison system was encouraged to abandon the board-reviewed parole process and replace it with the existing, but less-utilized, system of court-reviewed probation.

In this system, inmates are brought before a federal court judge who reviews the case and the PSI, which was prepared by the federal probation officer. Based on the recommendations of the members of the justice system, the statements of the offender, and the opinions of the families of the offender and the victim, the judge decides whether the offender is appropriate for release on probation. Like probation at the county level, the court approves a set of guidelines and rules for the offender to follow, and the proba-

tioner is bound by an order of the court to follow them.

Today, federal probation officers do a job that is in many ways different from the old parole model. The **Federal Probation Service** realized that its officers were ill prepared to provide the counseling and therapy that its clients needed to avoid relapse into criminal behaviors. Instead of trying to have officers do something they were not trained to do, it opted to work toward a Community Resource Management Team model. This approach to probation allows the officer to utilize resources in the community to assist with the reform and reintegration of the probationer. In this model, the probation officer would send the probationer out to a clinician in the community to assess the needs of the probationer. Then, based on the report of the clinician, the offenses committed, and the PSI, the officer would create a therapy plan, designed to compensate for the weaknesses and address the needs of the probationer. This plan would be carried out in the community, using clinical and therapeutic resources available in that community. The

Table 3-6   Characteristics of Adults on Probation, 1990 and 1998

Characteristic	1990	1998
Gender		
Male	82	79
Female	18	21
Race		
White	68	64
Black/African American	31	35
American Indian/		
Alask Native	1	1
Asian/Pacific Islander[a]	—	1
Hispanic origin		
Hispanic	18	15
Non-Hispanic	82	85
Status of supervision		
Active	83	77
Inactive	9	9
Absconded	6	10
Supervised out of state	2	2
Other	**	2
Adults entering probation		
Without incarceration	87	77
With incarceration	8	17
Other types	5	6
Adults leaving probation		
Successful completions	69	59
Returned to incarceration	14	17
With new sentence	3	9
With the same sentence	11	9
Absconder	7	3
Other unsuccessful	2	9
Death	—	—
Other	7	11
Status of probation		
Sentence suspended	41	27
Imposition suspended	14	10
Direct imposition	38	51
Split sentence	6	10
Other	1	2

Note: For every characteristic there were persons of unknown status or type.
Detail may not sum to one hundred because of rounding.

** = Not available.

— = Less than 0.5%

[a]Includes Native Hawaiians.

Source: Thomas P. Bonczar and Lauren E. Glaze, *Probation and Parole in the United States, 1998* (Washington, D.C.: U.S. Department of Justice, Bureau of Justice Statistics, 1999).

probation officer would not provide these services directly but instead would place the probationer in these services, monitor compliance and participation, and report to the court the progress of the probationer.

The Federal Probation Service had 33,254 offenders under supervision at year-end 1998. This represents a decrease of 0.8 percent for the year and calculates to a rate of 17 federal probationers per 100,000 citizens.

Research on Probation

Outcome Measures

Assessment of probation has become a major issue in modern corrections. Program performance must be monitored to determine if the program is achieving its goals and if the program is cost-effective in comparison with other forms of correctional disposition. A typical problem with this field involves the definition of both goals and success. Well-conceived and well-designed assessment measures provide specific and useful indicators of program performance, and multiple indicators as opposed to single indicators provide a more accurate assessment of a program's performance and effectiveness. The indicators also serve to provide managers with useful information with which they can enhance the efficiency and effectiveness of programming initiatives.

In corrections, **recidivism** has been relied upon as the sole measure of effectiveness. Recidivism as an outcome measure does not provide much assistance to correctional managers in determining the day-to-day impact of correctional programming. Historically, recidivism represents a single measure used to assess the long-term effect of a correctional program. Several problems are associated with using recidivism as the only measure of a program's effectiveness. These include the wide range of operational definitions for recidivism, the lack of control over postrelease conditions that may unduly influence the effect of a program on an offender, and the lack of consideration of participation in postrelease programming that may positively impact the outcome of the correctional process.

Defining Recidivism

Depending on the definition of recidivism used, the success rates of a recidivism-based study may vary from 30 to 65 percent. Some examples of recidivism used are simple recidivism, specific recidivism, rearrest, reconviction, and reincarceration.

Simple recidivism is based on the idea that any contact with the criminal justice system constitutes a failure of the correctional program. For those that use this outcome measure, success will occur only if the offender manages to stay out of trouble of any form for the duration of a certain period of time following the correctional process. Traffic citations, arrests for crimes unrelated to the original offense, being in the presence of or place where others are being arrested will all constitute a failure of the person and the program. This conservative perspective on recidivism and failure can make otherwise successful programs seem unsuccessful in the final analysis.

Specific recidivism considers the program a failure only if the person commits a crime similar to the original offense. This allows the person who was arrested for drug possession and who subsequently participated in a drug rehabilitation program to be arrested for battery without considering the drug rehabilitation to be a failure. A problem is that the program can define "similar to the original offense" in a manner that makes it virtually impossible for failure to occur. This style of assessment can make a marginal program seem successful, but it can also make the program operators seem unscrupulous if the unusual or creative definition of failure is made public. Is it appropriate to consider a person's drug rehabilitation a failure if he or she is arrested for drunk driving? The answer depends on the social definition of a drug and if the person in question went from drugs to alcohol as a result of the rehabilitation process.

Rearrest, as the term implies, considers the person a failure in the program if he or she is rearrested. The second arrest can be for any crime, simply because the terms of probation usually call for the person to remain law abiding and to engage in only legal activities.

Issues in Community Corrections

ROBO-PO: The Life and Times
of a Federal Probation Officer

Edward J. Cosgrove
United States Probation Officer,
Eastern District of Pennsylvania

U.S. Probation officer Mike Sterling is going into the field on Tuesday. It's a routine day. Anticipated issues to be encountered that day include: assessing the ability to pay and arranging a payment schedule for a sophisticated financial offender, a home inspection of a recently released individual with a history of violence, monitoring some chemical abuse cases, verifying some employment schedules, and rapport building with a few "significant others" who are involved with his clients. He may have time to stop at the local police station and the county courthouse to check some records.

Getting dressed, he dons his bullet-proof vest and appropriate loose fitting clothing to cover it. He checks his weapon, slips it into the holster, and drops the "speed loader" into his pocket. On the other side of the belt is the pager and "capstun." The latter also requires the officer to keep on his person a "Material Data Safety Sheet," which contains information about the chemical properties of this product and concomitant safety instructions.

Before leaving home, he checks his briefcase. There are maps, monthly report forms, financial questionnaires, pay stubs to be returned, criminal extracts ("rap" sheets), his field book, calculator, laptop computer, breathalyzer unit, and miscellaneous stationery. In a separate box are urine bottles, rubber gloves, and the laboratory documentation sheets. In the back seat of the car Mike keeps a copy of the current Sentencing Guidelines and a copy of titles 18 and 21 of the U.S. Code. In any event, the day begins.

In a sense, the tools of our trade have always defined who we are and what we do. It used to be easier. When Gannon and Friday were the role models for police officers, probation officers were an extension of the law. We kept "order" by seeing that people just did the right things. In the '70's, rehabilitation was the goal of supervision. The medical model taught us to diagnose a problem then provide treatment. Help meant counseling; understanding the hardships of poverty, illiteracy, and broken homes; rendering the necessary support to address these symptoms; and coping with the bad feelings and making changes.

As client needs seemed ever expanding, the '80's brought us the philosophy of reintegration. Probation officers could not expect to service all needs; so, the answer became brokering services: identify the problem and make the appropriate referral.

By the end of the '80's the pendulum had swung from primary care to clients to listening to the needs of the community. Mercy was not to be forgotten, but disparity must be eliminated. Guidelines achieved this with a focus on retributive justice, with scant atten-

Therefore, by default, a person who is rearrested has violated these general requirements placed upon him or her by the probation authorities. This perspective, however, is flawed in that society recognizes that many of those in jail will eventually be released and the charges against them dropped. Does this make them innocent? No, but in the eyes of the law they

tion focused on rehabilitation of the individual. The offender will be held accountable. Society will be protected. The probation service responded with the development of Enhanced Supervision. The goals were ranked: enforce court orders, provide risk control, address the correctional treatment needs of the offender.

What does a probation officer do? To this day, I suffer a violent visceral pain whenever I hear some visiting academic discuss the "two hats" of the probation officer: cop or counselor. At last count, we are at 33 hats and the number is growing.

Recording incidents has not proven a good way to explain what we do. We suffer from the "that's different" syndrome. A probation officer interviews a hostile police officer who has just learned that his best informant is being charged with acting as an informant without approval by the court; takes urinalysis tests on offenders suffering from AIDS [acquired immune deficiency syndrome]; instructs a probationer to cease work as a truck driver because of active alcohol abuse and a history of driving under the influence; analyzes corporate finances; or receives a 2:00 A.M. phone call giving notice of a home confinement violation. To each of these, most answer: "That's different." These events are situational, not indicative of the routine. And, of course, they're right. I don't know what's going to happen today; I only know that it's my job to address it.

Requirements for the job used to be listed as good writing skills and the ability to investigate, counsel, and interview. If training speaks the employer's perceptions of what workers need to know, then consider the following programs, which are offered to probation officers: Mental Preparation for Violent Confrontations, Dual Diagnoses, Child Abuse, Hate Groups, Sexual Deviance, Cultural Diversity, Negotiating Skills, Assertiveness Training, Fingerprinting, Ethics, Financial Investigation, Infectious Diseases, Chemical Abuse Seminars, Organized Crime Groups, Lexis/Nexis training. Is this competence or schizophrenia?

A good officer pays attention to the needs of the court, society, and the offender. We best serve the court when conditions imposed are realistic. Ask the average citizen what a probation officer does and you will still hear a comment about caring for juveniles. Offenders have yet to get the picture that their needs are not primary. In the midst of this confusion as to whose expectations we must meet, we still do our best to address the needs of all. The requisite personal and professional growth to meet these multifarious needs makes this an often misunderstood, but nonetheless challenging and rewarding, career.

Source: Edward J. Cosgrove, "ROBO-PO: The Life and Times of a Federal Probation Officer," *Federal Probation*, 58 (3), 1994. This article originally appeared in *Third Circuit Journal*, 12 (2), spring 1994.

are not guilty. Consequently, should rearrest constitute a failure of the person or the program? The answer depends again on the perspective of the program and the society.

Reconviction is similar to rearrest in that they both involve the actions of the criminal justice system. They differ, however, in the individual's degree of guilt. While almost anyone can be arrested for a crime at almost any time, the burden falls to the court to justify the arrest and to make the case that it was deserved by following up the arrest with a conviction. Absent the conviction, an arrest simply constitutes suspicion, a status that defines most persons already on probation. If reconviction is to be viewed as a failure of the probation program, then it must be decided based upon the seriousness of the most recent offense and the relationship of the most recent offense to the original offense.

Finally, there is reincarceration. While more serious than the other definitions for recidivism, it calls into question the efficacy of the probation process for the specific offender. Before a conclusion can be drawn about whether this constitutes a failure of the probation program, two questions must be answered. First, was the later offense related to the earlier offense, which resulted in the probation sentence, and second, was the incarceration in any way related to the offender's status as a probationer? If the probationer status had no impact on the sentence, and if the second offense was the result of unsuccessful programming, then considering the person a programming failure seems appropriate. Absent those conditions, it becomes a judgment issue.

Petersilia and others noted in 1985 "that the success of community corrections should not be based solely on some post-program assessment of behavior."[19] An alternative, as a complement to recidivism, is the use of performance-based **outcome measures.** These measures offer many advantages over the traditional reliance on a postrelease assessment indicator.

Before looking at the available research studies on probation, it is first important to consider their limitations. Although no correctional strategy is easy to evaluate, probation (and parole) poses some special difficulties because of ambiguity surrounding the appropriate measures of success.

The effectiveness of most correctional programs is measured by recidivism. In addition to recidivism, there is also the issue of probation revocation, which may be for the violation of a condition of probation, rather than a violation of the laws that apply to all members of a given society. Furthermore, violations of probation conditions do not automatically and unquestioningly result in probation revocation. An offender may commit a violation, or even a new crime, and still not have his or her probation revoked. Nevertheless, probation violation and revocation are frequently used as measures of probation success.

Probation officers have considerable discretion regarding their responses to violations of a probation condition. If an officer feels that continued community supervision is preferable to an arrest, he or she may choose to reprimand and warn the offender but to take no formal action. Similarly, revocation is an administrative decision. Within the bounds of due process, probation supervisors are permitted to individualize their judgments regarding the offender's need for incarceration. If a probationer is making substantial progress and does not seem to warrant imprisonment, he or she may continue to function in the community. Because probation staff may differ in their willingness to initiate the revocation process and because official and informal policy may vary from jurisdiction to jurisdiction, it is difficult to determine whether probation is working or if probation supervisors are tolerating violations and minor offenses in a special effort to maintain offenders in the community.

Studies on Recidivism

In the largest follow-up study of its kind, the Bureau of Justice Statistics found that 43 percent of a sample of felons sentenced to probation were rearrested within three years on a new felony charge. Approximately one-half of these arrests were for violent crimes or serious drug offenses.[20] Other findings of the study were 12 percent probation for a felony offense; 34 percent, property offense; 34 percent, drug offenses; and 20 percent, other.

Sixty-two percent of the probationers either experienced a disciplinary hearing or were re-arrested for a felony within three years; 46 percent had been sent to jail or prison or had absconded. Twenty-one percent of the probationers were allowed to return to the community even though probation officials had recommended against their release. Eighty-four percent of the probationers had been required to pay a financial penalty as a condition of probation, including victim restitution (29 percent), court cost (48 percent), and a supervision fee helping to defray the costs of their confinement (32 percent). The average assessment was $1,900; almost half of the offenders satisfied their financial penalties in three years. This study also found that, of 583,000 felons sentenced in state courts, 31 percent received straight probation involving a periodic visit with a probation officer, 21 percent received probation with confinement (jail or prison), 40 percent received a prison term, 6 percent received a jail term, and 2 percent received other dispositions.

Federal probation reported that 88,189 persons were on federal community supervision in 1996. Of these, approximately 84 percent completed their probation successfully, and 17 percent or 17,443 persons had their probation terminated. Fourteen percent were terminated because of violations of probation (3.8 percent for new crimes and 10.3 percent for technical violations).[21]

The first major assessment of probation effectiveness was undertaken more than fifteen years ago. In 1979, the National Institute of Law Enforcement and Criminal Justice (NILECJ) reported the results of a review of the probation evaluation literature.[22] For analytical purposes, it divided the literature into three groups: studies that compared the effectiveness of probation with that of alternative sentencing options, studies that measured probation outcome without any form of comparison, and studies that attempted to isolate the factors that enhance the likelihood of probation success.

Surprisingly, only five methodologically sound studies attempted to compare the effectiveness of probation with that of other sanctions. Three of the evaluations compared probation with incarceration by examining the experiences of probationers and similar offenders who had been incarcerated and were subsequently paroled. All three studies defined recidivism as a new offense or a technical violation. Two of the evaluations, one of which included a mixed group of offenders and one of which included only burglars, found that probation did produce lower recidivism rates except for mixed offenders with two or more prior felony convictions. The third study, which focused on female offenders, found no differences between probation and incarceration. Because probationers were compared with parolees, the benefits of parole might be expected to mitigate some of the negative effects of imprisonment, thus muddying the comparison of probation and prison.

A fourth study compared probationers, persons sentenced to probation following a jail term, and persons sentenced only to jail. Each group was followed for one full year in the community. The probation group produced the lowest rate of recidivism; almost two-thirds of the probationers had no subsequent arrests for technical violations or new offenses. Half of the shock probationers and 47 percent of those sentenced only to jail had no further violations during their year in the community.

The fifth comparison of probation supervision with an alternative sanction examined misdemeanant probationers. The subjects were randomly assigned to experimental and control groups. The probationers in the experimental group received supervision; those in the control group did not. Considering only a conviction for a new offense as the criterion for success, 22 percent of the supervised probationers and 24 percent of the nonsupervised probationers recidivated.

One can conclude little from the findings of these five studies. No two studies examined the same types of offenders under similar circumstances. At present, except for those persons with several prior felony convictions, probation seems to be at least as effective as alternative dispositions for persons normally jailed or imprisoned.

The NILECJ study examined a number of studies that reported recidivism rates for probation.[23] This assessment also produced no general conclusions about probation effectiveness because the studies examined diverse groups of offenders and employed varying definitions of success and follow-up periods. From an examination of the individual researcher's conclusions, a failure rate of 30 percent or less was generally viewed as demonstrating the effectiveness of probation.[24] Attempts to identify factors that enhance probation effectiveness are limited by the same methodological difficulties that plagued the preceding five studies. Nevertheless, of the ten studies reviewed by the NILECJ, over half produced significant correlations between recidivism and the following offender characteristics: previous criminal history, youth, status other than married, unemployment, low income, education below fourth grade, abuse of alcohol or drugs, and property offender. Previous criminal history was most frequently found to be a significant factor influencing recidivism. This finding supports another study's conclusion that persons with several prior felony convictions were less successful on probation than other offenders.

Evaluations of Specific Treatment Strategies

The NILECJ study identified approximately twenty studies of particular probation strategies and categorized them according to their principal focus: vocational or employment counseling, group or individual counseling, and drug treatment.[25] Regarding employment, only tentative evidence was found to support the proposition that employment counseling, including diagnostic services, vocational evaluation, referral services, job coaching, and stipends, can lower recidivism. Although employment and probation success undoubtedly are related and these services certainly can enhance the offender's employment status, employment counseling alone seems insufficient to reduce recidivism.

Support for the effectiveness of individual and group counseling is similarly mixed. Some success has been reported in treating sexual offenders and mixed offender groups whose participants actively engage in group activities, jointly develop treatment strategies with staff, and provide help and support to fellow group members. Other programs have shown no significant differences between counseled and noncounseled probationers. Poor research methodology is especially problematic in this area. In addition to all the previously mentioned difficulties, most evaluations have failed to define and describe adequately the treatments being offered, making a test of their effectiveness virtually meaningless.

Probation staff may treat drug addiction in various ways. They can view it as a disease requiring methadone maintenance; they can approach it using **casework** techniques and referrals to appropriate social services; or they can attack it using behavior modification strategies. Data support the positive impact of each of these strategies. Dole and Joseph have reported findings of dramatic reductions in arrest rates of probationers receiving methadone.[26] Comparing pretreatment and post-treatment arrest rates, subjects receiving methadone experienced a reduction from 120 to 55 arrests; a comparison group experienced 134 arrests.

A Philadelphia study randomly assigned drug-using probationers to regular supervision and drug counseling, which included intensive supervision, education, referrals, and rehabilitative treatment. The experimental group demonstrated lower recidivism rates than the drug users assigned to regular supervision and non-drug users under regular supervision.[27]

A behavior modification program that provided verbal encouragement and reductions in time on probation to drug users who performed specific behavioral tasks has also shown positive results. Not only did the number of arrests and probation violations decrease, but this group also demonstrated a higher rate of employment and attendance at group meetings than a control group.[28] The evaluations of specific treatment strategies show that probation can have a demonstratively positive impact on certain groups of offenders. When the offender's problem is well defined and the rehabilitative strategy is clearly articulated, comprehensive, and directly related to criminal behavior, the results can be impressive.

The RAND Study

The RAND Corporation in 1985 reported the results of a study, sponsored by the National Institute of Justice, of felony probation.[29] The RAND study used data from more than sixteen thousand offenders convicted of felonies in California as well as recidivism data on probation felons in Los Angeles and Alameda counties. The purpose of the research was to answer the following questions: What criteria are used by the courts to determine which offenders will be imprisoned and which will be granted probation? How many of these probationers are ultimately rearrested, reconvicted, and reimprisoned? How accurately can one predict which felons will recidivate and which will not?[30]

The examination of sentencing criteria indicated that, within each crime category, prior record, being a drug addict, being on community supervision at the time of the arrest, being armed, using a weapon, and seriously injuring a victim were all associated with being sent to prison instead of being placed on probation.

The manner in which the case was processed was also a significant factor. In general, offenders with private attorneys, those who had obtained pretrial release, and those who pleaded guilty were more likely to receive probation.

Although these criteria were highly correlated with the nature of the sentence, about 25 percent of sentences were not predicted by these factors, indicating that many probationers were indistinguishable from prisoners, in terms of their crimes and prior record. Not surprisingly, those probationers with histories and offenses comparable to prisoners were about 50 percent more likely to be rearrested than were other probationers.

The research concluded that felony probation in the jurisdictions studied presented a significant threat to public safety. Two-thirds of the probationers were rearrested during the three-year follow-up. More than half of the total number of probationers were reconvicted, and 34 percent were reincarcerated. The vast majority of the criminal charges against these offenders involved burglary or theft, robbery, or other violent crimes.

Predictions regarding reconviction based on type of crime, prior record, and substance abuse were found to be accurate in about two out of three cases. The nature of the presentence investigation recommendation, interestingly, was of little value in predicting recidivism. About two-thirds of those recommended for probation and two-thirds of those recommended for prison were subsequently rearrested. Using factors associated with probation success, the study found that only about 3 percent of prisoners could have been safely placed on probation as now administered.

The study concluded with a call for the expanded use of risk and needs assessment scales, the improvement of case management, and the development of intermediate sanctions and new strategies to better supervise and control offenders in the community. Although it is unclear whether felony probation in California accurately reflects felony probation elsewhere, the RAND study provided further impetus to efforts already under way to improve offender classification and to tailor community supervision to particular characteristics of offenders.

Summary

Probation, as both a concept and a practice, has a long history in Western societies. In the United States, it grew out of a need to do something that would assist the offender in remaining law abiding, while at the same time decreasing the population of the local jails. In more modern times, the role of probation has expanded to include supervision for the purpose of deterrence, as well as reform. A strength of probation is that it is made in a court, with a judicial officer presiding over the proceedings. This allows the person making the decision to be more aware of the local standards and values, and to make an individualized decision that reflects both the needs of the offender and the values of the community. For this judge to make the best decision possible, the probation office must create a report outlining the problems and needs of the offender prior to sentencing. The PSI report has a great deal of influence on the judge's decision and may reflect the beliefs and personal style of the probation officer as much as it reflects the needs and behaviors of the offender.

Probation is typically assessed using recidivism as the primary tool, but how jurisdictions and researchers define recidivism varies and, consequently, so does the reported effectiveness of the probation program. Studies of the effects of probation on both public safety and offender reform indicate that certain groups of offenders are inappropriate for probation consideration. For probation services to be more effective, there needs to be increased attention to, and evaluation of, those screening tools designed to assess risk to the public and the needs of the offender.

Key Words and Concepts

benefit of clergy

casework

community protection

Federal Probation Services

John Augustus

presentence investigation (PSI) report

recidivism

outcome measures

Questions for Discussion

1. What is meant by "probation is both a sanction and a sentence"?

2. What are some of the primary duties of a probation officer?

3. What are some of the primary goals of the probation process?

4. What are some of the methods used to place offenders on probation?

5. Who is seen as the father of American probation? When and where did he do his work?

6. How utilized is the sanction of probation?

7. What structural factors led to the abandonment of federal parole and the creation of the federal probation program?

8. How is probation success evaluated? What different forms can recidivism take?

For Further Reading

Abindinsky, Howard, *Probation and Parole: Theory and Practice* (Englewood Cliffs, N.J.: Prentice Hall, 1994).

National Advisory Commission on Criminal Justice Standards and Goals, *Corrections* (Washington, D.C.: U.S. Government Printing Office, 1973).

Tonry, Michael, and Kate Hamilton, *Intermediate Sanctions in Overcrowded Times* (Boston: Northeastern University Press, 1995).

United States Sentencing Commission, *Guidelines Manual,* November 1, 1995.

Chapter 4

Probation Supervision

Granting Probation
Probation Supervision
Innovations in Probation
The Future of Probation
Summary

Since its inception, probation has been viewed as a milder form of punishment, seen as getting a break or receiving a slap on the wrist. Criminal justice practitioners in other fields (such as traditional law enforcement) often viewed probation officers as more social worker than law enforcer, believing that they had little impact on public safety or crime control. The challenge today is to transform probation into a correctional service that protects the community, avoids unnecessary harm to the family of the offender, and at the same time assists in the reform of the offender.

Granting Probation

Sentencing Guidelines

The decision to sentence an offender to probation is an important one for both the offender and the community. From the offender's perspective, it is the difference between freedom and confinement. For the community, it is a question of protection from criminal behavior. The responsibility for this decision either rests with the sentencing court or is designated by legislatively imposed sentencing guidelines. A number of factors may influence the decision of the sentencing judge. Legislative provisions regarding who may be placed on probation vary considerably from state to state. Some states statutorily prohibit certain types of offenders from receiving probation. The most common offenses prohibited from probation are:[1]

Murder	(38 states)
Use of weapons	(29 states)
Sex offenses	(23 states)
Prior felony	(23 states)
Kidnapping	(17 states)
Drug crimes	(15 states)
Robbery	(13 states)
Repeat drunk driving	(3 states)

States that prohibit the use of probation for offenders convicted of certain crimes limit judges' discretion in sentencing those offenders by restricting the range of sentencing options.

From an organizational perspective, judicial decisions can be influenced by the availability of probation services and the judge's perception of the quality of those services. The use of probation at the practical level can be effected by four factors. First is lack of availability. In a particular state, probation may exist by statute, but some smaller or poorly funded localities may not have probation services available. In those areas, despite the judge's desires, probation is simply not an option. Second is the availability of supervision resources. In some other communities, probation caseloads may be so high that the ratio of probationers to probation officers renders probation supervision a form of suspended sentence. Judges who are aware of this problem may choose to impose alternative dispositions that require intensive supervision of the offenders rather than sentence an offender to a sanction that has neither supervisory nor therapeutic value.

Third is the offender's willingness to accept probation. Unlike being sentenced to a jail or prison term, defendants do have some say in the matter. They are given the choice of either agreeing to the conditions of probation or rejecting them and receiving an alternative punishment, generally imprisonment. Surprisingly, research conducted by Crouch has found that some offenders would rather serve a short prison term than a lengthy probation term under the supervision of a probation officer.[2]

Fourth is the judge's perception of the appropriateness of probation for a particular offender. The judge may be assisted in this determination by the **presentence investigation (PSI) report** and the probation officer's recommendation.

The American Bar Association (ABA) has provided guidelines to assist sentencing judges with the probation decision. It recommends that probation be the preferred sentence except when confinement is necessary to protect the public from further criminal activity by the offender; when the offender is in need of correctional treatment that can most effectively be provided if he or she is confined; and when the imposition of a sentence of probation would unduly deprecate the seriousness of the offense.[3]

The ABA also recommends that the court consider "the nature and circumstances of the crime, the history and character of the offender, and the available institutional and community resources."[4] In effect, it is suggesting that the judge consider three sets of factors: the offense, the offender's personal characteristics and background, and community correctional resources. Judges by and large follow the recommendations of the probation officer in the PSI. After all, the probation agency serves the court, and probation officers report either directly or indirectly to the judicial branch of government.

The factors influencing probation officers' judgments help explain why their recommendations are so important. An early study of probation decision making that was designed to study the probation decision and helped inform a generation of criminal justice researchers was the San Francisco Project. This federally funded study found that the probation recommendation was positively related to the following offender characteristics: educational level, monthly income, occupation level, marital and employment stability, participation in religious activities, and military record.[5] Recommendations against probation and for imprisonment were more likely when offenders exhibited any of the following characteristics: homosexuality, alcohol involvement, weapon use, violence associated with the present offense, family criminality, and drug abuse.[6]

The San Francisco Project also attempted to determine whether probation officers and judges agreed or differed in their ranking of the factors considered most important in the probation decision. Probation officers and judges participating in the study were asked to rank, in terms of their significance, the factors they believed influenced their decision regarding the dispositions of offenders. The judges and probation officers seemed to share similar perspectives, although they differed in the relative emphasis placed on each item. Both groups ranked prior record, confinement status, number of arrests, offense, and longest term of employment as the most significant factors in the sentencing decision. Considerable agreement was found on the factors that qualify a defendant for probation. When probation officers work with judges over extended periods of time, they are probably influenced by the judges' perspectives. Probation officers may make recommendations that are in accord with the judges' views and are therefore likely to be followed.

The Impact of Sentencing Guidelines

Sentence guidelines are now used in some jurisdictions to assist judges with their decision making. These guidelines are standardized instruments designed to provide clear and explicit direction to the court in determining the appropriate punishments. Their purpose is to reduce the incidence of arbitrary decision making and to encourage consistency in sentencing within a jurisdiction. Guidelines are legislatively imposed on the sentencing process, and many judges are critical of the guidelines because they remove judicial discretion in sentencing.[7] Where sentencing guidelines are in use, the need for PSIs is minimized. Most guidelines focus on two sets of factors in determining an appropriate sentence: the seriousness of the present offense and prior criminal record.

Standardized Sentencing Instruments

Table 4-1 presents a copy of the sentencing table used by the United States Sentencing Commission.

Several states use a variant of the guidelines, an offense score (based on the seriousness of the charge), and a criminal history score (based on prior records, which must first be computed for each offender). The second step requires the user to refer to the sentencing grid and identify the appropriate disposition. To illustrate the use of this instrument, consider an offender with no prior felonies who committed second-degree murder. The federal sentencing guidelines specify the base offense level as a 33. Using the sentencing guidelines grid, the sentence would be 135–168 months in prison.

Presentence Investigation Report

One of the primary functions of probation organizations is the preparation of the presentence investigation report. The PSI report serves at least five purposes in the sentencing and correction phases of criminal justice. Its primary purpose is to assist the judge in making an appropriate sentencing decision by providing supplemental information not revealed at the trial regarding the offender's personal and social circumstances. Utilizing this information, the judge can tailor a punishment that satisfies the purposes of justice and meets the offender's needs.

A second PSI objective is to provide a basis for an offender's probation plan. Treatment and supervision needs are identified during the course of the investigation so that appropriate services can be provided. A third function of the PSI is to assist institutional correctional officials if the offender is sentenced to a prison term. The PSI provides information that facilitates the classification of the offender for custody, work, education, and other prison programs. A fourth purpose of the PSI is to provide information about the offender to the parole board for use in release decision making. The PSI serves as a

Table 4-1   Sentencing Table (in Months of Imprisonment)

Zone	Offense Level	Criminal History Category (Criminal History Points)					
		I (0 or 1)	II (2 or 3)	III (4, 5, 6)	IV (7, 8, 9)	V (10, 11, 12)	VI (13 or more)
	1	0–6	0–6	0–6	0–6	0–6	0–6
	2	0–6	0–6	0–6	0–6	0–6	1–7
	3	0–6	0–6	0–6	0–6	2–8	3–9
	4	0–6	0–6	0–6	2–8	4–10	6–12
Zone A	5	0–6	0–6	1–7	4–10	6–12	9–15
	6	0–6	1–7	2–8	6–12	9–15	12–18
	7	0–6	2–8	4–10	8–14	12–18	15–21
	8	0–6	4–10	6–12	10–16	15–21	18–24
Zone B	9	4–10	6–12	8–14	12–18	18–24	21–27
	10	6–12	8–14	10–16	15–21	21–27	24–30
Zone C	11	8–14	10–16	12–18	18–24	24–30	27–33
	12	10–16	12–18	15–21	21–27	27–33	30–37
	13	12–18	15–21	18–24	24–30	30–37	33–41
	14	15–21	18–24	21–27	27–33	33–41	37–46
	15	18–24	21–27	24–30	30–37	37–46	41–51
	16	21–27	24–30	27–33	33–41	41–51	46–57
	17	24–30	27–33	30–37	37–46	46–57	51–63
	18	27–33	30–37	33–41	41–51	51–63	57–71
	19	30–37	33–41	37–46	46–57	57–71	63–78
	20	33–41	37–46	41–51	51–63	63–78	70–87
	21	37–46	41–51	46–57	57–71	70–87	77–96
	22	41–51	46–57	51–63	63–78	77–96	84–105
	23	46–57	51–63	57–71	70–87	84–105	92–115
	24	51–63	57–71	63–78	77–96	92–115	100–125
	25	57–71	63–78	70–87	84–105	100–125	110–137
	26	63–78	70–87	78–97	92–115	110–137	120–150
	27	70–87	78–97	87–108	100–125	120–150	130–162
Zone D	28	78–97	87–108	97–121	110–137	130–162	140–175
	29	87–108	97–121	108–135	121–151	140–175	151–188
	30	97–121	108–135	121–151	135–168	151–188	168–210
	31	108–135	121–151	135–168	151–188	168–210	188–235
	32	121–151	135–168	151–188	168–210	188–235	210–262
	33	135–168	151–188	168–210	188–235	210–262	235–293
	34	151–188	168–210	188–235	210–262	235–293	262–327
	35	168–210	188–235	210–262	235–293	262–327	292–365
	36	188–235	210–262	235–293	262–327	292–365	324–405
	37	210–262	235–293	262–327	292–365	324–405	360–life
	38	235–293	262–327	292–365	324–405	360–life	360–life
	39	262–327	292–365	324–405	360–life	360–life	360–life
	40	292–365	324–405	360–life	360–life	360–life	360–life
	41	324–405	360–life	360–life	360–life	360–life	360–life
	42	360–life	360–life	360–life	360–life	360–life	360–life
	43	life	life	life	life	life	life

Source: United States Sentencing Commission, *Guidelines Manual,* November 1995.

criminal dossier and provides information about the crime and the circumstances associated with it. This is particularly important when, after serving several or more years of a prison term, the offender comes before a parole board and may be the only living witness to the crime. Finally, the PSI plays an important role as a source of information for research in the field of corrections. The PSI represents a primary source document regarding offenders' background characteristics and personal attributes.

PSI Preparation   In most jurisdictions, probation officers prepare the PSI report. However, no single procedure or set of guidelines governs the preparation of the document and the identification of the items of information appropriate for inclusion in the report. Practices vary from jurisdiction to jurisdiction according to whether the report is required by statute or is optional at the judge's discretion. A study conducted by the Department of Justice found that, in twenty-four states and the federal government, the PSI was mandatory for virtually all felony cases; the PSI was discretionary for felony cases in fourteen states. In several states, the defendant was permitted to waive his or her right to a PSI.[8] PSIs are rarely prepared for misdemeanants although two states require them to be submitted prior to sentencing.

Probation agencies are usually responsible for the submission of the PSI. In some cases the defendant may hire a private agency to conduct a presentence investigation report and submit it to the sentencing judge for review. The National Institute of Corrections has concluded, based upon its survey of state agencies, that private for-profit agencies have not made major inroads in this area.[9] Most likely this has to do with defendants' ability to pay for this service.

Report Purpose and Content   The PSI is usually prepared after conviction and before sentencing, although some states leave the timing of the report up to the individual judge. Timing is somewhat controversial because the amount of information gathered is influenced by the amount of time available for preparation. One view maintains that a lengthy and detailed investigation should be initiated as soon as possible so that the report will be ready when needed. However, beginning the report before conviction presupposes the offender's guilt and may damage his or her reputation when the field investigation is conducted. Also, if the defendant is found not guilty, the probation agency's resources would have been wasted.

In most jurisdictions, probation officers are aided in their investigation by standardized forms that are usually referred to as either short or long forms. Their purpose is to guide the probation officer in collecting information regarding certain characteristics of the offender. The long form provides for a more in-depth investigation of a person's social and personal background, motivations, and characteristics. The short form is utilized when less detailed information is required or when probation resources are too limited to permit lengthy, in-depth investigations.

PSI preparation and utilization vary with the type of information collected. The primary purpose of this report is to assist the judge in determining an appropriate sentence for a convicted offender. Although the PSI plays a critical role in the entire criminal justice process, the type of information collected reflects a principal concern with factors considered relevant to the purposes of punishment. To illustrate the range of factors included in the PSI, consider the information state probation officers include in the standard investigation report: offense, defendant's version of the offense, prior record, family history, marital history, home and neighborhood, education, religion, interests and leisure activities, health, employment, military service, and financial condition. The information is summarized at the conclusion of the report and a recommendation regarding disposition is offered. In some jurisdictions, the recommendation is offered only when the sentencing judge specifically requests it. Research suggests that a high rate of agreement exists between the probation officer's recommendation and the judge's final decision.

Privately Prepared Presentence Reports

Agencies began appearing in the late 1960s to create **privately prepared presentence reports**.[10] These reports are usually commissioned by defense counsel in an attempt to develop alternatives to confinement in cases where incarceration seems likely. A variety of individuals and organizations are involved in such efforts. Former probation officers may offer such a service for a fee as a profit-making venture.

Not-for-profit organizations are also involved, as part of their advocacy for alternatives to confinement. The largest such organization is the National Center on Institutions and Alternatives (NCIA). NCIA developed in Washington, D.C., and now has branches in California, Florida, Nebraska, New York, and North Carolina. NCIA refers to its reports as client specific plans (CSPs). CSPs are individualized sentence recommendations that address defendant, victim, and criminal justice system concerns through a combination of treatments and conditions. Provisions are usually made for counseling, education, community service, restitution, employment, and some form of supervision. Because the program deals primarily with felonies, short periods of confinement—such as jail, weekend jail, and work release—are often advocated. CSPs generally arrange for treatment prior to sentencing and provide a more complete diagnostic approach to the offender's criminality than the more descriptive PSI. Overburdened probation officers are frequently responsible for preparing PSIs as well as the supervision of a caseload of offenders. The crowding of probation has resulted in PSIs that are not as in-depth as the offender or the defense counsel may desire. The privately prepared PSI provides an alternative source of information to judges. These privately commissioned plans are in demand by white-collar offenders who desire to avoid prison terms.[11] Today there are approximately

115 defense-based programs in the United States.[12] These programs handle more than sixteen thousand cases a year.[13]

Research indicates that although there is variation from jurisdiction to jurisdiction, CSP recommendations tend to be accepted in full or in part by the sentencing judge. The National Center on Institutions and Alternatives reports that over two-thirds of its cases have resulted in sentencing plans accepted by the courts. Other programs report similar success. One superior court judge, Coy E. Brewer Jr. of Fayette, North Carolina, commented that

the greatest concern I have had in sentencing is the paucity of sentencing options that I would face in a particular situation. These programs create a continuum of punishment options with more gradation in them, so that we have the possibility of meaningful community-based punishment.[14]

Probation Supervision

In addition to the PSI, probation agencies' second major function is in supervising offenders placed on probation by the court.[15]

Probation supervision involves at least three sets of activities: intervention, surveillance, and enforcement. Intervention refers to providing offenders access to a wide variety of treatment services, including drug and alcohol treatment, job skills training, and educational enrichment. Surveillance refers to the law enforcement aspects of a probation officer's job. It frequently involves monitoring the activities of the probationer through office and field visits, drug testing, and contacts with employers and family members. Enforcement involves holding probationers accountable for their behavior and entails a variety of strategies designed to control the offender.

Supervisory Styles

The **supervision styles** of offenders is influenced by two sometimes conflicting duties:

controlling the offender and providing social services. The first function places probation officers in a law enforcement role. They monitor the probationer's activities and ensure that the conditions of probation set forth by the court are met. When these conditions are violated, probation officers must take the offender into custody and initiate a revocation proceeding. However, little proactive monitoring takes place because of the massive standard supervision caseloads for which individual probation officers are responsible. Most of the monitoring is reactive—probation officers respond to official and unofficial reports of misconduct. Some probation offices make periodic checks of local police and jail booking records to see if any of their clients were arrested recently.

The provision of social services by probation officers is essentially a helping function. They attempt to deal with the offender's problems directly (by providing such services as counseling) or indirectly (by serving as a referral source). Individual probation officers vary in terms of their relative commitment to both the duties of control and service provision. Some officers prefer the law enforcement approach; others view themselves more as social workers.

Research on the subject of probation supervision indicates that probation officers choose one of several adaptive orientations to the supervision function.[16] One classic study suggests that probation officers fit into one of five personal and operational styles: Team Player, Mossback, Hardliner, Bleeding-Heart Liberal, and Maverick. While these officers differ in their personal styles, they each have personal and professional goals, and they work within the flexibility of their jobs to achieve these goals as best as possible (Table 4-2).

Team Players are the officers who seek to follow departmental policies as closely as possible, to follow the guidance of the superior officers in the office, and to avoid making decisions that create controversy. By following this set of personal standards, Team Players do nothing that places themselves in a difficult position; all decisions are backed by policy. At the same time, this stance eliminates one of the best elements of modern probation—the chance to create change by being creative with the caseload.

Mossbacks are typified by an old style of supervision. They are seen as just serving their time until retirement, making no extra efforts on behalf of their cases, and doing a minimal level of acceptable work. While this style of supervision is more common among older officers, it is certainly not unique to this group. Occupational burnout causes many young officers to become Mossbacks to cope with a job they no longer care for. They try to take a middle-of-the-road perspective and avoid actions that will be noticed by their superiors.

In contrast to the Mossbacks, the Hardliners believe that probation is serious business and that enforcing the rules set forth by the court constitutes serious punishment. The Hardliners would never allow the offender to commit a violation without receiving an appropriate response. They believe that the goal of probation is punitive, but they consider themselves fair. They maintain that the court set the conditions and the offender knew that violating these conditions would result in punishment, so therefore punishment is expected and appropriate.

At the opposite end of the spectrum are the Bleeding-Heart Liberals. These officers believe that the offender is in many ways also the victim. The economic, social, and criminal justice systems are so biased against the offender that their role is to work to even the playing field by assisting the offender. These officers are strong advocates of rehabilitation and believe the goal of probation should be to assist in reforming the offender.

The Mavericks do not adhere to a single personal philosophy, instead opting to work in any of the above styles, as situations re-

Table 4-2 Typology of Presentence Probation Investigators

Type of Investigators (Percent)	Assumed Role	Purpose of Sentencing	Presentence Recommendation
team player (30%)	facilitating department policies	reflect society's values	noncontroversial
mossback (30%)	following the rules	resolve the matter	middle of the road
hardliner (20%)	upholding traditional values	deter others	strict
bleeding-heart liberal (10%)	sticking up for the underdog	rehabilitate the defendant	lenient
maverick (10%)	weighing the case's individual merits	see that justice is done	varied

Source: John Rosecrance, "A Typology of Presentence Probation Investigators," *International Journal of Offender Therapy and Comparative Criminology,* 31 (2), 1987.

quire. These officers believe in individualized justice and will adopt a Hardliner or Bleeding-Heart Liberal style, as needed. This is a successful personal strategy, but it can create administrative problems. When an administrative supervisor assigns a case to an officer, the supervisor usually has some idea what the offender needs and what the officer will provide. Mavericks tend to be unpredictable, and the supervisor could be expecting a Bleeding-Heart Liberal but instead get a Hardliner.

Service Delivery Strategies

Two service delivery strategies are currently utilized in probation supervision: the caseworker model and the **resource broker** model. The caseworker approach utilizes a social work orientation that stresses a one-to-one relationship between the probation officer and the offender. The establishment of rapport leads to the development of a meaningful relationship between the officer and the client. That relationship is used as a leverage in changing the offender's behavior. This model has long been associated with probation and can probably be traced back to John Augustus's early humanitarian efforts. However, in recent years, this approach has been criticized as unrealistic. Huge numbers of offenders are being sentenced to probation terms with numerous conditions to obey. Probation officers are overburdened with administrative concerns for ensuring that conditions are adhered to, including restitution and drug testing.

Today an alternative to the caseworker approach is available. Under the resource brokerage model, the probation officer is no longer required to have the time or skills necessary to help all offenders with every problem. Instead, the probation officer refers clients to appropriate community resources. Serving as a broker, the probation officer attempts to identify the offender's unique needs and match them with available community resources. The probation officer continues to supervise the offender and monitor his or her progress in community programs (Figure 4-1).

Figure 4-1   Presentence Investigation Options

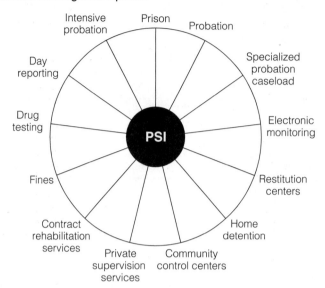

Generally, an eight-step plan is followed in resource brokerage. Probation officers are required to perform the following steps:

1. Inventory resources.

2. Develop resource banks.

3. Prepare the community.

4. Develop client contracts.

5. Develop plans.

6. Refer to community resources.

7. Purchase services.

8. Follow-up and evaluate.[17]

Probation Teams   A variation of the **casework** and resource brokerage approaches involves the establishment of teams of probation officers who are jointly responsible for managing caseloads. Each probation officer is expected to have specialized skills. The team brings together the precise skills individual offenders need. Supervision teams can therefore provide multiple services to probationers. These specialized teams focus on offenders who pose

a serious threat to society (for example, sex offenders, domestic batterers) or represent a high risk of reoffending (drug offenders).

Caseload Management

Caseload management refers to the strategies probation organizations use to assign cases or clients to probation officers in a manner that ensures the efficient use of probation resources. Caseload management typically involves four interrelated functions. The first function involves a needs assessment, which identifies the problems the offender presents. The second function involves referral, where the probation officer matches the needs of the offender with the appropriate treatment resources in the community. The third function involves the coordination of services provided to offenders. The fourth function involves serving as a broker for services. The probation officer is responsible for using his or her influence to bring the needed services and offenders together.[18] Probation agencies currently employ a number of techniques to assign caseloads. Offenders can be assigned to caseloads randomly, alphabetically, by certain personal traits or offense characteristics, or by the geographic area of the probationer's residence.

The level of supervision provided to individual offenders varies. Some offenders require intensive supervision and assistance; others require minimal supervision. In some agencies, special intensive supervision caseloads are utilized; in others, an attempt is made to assign each probation officer some clients who require minimum intervention and others who need intensive supervision to achieve a balanced caseload.

The choice between a generalized and specialized caseload system requires a probation agency to determine whether the resources are available to assign probationers to caseloads on the basis of some particular trait and to permit a probation officer to specialize with a certain type of offender or whether undifferentiated caseloads must be maintained. When probation officers are especially skilled in some area of assistance (for example, drug or employment counseling) and when a significant number of clients need assistance, specialized caseloads consisting of similarly troubled offenders are often utilized. When staff resources are limited or when greater diversity exists in client needs, generalized caseloads that include offenders with varying needs are utilized (Figure 4-2).

Conditions of Probation

Offenders placed on probation must agree to abide by certain rules and regulations prescribed by the sentencing court. This set of rules and regulations is generally referred to as the **conditions of probation.** In some states, these conditions are established by the legislature and written into law. In other states, judges have the discretion to impose specific conditions on a case-by-case basis. In still other jurisdictions, the discretion to impose conditions is left to the probation organization. In most communities, probationers must comply with both general and individualized conditions of probation.

The National Advisory Commission on Standards and Goals recommends against applying standard conditions to all offenders. Instead, it suggests a more flexible approach involving three considerations: (1) that the conditions be tailored to fit the unique needs of the offender; (2) that the conditions imposed be reasonably related to the offender's correctional program; and (3) that the conditions imposed be not unduly restrictive or conflict with the offender's constitutional rights (Figure 4-3).[19]

The Federal Sentencing Commission recommends that the conditions imposed are reasonably related to the nature and circumstances of the offense and the history and characteristics of the offender and involve only such deprivations of liberty or property as are reasonably necessary to effect the purposes of sentencing.[20]

The federal sentencing guidelines also mandate that the court impose the condition that the offender not commit another crime during the term of probation. Federal guidelines also require that if the offender is convicted of a felony the court shall impose at least one of the following as a condition of probation: a fine, restitution, or community service. The court may also order intermittent confinement as a condition of a probation term.

Other recommended conditions of release include:

1. The defendant shall not leave the judicial district without the permission of the probation officer or court.

2. The defendant shall report to the probation officer as directed and shall submit a truthful and complete written report.

3. The defendant shall answer truthfully all inquiries by the probation officer and follow his or her instructions.

4. The probationer shall support his or her family.

5. The probationer shall attend work training.

Figure 4-2   Resource Brokerage Client Contact

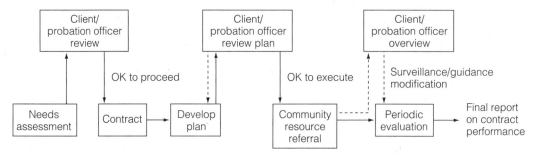

Source: James J. Dahl and Michael Chapman, *Improved Probation Strategies: Trainers Handbook* (Washington, D.C.: U.S. Government Printing Office, 1980), p. 177.

6. Notification must be made of changes in address within seventy-two hours.

7. The defendant shall refrain from the excessive use of alcohol and be prohibited from the use of controlled substances.

8. The defendant shall not frequent places where controlled substances are used.

9. The defendant shall not associate with criminals.[21]

Probation conditions imposed on offenders tend to fall into two categories. They are oriented toward either reforming the offender or controlling behavior. Reform-oriented conditions might require the offender to attend school, receive drug treatment, or undergo psychiatric treatment. Control-oriented conditions might include reporting requirements, restrictions on geographic mobility, and prohibitions from hanging around with certain types of persons or frequenting inappropriate places.

About two-thirds of the probation agencies collect supervision fees as a condition of probation.[22] These fees account for as much as 60 percent of probation budgets in some jurisdictions. Fees generally range between $10 and $40 per month. Although the fees have received some criticism, there is general agreement that they represent an important source of revenue and can be used to help teach offenders to pay their own way. Furthermore, fees encourage offenders to participate in programming; free programs are often taken for granted and may fail because the offender has not bought into the idea of reform.

Most professionals in the field of probation services seem to agree that a flexible approach should be taken with regard to probation conditions. The conditions should be clear and specific. The offender must also be capable of following and obeying them. Conditions that are vague, ambiguous, or unenforceable should be discouraged.

The probation officer plays an important role in ensuring that the offender understands and follows the conditions of probation. The probation officer generally has the responsibility for explaining the conditions to the offender to ensure that he or she understands them and to inform the offender of the consequences—that is, revocation of probation—of violating them.

Probation revocation is not automatic or recommended in every case. A probation officer has a number of disciplinary options available. These include:

Verbal reprimands;

Increased levels of supervisory contacts;

Increased drug or alcohol testing;

Figure 4-3   Resource Brokerage

Source: James J. Dahl and Michael Chapman, *Improved Probation Strategies: Trainers Handbook* (Washington, D.C.: U.S. Government Printing Office, 1980), p. 176.

Community service requirements;

Curfews;

House arrest;

Electronic monitoring; and

Short-term detention in a jail.[23]

Revocation

Probation **revocation** is a multistage process, involving at least two sets of decision makers. The probation officer has the authority to initiate the revocation process, but the decision to revoke an offender's probation rests with the sentencing judge. The probation officer has the power to arrest, but once the offender is in jail, many jurisdictions require someone besides the arresting officer (usually a judge or a probation supervisor) to review the case to determine if continued detention is warranted. Considerable flexibility exists throughout the revocation proceeding and, even though an ar-

rest has occurred, revocation is not automatic. Generally, there are two types of violations: legal violations, which involve the commission of a new crime, and technical violations, which involve no criminal conduct but a violation of the conditions of probation. When a violation occurs, the probation officer has the discretion either to take formal action and report the violation or to ignore or tolerate minor misbehavior. If the decision is made to invoke the formal revocation process, certain guidelines provided by case law must be followed.

Two Supreme Court cases have shaped the revocation proceeding. *Morrissey* vs. *Brewer,* 408 U.S. 471 (1972), directly addressed parole revocation proceedings. The due process protections established for parolees were subsequently extended to probationers in *Gagnon* vs. *Scarpelli,* 41 1 U.S. 778 (1973). These cases provided probationers with the right to a two-stage hearing that includes minimum due process protection during a revocation proceeding. In the first, preliminary hearing, a determination is made as to whether probable cause exists to revoke probation. Provided at this stage of the proceedings are the right to prior notice of the hearing, the right to written notice of the charges, the right to be present at the hearing, the right to present evidence and witnesses, and the right to a hearing before a detached and neutral hearing officer.

These same rights apply at the second stage of the revocation proceeding, where the revocation decision is made. In certain special circumstances, such as when a probationer is incapable of speaking effectively for himself or herself and has requested counsel, the advice of counsel may also be provided.

Federal courts consider the status of probation seriously. Given that the offender is not incarcerated, the decision to incarcerate and remove the offender's ability to move freely in society (with the understood limitations of the conditions of probation) is taken with extreme gravity. Incarceration as a result of probation revocation is seen as a grievous loss of liberty, and the decision to place someone in this state because of a probation violation must be made with due care and due process.

Statistics compiled by the Bureau of Justice Statistics indicate that 67 percent of offenders completed their probation terms successfully; 16 percent were returned to incarceration. Of these, 4 percent were returned with a new sentence, and 12 percent were returned to serve out the remainder of their sentence.

A Bureau of Justice Statistics survey of probation violators returned to state prison found that the most common reason for recommitment was an arrest for a new offense. This was followed by failure to report to a probation officer or absconding, followed by failure to pay fines, restitution, or other financial obligations.

Innovations in Probation

The 1980s–1990s was a period of great change in both the structure and delivery of probation services. Probation experienced unprecedented growth and further criticism. This criticism focused on the public safety as well as probation's failure to adequately control and supervise offenders. As a result of this criticism, probation agencies throughout the United States have been busy reinventing and reengineering themselves to reflect the public's demand to toughen the use of community sanctions. Numerous types of programs designed to enhance control were developed—drug testing, shock probation, intensive supervision, and electronic monitoring and house arrest, to name a few.

Probation Classification Systems

Classification systems became widely used in the 1980s as probation departments were confronted with the need to allocate increasingly scarce resources while client populations had begun to include more and more serious offenders. Research had indicated that clinical judgments alone often produced inconsistent decisions. The use of a structured instrument yielded better and more consistent judgments.

Risk and needs classification systems assess items of information proven to be related to the level of risk posed by offenders' release to the community and their particular needs during supervision (Figure 4-4). Offenders with high levels of risk and needs are provided with more intensive levels of supervision and service. Cases are normally reassessed at regular intervals, and levels of supervision are modified as appropriate.

Domestic Violence

Cook County, Illinois, has a specialized domestic violence court with a specialized probation supervision team whose mission is to rigorously enforce court orders (protective orders) and enforce conditions of probation. The American Probation and Parole Association provides guidelines for domestic violence intervention. According to Cook County chief probation officer Nancy Martin:

I felt the offenders needed some specialized treatment to deal with issues that lead them to be batterers in the first place, typical probation strategies were not working. . . . [W]e need to address special needs. . . . [W]e desire to have strict enforcement of conditions and court orders, random drug testing, mandatory attendance at batterers counseling sessions.[24]

The conditions in Cook County included a mandatory probation reporting schedule, random drug testing, and participation in counseling. Offenders are held accountable and make full restitution to the victim for hospitalization, medical expenses, and therapeutic counseling. Probation serves as a direct link between the criminal justice system and the offender. "The hope is that you're going to change the mindset, change the behavior that led to battery, and that you're not going to see incidences in the future."[25]

The Future of Probation

At present, the vast majority of offenders are sentenced to probation instead of prison. This pattern is unlikely to change in the future. Recent years have seen an increased acceptance of retribution as a correctional objective and determinate sentencing as the method by which to achieve equal punishment. These factors may reduce probation populations in some jurisdictions. However, the economic and human costs of incarceration are so great and so widely acknowledged that it is doubtful these population reductions will be more than temporary. It is more likely that the search for more efficient and effective probation strategies will continue. To date, no alternative sentence seems to offer as much flexibility and potential for both offender control and offender change.

Perhaps the greatest challenge to probation is the challenge to implement effective change. This is no easy task, as indicated by the results of an effort funded by the Bureau of Justice Assistance (BJA) to expand the use of intensive supervision programs. BJA funded eleven jurisdictions to field-test a model ISP based on the Georgia program. Sites were instructed to implement the Georgia model but to tailor it to local needs.

The evaluation continues for those programs that still exist. Some programs are thriving, while others have terminated or drastically curtailed their efforts. What accounts for the ability to implement a new program in a successful fashion? Joan Petersilia, principal investigator of the study, identifies the following factors as necessary for accomplishing change.

1. The project addresses a pressing local problem.

2. The project has clearly articulated goals that reflect the needs and desires of the customer.

3. The project has a receptive environment in both the parent organization and the larger system.

4. The organization has a leader who is vitally committed to the objectives, values, and implications of the project and who can devise practical strategies to motivate and effect change.

5. The project has a director who shares the leader's ideas and values and uses them to guide the implementation process and ongoing operation of the project.

6. Practitioners make the project their own, instead of being coerced into it; that is, they buy into it, participate in its development, and have incentives to maintain its integrity during the change process.

7. The project has clear lines of authority; there is no ambiguity about who is in charge.

8. The change and its implementation are not complex and sweeping.

Figure 4-4   Risk Assessment and Needs Assessment

RISK ASSESSMENT

			Score
1. Number of address changes in the last 12 months:	0	None	
	2	One	
	3	Two or more	2
2. Time employed in last 12 months:	0	More than 8 months	
	1	4 to 7 months	
	2	Under 4 months	
	0	Not applicable	2
3. Alcohol usage problems:	0	No interference with functioning	
	2	Some disruption of functioning	
	4	Serious disruption; needs treatment	4
4. Other drug usage problems:	0	No usage of illegal drugs	
	1	Occasional use	
	2	Frequent use; needs treatment	1
5. Attitude:	0	Motivated to change; receptive to assistance	
	3	Dependent or unwilling to accept responsibility	
	5	Rationalizes behavior; negative; not motivated to change	5
6. Age at first conviction:	0	24 or older	
(or Juvenile Adjudication in the last five years)	2	20–23	
	4	19 or younger	4
7. Number of prior periods of probation/parole supervision:	0	None	
(Adult or Juvenile)	2	One	
	4	Two or more	2
8. Number of prior probation/parole revocations:	0	None	
(Adult or Juvenile)	4	One or more	0
9. Number of prior felony convictions:	0	None	
(or Juvenile Adjudications in the last five years)	2	One	
	4	Two or more	0
10. Adult convictions/juvenile adjudications for:	0	Not applicable	
(Select applicable offenses and add for score. Do not exceed a total of 5. Include current offense.)	2	Burglary, theft, auto theft, or robbery	
	3	Worthless checks or forgery	0
11. Adult convictions/juvenile adjudications for assaultive offense within last five years:	15	Yes	
(An offense which involves the use of a weapon, physical force, or the threat of force.)	0	No	15
		Total Risk Score	**35**

(continued)

Figure 4-4   *(continued)*

NEEDS ASSESSMENT

Score

1. Academic/vocational skills	0	Adequate skills; able to handle everyday requirements	+2	Low skill level causing minor adjustment problems	+4	Minimum skill level causing serious adjustment problems _____
2. Employment	0	Secure employment; no difficulties reported; or homemaker, student or retired	+3	Unsatisfactory employment; or unemployed but has adequate job skills	+6	Unemployed and virtually unemployable; needs training _____
3. Financial management	0	No current difficulties	+3	Situational or minor difficulties	+5	Severe difficulties; may include garnishment, bad checks or bankruptcy _____
4. Marital/family relationships	0	Relatively stable relationships	+3	Some disorganization or stress but potential for improvement	+5	Major disorganization or stress _____
5. Companions	0	No adverse relationships	+2	Association with occasional negative results	+4	Associations negative _____
6. Emotional stability	0	No symptoms of emotional instability; appropriate emotional responses	+4	Symptoms limited but do not prohibit adequate functioning; e.g., excessive anxiety	+7	Symptoms prohibit adequate functioning; e.g., lashes out or retreats into self _____
7. Alcohol usage	0	No interference with functioning	+3	Occasional abuse; some disruption of functioning	+6	Frequent abuse; serious disruption; needs treatment _____
8. Other drug usage	0	No interference with functioning	+3	Occasional substance use; some disruption of functioning	+5	Frequent substance use; serious disruption; needs treatment _____
9. Learning ability	0	Able to function independently	+3	Some need for assistance; potential for adequate adjustment	+6	Deficiencies severely limit independent functioning _____
10. Health	0	Sound physical health; seldom ill	+1	Handicap or illness interferes with functioning on a recurring basis	+2	Serious handicap or chronic illness; needs frequent medical care _____
11. Sexual behavior	0	No apparent dysfunction	+3	Real or perceived situational or minor problems	+5	Real or perceived chronic or severe problems _____
12. Officer's impression of client's needs	0	Minimum	+3	Medium	+5	Maximum _____

Total Need Score   _____

Level of Supervision	Risk Score	Need Score
Maximum	18 and above	30 and above
Medium	7 to 17	15 to 29
Minimum	6 and below	14 and below

Source: Harry Boone, Betsy Fulton, et al., American Probation and Parole Association, 1995. Used by permission.

9. The organization has secure administrators, low staff turnover, and plentiful resources.[26]

Probation will continue to be the most widely used correctional disposition because it is less costly, more humane, and no less effective for most offenders than incarceration. Good reasons certainly exist for using probation, but, in a sense, probation strategies seem to win over existing alternatives by default: No better option is currently available. If something more than this is desired from probation, then current practices must be studied, serious consideration must then be given to what probation should be achieving, and the changes necessary to make probation an effective strategy in its own right should be implemented.

Summary

Probation is currently the most widely utilized postconviction correctional disposition. In the United States, it originated in the altruistic efforts of a shoemaker who felt that friendly supervision would do more to rehabilitate offenders than a jail sentence. Today probation is the most useful reintegrative strategy because it permits offenders to remain in the community while they receive counseling and assistance. At the same time, probation attempts to ensure **community protection** through the monitoring of offender behavior.

Although most observers have concluded that probation can be most effectively administered by the executive branch of state government, probation granting is a judicial function. The sentencing judge grants probation after determining that an individual offender is suitable for community supervision. This judgment is reached by referring to statutory eligibility requirements and by assessing the offender's background report, known as the presentence report. The preparation of presentence reports is one of the major responsibilities of probation

officers, whose other major function is supervising offenders.

Preparing presentence reports is difficult, sometimes involving gathering and verifying information on the offender's crime, prior record, attitude toward the offense committed, family life, employment and educational history, and early years. When probation officers are asked to make recommendations for or against the granting of probation, judges usually follow their recommendations.

Probation supervision typically involves a synthesis of law enforcement and counseling activities. Because of their large caseloads, which make individual casework virtually impossible, and the need to assist the offender in establishing long-term community ties, probation officers serve as resource brokers. These brokers of community services assess inmate needs, refer offenders to appropriate agencies, and monitor their progress in the community.

Probation conditions serve both reform and control objectives. They should reflect individual needs and capabilities rather than standardized rules. The violation of probation conditions may or may not lead to the revocation of probation and the incarceration of the offender. Before revocation can occur, either following a technical violation (of a condition) or a new crime, a two-stage revocation proceeding must be conducted to assess (1) probable cause that a violation occurred and (2) the desirability of revocation. This two-stage proceeding is designed to protect the offender from arbitrary and unnecessary incarceration.

Research on probation indicates that probation programs can be improved through the use of risk and needs assessments. Such classification schemes tailor supervision levels to the particular characteristics of individual offenders. At present, indications are that many persons on probation may require more supervision than they are getting. Yet these persons may not require incarceration. The benefits of intermediate punishments seem apparent. Intensive supervision programs, house arrest, electronic monitoring, and shock incarceration are all means of addressing the need for mid-range options in the correctional continuum. While they may serve as more punitive dispositions than standard probation, they may also provide the increased contact and guidance necessary to make probation a truly reintegrative strategy. Surprisingly, some offenders would prefer a short prison term to a long probation term with numerous conditions and requirements. Recently one Texas judge remarked, "Not in my wildest six years on the bench has this ever come up before. . . . I've had offenders ask for probation instead of prison, but I've never had one . . . ask me to do away with probation and go to prison."[27]

Key Words and Concepts

caseload management

casework

community protection

conditions of probation

presentence investigation (PSI) reports

privately prepared presentence reports

resource broker

revocation

supervision styles

Questions for Discussion

1. What are some reasons (other than seriousness of the crime) that an offender might not receive a sentence of probation?

2. What were some of the similarities and differences, noted by the San Francisco Project, between judge and probation officer?

3. Which different players and agencies use the presentence investigation (PSI) report to assist their decision making?

4. Why would an offender want to pay a private agency to prepare a PSI report?

5. What are the different operational styles that a probation officer can assume, according to Rosecrance? What role would you assume if you were a probation officer?

6. Consider a crime that is common in your geographic area. What conditions would you place on a probationer convicted of that specific crime? Why would these conditions be important?

7. What are the different categories of violation that can result in revocation?

8. How does the process of revocation operate, given the impact of the *Morrissey* and *Gagnon* decisions?

For Further Reading

Abindinsky, Howard, *Probation and Parole: Theory and Practice* (Englewood Cliffs, N.J.: Prentice Hall, 1994).

National Advisory Commission on Criminal Justice Standards and Goals, *Corrections* (Washington, D.C.: U.S. Government Printing Office, 1973).

Tonry, Michael, and Kate Hamilton, *Intermediate Sanctions in Overcrowded Times* (Boston: Northeastern University Press, 1995).

United States Sentencing Commission, *Guidelines Manual,* November 1, 1995.

Chapter 5

Parole and Other Prison Release Programs

What Is Parole?

Justice Objectives

Societal Objectives

Historical Development

Contemporary Parole

The Future of Parole

Summary of Parole

Temporary Release Programs

Summary of Temporary Release Programs

Parole is one of the most controversial correctional programs because it involves the early release of inmates from prison. It was once viewed as a necessary transition phase between prison and freedom, a period when correctional authorities could supervise newly released offenders and offer them the assistance needed to get back on their feet. The parole-granting process was established both to encourage rehabilitation and to ensure community protection. Parole supervision was expected to control and rehabilitate the offender. Parole review was purposely designed to be an informal and subjective administrative process in which qualified professionals could review an inmate's criminal offense, personal background, and prison record in an effort to determine readiness for release. Initially, this release process assumed that incarceration was essentially a rehabilitating experience. By releasing the offender when the prison experience had achieved its maximum benefit, and when the offender was no longer a threat to the community, parole could facilitate the offender's adjustment to freedom and use with maximum efficiency those scarce correctional resources.

In recent years, this view of parole has been repeatedly challenged. Critics of parole have argued that it does not work, that its underlying assumption of offender rehabilitation during incarceration is fallacious, that the parole release decision-making process is arbitrary, and that the surveillance and supervision of offenders in many jurisdictions are dangerously inadequate.[1]

While the debate over the fairness and effectiveness of parole practices continues, parole is still evolving. Two major forces are re-shaping parole: the continuing trend toward limiting judges' sentencing authority and the reduction of parole authorities' discretion to release offenders. Today more than three-quarters of the states have enacted determinate or mandatory sentencing laws that provide fixed prison terms for offenders. Many other states have begun using **parole guidelines** that limit parole boards' decision-making authority.

These developments represent major changes in the sentencing and parole decision-making processes. Parole has traditionally been linked to an **indeterminate sentencing** model—that is, sentences that include a maximum and minimum term of confinement, set by a judge, with parole authorities making their release decision within those predetermined boundaries. States placed only general restrictions on parole decision making, such as requiring offenders to serve the minimum of an indeterminate sentence. Good-time statutes, which permit offenders to have time deducted from their sentences for good behavior, often reduced the time served even beyond these limitations. This reduction of judicially imposed sentences by correctional officials is only one of the concerns of parole critics.

What Is Parole?

Parole is a method of releasing offenders from prison prior to the expiration of their sentence. Inmates are screened for their suitability for release based upon the risk they pose to the public. Once released to the community, inmates become parolees and are subject to both conditions and supervision performed by a parole agency. The parolees may have their parole revoked and returned to prison if their performance on parole is unsatisfactory. Parole is a more serious condition than probation, partly because most parolees have spent time in prison prior to parole release, and partly be-

cause of the more serious nature of the crimes required to be sentenced to prison. Parole includes several components.[2]

- A process for considering the appropriateness of an eligible offender's release from prison to community supervision prior to the expiration of his or her sentence.

- A period of community-based supervision after a prison term, through which the corrections system can maintain control over the offender, provide assistance in his or her transition to the community, provide continued treatment programming, and monitor his or her successful adjustment to life outside the institution or return him or her to prison if public safety is threatened.

- A power vested in a person or group to make informed release decisions for individual offenders, once the offender has reached parole eligibility.

Today parole is still the primary mechanism by which inmates are released from prison. Almost one-half of all offenders who have been returned to society are released via parole. The next largest single category is those inmates returned via **supervised mandatory release.** These offenders are also subject to parole supervision, but not the traditional parole release process. To highlight the changes in the parole process, in 1997 over 78 percent of all adult felons who were released from prison were released on parole.

Inmates who are not granted parole may be released in one of two other ways. First, they may receive a conditional or **mandatory release.** This form of release is based on the accumulation of **good-time credits,** which are deducted from the sentence because the inmate has conformed to institutional rules and regulations (statutory good time) or because he or she has performed some outstanding service during incarceration (meritorious good time). A second type of release is unconditional; it occurs through the **maximum expiration of sentence.**

Issues in Community Corrections

Molester Seeks Castration; Texas Agrees

Sam Howe Verhovek

HOUSTON, April 4—Larry Don McQuay describes himself as "scum of the earth" and claims to have molested young children at least 240 times.

Without treatment, the former bus driver wrote to a victims-rights group last year, "I am doomed to eventually rape then murder my poor little victims to keep them from telling on me."

The treatment that Mr. McQuay wants is castration. And now that he is days away from a mandatory release from prison, the State of Texas, which has repeatedly denied his request on the ground that it was elective surgery, has undergone an extraordinary turnabout.

The chairman of the state's Board of Pardons and Paroles, Victor Rodriguez, said today that Mr. McQuay could choose to have his testicles removed, and added that the board would encourage him to do so.

The Texas Attorney General, Dan Morales, offered a legal outline for how Mr. McQuay could go about becoming the first man on record to be castrated under state auspices. Or he could do it without any taxpayer money: a Louisiana businessman has offered to pay for the entire operation.

The state's comments today represent the latest twist in a bizarre and often grotesque saga focused on the question of what to do with the 32-year-old Mr. McQuay. A troubled man who may or may not have committed all the sex crimes he seems to enjoy describing in detail, he has commanded center stage as an avowed pedophile whom Texas says it must let out of prison.

On Tuesday, Mr. McQuay was literally on the verge of being released from prison with a $50 check and a bus ticket out of Huntsville, Tex. He would have been required to report to a halfway house here.

"He was two hours from walking out the door and they were saying, 'Adios, report in Houston 24 hours from now,'" said Dianne Clements, the president of Justice for All, a victims-rights group to which Mr. McQuay sent a half-dozen letters last year that included descriptions of his sexual fantasies about young children. "That's frightening."

Another member of the group calls Mr. McQuay "a ticking time bomb with a malfunctioning timer."

Under a gathering storm of public outrage and media attention, the pardons and paroles board managed to hold up Mr. McQuay's release while his case was reviewed and the board's chairman met with Mr. McQuay for 90 minutes.

On Wednesday, Mr. Rodriguez announced that the board had reluctantly concluded that it had no choice but to release Mr. McQuay, who had served six years of an eight-year sentence for indecency with a child in San Antonio in 1989. Under state laws, Mr. McQuay had earned a mandated release because of his accumulation of credits for good behavior in prison.

Moreover, despite passage of a law last year requiring that local law-enforcement agencies be notified when a convicted child molester is moved to their area, Mr. McQuay would not be covered by the law because his offense took place before it was passed.

Source: Sam Howe Verhovek, "Monster Seeks Castration; Texas Agrees; Soon to Leave Prison, Man Wants Testicles Removed as Precaution," *New York Times,* April 5, 1996, p. A9. Copyright © The New York Times Co. Reprinted by permission.

Inmates who max out serve their entire prison terms without benefit of parole or the accumulation of good-time credits. Most inmates sentenced to relatively short terms in county or city jails serve out their entire sentences because early release procedures are unavailable or underutilized. Parole release is generally available only to felons serving time in state or federal prisons. It is ironic that society provides the opportunity for early release principally to more serious, long-term offenders.

To complicate matters, parole is frequently confused with probation in the eyes of the general public. This confusion probably stems from the similarities between the two: Both require the offender to adhere to specific conditions of release and to accept community supervision. In some states, probationers and parolees are supervised by the same agency. However, the differences between the two client statuses are significant. Parole represents a form of release from prison; probation is a form of sentence that does not usually include a sustained period of incarceration in a state or federal prison. **Split sentences,** which provide for a short period of incarceration followed by probation, are an exception to this rule. An administrative agency, usually referred to as the **parole board,** makes parole decisions. In contrast, the probation decision is a judicial function and is made by a sentencing judge. Probationers and parolees also face different problems of adjustment. Probationers are not removed from the community, but parolees may have been isolated from the free world for many years before their release from prison. As a result, parolees often confront many serious difficulties during their transition from prison to the community.

As an organizational component of corrections, parole represents the final stage of the criminal justice system. By the time offenders are eligible for parole, their status has changed several times since their initial contact with the criminal justice system. They have been defined and treated as free citizens, suspects, arrestees, detainees, defendants, convicts, and inmates. If they are released on parole, they are placed under correctional supervision in the community and are referred to as parolees. The community regards individuals who have done their time not as free citizens but as ex-offenders. Although they have paid for their crime through punishment, those convicted of a felony lose many of their privileges as citizens. They may be denied the rights to vote, hold public office, obtain license for an occupation, or enter into civil contracts. These losses are generally referred to as the collateral consequences of conviction or civil disabilities. Some of these rights may be restored, but only if offenders apply to the appropriate state or federal authority.

Inmates returning to the community face more than a loss of rights. Their most immediate need is to survive—to find housing and feed and clothe themselves while searching for employment. If offenders have no family or friends to assist them and no money to tide them over until they obtain employment, their search for self-sufficiency may become desperate. Most offenders leave prison with the same problems with which they entered: drug, alcohol, emotional, interpersonal, educational, and employment problems that may stand as obstacles to law-abiding independence. Parole is expected somehow to help newly released offenders manage all these difficulties while protecting the community from ex-offenders who may be tempted to return to crime.

Justice Objectives

The changing nature of parole makes the identification of systemwide parole objectives difficult. Because many parole systems are in a state of flux, the objectives vary from jurisdiction to jurisdiction. However, consensus appears to have been reached over four objectives: (1) community protection, (2) the achievement of fairness and propriety, (3) the imposition of appropriate sanctions reflecting public expectations, and (4) the maintenance of the justice system.

Most, if not all, correctional systems share the first objective of community protection. Parole systems and parole boards both screen offenders for suitability for early release and supervise offenders while on release to ensure law-abiding behavior. The possibility that an offender might return to a life of crime is addressed by the parole release decision-making process, which is expected to screen out dangerous offenders, and by parole supervision. This supervision consists of two components: controlling the offender's behavior through surveillance strategies and providing social services and assistance.

The objective of ensuring fairness and propriety reflects a number of concerns, ranging from providing procedural rights to parolees to equalizing some of the perceived injustices associated with sentencing disparity (for example, when two offenders are convicted of similar crimes but receive vastly different sentences). Parole boards can minimize such disparities.

The use of appropriate sanctions reflecting public expectations requires parole authorities to be responsive to the community. The impact of the perceived community demands or pressures can be considerable. Community reaction may lead to reductions in the release rate or to the removal of a particular offender from parole consideration because of the notoriety of his or her crime or the status of his or her victim(s). Another side of public reaction is the community's role in welcoming the parolee upon his or her return to freedom. Community hostility and outright rejection can make the provision of services and assistance difficult at best.

The final major objective of parole is the maintenance of the justice system. As the prison-crowding crisis in the nation's prisons has demonstrated, parole boards act as a kind of system regulator. Because parole boards control the flow of ex-inmates into the community, they influence all other parts of the justice system, from police to prison. Within the correctional institution itself, parole's impact is extensive. Parole board policy not only influences the length of time inmates will serve, but parole board actions also influence the types of programs inmates will participate in. If parole boards look favorably upon prisoners who acquire educational credentials, this concern will rapidly spread to the inmate population and participation in educational programs will significantly increase. Parole board actions may also affect prisoner morale, which may be negatively affected, especially if the decision making appears arbitrary.

Societal Objectives

Society has some expectations regarding the effects of parole that go well beyond simple supervision. If it can be reasonably assumed that the court process reflects the beliefs of the citizenry and that judges within these courts act in support of the constituency that elected them, then it is possible to look at court decisions regarding parole as a barometer of public opinion.

What is the ultimate goal of parole, according to the courts? Parole is seen as social control; the conditions placed upon the offenders clearly indicate that, but what function does parole serve from the perspective of the court? The Latin term *parens patriae*, which is used to justify many of the actions of the juvenile court, helps to explain the legal goals of parole. Specifically, parens patriae states that the government has both the power and the duty to act as the "parents of the country." This implies that the courts, through the disposition and definition of parole, are expecting that parole will serve the interests of the offender, as well as the society. Society seems to share that sentiment. The public considers a person on parole who re-offends not just a danger to society, but also a failure of the parole process. Parole, like prison, is supposed to change the person, making them less likely to re-offend and more likely to survive in society.

The decision in *Greenholtz* vs. *Inmates of the Nebraska Penal and Correctional Complex,* which primarily effected the operations of the state as they pertain to the granting or parole release, stated that parole was—and continues to be—a rehabilitative device. The fact that it has not been completely successful in every case does not diminish the objective; parole is intended to be rehabilitative. Furthermore, the *Greenholtz* decision went on to state that parole can be considered a right, depending on the wording of the state statutes. Again, this belief reflects the tenets of parens patriae, which, if applied to parole, would argue that the state has a duty to provide services that will assist the offender in remaining law abiding. If a state writes in its parole legislation that an inmate "may" be paroled after serving a certain percentage of his or her sentence, then the inmate has the right to a hearing, but not to release. The discretion is in the hands of the state; parole is an option but is not automatic. If, however, the state law is written that the inmate "shall" receive parole after successful completion of a certain percentage of his or her sentence, then the parole is assumed to be automatic and the state is bound to show just cause for not allowing the inmate to be released. This occurs in some states where the role of the parole board is not to release, but to show why an inmate should not be released. According to the *Greenholtz* decision, inmates have the right to be considered for parole, but parole is not automatic unless the state law is written in that manner. If it is, then the role of the parole board is to retain, not release.

Historical Development

The word *parole* comes from the French term ***parole d'honneur,*** which means "word of honor." Parole can be traced back to the United States' English heritage. Three British correctional practices played an especially important role in the emergence of parole in the United States in 1876: the **policy of trans-** **portation,** the use of the conditional pardon, and the **ticket of leave.**[3]

The transportation of criminals by the British, which has its roots in the ancient practice of banishment, began in the 1600s.[4] The English experiment with transportation was designed to deal with some troubling socioeconomic problems that plagued England at the time. The country was experiencing high levels of unemployment along with the related social problems of crime and poverty. At the same time, the English were suffering a shortage of manpower in their American colonies. Transportation directly addressed all these social problems.

Initially, criminals were granted reprieves or stays of execution if they were able bodied and fit for work. Those persons granted reprieves were subsequently transported to the colonies for work. Because the transported felons sometimes surreptitiously returned to their homeland, restrictions were eventually placed on the transportees, prohibiting them from returning to England. This practice became known as conditional parole. Prisoners who violated the conditions would have their reprieve or pardon withdrawn and their original sentence imposed; offenders who remained in the colonies had their sentences suspended. The mechanics involved in transporting criminals were relatively simple.

When transportation was just beginning, the government paid a fee to the contractor for each prisoner transported. However, in 1717, a new law was enacted and this procedure was discontinued. Under the new procedure, the contractor or shipmaster was given "property in service" of prisoners until the expiration of their full term. After prisoners were delivered to the contractor or shipmaster, the government took no interest in their welfare or behavior unless they violated the conditions of the pardon by returning to England prior to the expiration of their sentence.

When the pardoned felons arrived in the colonies, their services were sold to the highest bidder and the shipmaster then transferred the "property in service" agreement to the new master. The felons were no longer referred to as convicted criminals but became **indentured servants.**[5]

The American Revolution ended the transportation of criminals to the British colonies in North America. However, the English crime problem did not abate, nor did the English find they had adequate resources to deal with their prisoner population at home. A search for solutions resulted in the transportation of convicted felons to Australia. This practice began in 1787 and continued until 1867, when the Australians' strenuous objections ended this penal practice.

The mechanics of transporting criminals to Australia differed somewhat from those of transporting them to America. The government met all the expenses incurred in transportation. The offenders did not become indentured servants but remained prisoners under the control of the British, who assumed responsibility for their behavior and welfare.[6]

In Australia, the colonial governor was responsible for the felons and had the authority to assign convicts to free settlers. Convicts assigned to settlers were expected to serve out their sentences, performing various tasks for their civilian supervisors. After a period of **penal servitude,** the transportees were granted pardons, which released them from their enforced labor. These pardons became known as tickets of leave, which generally read as follows:

It is his Excellency, the Governor's pleasure to dispense with the government work of _____ tried at _____ convicted of _____ and to permit _____ to employ (off government stores) in any lawful occupation within the district of _____ for his own advantage during good behavior or until his Excellency's further pleasure shall be made known.[7]

The method by which tickets of leave were granted underwent several changes. In the beginning, they were awarded to inmates for a variety of reasons, including good behavior, mer-

itorious service, or marriage.[8] Later, the ticket of leave was granted only after inmates had served a specific portion of their sentence. As per the English Penal Servitude Act of 1853, prisoners sentenced to terms of fifteen years or more were required to serve a minimum of six years before they could be considered for release. This was similar to the contemporary U.S. practice of specifying minimum terms of imprisonment to be served prior to release on parole.

In 1854, Sir **Walter Crofton** introduced three stages of penal servitude into the Irish convict system. Crofton's work was influenced by Captain **Alexander Machonochie,** who had experimented with these penal practices in New South Wales. Underlying these experiments was the objective of providing offenders with a graduated release experience. In Crofton's Irish system, offenders passed through three stages of confinement. After an initial stage of hard labor in isolation, offenders were provided with an opportunity to perform congregate labor. When they progressed to the third stage of penal servitude, offenders were placed in a transitional setting where they lived and worked under relaxed security conditions. If offenders successfully reached the third penal stage, they were granted a ticket of leave, which permitted a return to the community. This freedom, however, was conditional. If they misbehaved, they would be returned to prison to serve out their unexpired term.

In the United States, these correctional reforms came to the attention of **Zebulon Brockway.** Brockway, who became superintendent of the Elmira Reformatory in 1876, incorporated the concepts of the indeterminate sentence, parole, and the earning of good-time credits into his program for youthful offenders at Elmira.[9] He also persuaded the New York state legislature to pass an indeterminate sentencing law, which shifted the authority for determining the time prisoners served from the judiciary to correctional officials. Correctional authorities were to evaluate inmate behavior and conformity to institutional discipline. When officials believed that an inmate was fit for freedom, he or she was released for a six-month period of parole supervision by a volunteer-based guardian. These guardians were ordinary citizens who contributed their time and energies freely. Later, supervision was also provided by volunteer-based prison societies, which were concerned with the social welfare of newly released offenders. By 1900, parole was available in some form to inmates in twenty states. Less than twenty-five years later, only a few states had failed to adopt parole procedures.

Another correctional innovation of the 1800s was good-time credits, which attempted to provide inmates with incentives to improve themselves while under correctional custody. The belief was that no better way existed of achieving inmate commitment to institutional objectives than to provide credits for sentence reduction for good behavior. New York passed the first good-time statute in 1817; every state had authorized a good-time law by 1916.[10] Release based on the accumulation of good-time credits is referred to as supervised mandatory release. The release is automatic and does not require parole board approval. In some instances, offenders who present a clear and present danger will be released via this early release mechanism. These releasees are supervised by parole officers.

Good-time practices have continued to the present. Institutional administrators are among the strongest proponents of good time because it gives inmates incentives to obey prison rules and regulations. It also helps them make the most of their incarceration experience. This type of release provides prison administrators another mechanism by which to reduce crowding in correctional facilities. A survey by the National Institute of Corrections in 1995 revealed that major changes have taken place in the area of mandatory release. Nineteen jurisdictions have abolished mandatory release based on good-time credits for inmates.[11] This represents a major shift in correctional policy. What effect this will have on the operation of prisons that rely on the use of good-time credits to control inmate behavior is unknown.

Table 5-1 Characteristics of Adults on Parole, 1990 and 1998

Characteristic	1990	1998
Gender		
Male	92	88
Female	8	12
Race		
White	52	55
Black/African American	47	44
Other	1	1
Hispanic origin		
Hispanic	18	21
Non-Hispanic	82	79
Status of supervision		
Active	82	81
Inactive	6	5
Absconded	6	8
Supervised out of state	6	5
Other	**	—
Adults entering parole		
Discretionary parole	59	41
Mandatory parole	41	53
Reinstatement	**	5
Other	**	1
Adults leaving parole		
Successful completion	50	45
Returned to incarceration	46	42
With new sentence	17	13
Other	29	29
Absconder	1	9
Other unsuccessful	1	1
Transferred	1	1
Death	1	1
Other	**	1

Note: For every characteristic there were persons of unknown status or type. Detail may not sum to one hundred because of rounding.

** = Not available.

— = Less than 0.5%.

Source: Thomas P. Bonczar and Lauren E. Glaze, *Probation and Parole in the United States, 1998* (Washington, D.C.: U.S. Department of Justice, Bureau of Justice Statistics, 1999).

Contemporary Parole

As of December 31, 1997, 685,033 offenders were under parole supervision, which represents a rate of 346 per 100,000 and an increase of 1.3 percent over January 1, 1997. Of the 73 percent under active supervision, 61 percent were new parole placements and the remaining were existing parole placements (Table 5-1). Of the 504,289 prison releases in 1996, 369,808 (73 percent) were released from prison via

Table 5-2   Adults on Parole, 1998

Region and Jurisdiction	Parole Population, 1/1/98	1998 Entries	1998 Exits	Parole Population, 12/31/98	Percent Change in Parole Population during 1998	Number on Parole per 100,000 Adult Residents, 12/31/98
U.S. total	694,787	434,209	423,661	704,964	1.5	352
Federal[a]	63,512	24,895	21,238	66,761	5.1	33
State	631,275	409,314	402,423	638,203	1.1	318
Northeast	162,782	72,626	69,713	165,313	1.6	422
Connecticut	996	1,449	1,260	1,185	19.0	48
Maine[b]	67	2	4	65	–3.0	7
Massachusetts[a]	4,596	3,718	3,443	4,489	–2.3	96
New Hampshire	1,083	565	507	1,141	5.4	129
New Jersey[b]	16,903	16,281	18,627	14,557	–13.9	238
New York	59,670	25,096	25,218	59,548	–0.2	436
Pennsylvania[b]	78,264	24,726	19,822	83,168	6.3	910
Rhode Island	526	532	589	469	–10.8	62
Vermont	677	257	243	691	2.1	154
Midwest	89,860	69,798	65,939	93,719	4.3	201
Illinois	30,348	23,773	23,689	30,432	0.3	344
Indiana[c,d]	4,044	4,681	4,467	4,258	5.3	97
Iowa	2,037	2,608	2,451	2,194	7.7	103
Kansas[c]	6,150	4,982	5,107	6,025	–2.0	312
Michigan	14,351	10,503	9,523	15,331	6.8	211
Minnesota	2,446	3,011	2,462	2,995	22.4	86
Missouri[e]	12,514	5,034	7,182	10,366	–17.2	257
Nebraska	688	710	774	624	–9.3	51
North Dakota	116	338	279	175	50.9	37
Ohio	6,803	9,275	4,774	11,304	66.2	135
South Dakota	823	825	560	1,088	32.2	203
Wisconsin	9,540	4,058	4,671	8,927	–6.4	231
South	236,743	99,334	109,084	227,473	–3.9	321
Alabama[a,b,f]	6,356	2,423	2,059	6,785	6.7	208
Arkansas[e]	5,719	5,415	4,763	6,371	11.4	338
Delaware[a,b,g]	591	:	192	572	–3.2	101
District of Columbia[a,b]	7,761	1,553	2,975	6,625	–14.6	1,577
Florida	8,477	4,315	5,371	7,421	–12.5	65
Georgia[a]	21,915	10,360	11,749	20,482	–6.5	364
Kentucky	4,233	2,938	2,663	4,508	6.5	153
Louisiana	19,927	13,533	14,701	18,759	–5.9	590
Maryland	15,763	8,459	8,694	15,528	–1.5	404

discretionary parole release, while 20 percent (103,435) were unconditional releases. Of the 63,907 offenders who violated parole in the same year, only 40 percent received a new sentence for their actions. The remaining offenders, while parole violators, did not result in new convictions. Some states are more willing to be flexible when it comes to parole violations. Sometimes this stems from internal factors—such as prison crowding, which discourages readmissions—and sometimes it stems from administrative pressures to keep the failure rate low to appear in control of the paroled population (Table 5-2).

Factors influencing parole release include the state's parole law, eligibility criteria, formal and informal practices of the parole board, the community's attitude toward parole practices, and various problems affecting institutional corrections (for example, prison riots, overcrowding, and court orders). From a system perspective, such factors as the political environment—especially legislative action and election-year politics, law enforcement policies, and judicial behavior—influence the use of parole within a particular state.

An examination of national parole population trends suggests that more and more of-

Table 5-2 *(continued)*

Region and Jurisdiction	Parole Population, 1/1/98	1998 Entries	1998 Exits	Parole Population, 12/31/98	Percent Change in Parole Population during 1998	Number on Parole per 100,000 Adult Residents, 12/31/98
Mississippi[c,d,h]	1,378	1,094	983	1,489	8.1	75
North Carolina[b]	8,148	6,923	9,331	5,740	−29.6	102
Oklahoma[b]	1,928	317	713	1,532	−20.5	62
South Carolina	4,813	939	1,393	4,359	−9.4	152
Tennessee	8,693	3,086	4,174	7,605	−12.5	186
Texas[e]	109,437	32,189	29,604	112,022	2.4	793
Virginia	10,710	5,115	9,125	6,700	−37.4	130
West Virginia	894	675	594	975	9.1	69
West	141,890	167,556	157,687	151,698	6.9	346
Alaska[e]	472	313	293	492	4.2	117
Arizona	3,378	6,207	5,843	3,742	10.8	110
California[c,f]	104,412	140,724	134,519	110,617	5.9	466
Colorado	4,139	4,421	3,356	5,204	25.7	178
Hawaii	1,827	791	609	2,009	10.0	225
Idaho	820	832	378	1,274	55.4	145
Montana[a,e]	755	:	:	667	−11.7	102
Nevada[b]	3,463	2,606	2,014	4,055	17.1	317
New Mexico	1,626	1,671	1,524	1,773	9.0	144
Oregon	16,815	7,010	6,555	17,270	2.7	703
Utah	3,281	2,686	2,195	3,772	15.0	270
Washington[a,e]	480	23	155	375	−21.9	9
Wyoming[b]	422	272	246	448	6.2	127

: = Not known.

[a]Because of incomplete data, the population on December 31, 1998, does not equal the population on January 1, 1998, plus entries, minus exits.

[b]Some data are estimated.

[c]Data do not include absconders.

[d]Data do not include out-of-state cases.

[e]All data are estimated.

[f]Multiple agencies reporting.

[g]Data are for period beginning March 30, 1998, and ending December 31, 1998.

[h]Data do not include inactive cases.

Source: Thomas P. Bonczar and Lauren E. Glaze, *Probation and Parole in the United States, 1998* (Washington, D.C.: U.S. Department of Justice, Bureau of Justice Statistics, 1999).

fenders are being released to parole supervision every year. Although the shift toward limiting sentencing judges' and parole authorities' discretion may have an impact on this trend, it appears that, as prisons become more overcrowded, correctional authorities searching for relief will increasingly utilize parole or other early release procedures. However, the mood of the electorate is increasingly concerned with predatory and repeat criminals, and many states are taking action to permanently remove these offenders from society via "three strikes (or two strikes) and you're out" laws, which mandate life sentences. The im-

pact of these changes will be significant and long term.

More than 80 percent of inmates released from prison in the United States are subjected to some form of parole supervision. A major shift, however, has occurred in the method of releasing inmates from prison to correctional supervision in the community. Any increased use of parole would strain the resources of already overburdened parole agencies. If additional resources are not provided, parole agencies likely will come under new criticism for not supervising offenders adequately. In the past, such criticism has led to a "lock 'em up" approach to crime control, which only exacerbates prison overcrowding. Taken together, the preceding steps produce what some observers have called "the revolving door of justice."

Administrative Structure

Over the years, three organizational models for the administration of parole services have emerged—the institutional, the autonomous, and the consolidated models.

The institutional model invests institutional officials with the paroling decision. The rationale for this practice rests on the belief that, because prison officials are in day-to-day contact with the offender, they are the most knowledgeable regarding the offender's fitness or readiness for release. This model has been criticized because it is feared that the parole decision might be compromised and affected by factors unrelated to the offender's fitness for parole (for example, prison overcrowding). The institutional model has not gained much of a foothold at the adult level of corrections, but it appears to be the preferred method for placing juveniles on aftercare services following a period of more intensive incarceration (the equivalent of adult parole). This is referred to as youth parole in some states to distinguish it from juvenile probation.

The autonomous model places the authority for parole decisions in the hands of an agency that is independent from the organization that administers the prison. Supporters of this model argue that the parole decision process will be more objective under this strategy than under the institutional model. They suggest that the independent agency is less likely to be influenced by issues related to prison management. Critics of the autonomous approach argue that it interferes with the concept of a unified and consistent correctional process. That is, parole decisions may not be consistent with institutional treatment objectives and may even be at odds with prison programming.

The consolidated model represents a compromise between the institutional and autonomous models. It combines the best features of both strategies. A quasi-autonomous parole board is created within a larger corrections department. Institutional officials provide input into decision making but do not have the authority to release inmates early. This appears to be the preferred model in adult corrections today.

Essential Elements of Parole

The American Correctional Association outlined the essential characteristics of an effective and efficient parole system. An examination of some of them provides an overview of contemporary parole operations:

1. Flexibility in the sentencing and parole laws.

2. A qualified parole board.

3. A qualified parole staff.

4. Freedom from political or improper influences.

5. Parole assigned to a workable position in the governmental administrative structure.

6. Proper parole procedures.

7. Rerelease preparation within the institution.

8. Parole search.

9. A proper attitude by the public toward the parolee.[12]

Sentencing Flexibility

The structure and function of parole is inextricably tied to the sentencing model used within a particular jurisdiction. The structure of the sentencing laws determines to what extent the parole board is empowered to release inmates from prison prior to the expiration of their court-imposed sentences. The National

Advisory Commission on Criminal Justice Standards and Goals acknowledged the significance of sentencing models when it stated:

All parole systems, no matter how autonomous, are part of a larger process—not only of corrections generally, but also of a complex sentencing structure involving trial courts and legislative mandates. The structure and functions of parole systems and their relative importance in the jurisdiction's total criminal justice picture all depend largely on the sources of sentencing authority and limits on sentencing alternatives and lengths.[13]

A number of sentencing models (determinate, indeterminate, mandatory minimum, presumptive sentencing guidelines, and voluntary/advisory sentencing guidelines) are in use today, which have their own implications for parole.

The indeterminate sentence has been linked with parole since its inception and appears to be the model most consistent with the objectives of parole. Under this model, the legislature is responsible for setting the minimum and maximum prison sentence for a particular offense; the judge specifies a prison term within the parameters provided by the legislature; the parole board determines the actual time to be served. Under this model, three sources of authority—the legislature, the court, and the parole board—influence the sentencing and paroling practices of a particular jurisdiction.

The range of discretion provided to the parole board under the indeterminate sentencing model varies across jurisdictions. If the parole board is provided with total discretion regarding the release decision, then time served could range from one day to life. Such a policy would invest the parole board with almost total responsibility for the release decision, but political realities have prevented the widespread adoption of this practice. Today its use appears to be on the decline. Judges and legislators are extremely reluctant to give up their authority and place total discretion in the hands of parole board members, who are generally the governor's appointees.

As an alternative, the American Correctional Association recommends a sentencing model that is consistent with the objectives of parole but provides some limits on discretion.[14] Under this model, the sentencing judge specifies a maximum sentence but sets no minimum term, thereby empowering parole authorities to release inmates at any point up to the maximum term set.

In contrast to the position of the American Correctional Association, which generally encourages flexibility in the sentencing process, significant steps have been taken in many jurisdictions to reduce the discretion available to judges and parole authorities. Although many explanations have been offered for this trend toward reduced flexibility in the sentencing process, one important consideration is the disparity that can result from the wide latitude given to judges and parole decision makers. Parole was originally viewed as a means of reducing sentencing disparity, but many observers of the correctional process think that parole often falls far short of this goal and instead may introduce greater disparity into release decision making. Ideally, a parole system must be flexible enough to permit individualization of judgments but equitable and consistent enough to promote confidence in the fairness of the process. A second significant concern is the extent of sentence reduction achieved through parole and good-time procedures. Considerable feeling exists among the general public that parole has gone too far and that sentences need to be made more definite, both for punitive and deterrent purposes.

Changes in Parole Powers

The discretionary release powers of parole boards have changed over the last several years. Reflecting the get-tough attitude exhibited toward criminals by legislatures, parole has been abolished in seventeen states. Jurisdictions that have abolished parole include, pre-1990: Florida, Illinois, Indiana, Maine,

Issues in Community Corrections

Sentencing Models

Determinate

Sentence of incarceration in which an offender is given a fixed term that may be reduced by good time or earned time. There are usually explicit standards specifying the amount of punishment and a set release date with no review by an administrative agency (parole board). Postincarceration supervision (parole) may be a part of the sentence.

Indeterminate

Sentence in which an administrative agency, generally a parole board, has the authority to release an offender and determine whether an offender's parole will be revoked for violations of the conditions of release. In one form of indeterminate sentencing, the judge specifies only the maximum sentence length; the associated minimum duration is automatically implied but is not within the judge's discretion. In the more traditional form of indeterminate sentencing, the judge specifies a maximum and minimum duration that is set by statute. The sentencing judge has discretion on the minimum and maximum sentence.

Mandatory Minimum

A minimum sentence that is specified by statute and that may be applied for all convictions of a particular crime or a particular crime with special circumstances (e.g., robbery with a firearm or selling drugs to a minor within 1,000 feet of a school).

Presumptive Sentencing Guidelines

Sentencing that meets the following conditions: (1) the appropriate sentence for an offender in a specific case is presumed to fall within a range of sentences authorized by sentencing guidelines that are adopted by a legislatively created sentencing body, usually a sentencing commission; (2) sentencing judges are expected to sentence within the range or provide written justification for departure; (3) the guidelines provide for some review, usually appellate, of the departure. Presumptive guidelines may employ determinate or indeterminate sentencing structures.

Voluntary/Advisory Sentencing Guidelines

Recommended sentencing policies that are not required by law. Usually based on past sentencing practices, they serve as a guide to judges. The legislature has not mandated their use. Voluntary/advisory guidelines may employ determinate or indeterminate sentencing structures.

Source: National Assessment of Structured Sentencing (Washington, D.C.: U.S. Department of Justice, Bureau of Justice Assistance, February 1996).

Minnesota, New Mexico, Oregon, Washington, and the U.S. Parole Commission; post-1990: Arkansas, Arizona, Delaware, Kansas, Mississippi, North Carolina, Ohio, and Virginia.

Changes in Sentencing Affecting Inmate Eligibility Citizens and their legislative representatives are concerned with those who are serious violent offenders or repeat offenders

Issues in Community Corrections

The Truth About Polly Klaas

Richard Allen Davis was a dangerous violent felon. He was sentenced to life in prison in 1976 for kidnapping and other violent crimes. His criminal record was littered with instance after instance of predatory behavior. The paroling authority in the State of California knew this. His disregard for human life and safety, even while in prison, was a profound reminder of the need to keep this individual isolated from the community as long as possible. While in prison, the parole board reviewed his case six times, and six times the parole board rejected any possibility of release.

But the forces of change were at work in California. Politicians pledged to be "tough on crime." The obvious answer—"Abolish parole." And they got their wish. The requirement of earning the approval of the parole board before even a dangerous offender could be released was abolished. New standard sentences mandated automatic release after service of a set portion of the sentence. Offenders already incarcerated came under the provisions of the new law. Release dates were churned out by the prison system's computers for thousands

of prisoners then in custody. When the computers had done their job, there was no turning back. Richard Allen Davis had already served the amount of prison time that the new law and its mandatory release provisions demanded. He had a mandatory sentence alright—including a mandatory release. On the night of June 27, 1993, Richard Allen Davis walked out of prison, a free man. Less than four months later, in the safe darkness of a girlhood slumber party, Richard Allen Davis is alleged to have kidnapped and brutally murdered a little girl. Her name was Polly Klaas.

No one can say with certainty all that would have happened to Richard Allen Davis if parole had not been abolished in California. But there is overwhelming evidence that if the parole board had still been in control of release, Richard Allen Davis would have been in prison the night that Polly Klaas was murdered.[a]

[a]Information from California Board of Prison Terms.
Source: Abolishing Parole: Why the Emperor Has No Clothes (Lexington, Ky.: American Probation and Parole Association, 1995). Used by permission.

getting out of prison early. As a result, many state legislatures have taken steps to ensure that offenders serve a greater portion of their sentence. In many states, legislatures have passed truth-in-sentencing statutes, requiring certain more serious offenders to serve 85 percent of their sentences, established new minimum mandatory sentences, and eliminated good-time credits in many states.[15]

Some of the Most Noteworthy Changes
Missouri, Montana, Nebraska, and Texas passed

laws requiring inmates to serve a certain percentage of their sentence before being considered for early release. The federal Violent Crime Control and Law Enforcement Act of 1994 mandated that inmates serve 85 percent of their sentence prior to being considered for early release. California passed the three strikes law, which mandates life sentences without the possibility of release for third-time serious offenders. Five states and the District of Columbia have established life without parole statutes for certain types of offenders.[16]

Qualified Parole Board

Given the responsibilities of their office, parole board members need to be well qualified. However, few states have created and enforced guidelines that would ensure the selection and appointment of qualified individuals to these important positions.

To address the qualifications of parole board members, what they do must be examined and understood. Their responsibilities lie in two areas: general policy making and individual decision making regarding specific cases. Policy making includes interpreting parole to the public and promoting sound parole legislation as well as formulating regulations and guidelines on all matters related to the work of the parole board. Parole decision-making functions include reviewing cases to fix parole eligibility dates, granting and revoking paroles, discharging offenders from parole when supervision is no longer required, and determining the conditions of parole. In about half of the states, the parole board is also responsible for recommending commutations of sentence.[17] Where the workload is heavy, many agencies appoint a full-time administrator who is responsible for the details of day-to-day parole agency management.

The American Correctional Association suggests that prospective candidates for appointment should not be political officials and should have the following qualifications: good character, academic training in corrections or a closely related discipline (criminology, sociology, social work, or law), and experience with and an understanding of the offenders and their problems.[18] The National Advisory Commission on Criminal Justice Standards and Goals suggests that members should also have a high degree of skill in comprehending legal issues and statistical information.[19] A critical factor in selecting individuals for the parole board is the process by which members are appointed. In a majority of states, the governor has the power to appoint members to the parole board. Most appointments are for terms of six years or less. One survey of the appointment process reported that at least two-thirds of the states had either no criteria or standards so vague as to render them meaningless.[20]

Qualified Parole Staff

The quality of parole services will only be as good as the quality of employees working in the field of parole. In addition to the members of the parole board, there are several types of parole employees: administrators, field parole officers, and clerical workers. In some agencies, paraprofessionals (often ex-offenders) may also be employed as parole aides.

Parole officers are responsible for a variety of law enforcement and social service tasks. These include preparing inmates for parole; assisting in parole hearings; periodically meeting and communicating parole policy to offenders; counseling, advising, and assisting inmates regarding a variety of issues ranging from personal problems to employment needs; handling paperwork associated with parole casework; and making decisions regarding the offender's status on parole—that is, is he or she making a successful adjustment or should parole be revoked?

Parole supervision requires a blend of social service and law enforcement responsibilities. Law enforcement tasks include surveillance, field interviews, liaison with other law enforcement agencies, searches, and arrests. Social service tasks include counseling, crisis intervention services, and resource brokerage of community resources. The selection of individuals for parole fieldwork should be based on merit. Some consensus exists that the qualifications for a professional position should include graduation from an accredited university with a concentration in a corrections-related area. In addition, one year of supervised experience with a social service agency or one year of graduate study also seems desirable. At present, most states require a college degree but do not require any particular field of educational study.

In the state of Georgia, all parole officers hired since 1970 must have a four-year college degree and meet the training requirements set forth by the Georgia Peace Officers Standards and Training Act. This includes six weeks of basic training in such subject areas as investigation and supervision strategies, surveillance techniques, interpersonal communications, arrest procedures, constitutional law as it applies to parolees, firearms instruction, and ethics.

Freedom from Influence

Many important correctional decisions involve discretion. In terms of impact, these decisions can have serious implications for the offender (continued incarceration) and for the community (crime control). The exercise of discretion can also have a major impact on the organization and function of corrections. Therefore, decisions must not be influenced by partisan politics or considerations of personal gain. For example, the distribution of corrections jobs as rewards for political loyalty is not an uncommon practice, but it impedes professionalization in corrections. Political officials have also attempted to intervene in release decision making to obtain favorable treatment for specific offenders or to bar the release of inmates perceived as threats to the community. These actions undermine staff, inmate, and community commitment to the goals of corrections and can have disastrous consequences for parole system operation.

Effective Parole Administration

Currently, four organizational structures are used to administer parole in the United States. In most states, the parole board administers the combined probation and parole system. Under the second model, probation and parole are not unified; the parole board administers only parole services. In other states, parole and institutional corrections are unified. The

fourth administrative structure unites probation, parole, and institutional corrections in one superstructure.

The ideal structure for parole services administration is a subject of debate. Service continuity and coordination are enhanced by combining services under one organizational umbrella. But separating probation and parole from institutional corrections may permit these services to be more responsive to the orders of the courts and parole board, respectively. The problems of institutional corrections may divert administrative attention and subsequent funding from community-based services to prisons in a unified structure. The objective is to coordinate services without sacrificing recognition of the unique and sometimes conflicting problems of probation, prison, and parole administration.

Proper Parole Procedures

Providing a comprehensive and effective parole system requires considering several interrelated steps. These include providing offenders in prison with information concerning parole purposes, requirements, and expectations; preparing preparole reports for subsequent parole hearings; conducting various types of parole-related hearings; assisting inmates with developing satisfactory parole plans involving employment and a residence; providing graduated release experiences for inmates preparing for release; and providing services to parolees in the community. In addition, an adequate parole system is responsible for the parole revocation process and for the discharge of parolees no longer in need of supervision. These activities reflect the three basic functions of the parole process: preparole preparation, parole-related hearings, and postrelease services and responsibilities.

Preparole Activities   Preparole activities include education, planning, and preparation. Education involves informing inmates of how

Program Focus

The Iowa Parole Board

The Iowa Board of Parole consists of five members appointed by the Governor for four-year staggered terms.

The fulltime Chair is selected by the Governor from among the five members. The other four board members serve on a per diem basis.

Iowa law states that the membership of the Board must be of good character and judicious background, must include a member of a minority group, may include a person ordained or designated a regular leader of a religious community and who is knowledgeable in correctional procedures and issues, and must meet at least two of the following three requirements:

a. Contain one member who is a disinterested layperson;

b. Contain one member who is an attorney licensed to practice law in this state and who is knowledgeable in correctional procedures and issues; and/or

c. Contain one member who is a person holding at least a master's degree in social work or counseling and guidance and who is knowledgeable in correctional procedures and issues.

Board of Parole Membership

WALTER L. SAUR, Chairperson, Oelwein.
Walter Saur has served as Fayette County Attorney for seventeen years, and was president of the Iowa County Attorneys' Association prior to his appointment to the Board of Parole in 1978. He has degrees from Coe College, Drake University, and the University of Iowa, and has been honored with many awards, including Prosecutor of the Year from the National District Attorneys' Association, and the Distinguished Service Award from the Iowa Jaycees. He served in the U.S. Navy during World War II. A pilot in the U.S. Air Force during the Korean War, Saur is a retired Brigadier General.

BARBARA BINNIE, Vice Chairperson, Des Moines.
Governor Terry Branstad appointed Barbara Binnie to the Board of Parole in 1985. Barbara was Field Representative and Caseworker for Senator Charles E. Grassley's Des Moines Congressional Office, and has been Administrative Assistant and Scheduler for two U.S. Senate campaigns. For many years, she has

they can earn parole and what will be expected of them. Planning and preparation for parole involve both staff and inmates. Inmates, usually with the assistance of staff, attempt to set up an institutional program designed to prepare them for parole release. Ideally, this program begins the day the offender enters the institution, but practice suggests otherwise. Institutional administrators and personnel are frequently preoccupied with the

present rather than the future. Their primary concern is to encourage the offender to adjust to prison living rather than to begin preparation for release. Because of this problem, many correctional agencies have adopted short-term, intensive, institutional rerelease or preparole programs. These programs are usually sixty to ninety days in length and are provided to offenders as they near their release dates. They are often designed as much

been involved with ice sports activities for young people, and has served on the Board of Directors of the Des Moines Figure Skating Club and the Greater Des Moines Ice Sports Association.

ROBERT A. JACKSON, SR., Des Moines.
Robert Jackson was appointed to the Board of Parole by Governor Terry Branstad in 1985. Robert, a community organizer, has been a member of the Des Moines Human Rights Commission, the Polk County Senior Citizen Advisory Council, and the Polk County Mental Health Center Board. He was a construction laborer for many years and was involved in union activities, holding offices of Business Agent and Secretary/Treasurer. He is also a veteran of the U.S. Army, having served in World War II.

JOANNE C. LORENCE, Atlantic.
Joanne Lorence was appointed by Governor Branstad in March, 1989. She has been admitted to the bar in the States of Iowa, Kansas, and Missouri. Joanne has degrees from Central College (B.A.), Indiana State University (M.S.), and the University of Iowa (J.D.). She is also a member of the Cass County, Southwest Iowa, Iowa State, and American Bar Associations.

ELIZABETH WALKER, Davenport.
Elizabeth Walker was appointed by Governor Terry Branstad in November 1994. She is currently an Administrative Assistant with the Scott County Decategorization Project. Past government experience includes Administrative Assistant, City of Shreveport, Louisiana, and Records Specialist, Shreveport Police Department. She is a member of the Minority Chamber of Commerce, Iowa Invests Mentor Project, Juvenile Justice Committee, Big Sisters, and United Way and past participant of Voter Registration efforts. Elizabeth holds an Associate Degree in Applied Sciences from South University, Baton Rouge, Louisiana, and a degree in Business Administration/Accounting from Commercial Business College, Alexandria, Louisiana.

Source: Iowa Board of Parole, state of Iowa, 1996.

to undo the effects of incarceration as to prepare inmates for their return to society.

Another important task involved in the preparole planning process is the preparation of a case file on the inmate by the institutional parole officer or other institutional personnel. This file, usually referred to as the preparole report, is given to the parole board prior to the offender's hearing and should provide adequate information to allow the board to reach a reasonable decision regarding the inmate's prospects for parole. In many cases, this document is the sole basis for the parole decision. As a result, it must include relevant and pertinent information regarding the offender, his or her past, and future plans.

In practice, the quality and comprehensiveness of parole reports vary from one system to another, but most contain several basic elements:

1. Information regarding the offender's present offense, including arrest and conviction.

2. Information regarding the offender's individual and social characteristics.

3. A copy of the offender's presentence investigation report.

4. Institutional reports regarding the offender's adjustment to prison, participation in programs, institutional disciplinary infractions, and any recommendations by the institutional staff.

5. The offender's parole plan. (Usually, this must include the residence in which the offender will be staying upon release and a job. Most states require either a confirmed employment offer [job in hand] or a letter of assurance from an employer that the prospective parolee will be provided a job once he or she is released on parole.)[21]

In addition to these items, some parole boards permit statements or recommendations from the offender's sentencing judge and prosecutor or information regarding the victim's attitude toward the offender's release to be included in the parole report.

Parole-Related Hearings   There are several types of parole-related hearings. In some states where indeterminate sentences are used, the parole board sets the offender's minimum parole eligibility date. In other jurisdictions, the parole eligibility date is set by statute or by court order. After the eligibility date has been fixed, the parole board may conduct additional hearings to review cases on an annual basis to assess inmate progress.

Parole boards are responsible for presiding over hearings in which they determine prisoners' readiness for release. Although these hearings determine the time to be served by inmates, legal counsel and the presentation of witnesses are not permitted and hearings are often less formal than a judicial proceeding. They normally involve an interview with the inmate as well as a review of the preparole report. Although the intent is to gain insight into the inmate's character, these interviews often last only a short time and can become superficial and routine. Most states require the parole board to determine to the best of its ability that the prisoner will not violate the law again.

The Model Penal Code, drafted by the American Law Institute, recommends consideration of the following factors:

1. The prisoner's personality, including his or her maturity, stability, sense of responsibility, and any apparent development in his or her personality that may promote or hinder his or her conformity to law.

2. The adequacy of the prisoner's parole plan.

3. The prisoner's ability and readiness to assume obligations and undertake responsibilities.

4. The prisoner's intelligence and training.

5. The prisoner's family status and whether he or she has relatives who display an interest in him or her or whether he or she has other close and constructive associations in the community.

6. The prisoner's employment history, occupational skills, and the stability of past employment.

7. The type of residence, neighborhood, or community in which the prisoner plans to live.

8. The prisoner's past use of narcotics or past habitual and excessive use of alcohol.

9. The prisoner's mental or physical makeup, including any disability or handicap that may affect conformity to law.

10. The prisoner's prior criminal record, including the nature, circumstances, and frequency of previous offenses.

11. The prisoner's attitude toward law and authority.

12. The prisoner's conduct in the institution, including particularly whether he or she has taken advantage of the opportunities for self-improvement afforded by the institutional program, whether he or she has been punished for misconduct within six months prior to his or her hearing or reconsideration for parole release, whether he or she has forfeited any reductions of term during the period of imprisonment, and whether such reductions have been restored at the time of hearing or reconsideration.

13. The prisoner's conduct and attitude during any previous experience of probation or parole and the recency of such experience.[22]

In addition to these prisoner characteristics, a consideration of the community's readiness for the offender's return is often regarded as an important component of the release decision-making process. A decision not to release an inmate should be fully explained to the offender so that he or she can make the necessary improvements to gain release at a subsequent date.

In some states, the parole board does not physically preside over the parole hearings. Instead, parole examiners, who are employees of the board, conduct the hearings. They hear the cases and make recommendations to the board. In some states, the board is still responsible for all release decisions; in others, the board reviews only those cases in which the inmate or the correctional authority is dissatisfied with the hearing examiner's decision. The use of parole examiners can be an effective means of reducing the parole board's workload. Properly recruited and trained, examiners can conduct in-depth professional investigations and interviews, freeing parole board members to devote more time to issues of policy making.

The parole board is also responsible for parole revocation procedures and must approve the revocation of an offender's parole. Similarly, the parole board is responsible for determining discharge procedures for offenders who no longer need parole supervision and issuing final discharges to deserving parolees.

Postrelease Services   The final major activity of parole is the provision of postrelease services. The principal activity of this phase of the parole process is the supervision of parolees. As with the probation function, the supervision process includes two components: providing social services and monitoring the parolee's behavior. The service-delivery systems for probationers and parolees are similar; in some jurisdictions, the same agency deals with both types of offenders. However, parolees' adjustment problems are usually significantly greater than those of probationers. The person placed on probation usually remains in the community, and ties to family, job, or school remain essentially intact. This is not the case for the parolee, who must establish or reestablish ties to a community from which he or she has been forcibly removed for several months or several years. The longer offenders have been in prison, the less likely they will be to have a support group waiting for them in the community.

The conditions of parole the parole board establishes are important tools in the supervision process. Like probation conditions, parole conditions help the offenders when they need reform (offenders might be required to undergo drug treatment or counseling or to continue their education). The conditions also assist parole officers in their attempt to monitor and control the parolee's behavior by requiring the offender to report to them regularly, inform them about changes in residence or employment, refrain from associating with known offenders, and so on. Prior to parole, offenders are required to agree in writing to abide by all parole conditions. Should they fail to fulfill this agreement, parole can be revoked and they can be returned to prison.

The conditions placed on the offenders vary from state to state. The Model Penal Code provides guidelines for states considering a review and possible revision of parole conditions. It recommends the following conditions for parole: When prisoners are released on parole, the parole board shall require as a condition of parole that they refrain from engaging in criminal conduct, adhere to any reporting requirements, obtain and maintain employment, support their family, and participate in any treatment programs if directed. To protect the community, parole services have adopted many of the control-oriented programs used by probation agencies. These include intensive treatment, halfway houses, day reporting centers, intensive supervision, electronic monitoring, drug testing, supervision fees, and restitution.[23]

Revocation   There are two types of parole violations: a legal violation, which consists of a new crime committed by the parolee, and a technical violation, which is a violation of one of the parole conditions. Revocation is not automatic upon the commission of a violation. The parole officer has the discretion to initiate the revocation proceeding. The officer may overlook isolated technical violations. If the violation involves a new offense, the revocation proceeding is generally begun, but the return of the parole violator to prison is still not automatic.

As with the probation revocation process, the parole revocation proceeding must provide certain due process protections to the parolee. These protections include a two-stage hearing procedure. At the first stage, a preliminary hearing is held before an uninvolved person or impartial officer—not necessarily a judicial official—who determines if reasonable cause exists to believe that parole conditions were violated. The offender is provided notice of the hearing and a full description of the charges. At the second stage, the formal revocation proceeding takes place before the parole board or its representative. Minimum due process protection provided to offenders at this stage includes:

1. Written notice of the charge.

2. Disclosure of evidence against them.

3. The right to be heard in person and present witnesses and evidence in their own behalf.

4. A right to confront and cross-examine adverse witnesses (unless good cause is found for not permitting the interaction).

5. A neutral and detached hearing body (such as a parole board).

6. A written statement by the fact finders explaining the decision.

Revocation does not automatically lead to return to prison (Table 5-3). Because of prison crowding, many correctional systems are exploring the use of alternative punishments. These include revoking but returning to the same level of supervision (which results in a loss of time served on parole) and the addition of enhanced control options (drug testing, increased reporting, electronic monitoring, or the use of residential placements other than prison).

Promising Parole Strategies

Parole has undergone many changes in the past few years. Many states have modified or are in the process of modifying the paroling process. Several general observations may be made regarding the current status of parole (and probation) services.[24] First, despite extensive criticism, the rehabilitation ethic is not dead; many parole programs are still designed to change and assist the offender. In many states, specialized programs specifically targeted for parolees have been developed. They deal with offenders with specific problems (for example, sex and drug offenders). Second, the problems created by the conflicting roles assumed by parole officers, who must act as both police officers and social workers, remain unresolved. Third, there is an increasingly pervasive public perception of the threat of crime, which is often translated into a demand that parole agencies emphasize their control function. Fourth, during the past years, parole populations have increased dramatically. The number of staff assigned to parole agencies, however, has not kept pace with the rapid increase in caseloads. Thus, parole resources are seriously overburdened. Fifth, considerable growth has been seen in private sector involvement in the provision of services to parolees. At the same time, some parole agencies have been experimenting with the use of volunteers in parole. Finally, the use of halfway houses and work-release centers for parolees have continued to grow. All these trends affect the formulation and delivery of parole services. Innovations in parole may be grouped according to their principal focus: improving parole decision making or improving parole supervision.

Parole Decision Making   In terms of decision making, one of the most significant innovations is the development and use of parole guidelines, which structure the discretion of parole decision making and ensure that the decisions reached are fair and just. The advantage of guidelines, as one study suggests, is that they facilitate the attempt "to achieve a balance between the evils of completely unstructured discretion and those of a totally fixed and mechanical approach."[25]

The U.S. Parole Commission developed an actuarial tool known as the Salient Factor Score.[26] Designed to facilitate the parole decision-making process, it also illustrates the use of parole guidelines. This device helps the commission determine the period of confinement offenders should serve on the basis of two factors: offense severity and parole prognosis (based on the offender's personal characteristics). Fourteen states, the District of Columbia, and the federal system have adopted similar instruments.

The Salient Factor Score is based on the points assigned to an offender on seven items. When these points are totaled, a composite score ranging from 0 to 11 is obtained. Parole researchers have found that persons with high scores are generally good risks for parole. Figure 5-1 illustrates the salient factor scoring device in determining parole release. Whenever the board decides not to follow the guidelines, it must justify this action in writing. The case of John Wilkes illustrates the use of the Salient Factor Score and parole guidelines.

At age thirty-two, John Wilkes was convicted of illegally transporting Mexican citizens across the border into Texas. At the time of the offense, he had been employed for ten of the previous twenty-four months and had no history of drug or alcohol abuse. His prior record consisted of a conviction for burglary at age twenty-two. He was committed for that offense and then successfully paroled. Using the Salient Factor Score, the parole board determined that Wilkes was a good risk for parole. His score was 8, and he would normally be paroled after fourteen to eighteen months of incarceration.

One of the most promising strategies developed but unfortunately not in use today is **mutual agreement programming (MAP),** which is essentially a contract between the state and the offender regarding the date of release from prison.[27] It requires the cooperation and involvement of the offender, prison officials, and parole authorities. The offender agrees, usually at the beginning of the prison term, to participate in specific programs that are designed either to change his or her behavior (for example, Alcoholics Anonymous) or to provide new skills (for example, vocational training). The prison's role in this contract is to provide the mutually agreed upon resources. The parole authority in turn agrees to release the offender if he or she successfully completes the program obligations. The release date is a critical factor in the contract. The parole board's full cooperation is required if the MAP concept is to be realized. This cooperation is not always easily achieved because parole boards are reluctant to give up any of their discretion.

The mechanics of the MAP process begin with a statement of expectations signed by the three parties early in the offender's prison

Table 5-3 Sentenced Prisoners Admitted to State and Federal Institutions for Violation of Parole or Other Conditional Release, by Whether New Sentence was Imposed, Gender, Region, and Jurisdiction, 1996

Region and Jurisdiction	Total	Parole Violators					Other Conditional Release Violators				
		Total	New Sentence		No New Sentence		Total	New Sentence		No New Sentence	
			Male	Female	Male	Female		Male	Female	Male	Female
U.S. total	175,305	63,907	24,180	1,803	35,087	2,837	111,398	29,979	2,403	72,112	6,904
Federal	2,672	1,366	NA	NA	1,303	63	1,306	NA	NA	1,231	75
State	172,633	62,541	24,180	1,803	33,784	2,774	110,092	29,979	2,403	70,881	6,829
Northeast	19,887	15,887	1,204	44	13,593	1,046	4,000	379	19	3,477	125
Connecticut[a]	238	105	3	0	96	6	133	1	0	121	11
Maine	267	70	67	0	3	0	197	62	3	129	3
Massachusetts[b]	883	688	NA	NA	652	36	195	94	11	NA	NA
New Hampshire[b]	340	340	NA	NA	321	19	NA	NA	NA	NA	NA
New Jersey[c,d]	5,617	5,344	464	16	4,432	432	273	NA	NA	251	22
New York	8,240	7,231	NA	NA	6,765	466	1,009	NA	NA	996	13
Pennsylvania	3,770	1,675	452	20	1,136	67	2,095	78	2	1,940	75
Rhode Island[a,d]	283	185	73	6	100	6	98	54	3	40	1
Vermont[a,b,e,f]	249	249	145	2	88	14	NA	NA	NA	NA	NA
Midwest	21,597	12,543	3,736	182	8,037	588	9,054	4,356	279	4,028	391
Illinois[c,d,f,g]	5,224	NA	NA	NA	NA	NA	5,224	3,959	240	989	36
Indiana	769	769	214	9	505	41	NA	NA	NA	NA	NA
Iowa[f]	792	534	270	28	210	26	258	114	18	122	4
Kansas	1,298	1,225	219	6	918	82	73	14	0	58	1
Michigan[f]	3,606	3,606	968	60	2,402	176	0	X	X	X	X
Minnesota	826	8	1	0	7	0	818	136	11	638	33
Missouri	3,336	1,913	443	40	1,301	129	1,423	52	4	1,200	167
Nebraska[b]	335	335	NA	NA	298	37	0	X	X	X	X
North Dakota[b,c]	92	36	NA	NA	31	5	56	NA	NA	55	1
Ohio[d]	3,742	2,838	1,216	20	1,551	51	904	NA	NA	762	142
South Dakota	192	150	3	0	137	16	42	2	0	38	2
Wisconsin	1,385	1,129	402	19	677	31	256	79	6	166	5
South	44,080	27,148	17,748	1,449	7,241	710	16,932	8,384	658	7,224	666
Alabama	1,840	1,332	95	9	1,153	75	508	474	34	NA	NA
Arkansas	1,878	1,554	625	7	807	115	324	53	0	256	15
Delaware[a,d,e,g]	363	32	30	2	NA	NA	331	305	26	NA	NA
District of Columbia[a,d]	1,949	1,882	1,776	106	NA	NA	67	NA	NA	62	5
Florida[f]	3,722	121	12	0	109	0	3,601	731	53	2,632	185
Georgia[e,f]	3,042	3,042	2,449	142	377	74	NA	NA	NA	NA	NA
Kentucky	1,854	1,518	110	10	1,270	128	336	39	0	263	34
Louisiana	7,435	838	384	43	363	48	6,597	2,523	184	3,510	380
Maryland[h]	1,623	1,621	747	39	793	42	2	0	0	2	0
Mississippi	322	148	41	5	92	10	174	150	24	0	0
North Carolina[d,e]	4,579	4,579	4,194	385	NA	NA	NA	NA	NA	NA	NA
Oklahoma[d]	225	225	111	27	75	12	NA	NA	NA	NA	NA
South Carolina	2,259	1,402	235	14	1,082	71	857	292	20	499	46

career (usually at prison reception).[28] The agreement reached specifies a program designed to meet the offender's needs with objectives identified in incremental steps. Two strategies are utilized to induce the offender's participation and commitment to the change process. First, the offender is actively involved in the planning process for the program, and, second, rewards are used to reinforce his or her behavior. The ultimate reward is release from prison on parole. Rewards are not automatically provided to inmates; they must be earned. At regular intervals during their prison term, the offenders' progress is reviewed to determine if they are continuing to fulfill their part of the agreement. When a MAP program is adopted, the parole decision-making process becomes an individualized and therapeutic process whereby

Table 5-3 *(continued)*

Region and Jurisdiction	Total	Parole Violators					Other Conditional Release Violators				
		Total	New Sentence		No New Sentence		Total	New Sentence		No New Sentence	
			Male	Female	Male	Female		Male	Female	Male	Female
Tennessee[d,e,g]	3,623	2,152	1,983	169	NA	NA	1,471	1,327	144	NA	NA
Texas[d,g,h]	7,566	4,903	4,478	425	NA	NA	2,663	2,490	173	NA	NA
Virginia	1,632	1,632	458	63	982	129	0	X	X	X	X
West Virginia	168	167	20	3	138	6	1	0	0	0	1
West	87,069	6,963	1,492	128	4,913	430	80,106	16,860	1,447	56,152	5,647
Alaska[a]	782	234	14	2	213	5	548	65	9	412	62
Arizona[f]	2,005	531	126	12	330	63	1,474	296	17	1,031	130
California[c,g]	75,785	NA	NA	NA	NA	NA	75,785	16,161	1,380	53,011	5,233
Colorado	1,360	1,220	246	23	873	78	140	56	0	81	3
Hawaii[a,h]	916	416	41	16	349	10	500	186	37	226	51
Idaho	542	289	31	5	225	28	253	54	3	179	17
Montana[d]	341	125	5	1	118	1	216	NA	NA	200	16
Nevada[b,d]	636	636	59	11	532	34	X	X	X	X	X
New Mexico[b,c]	1,153	737	NA	NA	657	80	416	1	NA	376	40
Oregon	1,469	1,469	748	34	637	50	0	X	X	X	X
Utah	1,224	1,224	219	24	903	78	0	X	X	X	X
Washington	774	44	3	0	40	1	730	42	1	592	95
Wyoming	82	38	0	0	36	2	44	0	0	44	0

Note: Most, but not all, states reserve prison for offenders sentenced to one year or more.

NA = Not available.

X = State does not offer sanction, or total was zero so numbers under zero are listed as "X."

[a]Figures include both jail and prison inmates; jails and prisons are combined in one system.

[b]Parole violators with no new sentences may include inmates from other admission categories.

[c]Other conditional release violators with no new sentences include inmates from other admission categories.

[d]Data may include inmates sentenced to less than one year.

[e]Parole violators with new sentences may include inmates from other admission categories.

[f]Data are custody rather than jurisdiction counts.

[g]Other conditional release violators with new sentences include inmates from other admission categories.

[h]Some or all data for the admission categories are estimated.

Source: U.S. Department of Justice, Bureau of Justice Statistics, *Correctional Populations in the United States, 1996,* NCJ-170013 (Washington, D.C.: U.S. Department of Justice, 1999), p. 94.

the release decision is totally based on the offenders' progress toward self-improvement. If they do not take affirmative action to change their behavior, they are not released.

Although mutual agreement programming appears to be a rational process that permits offenders to use their time in prison profitably, few states have embraced the concept, and none currently uses it. The reasons are varied.[29] Several obstacles are the result of a lack of cooperation between parole boards (particularly autonomous ones) and corrections departments. Frequently, the parole board views MAP as usurping its release decision-making authority because prison officials are given a more significant role in the parole release process. Another impediment to successful MAP adoption is correctional system failure

Figure 5-1   Salient Factor Score (SFS 81)

Item A: PRIOR CONVICTIONS/ADJUDICATIONS (ADULT OR JUVENILE)

None	= 3
One	= 2
Two or three	= 1
Four or more	= 0

Item B: PRIOR COMMITMENT(S) OF MORE THAN THIRTY DAYS
(ADULT OR JUVENILE)

None	= 2
One or two	= 1
Three or more	= 0

Item C: AGE AT CURRENT OFFENSE/PRIOR COMMITMENTS

Age at commencement of current offense

26 years of age or more	= 2
20–25 years of age	= 1
19 years of age or less	= 0

***Exception: If five or more prior
commitments of more than thirty days
(adult or juvenile), place an "X" here _____
and score this item   = 0

Item D: RECENT COMMITMENT FREE PERIOD (THREE YEARS)

No prior commitment of more than thirty days
(adult or juvenile) or released to the community
from last such commitment at least three years
prior to the commencement of the current
offense = 1

Otherwise   = 0

Item E: PROBATION/PAROLE/CONFINEMENT/ESCAPE STATUS VIOLATOR
THIS TIME

Neither on probation, parole, confinement, or escape
status at the time of the current offense; nor committed
as a probation, parole, confinement, or escape
status violator this time   = 1

Otherwise   = 0

Item F: HEROIN/OPIATE DEPENDENCE

No history of heroin/opiate dependence	= 1
Otherwise	= 0

TOTAL SCORE

Source: U.S. Department of Justice, *U.S. Parole Commission Rules and
Procedures Manual,* January 1, 1995.

to deliver the resources or programs that it has agreed to provide. The prison system can usually point to legitimate reasons that programs cannot be provided, such as budget cuts, prison overcrowding, and so on. However, the result is that inmates work to meet their commitments, but the state fails to fulfill its side of the bargain.

A final obstacle to the introduction of MAP programming concerns its effectiveness in terms of reducing recidivism. Evaluations of MAP in Wisconsin, a state that pioneered its use, and Michigan have revealed that, when MAP was compared with traditional forms of parole release, significant differences in recidivism were not apparent.[30]

Parole Supervision   One of the most challenging problems in both probation and parole is the classification of offenders regarding their need for services and supervision. Without an effective classification scheme, scarce resources can be wasted. Some clients will be underserved, others will be overmonitored, and staff will be chronically overworked. Wisconsin's case management and classification system represents one state's apparently effective approach to this problem.

The Wisconsin system has four basic components:

1. *Risk and Needs Assessment.* This evaluation involves the use of a risk scale that discriminates between high-, moderate-, and low-risk individuals and a needs assessment instrument that focuses on academic or vocational needs, employment, financial management, marital or family problems, companions, emotional stability, alcohol usage, other drug usage, mental ability, health, and sexual behavior. Risk and needs assessments are used to assist staff in determining the level of supervision an offender requires.

2. *Case Management Classification.* This component involves the use of an interview guide to assist the staff in determining the type of supervision an offender requires. Four supervision strategies commonly utilized are selective intervention, casework and control, environmental structuring, and limit setting.

3. *Management Information System.* This system provides for the routine collection and systematic organization of information obtained on offenders at admission, reevaluation, and termination. These data provide a before, dur-

ing, and after record for each client and can be used to identify trends, project populations, examine usage of community resources, plan future purchase of services priorities, and answer special requests for information.

4. *Workload Deployment and Budget Procedure.* This procedure provides information on each supervising staff member's workload. This information facilitates the deployment of staff and the budgeting of new positions.[31]

A two-year follow-up of the implementation of Wisconsin's classification system yielded the following results. Assignment to different levels of supervision based on assessments of needs and risk appears to have had a significant impact on probation and parole outcomes. Increased contacts with high-need and high-risk cases resulted in fewer new convictions, rule violations, abscondences, and revocations. At the same time, decreasing contacts with low-risk clients had no perceivable adverse effects.

The Wisconsin Risk Assessment Scale has demonstrated effectiveness in predicting success or failure in completing probation or parole terms. In a sample of 8,250 clients, the percentage of individuals rated low risk and later had their parole revoked was 3 percent, while 37 percent of the cases rated high risk subsequently had their parole revoked.

Maximum supervision clients in Wisconsin require an average of three hours of agent time per month; medium supervision clients, 1.25 hours per month; and minimum supervision cases, 0.5 hours per month. Hence, an agent can supervise about six low-risk and low-need clients in the time required to supervise a single high-risk and high-need individual. Emphasis on proper implementation of the classification process and controls on paperwork and information flow were essential to the success of the Wisconsin system.[32]

Public Attitudes   If parole is to be an effective means of reintegrating offenders into the community, then the community must be receptive to the parolee's efforts to establish essential community ties. The general public must be willing and able to view the parolee with fairness and to offer assistance as needed. To accomplish this objective, parole agencies need to evaluate, release, and supervise offenders in a manner that merits the pride and respect of the community. The community in turn must understand the parole process and its function in the correctional system. Today, public understanding of parole seems to be at a low point. The media draw attention to failed parolees who commit new crimes while ignoring the majority who successfully complete parole. In states where early paroles have been granted to large numbers of inmates to relieve overcrowding, the press has sometimes appeared to fan the flames of community outrage rather than to assess the alternatives and examine the impact of such releases on crime rates. Parole too often is portrayed as a giveaway, as freedom granted to the undeserving solely because corrections officials lack the will to do otherwise.

Although current public attitudes toward parole have been influenced by newspaper, television, and radio accounts, the media cannot be singled out as the only guilty party in the misrepresentation of parole. State legislators establish parole criteria and standards, determine parole board member eligibility requirements, and, most important, fund all correctional agencies. However, they are rarely heard from when parole is attacked. In most states, parole board members have adopted a low profile, perhaps in an attempt to avoid scrutiny of a decision-making process that often falls short of the goals of fairness and impartiality.

Parole agency administrators and parole officers have generally chosen not to bring the parole process to public attention, perhaps in the belief that any attention can only yield negative results. In many ways, the media have simply stepped in to fill an information gap, a gap that could be better filled by those who legislate, administer, and deliver parole services.

The American Correctional Association suggests several strategies for the fostering of better public attitudes.

1. Parole personnel should work with community organizations such as the Salvation Army and other organizations that have an interest in parolees' adjustment problems.

2. An organized public information program is a necessity. Parole personnel should seize every opportunity to address civic organizations, church groups, and other interested bodies.

3. Potential employers, civic leaders, and other responsible citizens should be invited to the prisons to observe the correctional process at work.

4. Law enforcement and business executives should be invited to participate in institutional prerelease programs.

5. The parole board should invite representative law enforcement officials, judges, adult students, interested citizens, and responsible members of the press to attend parole hearings.[33]

These and other efforts to inform the public may create temporary problems for administrators as the public attempts to digest and evaluate new information. There has been too much confusion for too long for any informational program to achieve immediate success. But in the long run, an informed citizenry will be more amenable to correctional innovation and the funding of necessary correctional programs if a comprehensive and candid presentation is made of the issues. Correctional administrators must have confidence in the community's ability to respond justly to correction's needs. Correctional efforts can build this confidence through information dissemination.

The American Probation and Parole Association has adopted a proactive stance toward dealing with the issues and recently published a monograph: *Abolishing Parole: Why the Emperor Has No Clothes.*

The Future of Parole

Parole may change form in the future, but it can be expected to remain a widely used correctional strategy. Although the federal government and some states have abolished parole, they have maintained some form of community supervision of released offenders. The increasing number of mandatory releases supervised by parole agencies support this point. For example, when parole was abolished in North Carolina, a new program known as PRAC (Pre-Release and After Care) was created. PRAC provides for the supervision of all prisoners for ninety days after release by PRAC officers, many of whom were formerly parole officers. What has been abolished in North Carolina is the parole release decision-making process. Similarly, in the federal system, parole has been abolished but supervised release has been maintained. This component of parole is most likely to be rethought and restructured in future years; persons released from prison can benefit from community supervision. Parole, to be effective and to maintain the public's confidence, must have more and better programming options available to those offenders in need of community-based treatment, rather than supervision. In addition, and equally important, parole services must create and validate more specific and accurate assessment devices. As programming options increase, the assessment tools must keep pace to match the specific problems of each offender with the treatment options available. Even Robert Martinson, father of the "nothing works" perspective in correctional programming, acknowledged the need for postrelease community supervision, both to facilitate offender reintegration and to protect the community.[34] Later evaluations of Martinson's perspective indicated that it is not that "nothing works" but that "nothing works all the time with all offenders." While the best way to determine the length of time an offender should serve in prison is not yet apparent, greater efforts in this area could yield a parole system that is both behaviorally and economically effective and has the support of the public. At present, the confusion over legislative, judicial, and executive responsibility for sentence determination has mistakenly led to a call for parole abolition. What is needed instead is a continued examination of the release decision-making process so a formula can be devised that meets the concerns for fairness, equality, and individualization of case management. The search for such a process will probably continue for years to come.

Summary of Parole

Parole is the supervision of offenders granted release from prison by a parole board. Inmates may alternatively be released through the maximum expiration of their sentence or upon the accumulation of good-time credits. Parole may be distinguished from these forms of release by the manner in which it addresses the twin concerns of rehabilitation and control. The parole model assumes that inmates will be released when incarceration has achieved its maximum benefit and that community-based guidance, counseling, and behavior monitoring will both assist the ex-offender in his or her attempt to avoid future crime and protect the community during the adjustment period.

Like several other contemporary community-based programs, parole can be traced to English origins and to Crofton's stages of penal servitude. Today it is the most widely utilized prisoner release mechanism, although considerable variability still exists in the use of parole from state to state. Prison overcrowding is one factor that has encouraged an increase in the use of parole. Parole is a controversial correctional program, and it is easy to see why. If parole is to achieve its objectives of rehabilitation and control, sentencing practices must be flexible enough to permit the release of individuals at the optimum point during their prison term. But today a trend is apparent toward minimizing flexibility in the sentencing process. A qualified parole board is needed to make the difficult decisions called for in evaluating an inmate's readiness for release. Few states, however, have established requirements for parole board members. To serve offenders and protect the community, parole field staff need education in the area of criminal justice and must be able to understand their clients' problems. In most states, caseload size has increased far beyond the resources of parole field staff. Parole appointments and release decision making must be free from political influence if they are to maintain credibility. Too often parole board memberships are merely political plums.

Parole must be coordinated with other correctional services if it is to function effectively. Parole's essential elements are threefold: (1) preparing inmates for release and developing preparole reports on prisoners; (2) conducting hearings regarding parole eligibility, granting parole, and revoking parole and terminating parole supervision; and (3) supervising parolees in the community.

Innovative strategies in parole decision making include the use of parole guidelines and mutual agreement programming to facilitate and clarify the release decision-making process. Parole supervision can be improved through the use of well-validated classification schemes, comprehensive employment services for ex-offenders, and the involvement of ex-parolees in parole supervision through the creation of parole aide positions. If parole is to meet its difficult objectives, citizen awareness and support of parole are essential. Parole board decisions are too important to be made

behind closed doors. Parole supervision is too big a job to be accomplished in a hostile environment in which employers and citizens stigmatize and avoid the ex-offender.

Parole will probably continue to serve as the most widely used form of release, but concern remains that it will become more like the arbitrary opening and closing of floodgates than a meaningful crime control and offender-rehabilitation strategy. Legislators and parole and correctional authorities must work diligently to make the best use of parole, a program that is now more essential than at any other time in U.S. history. Crowded prisons must be relieved and the released prisoners must be reintegrated into society if the creation of prisons with rapidly spinning revolving doors is to be avoided.

Temporary Release Programs

The vast majority of offenders will be released from prison some day. Present trends in sentencing suggest that inmates will be required to serve a greater percentage of their sentence in prisons but will still be released from custody to live in the free world. The problems caused by this increasingly prolonged incarceration are diverse. Vocational and social skills deteriorate; independence and self-esteem decline; family and community support systems disappear. Temporary release programs permit inmates to work or study in the community prior to release or to visit the community for a specified number of days for any of a number of purposes. The primary objective of temporary release programs is to combat the effects of institutionalization and to prepare inmates for their eventual return to society.

Although all such programs are designed to prepare inmates for final release from prison, each can serve additional or alternate functions. For example, **work release** is sometimes used as a sentencing disposition. Inmates receiving such sentences are placed on work release immediately after imprisonment, instead of during the last part of their sentences. Study release can be used to supplement institutional educational programs. Furlough programs can be used as alternatives to conjugal visiting.

Each form of temporary release can also be part of halfway house programming. An offender can live in a community correctional facility and work or study in the community during the week and visit his or her family (on furlough) on weekends. Incarceration in a traditional prison is not a prerequisite for work release, study release, or furlough. But an offender's residence in a traditional prison, and the problems it causes, link these diverse programs as they attempt to meet a common objective. Temporary release programs provide a critical link between the imprisoned offender and the community. They are the primary means of bridging the confinement and community gap. As Walter H. Busher said:

The suspicion that unrelieved confinement cannot adequately prepare prisoners to function as responsible citizens after their release has been nagging serious men for at least 100 years. Yet, those whose business it is to confine society's offenders seldom seem able to acquire the strength of conviction, muster the courage, or mobilize the public support required to abandon or modify what they widely suspect to be sterile practice and, instead of pursuing courses of action more in keeping with their suppositions, these administrators tend to complacently repeat the errors of the past. At the base of this lies the average man's deep-seated and largely unresolved conflict concerning the proper means and ends of criminal justice.[35]

Types of Contemporary Programs

Temporary release programs are designed to prepare inmates for their eventual return to the community by releasing them for specified periods of time. During the release period, the inmate may work, attend school, visit with family, or make other preparations for final release.

Work Release   Work-release programs have been referred to by many names—work furlough, day parole, day pass, and community work. Regardless of the specific term employed, any program that provides for the labor of prison or jail inmates in the community under conditions of relaxed supervision for which inmates are paid prevailing free-world wages may be defined as work release. During nonworking hours, inmates on work release serve time like any other offenders. While at work, however, they labor under conditions similar (and in many cases, identical) to those of free persons. They must meet the same job requirements set for other employees, and they work with and are supervised by civilians.

A nationwide survey found that thirty-seven correctional agencies placed 64,610 inmates in work-release programs in 1994. New York state reported the largest number of inmates on work release with 24,055.[36] Factors such as prison overcrowding and historical events, as well as commitment to offender reintegration, have affected work-release utilization across the nation.

In most jurisdictions, work-release inmates labor under conditions identical to those experienced by free citizens. In most cases, these inmates locate their own job and arrange for transportation to and from their place of employment. In such programs, correctional authorities may have little or no involvement with the inmate's employer. In other settings, the correctional agency or institution may employ a work-release coordinator to identify potential jobs for offenders, negotiate official agreements or informal relationships with prospective employers, and arrange for employment interviews for carefully selected inmates. In some jurisdictions, long-standing agreements between correctional authorities and large-scale employers make employment interviews unnecessary. Any inmate that correctional authorities screen and recommend for the work-release program is accepted without question. In this case, the correctional authorities may provide inmates with transportation to and from the workplace. In some specific instances, the employer may transport a large number of inmates to industrial or agricultural jobs.

The type of institution and its location are important influences on work-release programs. Those located near urban areas generally have access to a wide variety of employment opportunities. A rural setting may not only restrict job opportunities but may also make it more difficult for inmates to blend unnoticed into the workforce of a small and tightly knit community.

Inmates confined in maximum security institutions may be expected to experience considerable internal conflict as they attempt to reconcile the two drastically different roles of inmate and free citizen. In addition, because few inmates in maximum security institutions are likely to be eligible for work release, institutional security demands and limited resources may restrict the use of such a program with these specific inmates. Medium or minimum security institutions are more likely to provide the staff and other resources necessary to operate a smooth-functioning work-release program. Custody concerns are less important in these settings, and more inmates are eligible for work release. More institutional resources can therefore be diverted to work-release programs. These resources may include work-release coordinators and special counseling and security staff.

In most jurisdictions, inmates are paid directly by their employers but are required to turn their checks over to correctional authorities. Correctional officials make deductions from the inmate's wages to cover the cost of confinement. Usually 5 to 10 percent of the inmate's pay is used to reimburse the state for room and board. Deductions may also be made to repay welfare agencies for the cost of supporting the inmate's family during his or her absence, to pay debts, to make restitution, or to cover the costs of transportation to and from employment. The remainder of the inmate's check is then deposited into a savings account. Offenders are usually required to

save a specific percentage of their earnings for final release. Limited withdrawals, however, can be made during incarceration, usually to purchase cigarettes, toiletries, radios, and other personal items. This is an important feature of work-release programs. Most inmates, because of the realities of prison, have forgotten the skills necessary to keep and follow a financial budget. Some offenders never developed those skills on the outside. The opportunity to earn a wage and use that wage to support oneself is rehabilitative on several levels and parallels life on the outside for those who eventually qualify for total release.

Study Release   Study-release programs are similar to work-release programs. Differences are a result of the type of placement inmates receive. Study-release inmates are students, not workers and employees. Like work-release inmates, however, they fulfill two roles: student by day and inmate by night.

Inmates on **study release** can attend a variety of instructional programs, including vocational and technical schools, high school, high school equivalency classes, adult basic education courses, colleges, and universities. Like other students, study-release candidates must meet the entrance requirements of their chosen educational program and must maintain the same academic standards set for all students.

Study-release program operation is influenced by the same factors that influence work-release programs. The institution's location determines the availability of educational programs. Urban environments generally offer programs for students who share common cultural backgrounds with offenders. Educational programs in rural areas generally have a more restricted student body. Because few of their residents are generally eligible for study release, maximum security institutions are generally unable to devote significant resources to the programs. Needed resources include physical facilities, such as quiet areas for late night study, and counseling and support services.

The major distinction between work and study release appears to be a product of the economic issues surrounding temporary release. Work-release programs can reduce the costs of incarceration and provide inmates with funds. Study-release programs create expenses because student tuition generally must be paid for each course undertaken. Unless inmate students can obtain financial aid or have their own personal financial resources, study release seems a financial liability when compared with work release. Financial aid, including veterans' benefits, vocational rehabilitation funds, and basic opportunity grants, is often available to prospective study-release participants. A few states, such as South Carolina, permit inmates to earn the necessary educational funds through part-time work programs. Some states allow inmates to apply for student-aid grants like their nonincarcerated counterparts.

In most jurisdictions, funding and public support for study-release programs are limited, so study release is not extensively utilized. Educational programs operated within institutional walls are made to serve the needs of inmate students. But financial restrictions are not the only factors limiting inmate participation in community study. Given a choice between work and study release, most inmates would probably select the employment option. Work provides an immediate financial return.

Study can provide only long-term and uncertain benefits. In addition, many states require an inmate to have a job lined up to be considered for parole. Inmate students who do not have sufficient resources for self-support will find that they will be encouraged to find employment to be considered for release on parole. Work may provide a feeling of personal satisfaction and self-worth. For most inmates, the educational process has provided only feelings of incompetence and failure. Thus, inmate demand as well as program costs may be expected to restrict the establishment and utilization of study-release programs.

In 1994, seven correctional agencies provided approximately 355 inmates with access to study-release programs.[37] This low figure, in comparison with the total inmate population, may be attributed at least partially to punitive public attitudes toward the treatment of prisoners as well as to the reluctance of prison administrators to stir up controversy within their state by offering convicted felons the opportunity to attend class with free citizens.

Furloughs   **Furloughs** are authorized, unescorted leaves from confinement granted for specific purposes and for designated time periods. Most furloughs are for twenty-four to seventy-two hours, although they may be as short as only a few hours or as long as several weeks. Inmates are usually eligible for furloughs at regular intervals. Furloughs may be as frequent as every one or two weeks or as rare as once or twice a year. Statutes, administrative regulations, and the inmate's custody status and individual need usually determine furlough duration and frequency. Virtually all overnight furloughs are to the inmate's home or to that of a family member.

Furloughs may be granted for a variety of purposes, the most common being the following:

1. To maintain or reestablish family ties.

2. To solve family problems.

3. To prepare for final release, to attend employment interviews, to search for housing, to obtain a driver's license, and so forth.

4. To attend a short-term educational or vocational program.

5. To attend a special event in the community (for example, to speak to a civic or student group).

Underlying all these specific purposes of furlough is the reintegrative function that these temporary leaves serve. Furloughs allow inmates to get a taste of freedom prior to release into society.

In some jurisdictions, the inmate and his or her counselor conscientiously plan furloughs in detail. They outline specific objectives for the leave, and the inmate is expected to complete each one. These structured furloughs are frequently used in prerelease planning. In other jurisdictions, furloughs are not planned or structured at all. Inmates are permitted to visit their families in the community and to relax and enjoy their freedom from incarceration. These home furloughs permit inmates to become reacquainted with family and friends, to resolve potential conflicts, and to demonstrate to themselves and others that they can make it "this time."

Like work-release and study-release inmates, furloughees face transportation problems. Inmates returning to homes many miles from prison often have difficulty negotiating and financing travel arrangements. Some institutions provide funds to hardship cases, but, in many instances, the inmates must work out their own solutions to the problem. Such difficulties are minor compared with those of the inmates who have no family to visit on furlough. Friends are rarely permitted to receive furloughees as temporary guests. For more than a few inmates, no friends are available in any event.

To permit inmates with no community ties an opportunity to spend some time in the community prior to release, volunteers are sometimes permitted to provide housing for inmates on furlough. A furlough volunteer may be a person who has visited, counseled, or tutored the inmate on a regular basis during his or her confinement or a representative of a civic or social group that wants to sponsor an inmate. Social service and charitable organizations are also sometimes permitted to receive inmates on furlough. For example, in New York, female inmates who have no family are often furloughed to a convent outside of New York City.

Accurately determining the number of inmates who receive furloughs annually is difficult. Some correctional systems maintain statistics only on the number of furloughs granted per year and not on the number of inmates released. Because many eligible inmates receive furloughs as frequently as three to six times a year, these statistics overrepresent the number of inmate furloughees. Nevertheless, the fact that thousands of furloughs are granted annually indicates that many inmates are regularly receiving temporary leaves from confinement. Generally speaking, one inmate is participating in a furlough program for every three inmates on work release.[38]

Objectives

Offender Reintegration   The primary objective of temporary release programs is to prepare inmates for final release and to facilitate their successful adjustment to the community. Temporary release programs attempt to accomplish this aim by briefly exposing the offenders to the demands and responsibilities of freedom while they are still within the custody of correctional authorities. The inmates may work or study in the community, renew ties with family and friends, and make specific preparations for final release. At night or after a few days of release on furlough, inmates return to the confines of the institution. Support services and counseling available within the institution can help them deal with role conflicts and family problems and assist them in managing increasing amounts of trust and responsibility.

Temporary release programs can be employed regardless of the offender's proximity to release. In the early stages of incarceration, participation in temporary release programs may help inmates maintain contact with the free world and minimize the effects of institutionalization. As the offender nears final release, temporary release programs can more directly focus on postrelease realities and demands. All methods of employing temporary release programs serve the same basic objectives of offender reintegration. Inmates who maintain family ties and community contact throughout incarceration face a less difficult adjustment when they are finally released.

Behavioral Management   Participation in temporary release programs is one of the most highly desired privileges available within prison. For this reason, work- and study-release assignments and home furloughs are often used for management purposes in correctional institutions. Consistently good inmate behavior can be rewarded with temporary release opportunities. Likewise, violations of institutional regulations, failure to make a positive adjustment to institutional routine, an uncooperative attitude, or unwillingness to participate in institutional programs can be met with a denial of temporary release privileges. In this way, the incentive of an approval for temporary release can be used to control and manage inmate behavior.

Humanitarianism   Temporary release programs serve humanitarian purposes. Offenders are provided with respites from the pains of imprisonment and are given opportunities to regain their feelings of self-worth through involvement in the normal human pursuits of work, study, and family interaction. Temporary release programs acknowledge the prisoner's basic human dignity, and they offer an opportunity to temporarily undo the essentially brutalizing effects of imprisonment.

Evaluation   Temporary release programs also serve evaluative functions. Inmates placed on temporary release have an opportunity to demonstrate to parole authorities that they can conduct themselves responsibly in the community. After evaluating offenders' behavior on temporary release, parole officials are better able to assess their readiness for release. Without opportunities to evaluate offender behavior in free-world settings, parole authorities must rely on an inmate's institutional adjustment as a measure of appropriateness for release. While no association necessarily exists between an ability to adjust to prison routine and a capacity to live responsibly in the community, these programs allow a glimpse of the offender's behavior in an environment devoid of gun towers and wire-topped fences.

Each form of temporary release has its own objectives, and they are the same as those for work release, study release, and furlough programs.

Problems and Issues

All temporary release programs are subject to the same three basic problems: violations of program rules and regulations, absconding, and temporary release crime. Although none of these difficulties is severe in terms of the numbers of inmates involved, the community response to these problems may be of tremendous importance. Citizen outrage is particularly vehement when crimes are committed by inmates assigned to work or study release or released on furlough.

Violation of Regulations   Late returns from work, school, or furloughs, excessive use of alcohol, and use of illicit drugs and contraband are generally the most common serious temporary release rule violations. Work releasees may stop at a bar between work and prison; inmate students may use marijuana, narcotics, or barbiturates after school; furloughees may try to spend a few extra hours with family members or bring contraband back to the correctional facility. The official reaction to these violations is generally to withdraw temporary release privileges from the inmate. In some instances, the inmate may lose good time or may be placed in administrative segregation as punishment. The particular correctional response will reflect institutional and departmental policy and the nature and circumstances of the violation. Inmates may have transportation difficulties that cause them to return late to the prison through no fault of their own. In some prisons, these circumstances would be viewed as mitigating; in others, the inmate would be charged with absconding. Some institutions are not concerned with whether a man drinks on furlough as long as he does not return to the prison intoxicated. If the contraband was nondangerous and was mistakingly brought in to the facility (a huge number of items are not allowed in a correctional facility), the administration will deal with it differently from a volitional attempt to smuggle in drugs or weapons.

The prison officials' only means of determining drug or alcohol use is to require urinalysis, breathalyzer, or other tests. However, these tests are of limited utility unless the drug or alcohol intake has been fairly recent. Enterprising furloughees have been known to schedule their narcotics use so that no trace of the substance is left in their system on their return to prison. The extent of temporary release rule violations is difficult to assess. Most drug and alcohol violations are probably not discovered. Late returns may be ignored, moderately disciplined, or charged as abscondences. This rate, however, includes removals for minor as well as serious violations. Even if the proportion of rule violations is high, many proponents of temporary release programs would argue that late returns and alcohol use are manageable problems. These actions may reflect little more than inmates responding to the difficulties of being half prisoner and half free citizen.

Absconding   In most jurisdictions, inmates who abscond from temporary release are classified as escapees. If convicted of escaping, they frequently receive lengthy prison sentences in addition to their original terms. The severity of the penalty for absconding and the rigorousness of the temporary release selection process have worked to keep absconder rates low. An average of approximately 5 percent of inmates on temporary release will abscond. This number includes inmates who return voluntarily after a short absence as well as offenders who are never found. Research has indicated that a temporary release program's escape rate is influenced by (1) criteria and care used in case selection; (2) constraints as to work sites (for work-release programs); (3) transportation arrangements; (4) nature and extent of services, such as surveillance and

supportive counseling; and (5) level and consistency of rule enforcement.[39]

One other factor may influence the escape rate in work- and study-release programs. Inmates who enter the community on a regular basis to work or attend school may be sorely tempted to visit family or friends when they are supposed to be attending their placement. If home furlough opportunities are not frequently available, this natural temptation may unfortunately prove to be overpowering.

Crime   The most significant problem in the area of temporary release is crime. When an inmate commits a crime while visiting the community on work or study release or on a furlough, citizens are invariably outraged. Political pressure is brought to bear, and, not infrequently, the entire temporary release program is held accountable for the acts of a few people.

These problems are not the only important issues in temporary release; they are only the most threatening ones. Three critical needs still remain. Appropriate eligibility criteria and selection procedures for participation must be developed. Cooperative relationships between prisons and employers and schools must be established. Supportive services for inmates who live in both the prison and the free world must be provided if temporary release is to aid an offender's reentry into the community.

Perhaps the most critical issue is the community's willingness to accept offenders. Such acceptance requires that inmates be given every chance to prepare themselves for final release. It requires a willingness to permit inmates to work and study and visit with their families prior to final release and a readiness to go behind prison walls to help prepare the remaining offenders for their eventual return to society.

New Directions

Two trends may be expected to influence the future of temporary release programs. The first is the movement toward determinate sentenc-

Issues in Community Corrections

Willie Horton and the
1988 Presidential Election

Willie Horton, a convicted murderer serving a life term in the state prison system of Massachusetts, was released on a furlough from which he did not return. His escape and subsequent crimes became a major campaign issue in the 1988 presidential election. Horton was released on a pass from prison, escaped, and went on a crime spree. While on the run, he kidnapped and raped a Maryland woman and assaulted her fiancé. Shortly thereafter he was arrested and tried for the attacks.

In a series of print and video ads, President [George] Bush's campaign suggested the responsibility for Horton's crime spree lay with the liberal prison release policies supported by Michael Dukakis, the governor of Massachusetts and the Democratic nominee

for president. These liberal release policies, it was alleged, permitted dangerous offenders (like Horton) serving life sentences in prison an opportunity for temporary release to taste the fruits of freedom by visiting the community. Bush's campaign published photographs of Horton, a black, along with information about his rape victim, a white female. At the time, campaign watchers pointed out that the ad was racist and preyed upon the fears of white women. The Willie Horton issue dogged Dukakis and his supporters during the remainder of the campaign, and many observers believed that this issue was at least partially responsible for Dukakis's defeat in the presidential election.

---

ing. More and more states seem to be evaluating their sentencing practices and concluding that problems resulting from disparity of sentencing and the perceived failure of parole require a change. In a number of states, the changes have included an adoption of determinate sentencing in which the nature of the offenders' crime determines the sentence they receive, and relatively little emphasis is placed on the offenders' background or the specific circumstances of the offense. Once the offenders are incarcerated, their institutional behavior has relatively little influence on the length of time they serve. In some states, parole has also been abolished or greatly curtailed; inmates must then serve their time with sharply reduced opportunities for early release.

Under such conditions, the released offenders may receive little assistance in their efforts

to adjust to freedom. Whatever aid parole officers formerly provided will be lost. Correctional officials wishing to facilitate inmate reintegration may choose to employ temporary release programs as a means of filling in the gaps left by the shrinkage of parole opportunities. Temporary releases may be granted so that inmates can achieve the graduated release that parole was once designed to provide.

The abolition of some parole programs may also encourage correctional authorities to use temporary release programs in a different way. Because parole will no longer be available as an incentive for good inmate behavior, temporary release programs may come to play an even greater role in institutional management. Temporary release privileges may be granted to deserving inmates and denied to offenders who manifest a poor institutional adjustment.

A second trend is the development and use of work-release facilities as a means of defusing overcrowding in major institutions. Some prison systems have developed work-release centers as a low-cost alternative to the expanding of major correctional institutions. The development of these program facilities permits prison administrators to transfer the less dangerous offenders, or those nearing the end of their prison terms, to these less secure programs, thereby freeing up bed space for more serious offenders.

Summary of Temporary Release Programs

Temporary release programs were established in American prisons to meet a critical correctional need—preparing the incarcerated offender for final release or parole to the community. Although the programs had diverse origins, the 1960s witnessed their linking both conceptually and administratively. The growing acceptance of the goals of community-based corrections was responsible for this new direction, as prison officials began to address postrelease realities in their development of correctional programs. Temporary release programs accomplish this aim by providing inmates with brief exposures to the community prior to final release.

Perhaps the most critical stage in temporary release programming is the selection of inmates for work or study release or furloughs. Eligibility criteria and selection procedures should be broad enough to allow inmates who may benefit from the programs to participate, while ensuring that no offender who poses a threat to the community is released. This is a difficult task. Most programs tend to be cautious in their selection process because the criminal activities of a few persons may severely damage an entire program. Another factor that may also restrict temporary release program participation is that temporary release is viewed as a privilege, so only inmates who show a positive institutional adjustment are generally approved for it.

Work-release programs have a number of advantages. The biggest asset is the economic benefit to inmates, their families, the victim, and the state. However, potential inmate employees face a number of problems as well: lack of jobs, reluctant employers, low pay, and generally unskilled, unrewarding work. Study-release programs can provide offenders with needed education in a normal community setting—high school, vocational school, or college. When well-planned programs are available, inmates may benefit from study release in nonacademic as well as academic ways. Furloughs help offenders maintain family and community ties. When they are used to permit inmates nearing final release or parole to obtain jobs or arrange housing in the community, inmates can experience both the practical and psychological benefits resulting from successful accomplishment of a task.

The future outlook for temporary release programs is mixed. Determinate sentencing, temporary release crime, and administrative problems will have competing influences on temporary release programs. Because virtually all inmates are eventually released, prerelease preparation of a useful nature needs to be made available to offenders.

Key Words and Concepts

Alexander Machonochie

furloughs

good-time credits

indentured servants

indeterminate sentencing

mandatory release

maximum expiration of sentence

mutual agreement programming (MAP)

parole

parole board

parole d'honneur

parole guidelines

penal servitude

policy of transportation

split sentences

study release

supervised mandatory release

ticket of leave

Walter Crofton

work release

Zebulon Brockway

Questions for Discussion

1. What is the role of parole in the administration of corrections? How has this changed since the 1980s?

2. What other methods of release exist for persons confined to prision?

3. What is a split sentence? How has its use resulted from increased crowding in prisons and jails?

4. What history and practice link the parole system to the English practice of transportation of criminals?

5. How have parole statistics changed in the past decade? What does this say about the use of parole and the success rate for those persons who receive parole?

6. How are the members of most parole boards chosen? What factors do these board members consider in the decision-making process? How would you make similar decisions if you were a parole board member?

7. How do most communities respond to parolees? What impact does this have on the parolee's chances of successful parole?

8. What creative methods of release have prisons used to both decrease their populations and remove less-dangerous persons from their facilities?

For Further Reading

Broad, R. A., *A Punishment Under Pressure: The Probation Service in the Inner City* (United Kingdom: Taylor and Francis, 1991).

Clear, Todd, and Harry R. Dammer, *The Offender in the Community* (Belmont, Calif.: Wadsworth, 2000).

Ditton, Jason, and Rosylyn Ford, *The Reality of Probation: A Formal Ethnography of Process and Practice* (London, England: Avebury Press, 1994).

Gangon vs. Scarpelli, 411 U.S. 778, 92 S.Ct. 1756 (1973).

Morrissey vs. Brewer, 408 U.S. 471, 92 SC 2593, 33 L. Ed. 2d, 484 (1972).

Part Two

Case Management and Supervision

Chapter 6   Offender Supervision: Control
and Public Safety Issues

Chapter 7   Economic Sanctions: Fines, Fees, Restitution,
and Community Service

Chapter 8   Community Residential Centers
(Halfway Houses)

Chapter 6

Offender Supervision: Control and Public Safety Issues

Objectives of Intermediate Sanctions

Scaling Correctional Options and the Correctional Continuum

Intensive Supervision Programs

Boot Camps

Home Confinement and Electronic Monitoring

Day Reporting Centers

Residential Programs

Summary

There have been essentially three eras in community corrections. The first period began with the origin of probation and lasted until the middle of the twentieth century; the second lasted up until the 1980s. The current third era is characterized by enthusiasm and support for intermediate sanctions. This support, which is recent considering the repeated historical rejection of early release for offenders, carries with it a cost. The public has been willing to support intermediate sanctions only if the programs could guarantee that public safety was a primary consideration in the release decision.

Objectives of Intermediate Sanctions

The current era of community corrections is defined by **intermediate sanctions.** Although most states report that a variety of intermediate sanctions are in use in their jurisdictions, the vast majority of offenders continue to be placed on probation or parole rather than assigned to the newer intermediate punishments. Recognition of the values underlying intermediate sanctions is essential to an understanding of contemporary community corrections. Those values are best understood by an examination of the objectives of intermediate sanctions.

Intermediate sanctions have three basic aims: to protect the community, to create a continuum of correctional punishments that provide a better fit between the offender and his or her sanction than can be achieved by probation or prison, and to reduce correctional costs.

Community Protection

Today, the first and foremost objective of all correctional programs is to provide for a safe community. As a result, great emphasis is placed on ensuring appropriate incapacitation of offenders, accompanied by a willingness to utilize **collective incapacitation** to achieve that end. Collective incapacitation requires the confinement of broad categories of offenders for lengthy periods of time to ensure that the community is safe from the offenders within that group. Overuse of incapacitation, or the confinement and restriction of individuals who pose relatively little danger to the community, is of lesser concern to the public than underuse. Underuse creates the potential for an offender to be sanctioned in a manner that would provide him or her an opportunity to offend again. This should not be interpreted as meaning that overuse of incarceration is of no concern to the public. Society has recognized that prisons are expensive institutions to build and operate, but most seem to agree (if bond support is any indication) that the costs are acceptable if the benefit is increased public safety.

Viewed from this perspective, the appropriate strategies to achieve community protection are clearly evident. Minimum and mandatory sentences to incarceration are necessary to guarantee that all offenders targeted for incapacitation receive that sanction. Violent offenders and criminals with multiple convictions are generally required to serve lengthy prison sentences as a result of this strategy. Depending on the jurisdiction, lesser offenders may also be the focus of these broad-based incapacitation strategies.

Today, community correctional programs must also place high emphasis on community protection. While traditional probation and pa-

role programs (with standard caseloads of one hundred or more offenders) are generally recognized as limited in their ability to supervise offenders, intermediate sanctions are specifically designed to impose significant restrictions on their participants. This is achieved by utilizing risk assessment as a means of selecting offenders for community alternatives and rigorous offender monitoring as a means of maintaining tight supervision.

For example, intensive supervision programs are designed to achieve both these goals through their selective admission requirements and tight management of offenders. **Home confinement** (also known as **house arrest**) programs achieve incapacitation within the community by requiring offenders to remain within their residence for many hours of each day. Electronic monitoring is sometimes used to assist in the supervision of offenders on home confinement (boot camps and other residential community correctional programs provide significantly greater restrictions than probation or parole). Even day treatment and residential centers can be seen as attempts to impose enhanced monitoring—regular daily supervision—on offenders in the community.

Enhancement of the Correctional Continuum

While the 1960s witnessed a development of community corrections programs across the entire system of justice (from diversion to prerelease programs), the current era focuses on expanding the range of punishments for convicted offenders. The earlier era saw programs develop in an attempt to avoid offender labeling, in the belief that offenders might increase their criminality as a result of the stigma attached to criminal processing, conviction, and sanctioning. Intermediate sanctions developed in an effort to better articulate the degree of sanction with the severity of crime (punishment dimension) and the individual aspects of the criminal (risk dimension). Instead of trying to avoid labeling (an old goal), today's intermediate sanctions programs focus on the control and punishment objectives. Recognizing the appropriateness of both punishment and community protection as necessary correctional objectives, intermediate sanctions incorporate these goals into the more rehabilitative and reintegrative goals of traditional community corrections. The results are programs that may attempt to assist offenders but always attempt to punish and restrict them.

Intermediate sanctions seek to calibrate the right kind of punishment with the level of offender dangerousness, which requires consideration of both treatment potential and the need for incapacitation, and the nature of the offender's act, which requires a consideration of the level of punishment deserved by the individual and that which is necessary for the more general achievement of deterrence. Intermediate sanctions provide necessary options to fit the degree of restriction and incapacitation an offender requires with the severity of punishment that should be meted out. All intermediate sanctions are considered significantly more punitive and restrictive than traditional probation or parole.

In many ways, intermediate sanctions provide a means of slowing the trend toward mandatory minimum prison sentences, while still providing an emphasis on public safety and punishment. Many reasons may be cited to limit the use of incarceration, but the most critical and broadly supported rationale is economic.

Economic Objectives

The economic crisis facing most states as a result of their reliance upon incarceration as a correctional strategy is well documented. Prisons are taking an exceedingly large share of most states' general revenues. Given that mandatory minimum sentences require almost a decade to reach their full impact on a prison system, the forecast is for even greater correctional demand on state budgets. The search continues for less

costly alternative sanctions that demonstrate both a get-tough approach to crime and a concern for public safety.

Whether intermediate sanctions will be allowed to serve this purpose remains to be seen. The vast majority of intermediate sanctions do cost less than imprisonment. Furthermore, many such programs established to reduce costs by serving prison-bound offenders have instead been utilized for would-be probationers by judges and others looking for more punitive options to traditional supervision. Placing probation-bound offenders in programs designed for prison-bound criminals is a costly and potentially counterproductive practice. Clearly, the desire for community safety and punishment is often at odds with the desire to reduce correctional costs.

In California, for example, when given the choice to follow less costly but equally effective sentencing policies, voters chose the more costly tough-on-crime approach. However, it remains unclear how well informed voters were in that situation, or how well informed they might need to be, to better weigh the advantages and disadvantages of different correctional policies.

In the coming years, much more research like that conducted by Petersilia for the California Policy Seminar will likely be done.[1] In 1995, she reviewed California prison admissions to determine who might be divertable and at what cost. She isolated eight potentially divertable groups of offenders (Figure 6-1) and then examined the costs of confining such individuals given their proportion within the prison population and their average length of sentence (Table 6-1). She found it was cost-effective to divert minor drug offenders to any program with a price tag of less than $14,412. An examination of intermediate sanction costs indicated that this could include drug-free homes as well as even less costly outpatient and methadone maintenance programs (Table 6-2). Parolees who committed technical violations or minor property offenses could be cost-effectively diverted to any program costing under $12,712 per year, which would include

Figure 6-1   Candidate Groups for Prison Diversion

Candidate Groups for Prison Diversion

Option 1:   Administrative, noncriminal (true technical violators).

Option 2:   Administrative, noncriminal, and less serious property (e.g., grand theft, receiving stolen property, petty theft with prior, forgery, fraud).

Option 3:   Administrative, noncriminal, less serious property, and minor drug (use and possession).

Option 4:   Minor drug (use and possession).

Option 5:   All drug (use, possession, sale, manufacturing).

Option 6:   Administrative, noncriminal, less serious property, and all drug (use, possession, sale, manufacturing).

Option 7:   Less serious property offenses (petty theft, receiving stolen property).

Option 8:   Persons serving six months or less in prison.

Source: Joan Petersilia, "How California Could Divert Nonviolent Prisoners to Intermediate Sanctions," *Overcrowded Times,* 6 (3), 1995, p. 4. Used by permission.

Table 6-1   Impact on Prison Admissions and Corrections Costs Achieved by Eliminating Prison for Selected Nonviolent Offenders, California Department of Corrections

Eliminate Prison for	Percent of Prison Admissions	Average Prison Months Served	Average Cost Per Inmate[a]	Total Spent on Group (millions)	Percent Spent on Group
1. Technical violators	4	4.00	$ 7,272	$ 22.7	1
2. Technical violators, minor property	16	6.99	12,712	167.3	9
3. Technical violators, minor property, minor drugs	26	6.08	11,047	237.9	13
4. Minor drugs (use and possession)	25	7.93	14,412	302.3	17
5. All drugs (use, possession, sales)	32	9.71	17,644	479.4	26
6. Technical violators, minor property, all drugs	46	8.78	15,955	620.3	34
7. Minor property	25	9.02	16,391	342.9	19
8. Persons serving six months or less	17	4.77	8,667	124.1	7

[a]Based on average annual California prison cost of $21,800.

Source: Adapted from Joan Petersilia, "How California Could Divert Nonviolent Prisoners to Intermediate Sanctions," *Overcrowded Times,* 6 (3), 1995, pp. 5, 7. Used by permission.

Table 6-2 Average Annual Cost of
Intermediate Sanction and Treatment Options

Intermediate Sanction and Treatment Options	Cost
California state prison	$21,800
California county jail	19,700
Boot camps (121 days prison, plus 244 days ISP)	11,700
House arrest with electronic monitoring	3,500–8,500
Intensive supervision probation/parole	4,000–8,000
Routine supervision probation/parole	200–2,000
Substance abuse treatment programs	
Residential	22,400
Social model (drug-free home)	12,500
Outpatient	2,900
Methadone maintenance	2,500

Note: ISP = intensive supervision probation and parole.
Source: Joan Petersilia, "How California Could Divert Nonviolent Prisoners to Intermediate Sanctions," *Overcrowded Times,* 6 (3), 1995, p. 6. Used by permission.

every intermediate sanction in operation in California except residential drug treatment.

The California analysis does not include the start-up costs of new prisons or intermediate sanction programs. It also provides only a limited assessment of the fiscal costs and benefits of various sanctions (leaving out considerations of the social costs of prison, the potential costs of crime by intermediate sanction participants, and the recidivism costs of all offenders). At the same time, it provides a fruitful first step toward the kind of data needed by policy makers, politicians, and informed citizens if they are to weigh the relative value of state dollars spent on corrections or other public services such as education, health care, and social services.

Scaling Correctional Options and the Correctional Continuum

Programs typically identified as intermediate sanctions include intensive supervision pro-grams, boot camps, home confinement, and electronic monitoring (Table 6-3). The list also includes community correctional programs such as restitution and community service, fines—both traditional and means-based day fines—and residential programs such as halfway houses. Virtually any sanction between probation and prison can be considered an intermediate sanction. The policy of intermediate sanctions, however, is to attempt to scale sanctions in terms of the objectives they may achieve and utilize them accordingly.

The scaling of sanctions is no easy matter. The appeal of intermediate sanctions lies in their ability to accommodate concerns with both individual risk (recidivism) and punishment. A broader examination of the correctional objectives that may be achieved by such programs includes general crime reduction, reparation, economic cost, and public satisfaction. The importance of understanding any particular correctional sanction in terms of its fit in the overall continuum should be clear: Every sanction is capable of meeting multiple objectives. The objectives attempted by any particular program are a reflection both of its

Table 6-3 Summary Listing of Coercive
Measures and Sanctioning Options

Coercive Measure	Sanctioning Options	
Warning measures [Notice of consequences of subsequent wrongdoing]	Admonishment/cautioning [administrative; judicial] Suspended execution or imposition of sentence	
Injunctive measures [Banning legal conduct]	Travel [e.g., from jurisdiction; to specific criminogenic spots] Association [e.g., with other offenders] Driving Possession of weapons Use of alcohol Professional activity [e.g., disbarment]	
Economic measures	Restitution Costs Fees Forfeitures Support payments Fines [standard; day fines]	
Work-related measures	Community service [individual placement; work crew] Paid employment requirements	
Education-related measures	Academic [e.g., basic literacy, general equivalency degree] Vocational training Life skills training	
Physical and mental health treatment measures	Psychological/psychiatric Chemical [e.g., methadone; psychoactive drugs] Surgical [e.g., acupuncture, drug treatment]	
Physical confinement measures	Partial or intermittent confinement	Home curfew Day treatment center Halfway house Restitution center Weekend detention facility/jail Outpatient treatment facility [e.g., drug/mental health]

placement in a particular jurisdiction's continuum and its own unique correctional orientation, as well as basic programmatic features. Jurisdictional variations in the sanctioning continuum and unique features of individual programs will always influence program operations and impact at the local level.

Intensive Supervision Programs

Intensive supervision programs (ISPs) provide close monitoring of convicted offenders and impose rigorous conditions on release.[2] The primary purpose of program restrictions and surveillance is to protect the community and deter the offender from lawbreaking or violation of the conditions of release. To achieve

this end, most ISPs provide small caseloads with multiple face-to-face contacts with offenders, random and unannounced drug tests, and stringent enforcement of probation (or parole) conditions. Curfews are frequently required, and house arrest with or without electronic monitoring may also be utilized.

Most ISPs also attempt to enhance offender accountability and encourage activities that will promote a crime-free lifestyle. Employment, employment-seeking activities, or school are typical program elements. Community service and restitution requirements are designed to enhance offender accountability.

Many ISPs also require treatment, counseling, or other interventions. The degree of emphasis on such activities varies considerably from program to program. Some jurisdictions actively attempt to rehabilitate offenders under

Table 6-3   *(continued)*

Coercive Measure	Sanctioning Options	
Physical confinement measures (continued)	Full/continuous confinement	Full home/house arrest Mental hospital Other residential treatment facility [e.g., drug/alcohol] Boot camp Detention facility Jail Prison
Monitoring/compliance measures [May be attached to all other sanctions]	Required of the offender	Mail reporting Electronic monitoring [telephone check-in; active electronic monitoring device] Face-to-face reporting Urine analysis [random; routine]
	Required of the monitoring agent	Criminal records checks Sentence compliance checks [e.g., on payment of monetary sanctions; attendance/performance at treatment, work, or educational sites] Third-party checks [family, employer, surety, service/treatment provider; via mail, telephone, in person] Direct surveillance/observation [random/routine visits and possibly search; at home, work, institution, or elsewhere] Electronic monitoring [regular phone checks and/or passive monitoring device—currently used with home curfew or house arrest, but could track movement more widely as technology develops]

Source: Center for Effective Public Policy, *The Intermediate Sanctions Handbook: Experiences and Tools for Policy Makers* (Washington, D.C.: National Institute of Corrections, 1993), p. 38.

their supervision, while others focus specifically on offender monitoring. Treatment-oriented programs often require offenders to improve their lives on many dimensions over the course of program involvement and require promotion through a series of progressive phases or levels to achieve total, unrestricted release. These same programs often provide graduated responses should behavioral problems develop, revoking release only after other sanctions have failed. Surveillance-oriented programs take less note of offender performance on any dimension other than violation of release conditions.

Program Development

ISPs are the descendents of efforts from the 1950s and 1960s that attempted to improve offender rehabilitation by reducing probation and parole caseload size. Caseloads of one hundred or more permitted only superficial contact between the offender and his or her supervisor. The belief was that probation and parole officers with smaller caseloads would have more time to spend with their clients and would be able to have a greater impact on their reform. To study the matter, the San Francisco Project randomly assigned offenders to officers in four caseload levels, ranging from 20 to 130.[3]

The results showed no link between caseload size and offender rehabilitation as measured by violation rates. Probation and parole officers seemed unsure of how to use the opportunity to work with smaller caseloads in a way that promoted rehabilitation. In effect, they were uncertain how to use their increased available time with offenders. Other duties also interfered with the efforts the officers did try to make to assist their clients. However, the study also found that probation and parole officers who had fewer clients to supervise were better able to detect behavior that was in violation of release conditions. In general, smaller caseloads led to enhanced supervision and control (and correspondingly more violations), but not necessarily enhanced treatment.

This was somewhat shocking news given the era's focus on offender rehabilitation. The results provided further impetus to efforts to enhance the role of probation and parole officers as therapeutic agents, to develop strategies that would serve as effective tools to change offenders' lives. Heightened educational and training requirements and greater professionalism on the part of probation and parole officers were also pursued.

Research was undertaken to learn what strategies might be most effective in stimulating offender reform. Gradually these studies led to significant changes in probation and parole officers' expected orientation and duties. Their role changed from one that emphasized individual counseling to that of a service broker, whose duties were to work with clients in identifying problems and needs, setting objectives for change, and locating the community-based services that would assist in achieving desired objectives (Figure 6-2).

The 1974 Lipton, Martinson, and Wilks report proclaiming that "nothing works" in corrections dealt a severe blow to efforts to improve offender rehabilitation and ushered in a mindset that fostered proportionality of punishment to crime and equity in sentencing as the dominant focus of the correctional agenda. At the time, the changing emphasis was perceived to be a response to the failure of rehabilitative efforts, not the lack of desire to pursue offender reform.

A decade later the focus had shifted again with the changing political climate. Just-deserts proponents had argued that equity was all that a criminal justice system could hope to accomplish. While still stating a preference for reintegrative efforts (if they could be made effective), conservative politicians argued that rehabilitation was not only impossible, but it was also irrelevant to a system that should focus first on protecting the community and second on punishing wrongdoers. This position had widespread popular appeal and represents the current focus of correctional efforts. Today, any program that increases control over offenders and better protects the community is likely to flourish, and intensive supervision programs offer just such an opportunity. They provide the smaller caseloads that years ago were found to permit better detection of offender violations, and they add program restrictions, monitoring, and supervision elements to provide as much incapacitation and deterrence as is possible under community release. The result is a program that is both punitive and crime control-oriented in its implementation.

ISPs have expanded rapidly in the last decade, spurred by early research in Georgia that showed the programs to be effective in reducing both costs and recidivism. By 1990, all states had implemented intensive supervision and more than fifty-five thousand offenders were participating in them.[4] Today, about 2 to 4 percent of offenders are released to intensive supervision programs.

Program development in the federal system has proceeded less rapidly, largely as a result of sentencing guidelines that provided no special role for intensive supervision. Several federal probation districts have experimented with intensive supervision caseloads, however, providing enhanced contacts, increased support services, and team supervision to offenders in southern Florida, northern Ohio, and Maryland.[5]

ISP Goals

Perhaps more than any other intermediate sanction, the goals of ISPs directly parallel those of the broader intermediate punishment movement.

Figure 6-2   How Objectives Shape
Programs: The Day Reporting Center

A clear understanding of goals and objectives is an essential starting point for good program design. One implication of that tenet is that a program's goals and objectives will have a much more profound effect on the program itself than will the simple selection of a program type or title. Programs with similar names and outlines may be designed differently to achieve different goals. An illustration using a day-reporting center model is provided.

Program A	Program B
Program objective: **Punishment and control**	Program objective: **Rehabilitation**
Activities: are structured for minute-by-minute accountability and may include burdensome and unpleasant activities.	Activities: are designed to define and address the factors identified as contributing to the offender's criminal activity.
Staff: responsibilities are heavily weighted to security and monitoring activities.	Staff: responsibilities are heavily weighted to program and counseling activities.
Facility: is designed and located for maximum ease of surveillance and control of movement.	Facility: is designed to provide areas conducive to counseling, group discussion, and practice of positive leisure activities, and is located in the community to provide access to community resources.
Programming: is designed to fill all hours during which the center is open.	Programming: is therapeutic and educational, and allows the offender some choice; emphasizes modeling positive behavior in the community.
Progress: is determined by the time spent on, and compliance with, decreasing levels of control, as well as completion of tasks or assignments.	Progress: is determined by completion of specific programs and by achieving milestones in the community (e.g., securing work, going to school, supporting a family).
Interventions: occur for the purposes of achieving program compliance; interventions involve increasing control or imposition of unpleasant assignments.	Interventions: occur as a response to program failure; program adjustments are made to better meet the needs of the individual offer.

Source: Center for Effective Public Policy, *The Intermediate Sanctions Handbook: Experiences and Tools for Policy Makers* (Washington, D.C.: National Institute of Corrections, 1993), p. 116.

Community Protection   The enhanced restrictions and monitoring that ISPs provide are designed to better protect the community, through restricting opportunities to commit crimes and increasing the likelihood that violations will be quickly detected. Personal and telephone contacts with offenders and often their families and employers are greatly enhanced over traditional forms of community release. Such contacts serve both to deter violations and detect unacceptable behavior. Curfews limit opportunities for misconduct as do random drug and alcohol tests. The resulting program may be viewed as more punitive than short prison or jail terms.

Correctional Costs   ISPs reduce correctional costs when they provide diversion from prison

Program Focus

Georgia's Intensive Supervision Program

Georgia's ISP

Georgia implemented the first of the new wave of ISPs [intensive supervision programs] in 1982. The model, a front-end intermediate sanction program developed in response to prison crowding, has been duplicated across the country. The following information was taken directly from Georgia Department of Corrections' Operating Procedures for Intensive Probation Supervision.

Statement of Purpose. "The purpose of the ISP Program is to provide a publicly acceptable sentencing option for selected offenders, primarily felons, who may be supervised in the community in lieu of serving a prison sentence. ISP may also serve as a sentencing alternative for those offenders who need greater supervision than can be afforded under regular probation supervision."

ISP Staffing. Georgia's ISP uses a team approach to supervision. One probation officer and one surveillance officer are responsible for a caseload of 25 offenders. The Probation Officer's primary duties include: coordinating screening procedures to determine offender eligibility; identifying treatment needs and coordinating services; serving as court liaison; ensuring proper case documentation; collecting fines, restitution and fees; and supervising all team activities. The Surveillance Officer's primary duties include: enforcing the conditions of probation; providing 24-hour surveillance capabilities; conducting urinalysis and breathalyzers; and assisting the probation officer as directed. Team supervision was devised by Georgia and many agencies have adopted the method for their ISPs.

Offender Selection. Offenders can be placed in ISP at three impact points: at the time of the initial sentencing; in lieu of revocation; and through post-sentencing modifications. Placement in ISP is dependent on a judicial decision, which is often based on a recommendation from ISP staff. Primary consideration is given to non-violent felony offenders presenting no unacceptable risk to the safety of the community but who have

or jail. This may occur when intensive supervision is employed judicially—when ISPs are used as an alternative sanction to a prison or jail sentence—or when offenders are sentenced to prison and diverted by correctional authorities to intensive supervision as an alternative to confinement. These programs are known as **front-end approaches,** because the offender is sent to an ISP before incarceration occurs. Programs that provide early release to prisoners are referred to as back-end strategies. While **back-end approaches**

may be utilized to reduce correctional costs, the savings are less than would be achieved had incarceration been avoided entirely. ISP may not eliminate the need to build additional prison space, but it may delay the construction and thus produce savings, which are referred to as deferred costs instead of eliminated costs.

A third type of ISPs is not designed to reduce correctional costs but to provide a tougher sanction than traditional probation or parole. These are **enhancement programs,**

need or risk factors exceeding the resources of basic supervision.

Program Components. Georgia's ISP operates under a system of phases. The following chart shows the specific supervision activities and requirements for each phase.

Phase one actually includes two tracks, the Standard Track and the Home Confinement Track, with placement being determined by individual characteristics. In addition to the conditions imposed in the Standard Track, the Home Confinement Track requires offenders to be in their residence except for pre-approved activities including employment-related activities, attendance at treatment and counseling programs, and activities related to their personal welfare.

In addition to these supervision requirements, throughout the program officers must conduct: verification of employment, full-time enrollment in school, or job seeking activities; monthly record checks; and random urinalyses.

Offenders who show a positive response to supervision as exhibited by stable employ-

	Phases		
	One	Two	Three
Length	3 mos. min.	3 mos. min.	Optional
Weekly contacts	4–7	3	2
Curfew	10 P.M.	11 P.M.	Officer discretion
Community service hours	48	48	0

ment, program participation, absence of major violations, and improved control of substance abuse are moved to the next phase. Upon completion of phase two, the goals of each case are reviewed to determine if the offender requires placement in phase three or if a transfer to regular supervision is feasible.

Source: Betsy A. Fulton, Susan Stone, and Paul Gendreau, *Restructuring Intensive Supervision Programs: Applying What Works* (Lexington, Ky.: American Probation and Parole Association, 1994), pp. I-10, 11. Used by permission.

established to provide a more rigorous sanction and one better fit to meet the requirements of today's increasingly high-risk offenders. Although enhancement programs clearly meet other correctional objectives, their costs are invariably greater than the alternative of routine supervision.

The various points at which ISPs may be employed are illustrated in Figure 6-3. Cost savings of ISPs are entirely dependent upon the stage of criminal justice system processing at which they are employed and the alterna-

tives that otherwise would have been utilized in their absence.

Intermediate Sanction ISPs indisputably provide an intermediate punishment to traditional probation and prison. Research indicates that this goal is invariably and uniformly achieved by the implementation of ISPs, thus providing a sanctioning alternative that better fits the crime severity and risk of many offenders. ISPs do much to enhance the credibility of a criminal justice system too long criticized

Program Focus

New Jersey's Intensive Supervision Program

New Jersey's ISP

New Jersey followed Georgia's lead with the implementation of an ISP [intensive supervision program] in 1983. However, New Jersey developed a back-end program to ensure true diversion from prison. The following information was taken from a 1992 progress report from New Jersey's Administrative Office of the Courts and the ISP program operations manual.

Statement of Purpose. ISP is a component of the Probation Services Division of the New Jersey Administrative Office of the Courts. ISP was created to:

1. reduce the number of offenders serving state prison sentences by permitting them to be resentenced to an intermediate form of punishment;

2. improve the utilization of correctional resources by making additional bed space available for violent criminals; and

3. test whether or not supervising selected offenders in the community is less costly and more effective than incarceration.

New Jersey describes its ISP as a "realistic and unique form of punishment, designed around a concept of social control within the community."

ISP Staffing. Unlike Georgia, one probation officer is responsible for all case activities. Officers must be available on a 24-hour basis. ISP officers are actively involved in screening offenders for program participation and in determining their eligibility.

Offender Selection. Only those offenders sentenced to a state prison term are eligible for program consideration. Offenders convicted of a homicide, robbery or sex offense are ineligible. The program is geared toward offenders with self-motivation who are willing to make a personal investment in the program. To ensure that they capture the appropriate population, New Jersey has implemented the stringent selection process described below.

Applications stating basic identifying information and the offender's plans upon his or her release, must be submitted 30 to 60 days after execution of an offender's custodial term. Upon receipt of the application, ISP staff review the offender's presentence report to ensure eligibility based on the nature of the crime. Once eligibility is determined, applicants are interviewed by program staff. Program staff then contact various parties to gather and confirm information and to invite recommendations. Based upon the compiled information a case plan is devised and an assessment report is prepared. This information is provided to the *ISP Screening Board,* which consists of a representative of the Department of Corrections, the Director of ISP and a public member appointed by the Chief Justice. After determining eligibility based on the written materials, the Screening Board conducts an interview with the offender to ascertain his or her sincerity and motivation. If the offender is still deemed appropriate for the program, the materials are forwarded to the *ISP Resentencing Panel,* which includes three judges appointed by the Chief Justice. Once the panel has determined the offender's appropriateness for ISP it has the authority to conditionally release the offender from prison and place him or her in ISP for a 90-day period. If successful during that 90-day period, the offender is granted another 90-day trial period. If again successful, the Resentencing Panel resentences the offender to the original sentence of incarceration minus time served; suspends the imposition of the sentence; and officially places the offender in ISP.

This complex process is designed to ensure the selective placement of offenders in ISP. The two 90-day trial periods give the offenders an opportunity to prove that they can safely function in the community and achieve their personal objectives. If at any time during this process the offender is deemed ineligible or fails to comply with the conditions of ISP, the motion for release is denied or the offender is returned to prison.

Program Components. Like Georgia, New Jersey's ISP focuses on a high level of control. The standard program components include: 16 hours of community service per month; a minimum of two drug screens per month; required employment and verification; a curfew of 10:00 P.M.; twenty supervision contacts per month; the use of a community sponsor and network team; required treatment or counseling; and the occasional use of home detention.

New Jersey's ISP places an emphasis on meeting treatment needs and working with community members to enhance the offenders' chances for successful reintegration. Counseling is described as the cornerstone of the program. Offender needs assessments and referrals to counseling are ongoing processes for all ISP participants.

Community sponsors and network teams are unique to New Jersey's ISP. ISP offenders must identify an individual within the community to serve as their community sponsor and other citizens willing to assist them who become part of a network team. The goal of involving these citizens is "to help the participant achieve his or her goals, make the plan of supervision a reality, and assist the ISP officer in ensuring that the objectives of the program are met."

All violations are reported to the resentencing panel to determine the appropriate action. The most commonly applied sanctions are increased curfew restrictions, additional community service hours, increased treatment requirements, home detention and short-term incarceration.

New Jersey has developed re-entry guidelines that slowly reduce the controls and restrictions placed on the offender. This re-entry process is designed to wean the offender off of the system and to ensure successful reintegration.

Source: Betsy A. Fulton, Susan Stone, and Paul Gendreau, *Restructuring Intensive Supervision Programs: Applying What Works* (Lexington, Ky.: American Probation and Parole Association, 1994), pp. I-11–13. Used by permission.

Program Focus

Massachusetts's Intensive Supervision Program

Massachusetts's ISP

The Massachusetts ISP [intensive supervision program] was designed as a probation enhancement program. Thirteen pilot programs were implemented across the state in 1985. The following information was taken from *Research in Corrections* (Byrne, Lurigio and Baird, 1989).

Statement of Purpose. The purpose of Massachusetts's ISP is to provide better supervision to high-risk offenders already on probation. It is an administrative model designed to provide a case management/risk control technique.

Offender Selection. Offenders placed on probation in Massachusetts are placed in one of four supervision levels based on a risk/needs classification system. To be placed in ISP probationers must rate "high-risk."

ISP Staffing. Like New Jersey, one probation officer is responsible for all duties associated with his or her caseload. These duties include assessment, referral and surveillance.

Program Components. The Massachusetts ISP stresses both strict enforcement of conditions and referral for services to address offender needs. Officers are required to conduct a full investigation of each offender during the first 30 days on probation. Personal interviews with the offender and collateral contacts are conducted to determine the offender's needs. Specific problem-oriented case plans are then developed, which include referrals to services for all identified high need areas. Officers are required to have ten contacts per month with each offender and to conduct a record check every 30 days. Mandatory case review occurs four and ten months after ISP placement. Needs assessment, referrals to services and follow-up are emphasized in three main areas: substance abuse, employment and counseling. The Massachusetts ISP uses a strict four-step revocation process requiring administrative review and judicial sanctions for noncompliance.

Source: Betsy A. Fulton, Susan Stone, and Paul Gendreau, *Restructuring Intensive Supervision Programs: Applying What Works* (Lexington, Ky.: American Probation and Parole Association, 1994), pp. I-13–14. Used by permission.

---

for its slap-on-the-wrist approach to criminals or, conversely, its one-size-fits-all approach to punishment.

Research on ISPs

The Georgia Study The Georgia Department of Corrections was the first to conduct and widely disseminate an evaluation of its ISP.[6] The results, reported in 1987, were uniformly positive, demonstrating a reduction in correctional costs by lessening prison commit-

ments as well as a lowering recidivism. Georgia attributed a savings of $6,775 to each offender diverted from prison and reported that ISP offenders committed fewer and less serious crimes than regular probationers as well as prisoners.

The results of the Georgia experiment prompted many other jurisdictions to develop ISPs. Subsequent evaluations, however, yielded mixed results and also provided ample evidence of considerable variation in the implementation of intensive supervision.

Figure 6-3   Key Decision Points Where Intensive
Supervision Programs Are Being Used

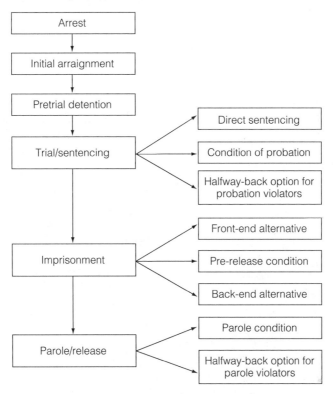

Source: Betsy A. Fulton, Susan Stone, and Paul Gendreau, *Restructuring Intensive
Supervision Programs: Applying What Works* (Lexington, Ky.: American Probation
and Parole Association, 1994), pp. 1–8.

GAO Survey   In 1989, the U.S. General Accounting Office (GAO) surveyed all corrections administrators to obtain data on ISP implementation and evidence of program effectiveness.[7] Forty-one states were found to have implemented ISPs. Detailed descriptions were available on thirty-four programs; evaluations had been conducted on only eighteen of them. Fourteen of the research reports addressed recidivism issues, nine of the studies considered the cost-effectiveness of ISPs, and nine looked at diversion—the impact of ISPs on prison and jail admissions.

Programs were found to vary considerably in the level of supervision they offered offenders. While approximately one-fifth of the pro-grams provided twenty-five or more contacts per month, 42 percent of the programs provided fewer than fourteen contacts and one in ten provided fewer than five. Evaluated programs tended to be somewhat more treatment-oriented than most, but the fact that less than a third of the programs required any form of counseling clearly indicates that the primary objective of the ISPs was offender control.

An examination of the eighteen studies revealed that ISPs do not reduce recidivism. As implemented, the programs provide significant community protection while the offender is in the program but offer little to assist the offender in reducing future criminality. The examination also showed that evidence of cost-effectiveness and diversionary impact was of such poor quality as to make any judgment on this matter impossible.[8]

National Institute of Justice Evaluation

In 1993, the results of a National Institute of Justice (NIJ) study of fourteen programs in nine states was reported. The study was conducted between 1986 and 1991 and included more than two thousand offenders.[9] The research was unique in that it utilized random assignment to place offenders either in ISP or traditional supervision, thus making it possible to better assess the effect of supervision characteristics on offender outcome.

All projects were part of a Bureau of Justice Assistance (BJA) demonstration project that provided funding for new program development as well as evaluation. All but two of the programs were probation or parole enhancement; the remaining two programs in Wisconsin and Oregon attempted prison diversion, with limited success in implementation.

Jurisdictions receiving the BJA funding had considerable latitude in designing programs to best fit local needs. The only requirement was that the offenders be adult, nonviolent criminals. Many of the programs attempted to focus their efforts on drug offenders, but they had difficulties placing the offenders in treatment. As a result, the programs studied were largely oriented toward surveillance and supervision.

The research revealed more about what ISPs cannot be expected to achieve than about their effectiveness. While the programs were able to provide an intermediate sanction that increased flexibility in sanctioning, they generally failed to reduce prison crowding, save money, or reduce recidivism. In summary:

1. Although the levels of contact varied considerably, the programs succeeded in providing enhanced surveillance. Surveillance alone, however, seemed to have little impact on recidivism. At the end of one year, 37 percent of ISP participants and 33 percent of controls were arrested, with the difference largely attributable to enhanced controls on the ISP offenders.

2. The ISPs truly provided an intermediate punishment. The programs were more coercive and limiting of personal freedoms than traditional supervision. The harsh response to technical violations was the most punitive aspect of the programs. Two-thirds of ISP participants had technical violations, versus 38 percent for controls.

3. The harsh response to technical violations minimized the cost-effectiveness of the ISPs. In one jurisdiction there were five times as many revocations of ISP participants for technical violations than controls; at the end of one year, 30 percent of ISP participants were in prison as compared with 18 percent of those under regular supervision.

4. Treatment activities, employment, and restitution payments were generally higher for ISP participants than controls, but the differences were relatively slight. No meaningful impact of these program elements could be discerned in the analysis.

Florida's Community Control Program

Florida's Community Control Program (FCCP) is the largest intensive supervision prison diversion program in the United States.[10] The program was implemented in 1983 and had served forty thousand participants by 1993. The FCCP provides a significant degree of offender control. Caseloads average about twenty to twenty-five offenders and permit more than two dozen supervisory contacts per month. FCCP participants receive drug and alcohol screening, and they are expected to perform community service, make restitution, and pay supervision fees.

The most unique feature of the Florida program is its integration into Florida's sentencing guidelines. In 1983, Florida implemented

Program Focus

The Experience of the BJA/NIJ Prison Diversion Programs

Prison diversion programs in this study did not provide data on the effect of ISPs [intensive supervision programs] on prison crowding. Of the two participating sites that implemented prison diversion programs in the demonstration, one had too few eligible offenders to yield usable results. In the other, the use of randomization was overridden by the jurisdiction, thereby foiling its purpose. The selection process at these two sites therefore makes it impossible to state with certainty the effect of ISPs in reducing prison crowding.

The experience of the two sites (Marion County, Oregon, and Milwaukee, Wisconsin) does reveal a number of insights into the issues jurisdictions face when making decisions about selecting convicted offenders for diversion into the community.

Marion County, Oregon

Marion County set eligibility requirements so stringent that few offenders could qualify for the prison diversion ISP. The study's mandated criterion of excluding offenders currently convicted of violent crimes was extended to exclude offenders with any prior record of violence. Examination of the Marion County data revealed that, in addition, a large percent of potential participants who had current burglary convictions was rejected. Although this offense is considered nonviolent, evidently Marion County did not wish to place burglars into ISP programs.

The three criteria—exclusion of violent offenders, people with any history of violence, and convicted burglars—shrank the pool of el-

igibles considerably. Furthermore, the local Marion County judge imposed the requirement of informed consent from the offender, producing a sample too small to yield statistically reliable results.

Milwaukee, Wisconsin

In Milwaukee, judges and probation/parole officers overrode the researchers' random assignment of offenders into the experimental and control groups. Milwaukee initially had two pools of eligibles: "front-end" cases consisting of high-risk offenders newly convicted of nonviolent felonies, and "back-end" cases consisting of probation or parole violators who were facing revocation. Regardless of the random designation made by the researchers, most front-end cases were sentenced to prison rather than diversion to an ISP. Of the back-end cases, more than half were sent to routine probation or parole.

That only two sites chose prison diversion suggests the level of concern on the part of the criminal justice system about the risks involved in sending convicted offenders into the community. Further evidence of this concern is the response of these two sites in placing additional restrictions on program implementation.

Note: BJA = Bureau of Justice Assistance; NIJ = National Institute of Justice.

Source: Joan Petersilia and Susan Turner, *Evaluating Intensive Supervision Probation/Parole: Results of a Nationwide Experiment,* Research in Brief (Washington, D.C.: National Institute of Justice, May 1993) p. 7.

sentencing guidelines that established up to two years of community control as an alternative to twelve to thirty months of prison—sanctions for mid-range severity offenders. Lesser criminals might receive probation or jail time, while more serious offenders could be sentenced to more than thirty months in prison.

Research on FCCP has focused on the program's impact on prison diversion and cost savings, as well as the effect on recidivism.

1. *Diversion.* An examination of FCCP participants found that the program had resulted in the diversion of some offenders from prison, but that other FCCP participants had come from the ranks of individuals who would have expected to receive lesser sentences to jail or probation. On the whole, FCCP accomplished more diversion than net widening.

2. *Correctional Costs.* As a result of its diversionary impact, the FCCP was able to reduce correctional costs. The FCCP participants cost the state $6.49 per day, while jail costs were higher ($19.52) and prison costs higher still ($39.05). Only traditional probation ($2.19) was less expensive than these other alternatives. An assessment of the numbers of FCCP clients drawn from each of these alternative sanctions (with net widening costing the state more dollars and diversion saving money) indicated that the FCCP saved approximately $2,746 for every program participant. This finding is especially dramatic given that the cost assessment also included the impact of the increased technical violations and revocations experienced by FCCP participants.

3. *Recidivism.* The FCCP was established as a statewide sentence and correctional sanction, not as a demonstration project. As such, the evaluation of the program was unable to employ random assignment of offenders to FCCP or alternatives. FCCP participants were presumably selected for the program because they were better risks than offenders who required prison. As expected, an examination of FCCP

participants and a carefully matched control group of offenders who received prison sentences did show that FCCP participants had lower conviction rates for new crimes. Drug offenders showed the greatest differences when matched with a control group. Twenty-seven percent of prison releasees were convicted for a new crime as compared with 11 percent of FCCP participants.

The Future of ISPs

Intensive supervision programs show great promise as a correctional sanction, enhancing the credibility of a criminal justice system that often offers offenders too little or too much punishment and control. The same may be said of the impact of ISPs on the profession of probation and parole. By providing a more meaningful sanction, the utility of community supervision is promoted, as is the stature of those whose role it is to provide community control. While different from that of the counseling and service-broker probation and parole officer of the past, the role is what most citizens and politicians wish to see played in community corrections. Still, many issues remain to be addressed.

Level of Control   On the one hand, there may be some advantage to further tightening restrictions and controls and further reducing opportunities for violations and crimes. Personal contact with offenders averaged only two hours per month in the programs studied by NIJ.[11] Enhanced supervision and controls might provide additional community protection and minimize program violations.

Technical Violations   On the other hand, a reduction in the response to technical violations may be in order. While certainty of revocation in response to violations is clearly punitive, no evidence shows that it has a deterrent impact, and it may be an overresponse to nonthreatening conduct. Greater targeting of conditions specifically to the individual offender's conduct, needs, and risk level may minimize the likelihood that offenders are needlessly returned to prison.

Treatment and Program Services As they are currently implemented, ISPs do not appear to reduce recidivism. Enhancing (or introducing) focused treatment elements in the programs may provide a means to achieve more than just the temporary control accomplished by enhanced surveillance while the offender is in the program. The interaction of treatment and control may provide more long-term results in recidivism reduction. While ISPs provide excellent monitoring, they seem to achieve no long-term gains in community safety and thus require a broader focus if they are to bring about more lasting results. More careful selection and targeting of offenders eligible for ISP participation should be equally valuable in this regard.

ISPs appear to be very good at what they do. Like all correctional programs, they tend to be oversold and raise expectations beyond what is reasonable given implementation limits. The potential of these programs is considerable. Given the will to refine and retarget these programs, they may provide much of what is needed to better serve both short- and long-term crime control objectives.

Boot Camps

The contemporary **boot camp** movement originated in Georgia in 1983. The fifty-bed, ninety-day program was established as one of an array of sentencing options designed to avoid a federal takeover of Georgia's overcrowded state prison system.[12] Five years later, fifteen programs had been established in nine states. Today, boot camps operate in more than half the states, serving adults and juveniles, men and women, in both state and local jurisdictions.

Definition

The term *boot camp* is sometimes used interchangeably with the terms *shock incarceration, shock probation,* or *shock parole.* While all of these programs include a period of confinement designed to provide a deterrent jolt to the offender and perhaps stimulate a readiness for rehabilitation, boot camps employ a distinctive approach to accomplish the shock. This strategy includes living conditions, a program structure, and emphasis on discipline and physical fitness that are clearly military in origin.

Program Objectives

Because boot camps seem to have universal appeal, they have expanded rapidly. The programs incorporate all the goals of other intermediate sanctions, including community protection, the provision of a mid-range sanction that is both more severe than probation and less punitive than incarceration, and the potential for cost savings.

In addition, boot camps have special appeal because they uniquely incorporate an environment that is punitive enough to warrant expectations of deterrence and sufficiently structured and focused to validate hopes for rehabilitation. Boot camps do this by targeting young offenders thought to be more capable of reform and more easily deterred than their more hardened peers and by providing a highly structured and strictly disciplined regime expected to remedy the personal and environmental deficiencies of these offenders and, at the same time, providing an environment sufficiently unpleasant to have a deterrent effect. Boot camps ideally fit a popular view of offenders and an explanation for their offending. Offenders are perceived to be persons who are soft and incapable of a productive lifestyle because of personal weakness and inadequate discipline and training. Boot camps shape up offenders both physically and mentally, providing them with the discipline necessary to achieve their objectives.

Issues in Community Corrections

Inmate Preferences for Incarceration over Intermediate Sanctions

"Probation Is a Trap"

Of the 98 offenders who believed some intermediate sanction was more severe than a short incarceration term, 20 (20%) said that short jail terms were not very difficult. As an experienced Houston con artist put it, "Three months in jail is a summer vacation." A similar sentiment was expressed by a San Antonio burglar, interviewed in Bexar County jail: "You get jail time over with right away. You just want to take care of the time as fast as you can." Short jail terms are not only short, they are final. From a Harris County burglar: "In jail, once you're gone [released], you're gone. Then there's no reporting. It's easier on your work and lifestyle." Some respondents felt jail or prison might teach them a lesson they would not get on the street. A Harris County DWI [driving while intoxicated] offender, now serving an ISP [intensive supervision program] term, argued the uselessness of regular probation:

In jail, you might learn something, straighten your life out. It's better to spend a little time in jail and learn something than spend 5 years on bullshit probation.

These respondents tended to be experienced offenders who had been on ISP and in jail or prison and had an idea as to how difficult they were.

Among the offenders, 30 (31%) regarded stiff fines as the most severe of the intermediate sanctions, and they argued that money was difficult to obtain. A Harris County cocaine user, now doing time in jail, told us, "$5,000 is $5,000. In today's economy, that's tough to come up with." Others, certain they could raise the money given the time, preferred to save

time by going to jail. A Harris County rapist, interviewed in prison, had such a pragmatic viewpoint: "To pay back $5,000 would take too long. Do the time and get it over with."

Fines were especially problematic because many of the respondents were out of work and had limited legitimate sources of income. An experienced Houston pickpocket, interviewed in jail, explained, "You steal because you haven't got any money, so they fine you and that causes more problems. Where do you get the money? You steal it." For some of our respondents, at least, fines were not only stiff penalties; they might do more harm than good.

But the strongest sentiments were reserved for intensive probation. Most respondents regarded a 2-year ISP term as even more stringent than a $5,000 fine or a 3-month jail term, and many regarded it as more severe than a 1-year jail term. A total of 50 respondents (51%) cited the difficulties of ISP as a reason for preferring a short jail term.

The problem cited most often was the level of supervision. A Bexar County drug courier, now in jail awaiting transfer to prison, was typical:

It's the amount of supervision that gets you down. When you're an addict, it's just impossible. You feel as though you're under watch all the time. In prison, you may never talk to somebody until you're leaving. . . . That's why many prefer the joint to probation.

From a Bexar County auto thief:

On [strict probation], you see the officer five times a week. Every day—that's outrageous! It's like prison. You spend most of your time with the probation officer.

A Dallas County jail inmate, convicted of drug possession, was even more direct: "If I've got to meet my PO [probation officer] five times a week, I'd rather be in jail."

Blacks and Hispanics were more likely to prefer jail to intensive supervision, and their comments suggest that differences in supervision may be one reason. A Houston drug dealer, interviewed in prison, told us, "Intensive supervision is hard on a Black man. Blacks get treated worse, even by Black POs." A Dallas man, convicted of welfare fraud, also felt that ISP officers were tougher: "I don't like POs to visit me very often. They don't always understand my personal problems at home." And a Dallas man, doing a life sentence for homicide, argued that "POs can be arbitrary and hold personal grudges."

Many respondents cited the difficulty of holding down a job on intensive probation. As a Bexar County drug courier put it, "Six months on Level 1 disrupts your whole life. You can't hold a job like that." A San Patricio County man, doing jail time for DWI, was even more blunt:

One year in prison is 1 year out of your life, but 2 years of probation is 2 years and you could lose your job. If you lose your job, you may as well be in prison.

Our respondents described a variety of problems that intensive supervision poses for workers. Some cited the time they need to take off from work to visit their POs and attend drug treatment sessions; some argued that they could not make enough to pay the probation fees. Others described the stigma associated with electronic monitoring devices and work visits by their POs. According to a Dallas pickpocket on Level 2 supervision,

Intensive supervision is fine. Weekly visits, the visits to your home—I can handle that. But if they meet you at your workplace, it makes work difficult.

Our respondents cited a final problem with intensive supervision—the threat of revocation. According to a San Patricio County drug dealer interviewed in jail,

Probation has too many conditions. If you can't meet them, you end up in jail anyway. I'd rather just do the time and pay off my debt to society that way.

From a Bexar County jail inmate, doing time for burglary: "On probation, you're on a short leash. If you cross over the line, they give you more time." And from a Harris County heroin addict: "The longer it lasts, the more chances you have to mess up. If you break [probation conditions], you'll do longer than a year in jail." Many had a fatalistic attitude about intensive supervision. Respondents believed that they had limited control over their ability to succeed on the street. Success was largely up to "arbitrary" POs who "didn't understand" and "held personal grudges"; holding down a job was difficult due to the time requirements and the stigma of supervision; and several respondents confessed that they were too disorganized to meet even the minimal requirements of regular probation. All this made intensive supervision risky and stressful compared to the certainty of incarceration. A Harris County con man, now doing time in jail, summed up the prevailing sentiment: "Probation is a trap. Do the time and get it over with."

Source: William Spelman, "The Severity of Intermediate Sanctions," *Journal of Research in Crime and Delinquency,* 32 (2), May 1995, pp. 124–126. Reprinted by permission of Sage Publications.

Program Development

The growth of boot camps is a result of considerable federal support as well as their unique fit with popular perceptions of crime and criminals. Federal funding to support the growth of new prisons has particularly identified boot camps as a correctional alternative that can be supported with new federal dollars. The Office of Juvenile Justice and Delinquency Prevention (OJJDP) funded three demonstration projects—juvenile boot camps—in 1991. A year later Congress authorized additional juvenile boot camps when it extended the Juvenile Justice and Delinquency Prevention Act.

Boot Camps Today

A national survey of boot camps conducted in 1994 identified fifty-nine programs in twenty-nine state correctional systems, representing a total program capacity of more than ten thousand participants.[13] Fifteen states made boot camp participation available to women as well as men. In addition, a half-dozen states had programs administered by local authorities, most frequently sheriff's offices or probation authorities. The national survey also found nine programs serving juvenile offenders. At that time, the federal prison system operated two boot camps, with a total capacity of about 350.

Perceived Objectives   A national survey of correctional officials revealed that current programs emphasize a diversity of goals. The most frequently cited goals were deterrence, rehabilitation, protecting the public, and lowering recidivism. Punishment was the least frequently cited goal by correctional administrators. This finding is consistent with other reports that describe correctional authorities as uncomfortable with an explicit focus on punishment as an end in itself, although its use as a deterrent is not perceived as problematic. Most of the administrators also indicated that the boot camps were designed to serve as an alternative to prison.

Eligibility Criteria and Selection   Most boot camps target young, healthy, nonviolent offenders with no prior prison experience. Most programs are voluntary, but the incentive of a shortened sentence is a significant factor in participation. Most programs now take offenders over twenty-five, and some over thirty. The definition of first-time offender differs from jurisdiction to jurisdiction, as does the interpretation of nonviolent crime. Most programs do weed out serious criminals. Seventeen states specifically designed their boot camps for drug offenders.[14]

Offenders are usually selected for boot camps by correctional authorities after sentencing to incarceration. In eight states, judges may sentence offenders directly to boot camp. In other states, judges, correctional authorities, and sometimes probation and parole agencies share in decision making.

Program Characteristics   All boot camp programs rest on a core rationale:

- Offenders selected for boot camp are still young enough, or insufficiently committed to criminal lifestyles, to change.

- Offenders enter boot camps without basic skills, in poor physical condition, and without having experienced success or pride in conventional pursuits such as employment and education. Offenders may lack self-esteem, or their self-esteem may be based on criminal exploits and the approval of criminal peer groups.

- Offenders lack self-discipline, respect for authority, and the ability or motivation to take responsibility and be accountable for their actions.

- A relatively short, intensive experience with military structure and discipline can ameliorate some of these deficits. Like new recruits in military boot camps, offenders can learn self-discipline, responsibility, self-esteem, and teamwork. These skills can help set offenders on the path to new lifestyles.[15]

Critics of boot camps say this objective is flawed, that military boot camps provide a foundation for the real training that lies ahead—the boot camp experience is not an end in itself. In response to such critics, newer programs have tended to adopt a more service-oriented agenda, providing greater assistance to inmates both during and after boot camp confinement.

The programs remain highly militaristic. Correctional administrators identified military titles, military-style protocol, barracks-style housing, drill instructors, the use of platoons, **summary punishment** (on-the-spot punishment for misbehavior), and a public graduation ceremony as elements in use in at least 80 percent of the states. Drug and alcohol counseling are available in all states, with four out of five also providing education and other counseling. Military drill and discipline as well as physical labor and training are present in twenty-eight of the twenty-nine states. Military activities clearly predominate in the schedules of boot camp participants.

The average boot camp experience lasts between 90 and 120 days. Most states allow offenders to quit the program, which normally results in imprisonment. About half the states provide intensive supervision to those who successfully complete the boot camp experience. New York's program is highly regarded for the quality of its postrelease supervision of boot camp graduates. Two-person parole officer teams supervise thirty-nine offenders for six months before the graduates are released to traditional supervision. Educational and vocational training, employment assistance, relapse prevention, and peer group counseling are arranged through community-based agencies.[16]

Most state-run boot camps are located on the same grounds as a larger correctional facility, a practice that allows for the sharing of some services and programs, even though offenders are segregated. In general, boot camps cost more than regular incarceration, because of the intensity of programming. The savings boot camps are expected to achieve result from the shortened sentences of program participants.

Other Boot Camps   Many locally authorized boot camp programs are operated by sheriff's offices or county corrections. These programs tend to be smaller and shorter in length than state programs. Most have a capacity of under fifty beds and programs that last less than ten weeks.

The two programs administered by the Federal Bureau of Prisons have a capacity of fewer than 350 offenders. Federal boot camp participants tend to be somewhat older offenders. The programs are more treatment- and services-oriented than other boot camps, and they avoid summary punishment and confrontational strategies.[17] Federal boot camp participants are released to halfway houses and expected to work, and then later released to home confinement.

Juvenile boot camps share many characteristics with other programs, but they place greater emphasis and more programming time on education and treatment. This practice is consistent with the philosophy of juvenile corrections and broader state mandates for educating juvenile delinquents.

Research on Boot Camps

Two major multiprogram evaluations of boot camps have been done. The first review was conducted by the General Accounting Office, and the second by Mackenzie and Souryal for the National Institute of Justice. The former study reviewed all existing program evaluations conducted up until 1992 and included site visits to several boot camps. The latter evaluation built on the first and examined projects funded by the Bureau of Justice Assistance and developed specifically to test program effectiveness.

General Accounting Office Study   The GAO concluded that boot camps can be utilized in a manner that reduces costs and crowding, but that program impact on recidivism was still an unknown.[18] The impact of boot camps on prison crowding was found to be a function of:

- The size of the program;

- The probability that boot camp participants would have been imprisoned;

- The rate of program completion;

- The difference in boot camp time served and time that would have been served in prison; and

- The rate of return to prison of both boot camp participants and prisoners who do not participate in boot camps but were eligible to do so (used as an estimate of the return-to-prison rate that boot camp participants would have had if they had not entered boot camp).

Many of the states felt that their programs did reduce crowding and saved considerable dollars. New York, with a large program, estimated the savings at $2.02 million for every one hundred inmates released from boot camp, while Louisiana and Florida put their savings at $1.6 million and $1.2 million, respectively.

The National Institute of Justice Study   The purpose of the NIJ study was to determine if boot camp programs were fulfilling their goals and to determine which particular aspects of boot camp programming were most effective.[19] Components of the study included a qualitative description of eight programs based on staff and inmate interviews, official materials, and observation; studies of inmate attitudinal change during incarceration, offender recidivism, and positive adjustment during community supervision (as measured by indicators such as employment and educational status); and an analysis of prison bed space savings.

The programs studied were in Florida, Georgia, Illinois, Louisiana, New York, Oklahoma, South Carolina, and Texas. The programs were selected based on their adherence to basic elements of boot camp programming: the development and enforcement of rules, strict discipline, boot camp-like atmosphere, drills, and physical training. They were also selected because of their differences on selected items: primary entry decision-making responsibility, rehabilitation focus, voluntary entry and dropout, release supervision level, and location in or outside a larger prison.[20] It was hoped that such variation would permit an assessment of the differential effectiveness of such elements on offenders.

Interviews   Correctional officers (COs) generally reported that they thought the programs were beneficial. The programs offered offenders a second chance; removed them from the general prison population; and gave them an opportunity to improve their work habits, get off drugs, and develop some self-esteem. For many of the COs, the job provided a sense of accomplishment. The work was described as stressful, however, and a number of programs reported high staff turnover. This was particularly true in regard to the drill instructor position, for which staff were often selected based on their military background rather than their correctional experience.

Inmates reported some surprise over the intensity of the program, particularly the amount of physical exercise and the confrontational approach. Most of them had chosen the program over traditional confinement because of its shorter sentence and the greater safety and improved living conditions. Generally, they reported the experience as positive. They described improved conditioning, getting off drugs and cigarettes, and better discipline, self-control, and self-confidence as the benefits of boot camp programming. On the negative side, verbal abuse, inferior food, harsh treatment, and lack of control over time were seen as unpleasant aspects of the program.

Those who dropped out did not like the program, but most said they would still recommend it to others who faced sentences of five years or more.

Probation and parole officers were the most skeptical about the programs. While they found the boot camp offenders to have a better appearance, more enthusiasm, greater ability to follow directions, and increased readiness for job seeking, they were suspicious of the ability of offenders to maintain these attributes when back in the community. As one experienced parole officer in New York stated: "While they are in the boot camp they are told, 'You are somebody. It's important to us that you do well, that you are fed well, and that you are clothed well.' . . . Then they go back to utter depravity. It's like throwing them down a well."[21]

Deterrence and Rehabilitation   Three-quarters of the programs listed rehabilitation and deterrence as program goals. The highly demanding program is expected to inspire a sense of accomplishment that can generalize to other activities. The regimen promotes physical health and provides a structured lifestyle. But the authors concluded that the long hours of menial labor did little to promote work skills and that, without such skill development, the offenders are unlikely to be successful in their postrelease lives.

While **shock incarceration** provides a catalyst for change, without sufficient rehabilitative programming graduates will lack the substance to support and maintain their new lifestyles. Within the boot camp, all decisions are made for offenders, and their days are highly structured, with rewards and punishments providing immediate responses to behavior. Returned to the unstructured, crime-ridden environments from which they came, where there is little from which to derive a sense of achievement, the graduates are unlikely to be able to overcome the same obstacles they confronted prior to the boot camp experience. While the participants may feel better about

themselves, they possess the same levels of skills and abilities with which they entered the program.

The boot camp experience can be viewed as a somewhat cruel hoax. It provides just enough of a boost to the individual to inspire a willingness and greater readiness to change, but little of the tools necessary to accomplish the long-term effort required to become a more productive citizen. The three to four months of boot camp programming may be valuable to the offender, but the achievements won over this relatively short time period need to be enhanced and supported if they are to provide a true foundation for the future.

Attitude Change   Boot camp participants became more positive about the program over time, but the antisocial attitudes of offenders showed little change except in the more treatment-oriented programs. This finding supports the preceding qualitative assessment. Truly "winning the offender over" may require providing a helping hand as well as a stern disciplinary environment.

Recidivism and Adjustment to the Community   Only three states achieved recidivism rates for boot camp graduates that were lower than those of a comparison group of offenders. In Florida, the boot camp graduates did as well as those who dropped out of the program, demonstrating that the characteristics of offenders selected for the program accounted for all the differences in recidivism; the boot camp experience added nothing to reduce further crime. Those programs that were effective—in Illinois, Louisiana, and New York—had intensive community supervision following release. The NIJ researchers concluded that this supervision, alone or in conjunction with boot camp programming, may have been responsible for the differences in participant recidivism. At the same time, measurements of offender adjustment to community supervision showed no differences for boot camp graduates and others, although

Issues in Community Corrections

Program Variation Within the NIJ Study: The Examples of Georgia and New York

Georgia

To avert a Federal takeover of its extremely crowded prison system, Georgia developed an array of sentencing options throughout the 1980s aimed at saving costly prison space. Implemented in November 1983, Georgia's 90-day boot camp program was one such option.

When the program was selected for participation in this study, program capacity was 250. Legal eligibility criteria restricted participation to 17- to 25-year-old males who were convicted of a felony, sentenced to at least 1 year, and had not been previously incarcerated. Offenders were placed in the program by the judiciary as a condition of probation. The sentencing judge retained case control until offenders were terminated from probation.

Although initial participation was voluntary, inmates were not permitted to drop out of the program voluntarily. Inmates did leave the program though for medical or disciplinary reasons prior to graduation. These offenders were discharged through a revocation process and served the remainder of their sentence in prison. During calendar year 1989, approximately 91 percent of the offenders who entered the program graduated.

The focus of the program in 1989 and 1990 was on work detail. Inmates were required to work approximately 7 hours per day (5 days per week). Two hours per week were devoted to rehabilitative activities that consisted mainly of life-skills classes. Upon release, offenders received regular probation.

Interviews with correctional officers and judges revealed that they strongly supported the program. In general, correctional officers were proud to be associated with the program and

judges believed that it was one of the best programs for young offenders. Probation officers were more skeptical. Boot camp participants reported improved physical conditioning as one positive aspect of the program. Some inmates reported that they had been verbally abused.

New York

Established in 1987 as part of an Omnibus Prison Crowding Bill, the program was the largest in the Nation at the time of multisite data collection. In 1990, New York State operated 5 shock incarceration facilities with a total capacity of 1,500, including approximately 100 beds for female inmates. Program length was 180 days.

Offenders were selected for participation in the program from a pool of offenders already sentenced to the New York Department of Correctional Services (NYDOCS). Primary placement authority rested with NYDOCS with one exception (placement of offenders between the ages of 26 and 29 had to be approved by the sentencing judge). Eligible offenders had to be between the ages of 16 and 30, sentenced to an indeterminate term, and eligible for parole within 3 years. (A recent legislative change raised the age limit to 34 years of age and younger, effective April 14, 1992.) Conviction of felony violent offenses rendered an offender ineligible. Offenders could also be deemed ineligible based on medical or psychiatric conditions, security classification, and criminal history.

Participation in the program was voluntary. Inmates retained the right to drop out of the program at any time. In this event, they were returned to prison to serve the remainder of their sentence. During calendar year 1988, approximately 69 percent of the offenders who entered the program graduated.

Beyond the common core of military-style discipline, training, and hard work, New York's program was noteworthy because it was structured as a therapeutic community and because it heavily emphasized substance abuse treatment. Participants spent approximately 4 hours per day involved in therapeutic programming and 1.6 hours per day in academic education. For example, each platoon formed a small "community" and met daily to problem solve and discuss its progress in the program. Inmates also learned decision-making skills (called the Five Steps to Decision-making) as well as life-skills. A total of 200 hours were additionally devoted to Alcohol and Substance Abuse Treatment (ASAT) program activities.

During the in-prison phase, parole staff worked closely with the inmate and the inmate's family to develop a residence and employment plan for implementation upon release from prison to a 6-month intensive community supervision program. High supervision standards included increased home visits, mandatory substance abuse counseling, weekly curfew checks, and random urinalysis. Other supervision objectives included enrollment in an academic or vocational program within 2 weeks of release and employment (at least part-time) within 1 week.

Interviews with corrections officers revealed that they considered working in the boot camp to be a rewarding experience because they believed they were accomplishing something worthwhile. Boot camp participants reported learning the most from the ASAT program and were most concerned about finding a job upon release from the program. Parole officers were aware of the difficult family/community environments to which many boot camp parolees were forced to return. They believed that the smaller caseloads and more intensive supervision allowed them to do a better job.

Program Contrasts

To summarize, Georgia's program capacity was 250, and program length was 90 days. Participation in the program was limited to young, first-time incarcerated offenders sentenced to the program as a condition of probation. Case control remained with the sentencing judge. Approximately 91 percent of the offenders who entered the program graduated.

In contrast, New York's program capacity was 1,500, and program length was 180 days. Eligibility criteria permitted offenders up to 30 years of age to participate. Participants were chosen from a pool of prison-bound offenders already sentenced to NYDOCS. Participation in the program was completely voluntary. Approximately 69 percent of the offenders who entered the program graduated.

Offenders in Georgia spent 2 hours per week involved in rehabilitative activities as compared with offenders in New York who spent 5.6 hours per day involved in rehabilitative activities. Upon release, program graduates in Georgia received regular community supervision, while graduates in New York began a 6-month period of intensive community supervision.

Source: Doris Layton Mackenzie and Claire Souryal, *Multisite Evaluation of Shock Incarceration,* Final Summary Report submitted to the National Institute of Justice (NIJ), November 1994, pp. 6–8.

positive adjustment was somewhat enhanced by more intensive supervision.

Reduction of Prison Crowding Like the GAO study, the NIJ evaluation found that carefully designed programs could reduce prison costs. The level of reduction was a function of program capacity, direction of imprisonment, program dismissal, and recidivism rates.

The Future of Boot Camps

Boot camps can be expected to continue to expand because of their widespread support. Indications to date are that the programs can reduce prison crowding and can provide a meaningful alternative to incarceration. Much remains to be addressed in the area of boot camp programming, however, if the programs are to achieve a lasting impact on the individuals they serve. Challenges that need to be addressed include:

1. Which offenders can most readily benefit from the short-term impact of the boot camp experience?

2. What elements of programming are most effective with which subgroups of offenders?

3. What is the appropriate balance between discipline and regimentation and counseling and skill development in boot camp programming?

4. What is the optimum length of boot camp participation? At present, program savings result from the short period of boot camp confinement, yet more services and longer periods of assistance may be necessary to achieve reductions in recidivism.

5. What are the attributes of effective boot camp staff, and what type of training should these individuals receive?

6. Almost half of boot camp participants drop out of many programs. Are there ways to better predict or enhance program completion?

7. Community supervision seems to play a major role in boot camp effectiveness. How can this supervision be paired with the boot camp experience and build on its foundation for long-term offender gains?

As more is learned about boot camps and their impacts, these programs will likely continue to play an increasingly meaningful role in community-based corrections.

Home Confinement and Electronic Monitoring

Home confinement (sometimes referred to as house arrest) is a sanction that requires the offender to be within his or her place of residence for specified periods of every day. Release is permitted for purposes of employment, schooling, or counseling, but little else. Home confinement may be utilized as a stand-alone sanction or as a condition of supervised release. Often it is utilized as a condition of intensive probation or parole supervision. Today, home confinement is used in every state, at every stage of the criminal justice system, for both adults and juveniles.

Home confinement conditions may be enforced manually, through telephone calls and field visits, or electronically. Electronic surveillance is available in two forms: **continuous contact** and **programmed contact.** Continuous contact models require the offender to wear a device that transmits a signal to a receiver connected to his or her home phone. The receiver or dialer alerts (through the phone line) a central computer when the offender moves outside the reception area of the receiver. Programmed contact approaches consist of random phone calls to the defendant requesting verification of his or her presence in the home. Verification may be provided electronically, through use of a key strapped to the offender, or through voice or video analysis.

Examining home confinement as a sanction without also examining **electronic monitoring (EM)** is difficult. Most studies of home confinement have focused on electronically monitored supervision, because EM was expected to provide an especially useful form of incapacitation and because the use of EM raised questions that merited special investigation and study. Home confinement used without EM looks much like community supervision with a restrictive **curfew,** a sanction not too different from traditional community release. With EM, home confinement better meets the criteria for intermediate sanctions—providing a greater emphasis on community protection, cost savings, and punishment. This is not to say that the advantages of electronic monitoring over manual approaches have been demonstrated; they may be more apparent than real.

Objectives

Reduction of Correctional Costs   Home confinement is most frequently supported for its potential to reduce costs. This is because home confinement proposes simple goals. It provides no directed effort at behavior change, and it permits offenders to carry on much of their lives as if unsanctioned. What it does attempt to do is provide an alternative no-cost residence for offenders who do not require incapacitation, in a manner that is restrictive for individuals who can handle the inconvenience of being homebound. In virtually every assessment of home confinement, the primary value of the program consists in the number of jail or prison days avoided.

Electronic monitoring is expected to be less costly than manual monitoring because of reduced personnel costs and because costs can be more easily passed along to the offender. It is not clear whether either of these propositions is true. While EM is less personnel intensive than a high-contact manual monitoring program, how many manual contacts are necessary to enforce home confinement is not known. In addition, EM does require personnel to install the communications system, input and update offender schedules, and monitor alarms. While the EM equipment is an additional expense, most jurisdictions provide means of recouping program costs, because offenders are required to pay for use of the monitoring equipment; that same fee may be used to cover the cost of manual supervision in nonelectronic programs.

The cost savings of home confinement are much like those of other intermediate sanctions. When utilized in a manner that serves as an alternative to incarceration, the programs save money. When utilized with nonincarceration-bound offenders, or for longer periods of time than offenders would have spent in jail, or in a manner that produces many revocations and lengthy subsequent incarcerations, the programs lose their cost-effectiveness.

Community Protection   Home confinement is not incarceration; even with EM, there is no electronic jail. Monitoring the offender on home confinement does, however, permit the detection of violations more rapidly than would be observed in less structured settings. This allows the program to quickly identify offenders who cannot abide by program restrictions and revoke their release. Home confinement thus provides a measure of protection that unsupervised release cannot.

Whether EM provides greater security than manual supervision is unclear. EM may appear to do so, as a result of its employment of sophisticated technology. To the extent that EM provides more frequent contacts, or continuous contact with the offender, the level of supervision is enhanced and violations can be detected more readily. EM does provide more of a deterrent to violations than manual supervision, although the constant presence of the electronic device may prove inhibiting to offenders.

Intermediate Punishment   Home confinement is less punitive than incarceration, but more harsh than traditional community release. The inconvenience of the sanction should not be minimized. It requires offenders to be within their residences up to twenty-four hours per day, seven days a week, with release only for the essentials of work, school, religious services, and programmed assistance. Duties as mundane as getting the car fixed or picking up laundry must be done by others or remain undone. The offender is homebound and suffers the same impacts of boredom and cabin fever suffered by those who are immobile for other reasons. For good or ill, family relationships are affected by the constant presence of the offender as well as his or her need to depend on others for assistance in negotiating the services of the outside world. EM has an additional punitive element: The bracelet the offender must wear can be both an annoyance and a humiliation, a constant reminder of his or her diminished status.

The family, too, may experience some of these effects. Programmed contact EM systems have been particularly bothersome because of the random phone calls engineered at all hours of the day. Manual contacts seem to be less bothersome, perhaps because they are less inconveniently timed. Continuous contact EM programs are the least intrusive in this regard.

Some of the enthusiasm for electronically monitored home confinement is a result of its origins as a device that some expected to have behavior-modifying as well as surveillance potential. There is continued interest in this aspect of electronic monitoring and the potential of home confinement to affect offender behavior.

Program Development

Home confinement was in use as a correctional sanction before electronic monitoring was introduced. Florida's Community Control Program has utilized home confinement as part of its intensive supervision strategy since its inception in 1983. That program implemented EM in 1987.[22] FCCP had almost eleven thousand participants in 1990. Only about nine hundred of these individuals were subject to electronic monitoring.[23]

The origins of electronic monitoring can be traced back to the Harvard University studies of Ralph Schwitzgebel and his colleagues.[24] In the 1960s, they devised a belt-worn transceiver and established a network of repeater stations in the Boston area linked to a central monitoring station. This equipment allowed a subject to be tracked over several blocks. Schwitzgebel hoped that the device would eventually be used to facilitate therapeutic as well as crime control objectives. He envisioned a system in which tones might be sent to warn offenders when they approached inappropriate settings or engaged in illicit actions, and praise could similarly be communicated in response to positive activities.

In the early 1980s, two judges experimented with equipment that provided a means to monitor offenders in their own homes. Although the first experiment ended after five trials because of equipment problems, the second, in Key Largo, Florida, was more successful and grew into a countywide program managed by Pride Inc. (a private contractor).[25] At about that same time, the Florida Department of Corrections began experimenting with electronic monitoring as part of its FCCP initiative.

Home confinement with EM grew throughout the 1980s from small experimental programs into statewide initiatives. In 1986, there were only ninety-five offenders on EM; four years later, there were more than twelve thousand spread across every state in the country.[26] Today, more than ninety thousand local, state, and federal offenders are being supervised on EM.[27]

During the 1980s, more than twenty-five hundred news-related articles were published on EM each year, most of which highlighted the cost savings of this innovative new technology.[28] In the 1990s, a shift in perspective began to occur, even as programs continued to expand. Articles about equipment problems began to appear, and questions began to be raised about the degree to which EM could live up to claims that it was a magic bullet for corrections. The value of the technology per se began to be examined, even as efforts continued to resolve equipment problems and enhance personnel training. Correctional agencies gradually realized that EM, like any new technology, provides both costs and benefits.

Unlike other correctional initiatives, the growth of EM is supported by an active and clearly defined private sector constituency: the manufacturers and vendors of EM equipment. Marketing at correctional trade shows, they encouraged experimentation with EM that led to rapid adoption of the innovation as well as continued efforts at equipment improvement. Many of the early radio interference and weather-related problems in transmission have been resolved, and the development of mobile units enables probation and parole officers to monitor the offender's presence from their vehicles. Cellular technology allows offenders without phones to participate in EM. Equipment has been miniaturized, battery life enhanced, and the bands worn by offenders made stretchable and tamper resistant.[29] New technology includes the use of visual phones combined with continuous radio frequency EM—when a violation is noted, the computer calls home and requests a visual.

Despite these innovations, a number of issues surrounding program utility and implementation remain to be addressed. These questions are particularly relevant to stand-alone programs that provide no other supervision or programming beyond the enforcement of home confinement. While this correctional option provides the least costly utilization of the home confinement sanction (as opposed to ISPs, which provide much greater supervision at greater cost), it also raises new questions for correctional policy makers, administrators, and managers.

Implementation Issues

Offender Selection   One of the most challenging issues is the selection of EM program participants for stand-alone home confinement and electronic monitoring programs. The question is: For whom is the sanction most appropriate? In the absence of national evaluations, jurisdictions have been left to their own devices to experiment as they see fit. At present, older offenders, with stable home environments, including steady employment, and no significant history of contact with the criminal justice system, seem to make ideal EM participants.

A seven-year study of offenders convicted of driving under the influence or driving with a suspended license found that 97 percent of these individuals completed the EM phase of a longer period of probation supervision successfully.[30] These same offenders encountered greater difficulty while under traditional probation supervision following EM. About one-third of the offenders committed a new offense (usually involving driving without a license or under the influence) or a technical violation. Almost one-fourth of the offenders failed to complete probation successfully. EM may provide some community protection, but the results probably will be limited to the period of active monitoring. Whatever the benefits of EM, they are short-lived.

It has been suggested that EM and home confinement can have a stabilizing effect on the offender, requiring the keeping of regular hours and leading to better work performance. The avoidance of substance abuse may be facilitated by requiring the participant to stay home instead of seeking entertainment elsewhere. Closer contact also may enhance family relations. While these expectations are logical, offenders should not be selected for the program with rehabilitative objectives in mind, unless some significant effort is made to support and maintain these changes following EM.

Likewise, research with pretrial releasees has indicated that these offenders may not do well on EM, simply because successful EM participation offers no incentive to those who face the threat of greater punishment upon conviction. EM requires that motivated offenders have adequate support systems to encourage them to adhere to program restrictions. While this group could include individuals charged with serious crimes, it is questionable whether recent moves to place increasingly serious offenders on EM is fully warranted.

The earliest stand-alone programs targeted only minor offenders, including significant numbers of major traffic offenders. The most recent report indicates that today about one-third of all EM participants (in both stand-alone and enhanced probation and parole programs) are property offenders, 22 percent are drug offenders, and 12 percent have been convicted of violent crimes. Both domestic violence and sex offenders have been placed on EM.[31] Those who are appropriate for stand-alone home confinement—persons who would otherwise have been incarcerated—are likely to be a select group of offenders. Little is known about how to target them in a manner that achieves both community protection and cost savings.

Technological Problems   Many of the original problems that hampered technology have been resolved, but others remain. Incompatible phone lines provide perhaps the most widespread challenge. Unreliable power supplies and the sensitivity of tamper alarms are continuing issues. Radio frequency (continuous) programs provide special challenges. Because the systems search for a signal from a transmitter attached to the offender, interference affects the reliability of alarms generated by the system. Interference can come from a wide array of sources, including sleep patterns, housing construction, cast-iron bath tubs, FM radio stations, and terrain.[32] Programmed contact systems have more everyday sources of difficulty—busy telephone lines make it impossible to reach offenders and obtain a response.

At present, more false negatives (the offender is reported absent when he or she is not) than false positives (the offender is reported present when he or she is not) are reported. While this means that the community is protected more often than not, false negatives require significant personnel follow-up and affect the perceived integrity of the program from both offender and supervisor perspectives.

Organizational Issues   The implementation of EM requires considerable staff training and preparation.[33] A computer-skilled employee is required to enter and remove clients from the system, input schedule modifications, and produce summaries of EM contact records. Additional work is involved in the training and orienting of clients, connecting of equipment, updating of offender schedules, keeping track of excused absences, reviewing and interpreting system messages, following up on suspected violations, and conducting independent field checks of the offender and equipment. When the system is out of order, the tasks must be performed manually.

Electronic monitoring is part of the information age. The systems provide much more information than traditional supervision, so organizations and their personnel must be prepared to monitor and act upon that information. A substantial portion of all messages received by EM systems requires action.[34] About two-thirds of all EM programs make provisions for round-the-clock responses. Without such strategies, the value of EM is limited.

Offender Perspectives   Offenders tend to view EM programs as moderately difficult and somewhat punitive, but better than jail.[35] Available data indicate that no meaningful distinctions are made between manual and electronic monitoring. Offenders are generally challenged by an initial adjustment to the program, followed by a period of domesticity, in which they search for at-home projects and sources of entertainment (or second jobs, if allowed). Boredom sets in later and generally lingers until the completion of the period of supervision. Because the periods of supervision are generally short (less than three months), little opportunity exists for long-term adjustments to be initiated.

Family member reactions vary according to the particular program examined. Family members can enjoy having the offender home, or at least they appreciate knowing where he or she is. They do not enjoy having to assume the routine chores of the homebound offender or having to endure persistent telephone contacts at inconvenient times.

Program Effectiveness

In the absence of nationwide studies, one can only assess program effectiveness anecdotally. Existing research has lacked any serious effort at random assignment of subjects to EM or other sanctions. Comparison groups and significant periods of follow-up are largely absent. Depending on the characteristics of subjects assigned to EM and the level of tolerance for violations (real or system produced), on average about 90 percent of offenders seem to complete the programs successfully. At the same time, few offenders complete their sentences without some number of unsuccessful contacts.[36] Almost half of the participants have at least one violation. A study of the self-reports of seventy-eight offenders who had successfully completed their programs revealed that almost half admitted they had violated program restrictions, generally to accomplish a short errand. New arrests while under EM are relatively uncommon.[37]

The Future

Home confinement programs with electronic monitoring are likely to continue to expand. Agencies are increasingly scrupulous in their assessment of vendors and equipment before adopting the technology, and they are finding innovative ways to cover program costs and establish partnerships with the private sector. Remote reporting and computing centers allow agencies to contract with service providers in other states and be assured that the service will in no way be jeopardized by the distance.

Technological Advances   Technological advances are also continuing at a rapid pace. A proposed second generation of systems would track offenders over a wider area and keep participants under constant surveillance. In 1994, Westinghouse received a half-million-dollar grant to develop a prototype system to track offenders over a citywide area—the system is to be tested in Pittsburgh.[38] More accurate and reliable alcohol testing and voice confirmation units are already in use, and the technology exists to combine blood pressure checks and the monitoring of other bodily functions with EM—to monitor for sexual urges, violence, and drug use. Technological improvements will continue to outpace the ability to integrate them effectively into correctional agencies. The need to contain correctional costs will continue to motivate efforts to achieve that integration.

Use as a Sanction for Technical Violations
Home confinement with EM provides clear indications of benefit as a sanction for individuals who violate probation or parole. As a low-cost alternative to revocation, EM provides a punishment that can also enhance community protection. Because the family of the offender is affected as well by the EM experience, increased support may be marshaled to assist the EM participant in meeting his or her obligations.

Such utilization requires that EM use be carefully monitored and not routinely imposed without explicit purpose and focus. Requiring EM of all offenders under intensive supervision (as is often the case) limits the utilization of EM as an alternative to revocation when violations occur and probably enhances the number of technical violations identified. A more targeted use for those offenders showing difficulty in ISP participation may yield an added deterrent benefit.

Research Needs   Home confinement and EM programs are difficult to study in isolation because they are often combined with other sanctions. Because their use is often individualized, to specific small projects and groups of offenders, well-designed experiments are difficult to achieve. Without such research, the utility of home confinement and EM cannot be fully realized. Technological advances, the need to reduce costs, and the desire to explore program effectiveness with a more varied offender population probably will stimulate further study of program impacts and offender outcomes.

Day Reporting Centers

Day reporting centers (DRCs) are among the newest of intermediate sanctions. Although they originated in the United States at about the same time as house arrest and electronic monitoring, their growth was much slower. In 1990, only thirteen day reporting centers had been established in the United States. By the end of 1994, however, that number had increased by more than one hundred and the programs were operating in twenty-two states.[39]

The rapid growth of DRCs in the 1990s seems to be a result of the search for different organizational strategies for the provision of community sanctions as well as an effort to provide innovative programs. DRCs are facilities that offer surveillance, treatment programs, and other services to offenders on community release. They allow offenders to live at home or in community correctional residences, but they require regular attendance at the center for monitoring as well as for personal assistance, education, and counseling. Some programs provide virtually all services through the use of their own personnel, while others make extensive referrals to community agencies. A number of programs **co-locate the services** of other organizations, including private nonprofit agencies, within the grounds of the DRC, granting free space in return for assistance to clients.

Objectives

The goals of day reporting centers are no different from those of other intermediate sanctions. The programs are designed to protect the community, while saving money and providing a punishment more onerous than traditional probation but less severe than incarceration. The programs originated from the efforts of several jurisdictions to overcome their prison and jail crowding problems. They hoped that the regular supervision of offenders would provide sufficient community protection to permit their release from incarceration, while saving the jurisdiction the costs of confinement.

Day reporting centers are unlike some other intermediate sanctions, however, in that the vast majority of the DRCs make extensive use of therapeutic, educational, vocational, and life skills development programs. Although the monitoring requirements of DRC participation make clear that surveillance and community protection are important elements of the sanction, the heavy service emphasis reflects a definite rehabilitative side as well. DRCs provide an approach to community protection that is definitely more reintegrative in emphasis than other sanctions. In many ways, DRCs are principally a means of efficiently organizing **service delivery** from the perspective of both providers (treatment, counseling, and educational programs) and consumers (offenders on community release). DRCs can provide one-stop shopping for the multiproblem offenders that typify today's criminal.

Development of Day Reporting Centers

The rehabilitative orientation of DRCs is a direct outcome of their origins. While DRCs

Program Focus

A Composite Day Reporting Center

As this report discusses, while American DRCs [day reporting centers] share a few basic characteristics, they also vary to a large degree in terms of a number of other features. Based on the research findings, however, it is possible to create a composite picture of the DRCs that responded to the mail survey. Certainly not every DRC has all of the following features, but in general these characteristics are representative of a typical day reporting program:

- Was established only two or three years ago by a local public (judicial) agency.

- Accepts primarily male offenders who are on probation or have violated conditions, who abuse alcohol and other drugs, and who pose a low risk to the community.

- Aims primarily to provide treatment and other needed services to offenders and to reduce jail or prison crowding in its community.

- Is open five days (about 54 hours) each week and has a program duration of about five months.

- Serves fewer than 100 offenders at any one time.

- Maintains a strict level of surveillance and requires more contacts with offenders than is required by the most intensive form of community supervision otherwise available in the jurisdiction.

- Directs successful offenders through three phases with increasingly less stringent requirements, requires five on-site contacts during the most intensive phase, also monitors offenders off-site through telephone and field contacts and electronic surveillance, monitors offenders for a total of nearly 70 hours per week.

- Tests offenders for drug use at least five times each month during the most intensive phase.

- Provides numerous services on-site to address clients' employment, education, and counseling needs, refers offenders off-site for drug abuse treatment.

- Requires offenders to perform community service.

- Has one line staff for about every seven offenders and has a relatively low staff turnover rate.

- Costs about $20 per day per offender.

Private programs differ from this composite in that they provide more services, have fewer staff and higher staff turnover, are slightly larger and more expensive, and recruit more offenders released early from jail or prison.

Similarly, older programs diverge from the composite because they have fewer admissions, they recruit more offenders released early from jail and prison, and they require more offender contacts.

Source: Dale Parent, Jim Byrne, Vered Tsarfaty, Laura Valade, and Julie Esselman, *Day Reporting Centers* (Washington, D.C.: National Institute of Justice, 1995), p. 40.

were first used in the United States in the 1970s for juvenile offenders and the deinstitutionalized mentally ill, they were introduced to community corrections through the influence of programs established in Great Britain.[40] In 1972, British probation officials persuaded Parliament to establish four centers for nonserious but chronic offenders. At the time, the only option for these individuals was confinement, not because of any threat posed to the community, but because they lacked the life skills to survive in a law-abiding manner. The vast majority of these offenders were substance abusers as well. Within ten years, eighty such programs had been established in England and Wales.

In 1985, Connecticut correctional officials searching for strategies to reduce the state's prison-crowding problem learned of the British centers and developed a prototype in Hartford.[41] Massachusetts justice officials were visiting Great Britain at about the same time and independently decided to introduce DRCs to that state through the establishment of a facility at the Hampden County Jail in Springfield.

The early U.S. day reporting centers were primarily private entities. Many of the programs were linked to residential community corrections facilities, which made possible the sharing of space as well as joint use of the services required by both residential and nonresidential populations. For some offenders, involvement in the DRC followed release from the residential facility; other offenders were recruited from among jail and prison-bound populations; and other participants were probationers and parolees believed to require the greater supervision and assistance a DRC provided.

Today, DRC participants are drawn from all stages of the criminal justice system. Most of the newer centers are public facilities, reflecting the growing interest of correctional authorities in strategically incorporating DRCs into community correctional systems. Many of the programs are also much larger than the original centers. While the average size is about

eighty-five participants, the largest centers serve two thousand offenders on any one day.

Program Characteristics

Virtually all that is known about DRCs is drawn from a National Institute of Justice survey of programs reported in 1995.[42] That study identified 114 programs in twenty-two states and was able to gather data about program objectives, characteristics, and participants from fifty-four centers. To enrich the survey, the researchers also conducted site visits to four major DRCs.

The study found that although DRC program operations varied greatly, the programs shared similar goals. Providing offenders with access to treatment and services was the highest-rated objective identified by the fifty-four centers.

Surveillance   All programs had strict requirements for offender monitoring. Most DRCs initiate program participation with a relatively high number of required DRC contacts, field visits, and telephone contacts per week. Participation in counseling, educational, and training programs is also extensive. Offenders normally progress through three or four successive stages of program involvement, with requirements decreasing with successful treatment and monitoring experiences.

Most programs require participants to complete and submit a daily itinerary. Many of the offenders are also subjected to a curfew. Two-thirds of the programs require five visits to the DRC per week at program entry. Average DRC participation lasts five to six months, during which time the offender averages eighteen hours on site and more than sixty hours of collateral contacts per week. Virtually all programs test for substance abuse.

Services, Staffing, and Cost   Day reporting centers provide a wide array of services: assisting offenders with job seeking and place-

Table 6-4 Types and Locations of Services
Offered by Day Reporting Centers (DRCs)

		Location of Service		
Type of Service	DRCs that Provide Services	At DRC	Elsewhere	Both
Job-seeking skills (N = 53)	98%	79%	13%	8%
Drug abuse education (N = 52)	96	69	17	14
Group counseling (N = 51)	96	80	12	8
Job placement services (N = 50)	93	62	34	4
Education (N = 49)	93	55	31	14
Drug treatment (N = 48)	92	31	54	15
Life skills training (N = 49)	91	92	6	2
Individual counseling (N = 47)	89	72	17	11
Transitional housing (N = 32)	63	13	81	6
Recreation and leisure (N = 31)	60	74	16	10

Source: Dale Parent, Jim Byrne, Vered Tsarfaty, Laura Valade, and Julie
Esselman, *Day Reporting Centers* (Washington, D.C.: National Institute of Justice,
1995), p. 13.

ment, educational needs, substance abuse education, and treatment, and life skills training (Table 6-4). Most of the services are provided on site; drug treatment is most likely to be provided elsewhere. All DRCs provide services five days a week; about one-third are open for at least one additional day.

Offenders in two-thirds of the programs participate in community service. In some programs the emphasis on community service is considerable, with DRC vans transporting participants to worksites, where they are supervised by DRC staff.

On average, DRCs employ one staff member for every seven offenders, but the largest programs may have a much higher ratio of offenders to staff. Most staff receive the equivalent of about seven weeks of training during the first year of their service.

Program costs are a direct function of the level of services and surveillance provided by the center. The average cost per offender per day is $35.04, but that amount varies from $10 to $100. In general, the cost of DRCs is less than incarceration but more than probation. DRCs may even cost more than surveillance-oriented intensive supervision programs.

Eligibility Criteria and Participant Success

DRCs provide services to a wide variety of offenders on community release. While an important goal of DRCs is to reduce the costs of confinement, the NIJ survey found that most offenders are recruited into DRCs from probation and parole, not directly from incarceration. While it is impossible to determine if some of these offenders would have remained incarcerated without the presence of the DRC, it is more likely that DRCs provide enhanced treatment and surveillance to offenders who would otherwise achieve community release. However, DRCs clearly provide an alternative to revocation for probation and parole violators. Almost three-quarters of all DRCs admit such offenders. Because offenders are referred to DRCs after already obtaining release, DRC screening is more likely to focus on the need for treatment and supervision than offense seriousness. Some programs do target offenders with special needs, however, such as women with children and individuals with mental problems.

Perhaps because of the wide array of offenders who are served by DRCs and the heavy presence of those having difficulty on community supervision, DRC program completion rates are not high. The average DRC reports that half of all participants do not successfully complete the program, and although the range of termination rates is considerable (programs vary from 14 percent to 86 percent negative terminations), many individuals in DRCs cannot function successfully under their supervision. Other factors also seem to affect completion rates. Private facilities are more likely to terminate offenders unsuccessfully, as are programs with a high level of service. Public agencies may be more tolerant of violations and less likely to attempt to resolve offender problems (or remove problem offenders) by revocation. Higher levels of service also mean greater expectations for offenders, another factor that could enhance violations. Programs with curfews tend to report fewer unsuccessful terminations.

Program Illustrations

Harris County (Houston) Community Supervision and Corrections Department (HCC-SCD)

Day reporting is one of several options in the four-tier continuum of sanctions used in Houston, Texas.[43] Tier one is total confinement in a local jail or other secure facility, tier two consists of other residential sanctions, tier three includes day reporting and other levels of community supervision, and tier four is unsupervised probation. Day reporting is the most intensive form of community supervision and is referred to as SIPP—the Super Intensive Probation Program.

Although the program was established to reduce jail crowding, judges resisted constraints on their sentencing discretion. SIPP is now used as a reentry program for graduates of residential programs and at decision points where confinement is a likely outcome, as in revocation hearings.

Because of the scale of the program, which can serve more than two thousand offenders

in a single day, SIPP has developed several specialized caseloads.

Mentally Ill and Mentally Retarded Offenders The SIPP programs can serve 250 mentally ill or mentally retarded offenders. These cases come from three sources: (1) as referrals from Project Action, a residential treatment program for mentally ill or impaired offenders, (2) as the result of direct court sentences, and (3) as an alternative to revocation from a tier two or tier three placement. For this group, staff emphasize crisis intervention more strongly, monitor offenders' intake of prescribed medications, make more frequent referrals for services, and exercise more patience in dealing with offenders.

Stalkers This group, which consists of offenders who are subject to restraining orders, has a higher level of field contacts as well as more intensive and lengthy curfew requirements.

Sex Offenders About 125 positions are available for sex offenders who are in community-based treatment.

Graduates of Institutional Drug Treatment Programs The Texas Department of Corrections operates substance abuse felony punishment facilities, which provide treatment for drug-involved offenders. Probationers who do not adjust satisfactorily to supervision can be placed in these low-security facilities for up to one year while still on probation.

Probationers in an Alternative Campus The public schools have created alternative campuses for seventeen- to nineteen-year-old felony probationers who are still in school.

Boot Camp Graduates Each platoon of graduates participates in weekly group meetings at the SIPP and performs group community service. The program's intent is to prolong the esprit de corps generated in the boot camp.

Offenders on Both Probation and Parole All parolees who are also on probation are on a specialized SIPP caseload.[44]

There are two SIPP units. SIPP North is located next to a freeway in a black and Hispanic low-income area. It shares a county office building with several human service agencies. SIPP South is located in an older commercial area on the edge of downtown Houston in what used to be a used-car dealership.

In phase one of the program, offenders must report daily, unless they are working, in which case phone or field visits are utilized. Contact is reduced to three times a week in phase two, and once a week in the final phase. Offenders take a drug test during their first visit and are subjected to random testing thereafter. Offenders must pay fines, fees, and restitution and perform community service if ordered by the court. Most offenders remain in SIPP three to six months. Every effort is made to avoid offender revocation, by moving offenders from one supervision level to another, until all means fail.

SIPP provides an extensive array of services:

Substance Abuse Evaluations and Assessments A certified substance abuse counselor is on site twice a week to evaluate offenders, and a licensed therapist is on site one day a week to evaluate mentally impaired offenders for substance abuse programming.

Education Lab If offenders read below a sixth-grade level, they are required to attend the education lab, which has fifteen computer stations and is open daily until 8 P.M. Education labs also are provided in all HCCSCD residential programs, so offenders who enter SIPP as residential program graduates can continue working on their educational objectives.

Support Group Meetings Graduates of residential programs who (before discharge from the residential facility) were deemed at high risk for recidivism attend weekly support group meetings. Facilitated by licensed counselors, these meetings are intended to reinforce behaviors learned in the residential facilities.

Individual and Group Therapy One licensed therapist is on site one day a week at each SIPP office to provide group and individual therapy. A psychologist is on site all week at each location to conduct psychological evaluations and to conduct individual and group therapy.

Vocational Intervention Program HCCSCD contracts with the Texas Employment Commission to provide employment readiness classes for offenders and to make employment referrals.

Urinalysis Each SIPP office has trained monitors who conduct on-site testing.

Life Skills Training Each SIPP office (and all residential programs) offer a core program to help offenders overcome patterns that contributed to their criminal behavior. In addition, the program teaches employability and job retention skills.

Intensive Mental Health Case Management Project Action caseworkers (funded by the Texas Council on Offenders with Mental Impairments) work closely with SIPP counselors to help mentally impaired offenders use community mental health services, Medicare and Medicaid services, inpatient hospitalization, community health care, substance abuse counseling, job placement and assistance, and crisis intervention.

Health and Personal Growth Education HCCSCD provides educational information to offenders using a variety of media, including videos or speakers on such topics as acquired immune deficiency syndrome (AIDS) awareness, conflict resolution, parenting skills, nutrition, addiction, and employment skills.

Community Service HCCSCD's community service program encompasses more than just SIPP participants. HCCSCD has more than forty-five hundred offenders on community service crews (and many more performing individual community service) at any given time.

Program Focus

Local Jurisdiction Boot Camp:
Harris County (Houston), Texas

The Harris County CRIPP facility (boot camp) began operation in May of 1991. The facility is located outside of the Houston, Texas, city limits in Humble, Texas. The CRIPP facility is designed for both young male and female offenders sentenced to the **Courts Regimented Intensive Probation Program** as a term of their probation. The facility houses approximately 400 male probationers at any one time. The males are housed, in cohorts of approximately 48, in various Quonset hut style barracks. Female probationers are housed separately in only one barracks (Bravo) and make up fewer than 48 in number.

Life at the CRIPP: The Alpha Barracks

. . . Upon arrival at the CRIPP facility, probationers are taken to the Alpha barracks for their initial shock. This process involves being subjected to military-type discipline. The probationer is then informed of the rules. Barracks run on a Marine model (e.g., as if the building were a ship), the right side is "starboard," the left side is "port," walls are "bulkheads," toilets are "the head," and the floor is the "deck." Each barracks has its own individual chain of command. Select probationers are assigned as guide, or leader, of the entire barracks, and additionally four or more squad leaders are chosen who are subordinate to the guide. Each probationer must use the chain of command (e.g., his squad leader, then the barracks guide, and finally the drill instructor) to make requests, etc. The probationer is given a crew cut, and a booklet containing orders, which he must learn. All personal clothing is taken away and he is issued a pair of old, torn, usually oversized pants and shirt; this clothing is recycled from Alpha group to Alpha group. The probationer keeps his own footwear for the time being. He will remain in this clothing (with a few laundry runs) until he is moved to a program barracks. Because of its function (staging), probationers in the Alpha barracks spend the majority of their time (non-program time) doing physical training, and learning general orders. The daily schedule maintained by the probationers in the Alpha barracks is, in all other regards, the same as for the program barracks.

Probationers rise at 3:00 A.M. for breakfast, after which they run their "daily" physical training. Lunch is served at 11:00 A.M., followed, in the case of Alpha probationers, with barracks cleanup and quizzes by the drill instructor on general orders, then more physical training. Dinner is served at approximately 3:00 P.M. with more barracks maintenance and physical training following. Lights out occur at 10:00 P.M.

Program Status

Once the probationer has progressed through the Alpha barracks, he is moved to a program barracks (program time starts now). Within the first week in the program barracks he is issued a different uniform—a desert pattern BDU (battle dress uniform). This uniform helps (in CRIPP theory) to instill pride in the individual and to add as his first privilege (real clothing). While in the first stage of the program, barracks probationers start their life skills and vocational training. As they move through the stages of the program barracks they are increasingly given more freedom. However, freedoms can be revoked for any infraction of the rules or disrespecting any CRIPP personnel.

Final Phase

Once the probationers enter the final stages of the program barracks (last two weeks), they are again issued a different uniform: a woodland "camo" BDU and a pair of combat boots. This uniform (in CRIPP theory) further distances them from probationers in the Alpha barracks (torn up clothes) and other program barracks (desert "camo"), and instills in them a further sense of pride. The probationers wear this clothing on graduation day as they march and perform various drills and ceremony maneuvers for family, CRIPP personnel, and visiting politicians. Often a Harris County judge will be present at the graduation ceremony, and will speak to the graduates about their new lives as productive citizens.

Life Skills Training

CRIPP probationers are exposed to a wide variety of life skills and regimented paramilitary-type training. Life skills training includes general health and AIDS [acquired immune deficiency syndrome] awareness counseling; probationers are encouraged to take a voluntary AIDS test. There is counseling of the probationer both prior to and after any AIDS testing, a service provided by Harris County Health Department. Vocational training is provided in the form of computer skills training—a computer lab is located at the facility.

Physical Training

Paramilitary training [PT], primarily physical training, occupies the largest part of the probationer's time: probationers are encouraged to attain excellent physical achievement through extensive PT drills. The CRIPP administrative cadre follow the U.S. military's training manual for all PT exercises, and probationers are given numerous PT tests throughout their stay at the CRIPP facility. PT tests consist of a two-mile run, sit-ups, and push-ups. PT is used by the cadre as a builder of both individual and company (barracks) esteem, and the results of PT tests are utilized as a longitudinal measure of both individual and group performance.

Physical training is also used by the CRIPP cadre as punishment. Probationers are often told to "drop" and do 25 push-ups for minor rule infractions. This type of punishment is administered on both an individual and a group (barracks) level. Physical training as punishment is not limited solely to push-ups. Gorilla jumps (jumping from a squatting position with arms reaching above the head), sit-ups, or in the case of group punishment, a tour of the CRIPP facility's confidence course (obstacle course) can also be used. The CRIPP obstacle course consists of numerous eight-foot-high walls, rope climbs, horizontal rope ladder, and slanted log ladder obstacles. Runs on the obstacle courses are conducted by the drill instructor, who leads the probationers by example.

Additional paramilitary training includes general "military bearing" (e.g., attention to personal appearance, tidy uniform, shined boots, etc.), and drill ceremony (marching in formation). These are the primary tools used by the CRIPP cadre to instill a sense of pride, self-esteem, and teamwork into the probationers.

Source: Robert J. Hunter, "Locally Operated Boot Camp: Harris County (Houston), Texas," *American Jails,* July/August 1994, pp. 13–15. Reprinted by permission.

Figure 6-4 Superior Court in Maricopa County, Arizona, Sentencing Continuum

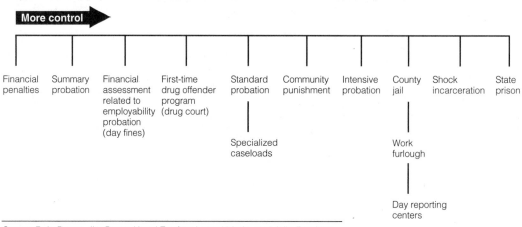

Source: Dale Parent, Jim Byrne, Vered Tsarfaty, Laura Valade, and Julie Esselman, *Day Reporting Centers* (Washington, D.C.: National Institute of Justice, 1995), p. 3.

HCCSCD has sixty twelve-passenger vans, stored and maintained at SIPP South, to transport community service work crews. Skilled workers constructed a large portion of HCCSCD's new community corrections facility, for example, and also helped to build a new nature center in the county park system. Unskilled offenders typically perform cleanup tasks.[45]

Maricopa County (Phoenix) Adult Probation Department Day Reporting Centers Day reporting was established in Phoenix in 1992 and quickly became an integral component of the local correctional continuum of sanctions (Figure 6-4).[46] DRCs were established in an effort to reduce jail overcrowding in response to a federal court order. The programs were funded by increasing the charges to the federal government for housing federal prisoners, a bond issue, and Bureau of Justice Assistance support, and by creating a unique co-location strategy with a wide range of local treatment providers. DRC developers offered free rent to treatment providers in exchange for slots for DRC clients in counseling and educational programs.

The initial target population for the DRC consisted of nonviolent offenders with identifiable treatment needs who were serving split sentences—jail followed by probation. About six hundred offenders meet the general criteria each month, but a restrictive selection and review process reduces this number to about fifty program participants (Figure 6-5). To be selected for the program, an individual must not pose a risk to the community or be in need of long-term residential treatment. He or she must have a verifiable address and access to transportation and cannot have any pending charges that would prohibit participation. Typical reasons for DRC rejection include a history of violence, use of a weapon, a history of sex offenses, pending court appearances, and escape risk.

Maricopa's DRC has three neighborhood offices. The Eastern Center, located in Mesa, shares facility space with an ISP, field service program administrators, the community punishments program, and the community services program. The Central DRC is located in the Garfield Adult Probation and Community Center, an area with a significant gang

Figure 6-5   The Caseflow Process in Maricopa County, Arizona

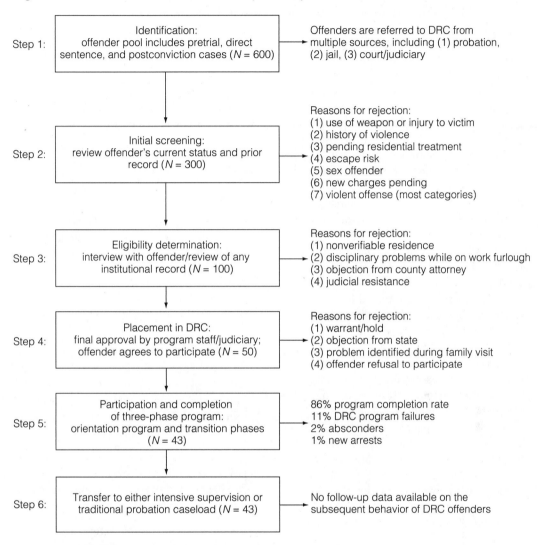

Step 1:
Identification: offender pool includes pretrial, direct sentence, and postconviction cases ($N = 600$)

Offenders are referred to DRC from multiple sources, including (1) probation, (2) jail, (3) court/judiciary

Step 2:
Initial screening: review offender's current status and prior record ($N = 300$)

Reasons for rejection:
(1) use of weapon or injury to victim
(2) history of violence
(3) pending residential treatment
(4) escape risk
(5) sex offender
(6) new charges pending
(7) violent offense (most categories)

Step 3:
Eligibility determination: interview with offender/review of any institutional record ($N = 100$)

Reasons for rejection:
(1) nonverifiable residence
(2) disciplinary problems while on work furlough
(3) objection from county attorney
(4) judicial resistance

Step 4:
Placement in DRC: final approval by program staff/judiciary; offender agrees to participate ($N = 50$)

Reasons for rejection:
(1) warrant/hold
(2) objection from state
(3) problem identified during family visit
(4) offender refusal to participate

Step 5:
Participation and completion of three-phase program: orientation program and transition phases ($N = 43$)

86% program completion rate
11% DRC program failures
2% absconders
1% new arrests

Step 6:
Transfer to either intensive supervision or traditional probation caseload ($N = 43$)

No follow-up data available on the subsequent behavior of DRC offenders

Note: The caseflow process can be described separately for the young adult offender population, for step program offenders (step = short-term enhanced probation), and for offenders referred from the jail/work furlough program. The population estimates are based on monthly totals provided by Maricopa County's DRC director (June 1994). DCR = day reporting center.

Source: Dale Parent, Jim Byrne, Vered Tsarfaty, Laura Valade, and Julie Esselman, *Day Reporting Centers* (Washington, D.C.: National Institute of Justice, 1995), p. 35.

presence. The Western Center is expected to relocate from temporary facilities to a forty-thousand-square-foot mall purchased to house the program.

The Phoenix DRC participant moves through a three-phase program, with each successive phase reducing the level of surveillance and treatment contact. Each DRC supervision team has a caseload of approximately thirty offenders. During the day, participants normally follow an hour-by-hour schedule of activities at the DRC until they are employed. The team works carefully with offenders, varying both treatment and surveillance activities to match offender needs and to response to progress or problems.

DRC services include job placement and job readiness, educational and literacy programs, self-help support groups (Alcoholics Anonymous and Narcotics Anonymous), intensive counseling for chemical dependency, community service, and other counseling and treatment. Many of the services are provided by nonprofit agencies located at the DRC.

Although no formal evaluation of the program has been conducted, data are available on offender outcome. Eighty-six percent (673) of the 780 offenders terminated from the program successfully completed all phases. There had been only five new arrests, sixteen absconders, and eighty-six persons returned to jail. Given the high level of supervision and treatment services required in the program, the 11 percent failure rate was considered to be a positive accomplishment.

The Phoenix program costs about $16 per day. Given that the offenders are drawn from the jail-bound population sentenced to both jail and probation, and that a day of jail confinement costs more than twice that amount ($37), the county estimates a savings of more than $1.3 million since the program began.

Future of Day Reporting Centers

Day reporting centers have an excellent future as intermediate sanctions. Their attempt to consolidate services in a single location is both an effective and efficient approach to service delivery. Their potential impact on the quality of community-based corrections within a jurisdiction is considerable, for they offer the opportunity to enhance treatment and services to a broad constituency of offenders.

They have also proved to be a means of creatively involving the nonprofit sector in the delivery of needed assistance to correctional clients. In addition, if efforts are made to target incarceration-bound offenders, DRCs will prove cost-effective.

Less is known about DRC impact than about other forms of intermediate sanctions. Research is needed to examine:

- The extent to which DRCs achieve their stated goals, and the extent to which those goals changed as the programs were implemented and evolved.

- The actual versus the planned operation of the programs, to determine if the intended levels of surveillance and services were delivered.

- Offender selection processes, to describe any variations from the intended models and to assure that random assignment of offenders was maintained during the study period.

- Important features of the programs, such as the numbers of offenders who obtained and held employment, the numbers of participants who completed treatment programming, the numbers of hours of community service rendered, and so on.

- Reasons that offenders failed in the programs, including removals for violations of DRC rules or failure to complete other required conditions, treatments, or services.

- The impact on public safety, including a comparison of recidivism rates for DRC participants and graduates with those of the control group.

- The cost of DRCs and, particularly, total system expenditures, including costs of confining persons who fail to complete the program.[47]

NIJ has funded research on three DRCs in Wisconsin. If the results show that they are living up to their potential, much further expansion of these programs can be expected. Even if the impact on offenders is found to be less than hoped for, the reasonableness of combining services and supervision under one roof makes DRCs a likely component of the future of community corrections.

Residential Programs

Residential programs or centers have been created in an attempt to achieve several goals of the criminal justice system. These programs operate with the intent of rehabilitating, stabilizing, and reintegrating the offender, and they are best suited for offenders with specific needs and from specific backgrounds. Residential programs are similar in both structure and operations to programs such as halfway houses and work furloughs. These programs, however, differ in two important ways: They are designed to address a set of problems unique to the specific offender, and the offenders in the program are usually similar in regard to their problems and current state. Residential programs have been created in response to the complexity of the lives of some offenders, and the need for progressive responses to current social problems.

Objectives

Because many residential programs focus on a specific type of offender with a specific set of circumstances and needs, the specific objectives are highly individualized and differ among programs. For instance, a specific residential program might focus on drug-related crimes, committed by women, who have young and dependent children living outside the correctional facility. The objectives of this program would address these three areas. The program would seek to provide drug counseling and support groups to keep the clients drug-free and provide drug testing to make certain that the clients were not using drugs when they were not under the supervision of the facility. The pro-

gram might encourage (or require) the clients to remain gainfully employed and allow them to visit, or perhaps share a room, with their children once the clients had earned the privilege. The program would provide, either in-house or through an external service provider, skills training and improvement to enhance the chances that the clients will be able to survive in the society in a law-abiding manner.

Program Characteristics

These programs are usually small, typically housing from five to twenty participants. The operators of these programs seem to prefer locations outside the city, primarily in residential areas. These programs are usually highly structured at first, mostly to ease the transition from a totally incarcerative environment to one with more autonomy and less control. As participants earn credits and are promoted, they receive more freedom and are allowed more time out of the house. These homes are usually indistinguishable from the surrounding homes, except that they generally lack garage space (because the clients are not allowed to own cars, the space is usually converted to living areas) and have electronic locks on the front door. Often the windows are secured to control attempts to leave the facility without obtaining proper release. To be effective, operators of these facilities have found that they need to be located in an area of slightly higher socioeconomic status than the typical program participant is accustomed to. This helps to make the participant aspire to achieve more, because it becomes possible that they could, with time and effort, live in a similar place without external support.

To achieve the goals set out by these agencies, guaranteeing timely access into counseling programs also becomes necessary. For this goal to be achieved, the facility must be located with convenient access to public transportation. Given that the participants will likely need to work and attend counseling and skills training, access to transportation becomes critical for the success of the program and the participants.

Participant Characteristics

These offenders usually have specific problems of the type that can be effectively addressed in a community setting. They usually have other issues that make their return to society more problematic (no home, dependent children), and they also tend to have a strong desire to survive on the outside in a law-abiding manner. Most often these are nonviolent offenders, and their crimes were the result of a set of circumstances that can be effectively addressed by treatment, counseling, or education options. Often these are first-time offenders who have committed crimes that are too serious for probation, but for whom the criminal justice system still holds out some hope for reform.

Summary

Much of the current focus in community corrections is on the use of intermediate sanctions. Although the vast majority of offenders participate in traditional probation and parole, these new programs highlight the present correctional emphasis on community protection, provide a means of reducing the costs of punishment, and offer new options to better fit the punishment to the offender and the offense.

Intensive supervision programs utilize small caseloads, multiple face-to-face contacts, drug testing, and the enforcement of conditions to restrict offenders and provide for the early detection of violations. Some programs also provide some enhanced treatment opportunities. To date, the ISPs are effective at providing an intermediate punishment but are less useful in accomplishing behavior change. The cost-effectiveness of the programs is a function of their use as an alternative to confinement or as an enhancement to traditional community supervision. One of the greatest challenges to ISPs is the need to determine the appropriate conditions, monitoring, and response to violations for various subgroups of offenders. At present, ISPs do an excellent job of detecting technical violations but show no impact on recidivism. The utility of surveillance under such conditions is unclear.

Boot camps combine a stern, well-disciplined military-type environment with a focus on physical fitness in an attempt to jolt offenders out of their prior patterns of conduct. A short-term experience that builds health as well as self-esteem presumably can assist offenders in overcoming the obstacles that precipitated criminal conduct. Most boot camp participants are relatively young offenders without lengthy criminal records, who are perceived to be more amenable to change than more hardened criminals. Boot camps may accomplish the shock to the system they are intended to accomplish, and short-term attitude change and patterns of conduct may be effected. In the absence of any skill-enhancement programming, however, boot camp influence can be expected to fade upon the offender's release. Successful programs have accomplished more long-term change as a result of intensive community assistance provided upon release. Boot camp participation can save money, when programs are used as short-term alternatives to longer periods of incarceration.

Home confinement and electronic monitoring are designed to save money and to release the offender under conditions that are expected to be both punitive and restrictive enough to protect the community. EM is expected to be less costly than manual monitoring of home confinement, but this benefit has not yet been demonstrated. EM is the most high-tech of the intermediate sanctions, a factor that has assisted in marketing the program

Program Focus

Prison Without Walls:
A Typical Day Reporting Experience

John, 28 years old and unemployed, is arrested for possession of cocaine. He is sentenced to probation, but during that time he misses several meetings with his probation officer and tests positive for drug use. Rather than punishing John for this probation violation by sending him to the State prison, which is already 10 percent over capacity, the judge assigns him to a nearby DRC [day reporting center]. The DRC, which the State judicial department began operating two years ago, accepts John because, based on his history and offense, he is of small risk to the community and is in need of drug abuse treatment and other services. Furthermore, by keeping John under community supervision, the judge avoids adding to the already high prison population.

John begins the first phase of the three-phase program in June. For the first three weeks, he must report to the DRC five times each week, where he twice is tested for drug use. The program is open from 8 A.M. to 6 P.M. Monday through Friday and from 9 A.M. to 1 P.M. on Saturdays. When he is not at the center, John must remain at home except to do errands that he has already planned on a weekly itinerary, on record at the DRC. Program staff telephone John several times during the day to monitor his whereabouts and ensure that he is abiding by his 8 P.M. curfew. Once a week, staff also make an unannounced visit to his home. John also begins to attend drug abuse education classes, GED [general equivalency diploma] classes, job skills training, and group counseling sessions, conducted on-site by program staff. In addition, twice a week he goes to a drug abuse outpatient clinic, referred by the DRC.

In the middle of his second week, John misses a counseling session and a GED class. Instead of moving to the second, more lenient phase at the end of the third week, John must remain under the more intensive form of supervision for an additional week. Informed that another violation might land him in the State correctional facility, he subsequently commits no other violations. By the end of June, he is ready to begin the second phase, during which he must continue with his drug abuse treatment and classes but report to the DRC only twice a week. In addition, he joins many of the other 90 offenders in performing several cleanup and construction projects around the city.

After three months without violating any regulations, John begins the third and final phase of the program, during which he reports to the DRC only once a week. With assistance from a job placement agency that offers its services at the DRC, he finds employment with the State parks system. By the end of November, he has been released from the DRC. The cost to the State of his placement in the DRC has been half of what it likely would have been had he been incarcerated, and John seems on his way to making a more productive contribution to society.

Source: Dale Parent, Jim Byrne, Vered Tsarfaty, Laura Valade, and Julie Esselman, *Day Reporting Centers* (Washington, D.C.: National Institute of Justice, 1995), p. 23.

and that offers unique challenges and benefits. Many of the early technological problems with EM have been overcome, and research continues in the attempt to develop systems that are nonintrusive but effective in monitoring offenders over wide areas. The organizational challenges of EM are not to be ignored. The technology requires skilled personnel to input, revise, interpret, and respond to data generated by EM. Careful selection of offenders is essential for EM to be effective. Little is known about how to target the most appropriate subgroups of criminals for this sanction. However, home confinement and EM seem to be an appropriate sanction for community releasees discovered to have committed technical violations. As an alternative to revocation, EM provides a sanction that is both punitive and protective of community interests.

Day reporting centers provide a means of organizing service delivery and supervision to community releasees. Correctional systems have developed innovative means of co-locating therapeutic services at DRCs, thus providing offenders access to a multitude of services at a single location. Like other intermediate sanctions, DRCs are designed to save correctional costs through their utilization as an alternative to incarceration. They are also established as a means to provide greater rehabilitative programming to offenders who would otherwise experience only community surveillance. At present, many individuals assigned to DRCs are unable to complete the programs successfully. The explanation for high failure rates is unclear. Is monitoring too limited or too restrictive? Are services inadequate or simply focused on offenders for whom more or different efforts are needed? More research is needed to address these questions. In any event, DRCs are likely to continue to expand based on the efficiency they provide to a system that offers little in the way of services to the vast majority of offenders.

Residential programs, while not for all offenders, can provide specialized programming and living arrangements to better reintegrate the offender into society. These programs offer some benefits that could serve to motivate the offender to remain law-abiding, while providing the offender with skills that could serve to make life on the outside more successful and stable.

Intermediate sanctions provide means of reducing correctional costs and expanding sentencing options. They can serve as alternative punishments for offenders having difficulty on traditional community release. In the future, one can expect their utilization to increase, reflecting perceptions of crime severity, correctional costs, available remedies, and the willingness of judicial authorities and corrections professionals to adopt new patterns of response.

Key Words and Concepts

back-end approaches

boot camp

collective incapacitation

co-location of services

continuous contact

curfew

day reporting centers (DRCs)

electronic monitoring (EM)

enhancement programs

front-end approaches

home confinement

house arrest

intensive supervision programs (ISPs)

intermediate sanctions

programmed contact

service delivery

shock incarceration

summary punishment

Questions for Discussion

1. Given the research that shows how cost-effective diversion programs can be, why does the public resist the increased use of these programs?

2. Why was it found that decreasing officer caseloads did little to increase the effectiveness of probation?

3. Why would an offender avoid placement in an intensive supervision program, preferring instead to remain in prison or jail?

4. What factors have been found to improve the effectiveness of boot camps? Why are these follow-up programs not in greater use?

5. How do federal boot camp programs differ from those operated at the local level?

6. Which type of offender would be most appropriate for electronic monitoring? Which type would be least appropriate?

7. What makes day reporting centers different from other forms of intermediate sanction? Do these differences reflect the offender, the offense, or both?

For Further Reading

Harris, Robert, *Crime, Criminal Justice, and the Probation Service* (New York: Routledge, 1991).

May, Timothy, *Probation: Politics, Policy, and Practice* (Bristol, Pa.: Taylor and Francis, 1990).

Stenson, Kevin, and David Cowell, *The Politics of Crime Control* (Newbury Park, Calif.: Sage, 1992).

Zvekic, Ugljesa, ed., *Alternatives to Imprisonment in Comparative Perspective* (Chicago, Ill.: Nelson-Hall, 1993).

Chapter 7

Economic Sanctions: Fines, Fees, Restitution, and Community Service

Fines

Day Fines

Fees and Surcharges

Debt Collection

Restitution and Community Service

Summary

The need to expand the continuum of correctional sanctions has led to a vigorous search for new and different intermediate sanctions. At the same time, traditional penalties are being revisited to determine how they might meet contemporary needs. Economic penalties look particularly attractive in this context, because their principal objectives are in agreement with the public's current view of corrections. These sanctions are clearly punitive, offering significant opportunities for retribution and deterrence. They also generate revenue, a real concern in the current period of skyrocketing criminal justice costs. Offender dollars may be distributed to the court, funds may be used to help cover the costs of criminal justice system operation, or monies may be contributed to the victim, in a form of restitution or compensation. Economic penalties that extract labor from the offender may even be used to benefit the community through service programs.

Fines are one of the oldest means of punishing offenders, dating from the Code of Hammurabi. In the United States, they have traditionally been used only with minor offenders. Their limited use stems from problems in the collection of penalties and the failure of these sanctions to make provisions for variation in offender income and wealth. Efforts to improve collection processes and structured, or day fine, programs can be expected to increase the utility of fines as a correctional sanction.

The imposition of fees and surcharges that cover part of the costs of criminal justice system operations is already on the rise. These charges are imposed at sentencing, alone, or alongside other penalties such as probation. These fees provide an opportunity to enhance punishment, to recoup some of the costs of program operation, or to provide funding for victim compensation or other worthy efforts. Everything from presentence reports to electronic monitoring is being in part charged back to offenders. From the offender's perspective, these fees may be indistinguishable from fines.

Restitution and **community service** programs differ from penalties and fees in that restitution payments are made to the victim, not to the criminal justice system. Community service programs extract labor that is paid to the community. Both restitution and community service programs are considered to be broader in focus than other economic sanctions. Proponents of the programs believe that restitution and community service sanctions are conducive to rehabilitation, an anticipated result of the learning opportunities provided by the exposure to victim circumstances and community needs.

Fines

If you asked the average citizen what offenses were appropriate for sanctioning by fines, the list of offenses given in response would probably include no serious crimes. In the United States, fines are generally viewed as more appropriate for traffic and other noncriminal violations than serious offenses. Few individuals consider fines to be anything more than a slap on the wrist—appropriate for minor offenses, but an inappropriate response for any significant wrongdoing. Yet in other parts of the world, fines are a meaningful correctional disposition. In West Germany, 81 percent of adult crimes and 73 percent of violent crimes are

punished by fines as the sole penalty. In England, more than one-third of all felonies and 39 percent of violent offenses result in fines.[1]

Although **fines** are used much less extensively in this country than elsewhere, a national survey of courts revealed that fines are utilized more extensively in this country than most people realize. They are also employed for a relatively broad range of criminal offenses (Table 7-1). This is especially true when the case involves a first offender with a known ability to pay. At least one-third of the judges surveyed reported imposing a fine in more than half the cases in which an adult first offender is sentenced for offenses such as:

- Sale of an ounce of cocaine.

- Fraud in a land deal.

- Embezzlement of $10,000.

- Assault with minor injury.

- Auto theft of $5,000 value.

- Harassment.

- Bad check.[2]

In situations involving nonfirst offenders, judicial willingness to impose fines is greatly reduced, as indicated by the responses of more than one thousand judges to a hypothetical case involving a defendant with several prior convictions charged with larceny and criminal possession of stolen property (Figure 7-1). Federal courts have also begun to use fines and restitution as a way of dealing with their increasing caseloads. Federal courts are sentencing a large percentage of certain nonviolent offenders to restitution or fines or both (Table 7-2).

Impediments to the Use of Fines

Upon further inquiry, judges indicated that there were two major impediments to the broader use of fines: the inability to set an appropriate amount and problems in the enforcement of

Table 7-1 Types of Offenses for Which
Fines Are Commonly Imposed, by Court Type

Type of Offense	Limited Jurisdiction (N = 74)	General Jurisdiction (Felony, Misdemeanor, and Ordinance, N = 28)	General Jurisdiction (Felony Only, N = 24)	Total (N = 126)
Driving while intoxicated/ driving under the influence	54	22	2	78
Reckless driving	30	9	0	39
Violation of fish and game laws and other regulatory ordinances	24	3	0	27
Disturbing the peace/breach of the peace/ disorderly conduct	32	8	1[a]	41
Loitering/soliciting prostitution	15	4	0	19
Drinking in public/public drunkenness/ carrying an open container	14	5	0	19
Criminal trespass	10	2	1	13
Vandalism/criminal mischief/malicious mischief/property damage	9	3	3	15
Drug-related offenses (including sale and possession)	23	10	11	44
Weapons (illegal possession, carrying concealed, and so on)	6	2	1	9
Shoplifting	17	3	0	20
Bad checks	14	2	0	16
Other theft	19	9	8	36
Forgery/embezzlement	2	3	2	7
Fraud	1	4	1	6
Assault	29	14	5	48
Burglary/breaking and entering	2	6	6	14
Robbery	0	1	3	4

[a]Superior Court, Cobb County—1 percent of caseload includes misdemeanors.
Source: Sally Hillsman, Barry Mahoney, George Cole, and Bernard Auchter, *Fines as Criminal Sanctions,* Research in Brief (Washington, D.C.: U.S. Department of Justice, National Institute of Justice, September 1987), p. 3.

fines; that is, collection rates.[3] Statutory limits on fines are generally so low that affluent offenders can simply buy their way out, while minimum fines are still too high for many poor offenders. Judges were interested in, but largely unaware of, options that would allow them to better fit the penalty to the offender based on income.

Most judges were also unaware of the many techniques that can be used to enforce fines. Research has indicated that the effective en-

forcement of fines can be achieved with relatively simple procedures, such as careful tracking of payments, prompt notice of failure to make a payment, and limited use of lengthy installment plans.[4] In the United States, such simple procedures are uncommon. More than two-thirds of the courts surveyed move immediately to arrest offenders when a payment is missed. This get-tough approach often fails to achieve its purpose because the mechanism for achieving an arrest—the serving of a warrant

Figure 7-1   Judges' Choice of Sanctions in
Hypothetical Larceny Case, by Type of Court

The hypothetical case: A twenty four-year-old male defendant is charged with larceny and criminal possession of stolen property. He is alleged to have removed a $40 pair of slacks from a department store, concealing them in a box that had a forged store receipt, and leaving without paying. He was arrested outside the store. The defendant pleaded guilty to the criminal possession charge, and the larceny charged was dropped.

Custody status: On $1,000 bail.
Family status: Single with no dependents.
Employment status: Janitor earning $160 per week.

Offender's record:	1979	Bad check	Convicted—restitution.
	1980	Bad check	Dismissed.
	1981	Larceny	Convicted—6 months probation.
	1982	Larceny	Convicted—1 year probation.

The instruction: On the basis of this information, we would like your estimate of the sanction you would likely impose.

Sanction	General Jurisdiction (N = 631 Judges)		Limited Jurisdiction (N = 478 Judges)	
	Percent	Number	Percent	Number
Jail/prison only	40	252	27	130
Jail/prison plus fine	15	92	27	130
Jail/prison plus fine plus other	18	112	23	111
Jail/prison plus sanctions other than fine	17	109	11	54
Fine only	2	15	4	20
Fine plus sanctions other than jail	5	34	6	28
Other sanctions, alone or in combination, not including jail, prison, or fine	3	17	1	5
Total	100	631	100	478

Source: Sally Hillsman, Barry Mahoney, George Cole, and Bernard Auchter, *Fines as Criminal Sanctions,* Research in Brief (Washington, D.C.: U.S. Department of Justice, National Institute of Justice, September 1987), p. 3.

for nonpayment—represents a very low priority for law enforcement. The harsh penalty fails to guarantee compliance because it is rarely enforced in an effective manner.

The answer to these problems comes in two forms: day fines and enhanced **collection procedures.** Structured or day fines have been utilized successfully in a number of jurisdictions to ensure that fine amounts reflect an offender's ability to pay. A number of other jurisdictions have developed innovative strategies to ensure fine enforcement. Most nonpayment results from easily addressed problems—improperly

set fines and the failure to monitor and enforce the collection of payments.

Day Fines

Day fines are economic sanctions tied to the offender's daily earnings. These penalties are frequently used in Europe and in South American countries but less often in the United States, where economic sanctions have been based on the severity of the crime instead of

Table 7-2 Fines and Restitution Ordered in U.S. District Courts for U.S. Sentencing Commission Guideline Cases, by Primary Offense, Fiscal Year 1997

Primary Offense	Total Cases	No Fine or Restitution Ordered		Restitution Ordered/No Fine		Fine Ordered/No Restitution		Both Fine and Restitution Ordered		Amount of Payment Ordered			
		Number	Percent	Number	Percent	Number	Percent	Number	Percent	Total Cases	Mean (Dollar)	Median (Dollar)	Total (Dollar)
Total	48,515	30,982	63.9	8,473	17.5	7,965	16.4	1,095	2.3	17,099	97,727	4,000	1,671,028,992
Murder	102	68	66.7	18	17.6	7	6.9	9	8.8	33	11,225	4,633	370,409
Manslaughter	53	22	41.5	27	50.9	2	3.8	2	3.8	30	5,098	2,720	152,942
Kidnapping, hostage taking	76	35	46.1	29	38.2	5	6.6	7	9.2	38	20,571	3,190	781,685
Sexual abuse	218	120	55.0	59	27.1	29	13.3	10	4.6	97	3,564	1,320	345,698
Assault	518	340	65.6	90	17.4	73	14.1	15	2.9	177	9,560	1,500	1,692,148
Robbery	2,011	673	33.5	1,181	58.7	74	3.7	83	4.1	1,283	15,769	4,000	20,231,925
Arson	104	38	36.5	55	52.9	7	6.7	4	3.8	65	383,050	40,000	24,898,275
Drug offenses													
Trafficking	18,019	15,164	84.2	127	0.7	2,705	15.0	23	0.1	2,847	55,378	2,000	157,661,348
Communication facility	397	307	77.3	1	0.3	89	22.4	0	X	90	3,531	2,000	317,810
Simple possession	626	299	47.8	2	0.3	325	51.9	0	X	324	969	1,000	313,926
Firearms	2,313	1,722	74.4	191	8.3	383	16.6	17	0.7	578	24,350	2,000	14,074,045
Burglary, breaking and entering	61	15	24.6	36	59.0	5	8.2	5	8.2	46	5,041	2,233	231,900
Auto theft	146	46	31.5	69	47.3	27	18.5	4	2.7	95	31,388	10,832	2,981,824
Larceny	2,817	675	24.0	1,202	42.7	737	26.2	203	7.2	2,097	22,927	2,048	48,078,550
Fraud	6,903	1,826	26.5	3,901	56.5	755	10.9	421	6.1	4,858	230,249	14,000	1,118,551,707
Embezzlement	832	143	17.2	569	68.4	72	8.7	48	5.8	676	45,850	7,569	30,994,754
Forgery, counterfeiting	663	296	44.6	222	33.5	91	13.7	54	8.1	352	25,239	1,220	8,883,996
Bribery	275	98	35.6	53	19.3	110	40.0	14	5.1	175	83,517	7,709	14,615,427
Tax	991	373	37.6	150	15.1	420	42.4	48	4.8	607	51,059	6,500	30,993,111
Money laundering	892	479	53.7	161	18.0	229	25.7	23	2.6	396	344,374	11,155	136,371,981
Racketeering, extortion	603	418	69.3	75	12.4	95	15.8	15	2.5	179	136,056	7,500	24,354,104
Gambling, lottery	181	77	42.5	1	0.6	100	55.2	3	1.7	104	9,386	2,200	976,155
Civil rights	161	79	49.1	23	14.3	53	32.9	6	3.7	80	7,458	2,445	596,667
Immigration	6,669	6,226	93.4	10	0.2	429	6.4	4	0.1	441	5,359	700	2,363,530
Pornography, prostitution	287	167	58.2	3	1.0	113	39.4	4	1.4	120	4,955	3,000	594,563
Prison offenses	302	263	87.1	10	3.3	29	9.6	0	X	39	2,643	1,000	103,067
Administration of justice offenses	876	614	70.1	70	8.0	176	20.1	16	1.8	259	57,785	2,000	14,966,287
Environmental, wildlife	115	30	26.1	24	20.9	42	36.5	19	16.5	84	7,124	2,942	598,406
National defense	22	16	72.7	1	4.5	5	22.7	0	X	6	7,542	4,000	45,250
Antitrust	11	1	9.1	3	27.3	7	63.6	0	X	10	59,171	35,000	591,710
Food and drug	61	17	27.9	1	1.6	43	70.5	0	X	44	7,325	5,000	322,318
Other	1,210	335	27.7	109	9.0	728	60.2	38	3.1	869	14,929	500	12,973,474

Note: Of the 48,848 guideline cases, 333 cases were excluded because of one or both of the following conditions: missing primary offense category, 167; and missing information on type of economic sanction for cases in which orders were made, 169. A total of 17,099 cases were used to calculate amount of payments ordered. This differs from the 17,533 cases in which fines and/or restitution were ordered because of the exclusion of cases in which the amount of fine and/or restitution was not specified. Fine information includes either fines and/or cost of supervision.

Source: U.S. Sentencing Commission, *1997 Sourcebook of Federal Sentencing Statistics* (Washington, D.C.: U.S. Sentencing Commission, 1998), p. 33.

Table 7-3   Comparing Conventional Fines
with Day Fines, the Milwaukee Experience

| Offense | Conventional Practice | | Day Fine Project | |
	Fine	Maximum Deposit	Median Benchmarks	Maximum Benchmarks
Disorderly conduct	$200	$109	5	10
Retail theft	500	319	16	25
Vandalism	500	319	16	25
Loitering/prowling	500	139	7	25
Carrying concealed weapon	500	265	13	25
Assault and battery	500	319	16	25
Abandoned auto	200	79	4	10
Obstructing issuance of citation	250	109	5	13
Theft	500	319	16	25

Source: Douglas C. McDonald, Judith Greene, and Charles Worzella, *Day Fines
in American Courts: The Staten Island and Milwaukee Experiments* (Washington,
D.C.: U.S. Department of Justice, National Institute of Justice, 1992), p. 66.

the offender's ability to pay. Because traditional fines are impossible to implement in an equitable fashion, given the variation in economic status among offenders, they are used much less frequently in the United States. In the search for intermediate punishments, day fines present meaningful options to traditional sanctions.

Objectives of these fines are:

- To lower the cost of punishment.

- To achieve equity.

- To enhance or mitigate the severity of punishment.

- To expand the range of offenses for which fines are utilized.

- To enhance the collection rate of fines.

Day fines were developed to overcome problems associated with traditional fines. Like all economic sanctions, day fines are designed to be punitive. They achieve this punishment at a very low rate of cost for administrative services and generate revenue that can be utilized to support other criminal justice system operations.

Unlike traditional fines, which are based only on the severity of the offense, day fines also consider the offender's ability to pay. Thus with a day fine it is possible to achieve the same relative economic impact on a rich offender as a poor one by taking the same proportion of income and wealth from each individual—that is, roughly a day's income.

Because offender income and wealth can be considered, day fines can be used in situations where a standard fine would not be appropriate. For example, fines for the most frequently charged nontraffic offenses in the Milwaukee Municipal Court range from a high of $500 for assault and battery to a low of $200 for disorderly conduct (Table 7-3). For a low-income first offender, these penalties might be too severe, but for the repeat offender with legitimate or other sources of funds, the sanctions would provide insufficient punishment. By relating the fine to offender income level, the fine can be lowered or raised to meet the means of the defendant. With this flexibility, day fines are appropriate in many circumstances where traditional fines would provide too much or too little punishment.

Finally, research has indicated that one of the principal barriers to the collection of fines is the setting of fines that are inappropriately high and thus require lengthy installment plans that are impediments to compliance. Evidence shows that the setting of a reasonable fine amount is one of the most effective methods of increasing the collection rate of economic penalties.

How Day Fines Are Calculated

With day fines, determining the amount of punishment is separated from a consideration of how much money must be paid. The first step in the process requires courts to define a unit of punishment, and then establish the number or range of units to be imposed for all types of offenses covered by the system. A calculus then has to be developed that permits the court to translate these units into dollars. The new system must then be accommodated into existing habits, customs, and laws regarding the determination, imposition, and enforcement of fines.

The central issue to the creation of day fines is ranking the severity of crimes by the number of newly established units. After ranking is achieved, proportionality must be attained, so that an offense that is twice or three times as serious as another crime yields two or three times the units of the other offense.

Determining how many punishment units to assign to each type of offense involves a process similar to the development of sentencing guidelines. These are normative judgments. Decision makers must consider issues relative to the development of any system of sanctions. These include questions such as whether to provide a range of sentencing options or simply identify a presumptive sentence, and whether to identify enhancements or reductions in units for aggravating and mitigating conditions, or characteristics of the offender, such as prior record.[5] While some courts have developed new punishment scales to match day fines with offenses, others have utilized past practice as a guide in the development of day fines.

The Staten Island Experiment

In 1987, the Vera Institute of Justice funded the first project to implement and evaluate day fines. The first day fine was imposed in the Richmond County Criminal Court in Staten Island in 1988.[6] The Staten Island court system developed a new model to assign penalty units to offenses. A scale was created with 120 day fine units, and a range of recommended units was assigned to selected offenses (Table 7-4). In those instances where a range was provided, guidelines were presented to assist the judge in determining the precise number of units to assign. For example, in the case of offenses involving personal harm, the level of victim injury was an aggravating factor; the value of property stolen had a similar effect in theft and other property offenses (Table 7-5).

The next task was to convert the units into dollars based on the offender's ability to pay. The offender's net daily income was utilized, with adjustments for family responsibilities and poverty status. While legitimate income could be determined through the utilization of paycheck stubs and income tax records, determining wealth and criminal income was more complicated. In Staten Island, judges were given latitude to assess the offender's resources at a higher level than indicated by salary and wages. The project's planners viewed this ability as part of the inherent and routinely exercised powers of the judiciary, already utilized in setting bail or assessing whether counsel should be provided by the state. In this jurisdiction, judges had long-standing practices of setting stiff fines for offenders whose offenses were particularly economically motivated, such as small-time gamblers and seasonal vendors of firecrackers. Factors such as evidence of the offender's lifestyle, dress, personal appearance, and criminal record were routinely taken into account. Techniques such as those commonly used by law enforcement to conduct net worth investigations were occasionally necessary, but in general the experienced judge was expected to have little difficulty in assessing the offender's true ability to pay.

Although New York had a high collection rate before the creation of day fines (almost 75 percent of fines were collected within one year of imposition), the planning group added to this effort by creating enhanced collection procedures. The group appointed a day fine officer to monitor the collection of fines and

Table 7-4   Classification of Offenses into Day
Fine Severity Levels, the Staten Island Experience

Severity Level/ Penal Law Number	Behavior	Offense and Degree	Day Fine Units
Level 1 (95–120 day fine units)			
130.20	Harm persons	Sexual misconduct	90–120
120.00	Harm persons	Assault 3	20–95
Level 2 (65–90 day fine units)			
260.10	Harm persons	Endangerment of child welfare	20–90
215.50	Obstruction of justice	Criminal contempt 2	75
120.2	Harm persons	Reckless endangerment 2	65
110–155.30	Property	Attempted grand larceny 4	20–65
Level 3 (45–60 day fine units)			
265.01	Weapons	Possession of weapon 4	35–60
155.25	Property	Petit larceny	5–60
165.40	Property	Possession of stolen property 5	5–60
165.05	Property	Unauthorized use of a vehicle	5–60
221.40	Drugs	Sale of marijuana 4	50
225.05	Misconduct	Promotion of gambling 2	50
220.03	Drugs	Possession of contraband substance 7	35–50
110–120.00	Harm persons	Attempted assault 3	10–45
Level 4 (30–40 day fine units)			
170.05	Theft	Forgery 3	40
221.15	Drugs	Possession of marijuana 4	35
110–140.15	Property	Attempted criminal trespass 2	30
245.00	Sex crime	Public lewdness	30
110–155.25	Property	Attempted petit larceny	5–30
110–165.40	Property	Attempted possession of stolen property 5	5–30
Level 5 (15–25 day fine units)			
240.37A	Sex crime	Loitering/prostitution	25
205.30	Obstruction of justice	Resisting arrest	25
110–221.40	Drugs	Attempted sale of marijuana 4	25
110–265.01	Weapons	Attempted possession of weapon 4	5–25
110–120.20	Harm persons	Attempted reckless endangerment 2	20
140.10	Property	Criminal trespass 3	20
240.25	Misconduct	Harassment	15
Level 6 (5–10 day fine units)			
165.09	Property	Auto stripping 2	10
221.10	Drugs	Possession of marijuana 5	5
230.00	Sex crime	Prostitution	5
190.05	Theft	Issuing bad check	5
240.36	Misconduct	Loitering 1	5
140.05	Property	Trespass	5
240.20	Misconduct	Disorderly conduct	5

Source: Douglas C. McDonald, Judith Greene, and Charles Worzella, *Day Fines in American Courts: The Staten Island and Milwaukee Experiments* (Washington, D.C.: U.S. Department of Justice, National Institute of Justice, 1992), p. 23.

Table 7-5 Day Fines Benchmarks for Aggravating
(Premium) and Mitigating (Discount) Circumstances

Offenses	Discount Number	Benchmark Number	Premium Number
Offenses involving harm to persons: 120.00 AM Assault 3 Range of 20–95 day fine units			
A. Substantial injury Stranger to stranger; or, where victim is known to assailant, he or she is weaker, vulnerable.	81	95	109
B. Minor injury Stranger to stranger; or, where victim is known to assailant, he or she is weaker, vulnerable; or altercations involving use of weapon.	59	70	81
C. Substantial injury Altercations among acquaintances; brawls.	38	45	52
D. Minor injury Altercations among acquaintances; brawls.	17	20	23
Property and theft offenses: 155.25 AM Petit larceny Range of 5–60 day fine units			
$1,000 or more	51	60	69
$700–999	42	50	58
$500–699	34	40	46
$300–499	25	30	35
$150–299	17	20	23
$50–149	8	10	12
$1–49	4	5	6

Source: Douglas C. McDonald, Judith Greene, and Charles Worzella, *Day Fines in American Courts: The Staten Island and Milwaukee Experiments* (Washington, D.C.: U.S. Department of Justice, National Institute of Justice, 1992), p. 24.

utilized a computerized system to track offenders and payments. In the enhanced collection model, automatic notices were sent out immediately upon nonpayment. Installment plans were utilized sparingly and involved only short time frames of no longer than three months. Payment dates were set in relation to the dates the offenders received wages. For welfare recipients, 10 percent of each grant was held back for fine payment. Enforcement efforts included letters and telephone calls, which were also useful in yielding information of relevance to the offender's situation. Jailing was utilized only for the willful nonpayment of a fine.

Here are typical offenders receiving day fines.

Richard Smith was prosecuted for threatening a police officer and resisting arrest. When stopped for a traffic violation, he told the officer that he knew where he and his family lived and threatened to get him. When placed under arrest, he refused to be handcuffed. He was arraigned for resisting arrest (a class A misdemeanor); harassment (a violation); and disorderly conduct (also a violation). He pleaded guilty to disorderly conduct.

Mr. Smith is twenty years old. He is single and lives with his mother. He works at the City Department of Transportation, where his take-home pay is $800 every two weeks. He is self-supporting and reported no dependents.

Mr. Smith was sentenced to pay a five-unit day fine. His unit value was fixed at $32, for a total fine of $160—which he paid in full at sentencing.

Joseph Burke was prosecuted for stealing a car. He was arraigned for grand larceny (a class E felony); possession of stolen property (a class E felony); and unauthorized use of an auto (a class A misdemeanor). He pleaded guilty to attempted unauthorized use of an auto (a class B misdemeanor).

Mr. Burke is twenty-one years old. He is single and lives with his mother, to whom he contributes support. He works at a restaurant and reports take-home pay of $180 per week. He was sentenced to pay a ten-unit day fine, and his unit value was set at $11.78. His fine totals $115. He was given an installment schedule for payment and has paid his fine in five payments over three months.

Louis Martini was prosecuted for falsely reporting the theft of a car to defraud his insurance company. He was arraigned on a charge of insurance fraud (a class D felony) and pleaded guilty to making a punishable false written statement (a class A misdemeanor).

Mr. Martini is thirty years old. He is married and lives with his wife and three children in a home they own. At his arraignment he claimed to be unemployed, but he was represented by private counsel, and it seemed apparent to the judge that Mr. Martini was not indigent and had significant assets. The judge suggested that he return to court with tax records so that a fair day fine unit could be estimated in his case.

He was then sentenced to pay a forty-unit day fine. On the basis of his tax records (which showed an annual income of about $35,000), the judge estimated his unit value at $23.10—resulting in a total fine of $924. Although he continued to assert that he was unemployed, Mr. Martini paid his day fine in full on the day he was sentenced.

Robert Silver was prosecuted for trying to prevent the arrest of his brother and for possession of a pellet gun. He was arraigned for obstructing governmental administration (a class A misdemeanor) and a related administrative code violation. He pleaded guilty to disorderly conduct (a violation).

Mr. Silver is twenty-three years old. He lives with his brother. When he was arrested, he was working as a stock clerk in a store, but at sentencing he said he was unemployed and living on savings. The judge assumed he could easily find another job and estimated his potential income at about $6 per hour.

Mr. Silver was sentenced to pay a five-unit day fine with a unit value set at $19.64—for a total amount of $100. He paid the day fine in two installments over a period of a month.[7]

Program Effectiveness The goal of the Staten Island Project was to determine if the availability of day fines would increase judicial willingness to impose fines and influence the severity of the fines imposed. The creation of an enhanced collection process also made it possible to evaluate the enforcement of day fines using both traditional and enhanced enforcement procedures. The research design was a comparison of felony and misdemeanor arrests disposed of before and after the creation of day fines. Almost five thousand cases were examined over a two-year period. The effectiveness of the enhanced collection procedure was tested by randomly assigning day fine cases to traditional collection methods versus the new approach.

Results of the research were extremely positive.[8] The day fines were easily integrated into judicial use, replacing the vast majority of the fixed fines previously utilized. The major impact of the day fines seems to be a 25 percent increase in the severity of fines. The increase would have been much higher if statutory maximums had not been reached in so many cases.

Day fines were found to be as collectable as traditional fines, even though they were significantly more severe. The new collection procedures did, however, improve the outcome, reducing the number of fines in which no payment was received from 22 to 6 percent. As expected, day fines did take longer to collect—on the average more than twice the length of time of traditional fines—because their amounts were greater than previous fines. Low-income offenders were no better or worse at complying with day fine sentences than with traditional sentences.

The Milwaukee Municipal Court Experiment

The Milwaukee Municipal Court conducted an experiment to determine if day fines could be substituted for conventionally structured fines for first offenders convicted of minor crimes.[9] The Milwaukee planners took a different approach to the calculation of the fines than the New York designers. The Wisconsin group began with the maximum and minimum dollar amounts permitted by the city ordinance for fines already authorized, and then converted those into day fine units. They chose as the presumptive sentence the dollar amount that could be paid if the violator chose not to contest the charges.

To create comparison groups, judges were asked to utilize day fines for two weeks followed by conventional fines for two weeks in alternating sequence for a period of twelve weeks. The results of the Milwaukee experiment differed from those produced in Staten Island. Perhaps because of the more limited nature of the experiment, no improvement was seen in the collection of fines even though the day fines imposed were lower than the conventional fines. Both conventional and day fines were unpaid after four months in 59 to 61 percent of the cases. The day fine system did, however, increase payment rates for low-income offenders and increased the number of fines that were paid in full.

Structured Fines Research

Given the varied outcomes of the Staten Island and Milwaukee experiments, additional study is needed to determine the specific benefits of day fine programs. Such **structured fines research** is now being conducted by the RAND Corporation.[10] The national study, funded by the Bureau of Justice Assistance, includes courts in four sites: Phoenix, Arizona; Des Moines, Iowa; Bridgeport, Connecticut; and the state of Oregon. The study will examine issues of program design and implementation as well as the impact of day fines on sentence severity, revenue collection, and replicability.

Fees and Surcharges

The idea of making the offender pay for the costs of administering the system of justice is an attractive one. It provides an additional punishment to the convicted while generating revenues to support an overburdened criminal justice system. The last ten years have witnessed an enormous proliferation of **fees** and **surcharges.** More than half the states authorize the imposition of court costs, a dozen states authorize a surcharge on fines, and many permit penalty assessments on offenders.[11]

Corrections Compendium, a newsletter that reports on current issues in corrections, recently published the results of a national survey of correctional fees. The study found that twenty-eight states charged a probation supervision fee and twenty-one states required a parole supervision fee.[12] Of the more than two dozen states that utilized electronic monitoring, half the probation agencies and about one-fourth of the parole organizations assessed clients for some of the monitoring costs. Amounts of the supervision fees ranged from $5 per month in Tennessee for parolees to $100 maximum for probationers in Louisiana. Most fees ranged between $10 and $30.

Additional fees that states charge convicted offenders are extensive, covering everything from presentence reports to the videotapes used in field sobriety tests. The proliferation of fees caused one judge to note that he now rarely used fines because "after paying $56 court costs, $10 fee to the Crime Victim Compensation Fund, $200 public defender fee, and $100 to $500 in probation supervision fee, the defendant will be sufficiently punished."[13]

The *Corrections Compendium* survey revealed these additional fees:

Reimbursement of defense counsel.

Treatment costs.

Crime lab assessment for drunk-driving convictions.

Jail fee or jail staffing fee.

Drug testing.

Pretrial application fee.

Pretrial service fee.

Interstate compact fee.

Community service fee.

Funds to support victim compensation, drug education, peace officer, and prosecutor.

Training, drivers education, crime stoppers.

Not surprisingly, given the costs of criminal justice system operations, states that do not presently impose such assessments are examining the matter for future action, and states that currently impose selected fees are considering additional surcharges. But some problems have arisen. A few states have rejected the issue of fees after closer examination. Other states have done away with them following implementation. An Alaskan respondent to the *Corrections Compendium* survey said, "We found it to be a great problem in collecting and much of the staff's time was spent in the process." A Kansas parole staff member who studied the matter concluded that supervisory fees were just "more trouble than they are worth." A Wyoming study revealed that "supervision fees would not be cost effective in terms of generating revenue vs. the cost of the program."[14]

Three general sets of questions must be addressed when correctional fees are being considered: How much revenue can fees generate? What is an appropriate fee schedule and how should it be administered? How will the fees be collected?

Revenue Generation

Wide variation exists in the amount of revenue that states and correctional agencies are able to raise through fee collection. Most of this variation seems to be a result of how fees are implemented, rather than offenders' ability to pay. While there is a concern about the ability of indigent offenders to pay fees, a number of jurisdictions have shown that even when fees are waived for truly indigent offenders, the amount of revenue that can be raised is significant. Texas, for example, raises more than one-half of all funds in its probation operating budget through fees (Table 7-6). Several other states raise at least 25 percent of their annual expenditures, while an additional half-dozen states raise between about 10 and 20 percent of their operating budgets. Research has shown that correctional fees are most likely to generate substantial revenue when:

- Officials emphasize program fees (mainly supervision fees and room and board fees) rather than service fees (for example, fee for drug testing);

- Fees are set at moderate levels and well within offenders' abilities to pay, given their total court-imposed obligations;

- Fee collection is accorded high priority, both by judges and correctional administrators;

- Fees are levied on a large proportion of the correctional population, including misdemeanants; and

- Persons truly unable to pay fees are screened out initially or upon first evidence of payment problems.[15]

Fee Schedules

Unlike fines, where the goal is to achieve the appropriate level of punishment through the determination of a suitable penalty, the judgment about the appropriate amount for a fee is much more arbitrary. While fees should be set high enough to generate meaningful revenue and make collection efforts worthwhile, they must also be set low enough to achieve a

Table 7-6 Correctional Fee Revenues as
Percent of Probation and Parole Operating Budgets

Probation and Parole Agency	Correctional Fee Revenue	Total Operating Budget	Fees as Percent of Total Operating Budget
Texas (probation only)	$45,677,784	$90,558,700	50.44
Florida	15,600,000	45,231,624	34.49
Alabama	2,700,000	8,900,000	30.34
Arkansas (probation only)	369,559	1,270,090	29.10
North Carolina	5,502,662	32,757,893	16.80
South Carolina	3,482,692	21,200,000	16.43
Arizona (parole only)	396,008	2,892,300	13.69
Louisiana	1,894,482	15,691,726	12.07
Idaho	442,649	4,000,000	11.07
Nevada	701,956	6,694,542	10.49
Oklahoma	969,704	9,851,251	9.84
Oregon	2,826,843	38,343,305	7.30
New Hampshire	166,671	2,500,000	6.67
Washington	1,193,076	27,374,885	4.36
Virginia	850,406	21,200,000	4.01
Kentucky	271,230	8,975,995	3.02
Colorado (probation only)	452,928	16,082,479	2.82
Total, state agencies	$83,498,650	$353,524,790	23.60

Source: Dale Parent, *Recovering Costs Through Offender Fees* (Washington,
D.C.: U.S. Department of Justice, National Institute of Justice, June 1990), p. 5.

high rate of collection. Waiving the fee for individuals who are truly unable to pay is a reasonable act that saves collection costs in the long run. Too liberal a waiver policy, however, decreases total revenue.

In the determination of fee schedules, most states rely on fixed schedules.[16] Instead of attempting to increase the fee for offenders with more income, agencies try to ensure that all fees are low enough to impose little hardship. Waiver policies vary considerably, with a few agencies reporting that almost one out of four offenders has his or her fee waived. Most states, however, report that more than 90 percent of offenders are ordered to pay fees. The most common justifications for waivers include employment handicap, hardship on dependents, indigence, inability to find a job, and student status.

Generally speaking, if fee programs are to be successful, it makes sense to impose fees on broad ranges of offenders, and not just the more serious ones. Surveys have indicated that lesser offenders may be better payment risks than more serious criminals.[17] For example, misdemeanants are generally considered to be good payment risks. The probability of nonpayment increases with offender prior record, with the frequency and seriousness of substance abuse, and with factors that diminish an offender's employability.

Finally, fee payments must be prioritized in the context of other court-ordered obligations that offenders must pay. If fees consistently receive lower priority than other payments, then the revenue generated may be insufficient to warrant collection efforts.[18] For example, if an offender is required to pay $40 each month for supervision, $50 in fines, and $150 in restitution, but in a particular month pays only $75, where should that amount be credited? A successful fee collection process requires that fee payment receive a high priority within the total scope of offender financial obligations.

Debt Collection

Problems of Enforcement

Problems of **enforcement** are much like the problems with fines.

Role Orientation   The role of fine and fee collector is an uncomfortable one for both courts and probation. These organizations do not see themselves as collection agencies.

Dispersion of Responsibility   The responsibilities of enforcement are widely dispersed, among courts, law enforcement, probation, and prosecution. This includes the judges who impose fees, the clerks who receive the funds owed the court, those who share enforcement roles through the use of revocation and arrest, and officials charged with the responsibility of prosecuting individuals for willful nonpayment.

Disincentives   Because the agencies doing the collecting often do not benefit directly from the revenues they collect, there are disincentives to engage in vigorous enforcement efforts.

Multiple Tasks   The courts are engaged in both the collection and disbursement of funds collected to a variety of agencies. These procedures and their proper execution are extremely complicated in many jurisdictions. They do not encourage enforcement efforts that can be seen as only adding to the volume of complex activity.

Enforcement Dependence   Finally, the entire enforcement process is interdependent.

Courts cannot effectively compel local law enforcement to enforce warrants. Probation is unlikely to be revoked for this purpose and prosecutors are generally unenthusiastic about prosecuting for even willful nonpayment. Thus the enforcement process possesses little of the coherence necessary to ensure the effective collection of revenue.[19]

To avoid the preceding problems, court and correctional officials need to maximize incentives and establish effective enforcement procedures. When fees are instituted, agency authorities must work with policy makers to ensure that revenues generated by fees will not result in the reduction of regular appropriations.

Certain and credible responses are needed for nonpayment. A national survey of the sanctions used to enforce payment reveals that the penalties range from no action to confinement (Table 7-7). For probationers, a first missed payment should probably evoke only counseling, while a second should result in a review of the offender's budgetary situation. An administrative hearing should be held if delinquencies persist, perhaps to restructure the payment schedule or to waive payment if appropriate. If delinquencies appear willful, the addition of a curfew or community service may be appropriate. Revocation and confinement are clearly responses of last resort. An effective management information system, as well as evaluations of employee performance that take collection efforts into account, are additional means of increasing enforcement effectiveness.

New Jersey's Model Collection Process

New Jersey is making a considerable effort to improve its process of collecting fees and surcharges.[20] The New Jersey Probation Agency has been responsible for collecting court-imposed payments since 1900. Fines and child support were the principal payments assessed in the early years. Today, the agency also collects penalties defined by the Violent Crimes

Table 7-7   Sanctions Used to Enforce Fee Payment

Types of Sanctions	Jails (n = 17)	Prisons (n = 17)	State Probation and Parole (n = 17)
Confinement	6	6	13
None	4	4	5
Reprimand	1	4	13
Increase payments	1	0	5
Prison disciplinary system	N/A	6	N/A
Extend supervision	N/A	N/A	8
Community service	0	N/A	10
Other	7	9	6

N/A = Not applicable.

Source: Dale Parent, *Recovering Costs Through Offender Fees* (Washington, D.C.: U.S. Department of Justice, National Institute of Justice, June 1990), p. 16.

Compensation Board and fees to the Victim/Witness Assistance Fund. A new fund, the Criminal Disposition and Revenue Collection Fund, was created in 1991 to finance improved collection practices and record keeping. In addition, the Comprehensive Drug Reform Act requires defendants convicted of drug offenses to pay a forensic lab fee to offset the cost of testing confiscated drugs, and it mandates a Drug Enforcement and Demand Reduction penalty to fund local drug education and prevention efforts.

Probation also handles pretrial intervention application fees, court costs, traffic penalties, mandatory surcharges, drug-testing fees, and, in some cases, fees for supervision. Between 1980 and 1991, the amount of fees for which the probation agency was responsible increased by sevenfold. To improve the quality of collection services, a consulting firm was hired to assess collection techniques in four counties and make recommendations for the development of a model statewide process. The research found that the success of a probation agency's collection efforts was not related to the economic health of the county in which collections were made, but instead depended upon the quality of collection services employed. The recommendations included a call for:

- Standardized and codified collection policies and procedures.

- Financial background investigations of the offender's ability to pay.

- Payment of some financial penalties at sentencing.

- Detention of individuals who demonstrate an ability to make an initial payment at sentencing but fail to do so.

- Incorporation of a specific payment plan into the sentence.

- Research to establish optimum fine, fee, and penalty levels based on the defendant's ability to pay.

- Rapid communication of sentences to the probation agency.

- Automated collection records that generate billing notices, dunning letters, and payment coupons.

- A structured approach to nonpayment based on a series of increasingly negative consequences to those in default.

- Adoption of techniques used successfully in the enforcement of child support.

The new model process is detailed in a policies and procedures manual that includes a flow chart of all procedures; citations of relevant statutes, case law, and administrative directives; detailed protocols for the use of specific collection techniques; and sample forms to be used by all departments. At the core of the manual is the model collection process, a detailed step-by-step description of the specific responsibilities of prosecutors, case managers, court administrators, judges, and probation staff. For example, the model specifies that prosecutors should recommend specific payment amounts, time schedules, and payment plans during the plea bargaining process. Authors of presentence and predisposition reports should verify offenders' ability to pay and develop specific plans for judicial review. Judges should play a central role in the collections process by establishing court orders, developing payment plans, requiring payment at the time of sentencing, and enforcing their own orders.

The Privatization of Collection Activities

Morris and Tonry have suggested that fine and fee enforcement represents an excellent opportunity for the privatization of a correctional process.[21] Fines that are unpaid for more than a week after imposition of a sentence could be referred to a commercial debt collection agency that would enforce fines on a commission basis. Courts could retain responsibility for very small or very large fines (for which it would be worth the court's effort to achieve full payment without sacrificing a commission). The cost of the commission, which might run between 25 and 30 percent of the fee, would more than cover the efforts that might otherwise be made by court or probation authorities at debt collection and should provide a reasonable incentive for the debt collection agency to obtain compliance. In addition, the higher rates of debt collection that should be achieved by the private agency would more than justify the payment of

a commission. The collection agency would have access to all routine means of debt collection at their disposal, including attaching the offender's property, garnishing wages, and taking any other legal action used in civil debt collection procedures.

Fines that could not be collected by the private agency could be written off, when the costs of collection began to outweigh the dollars to be gained or when the debtor is simply unable to pay. However, the court could choose to retain authority over all uncollected fines and could proceed with alternative punishments against those perceived to be willfully avoiding payment. In either case, the advantages of private sector involvement seem clear.

The single most important factor in enforcing payment of fines is prompt notification of the debtor whenever payments are in arrears. The employment of private debt collection agencies seems like an ideal opportunity for courts and probation offices to outsource an activity in which they have little expertise, experience, or interest.

Restitution and Community Service

Webster's dictionary defines *restitution* as "the act of restoring; especially the restoration of something to its original owner."[22] In contemporary correctional usage, *restitution* has been defined as "a requirement, either imposed by agents of the criminal justice system or undertaken voluntarily by the wrongdoer but with the consent of the criminal justice system, by which the offender engages in acts designed to make reparation for the harm resulting from the criminal offense."[23]

Galaway developed a typology of restitution based on the nature of the offender's payment, which may be in the form of money or service, and the nature of the recipient, who may be either the individual victim or the community as a whole.[24] In the United States, monetary payments from the offender to the victim and service provided by the offender to the community are the most common forms of restitution. This latter form is often referred to as **symbolic restitution** because restoration for the harm done is made in the form of good works benefiting the entire community instead of the particular individual harmed. Symbolic restitution is referred to here as *community service* and the term *restitution* is used to describe the monetary payments offenders make to individual victims.

Restitution programs can be distinguished from victim compensation projects. Although both plans provide financial reimbursement to crime victims, only restitution requires that the payments be made by the individual who committed the offense. Victim compensation programs normally draw upon funds raised by taxation or fees paid by all convicted offenders. The particular offender is not involved in the transaction and may not even have been identified. An independent victim compensation board or committee assesses the extent of the victim's losses and determines his or her eligibility for payment.

Contemporary Applications

Offense Categories   Restitution is almost invariably limited to use in economic offenses. The money or goods taken from victims and the damage done to their property is restored through financial payment. Restitution can be used in response to violent crimes, but the difficulty of putting a price tag on physical injury, which must include estimates of hospital fees, loss of income, and the financial effects of psychological trauma, limit its use even as a supplement to incarceration for violent offenders.

Community service is normally utilized for property offenders as well, although the various forms that service may take make it adaptable to a broad range of minor offenses. For example, a person convicted of cruelty to animals may be required to work a specific number of hours in an animal shelter. An individual found to have been driving while intoxicated may be required to work in treatment programs for alcoholics or a hospital emergency ward. However, the nature of the work required in service to the community does not have to be designed to instruct the offender in the error of his or her ways. The offender's characteristics and the nature of the good works may be unrelated. Because it is not always feasible or even desirable to place offenders in situations related to their criminal activity, the emphasis in community service is usually on the symbolic nature of the reparation—doing good in the community after having caused harm through crime.

Criminal Justice System Stages   Restitution and community service may be required of offenders at various stages of the criminal justice system. Unlike fines and fees, restitution is frequently used as an informal disposition prior to an arrest or criminal prosecution. Police or prosecutors, with the agreement of the victim(s), may permit shoplifters to return stolen merchandise or allow check offenders to pay off their debts in lieu of criminal proceedings. Similarly, restitution and community service frequently serve as formal conditions of pretrial diversion. Prosecution can be avoided if the defendant is willing to repay the crime victim or perform a specific number of hours of community service. Alternative dispute resolution programs frequently rely on restitution as an option in the mediation of citizen disputes.

Restitution and community service are often employed as conditions of probation. Statutes in many states permit courts to order payment of restitution as a requirement of probation. In other areas, courts use this sanction by virtue of their general power to establish probation conditions.[25] Courts are also experimenting with community service as a condition of probation, especially for juveniles, youthful offenders, first offenders, and misdemeanants.

Community service is rarely utilized for offenders who receive prison sentences or even persons required to live in halfway houses as a condition of diversion, probation, or parole. Restitution is commonly used for these individuals. Georgia operates a number of **community restitution centers** (now known as diversion centers), where probationers live as they complete court-ordered restitution. In North Carolina, inmates on work release are often required to use some of their earnings to make restitution as they serve out their sentences. South Carolina utilizes restitution centers for both probationers and parolees.[26]

Extent of Use

Hundreds of restitution programs are in operation throughout the United States at the adult and juvenile level.[27] A number of factors appear to be responsible for the tremendous growth of these programs, including an increased recognition of the need to address the losses suffered by the victim, the need to make offenders more accountable for their crimes, and the need to provide effective alternatives (from a punishment perspective) to the use of overcrowded prisons and jails.

Historical Perspective

The history of restitution can be traced back to pretribal man. Hudson and Galaway have described the development and modification of the concept of restitution as encompassing three broad stages.[28] Initially, each person acted individually to define the law and administer punishment. As human beings began living in tribes and kinship groups, the idea of collective social responsibility began to emerge and with it came the development of blood feuds between kinship groups for the purpose of resolving individual grievances. Then a system of mitigating and resolving blood feuds evolved—the offending family group compensated victims or their families for deaths or injuries inflicted. The family's central role in criminal matters was gradually displaced.

By the end of the twelfth century, the state (the king) was defined as the offended party whenever a crime was committed. It became the right and responsibility of the state (not the individual victim or his or her family) to punish offenders and collect damages (fines). The state thus came to represent the victim in criminal proceedings. The practice of offender restitution began to play an insignificant role in criminal justice.

Although it received only limited use as a penal sanction, the concept of restitution has remained alive and well throughout the years. In the sixteenth century, Sir Thomas More suggested that offenders be required to make restitution to the victims of their crimes and labor on public work projects. Two hundred years later, Jeremy Bentham described monetary restitution and the replacement of stolen goods as essential to efforts to fit the punishment to the crime. Another perspective was provided by Herbert Spencer, who viewed prison labor as a way for the offender to make restitution and contribute to the cost of incarceration. The length of an inmate's prison sentence, he argued, should be based on the amount of damage done and the offender's ability to work off his or her debt to the victim.[29]

In 1891, the International Penal Association Congress considered recommendations for the abolition of short prison sentences and the introduction of court-ordered restitution as a correctional alternative, but the proposal drew only limited attention. Almost fifty years later, the British penal reformer, Margaret Fry, resurrected the restitution concept and gave it a new twist—offender rehabilitation. "Repayment is the best first step toward reformation that a dishonest person can take. It is often the ideal solution."[30] Although her work contributed to the later development of victim compensation programs in several countries, a 1958 survey of twenty-nine nations revealed that restitution to crime victims was still almost nonexistent.[31]

Restitution programs gradually gained support throughout the 1960s. In 1962, the Model Penal Code developed by the American Law Institute proposed that a defendant placed on probation may be required to "make restitution of the fruits of his crime or to make reparation, in an amount he can afford to pay, for the loss or damage caused thereby."[32] The American Bar Association (ABA) later recommended that decisions regarding fines and their amount should take into account whether the imposition of the fine will interfere with the offender's ability to make restitution.[33] Both the ABA and the National Council on Crime and Delinquency (NCCD) supported the use of restitution as a condition of probation. NCCD's recommendation provided for restitution to victims and dependents of victims killed "for any money or property loss or compensation for injury directly resulting from the crime."[34] The 1973 report of the National Advisory Commission on Criminal Justice Standards and Goals viewed offender restitution as a factor mitigating the imposition of a prison sentence.[35]

Throughout the 1970s, legislation providing for the use of restitution as a component of sentencing and an objective of specific correctional programs was developed and implemented in many states. During that same period, Law Enforcement Assistance Administration grants provided funds to programs in eleven states, and the Office of Juvenile Justice and Delinquency Prevention funded more than forty restitution programs. Today most states have implemented restitution procedures, and many jurisdictions have subsequently experimented with community service as an alternative to confinement or monetary restitution.

Contemporary Support for Growth in Restitution and Community Service

Emphasis on Employment   Many of today's welfare and correctional reform efforts seem to focus on offender employment and labor.

Work is an essential element of an independent noncriminal existence. It is therapeutic and a constructive means of occupying one's time. Work benefits the individual, the family, and the community. Any correctional program that utilizes work as a central element is likely to achieve considerable support because program participation is viewed as time well spent. The aftereffects of a positive work experience can also be expected to generalize to postcorrectional employment efforts.

Universal Appeal   Restitution and community service can be all things to all people. The work (and financial payments) may be considered punishment by those who view punishment as the criminal justice system's appropriate response to crime. It may be viewed as rehabilitative by individuals who support treatment as a correctional objective. In restitution and community service projects, the offender is neither let off nor subjected to meaningless punishment, a balance that is difficult to obtain under more traditional sanctions.

Economic Benefits   Correctional programs must increasingly be sold on the basis of their financial benefits. Restitution and community service are normally less costly than imprisonment, even when residence in a community facility is a program component. Restitution is also less costly than victim compensation programs, which normally require taxpayers to contribute to victim aid.

The community derives economic benefit from labor performed in service projects. The hours of community service offenders provide may make new projects possible, supplement existing resources, or permit community activities to be accomplished more efficiently or with greater care. Offenders and their families benefit from the offender's opportunity to obtain or maintain employment and contribute to the family's support. All of these economic factors argue for the continued expansion of restitution and community service projects.

Victim Assistance   Americans' concern with victims has grown considerably in recent years. Research has attempted to determine the characteristics that identify persons as vulnerable to victimization and the influence of such factors as age, race, gender, socioeconomic group, and geographic area on the patterns of victimization. Victim assistance projects have been established across the United States to provide temporary shelter, food, clothing, legal services, counseling, and financial assistance. Victims of such crimes as rape, child abuse, and wife beating have received particular attention, as have elderly crime victims.

The victims of crime are the most direct beneficiaries of restitution efforts. Because many crime victims are, like offenders, financially disadvantaged, they are poorly equipped to manage the economic loss and related financial difficulties of crime. Reimbursement may be essential to the victim's financial recovery from criminal attack. Regardless of social status, most victims tend to rank the economic effects of crime as serious problems.

Financial aid also may facilitate the victim's psychological recovery from victimization. Of critical importance is the concept of **equity**— restoring what has been lost, attempting to undo the damage done. Restitution officially recognizes the injury done to the victim and promotes restoration. It brings victims into the criminal justice system as active participants. Their concerns do not fall on deaf ears but are heard and evaluated and provide the basis for sanctioning the offender. Such experiences should promote victims' feelings of self-worth, feelings that often receive low priority in contemporary criminal proceedings.

Restitution also facilitates victims' development of a realistic view of the attacker. They may learn about the offender's background, circumstances, and motivation for the offense. Seeing the criminal as a human being with problems and needs, as a person willing to make amends for his or her actions, may encourage victims to adopt a less punitive approach toward the immediate criminal proceedings. Victims come to view the offender as less of a predator and consequently to see themselves as less vulnerable to attack. They may thus be willing to accept a more moderate disposition for the offender. Restitution encourages victims to look toward the future and the financial payments they will receive, rather than to the past and the vengeance they may desire.

A Closer Look at Correctional Objectives

Restitution and community service have universal appeal because they promise something for everyone. Restitution and community service can serve the correctional objectives of retribution and rehabilitation, and they may be used to make the criminal justice process more humane. Restitution and community service programs also mitigate the community's views of the offender and can improve public views of the criminal justice system.

The humanitarian benefits of restitution and community service are closely linked to their rehabilitative objectives. Both forms of sanction can be directly or indirectly related to the offense committed, thus personalizing justice in a manner impossible when only imprisonment or community supervision is imposed. Making punishment more meaningful should promote the goals of rehabilitation because the offender comes to view the criminal justice system as responding to his or her particular behavior.

Fulfilling the conditions of restitution or community service orders may provide the offender with an enhanced feeling of self-worth. Paying off his or her debt and providing volunteer services to the community may give the individual a sense of accomplishment. For many persons, it may be the first time they have worked in a volunteer service capacity. This new learning experience could promote attitudinal changes in many offenders as they come to understand themselves and others better through their efforts. If nothing else, a well-designed community service project may broaden the offender's horizons. Restitution may provide a sense of achievement as the offender steadily approaches and meets the payment goal. Both restitution and community service should increase the participant's self-respect rather than denigrate it with meaningless punishment.

Restitution and community service may promote rehabilitation in other ways as well. Both procedures provide offenders with a means of expressing guilt for their conduct. Such feelings may become more manageable because the offenders are able to do something constructive following their offense, instead of repressing whatever remorse they may feel and attempting to rationalize their behavior. They may be able to express, accept, and resolve personal conflicts about their actions. Some therapists view the acknowledgment of responsibility that is required in restitution as a prerequisite for offender change.

Finally, restitution and community service programs may contribute to the development of personal discipline and good work habits among offenders. Because they make restoration payments and must complete specific hours of work, offenders are required to maintain good relations with supervisors and coworkers and achieve an acceptable level of job performance. To make restitution payments, they must budget and save personal income. It is hoped these skills can be maintained and extended to other areas of offender behavior after restitution and community service requirements have been fulfilled.

In addition to the goals of punishment, rehabilitation, and humanitarianism, restitution and community service may improve community attitudes toward offenders and the criminal justice system. Utilizing restitution and community service as an alternative or addition to penal sanctions may mitigate the public's desire for vengeance, much as it affects the victim's perspective. Requiring criminals to pay their debt to the community allows them to be readmitted to society, without the

lingering feeling that justice was not done, that the punishment was not enough. The label of having completed restitution or community service is clearly preferable from all perspectives to the stigma of having completed a prison sentence.

Community attitudes toward the criminal justice system may also improve with the increased use of restitution and community service. A survey of citizens' views regarding creative restitution, which includes the use of monetary payments, service to victims, and service to the community as alternative dispositions, indicated that program support is overwhelmingly strong.[36] Similar findings were reported by a study of the views of judges, solicitors, and practicing attorneys.[37] Nine out of ten persons questioned favored using creative restitution for various property crimes, drunk driving, and income tax evasion. These programs received considerably greater support than victim compensation plans. Restitution and community service may not only better serve the general public's view of what the criminal justice system should be doing, but may also facilitate greater agreement among the justice system, its personnel, and the community regarding the system's functions and goals.

Achieving these objectives requires careful program development and planning, especially in regard to the development of community service activities. Figure 7-2 contains guidelines for the development of service activities designed to benefit offenders and their communities.

The Restitution and Community Service Process

Eligibility Criteria   Eligibility criteria for participation in restitution or community service programs vary from jurisdiction to jurisdiction. Normally, participants are first offenders who have committed relatively minor economic crimes, offenses against the public order, or traffic violations. However, judges and parole

Figure 7-2 Balanced and Restorative Principles
for Community Service Project Design

1. Ensure that the service meets a clearly defined need and that this need is obvious to offenders. In most cases, the benefits of meaningful service work will be apparent or will take relatively little time to explain to the young offenders. For instance, prior to beginning a brush clearing project, the project leader could discuss the fire hazards caused by accumulated brush and highlight the fire prevention benefits of such a project.

2. The service activity should at least symbolically link offender with offense and victims, and, whenever possible, community service should be performed in the offender's neighborhood.

3. The activity should bring offender and conventional adults together. Especially with youthful offenders, service projects should provide opportunities for bonding and role modeling.

4. Probation staff and community service supervisors should view offenders as resources and focus on outcomes. When community service is most effective, the work itself, and its completion and quality, is the focus of attention, and workers are treated as essential resources to complete the job. When the approach focuses on tackling tough community problems, staff can convey to offenders that they are genuinely needed to solve the problem. Treated as a resource rather than a client of service, offenders may develop stronger self-images and be viewed by peers and the community in a different light.

5. Involve offenders in planning and executing projects. Involvement reinforces commitment and allows for a higher level of cognitive learning from the work experience.

6. Provide for a sense of accomplishment, closure, and community recognition. Whenever possible, community corrections staff should design projects that have a clear beginning and end. When offenders feel and directly witness the impact of their efforts, offenders' personal satisfaction is increased and the staff has opportunities to recognize workers.

Source: Gordon Bazemore and Dennis Maloney, "Rehabilitating Community
Service: Toward Restorative Service Sanctions in a Balanced Justice System,"
Federal Probation, 58 (1), March 1994, p. 30.

boards generally have considerable discretion to use the sanctions whenever they consider the offender an appropriate candidate. The only additional factor that invariably enters into the selection of offenders for restitution is the defendant's ability to afford financial payments to the victim. This consideration is of particular importance when decision makers view only **full restitution**—payment for all victim losses—as an appropriate requirement. Some jurisdictions avoid the all-or-nothing question by awarding partial restitution to victims based on the offender's ability to pay.

The length of time required to complete restitution payments is an important related concern. A low-income offender could pay off even a large sum of money if the payments were stretched out over twenty to thirty years, but a limited time frame may be more appropriate. Otherwise the payments may be so small as to be of little value to the victim but to represent a seemingly endless burden to the offender. In such cases, the entire procedure can easily become little more than a record-keeping nuisance. Those victims who are covered by insurance may prefer to recover their loss from the insurance company and be done with the matter.

Amount of Restitution or Community Service

The amount of restitution to be made is normally based solely upon the amount of financial loss the victim suffers as a direct result of the crime—the money taken or the monetary value of the stolen goods or damaged property. Additional indirect injuries, however, can also be calculated. The income lost through unemployment and the costs of hospitalization, medical and psychological treatment, and vocational rehabilitation may be considered whenever the victim is in some way debilitated by the criminal attack. Income lost because of time spent in court also may be considered. The final restitution order may be determined by any of these factors, viewed in the context of the offender's ability to pay.

The number of hours an offender is expected to contribute to community service can be calculated in two ways. The first approach specifies the fine an offender would normally be expected to pay or the potential loss associated with an attempted theft. It places a dollar value on volunteer work (for example, $10 a day) and requires the offender to work the number of days and hours necessary to earn the fine or make symbolic restitution for what was stolen. The second approach directly specifies the number of hours of work an offender should complete as penalty for the crime; for example, twenty-four hours might be required for possession of a small amount of marijuana.[38] The second method permits greater flexibility in the development of community service requirements because it is not tied to existing penal sanctions (fines) or the value of what was stolen if the crime attempted had not been completed. It may, however, appear somewhat arbitrary because no objective link exists between the crime and the number of hours that must be served.

Victim-Offender Relations   Victim involvement in community service projects is rare. Generally, community service is required when no specific victim can be identified or when the offense falls into the category of victimless crimes, such as drug or alcohol offenses. Restitution programs present a different picture. Victim involvement may be extensive and include active participation in decision making regarding the offender's appropriateness for restitution, the amount of restitution to be required, and the scheduling of payments. Personal contact between the offender and the victim may also be extensive during the payment period. Some victims may not desire to play such an active role in restitution efforts.

They may fear a reprisal from the offender or view such activities as merely bothersome and inconvenient. Other persons may prefer to trust a third party to negotiate the restitution agreement. Some victims share culpability for the criminal act and are reluctant to seek restitution. Others view punishment as preferable to restitution and refuse to involve themselves in negotiations designed to provide restitution as an alternative to imprisonment.

Although most research indicates that correctional administrators and probation and parole officers support direct victim-offender involvement in the restitution process, victim involvement is extremely limited. One study found that only 6 of 525 cases of restitution involved the face-to-face contact of victims and offenders.[39] Although victims often have input into the decision-making process regarding the extent of their financial loss, the court or restitution project staff members normally formulate the restitution order. Sometimes victims are not even adequately informed when restitution has been required of their offender.[40]

Research on victim participation in restitution reveals that insurance companies and large businesses are awarded a large percentage of all restitution payments.[41] These victims would be expected to show less interest in active participation in restitution negotiations than individual victims. Their predominance among restitution victims may partially explain victims' limited roles in the restitution process.

Enforcement of Conditions   Some offenders required to complete community service orders are virtually on their honor to fulfill their agreements. Others are supervised by staff at the agencies at which they work. Diversion project staff and probation and parole officers may also share in the monitoring of offender compliance with the service order. Failure to fulfill the terms of the agreement may result in the reinstatement of prosecution, revocation of probation or parole, or imposition of a fine.

Compliance with restitution orders is monitored and enforced in the same manner as community service, but additional alternative responses are available. Contempt citations or attachments of the offender's salary are sometimes utilized when the failure to make payments appears willful. When unemployment, income reduction, or increase in financial responsibilities seems to have caused the problem, the restitution order may be modified to reflect the offender's changed circumstances. A grace period of three months is normally allowed before any action, punitive or otherwise, is taken.

Community Supervision and Residential Alternatives

The Community Service Sentencing Project

The Community Service Sentencing Project (CSSP) was created in 1979 by the Vera Institute of Justice as an intermediate sanction for repeat misdemeanor offenders. The program requires seventy hours of community service in some of the poorest neighborhoods of New York City.[42] Unlike many community service programs that rely on offenders to find their volunteer agency and develop a schedule for service activities, the Vera program works with extremely disadvantaged offenders in a closely monitored setting.

To achieve a successful program, CSSP utilizes a selective intake criterion and enforces sentences through compliance activities, a warrant execution capacity, and resentencing procedures. Applicants to the program are largely unskilled, unemployed minority offenders with extensive prior records and personal problems, generally including serious substance abuse. Within this population, efforts are made to select those with the greatest potential for program completion. Individuals with outstanding warrants or prior failure to complete the program are generally not good risks. Individuals must truly desire program participation, as opposed to merely wanting

to avoid jail, and be physically and mentally capable of completing the sentence. Successful candidates also must have sufficient community ties to provide support for program completion and to make it possible for project staff to locate them in the event of failure to complete the sentence.

Once accepted into the program, the offender signs a contract detailing the work to be performed. The court then grants a conditional discharge, often specifying the amount of jail time the offender will receive if he or she fails to complete the program successfully.

Participants who arrive at the worksite on time receive breakfast and lunch. Many are malnourished, and food encourages attendance and discourages tardiness or leaving the worksite at lunchtime. Site supervisors call in worksite attendance, informing CSSP compliance and enforcement staff if they need to locate participants. Emergency help is provided to participants who need a detoxification program, immediate housing, or reinstatement of welfare benefits. This assistance is coordinated by the support services coordinators, who are at the worksites every morning at 9:00 A.M. to meet the newly sentenced participants. This unit also provides money for child care and food as well as job referrals. Referrals to jobs and drug programs are held out as an incentive for program completion.

Work is performed at various community sites, such as community centers, potential neighborhood garden sites, and homes for the elderly. The work performed is primarily unskilled labor: clearing vacant lots, painting, simple carpentry, and preparing garden beds for planting. Enormous skill is required of the site supervisors, who must organize a disparate crew unused to discipline or obeying orders.

Compliance rates were high in the early years of the CSSP. When they began to decline in the mid-1980s, the position of compliance officers was established to make home visits and otherwise track down missing offenders. When this approach failed to yield significant results, the position of enforcement officer was created, and former police and corrections officers were hired to fill these positions. Each office of the program now has a support services coordinator, a compliance monitor, and an enforcement officer. The compliance officer normally is the first to learn that the offender has disappeared, been hospitalized, or been evicted from his or her home. Information is then relayed to the enforcement officer, who visits the offender's hangouts before making home visits. Depending on the circumstances, the enforcement officer may bring the participant to the worksite; leave a severe message with the household reminding the offender of his or her obligations; or work with support services if a health, housing, or drug problem has developed.

Warrants are requested from the court only as a last resort. The program documents efforts to encourage completion of the sentence—the phone calls and home visits made and the assistance provided. The enforcement unit then executes the warrant, operating under a strict set of guidelines intended to govern the conduct of enforcement officers.

Between July 1, 1991, and June 30, 1992, 1,680 persons were sentenced to perform community service. Almost two-thirds of the offenders completed the program without violation. Six hundred and thirty-nine individuals did violate the terms of their community service and 401 were returned to court for resentencing. The majority of these resentenced offenders received jail sentences averaging 128 days.

South Carolina's Restitution Centers   Following successful efforts in many states, South Carolina opened its first restitution center in 1987.[43] The center was made possible by legislation that provided for a number of correctional innovations, including the creation of a community supervision alternative to prison. The objective of the center was to serve as an alternative to incarceration as well as to promote restitution.

The program serves nonviolent offenders who are sentenced to probation and parolees who enter the facility as a condition of release.

The restitution center also serves as an alternative to probation or parole revocation. To be placed in the center, offenders must be physically and mentally able to work and owe restitution or court-ordered fines or fees. While at the center, offenders must maintain employment and perform unpaid community service during their off hours. Residents turn their paychecks over to the restitution center staff, who apply funds toward offender obligations. In addition to restitution, fines, and fees, offenders must also pay for room and board at the center, as well as taxes and sometimes child support.

Most offenders in the restitution center have never held a steady job and have a history of alcohol or drug abuse, low education levels, and unstable residences. To address these problems, the center offers drug and alcohol awareness counseling, stress and money management classes, and life skills programs such as general equivalency diploma (GED) and job preparedness training.

In the first five years of program operation, the restitution centers collected more than $1 million from the offenders' wages to meet their financial obligations. South Carolina plans to extend the use of these centers to additional sites over the next few years.

Victim Compensation Programs

Restitution and **victim compensation** programs are the two major forms of financial assistance available to crime victims. Although both programs have similar basic objectives, they differ considerably in philosophy, procedures, and practical implications. In recent years, considerable attention has been focused on these programs' relative merits as local and state governments have attempted to develop more appropriate responses to crime and its victims.

Victim Compensation Programs   Restitution programs hold individual offenders responsible for their crimes, but compensation programs attribute that responsibility to the state. Compensation programs view the state as having failed to fulfill its obligation to protect the citizen from harm, and therefore it must reimburse victims for their injuries. In compensation programs, crime victims' interests override all other factors. Financial assistance is determined by victim needs, not by the ability of the criminal justice system to identify, arrest, and convict the offender; to determine his ability to make restitution; or to enforce a restitution agreement. It is generally argued that, if the predominant concern is victim assistance, compensation programs provide a more comprehensive means of providing financial aid.

Victim Compensation Program Operations

Most compensation projects follow the same basic procedures: (1) Victim claims are screened to determine eligibility, (2) supporting documentation is requested from claimants, (3) the case is investigated and the information provided is verified, (4) a recommendation is made to the program's award committee, and (5) the final decision to award or not award is made.

One study of victim compensation programs revealed that most programs provided compensation only to victims of violent crimes.[44] Most programs also made awards to a member of the victim's immediate family in the case of victim death. Claims normally had to be filed within one year after the crime. Only injuries resulting from crimes reported to police were eligible for aid in most programs. Medical expenses and loss of support or income qualified for reimbursement in all programs; funeral expenses and pain and suffering were less frequently eligible for compensation; property loss was not a legitimate claim in any state. Most programs required the victim to have suffered a minimum financial loss before qualifying for an award. The maximum award possible was generally $10,000. The programs differed widely in the number of claims they had received, processed, and awarded. During a year's operation, claims received ranged from 50 in one state (Alaska) to 2,341 in another (New York). Awards varied from about one-third to 95 percent of all claims received.

Costs and Benefits

One of the most critical issues in an evaluation of the merits of victim compensation and restitution programs is the economic costs and benefits the programs incurred. Compensation programs invariably operate at a cost to the taxpayer. Yearly costs may vary from a few hundred thousand to several million dollars, depending upon program size.[45] Restitution projects may involve financial savings to the taxpayer because they can provide community supervision or community residential alternatives to costly incarceration. Restitution payments do not necessarily involve special costs to the taxpayer because payments are made by offenders, and criminal justice officials (probation and parole officers), who would be supervising the offender even if restitution had not been required, generally supervise payment.

Determining the relative economic benefits of restitution and compensation programs to victims is difficult. Theoretically, compensation programs could serve all crime victims; restitution programs are inherently limited to cases where offenders can be identified and required to make restitution. However, no state has yet committed itself to the enormous cost of compensating all crime victims. Whether victims today receive greater payments from compensation or restitution programs is not clear.

Restitution programs are currently more popular than compensation programs because of their cost benefits, the focus on offender responsibility, and fears that victims or alleged victims who inflate their losses to attain large awards may misuse compensation programs. However, compensation programs still receive considerable support. Concern with the suffering of victims continues to grow, and few states are likely to take the politically unpopular step of ending the programs, even if restitution were to prove to be a clearly more desirable option.

Many states and the federal criminal justice system have attempted to combine the best effects of both restitution and victim compensation by charging offenders fees that are then paid into victim compensation funds. The first $100,000,000 in federal fines collected each year, for example, is paid into the Federal Victims Compensation Fund. Given the current focus of restitution programs on nonviolent property offenders and the emphasis on violent crime in compensation projects, the programs may continue to serve complementary goals and objectives for victim assistance and offender rehabilitation.

Rehabilitation, Restitution, and Community Service

Although much of the original interest in restitution and community service programs focused upon their rehabilitative potential, today's programs often are more concerned with the punishment of offenders. The question remains: Can restitution serve to rehabilitate even as it serves to punish? In most communities, restitution is used not as a sole sanction or alternative to imprisonment, but as an add-on to routine punishments. Although some evidence shows that victims prefer to see restitution used in conjunction with other sanctions, this practice may make offenders feel that they are receiving double punishments. A survey of victims and offenders from nineteen adult restitution programs found that offenders who were required to make restitution in addition to serving a prison sentence felt that such judgments were especially unfair.[46] Offenders viewed sole sanction or restitution plus probation as more appropriate dispositions.

Although voluntariness is viewed as essential if restitution is to exert a rehabilitative effect, it is difficult to make restitution truly voluntary. It is either used as an alternative to a more punitive disposition or added to a traditional sanction such as probation, incarceration, or parole. In both situations, restitution is at least somewhat coerced and its rehabilitative value may decline to the extent that the offender comes to view restitution as just a fine paid to a different party. When restitution becomes part of the plea bargaining process, this perspective seems inevitable.

There is also some question about the use of **partial restitution** as a disposition for offenders unable to make complete reimbursement within a reasonable time period. If an offender is permitted to pay back one-half or one-third of the money he or she stole or a small proportion of the value of goods stolen, restitution may encourage rather than discourage crime. It has been argued that such plans merely tax the criminal for his or her acts of thefts. The reparations not only do not restore equity, but they also mock the ideal of restitution and offer nothing in the way of deterrence.

The confrontation of the offender and victim and their negotiations regarding the restitution agreement are designed to facilitate mutual understanding and to encourage the offender to think twice before committing another crime. In reality, such occurrences are unlikely. Victim-offender contact is extremely limited, often by victim choice. Most victims fail to fit an image likely to discourage further crime. Department stores, insurance corporations, and other businesses that are awarded restitution payments may encourage the criminal's view that the rich get richer and the poor must manage any way they can.

The potential of community service sentencing also merits closer examination. After studying the current use of community service sentences, Harland concluded that they are generally

neither an alternative to incarceration nor a truly voluntary endeavor on the part of most offenders. In addition, there is doubt about the role, if any, that the possible rehabilitative effects of community service may play in sentencing decisions, and about the merit behind rehabilitative claims for service penalties. Rather, stripped of its euphemistic terminology, the "voluntary service alternative" bears a striking resemblance to the Thirteenth Amendment concept of involuntary penal servitude as a punishment for crime.[47]

The rehabilitative impact of community service sentences may be especially dubious when the nature of the service is unrelated to the offender's crime. When the offender convicted of driving while intoxicated is sentenced to pick up litter in a park, he or she may have difficulty understanding the symbolic nature of his or her actions and may view the disposition simply as forced labor. This situation is not unlikely, because volunteer work clearly related to the offender's crime is not always available or desirable. The focus is often understandably on community needs, not offender rehabilitation.

Neither restitution nor community service programs are inherently rehabilitative. To achieve the goal of offender change, the programs have to be designed and implemented with constant attention to therapeutic objectives. These objectives often conflict with other program aims because, like most correctional programs, restitution and community service do not provide simple solutions to the problem of crime.

Enforcement of Restitution Conditions   Because restitution is frequently a condition of probation or parole, the enforcement of restitution conditions through revocation proceedings is a common problem. Imprisonment for debt is a violation of the U.S. Constitution, so probation and parole officers are extremely reluctant to consider initiating revocation proceedings unless it is clear that the offender is able, but unwilling, to make restitution payments.

Most jurisdictions permit a three-month grace period to elapse before considering enforcement efforts. Income and expenses must then be verified to ensure that the offender is financially able to meet the payment schedule. If it appears that he or she is economically unable to maintain the agreement, attempts are usually made formally (through a modification of probation conditions) or informally (through an agreement negotiated between the offender and the victim) to reduce the amount of restitution payments. In such cases, the payments may be spread out over a longer period or partial restitution may be allowed.

Even when the offender's financial status has been verified and his or her failure to make restitution is clearly a result of a reluctance to make payments and not of a limited income, probation and parole officers may still attempt to avoid revocation. If the offender has committed no crimes or other violations of community supervision, revocation may not serve the objectives of offender rehabilitation, reintegration, or community protection, the traditional purposes of probation and parole. Such proceedings place the probation or parole staff in the role of agents for a debt collection agency. Imprisonment does not result in the payment of restitution, only punishment for an offender who may otherwise be making a positive adjustment to the community. To avoid such situations, probation and parole officers have been known to juggle the books to hide an offender's failure to meet the restitution schedule.

The enforcement of restitution conditions can place the staff of supervising agencies in a difficult position. Permitting a pattern of nonpayment is clearly not desirable, but the available alternatives often provide no suitable remedy. The problems of determining offender ability and intent, the desire to encourage whatever positive adjustment has been made, and staff members' discomfort as they attempt to operate as debt collectors limit the effectiveness of enforcement strategies.

Summary

Economic sanctions present great potential for enhancing the continuum of correctional sanctions. They are both punitive and revenue generating, a combination that much of the general public finds hard to resist. Restitution and community service sanctions have the additional potential of rehabilitative impact and mitigation of victim and community fear and rejection of the offenders.

The challenge of economic sanctions is to select appropriate amounts of money or labor for punishment and to develop a method to ensure that revenue is collected and work is performed. Setting penalties too high results in inflated projections of income and shortfalls in collection. This in turn diminishes the willingness of the system to employ economic sanctions. But if fines, fees, restitution, and community service penalties are set too low, they will be utilized only with very minor offenders, and the resulting incentive for monitoring and enforcement of punishments will be little. In addition, low rates of restitution may make profit-oriented crime more desirable, encouraging the offender to believe that crime does, in fact, pay.

Striking the right balance with these sanctions is a worthwhile objective. These programs present universal appeal and have been shown to generate sufficient revenue. The importance of careful program design, selection of participants, and reasonable goal setting cannot be overemphasized. Systemwide commitment to program success is equally important, because courts and correctional agencies must often rely on law enforcement and prosecutors to assist in enforcement efforts.

Key Words and Concepts

collection procedures

community restitution centers

community service

day fines

enforcement

equity

fees

fines

full restitution

partial restitution

structured fines research

surcharges

symbolic restitution

victim compensation

Questions for Discussion

1. Why is the criminal justice system again considering the option of fines for offenders? What has changed in the process of determining fines that makes them again seem attractive?

2. Are fines used more or less often in other nations? Do other nations use fines for crimes that would never be considered for fines in the United States?

3. Do surcharges for the use of the criminal justice system create additional punishment for the poor or place the costs of operating the system in the hands of those who use it? Think of some reasons that support and oppose the use of these charges.

4. What barriers exist to the collection of fines and fees? Who should be responsible for the collection of these fees?

5. Is using offenders to clear trash from roads or to clear weeds from vacant land an example of punishment or restitution? Does this process decrease recidivism or just improve society?

For Further Reading

Hillsman, Sally T., et al., *Fines as Criminal Sanctions,* Research in Brief (Washington, D.C.: National Institute of Justice, September 1987).

McDonald, Douglas, et al., *Day Fines in American Courts: The Staten Island and Milwaukee Experiments* (Washington, D.C.: U.S.

Department of Justice, National Institute of Justice, April 1992).

Morris, Norval, and Michael Tonry, *Between Prison and Probation: Intermediate Punishments in a Rational Sentencing System* (New York: Oxford University Press, 1990).

Parent, Dale, *Recovering Costs Through Offender Fees* (Washington, D.C.: U.S. Department of Justice, National Institute of Corrections, 1990).

Schneider, Anne L. (ed.), *Guide to Juvenile Restitution* (Washington, D.C.: U.S. Government Printing Office, 1985).

Chapter 8

Community Residential Centers (Halfway Houses)

Objectives

Historical Perspective

Program Planning and Operations

Problems and Issues in Halfway Houses

Program Evaluation

The Future of Halfway Houses

Summary

Residential community corrections or halfway houses are designed to help ex-offenders negotiate the critical transition from confinement to the community. They may also be used to aid other offenders who are being supervised in the community and who are in need of more structure and supervision in a community residential setting (for example, probation enhancement). The provision of a supportive environment; the **basic necessities** of food and shelter; and assistance in securing employment, education, and counseling services facilitate adjustment to the community and thus promote the correctional goal of reintegration.

In the past, a great variety of correctional facilities and programs have claimed the title of "halfway house." Some of these facilities are small, secure, community-based institutions that provide a full range of correctional programs. Others are loosely structured programs that provide shelter but little else to ex-offenders who live in the house on a voluntary basis.[1] Most halfway houses lie somewhere between these two extremes—they provide moderate levels of supervision and programming for various categories of offenders.

Today's halfway houses typically serve **prereleasees,** persons who are being permitted to serve the last portion of their prison sentence in the community, or parolees (Figure 8-1). In many jurisdictions, however, halfway houses serve other offenders as well. For example, defendants selected for diversion, pretrial release, or probation may be required to live in a halfway house as a condition of supervision. Inmates on probation or parole may also be placed in a

Figure 8-1 Three Models of Release
or Transfer from Prison to Halfway House

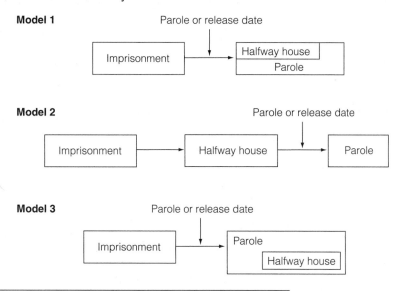

Source: E. Latessa and H. Allen, "Halfway Houses and Parole: A National
Assessment," *Journal of Criminal Justice,* 10, 1982, p. 156. Copyright 1982,
Pergamon Press, Ltd. Reprinted with permission.

halfway house as an alternative to probation revocation when they may be in danger of failing in the community. The type of population served varies from community to community and from halfway house to halfway house, depending upon the characteristics of the specific program and the services the halfway house provides. Some halfway houses are administered by correctional agencies and accept only offenders as residents. Others, especially those that provide special treatment programs for alcoholics, drug abusers, or persons with mental health problems, accept individuals referred from social service agencies and self-referrals as well as offenders. Still others focus the majority of their efforts on non-offenders and accept criminal justice clients only occasionally. Programs that accept both offenders and nonoffenders are often administered by public health or welfare agencies or by private organizations.

A national survey of correctional agencies reported that more than nine hundred halfway houses were operating across the United States.[2] Over 90 percent of the programs are privately administered, but these privately administered programs account for only 60 percent of the offenders in halfway houses nationwide. Most programs have an average capacity of about twenty-five residents, although they vary in size from 140 to only 6 beds. The average length of stay in a halfway house ranges from eight to sixteen weeks. In 1996, for the first time, privately contracted halfway houses cost more per day than their publicly funded and operated counterparts.

At least thirty-eight jurisdictions use halfway houses or community treatment centers for prereleasees or parolees. More than thirty-one thousand inmates were residing in halfway houses in 1995 (Figure 8-2).[3] Halfway houses are used as a **minimum custody** option in many prison systems where low-risk inmates are assigned. In this setting, it is considerably cheaper to house and supervise an inmate than

Issues in Community Corrections

Agency-Operated or -Funded Halfway Houses

- Eleven agencies operated 79 halfway houses as of January 1, 1997. West Virginia and Michigan operated the most halfway houses, 18 and 17, respectively.

- Twenty-three adult correctional agencies had 485 contacts with community treatment centers on January 1, 1997. The Federal Bureau of Prisons had the most contacts (260).

- On January 1, 1997, 15,463 inmates were in halfway houses in 26 agencies. Inmates in

agency administered houses comprised 31.4% of this total.

- Inmates in community treatment centers accounted for 2.3% of all inmates in the 27 reporting agencies. Alaska had the highest percentage of its inmates in community treatment centers (12.3%).

George Camp and Camille Camp, *The Corrections Yearbook* (South Salem, N.Y.: Criminal Justice Institute, 1997).

---

in a higher-security setting. In 1995, a minimum security bed cost on the average $32,000 to build; medium security bed, $54,000; and a maximum security bed, $80,000.[4]

Objectives

Halfway houses serve several objectives. As the director of the National Institute of Corrections remarked: "No single description can characterize the variety of residential programs currently in operation, as they serve diverse purposes for different components of the criminal justice system."[5] The traditional halfway house has expanded to include a number of offender types under its roof. Today, it is referred to as a **community residential center** or residential community corrections. Under this umbrella term exist a number of programs and functions, including halfway houses, **prerelease centers,** community correctional centers, community treatment centers, and restitution centers. These facilities

house probationers in need of more secure custody, inmates in prison who are in need of less secure custody, work release inmates, prereleasees, parolees, probationers and parolees whose freedom has been revoked, and drug and alcohol clients. They enhance the range of sanctions available to a sentencing judge (serving as an intermediate sanction), provide an alternative placement for prison systems, assist in controlling prison populations by providing a less costly housing setting, and provide a transitional setting for releasees. Finally, they provide a semisecure correctional setting in the community. Objectives include community protection and reintegration.

Community Protection   Halfway houses address the issue of **community protection** in two ways. First, they provide risk screening of inmates placed in low-custody settings. Second, they offer a semisecure correctional setting, through continuous direct or indirect monitoring of inmate, parolee, or client behavior and a supportive environment designed to

Figure 8-2   Inmates Located in Halfway
Houses on January 1, 1994–1997

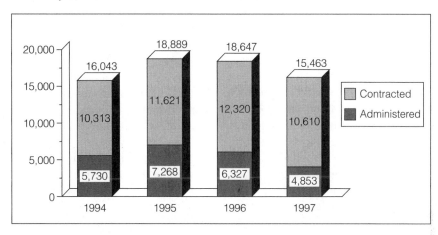

Source: George Camp and Camille Camp, *The Corrections Yearbook* (South
Salem, N.Y.: Criminal Justice Institute, 1997).

assist the offender in returning to a crime-free
lifestyle.

Reintegration   Halfway houses assist in the
reintegration of ex-offenders by increasing
their ability to function in a socially acceptable
manner and reducing their reliance on criminal behavior. To accomplish this objective, the
halfway house accepts ex-offenders released
from prison, provides the basic necessities of
room and board, and attempts to determine
each individual's reintegration problems, plan
a program to remedy these problems, and
provide supportive staff to assist the resident
in resolving problems and returning to society
as a law-abiding citizen.[6] By facilitating community adjustment, halfway houses can benefit both the offender and the community.

Benefits to the Offender

Providing ex-offenders with the basic necessities
of food, clothing, and shelter is undoubtedly
more humane than returning them to the community with no thought to their ability to locate
a job or a place to live. Most prison systems provide inmates about to be released from prison
gate money to help them get established. Many
prison systems today allow inmates to work and
to place the excess money earned into savings
to be used upon their release. In California, inmates receive $200 as gate money. This money
is not enough for a person to get established in
a community. Although parolees are required to
have a residence and employment plan prior to
release, these plans are often less than ideal and
sometimes unrealistic. The housing plan frequently identifies the ex-offender's family home
as his or her parole residence. Preexisting problems with family members may make these living arrangements difficult; the additional stress
of readjustment can make them impossible.
Similarly, the jobs identified by persons hoping
to make parole frequently consist of low-paying,
monotonous employment under poor working
conditions simply because the would-be parolee
is willing to accept any job to facilitate his or
her release. Once freed, the unattractive aspects of the work and the parolee's reactions
to these conditions may lead to early termination. Halfway houses can help avoid these
problems by providing ex-offenders with the

basic necessities while they locate housing and employment suitable to their needs and resources.

Halfway houses also provide the **emotional support** offenders need to manage the demands and pressures of readjustment. Informal counseling is available, and staff members are willing to listen to and discuss residents' personal dilemmas. Perhaps more important, the offender is in a setting where those who share the same predicament are at hand to provide understanding and support. For individuals who require more intensive interventions, halfway houses can offer more structured therapeutic programs. Drug, alcohol, or family counseling may also enable the offender to develop the skills and resources needed to meet community demands, while still in the semisheltered program environment.

Finally, halfway houses can help ex-inmates find and obtain **community services.** The halfway house staff can act as advocates for ex-offenders, providing them with support, security, and direct assistance while plans for education, training, employment services, financial assistance, and counseling from community agencies are being developed and implemented. Because community programs may have waiting lists or delays in service delivery, halfway house personnel can work to facilitate the bureaucratic process while the halfway house meets the individual's most immediate needs. Halfway house programs for those offenders who have not served a prison term provide an alternative to incarceration. Like programs for prereleasees and parolees, they provide a humane and supportive environment for meeting basic offender needs. Community resources are used to facilitate the adjustment of those persons who do not require imprisonment, but who need more assistance and supervision than a nonresidential program can provide.

Benefits to the Community

Halfway houses can serve the community in two ways. First, they provide a sufficiently secure environment to protect the community. Residents' activities and associations are monitored and support services, staff role models, and recreational pursuits are available. Persons supervised under these conditions should be less likely to engage in criminal behavior than offenders with less assistance and fewer opportunities.

Second, facilitating inmate adjustment to the community is expected to reduce recidivism following residence in the halfway house. The opportunity provided to offenders to get firmly on their feet, to achieve some success in negotiating the routine distresses and temptations of living and working, and to develop and implement realistic plans for the future should reduce postrelease criminal behavior.

Benefits to the Justice System

Halfway houses, community treatment centers, and other minimum security facilities provide a low-cost housing alternative to prison systems for handling nondangerous offenders. With many correctional systems experiencing unprecedented overcrowding in their prisons, combined with the active intervention of federal courts to force state correctional systems either to reduce their prison population to within constitutional (that is, manageable) limits or to expand capacity, halfway houses have been viewed as a reasonable and cost-effective way to rapidly house more prisoners and at less cost than constructing more secure facilities. These facilities, as temporary secure settings, may also serve as enhancements to probation and as another method of dealing with probation and parole violators.

Historical Perspective

The origin of halfway houses is unknown. Some writers suggest that they grew out of early acts of Christian charity. For example, St. Leonard established a monastery during the middle of the first century that provided room and board for convicts whose release he had been able to obtain from the king.[7] From the time of this early effort to the present, religious communities have frequently provided ex-convicts with food and shelter upon their release from prison.

Sir Walter Crofton's **Irish system** may also be responsible for the development of the halfway house. This system of penal servitude provided for incarceration in a maximum security prison followed by work in the free community and residence in an intermediate institution. This intermediate institution, with its emphasis on work in the community and preparing the offender for release, seems to be the most direct forerunner of the contemporary halfway house. Undoubtedly, it was the first modern attempt by correctional officials to create a special residence designed to facilitate the offender's transition from prison to freedom.

The first formal recommendation for the establishment of a halfway house in the United States was made in 1817. During the preceding year, a riot in a Pennsylvania prison prompted the legislature to establish a commission to study prison problems and suggest reforms. One of the commission's many recommendations reflected a concern for the ex-convict's well-being. The commission proposed a building

to be erected of wood, at a small expense, as it is only recommended by way of experiment. The convicts who are discharged are often entirely destitute. The natural prejudice against them is so strong, that they find great difficulty in obtaining employment. They are forced to seek shelter in the lowest receptacles; and if they wish to lead a new course of life, are easily persuaded out of it, and perhaps driven by necessity to the commission of fresh crimes. It is intended to afford a temporary shelter in this building, if they choose to accept it, to such discharged convicts as may have conducted themselves well in prison, subject to such regulations as the directors may see fit to provide. They will have a lodging, rations from the prison at a cheap rate, and have a chance to occupy themselves in their trade, until some opportunity offers of plac-

ing themselves where they can gain an honest livelihood in society. A refuge of this kind, to this destitute class, would be found, perhaps, humane and politic.[8]

This proposal was never implemented because many persons feared **criminal contamination.** It was believed that if ex-inmates lived together, they would spread their criminality from one to another like a disease. Solitary confinement within the halfway house was thought to be necessary to inhibit the spread of criminality. Because ex-offenders, as free persons, would probably be unwilling to accept such living conditions, halfway houses seemed impractical.

Opposition to halfway houses continued in corrections for many years. Even normally progressive prison reform organizations and proponents of parole rejected the idea that ex-prisoners could benefit from a transitional group residence prior to complete freedom. For the remainder of the century, private citizens made virtually all subsequent efforts to provide halfway houses for ex-offenders in the United States. In 1845, the Quakers established the Isaac T. Hopper Home in New York City. (It is still in operation today.) Almost twenty years later, a group of reform-minded Bostonians established a home for Massachusetts women released from prison or jail. For almost twenty years, their Temporary Asylum for Discharged Female Prisoners provided "shelter, instruction, and employment for discharged female prisoners who are either homeless or whose homes are only scenes of temptation."[9]

In 1889, the Philadelphia House of Industry was created. (It continues receiving parolees from Pennsylvania prisons today.) During the next decade, Maud Booth and her husband established Hope Hall for ex-inmates in Manhattan. Although police opposition repeatedly threatened the program, it survived, and similar facilities were subsequently established in California, Florida, Illinois, Iowa, Louisiana, Ohio, and Texas. All these shelters met considerable opposition from parole authorities because association with former prisoners was forbidden by parole regulations.

Little growth in halfway house development occurred during the next half century. A few mission-type homes were established, and the Salvation Army and the Volunteers of America continued to provide lodging for ex-offenders, as they did for other homeless men. The halfway house movement was not revived until the 1950s, when St. Leonard's and Dismas House, founded by clergy, and other facilities established by private citizens began to appear. Most observers seem to agree that "growing dissatisfaction with high recidivism rates, combined with a new awareness of the problems facing the released prisoner" sparked the renewal of interest in halfway houses.[10]

In 1961, Attorney General Robert F. Kennedy added his support for the growing halfway house movement and explained his objectives:

We wanted to develop a center where in addition to the basic needs of food and a room, the released inmate would be helped to find a job where he would be given the support and guidance to enable him to live with his emotional problems, and where he might make the transition from the institution to community life less abruptly, less like slamming into a brick wall. We wanted a center which would be his sponsor in the "free world," introducing him to community life gradually and withdrawing when the process was completed. Ex-prisoners in all age groups need this kind of assistance.[11]

His concerns persuaded Congress to appropriate funds to establish three experimental prerelease guidance centers for juvenile offenders. Following the success of these centers, the Federal Prisoner Rehabilitation Act of 1965 authorized the establishment of halfway houses for adult offenders as well as other community corrections programs.

During the late 1960s, halfway houses began to expand their functions to include half-in services for persons placed on probation and other offenders. For these individuals, halfway houses serve as an alternative to incarceration. Since that time, halfway houses have been serving persons in a variety of criminal justice statuses, offering half-in programming for persons diverted from the criminal justice system, placed on pretrial release, or sentenced to probation. At the same time, most halfway houses continue to function as half-out houses, providing counseling and other forms of assistance to prereleasees and parolees.

The growth of halfway house programs was strongly influenced by the organization of the International Halfway House Association (IHHA) in 1964. The IHHA promotes the establishment of halfway houses, encourages the development of high standards in their operations and management, and serves as a professional forum for the exchange of ideas. Since that time, interest in halfway houses has continued to grow, and the developing characteristics of halfway houses have reflected the diversity of public and professional interest. Halfway houses have become increasingly sophisticated in recent years. Although most continue to focus on the needs of the ex-offender (or soon to be), they provide an expanded range of services and their ties to correctional agencies and community resources have significantly improved.

Program Models

Although halfway houses vary considerably, most can be measured against a continuum of program objectives and services. The two opposing end points of the continuum are the supportive and the intervention programs; most halfway houses fall somewhere between these two models.[12]

Generally, **supportive programs** tend to have few professional staff members, offer few, if any, counseling services, and be geared toward resource identification for offenders. Supportive programs are based on the assumption that "the offender possesses sufficient motivation to utilize those community resources that meet his or her particular needs."[13] In these programs, staff functions primarily as an information service that refers offenders to appropriate community services. Program personnel assume that residents will take advantage of these services once they become aware of them and possess enough self-control to require only limited supervision.

Intervention programs have relatively large numbers of professionals and offer extensive counseling services. Intervention programs assume that offenders possess neither the motivation nor the personal resources to use the community services they require. The program's professional staff is responsible for remedying the deficiencies that inhibit utilization of needed community resources by providing prevocational, vocational, and psychological counseling on both an individual and group basis.

Regardless of the nature of the program, all halfway houses perform three basic functions: referral, intake, and programming.[14]

Referral **Referral** is the directing of potential residents to the halfway house. It does not guarantee acceptance into the program, but instead implies only "an interest in the program for a particular offender on the part of the offender himself, the halfway house or institutional staff, or an interested party."[15]

The halfway house's ties to the correctional institution(s) from which offenders are released is of critical importance to the referral process. A facility with close ties to a prison, such as those that serve as work-release or prerelease correctional centers, often has no control over the referral process—only the availability of bed space limits correctional referrals. Although such programs cannot pick and choose their residents, they avoid the necessity of recruiting.

Halfway houses that have no direct ties to the correctional system must depend upon informal relations with correctional authorities and social service agencies to recruit clients. Good relations are essential if the halfway house is to operate near capacity. Numerous referrals also permit the facility to select those individuals most suited to the program.

Intake **Intake** begins when halfway house staff members initiate their assessment of an individual referred to the program. The process includes the decision to accept or reject the candidate and all orientation efforts designed to acquaint newly accepted residents with the "rules, regulations, goals, and philosophy of the house program."[16] During this period, which ranges from two to thirty days, new residents are usually restricted to the house.

The intake process varies, depending upon the program's supportive or intervention focus. In supportive halfway houses, the focus is on determining if the offender can benefit from the services the program offers. An assessment is made of the individual's

1. Family and community ties,

2. Potential for employment and skill development,

3. Mental health,

4. Physical condition,

5. Level of motivation to seek and hold employment,

6. Desire to succeed in the community, and

7. Level of savings.[17]

Persons with few resources in these areas are usually considered unsuitable for supportive programs.

Intake in intervention programs utilizes clinical, diagnostic, and classification procedures to assess the individual deficiencies of personality and social adjustment. Depending upon the particular treatment program the halfway house offers, various techniques of personality, attitude, and behavior assessment may be employed to identify offender problems and needs. Persons found to be in need of the intervention the halfway house offers are generally accepted into the program.

Programming The **programming** process consists of five overlapping phases: plan development, service provision and resident

Program Focus

Montgomery County, Maryland, Prerelease Agreement

As a Voluntary Participant in the Pre-Release Program, I Agree to Follow the Program's Rules:

1. I agree to industriously work at my employment, training or educational program. I will go to and from its location by the most direct route in the least amount of time. After each day's approved activities I will immediately return to the Pre-Release Center. If any situation occurs which prevents me from returning at the prescribed time, I will immediately call the Pre-Release Center for instructions. I will not be absent from the approved day's activities without approval of a Center staff member.

2. I will not act as a strike breaker, or participate in any strikes, demonstrations, or similar activities and I will report any similar situations to the prerelease Center staff.

3. I agree to buy the necessary materials, clothing and/or equipment essential to my employment.

4. Prior to making any move to change my employment I will inform the staff of the Pre-Release Program and obtain their approval.

5. I agree to deposit with the Work Release Supervisor my earnings less payroll deductions and I further agree to pay the County 20% of my income for room/board, etc. while working and at the Prerelease Center. I also agree to pay my valid debts. Prior to borrowing money, incurring debts, opening bank or charge accounts, etc., I will obtain approval from Center staff.

6. I will arrange my own transportation to and from work. I understand that before operating a motor vehicle I must have a valid driver's license, automobile registration, and proper insurance coverage as required by Maryland law.

7. I agree not to leave the Pre-Release Center premises without prior authorization from Center staff.

8. It is, of course, understood that I will obey all laws of the State of Maryland. Should I have any contact with the police I will immediately notify a Center staff member.

participation, review of participation and progress, release decision and process, and follow-up.[18]

Plan Development The first step in halfway house programming is usually the development of a plan of action for the resident. This plan identifies objectives the offender should accomplish during residence in the program and often specifies how much time it may take. Usually both the resident and the halfway house counselor develop the plan. Working together, they discuss the offender's problems and attempt to achieve a mutual agreement regarding objectives and the best means to accomplish them. The plan is sometimes prepared in the form of a contract that specifies both offender and staff responsibilities; in other programs, the agreement is more informal.

9. I agree not to use, possess or introduce into the Pre-Release Center any weapons, alcoholic beverages, narcotics or drugs (unless under doctor's orders).

10. I agree to resolve the problems I confront in non-violent ways and I will not verbally or physically abuse another person.

11. I agree to submit to urinalysis or alcolyser tests when requested by Pre-Release Center staff.

12. I agree to participate in the Center's Social Awareness Program, in the group counseling program and (or) other community programs (i.e., alcohol or drug groups) dependent upon my problems, needs and goals.

13. If I earn home visitation privileges while in this program, I agree to spend my time at pre-arranged activities with my family or friends as approved by the Center staff, and I will conduct myself properly, obeying all laws as well as the rules of the program during my release into the community.

14. I have read the Pre-Release Center Guidebook and agree to follow the program activities and procedures of the Pre-Release Center.

I am committed to making those personal changes necessary for me to remain crime free. Thus, I am ready to become meaningfully involved in this program and the treatment opportunities made available to me. I am prepared to honestly accept responsibility for my own behavior and will demonstrate responsibility through my actions.

I realize that if I violate my part of this agreement I can be immediately removed from the program and placed in security confinement, and I will be subject to the penalties provided by law.

Resident's Signature   Date

Signature of Staff Member   Date

Source: Robert Rosenblum and Debra Whitcomb, *Montgomery County Work-Release/Pre-Release Program, Montgomery County, Maryland* (Washington, D.C.: U.S. Government Printing Office, 1978), p. 127.

Most programs attempt to develop individualized treatment plans. Some halfway houses, however, attempt to select similar residents and utilize one house plan for all residents.

Service Provision and Resident Participation
The halfway house or the community may provide services to residents, most frequently interpersonal counseling. Employment counseling and job placement are also frequently provided, but community agencies more often provide these services and other educational programs.

All halfway houses require clients to meet certain expectations for continued residency, often to:

1. Observe at least minimum security requirements (checking in and out is generally required),

2. Keep rooms and belongings in good condition,

3. Perform household duties,

4. Attend counseling sessions,

5. Secure and maintain employment, and

6. Demonstrate appropriate attitude and behavior.[19]

Review of Program Participation and Progress In most halfway houses, residents are reviewed on a regular basis. Reviews focus on program participation and progress and occur between one and four times per month. At such reviews, staff and employer reports of resident behavior are generally discussed. The residents' self-evaluation and information from social service agencies and schools that deal with them are also sometimes considered. The residents' future in the program depends upon the results of the evaluation and their criminal justice status. The unsuccessful residents may be evicted from the house and suffer the collateral consequences of renewed prosecution, jailing, or imprisonment. Residents with less serious problems may be punished by a reduction of privileges. Residents making satisfactory progress may have their programs modified or continued as before. Persons who have received as much benefit as possible from the program may be terminated.

Release Decision and Process When offenders have accomplished what they were expected to achieve, they are ready for release. Consideration for release is usually initiated by the clients' attainment of specific program goals or by their exceeding the average length of stay in the program. A final criterion for release is the client's ability to prepare for leaving the program. These preparations include locating appropriate housing and employment and developing financial plans for the future.

Follow-up Follow-up activities may include both services to the former resident and data-gathering efforts for the purpose of program evaluation. Efforts are made to prevent offenders from encountering further legal difficulties and to assist them if it appears that they were released too soon. Information about resident adjustment to the community, usually including employment status and subsequent criminal behavior, is gathered for periods ranging from three months to two years. Follow-up activities generally receive little emphasis in most halfway house programs because the limited staff and resources available are directed toward serving in-house residents.

Program Illustrations

Massachusetts Prerelease Centers Massachusetts provides a good example of a state committed to community residential assistance for ex-offenders.[20] In 1972, a correctional reform law requiring the establishment of community correctional programs was passed. The reform law permits transfer to prerelease facilities during the last eighteen months preceding an inmate's parole eligibility. One month after the law was passed, the first prerelease unit was established in a vacant building on the grounds of the Boston State Hospital.

Most inmates are transferred to prerelease programs when they are eight months from parole eligibility. They are given two weeks to find a job, after which they pay the state for their room and board, depending upon how much they earn. The inmates progress through the programs through a series of five phases. Entry to a phase depends upon appropriate behavior; with each phase comes additional furlough time, ranging from ten hours a week in phase one to forty-eight hours in phase five.

The inmates in the programs are usually older offenders who have spent three to four years in prison. They have little difficulty in locating jobs, although many of these jobs are menial and low paying. Employment coordinators assist them in obtaining employment, sometimes making as many as seventy-five attempts before a job is secured. Although it is against Massachusetts law to discriminate against offenders, many employers are not interested in hiring inmates on prerelease.

Minnesota PORT Programs   Minnesota's statewide **PORT** (Probational Offenders Rehabilitation and Training) **programs** began with a tri-county program in Rochester, Minnesota.[21] That program serves both adult and juvenile males referred from local courts. Their offenses range from truancy to armed robbery.

Entrance into the program is voluntary. Candidates undergo a three-week, live-in evaluation at the PORT facility prior to acceptance. During this time, the candidate and the screening committee—comprising a psychiatrist, a probation officer, a layperson from the community, the executive director, and representatives from both the resident and counselor groups—determine if PORT is the choice of both parties.[22] Candidates must identify and describe to the committee their reasons for wanting to enter PORT. This practice is designed to encourage the residents' desire to be helped by the PORT program. The executive director of the PORT program described the core of the program as

a combination of group treatment and behavior modification. The residents meet as a group Sunday, Wednesday, and Friday evenings with the program director and the two trainees. Confrontation, frankness, honesty, trust, care, reality-testing, and decision making are the ingredients of the group process. The quality of the culture at PORT is primarily affected by the success of this phase of the program. The behavior modification feature was added after a year of operation when we found that the group alone was insufficient. Group sessions were spending too much time on individuals' problems in school and job performance, inconsistencies developed in ascertaining acceptable levels of performance, and the newcomer's association with outside groups and their often varying value systems confused him. Also, the fact that the program was experiencing some failures led to the addition. A point system is used to mete out levels of freedom systematically, based upon measured performance in tangible areas. These include weekly school and

work reports, building cleanup, managing a budget, planning and carrying out social activities successfully, and similar accomplishments. Operationally the newcomer starts off at the bottom rung of a group-evolved classification system which has categories ranging from 1 (minimum freedom) to 5 (freedom commensurate with that of an individual of the same age in the community). Working up the ladder is accomplished through a combination of earning points and group decision. Through the process of demonstrating performance to the group and earnings on the point system, the resident gradually weans himself from PORT, increasingly gaining the freedom and responsibilities accorded the "normal" person of his age.[23]

PORT is sometimes used as an alternative to revocation for persons on probation or parole. The case of Roger, a fifteen-year-old with a chronic history of assault, illustrates the program's work with just such an offender:

Roger had been out of a state institution for three months when he again became involved in a number of fights and assaults. This, plus poor adjustment to home, school, and parole supervision, would have resulted in his return to an institution had PORT not been available.

During the initial several months at PORT his adjustment was poor. When frustrated, he cried, when collected, he "conned" the therapy group, which they pointed out to him. The fighting continued, culminating in his being expelled from school. When that occurred, instead of returning to PORT, he ran off, which he had done on two other occasions. Some days later, through the help of other PORT residents, he was picked up by the police and jailed.

The "group" and staff recognized that Roger's associates were the strongest force in his life, much stronger than PORT, and if we were going to interrupt this progression of negative behavior, it would be necessary to alter the nature of their influence. His associates were informed that Roger would not be released from jail until he met with the PORT program director, Jay I. Indgren, and members of the group at the jail and unless they promised that they would support only responsible behavior on his part. They appeared at the appointed time but the setting created so much tension that another session was scheduled for the next day at PORT.

Results were beyond expectation. For example, the leader of the group of friends turned to Roger during the meeting and said that Jay wasn't as bad a guy as he, Roger, had made him out to be.

At this writing some five months later, Roger is in class 5 and asking the group to leave PORT. He has been maintaining a "C" average in school where his adjustment has been satisfactory; he works part-time at a service station. A month ago he was picked up drinking with his friends. However, after [it] explored the behavior with him, the group concluded that the incident was more a learning experience than a regression. He spends less and less time at PORT and probably will be released soon. The question of PORT's being able to afford the necessary controls and help for Roger was raised several times during the course of his stay. If the special school operated by the public schools at Rochester State Hospital had not been available to take the boy when he was expelled, institutionalization would have occurred, because he was of school age. Each time he had a problem, help, care, pressure, and loss of freedoms emanated from the group and the program, and he emerged stronger after every experience.[24]

Federal Bureau of Prisons Overview   The mission of the Bureau of Prisons is to protect society by confining offenders in the controlled environments of prison and community-based facilities that are safe, humane, and appropriately secure and that provide work and other self-improvement opportunities to assist offenders in becoming law-abiding citizens. All federal inmates who are able must work and are paid a small wage, a portion of which some inmates use to make restitution to victims through the Inmate Financial Responsibility Program. About one-fourth of the inmates are employed by Federal Prison Industries Inc., a government corporation that produces a range of goods and services from office furniture to electronic cable assemblies for sale to federal government clients. Research has shown that inmates who work or receive vocational training adjust better to prison, are more likely to hold a job after release, and are less likely to commit new crimes. Most inmates serve the last few months of their sentence in a community corrections center, or halfway house, and often hold jobs in the community while preparing for their release. Several hundred halfway houses around the country are privately operated under contract and monitored by the bureau.[25]

Program Planning and Operations

Planning and operating a halfway house is no simple task, yet most in existence today developed with relatively little guidance. Subsequently, many programs have suffered from poor or incautious planning and administration. To remedy this problem, the National Institute of Law Enforcement and Criminal Justice (NILECJ) funded a study of halfway house program models. The project's objective was to identify critical issues in halfway house planning and operation and offer guidelines for addressing these issues. The final report was published in 1978. Today it serves as one of the best sources of information available on such issues as target population selection, location and site selection, personnel and training, treatment services, and security.[26]

Target Population Selection

One of the most critical questions in halfway house planning is who is to be served. Much of the success depends on the planners' ability to identify persons in need of halfway house services and to develop a program to meet those needs. Any planning effort should begin with a needs assessment designed to identify the number of offenders within a particular jurisdiction who might benefit from halfway house services and the types of problems they would require assistance in resolving.

The National Council on Crime and Delinquency has identified six factors that can be used to assist in the selection of a **target population**.[27]

1. *Geographic Location.* If the program aim is to reintegrate offenders into the community, then only persons who are residents of that community or who are willing to relocate to that community should be selected as residents.

2. *Age.* Residents should be able to utilize all services provided by the halfway house, so persons selected for the program should normally be between the ages of seventeen and sixty. Younger individuals might be expected to have difficulty entering the workforce; older persons may be too close to retirement age for gainful employment. Currently, over half of all halfway house residents are between the ages of twenty-one and thirty.

3. *Gender.* Gender is an important consideration only because it is necessary to ensure that enough people in the target population merit a halfway house. A halfway house may be single-sex or coed, although resistance to a coed facility may be encountered in some communities.

4. *Length of Stay.* The length of the client's sentence must be matched to the halfway house program. Individuals placed on community prerelease status for the last three months of their prison sentence cannot be expected to take full advantage of a program that requires six months to a year of residency. The model policy statement developed by the United States Bureau of Prisons for its community residential centers recommends that client selection should anticipate the following minimum lengths of stay for specific program services:[28]

Work release employment placement only	30 days
Work release to accumulate savings	90 days
Preparole and prerelease testing in the community	90 days
Marital and family counseling	30–60 days
Aftercare treatment for alcoholism	60 days
Vocational and special training	Open
Aftercare treatment for drug addiction	90 days

The average length of a residence in a halfway house is between eight and sixteen weeks.

5. *Offender Characteristics.* Dangerous, hostile, and emotionally disturbed offenders should probably be excluded from minimum security programs such as halfway houses. Any individual likely to jeopardize the other residents, the program, or the community should also be excluded. Most halfway houses do not take in persons with mental and emotional problems. Persons with physical disabilities and sexual deviancy are also frequently prohibited from participation.

6. *Drug-Dependent and Alcoholic Offenders.* The National Council on Crime and Delinquency recommends that these persons should be admitted to the program only if professional staff are available to work with them. Perhaps as a result of a lack of trained staff, many programs bar offenders with drug and alcohol problems. However, about one-third of all halfway house programs are specifically designed for such offenders.[29]

Location and Site Selection

If halfway houses are to facilitate offender reintegration into the community, they must be located in the community. The critical question is: Which community and what neighborhood? Citizen attitudes are one of the most important considerations in the selection of location—many houses have been forced to close or relocate because of unfavorable community response. Neighborhood residents are often concerned about danger to persons or property from halfway house residents, or about a decline in real estate values following the opening of a home for ex-offenders. Although research in a number of states indicates that crime rates do not increase and property values do not decline when a halfway house enters the neighborhood, public attitudes continue to be fearful and neighborhood problems rank as one of the most serious difficulties reported by halfway houses.[30]

The type of neighborhood suitable for the establishment of a halfway house is the subject of some debate. The American Correctional Association suggests that halfway houses should be located in as good a neighborhood as the community will permit.[31] Other observers suggest that the environment should be similar to the areas to which residents will be returning, which usually suggests a low socioeconomic neighborhood. "Commercial locations or those undergoing transition or redevelopment, marked by little neighborhood cohesiveness and a resultant anonymity" are sites favored by such advisers. They believe that halfway house residents need to be able to blend into the community and feel a part of it, "rather than being identified and stigmatized as being from a correctional center."[32] There is considerable opposition to locating the halfway house in a deteriorating area, but a "racially, culturally, and economically diverse community" is generally viewed as desirable.[33]

At present, halfway houses appear to be an urban phenomenon. Nine out of ten are located in urban areas and two-thirds are in counties with populations of 500,000 or more. The programs are usually located in areas zoned for multiple-family housing; only one in five has been established in a neighborhood restricted to single-family dwellings. Most of the facilities are in multiracial, lower-middle-class areas. The halfway house's approach to community relations is generally to keep a low profile, although some programs provide special services to the community, such as chaperoning senior citizens and sponsoring clean-up projects and social events.[34]

The final question pertaining to halfway house geographic location is accessibility to essential community resources. Although the program may be established in virtually any type of community, it must be located near public transportation, employment, and educational opportunities. Other community resources, such as medical and social services and recreational activities, must also be conveniently located.

A critical issue that may influence or supersede questions of geographic location is the type of facility desired and available for use as a halfway house. Old homes or unused public buildings are sometimes donated or made available virtually rent-free to halfway house administrators. Such actions often constitute unrefusable offers. Halfway houses have been located in abandoned military barracks, old hotels, newly constructed, specially designed correctional centers—every imaginable structure capable of serving as a communal residence.

Three-fourths of the halfway houses in operation today are relatively new, having developed during the 1970s. Former homes and hotels serve as the site of about half of the halfway houses; about 10 percent of the halfway houses utilize space rented from Young Men's Christian Associations (YMCAs), the Salvation Army, or apartment buildings. The remaining structures are so diverse as to resist classification. Most facilities require residents to share a bedroom with another participant. In 40 percent of the programs, three or more persons share rooms.[35]

Personnel and Training

Halfway houses originated with virtually all-volunteer staffs, but today they utilize a variety of personnel, including professionals, paraprofessionals, student interns, and ex-offenders, as well as volunteers. Ideally, professional people with graduate degrees or college plus experience are employed to fill the central roles of program director and treatment staff. Paraprofessionals, persons with a combination of background, education, and experience appropriate to halfway house employment, can supplement professional staff. Specially trained paraprofessionals can "provide links with community resources[,] . . . work with special problems, such as drug abuse and alcohol, or facilitate group or individual counseling."[36] Volunteers can serve in a great variety of capacities. Those persons from backgrounds similar to the residents may serve as role models. Volunteers from middle-class backgrounds can facilitate clients' entry into jobs and educational opportunities that might otherwise be closed to them. Student interns may be utilized similarly to volunteers or paraprofessionals, depending upon the involvement of their educational institutions in preparing them for their halfway house responsibilities. Ex-offenders can be employed by the halfway house, depending upon their education and work experiences. Ex-offenders can contribute much to the halfway house program. They may bring a special knowledge and understanding of offender problems and needs that can facilitate many aspects of program operation.

The average halfway house program today has between four and seven full-time employees; one or two persons may serve as administrators and two to five staff members may function in treatment capacities.[37] Almost half the programs employ between one and three part-time staff. Two-thirds of the halfway houses use volunteer services. As many as two hundred volunteers may be serving a single program. Volunteers are used in many capacities: leading group sessions, raising funds, transporting residents, organizing community events with residents, and substituting for evening staff. Relatively few programs employ ex-offenders. Those that do are more often private, not publicly administered, facilities.

The National Evaluation Program (NEP) survey indicated that three-fourths of halfway house administrators, but only half of treatment personnel, hold college degrees.[38] Their degrees are often in areas unrelated to their roles and responsibilities as treatment staff. Less than 40 percent of the program adminis-

trators and fewer than one in six treatment personnel hold graduate degrees.

A recent survey of halfway house administrators revealed that high staff turnover is one of their most significant problems. A variety of causes was said to underlie problems in staff retention: "low pay levels, few opportunities for advancement, and **burnout** due to frequent and intensive contact with residents" were the most frequently mentioned sources of employee distress.[39]

Treatment Services

Halfway houses may provide many services to their clients, either directly or through referral to community resources. The types of services the house offers should reflect resident needs and generally should complement, not duplicate, existing community resources. Some services, such as interpersonal counseling, must be available within the halfway house regardless of community offerings. Interpersonal counseling provides the core of the special support and understanding necessary to facilitate the ex-offender's adjustment to freedom. Basic employment and educational counseling can usually be offered to residents, depending upon the availability of qualified staff. More professional assistance in the areas of vocational and educational testing and placement may be obtained from community resources. In-house drug and alcohol counseling are essential if residents have substance abuse problems, but such services may be complemented by specialized community services.

Many halfway houses develop an individual treatment plan for each resident.[40] Most of the plans indicate specific objectives to be achieved and time frames for their accomplishment. Resident counseling receives the greatest emphasis in today's halfway house treatment efforts—one-third of the program is usually devoted to interpersonal counseling. Three out of four halfway houses offer family counseling, but considerably less program time is devoted to this form of service.

Employment and education are viewed as principal goals for halfway house residents. Nine out of ten programs offer some employment counseling within the house, and many facilities refer residents to community employment services. Half the programs provide educational counseling and placement and almost one-third offer in-house instruction. Financial assistance and counseling are available in most halfway house programs. Drug and alcohol counseling is the central focus of a number of programs and a major emphasis in many others. Between one-half and two-thirds of all facilities provide special treatment and counseling for residents with drug and alcohol abuse problems.

Major program services provided by contemporary halfway houses are listed in Table 8-1. Interpersonal and employment counseling and services account for over half of all treatment efforts. Forty percent of all halfway house residents also receive employment services from the community. Follow-up program services are routinely offered to many former halfway house residents. Interpersonal family and employment counseling are the most frequently offered services to ex-clients.

Resident Security and Community Protection

Although halfway houses are minimum security facilities and are designed to approximate normal community living conditions, they are expected to offer sufficient program structure. This does not mean that halfway houses should be run like mini-institutions located in community settings. Bars, locks, and constant surveillance are wholly inappropriate for halfway houses. However, the period of transition from prison to the community is a stressful phase of adjustment, often complicated by temptations to return to the companionship of former associates and previous behavior patterns. A halfway house program that provides some external controls over resident behavior can protect residents from injuring (in one

way or another) themselves, each other, and the community. Basic controls that most halfway houses can employ include (1) house rules of behavior; (2) curfews, night security, and supervision; and (3) logs of resident activities, sometimes subject to verification.[41]

The rationale behind each of these controls is the development of personal responsibility. House rules should be similar to the rules that govern conduct in the general society. Informal discussions with staff members should help residents conform to house rules. Residents should receive positive feedback for appropriate behavior, but they should also be frankly informed of failure to meet their responsibilities. All rules should be clearly specified to each resident when he or she enters the program. Both residents and staff should review rules and their enforcement whenever particular regulations appear problematic or enforced in a selective or arbitrary fashion.

Limiting the residents' time spent in the community during the evening hours and providing special security and supervision during this period is designed to reduce the residents' unstructured leisure time in the community, when temptations of various types may become particularly powerful. Such controls also provide the neighboring community with a feeling of safety and protection. Similarly, requiring residents to account for their time and efforts to verify the accuracy of resident activity reports are designed to ensure that residents do not find themselves in the wrong place at the wrong time.

The Federal Bureau of Prisons recommends that the development and implementation of controls should be guided by two considerations.[42] First, controls should be relaxed as residents demonstrate responsible behavior. The objective of the external controls is to provide sufficient structure only until the resident is able to develop and successfully utilize inner behavioral controls. Second, controls do not have to be applied equally to all residents. Persons with particular problems, such as alcoholism, may be reasonably restricted from certain ac-

Table 8-1 Summary of Treatment
Services Data, by Percentage

Treatment Service	Average Percentage of House Effort Devoted to Service	Average Percentage of Residents Receiving Service from Community Agencies	Percentage of Houses Offering Service to Ex-Residents
Interpersonal counseling	31.0	17.0	54.8
Family counseling	6.6	6.5	49.3
Vocational testing and assessment	2.9	26.9	25.0
Vocational skill training	1.8	20.8	23.1
Employment counseling	18.3	18.8	45.4
Educational testing	1.9	16.4	25.6
Education	2.2	16.9	32.6
Education counseling	5.3	12.5	35.7
Financial assistance and counseling	8.4	15.9	35.7
Physical rehabilitation	0.4	5.8	0
Alcohol abuse	6.0	15.9	17.6
Drug addiction and dependency	5.3	17.4	35.9
Recreation	6.0	19.4	36.4
Psychological testing	1.7	13.8	21.4
Psychological and psychiatric services	2.6	15.5	19.8
Total	100.4		

Note: Total exceeds 100 percent because the variance (from 125 to 152) in total
number of houses reporting on each service.

Source: R. P. Seiter et al., *Residential Inmate Aftercare: The State of the Art,*
Supplement A: *Survey of Residential Inmate Aftercare Facilities,* National
Evaluation Program Phase I (Columbus: Ohio State University, 1976), p. 43.

tivities not off limits to other residents. Similarly, some persons may be required to meet special program requirements designed to help them manage specific personal difficulties. For example, residents who are chronically in debt may be required to limit their cash on hand and increase their savings to levels beyond those expected for the average resident.

Problems and Issues in Halfway Houses

The Dilemma of Being Half-In and Half-Out

Few inmates would choose prison over life in a halfway house; yet living in a halfway house presents certain problems. Although halfway houses should offer inmates as much freedom as they can reasonably handle, disagreement exists about the amount of structure and security necessary to ensure that the transition from prison to the community is gradual. From the inmate's perspective, the halfway house sometimes seems to offer no more freedom or responsibility than prison. During incarceration, such restrictions might be more easily tolerated, but when they exist side by side with eight or more hours of freedom during work in the community, they are difficult to manage. Halfway house residents have frequently objected to being treated like children and required to obey what they believe are petty regulations. In an effort to demonstrate to wary citizens that appropriate security measures are being enforced, some programs have

Program Focus

Freedom: Halfway House Style

About 50 . . . inmates live in the Tallahassee Community Correctional Center, a U-shaped concrete building in a business section of the city and just next door to a fenced-in state "road prison" in a similar design.

Residents of the work-release center work as masons, cooks, plumbers, carpet installers, painters, demolition workers, roofers, septic tank cleaners, and warehouse loaders. Many make the minimum wage, but those with skills earn more. Residents pay for room and board on a sliding scale depending on their income, and must buy clothing, sheets, pillowcases, blankets, and all personal supplies. They pay $1.50 a day for transportation to and from work.

Some residents said it was difficult, after all the deductions were made from their paychecks, to save very much money. "It's not possible to save enough to get out and buy a car and put a down payment on an apartment," one man said. But most said they preferred the community center to the prison they had left behind. "We have screens on the windows instead of bars," said one, "and they're not searching you all the time." Many inmates, the men said, are returned to prison for breaking rules, and they blamed this on the frustration caused by the lack of furloughs. (Furlough eligibility is strict in Florida, but rules seem to vary from center to center.) "Work releasees," one inmate said, sometimes "try to get away with things. They leave their job, change their job, smoke pot, and drink. They get into trouble with women, like being with a woman in a car. If they'd let you go home on furlough every once in a while, you wouldn't have to do these things." Another resident added: "I don't see why I can be out there for eight hours a day among people and can't go out for a few hours on a Saturday. When you start going out and working, at first you're so happy, and then after a month or so you don't get a furlough and eventually you say, 'I owe this to myself,' and you end up in trouble."

Source: Joan Potter, "The Dilemma of Being Half In and Half Out," *Corrections Magazine*, 5 (2), 1979, pp. 67, 68. Copyright 1979 by *Corrections Magazine* and Criminal Justice Publications Inc., 116 West 32nd Street, New York, N.Y. 10001.

developed and implemented rules and regulations more strict than those in most contemporary institutions. The necessary balance between security and resident responsibility is often difficult to obtain.[43]

Furloughs   One of the greatest sources of conflict is the granting of furlough privileges. Many programs permit inmates to travel to and from their jobs independently and function freely in the community for up to ten hours per day, only to restrict them to the facility on evenings and most weekends. Such restrictions can be frustrating. The temptations of freedom are within reach but unattainable. Because many programs require all residents to spend a specific period of time in the program before furloughs are permitted, inmates who can handle freedom responsibly are sometimes unnecessarily restricted to quarters. The dilemma appears whenever attempts are made to separate the responsible from the less responsible residents. No scale has yet been devised to make such decision

Program Focus

The Mariana, Florida, Community Center

The community center in Mariana is in a flat, monotonous rural area out of sight of houses or businesses. It consists of a cluster of old white frame buildings, which are expected to soon be replaced by a one-story concrete structure that had been built on the same grounds. The wooden buildings were constructed as a "road prison" in 1934; so people who live in and around Mariana are used to seeing prisoners working on the roads. The facility was closed as a road prison in 1964 and reopened seven years later as a "study-release" center, with inmates attending classes at a local community college. The center was turned into a work-release facility about three years ago.

Residents work at a Coca-Cola bottling plant, a window shade factory, a furniture plant, and on construction jobs. They range in age from 18 to 64, and are serving sentences of from one year to life. Only 25 percent come from the area. Most earn the minimum wage and do manual labor. "They have a real good relationship with the community," said Herbert Melvin, a counselor. "People say they'd rather hire them than anyone else. They're on time and they show up every day." With a good record, men are usually paroled after six months, Melvin said.

Source: Joan Potter, "The Dilemma of Being Half In and Half Out," *Corrections Magazine*, 5 (2), 1979, pp. 67, 68. Copyright 1979 by *Corrections Magazine* and Criminal Justice Publications Inc., 116 West 32nd Street, New York, N.Y. 10001.

making foolproof. Unfortunately, the program's desire to err on the side of caution can place unnecessary pressures on halfway house residents.

Employment Problems   The problems of securing and maintaining employment plague many halfway house residents. Offenders sometimes spend months in the community without finding a job. Such delays often lead to offenders' return to prison for the violation of that specific condition of parole. If offenders are permitted to remain in the community, the effects of continued unemployment can be exceedingly demoralizing. Some programs restrict persons to the halfway house unless a job interview is scheduled in an effort to keep residents from roaming the streets. Such regulations led one halfway house resident to report: "It's a trick. . . . I can't get a social pass (permission to leave the center) because I don't have a job and I can't get a job because I am unskilled."[44] The jobs that are secured are often below the offenders' level of ability. Another inmate remarked: "Everybody knows that when they've got hard work to do and want cheap labor, they call here and we have to take it."[45] The low wages provided by such employment often make saving for final release difficult.

Halfway House Facilities   The facilities in which halfway house programs operate often cause additional problems. The structures are sometimes dilapidated buildings in decaying parts of the community simply because no other facilities can be readily secured. Small

Issues in Community Corrections

The Inmate Code in a Halfway House: A Source of Resistance to Constructive Reintegration

1. Above all else, do not snitch. Informing was regarded as an act directed not simply against an individual, but against the whole collection of deviant colleagues. Snitching would permanently jeopardize a resident's standing with other types, residents, and inmates. His reputation would be spread throughout the whole deviant community, and he would find that he could no longer operate with other deviants. . . .

2. Do not cop out. That is, do not admit that you have done something illegal or illegitimate. Someone who turned himself in willingly would be regarded as strange, "not like us," dumb, and probably not trustworthy, because to "cop out" was a form of defecting to the other side. To turn oneself in could be viewed as a form of defection, because it implied agreement with the standards that one had violated. To turn oneself in to a parole agent when one was about to be caught anyway or when one was "tired of running" and likely to get caught by the police, however, was not talked about as "copping out."

3. Do not take advantage of other residents. This maxim was principally directed against thievery among residents. However, if a resident had something stolen from him, it was his own responsibility to take care of the thief.

Unlike the case of the snitch, a resident could not count on others to negatively sanction the thief. Residents were prohibited by the code from appealing to staff for assistance in locating the stolen goods.

4. Share what you have. A regular resident should be relatively generous with other residents in terms of his money, clothes, and wine. If he used drugs, he should offer a "taste" to others that were around when he "geezed." He should share drugs with his closest friends and sell drugs to others, if he had more than he needed. He should share his "fix" (syringe and spoon) with others and "score" (purchase drugs) for those who could not find a connection (source of drugs).

5. Help other residents. This maxim was principally a directive to help one's fellows avoid detection and punishment. It included "standing point" for them (being a lookout for staff or the police when the other was involved in a compromising activity, such as injecting drugs), warning them about suspicions that staff had, telling staff that they were ignorant about the activities of other residents, so as not to help staff indirectly investigate another resident, providing cover stories for other residents, helping another resident sneak in to the house after curfew, etc.

dismal rooms, peeling paint, dirty torn carpeting, or floors smelling of disinfectant are typical of such programs. One female halfway house resident remarked: "This place projects an image, a dope-fiendish image. The neighborhood is kind of bad. By being in this kind of area the men around here know who we are and they'll stand in the doorway waiting for us

6. Do not mess with other residents' interests. A resident should not prevent others from enjoying their deviance, should not disapprove of it, and should not in any way draw staff's attention to it. This includes not "bringing the heat" by engaging in suspicious actions or by getting into an unnecessary altercation with staff. For example, one could "bring the heat" by leaving evidence of drug use around the house which would lead staff to suspect everybody.

7. Do not trust staff—staff is heat. This maxim simply says that in the final analysis staff cannot be trusted, because one of staff's principal occupational duties is to detect deviance. Anything a resident might let them know about himself or others could, in some presently unknown fashion, be used by them to send him or someone else back to the joint. So, if a resident has anything deviant going for him at all (like having a common-law wife, occasionally using heroin, having user friends in his house, or even using marijuana), he is well advised not to let his agent know his real residence and to give his mother's address instead. In this way he avoids letting his agent know anything that might lead to the discovery of his deviant doings. This advice holds even if a resident is on the best of terms with his agent.

8. Show your loyalty to the residents. Staff, in fact, is "the enemy," and a resident's actions should show that he recognizes this. He should not "kiss ass," do favors for staff, be friendly to staff, take their side in an argument, or accept the legitimacy of their rules. Any of these acts can be understood as a defection to their side, and makes a resident suspect of being the kind of "guy" that would snitch. It is not that being friendly to staff or complying with staff's regulations is intrinsically illegitimate, but these matters indicate what kind of person one is and that one, thereby, may not be trustworthy in protecting residents and their interests. If a resident makes it clear in other ways (as, for example, in his private dealings with other residents) that he indeed is on the residents' side, these signalizing activities may then be understood in other ways by the other residents. They may be understood as efforts to manipulate staff in some concrete way, e.g., a resident wants them to give him the best jobs they have, or wants to make the kind of impression on his parole agent that will lead the agent away from suspecting him when he otherwise might.

Source: D. L. Wieder, "The Inmate Code in a Halfway House," pp. 520–523 in *Justice and Corrections,* N. Johnston and L. Savitz (eds.) (The Hague, Netherlands: Mouton, 1974).

to come out."[46] Another inmate noted: "It's depressing enough going out every day and filling out applications . . . and hearing them say, 'We're not hiring,' or, 'I'll call you if a job is available,' and then having to come back and sit in an ugly room."[47]

The halfway house can draw upon the armory of community resources and services to encourage the resident who is unsure of where his or her loyalties lie. Staff can also tailor desired privileges to individual efforts at responsible behavior. By using its substantial resources, the halfway house is much better prepared to overcome inmate resistance than the traditional prison.

Overcoming Inmate Resistance   In many community-based facilities, the inmate code is alive and well. The inmate code, which encourages loyalty to residents and distrust of staff, often acts as a significant barrier to reintegration. Keeping offenders who could have been imprisoned in the community or moving inmates into the community from jail or prison does not always make them appreciative and receptive to rehabilitation. In some ways, resistance to authority (also part of the inmate code) may make obtaining and retaining employment more difficult, and the prospect of returning to prison even more likely.

Although inmates may be anxious to transfer to a halfway house and noninstitutionalized offenders may view a halfway house commitment as preferable to imprisonment, it would be unreasonable to expect the new resident's initial positive reaction to his or her placement to be retained throughout his or her stay at the facility. Some offenders may be less than pleased with halfway house placements. If halfway houses are widely utilized as prerelease centers, inmates may view such transfers as a right, not a privilege, and arrive disgruntled about delays. Other offenders may view halfway houses as a more severe disposition than they expected, having hoped for no more than probation supervision.

Many inmates attempt to settle into a halfway house as they would into a prison—adopting a "do your own time" ethic that resists any outside intervention. Staff must work to demonstrate that the resident can try new behaviors without fear of failure, that real support exists for the resident's efforts to change, and that meaningful guidance and assistance

are available. These ideas, coupled with the inmate's recognition that these changes can improve his or her future living conditions and overall contentment, can enhance motivation and increase the overall effectiveness of the community-based corrections program.

Halfway House/Community Relations

Although research has not indicated that the establishment of a halfway house in any way reduces neighborhood security or leads to higher crime rates, the public's fear of such occurrences is real and pervasive. Most citizens are extremely reluctant to have a halfway house established in their own residential area. Many programs have failed simply because they were unable to overcome community resistance. Considering the real problems that ex-offenders confront when they attempt to reestablish themselves in the community, citizen hostility is doubly damaging. It hurts the program and confirms offender suspicions about the good will of the community.

Although a certain amount of community resistance seems inevitable, halfway house program administrators can attempt to keep it at a manageable level, using various strategies to minimize public hostility and promote community acceptance. Many of these efforts must be initiated in the program planning stage to get the residents of the surrounding area to buy into the idea of a halfway house and to give them a voice in its operations and policies. This period is of critical importance in the process, and all attempts to establish a stable and enduring program should take the timing of neighborhood presentations into account.

The following sequence of activities is recommended in developing sound community relations:

1. Meet individually with local government leaders (planning boards; private and public social, health, and welfare agencies; fraternal, church, and neighborhood improvement groups). Local

police support is essential. If school-age populations are involved, school authorities should be contacted. This list is not inclusive and is only suggestive of the many important groups to contact.

2. Form a steering committee of local leaders. Having this group meet regularly is helpful to permit recognition and assurance of its mutual interest and support for the program.

3. Explain the program honestly. It is inadvisable and mistaken not to discuss the program in all its ramifications. This means difficulties and problems expected, as well as benefits and advantages.

4. The assistance of neighborhood leaders, whose support has been enlisted previously, will do much to temper community antagonism and help keep negative opposition forces from polarizing.

5. Regularly scheduled meetings should be held both during the planning stages and after the program opens. It is helpful to hold annual or semiannual community meetings (open houses) to which all who are interested may come to visit, meet staff, and learn of the progress, problems, and needs of the halfway house.[48]

Positive **halfway house/community relations** require the program to bring something to the community, not simply drawing upon its services and resources. The program's facility can be used as a meeting place for community organizations. Halfway house residents can provide services to local residents; social events can be sponsored by the program. Virtually no limit exists to what the halfway house can contribute if it views itself as an integral part of the community. This self-perception is imperative if the community is to adopt that same viewpoint.

Public involvement and support is the key to a successful community correctional policy. The National Institute of Corrections recommends that a proactive strategy be used to enlist the support of the community for correctional initiatives. They suggest using a checklist:

- A clearly defined mechanism or process.

- Commitment to the mechanism or process by all parties directly concerned.

- Direct access by citizen participants to the decision-making process.

- Representation of all appropriate segments of the community.

- A clear definition of the participating citizen's role.

- Adequate preparation and briefing available for citizen participants.

- In-depth information and staff help available for participants to carry out their assigned responsibilities.

- Well-defined procedures as to how and to whom citizen participants are accountable.

- Procedures for reporting back the disposition of citizen recommendations.[49]

Program Evaluation

In 1982, Latessa and Allen summarized the efforts of ten correctional systems to evaluate their halfway houses (Table 8-2). Prior to their assessment, the most comprehensive study of halfway houses had been conducted by the National Evaluation Program. This in-depth investigation of halfway houses merits a closer examination.

National Evaluation Program

In 1977, NEP reported the results of an extensive evaluation of prior research studies of halfway houses.[50] A total of fifty-five evaluative reports were reviewed. Despite numerous

Table 8-2   Evaluation Study Outcomes and Comments

Jurisdiction	Outcomes and Comments
Alabama	Law Enforcement Assistance Administration grant; higher-risk clients can be contained at half the cost.
California	In-house study; private houses are economically and operationally more feasible than state-operated houses.
Connecticut	In progress.
Iowa	Done by parole board a year ago; found no significant difference in outcome between halfway house residents and those released to the community directly, but did not consider differences among clients. The parole agency does not necessarily agree with the findings of the study.
Massachusetts	Informal assessment; showed halfway houses to be good for transition period.
Michigan	Found halfway houses to be effective for screening for parole release.
Mississippi	In progress.
Missouri	Compared halfway house and non-halfway house clients; no difference in number of later violations or problems, but halfway house clients had more severe problems to begin with.
District of Columbia	Evaluation in 1977–1978; found that halfway houses run by ex-convicts had a better track record than the others.
Federal	Found that halfway houses had no effect on recidivism but did improve employment.

Source: E. Latessa and H. Allen, "Halfway Houses and Parole: A National Assessment," *Journal of Criminal Justice,* 10 (2), 1982, p. 161. Copyright 1982, Pergamon Press, Ltd. Reprinted with permission.

methodological problems in many, if not most, of the research efforts, the following general conclusions were reached.

Recidivism   Almost two-thirds of the studies attempted to measure resident **recidivism.** Generally, residents' postrelease behavior was followed up for between twelve and eighteen months. Evidence on program impact is divided. About half the studies found lower recidivism rates for halfway house residents when they were compared with institutional parolees. The remaining studies found no differences between former halfway house residents and the comparison group.

Efficiency   Twelve of the fifty-five reports examined the efficiency with which services are provided to halfway house residents. These studies usually took the form of a cost analysis. Because halfway houses differ so greatly in the amount and quality of services they pro-

vide, generalizing about program costs is difficult. Existing evidence indicates that halfway houses can operate at a cost below, equal to, or greater than institutional costs. Halfway house services almost invariably cost more than probation or parole.

One problem that repeatedly seemed to raise program costs was low utilization. Halfway houses operated at between 21 and 76 percent capacity; ideal occupancy was reported to be 85 percent. **Per diem costs** (cost per resident per day) ranged from $13.19 to $70.50 (a program with 21 percent occupancy) (Figure 8-3).

Treatment Services   Halfway houses appear able to help ex-offenders locate and maintain employment during the period of their residency in the program. Evidence shows, however, that this employment is short-lived after the individual leaves the program. Little evidence is available that educational services

Figure 8-3 Halfway House Daily Cost per Inmate, 1990–1996

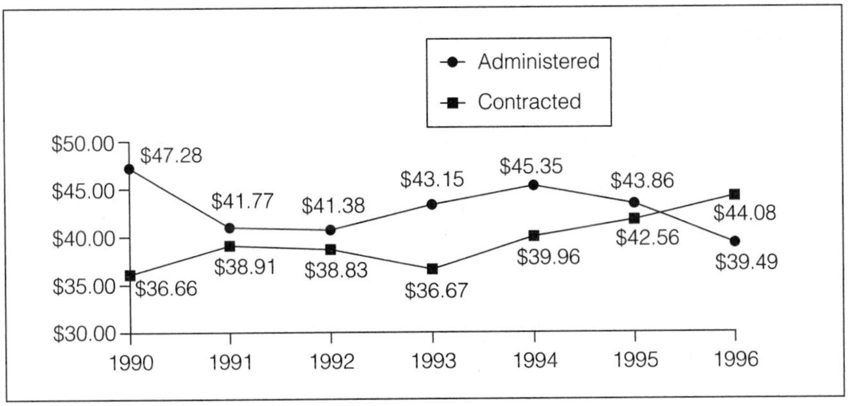

Source: George Camp and Camille Camp, *The Corrections Yearbook* (South Salem, N.Y.: Criminal Justice Institute, 1997).

influence residents' postrelease behavior. Surprisingly, virtually no research on the impact of interpersonal, drug, or alcohol counseling was found, even though these services provide the major focus of many halfway house treatment programs. The effects of family counseling, financial and housing assistance, and leisure time activities are similarly uncertain.

Program Security Only one measure of the impact of in-house security efforts was available—program noncompletion rates, which ranged from 30 to 50 percent. But they are difficult to evaluate because they include persons terminated because of failure to adjust to the program and job loss as well as residents evicted because of misbehavior. Studies of residents' in-program criminal behavior indicate that between 2 and 17 percent of all residents are charged with or convicted of new offenses during their program stay. About one-fourth of these offenses involve attacks on the person; another 25 percent involve property crimes; and the remainder generally consist of drug-related or public order offenses. There is no indication that real or perceived crime rates increase or that the public perceives a decline in

neighborhood security following the establishment of a halfway house.

NEP Recommendations

The NEP recommended that future research efforts focus on providing "systematic evaluative research that utilizes good design, randomization, control groups, adequately operationalized variables, and consideration of intervening variables."[51] Furthermore, research on halfway houses should not be limited to measures of client recidivism but should focus on broader issues of ex-offender adjustment to the community. One method of broadening the research focus is to use the **Relative Adjustment Scale** to measure program effectiveness in facilitating offender reintegration. The Relative Adjustment Scale consists of an index of the severity of nonresident criminal behavior used in conjunction with an index of social adjustment to measure program impact (Table 8-3). The scale was formulated in the belief that reintegration is not "a sudden change in behavior, but movement toward acceptable societal norms." Therefore, assessing various aspects of adjustment is important to gauge the true extent of an offender's movement toward appropriate behavior.[52]

The adjustment index emphasizes work and educational stability, self-improvement efforts, financial responsibility, probation or parole progress, and the absence of critical incidents or illegal activities. Used along with the index of criminal severity, it allows calculation of the offenders' relative adjustment. Persons may be considered to have made relatively positive adjustments even though they have been involved in minor delinquent acts. Individuals, however, with no criminal activity but no evidence of positive adjustment in other areas of life will not qualify as complete successes. The information this scale provides should be more realistic than efforts to classify offenders as successes or failures based upon only one aspect of adjustment.

GAO Survey

The General Accounting Office (GAO) conducted a different type of evaluation when it studied fifteen halfway houses in Florida, Missouri, Pennsylvania, and Texas to determine "whether the states had developed coordinated effective strategies for integrating halfway houses with their overall correction efforts."[53] The research concluded that halfway houses had considerably increased in number and could either become a valuable alternative for many offenders or could die out for lack of funds and public support. The states lacked well-organized systems for coordinating state and locally operated programs. No single agency had information about all halfway houses in any state. The states could not ensure that halfway houses were located in the communities that had the greatest offender populations and that were not already served by existing programs. They also had no means of determining if a community had sufficient resources to meet offender needs if a halfway house was established. Finally, the states had failed to coordinate halfway houses

with other parts of their correctional systems. Prisons and probation and parole agencies had no plans for determining the extent to which halfway houses could or should be used. These findings indicate that extensive planning and coordination of information is drastically needed if halfway houses are to reach their objectives. Otherwise, haphazard program development and isolation from the agencies charged with primary responsibility for offender rehabilitation may prove their undoing.

Minnesota Evaluation

One state has attempted to conduct a systematic evaluation of halfway houses established by both its Department of Corrections and local units of government. Minnesota evaluated all halfway houses for released offenders established in that state during a four-year period.[54] Its findings, reported in 1976, were less than encouraging—only about one-third of the halfway house residents were successfully terminated from their programs. Forty-five percent of the residents failed to complete the project because of absconding, failing to cooperate, or similar difficulties. The remaining residents generally withdrew from the programs voluntarily, were withdrawn by their referring agency, or were transferred to another program.

The research concluded that halfway houses were an inappropriate form of rehabilitation for most of the clients sent to them. Most of the clients in the PORT-type programs studied would have been placed on straight probation if the halfway houses had not been available. Although persons who successfully completed the halfway house programs demonstrated higher levels of postrelease success than residents unsatisfactorily terminated, there were so few successes that program impact was severely limited. The Minnesota study examined factors related to low program completion rates and proposed the following recommendations for halfway house development, integration, and administration:

Table 8-3 Adjustment Criteria Index

Assigned Score	Adjustment Criteria
+1	Employed, enrolled in school, or participating in a training program for more than 50 percent of the follow-up period.
+1	Held any one job (or continued in educational or vocational program) for more than a six-month period during the follow-up.
+1	Attained vertical mobility in employment, educational, or vocational program. This could be a raise in pay, promotion of status, movement to a better job, or continuous progression through educational or vocational program.
+1	For the last half of follow-up period, individual was self-supporting and supported any immediate family.
+1	Individual shows stability in residency. Either lived in the same residence for more than six months or moved at suggestion or with the agreement of supervising officer.
+1	Individual has avoided any critical incidents that show instability, immaturity, or inability to solve problems acceptably.
+1	Attainment of financial stability. This is indicated by the individual living within his or her means, opening bank accounts, or meeting debt payments.
+1	Participation in self-improvement programs. These could be vocational, educational, group counseling, or alcohol or drug maintenance programs.
+1	Individual making satisfactory progress through probation or parole periods. This could be moving downward in levels of supervision or obtaining final release within period.
+1	No illegal activities on any available records during the follow-up periods.

Source: Harry E. Allen et al., *Halfway Houses* (Washington, D.C.: U.S. Government Printing Office, 1978), p. 75.

1. No new halfway house programs should be established unless they are to be evaluated under strict research conditions.

2. A high priority should be placed on cost-benefit analysis.

3. Efforts should be made to increase resident program completion rates.

4. An investigation should be made into new nonresidential community correctional programs and institutional programs.

5. The training of halfway house staff should be improved.

6. Funds should be made available to replace halfway house staff members while they attend training programs.

7. Career ladders should be developed for halfway house paraprofessionals.

8. Continued efforts should be made to obtain the referral of felons to community residential programs as an alternative to incarceration.[55]

The Future of Halfway Houses

The future of halfway houses will inevitably be determined by the ability of the programs to improve the coordination of their services with correctional systems and community resources. The enhancement of halfway house internal organization and management strategies will be essential to this effort and will provide increased cost-efficiency as well. Three valuable administrative strategies are **management by objectives (MBO), management information systems (MIS),** and **mutual agreement programming (MAP).**

Management by Objectives

Management by objectives is a relatively simple technique designed to improve administration. It requires "the establishment and communication of agency goals and objectives, the setting of individual staff job targets supporting those goals and objectives, and periodic reviewing and evaluating of staff performance related to those job targets and the results achieved in light of the agency's goals and objectives."[56]

MBO permits program activities to be organized around specific goals and objectives. Three types of goals are normally developed: long range, short term, and job targets. Each type of goal is developed in each of the agency's key result areas, such as program delivery; staff training and development, community relations, and communication; records, reports, and research; facilities, equipment, and supplies; and finances.[57] For example, if a large number of repeat felony youthful offenders are not completing the halfway house program, the following plan might be developed for the key result area of program delivery:

Long-Range Goal—To have in operation . . . a residential treatment program from which 80 percent of the "hard core" young adult offenders successfully graduate.

Short-Range Objective—To have written . . . a residential treatment program for the "hard core" young adult offender.

Staff Job Target—. . . To have written the first draft of a residential treatment program for the "hard core" young adult offender.[58]

All goals are developed in terms of measurable activities to be accomplished within specific time frames. Staff job targets are ranked to permit efficient organization of tasks. Generally speaking, MBO permits the halfway house (or any other program) to know where it is going, where it has been, and, with considerable precision, the current status of program operations.

Management Information System

The management information system developed by Massachusetts Halfway House Inc. "functions as a communication mechanism, a tracking and monitoring system, and a vehicle used as an aid in the evaluation of employee job performance."[59] Utilizing a series of forms especially developed for halfway house administration, virtually all program activities are recorded on a continuing basis. At any given time, the halfway house is thus able to identify what information is being communicated within the organization, the status of task accomplishment, and each employee's job performance level. Such information is clearly an invaluable tool to program administration and evaluation.

Mutual Agreement Programming

Mutual agreement programming involves the development of individualized contracts by halfway house staff, parole authorities, and prospective halfway house residents. Each party agrees to honor certain commitments:

Residents must assume responsibility for planning (along with program staff) and successfully completing an individually tailored rehabilitative program in order to obtain release on parole on a mutually agreed upon date.

Parole board members must establish a firm parole date and honor it if the resident fulfills the explicit objectives and mutually agreed upon criteria stated in the MAP contract.

Program staff must provide the services and training sources required by the resident, as explicitly guaranteed in the contract, and must fairly assess their own performance in the program.[60]

MAP programs provide several advantages over more traditional parole plans: A specific release date and the conditions for release are clearly established for the offender, parole and halfway house obligations are made explicit, and any individualized treatment plan for the parolee is formulated and implemented.

Such developments seem imperative if halfway houses are to realize their potential for offender assistance. Although these new strategies may generate additional paperwork and somewhat bureaucratize the reintegration programs, their payoff may be considerable—particularly if the goals of the contract are achieved.

Summary

Today's halfway houses are as varied as the offenders they serve. The programs originally created by dedicated citizens and volunteers in an attempt to meet the basic needs of ex-prisoners returning to the community now provide food, shelter, counseling, and employment assistance to persons diverted from the criminal justice system, defendants awaiting trial, and convicted offenders, as well as ex-inmates. Halfway houses offer their residents services ranging from sophisticated diagnostic and clinical treatment programs to the identification, referral, and securing of community resources.

Halfway houses continue to serve principally ex-offenders. Their objective is to facilitate their reintegration into the community. By easing inmates' transition to the free world, halfway houses serve both offenders and the community. The ex-offenders are given a chance to adjust gradually in a supportive environment in which their basic needs can be met. The community receives both short- and long-term benefits from the supervision and assistance provided to ex-inmates returning from prison.

To accomplish their goals, halfway houses must carefully select their residents, facilities, and location. Treatment and control strategies must match the offenders' needs and resources and must reflect their capacity for responsible behavior. Staffing and training activities can make or break the program, so recruitment and selection procedures must be comprehensive and clearly linked to job descriptions. Orientation and in-service and academic educational experiences need to be used to ensure that capable employees grow and develop with their responsibilities.

Research indicates that halfway houses can reduce recidivism and serve as cost-efficient alternatives to incarceration. Halfway houses are not always successful, however. Poor planning and coordination with community resources and correctional agencies, programming difficulties, public fears and hostility, and dilemmas inherent in the half-in and half-out predicament of residents often prove the downfall of these facilities. In the future, some of these problems may be overcome by more comprehensive planning efforts and the introduction of various management strategies.

Key Words and Concepts

basic necessities

burnout

community protection

community residential center

community services

criminal contamination

emotional support

gate money

halfway house/community relations

intake

intervention programs

Irish system

management by objectives (MBO)

management information system (MIS)

minimum custody

mutual agreement programming (MAP)

per diem costs

PORT programs

prerelease centers

prereleasees

programming

recidivism

referral

reintegration

Relative Adjustment Scale

residential community corrections

Sir Walter Crofton

supportive programs

target population

6. Assume an inmate was going to be released into your community. How much gate money would be necessary to support this inmate while he or she became self-reliant? How would placement in a halfway house change that financial need?

Questions for Discussion

1. What structural and historical issues have made the halfway house so diverse and difficult to describe?

2. What are some of the many ways the halfway house can benefit the offender? How may these programs benefit the community as well?

3. What are the different models of operation for the halfway house? What do these models say about the goals of halfway houses?

4. Which type of offender is usually excluded from halfway house participation? Make arguments both for and against this practice of exclusion.

5. Why do many inmates resist the process of reintegration? How do they view the process?

For Further Reading

Allen, Harry E., et al., *Halfway Houses* (Washington, D.C.: U.S. Government Printing Office, 1978).

Keller, Oliver J., and Benedict S. Alper, *Halfway Houses: Community-Centered Correction and Treatment* (Lexington, Mass.: Lexington Books, 1970).

Parent, Dale, *Residential Community Corrections: Developing an Integrated Corrections Policy* (Longmont, Colo.: National Institute of Corrections, 1990).

Parker, Ann, et al., *So You Want to Start a Community Corrections Project* (Hackensack, N.J.: National Council on Crime and Delinquency, 1974).

U.S. Bureau of Prisons, *The Residential Center—Corrections in the Community* (Washington, D.C.: U.S. Government Printing Office, 1973).

Part Three

Supervising Special Populations

Chapter 9   Problems and Needs of Drug- and Alcohol-
             Abusing Offenders

Chapter 10   Special Problem Offenders: Mentally Ill and
             Sex Offenders in Community Corrections

Chapter 11   Problems and Needs of Female Offenders

Chapter 12   Programs for Juveniles

Chapter 9

Problems and Needs of Drug- and Alcohol-Abusing Offenders

Special Problems of Drug Abusers

Treatment of Drug Abusers

Special Problems of Alcohol Abusers

Treatment of Alcoholics and Problem Drinkers

Community-Based Correctional Programs for Alcoholic Offenders

The Effectiveness of Alcohol Treatment

Summary

Criminal offenders often abuse drugs or alcohol, and their drinking or drug-taking problems are usually closely associated with their criminal behavior. Law-abiding behavior can rarely be promoted among drug and alcohol abusers unless an effort is also made to help them manage and cope with their substance abuse. Community-based correctional programs are especially important in this effort because effective treatment must prepare drug abusers and problem drinkers to handle the pressures and responsibilities of freedom without resorting to substance abuse. To be meaningful, drug and alcohol treatment must prepare the offender for life in the community. Effective rehabilitation thus requires community-based programming.

Special Problems of Drug Abusers

Drug Abuse and Crime

One of the most significant and difficult problems facing the criminal justice system is the problem of the drug-abusing offender. Both violent and economic crime are linked to illicit substance abuse. Barbiturate and amphetamine use tends to be associated with assaultive behavior. Barbiturate use can produce the same type of violence that often results from alcohol intoxication.[1] Most directly linked to criminal behavior is the problem of narcotics use, which is associated with both violent and nonviolent forms of economic crime. Traditionally, narcotics

Table 9-1   Levels of Prior Drug Use by State Prisoners,
by Type of Drug and Frequency of Use, 1991 and 1997

Type of Drug	Ever Used in the Past		Ever Used Drugs Regularly[a]		Used Drugs in the Month Prior to Offense		Used Drugs at the Time of Offense	
	1991	1997	1991	1997	1991	1997	1991	1997
Any drug[b]	79.4%	83.0%	62.2%	69.6%	49.9%	56.5%	31.0%	32.6%
Marijuana/hashish	73.8	77.0	51.9	58.3	32.2	39.2	11.4	15.1
Cocaine/crack	49.4	49.2	31.9	33.6	25.2	25.0	14.5	14.8
Heroin/opiates	25.2	24.5	15.3	15.0	9.6	9.2	5.8	5.6
Depressants[c]	24.0	23.7	10.8	11.3	3.8	5.1	1.0	1.8
Stimulants[d]	29.7	28.3	16.6	16.3	7.4	9.0	2.9	4.2
Hallucinogens[e]	26.9	28.7	11.5	11.3	3.7	4.0	1.6	1.8
Inhalants	NA	14.4	NA	5.4	NA	1.0	NA	NA

Note: Detail adds to more than total because prisoners may have used more than
one type of drug.

[a]Used drugs once a week or more for at least a month.

[b]Other unspecified drugs are included in the totals.

[c]Includes barbiturates, tranquilizers, and Quaalude.

[d]Includes amphetamine and methamphetamine.

[e]Includes LSD and PCP.

Source: U.S. Department of Justice, Bureau of Justice Statistics, *Substance Abuse
and Treatment, State and Federal Prisoners, 1997,* Special Report NCJ-172871
(Washington, D.C.: U.S. Department of Justice, January 1999), p. 3, Table 2.

users have preferred income-producing crimes that require no violent confrontation, such as shoplifting or drug sales. Addicts also engage in prostitution when desperate to obtain funds. However, addicts have been known to resort to street robberies (muggings) and other crimes that run the risk of victim confrontation (for example, burglary).

Evidence shows that addict crime is becoming increasingly violent. One researcher noted after a review of recent studies: "Probably as many as two-thirds of all addicts now engage in crimes against persons (usually muggings and armed robberies) and as many as one-third of all addicts commit these crimes as their primary means of support."[2] The increasingly violent nature of addict crime seems to be the result of the younger addict's opportunistic approach to crime. Unskilled and impulsive, these offenders tend to pursue any activity likely to provide economic gain.

Unlike prior generations of narcotics users, a large proportion of today's addict population

engaged in criminal behavior before using narcotics.[3] After the onset of addiction, criminality tends to increase and to focus on income-producing activities.[4] One other factor distinguishes contemporary opiate users from previous generations of addicts. Many of today's narcotics addicts are **polydrug users,** persons who regularly use more than one controlled substance or who combine alcohol abuse with illicit drug use. Often these individuals can switch to other drugs with relative ease to regulate their habits or to deal with a temporary reduction in the narcotics supply. This ability to substitute one drug for another (usually methadone or barbiturates for heroin) may make the individual's addiction problem more difficult to treat. Polydrug users, when compared with street addicts, engage in criminal behavior at an earlier age and are subsequently more diverse in their criminal activities (Table 9-1).[5] The 1980s also witnessed the emergence of various new illicit drugs, such as crack (cocaine that has been processed into a rocklike substance) and ice.

Issues in Community Corrections

Fact Sheet: Methamphetamine

Ice *v.* Meth

Methamphetamine originated in Japan in 1919. Ice is a new, smokeable form of methamphetamine. While Ice and "Crystal Meth" are chemically the same, they are structurally different. Ice is a crystalline form of methamphetamine that is high in purity (90–100 percent). It is similar in size and appearance to quartz or rock salt. Crystal Meth, while it is called "crystal," is usually obtained in a powder form and in varying levels of purity. Both Ice and Crystal Meth can be smoked. While the effects of Crystal Meth last two to four hours, the duration of an Ice-high is said to last anywhere from seven to twenty-four hours. Crystal Meth is typically injected, snorted, or ingested orally (in pill form).

Use of any form of methamphetamine results in intense euphoria and tremendous energy. There have been reports of paranoid and violent behavior with prolonged usage. Because the purity of Ice is greater, these effects are intensified. Ice has also been reported to cause nausea, vomiting, rapid respiratory and cardiac rates, increased body temperature, and coma at high dosage levels. Overdoses are common since it is difficult for the users to control the amount of smoke being inhaled. Since 1985, there have been thirty-two deaths attributed to Ice in Honolulu. In the first six months of 1989, there were twelve deaths.

Availability of Ice   Current law enforcement intelligence indicates that Ice is primarily found in Hawaii. Within the last year, Ice has become available on the mainland of the United States. In San Francisco two seizures have been made. While there have been no seizures of Ice in San Diego or Los Angeles, Ice is re-

portedly available on a limited basis in these cities. The DEA [Drug Enforcement Administration] Seattle Division has also made two small seizures of Ice. In October 1989, DEA agents in New York seized 900 grams of Ice from two Korean traffickers, one of whom claimed that he was able to supply ten to twenty kilograms of Ice per month to the United States.

Ice Traffickers   While other forms of methamphetamine are primarily produced domestically, Ice is produced in Hong Kong, Korea, Japan, Taiwan, Thailand, and the Philippines. There have been no confirmed reports of domestic manufacture of Ice; however, DEA reports suggest that "Asian chemists" have operated a lab in Portland, Oregon, which later moved to the Los Angeles area.

The trafficking of Ice appears to be tightly controlled by a small group of Asians and affiliated gangs. The groups tend to be organized along ethnic lines. The principal trafficking groups are the Vietnamese, Filipinos, and Chinese. For these reasons, intelligence analysts suggest that states having large Asian communities will be among the first to report widespread availability and use. This can be monitored by tracking such indicators as methamphetamine-related treatment admissions and emergency room incidents and seizures of the drug by law enforcement agencies. Additionally, the National Institute of Justice-sponsored Drug Use Forecasting (DUF) program, a survey of drug use by arrestees, has added a section to the questionnaire designed to track Ice use.

Source: Bureau of Justice Statistics, *Drugs and Crime Data* (Washington, D.C.: U.S. Department of Justice, 1989)

Issues in Community Corrections

Emerging Drugs

Methamphetamine, LSD and the benzodiazepine Rohypnol are the emerging drugs also mentioned in Connecticut, Maryland, New York, and Washington, D.C.

Ethnographers and/or police in Los Angeles, Atlanta, El Paso, Denver, Newark, Trenton and D.C. mentioned problems associated with increased methamphetamine use. Some users are young, often middle income and use methamphetamine as part of a battery of "party drugs," which often include LSD, marijuana, Ketamine, and alcohol. Methamphetamine is available in powdered form and either injected or snorted like cocaine. While methamphetamine has been a serious problem in the West and Southwest for a number of years, its increasing availability from domestic laboratories and the abundant supply of the drug and/or its chemical precursors from Mexico, have encouraged markets outside those areas. In areas like New York, New Jersey, and Delaware methamphetamine use has in the past been confined to a small but dedicated group of older users, referred to as "bikers users" because of a frequent association with motorcycle clubs. In the past year, however, methamphetamine is reported as part of raves (all night dancing parties) and as part of a number of drugs used by college aged students.

Even in areas like Southern California, the popularity and availability of methamphetamine was still rising. Emergency room deaths in Los Angeles related to methamphetamine use have increased dramatically in the last year; and police sources in Los Angeles reported that the street-level price of methamphetamine has been dropping steadily as Mexican sources flood the market.

Hallucinogens continued to be popular among teens and young adults in New York, Denver, Newark, and Washington, D.C. The popularity of hallucinogens is particularly high in suburban areas and among young adults active in "the club scene," i.e., those who frequent music clubs catering to young adults. Drugs such as MDMA, LSD, and Ketamine ("Special K") may also be used as part of the "club scene" activity; and in Delaware, New York, Atlanta, and Chicago, heroin was mentioned as increasingly acceptable as one of the drugs used by this group. The Miami ethnographer noted that while LSD was popular among these young adults months ago, it has been replaced by MDMA and Rohypnol.

According to the Delaware ethnographer, LSD was still popular among teens and young adults in that area. LSD users there were reported to take two to five "hits" or doses at a time to achieve a drunken and highly hallucinogenic effect. They also were combining or sequencing LSD with MDMA ("candy flipping") to produce different effects over the course of an evening.

The Narcotics User: A Portrait in Diversity

The characterization of the criminality of narcotics users pertains only to chronic, habitual users who are addicted to narcotics. **Drug addiction** has been defined as a state of periodic or chronic intoxication produced by the repeated consumption of a drug (natural or synthetic). Its characteristics include

Police in the D.C. area reported that LSD is in limited supply in most parts of the district, but is plentiful in the surrounding suburban areas of Maryland and Virginia. It sells for approximately $5 a dose and is available in $100 units. D.C. police also reported the appearance of a new form of LSD paper, which is a variant on the more common blotter paper. The new "tape" on which doses of LSD are sold, is approximately 1/4 inch wide and twenty inches long; a single dose is contained on a 1/4 inch square of the tape. Maryland police noted that uncovering LSD dealers is particularly difficult given the nature of the market. Since most transactions occur among young, suburban users known to each other, older police officers working undercover automatically appear suspicious.

PCP (phencyclidine), a drug whose use had been generally confined to the D.C. area for several years, is reported by ethnographers and police contacts in the Northeast this quarter. In New York, PCP has appeared in $10 units with brand name markings like "Crazy Eddie." In D.C., police report that New York, Canada, and California are sources of PCP to their area. Prices in the D.C. area are stable at $3–5/treated cigarette, $30–40/gram, $300–500/ounce and $350–500/ounce of treated marijuana.

Ketamine hydrochloride (Ketamine, Ketalar or "Special K") is a tranquilizer used in veterinary medicine chemically similar to phencyclidine. While there are some uses in humans as an anesthetic, inappropriate doses produce sedation and hallucinogenic effects. In large doses it can produce vomiting and convulsions. While it has been reported in New York for over two years, it is now reported as a "club drug" popular in New Jersey, Delaware, D.C., Florida and Georgia.

According to police and DEA [Drug Enforcement Administration] sources, Ketamine is diverted to the illicit market from veterinary sources. It may be in liquid or powdered form, packaged in baggies or capsules for sale. While it is possible to inject Ketamine, it is generally snorted in a powdered form. Because of its appearance, Ketamine is often mistaken for cocaine or crystal methamphetamine. A "hit" or dose costs approximately $20.

Rohypnol, discussed in the last Pulse Check, is again reported in Texas, Florida and Delaware. Ethnographers in Texas and Florida report that local law enforcement agents are seizing more Rohypnol tablets, often still in the manufacturers' packaging. The Delaware ethnographer reported that area young users advertise the popularity of Rohypnol on T-shirts with the formula for Rohypnol and Ketamine emblazoned on the front.

Source: National Trends in Drug Abuse: Emerging Drugs (Washington, D.C.: National Office of Drug Control Policy, 1996).

(1) an overpowering desire or need (compulsion) to continue taking the drug and to obtain it by any means; (2) a tendency to increase the dose; (3) a psychic (psychological) and generally a physical dependence on the effects of the drug; and (4) an effect detrimental to the individual and to society.[6]

Two additional concepts are often used to define addiction. **Tolerance** refers to the addict's need to increase the dosage of the drug to continue to achieve its desired effects. **Withdrawal** refers to the onset of painful physical and psychological symptoms when drug use is discontinued. Addiction produces biological (tolerance and withdrawal), psychological (compulsion and dependence), and social effects.

Many misconceptions exist about both addiction and addicts. Contrary to popular belief, all narcotics users are not addicts. Many heroin users are only occasional users, referred to as **chippers.**[7] Chippers use narcotics in a recreational fashion, on weekends and special occasions, and are able to "regulate their use of heroin in much the way social drinkers regulate their intake of alcohol."[8] Many persons who first used heroin in Vietnam fit this pattern of use. Today, there are an estimated two or three occasional users for each narcotics addict.[9]

Addiction must be viewed as a process, "a sequence of experiences through which an individual acquires a meaningful conception of drug use behavior and its situational contexts."[10] One does not immediately become addicted to heroin after one euphoric experience. Many people experience nausea and considerable discomfort after their initial contact with the drug. Normally, prenarcotics addicts are introduced to heroin by drug users they admire; wishing to gain their respect, they try narcotics. In other cases, individuals who wish to experiment with narcotics seek out known drug users.[11] In either situation, would-be users must prove themselves to be cool and trustworthy to the established heroin users. They must also learn the mechanics of narcotics use, how to recognize and experience the high, and, finally, how to maintain a constant supply of narcotics when and if dependence develops. Continued regular use is required to achieve addiction.

Characteristics of Narcotics Addicts

Most narcotics addicts live in urban areas characterized by poverty, high crime and delinquency rates, and a high concentration of minority groups.[12] Although heroin use can be found in almost every American city, narcotics addiction tends to be concentrated in the northeastern United States.

The families of heroin addicts tend to be disturbed and severely troubled. Alcoholism and physical and mental illness are frequently present. In such families, children learn few prosocial values or interpersonal skills.[13] Chein et al., who conducted an intensive study of addicts and their families, report:

> In almost all addict families, there was a disturbed relationship between the parents, as evidenced by separation, divorce, open hostility, or lack of warmth and mutual interest. . . .
>
> The families of the addicts did not provide a setting that would facilitate the acceptance of discipline or the development of personal behavioral controls. The standards of conduct offered by the parents were usually vague or inconsistent; the addicts had characteristically been overindulged, over frustrated, or experienced vacillation between overindulgence and over frustration.[14]

Although most addicts possess normal intelligence, their educational backgrounds are similarly deficient. Most fail to complete high school, and many never attend.[15]

The Addict Personality

Although narcotics addicts share certain residential, familial, and educational disadvantages, no single addict personality has been identified. Studies of addicts' needs, values, attitudes, and self-concepts have yielded contradictory results. Although most addicts exhibit symptoms of various personality disorders, determining whether such personality traits preceded or resulted from addiction is rarely possible. No trait or combination of characteristics has been found to be unique to the addict. Individuals exhibiting personality disorders similar to those of addicts frequently live drug-free lives.

Causes and Purposes of Drug Addiction

Attempts to identify the causes of narcotics addiction have proven to be more successful than efforts to isolate the causes of crime or to describe the addict's personality. A number of theories have been proposed to explain certain aspects of addiction among certain types of narcotics users, but no single theory can account for every addict's problem.

The popular view is that heroin is used for one or more of the following reasons:

1. Its euphoric qualities.

2. Ignorance of the effects of long-term use.

3. The relief of pain, anxiety, or depression.

4. To escape from the demands of the real world.

5. To become part of the "in" group.

6. As a step up from other drugs.

7. Peer group pressure.[16]

The idea that narcotics addiction offers anything of value to the heroin user may seem somewhat farfetched, but this is the principal focus of learning theories. Drug abuse is a purposeful activity that is designed to achieve specific rewards. The range and complexity of what has been referred to as the purposes of addiction are not readily apparent, however, until one considers the addict as he or she functions in his or her world—the street.

Preble and Casey, who have studied not only black and Puerto Rican addicts but Irish, Italian, and Jewish drug users as well, report the following:

Addicts actively engage in meaningful activities and relationships seven days a week. The brief moments of euphoria after each administration of a small amount of heroin constitute a small fraction of their daily lives. The rest of the time they are aggressively pursuing a career that is exacting, challenging, adventurous, and rewarding. They are always on the move and must be alert, flexible, and resourceful. The surest way to identify heroin users in a slum neighborhood is to observe the way people walk. The heroin user walks with a fast, purposeful stride, as if he is late for an important appointment—indeed, he is. He is hustling (robbing or stealing), trying to sell stolen goods, avoiding the police, looking for a heroin dealer with a good bag (the street detail unit of heroin), coming back from copping (buying heroin), looking for a safe place to take the drug, or looking for someone who beat (cheated) him—among other things. He is, in short, taking care of business, a phrase that is so common with heroin users that they use it in response to words of greeting, such as "how you doing?" and "what's happening?" Taking care of biz is the common abbreviation. Ripping and running is an older phrase that also refers to their busy lives. For them, if not for their middle and upper-class counterparts (a small minority of opiate addicts), the quest for heroin is the quest for a meaningful life, not an escape from life. And the meaning does not lie, primarily, in the effects of the drug on their minds and bodies; it lies in the gratification of accomplishing a series of challenging, exciting tasks, every day of the week.[17]

Typical of the New York street addict is one who reported: "When I'm on the way home with the bag safely in my pocket, and I haven't been caught stealing all day, and I didn't get beat and the cops didn't get me—I feel like a working man coming home; he's worked hard, but he knows he's done something." This addict continued, "The feeling of hard work rewarded by accomplishment was strong even though I know it's not true."[18]

Only when one considers the strong appeal of **street life,** and the purposeful existence it provides to individuals who otherwise feel that their lives are meaningless, can the difficulty of drug treatment be fully understood. The overwhelming strength of the habit of addiction becomes apparent when this factor is added to other purposes of addiction, such as:

1. Removing the addict from an environment with which he or she cannot cope.

2. Decreasing anxiety and depression resulting from actual or perceived failure to cope with reality.

3. Establishing or enhancing self-esteem through membership and acceptance in an esteemed peer group.

4. Attempting to cope through the use of heroin as a crutch.[19]

Issues in Community Corrections

I Did Drugs Until They Wore Me Out, Then I Stopped

Mike Posey
San Diego, Calif.

I have to laugh at the debate over what to do about the drug problem. Everyone is running around offering solutions—from making drug use a more serious criminal offense to legalizing it. But there isn't a real solution. I know that. I used and abused drugs, and people, and society, for two decades. Nothing worked to get me to stop all that behavior except just plain being sick and tired. Nothing. No threats, no ten-plus years in prison, not anything that was said to me. I used until I got through. Period. And that's when you'll win the war. When all the dope fiends are done. Not a minute before.

Any real dope freak will continue to use drugs until he has had all the drugs he can take. Meanwhile, he either dies, goes crazy or goes to jail. Those are the options. Every addict knows where he's going. No surprises. But the seduction of the drugs is more powerful than anything that you, someone who has never done it, can ever begin to imagine.

One day, though, if you live, there comes the time when it doesn't work anymore. It just doesn't do it. The feeling is harder to get and harder to keep chasing. You've gotten old.

I was 40. Old and worn out. I used until I just couldn't anymore. Then, I said the only prayer I ever knew: "God, help me. . . ."

Unfortunately, most dope addicts never live to do that, and most don't want to. In all the more than twenty years of my insanity, I never once considered anything except where to get off on drugs and how much it might cost.

Obtaining the money wasn't a problem. I could always find the money. I spent many years in prison as a result of that obsessive search for the bread to get off. I spent many days in prison waiting to get out, to get off just that one more time, knowing that, after a few years, it would be really righteous. I didn't once consider the consequences, and even if I had, I would have done what I had to do. Dope is the most potent motivator known to my experience, and it looks like things haven't changed much since I stopped.

There is only a war if everyone is fighting. I don't see the average dope fiend fighting. If a dope fiend can get high without hurting anyone, that's nice. If he has to cut your throat,

Postaddiction Syndrome

A Consumers Union report on licit and illicit drugs offers a dramatic and explicit description of **postaddiction syndrome**—the discomforting symptoms that continue to plague narcotics addicts long after the physical effects of withdrawal have subsided:

Most addicts who mainline heroin, when asked what happens when they "kick the habit," describe the classic withdrawal syndrome—nausea, vomiting, aches and pains, yawning, sneezing, and so on. When asked what happens after withdrawal, they describe an equally specific "post addiction syndrome"—a wavering, unstable composite of anxiety, depression, and craving for the drug. The craving is not continuous but seems to come and go in waves of varying intensity, for months, even years, after withdrawal. It is particularly likely to return in moments of emotional stress. Following an intense wave of craving, drug-seeking behavior is likely to

well, that's fine too. But mostly a dope fiend doesn't want anything except to get high and get by. Nothing more. No place to stay, no job, no kids, no responsibility.

Just say no: What an idea! I wonder why I didn't think of that twenty-five years ago, when I started. I wonder where that thought went. The first time I shot dope and I felt that stuff hit my head and my body convulsed, the best feeling I ever had in my life came over me. I was on top for a couple of hours. No pain. No nothing. That's where the idea went. It went out with all the pain, and the other factors common to addicts.

I started a quarter century ago. I'm old now. I haven't taken a drink of alcohol or used a drug in some years. I had my prayer answered. I'm clean and sober. Sure, I feel better. I look better. I have a wife, and I write, and I am able to be a part of society. But I'm still a dope fiend at heart. And I know full well this "war" is a loser.

You can't expect every dope fiend in the U.S. to quit like I did and never use again. And until all of them quit, there will be a market.

I shot dope until a few years ago, unabated. Even in prison, I managed to stay loaded. Nothing can stop a dope fiend from getting stoned. The dope came in with guys' girls visiting. I saw them fiddle it out from under their dresses in the visiting room. We'd get up in our little cubicles and shoot that wonderful stuff with needles made from light bulb filaments.

When I was on the streets, I did $100 a day, every day. I managed to hustle that C-note every day. I woke up every morning needing to go cop some. Hustling and stealing and conning and boosting and rolling drunks, until I'd make it to the man's house and get the four bags I needed. From there I would go and get high and nod and forget how awful life was.

San Diego, New York City or Davenport, Iowa. A dope fiend is a dope fiend. Nothing changes except the stage. The players will always be there. Good luck on your war. I'm just glad I ain't fighting it anymore.

Source: Mike Posey, "I Did Drugs Until They Wore Me Out, Then I Stopped," *New York Times,* December 15, 1989, p. 31. Copyright © 1989 by The New York Times Company. Reprinted by permission.

set in, and the ex-addict relapses. When asked how he feels following a return to heroin, he is likely to reply, "it makes me feel normal again"—that is, it relieves the ex-addict's chronic triad of anxiety, depression, and craving.

It is this view—that an addict takes heroin in order to "feel normal"—that is hardest for a nonaddict to understand and to believe. Yet it is consonant with everything else that is known about narcotics addiction—and there is not a scrap of scientific evidence to impugn the addict's own view. The ex-addict who returns to heroin, if this view is accepted, is not a pleasure-craving hedonist but an anxious, depressed patient who desperately craves a return to a normal mood and state of mind.[20]

The ex-addict who seeks a return to normality is likely to relapse into narcotics use. This likelihood of relapse may be the greatest problem faced in drug treatment programs today. Having achieved the necessary motivation to abstain from narcotics long enough to pass through the withdrawal stage, the addict must then cope with a lingering craving for heroin. This craving may appear days, weeks, or months after the last use of the drug. Because it is unpredictable, it is almost impossible to control.

If long-term **abstinence** is to be achieved, a drug treatment strategy must contain counseling and support services designed to achieve two related goals: (1) reduce the addict's desire to seek out the purposes of narcotics use or to make these purposes seem less appealing and (2) promote the development of the internal controls necessary to withstand a continued desire for narcotics.

Treatment of Drug Abusers

According to the National Institute of Drug Abuse, approximately one million people are in treatment programs today. More than half of these people are receiving treatment as outpatients. The United States has several thousand drug treatment programs. The programs are operated by government and nongovernment agencies; some are hospital affiliated, many are not. Further, drug treatment programs can be divided into those that operate for profit and those that are nonprofit. The for-profit programs generally draw insurance-supported referrals, while the nonprofit programs accept a wide variety of clientele. The crack (rock cocaine) epidemic that swept through the United States in the second half of the 1980s overwhelmed the existing capacity of nonprofit programs, and in many cities long waiting lists still exist for admission to those facilities.

Five major forms of drug treatment are currently available: methadone maintenance, therapeutic communities, outpatient drug-free programs, detoxification programs, and correctional programs. Methadone maintenance and therapeutic community programs are the most widely employed narcotics treatment modalities. Outpatient drug-free programs primarily serve nonaddicts. Detoxification programs offer short-term medical assistance to narcotics addicts during the period of withdrawal. And community-based correctional programs are designed specifically for narcotics addicts.

Methadone Maintenance

Methadone is a long-acting synthetic narcotics substitute. After the appropriate daily dosage has been established, it blocks the effects of heroin taken by the methadone user. Methadone produces no side effects and can be orally self-administered, thus making its ingestion a simple matter. No needle and syringe that might remind the addict of his or her former heroin use are required.

Special outpatient clinics provide addicts with methadone. Medical personnel determine each patient's dosage and supervise daily drug administration. Methadone clinics normally consist of a medical unit, with offices for physicians, a common room for group therapy, and several smaller counseling rooms.

Methadone may be used to facilitate detoxification, as a permanent alternative to heroin use, or as a bridge to total drug abstinence. At present, more than seventy-five thousand former heroin addicts receive daily doses of methadone.[21] Whether used as a temporary or permanent alternative to heroin, methadone permits the addict to utilize the time previously spent securing drugs in a more constructive fashion. Research indicates that methadone users reduce their criminal behavior and increase their educational and employment achievement. **Methadone maintenance** appears to be more effective with older narcotics addicts and anxious, compliant, employable individuals from stable families. These persons seem to perform especially well in programs that emphasize middle-class values and productive behavior.[22]

Despite the effectiveness and low cost of methadone maintenance, the treatment has received considerable criticism. Some of this criticism is based on philosophical grounds. Objections have been raised to the concept of curing heroin addicts by helping them become addicted to a substitute narcotic. Critics suggest that the goal of treatment should be total abstinence, not enslavement to another drug.

Other criticisms of methadone maintenance are prompted by more practical concerns. Observers have noted that addicts often use methadone to regulate their habits. They can decrease their heroin consumption by taking methadone with wine and pills. The wine and pills reduce methadone's ability to block the effects of the heroin.[23] Because most methadone clinics require patients to submit urine specimens for testing for signs of heroin use, addicts wishing to use methadone while continuing their heroin habits must take special measures to avoid detection by program staff. Such addicts often pay nonaddicts for "clean" urine specimens to substitute for their own "dirty" ones.[24] Recent changes in collection procedures have made this substitution more difficult. Cups that change color when warmed by the urine betray those addicts who are attempting to fool the test. Some enterprising addicts have even resorted to using a catheter to pump clean urine into their bladder (a process known as doping) to fool some of the more strict urinalysis procedures.

The problems created by persons who enter methadone treatment for nontherapeutic purposes are particularly acute in large-scale methadone clinics that inadequately supervise their patients. The solution to these difficulties lies in efforts to screen prospective methadone patients more carefully and to supervise the urine testing and methadone administration more rigorously.

Although methadone maintenance is demonstrably effective in reducing in-treatment criminality, as many as 70 percent of all methadone users eventually return to illicit drug use.[25] Considering the purposes of addiction, this finding

is not surprising. Methadone maintenance treatment must be combined with supportive therapy if clients are to learn how to use their newfound time and energy. Methadone users must establish new personal goals and be offered guidance if they are to learn how to accomplish their newly defined objectives.[26] Without such aid, they may choose to return to the well-defined goals and highly structured life of the heroin addict.

Therapeutic Communities

Therapeutic communities are drug-free communes often staffed by former narcotics addicts. Separate dormitories or suites of rooms are provided for males and females. Additional facilities may include a family-oriented kitchen and dining room, recreational areas, and space for individual and group counseling.

In therapeutic communities, drug abuse is normally regarded as a symptom of a deeper personal problem. **Confrontational therapy** and peer pressure are often employed to change the attitudes, values, and behavior that promote drug dependence.[27] New residents are verbally attacked by fellow residents at group meetings and are criticized for any form of irresponsible behavior. Within the community, drug use is viewed as the height of irresponsibility. The objective of these confrontations is to strip away drug users' defenses and prohibit the rationalization of irresponsible behavior.

Following the tearing-down process, building up begins. After initially performing only menial chores in the community, more important (that is, responsible) tasks are assigned to residents who have learned to level with themselves and others. The residents develop self-esteem and feelings of personal worth as they gradually become accepted as functioning members of the community.

The most widely publicized therapeutic communities today are Daytop Village, Odyssey House, Phoenix House, and the Delancey Street Foundation. These programs share the approach

Prison: A Self-Contained Treatment Community

Intensive treatment programs are a way to stop the revolving door for drug offenders, and they only add about $4,000 a year to the cost of incarceration. The 1994 Crime Bill authorizes $382 million for drug treatment in state and federal prisons over the next five years.

The Amity Righturn program in the R. J. Donovan Correctional Facility in San Diego is the only therapeutic community in California's prison system. Recidivism among its graduates is 25 percent lower than among inmates who do not participate in the program.

The 200 prisoners in the Amity program are housed in a separate cell block for a year, but they eat and exercise with other prisoners. All participants are assigned daily responsibilities and some receive wages for holding important jobs. When they are released from Donovan, Amity inmates can continue treatment at a nearby residential facility.

Since 1980 Amity has been running a similar program for thirty jail inmates in Pima County, Arizona. More than two-thirds of those who complete treatment report that they have not used any drugs or alcohol for at least six months following their release from jail. This demonstrates a significant break with the past, since participants in the Pima County program reported having used regularly for an average of fifteen years.

Source: "Keeping Score: What We Are Getting for Our Drug Control Dollars 1995," *Drug Strategies*, 1996.

to drug treatment described here, although there are important distinctions between them. Phoenix House and Odyssey House encourage residents to reenter society following treatment and attempt to facilitate reentry during the latter months of treatment. Odyssey House, unlike the other programs, uses professional personnel and has established special programs for adolescent addicts, gifted addicts, addicted parents, mentally disturbed addicts, and Vietnam veteran addicts.[28] The Delancey Street Foundation requires a two-year commitment from applicants, who must take a vow of poverty before entering the program. The foundation owns and operates several businesses that earn a monthly gross of $30,000.

In recent years, with crack sweeping the nation, the demand for the services of therapeutic communities has been considerable. Although programs have enjoyed a rebirth in the early 1990s, two as-yet-unsolved problems continue to plague virtually all of them. First, only a small percentage of addicts are appropriate clients for therapeutic communities. These drug-free and self-help programs reach only an estimated 2 percent of all heroin addicts.[29] The vast majority of addicts who enter the programs quickly drop out, unwilling or unable to withstand the harsh regimen, menial tasks, and verbal abuse that are essential elements of treatment.

Second, many of the persons helped by the therapeutic communities seem to become dependent upon the programs. They either never leave the community or become staff members in offshoots of the original program. It is unclear why this dependency develops. Individuals who conquer their drug problem may be

Program Focus

Learning Life Skills Through Delancey Street

The 1,000 Delancey Street residents have had rough times. On average, they have been hard-core drug addicts for ten years and have been incarcerated four times. Most are functionally illiterate and unskilled.

Delancey Street Foundation, a self-help residential education center, turns them around. After four years, they leave Delancey with a high school equivalency certificate and the vocational, interpersonal and social skills necessary to live drug-free in society. The organization does not conduct follow-up studies, but does keep in touch with its graduates. Some have gone on to become stockbrokers, lawyers, mechanics, truck drivers, real estate agents and city officials, including a deputy sheriff and a deputy coroner.

All of this is accomplished at no cost to taxpayers. There are no paid staff; the older residents help the newer ones, and everyone works. Delancey Street's operating funds come from its printing, sales, baking, catering, automotive and other services, which are run by the residents. The foundation opened in San Francisco in the early 1970s and now has facilities in Los Angeles, New Mexico, New York and North Carolina. Daily group therapy helps each patient better understand themselves and their disease. By sharing personal experiences, patients learn—often for the first time—to trust and seek help from friends and loved ones. Group sessions on grief, women's issues, the Steps of Alcoholics Anonymous, and other topics help patients recognize and begin to resolve personal barriers to recovery.

In individual counseling sessions counselor and patient work together to identify personal problems and set specific goals that will lead to a better life. These goals might include overcoming resentment, developing trust in others, or identifying self-defeating behaviors.

Source: "Keeping Score: What We Are Getting for Our Drug Control Dollars 1995," *Drug Strategies,* 1996.

unable to find the same level of acceptance and status in the outside world that they find within the therapeutic community. Or they may simply be substituting one dependency for another. Although it may be argued that dependence upon a therapeutic community is preferable to dependence upon heroin, the fact that only a fraction of all addicts can ever achieve even this goal reduces the therapeutic community's utility as a drug-abuse treatment strategy.

Therapeutic communities have rarely been subjected to rigorous evaluation. It has been suggested that the paucity of evaluation data is the result of their unwillingness to permit outsiders to learn about their high attrition rates and the difficulty their clients have in achieving a drug-free existence outside the commune. Although therapeutic communities are probably no more reluctant to be evaluated than other types of rehabilitation programs, in the past the perceived tendency toward secrecy has inhibited research.

It is hoped that future research efforts will meet with greater success. In the realm of drug treatment, no strategy has proved completely successful in achieving total and permanent

Program Focus

Bureau of Justice Assistance Fact Sheet: Treatment Accountability for Safer Communities

Created in 1972 with Federal funding authorized under the Drug Abuse and Treatment Act, Treatment Accountability for Safer Communities (TASC) is a program model designed to break the addiction-crime cycle of nonviolent, drug-involved offenders by linking the legal sanctions of the criminal justice system with the therapeutic interventions of drug treatment programs. TASC manages drug cases by moving the offender through the criminal justice process and into drug treatment, simultaneously providing monitoring services as an adjunct to criminal justice supervision. TASC comprehensive case management services create a unique interface among the criminal justice system, the treatment service system, and the offender, thus allowing for effective and efficient outcomes.

From 1986 through 1995, the Bureau of Justice Assistance (BJA) awarded grant funding to National TASC, the national membership organization that advocates the improvement and expansion of the TASC model to provide training and technical assistance to jurisdictions implementing TASC programs.

The TASC Model The TASC model comprises four discrete activities:

- Identification of drug-involved offenders to determine their appropriateness for referral by the criminal justice system into the TASC case management system.

- Assessment of the offender's drug and alcohol treatment needs.

- Referral of the offender to the appropriate drug treatment placement.

- Continuous case management of the offender, through reporting protocols, urine monitoring, and ancillary requirements, to ensure compliance with criminal justice orders and the drug treatment regimen.

A unique benefit of the TASC model is its ability to provide case management and treatment linkages at any point in the criminal justice continuum—from pretrial service agencies, the courts, jail treatment programs, probation agencies, and community corrections agencies involved in intermediate sanctions to reintegration of the offender into the community. TASC programs work to establish treatment accountability by ensuring that offenders receive the appropriate type and level of treatment and that the offender is attending treatment regu-

abstinence. The evaluation of therapeutic communities, methadone maintenance, and all other rehabilitation strategies can yield valuable insight into the problem of narcotics addiction and facilitate the development of more effective treatment alternatives.

Community-Based Correctional Programs for Narcotics Addicts

The most widely utilized community-based correctional programs for narcotics addicts on probation or parole are specialized supervision

larly, treatment is progressing, and the agency to which TASC referred the offender is providing effective treatment services.

The TASC model can be replicated in urban, suburban, and rural jurisdictions, and it can be applied to unique requirements of special populations, such as female and juvenile offenders. The model is built around 10 critical organizational and operational elements that provide foundation and structure to link TASC to the criminal justice and drug treatment systems. These elements are as follows:

TASC Organizational Elements

- A broad base of support from the criminal justice system, with a formal system for effective communication.

- A broad base of support from the treatment community, with a formal system for effective communication.

- An independent TASC unit, with a designated administrator.

- Staff training, as outlined in TASC policies and procedures.

- A system of data collection for program management and evaluation.

TASC Operational Elements

- Explicit and agreed upon eligibility criteria.

- Screening procedures for the early identification of eligible offenders.

- Documented procedures for assessment and referral.

- Documented policies, procedures, and technology for drug testing.

- Procedures for offender monitoring with established success and failure criteria and procedures for regular reporting to the criminal justice referral source.

Source: U.S. Department of Justice, Bureau of Justice Assistance, Office of Justice Programs.

programs and halfway houses. In addition, more than fifty-five cities have established Treatment Alternatives to Street Crime projects that link criminal justice system clients and noncorrectional, community-based drug treatment programs.

Most community supervision programs share a common feature—an attempt to use the coercive force of the criminal justice system to encourage offenders to commit themselves to rehabilitation. Generally, offenders are required to provide urine samples to the

Issues in Community Corrections

Probation Work with Drug Offenders

Since I'm a drug testing officer, all my contacts with clients have to be on a surprise basis. I contact people in the office or their homes or on their jobs. Sometimes we meet at someone's house or a restaurant. I go out quite a bit. My theory is that you don't know what's going on until you get out there on the street and see where it's coming from.

Yesterday, I found that I had two people whose tests showed that they had been using heroin. I have to get these people into the office to find out how much heroin they have taken and what to do about it.

If the drug use is out of control, I'll try to get them into a hospital or a drug program. I'll try to get them off the street one way or another. Somewhere along the line I have to make a decision about what to do with a client.

Naturally, you have to get them drug-free one way or another. This can mean going to jail. But usually there are several choices besides jail. You put them into a hospital. You let the judge know what you're doing. If a person is a threat to other people, you get him into a position where he no longer is a threat.

When I get back from lunch, the office is usually full. I talk to spouses and parents of people in jail. They wonder how their relatives are doing. I study some new cases coming up. A lawyer calls me about what I intend to recommend on a certain case. I write another report and by now it's 3:30 P.M.

The first person whose tests showed he was on heroin comes in. Not only is he back on heroin, but he's gotten arrested in someone's home for burglary. A new offense takes away a lot of your choices. I tell him I can recommend to the judge that he either goes to jail or gets into a drug treatment program. He takes the drug treatment program.

Around four, my clients start coming in. I take urine specimens and do skin tests. The urine test only works if the drug has been used in the last three or four days. But a needle mark stays on for three or four weeks. I have a magnifying flashlight and I look at the veins in their arms. You become very skilled at knowing how a person uses drugs.

Most of the people on probation are just average people. But there are some on probation who are hardcore, repeat offenders. I like to work with this kind, the heavy offender, the one who's been in trouble a long time.

I like crisis. I'm a good problem solver. My work is different, exciting. It gives me a chance to have a lot of contact with people. I was born and raised on the streets. I like the streets and I like the people. I like doing something a lot of people can't do.

Source: Constitutional Rights Foundation, *Criminal Justice* (New York: Scholastic Book Series, 1978), pp. 180–182. Reprinted by permission.

supervising agency for testing for drug use. This monitoring effort and the threat of revocation are designed to encourage offenders to make a serious attempt at abstinence. In addition, most probation and parole programs for narcotics addicts emphasize the offenders' general need to develop a sense of responsibility. Abstaining from narcotics use is one element of responsible behavior. Securing employment, supporting one's dependents, and participating in education or vocational training programs are also viewed as essentials of responsible living.

The Narcotic Treatment and Control Unit of the Los Angeles County Probation Department supervises Los Angeles County felons who have narcotics problems.[30] The program's goal is to overcome the probationer's dependence on narcotics and make him or her responsible for his or her actions. This aim is pursued through honest and direct counseling efforts that demonstrate respect for the client while showing that irresponsible behavior will not be tolerated.

Chemical testing for drug use is employed on a regular and surprise basis, and probationers regularly receive skin checks for injection sites. For most offenders using narcotics when placed on probation, detoxification occurs in the community.

Sometimes a halfway house has a kick pad, a place to live while experiencing the symptoms of withdrawal. Probation officers in the unit are especially knowledgeable about drug abuse patterns and characteristics. Realistic limits are placed on the offender's drug-using behavior; sporadic use may be tolerated, but the reestablishment of a narcotics habit is prohibited. Addicts are encouraged to be truthful about their narcotics use and to inform their probation officers if they violate probation regulations and use narcotics. An attempt is made to understand the factors that precipitated the incident of use and to utilize that information to avoid similar situations in the future.

The program takes a step-by-step approach to rehabilitation, focusing first on immediate difficulties, such as housing, food, and clothing. Long-term goals, such as family stability, a crime-free lifestyle, and an improved self-image are later addressed using a problem-solving approach.

Staff in the Narcotic Treatment and Control Unit must be capable of becoming intensely involved in their clients' lives. They must be flexible individuals who can treat their clients fairly, based on each individual's strengths and weaknesses. A psychiatrist assists the staff in developing self- and unit-awareness on a monthly basis. These consultations also serve cathartic purposes. Staff members are encouraged to ventilate their feelings regarding their extremely demanding and frustrating work.

The Narcotics and Drug Abuse Rehabilitation Program, located in Los Angeles, provides various treatment services on a contract basis to federal probationers and parolees. Most of the clients are male minority group members who never finished high school, have at least one prior felony conviction, and have a history of hard drug use.

The program provides individual and group counseling; crisis counseling is available on a twenty-four-hour-a-day basis. Job placement services are also offered. Clients may choose from a range of treatment modalities, including methadone detoxification, methadone maintenance, and the therapeutic community. The program is staffed by professionals, paraprofessionals, and graduate students. As in many drug treatment programs, many of the staff members are former narcotics users.

A three-month evaluation of the program indicated that at least four out of five participants are remaining drug-free. Over half the probationers and parolees are working or attending school or both. Counselor ratings reveal that about two-thirds of the clients are doing well. A two-year program assessment indicated that 12 percent of program participants are convicted of new offenses.[31]

An attempt to explain program successes and failures led its director and associate director to describe a feature of their client population that makes them resistant to treatment—what they refer to as an ingrained, manipulative lifestyle:

> We have observed time and again that after a considerable amount of time certain of our patients reach a point where they are able to work and earn a satisfactory income, that interpersonal relationships improve, and significant progress is made in dealing with their drug needs. It then seems as

Issues in Community Corrections

Narcotics Addicts on Parole

Alice is beaming. "I shampooed the rugs this morning," she proclaims proudly, as if she had swum the English Channel.

Sitting across from Alice in the cramped living room of a small apartment in San Bernardino, Calif., Gary Pena glances around at the gleaming ashtrays and uncluttered table tops. "Yeah, and you don't have a pile of dishes and garbage around like you used to," Pena says. "I'm proud of you."

"My old man likes it neat," Alice says.

"You got yourself a nice place, a little money, an old man who comes home every evening—that's where it's at," says Pena. "How long you been in this rat race, anyway?"

"Since '73," Alice sighs. "You know, it gets tiring, running from the law. And the drugs ain't no good anymore, either, they cut them so much."

Pena is a parole officer, and Alice is a narcotics addict under civil commitment. He must make sure that she has not reverted to heroin or, more importantly, crime. Alice, he feels, is doing well. "She needs a lot of structure and support," he says as he drives away. "She calls me twice a week just to say hello. She's on methadone and seeing a psychiatrist. But at any time she can say to hell with things and go back to using." In his car, Pena carries a pair of handcuffs and a supply of preaddressed, postage-paid bottles for mailing urine samples to a laboratory. These are for surprise tests, given in the field; each addict is also required to come in regularly for scheduled tests. A test will disclose whether a suspect has used heroin (or amphetamines, PCP, cocaine, or codeine) within a three-day period. If Pena is particularly suspicious that an addict is using, he will have the person come in for two tests each week.

"I grew up with hypes," says Pena, 35. His youth was spent in a barrio where drugs were part of the fabric of life. "My neighbors were hypes." He shrugs. "Everybody's chosen a different way to go."

In the afternoon, Pena drives out to visit one of his problem cases. Paul owes $75 a month in child support to his former wife, his current girlfriend is pregnant, and he doesn't have a job.

"You need a job," Pena tells him sternly. "I don't care if it's making a dollar an hour. . . ."

"$3.25 is the minimum now," Paul interjects, with the trace of a smirk on his face. This does not go over well with Pena.

though the life-style characteristics that are so deeply ingrained strike out and the patient is unable to tolerate his new-found stability and success. He may suddenly commit a burglary, or receive stolen goods, or use heroin, even though the gain for any of these activities is extremely small. It is our hypothesis that these individuals become frightened by their stable life-style and the ensuing sense of boredom, which is akin to a depression state, and they feel the need to do something to relieve this growing tension. This may reflect an inability to tol-

erate the negative feelings the person has about himself, which his previous manipulative, hustling life-style enabled him to avoid. This occurs when the addict becomes involved with obtaining drugs, avoiding arrest, and coping with the recurrent illness resulting from withdrawal. His life centers upon his drug-related routine and not upon his own feelings of inadequacy. When those feelings do arise, they can be explained away by the effect of drugs, lack of drugs, or "persecution" by law enforcement. In our experience, individuals who are severely dis-

"How come you're not motivated?" Pena asks. "You say you don't have a car to look for work. Well, the bus runs every day and it's only 35 cents."

"Sometimes I don't have 35 cents."

"I tell you what, you come down to the office tomorrow. You got thirty days to get you a job. I'm gonna give you written instructions to get a job."

Paul begins to protest. Pena cuts him off. "Don't give me excuses," he says. "Just do it."

Pena is more sympathetic toward another addict, Norman, who is afflicted with a chronic skin disease that keeps him in excruciating pain. His legs are swollen to twice their normal size, and he can barely walk. To top it off, his mother is slowly dying of cancer. Norman uses heroin to kill the pain. Pena says he is satisfied if Norman sticks to alcohol. "He's a broken-down guy," Pena says.

On his other visits, Pena counsels a mother whose son and daughter are both addicts. ("The psychiatrist said I raised him [her son] as a girl," she says mournfully. "It's been a heavy thing.") He gives one of his charges a ride to work, and checks in on an addict burglar who is taking a welding course. He jokes with a former prostitute who has found a "Sugar Daddy" to keep her, and only protests mildly that she is drunk. "At least it isn't eight o'clock in the morning," he says. Another ex-addict is living in a religious group home, waiting to go to Bible school. "Hey, you've come a long ways," Pena says. "Stay clean two years and get off the program. No way you can't do it." Pena checks his arms anyway and tells him to come in for a urine test.

Jack Steinbrunn, the district administrator in charge of Pena's region, tells his officers that an occasional "dirty" test is not grounds for return to the institution. "The main thing is to curtail criminality," Steinbrunn says. "The easiest thing out here is to find a way to lock 'em up. But you have to be pretty creative to come up with ways to keep them out on the streets." That, Steinbrunn says, is what being a parole officer is all about.

Source: Stephen Gettinger, "For Addicts, Parole Is Tougher," *Corrections Magazine,* 6 (2), 1980, pp. 48–49. Copyright 1980 by *Corrections Magazine* and Criminal Justice Publications Inc., 116 West 32nd Street, New York, N.Y. 10001.

turbed psychiatrically, or persons who have great difficulty giving up their manipulative, hustling life-style, are most likely to fail in a rehabilitative program.[32]

A nationwide program of drug treatment services is available for federal offenders on community supervision status. The federal program, which began in 1979, contracts with over several hundred community drug treatment programs to provide substance abuse services. In addition, intensive supervision is available within federal probation caseloads, and community resources are utilized on a no-fee, case-by-case basis.

Halfway houses for narcotics addicts may be directly administered by criminal justice personnel, or they may provide services on a contractual basis. Generally, these programs offer more than simple support services to narcotics addicts because of the seriousness of the addiction problem. Halfway houses typically use a modified version of attack therapy when a confrontational counseling approach is employed. Because client motivation is required if attack therapy is to be successful, the lack of motivation typical of persons coerced into treatment necessitates a more encouraging and less demoralizing therapeutic approach.

Working with unmotivated narcotics addicts is extremely demanding. When these offenders share a communal residence, a good chance exists that the least motivated offenders will subvert the treatment of those persons who are considering a commitment to abstinence. This tendency can lead to the development of a thriving drug subculture within the halfway house program. The establishment and maintenance of a rehabilitation ethic in such an environment requires a well-structured and supervised program. In addition, vigilance by staff members who understand themselves and their clients and are strong enough to deal honestly and fairly with persons who often push them to the limit of tolerance is an essential program component. The East Los Angeles Halfway House is an example of what can occur if a halfway house is poorly planned and implemented.

The East Los Angeles Halfway House was designed to provide paroled addict felons with a therapeutic transitional residence prior to release into the community. The National Institute of Mental Health program evaluation indicated that this goal was never achieved.[33] The program's failure was attributed partially to the design of the experiment. Inmates who were expecting to be released directly into the community were randomly selected to enter the halfway house instead of being freed. The members of the experimental group showed considerable resentment at being helped in such a coercive manner. When they learned that they were to be charged for their room and board in the halfway house, their fury grew.

The program was located in a Mexican-American barrio with a high incidence of narcotics addiction. The easy availability of drugs proved too tempting for many halfway house residents, who were confronted on a daily basis with the signs and symptoms of heroin use. The site of the program within the barrio caused additional difficulties. Because the building that housed the halfway house also served as the district parole office, the program gradually assumed an authoritarian character. This led to the use of official action in situations that might have better been managed in a more flexible and informal manner.

The program attempted to function as a therapeutic community, but because residents were not motivated to change their behavior, this objective proved impossible to achieve. When residents failed to act responsibly, staff were often indifferent. The staff members viewed the residents as sick. This angered the residents, but because they were afraid that complaints might negatively affect their parole evaluations, they maintained a resolute silence. This silence extended to group counseling sessions and thus nullified whatever benefits counseling might have achieved.

The failure of treatment efforts such as happened in Los Angeles is avoidable. The Massachusetts Department of Correction recently began releasing a small number of inmates to drug contract houses. These programs were designed to assist inmates in the transition to total freedom in the community. A variety of halfway houses, using different treatment strategies, currently serves Massachusetts offenders on a contractual basis.[34] Although the sample of subjects included in this evaluation was small, a comparison of the halfway house residents with persons released directly into the community indicated that persons released directly into the community usually recidivate at three times the rate of halfway house residents.

Special Problems of Alcohol Abusers

Alcohol and Crime

Alcohol consumption is linked to many forms of criminal behavior. Approximately one-third of all arrests are for alcohol-related crimes such as public drunkenness, disorderly conduct, vagrancy, driving while intoxicated, and liquor law violations. In addition, a significant number of violent crimes involve a drinking victim or offender. Although determining exactly how many murders, robberies, rapes, and assaults involve alcohol abuse is impossible, drinking clearly influences criminal activity in many ways.

A special report to Congress by the Department of Health, Education, and Welfare (now the Department of Health and Human Services) stated: "Alcohol can be involved in forming intent for a crime, in aggravating the course of a criminal event (for example, by triggering excess violence), or in affecting the outcome of a crime already completed (for example, by inhibiting the offender's escape)."[35] Research on the relationship between alcohol and crime has necessarily been limited to studies of the drinking behavior of arrested persons and prison inmates. This research provides a general picture of the role of alcohol consumption in particular forms of violence.

Research on Arrested Persons

Studies of alcohol-related violent crime reveal that both offenders and victims of such offenses are often drinking at the time of the offense.[36] The rate of alcohol involvement varies according to the type of crime examined and the particular methodology employed in the research study (Table 9-2). For crimes of robbery, as many as three-fourths of all offenders and 69 percent of the victims may have been drinking.

Research shows even higher rates of alcohol involvement in homicide cases. Some studies have found that more than four out of five homicides involve a drinking offender or victim. Assault, rape, marital violence, child abuse and neglect, and child molestation situations have all included high numbers of alcohol-consuming offenders. Studies of homicide indicate that nonwhite victims, especially males, are especially likely to have been drinking at the time of the offense. Victim-precipitated homicides, stabbings, and excessively violent murders are all highly associated with alcohol consumption. The majority of serious offenders were under the influence of alcohol or drugs at the time their offense occurred.

Studies of Prisoners

Studies of prison inmates reveal that drinking often precipitates not only violent crime but also property crime. Depending upon the measure of alcoholism used and the particular inmate population under study, as many as 83 percent of all prisoners report having a drinking problem.[37] On the average, inmates report a higher rate of drinking problems than is found in the general population.

To understand the influence of alcohol on crime, the effects of alcohol on the human body must be considered. In doing this, one major distinction must be recognized between the alcohol and crime and drugs and crime problems. Drug users normally engage in the greatest amount of crime after addiction has occurred. The one-time or occasional user of narcotics poses no special crime problem (other than possession of an illicit substance). However, any person may be influenced by alcohol in such a way that crime results. The social drinker, the problem drinker, and the chronic alcoholic may pose equal crime problems. Most alcohol-related violence probably results not from the outburst of the chronic alcoholic, but from the social drinker or the problem drinker who is still functioning in

Table 9-2 State and Federal Prisoners Reporting Alcohol or Drug Use at Time of Offense, by Type of Offense, 1997

Type of Offense	Estimated Number of Prisoners[a]		Percent of Prisoners Who Reported Being Under the Influence at Time of Offense					
			Alcohol		Drugs		Alcohol or Drugs	
	State	Federal	State	Federal	State	Federal	State	Federal
Total	1,046,705	88,018	37.2%	20.4%	32.6%	22.4%	52.5%	34.0%
Violent offenses	494,349	13,021	41.7	24.5	29.0	24.5	51.9	39.8
Murder	122,435	1,288	44.6	38.7	26.8	29.4	52.4	52.4
Negligent manslaughter	16,592	53	52.0	B	17.4	B	56.0	B
Sexual assault[b]	89,328	713	40.0	32.3	21.5	7.9	45.2	32.3
Robbery	148,001	8,770	37.4	18.0	39.9	27.8	55.6	37.6
Assault	97,897	1,151	45.1	46.0	24.2	13.8	51.8	50.5
Other violent	20,096	1,046	39.6	32.2	29.0	15.9	48.2	37.2
Property offenses	230,177	5,964	34.5	15.6	36.6	10.8	53.2	22.6
Burglary	111,884	294	37.2	B	38.4	B	55.7	B
Larceny/theft	43,936	414	33.7	B	38.4	B	54.2	B
Motor vehicle theft	19,279	216	32.2	B	39.0	B	51.2	B
Fraud	28,102	4,283	25.2	10.4	30.5	6.5	42.8	14.5
Other property	26,976	757	36.0	22.8	30.6	16.4	53.2	34.6
Drug offenses	216,254	55,069	27.4	19.8	41.9	25.0	52.4	34.6
Possession	92,373	10,094	29.6	21.3	42.6	25.1	53.9	36.0
Trafficking	117,926	40,053	25.5	19.4	41.0	25.9	50.9	35.0
Other drug	5,955	4,922	29.9	19.7	47.1	17.1	59.2	29.0
Public-order offenses	103,344	13,026	43.2	20.6	23.1	15.6	56.2	30.2
Weapons	25,642	6,025	28.3	23.0	22.4	24.4	41.8	37.1
Other public-order	77,702	7,001	48.1	18.5	23.3	8.1	60.9	24.1

Note: The U.S. Bureau of the Census conducted the 1997 Survey of Inmates in State Correctional Facilities for the U.S. Department of Justice, Bureau of Justice Statistics (BJS) and the 1997 Survey of Inmates in Federal Correctional Facilities for BJS and the Federal Bureau of Prisons. Data were collected from June through October 1997. The samples were taken from a universe of 1,409 state prisons and 127 federal prisons enumerated in the 1995 Census of State and Federal Adult Correctional Facilities or opened between completion of the census and June 30, 1996. The sample design for both surveys was a stratified two-stage selection; first, selecting prisons, and second, selecting inmates in those prisons. For the state survey 280 prisons were selected, 220 male facilities and 60 female facilities. Of the 280 facilities, 3 refused to allow interviewing and 2 closed before the survey could be conducted. Overall, 32 male facilities and 8 female facilities were selected for the federal survey, and all participated. A total of 14,285 interviews were completed for the state survey and 4,041 for the federal survey, for overall response rates of 92.5% in the state survey and 90.2% in the federal survey.

Based on the completed interviews, estimates for the entire population were developed using weighting factors derived from the original probability of selection in the sample. Excluded from the estimate of federal inmates were unsentenced inmates and those prisoners under federal jurisdiction but housed in state and private contract facilities. Those prisoners who were under state jurisdiction, yet held in local jails or private facilities, were excluded from the estimated number of state prisoners. As a result, the estimated prisoner counts do not match those in other BJS data series.

The estimated prisoner counts vary according to the particular data items analyzed. Estimates are based on the number of prisoners who provided information on selected items.

[a]Based on cases with valid offense data.

[b]Includes rape and other sexual assault.

Source: U.S. Department of Justice, Bureau of Justice Statistics, *Substance Abuse and Treatment, State and Federal Prisoners, 1997,* Special Report NCJ-172871 (Washington, D.C.: U.S. Department of Justice, January 1999), p. 3, Table 1.

Issues in Community Corrections

Heavy Drinking: Long-term Effects

Chronic, excessive use of alcohol can seriously damage nearly every organ and function of the body. When alcohol is burned in the body it produces another, even more toxic substance, acetaldehyde, which contributes to the damage. Alcohol is a stomach irritant. It adversely affects the way the small intestine transports and absorbs nutrients, especially vitamins and minerals. Added to the usually poor diet of heavy drinkers, this often results in severe malnutrition. Furthermore, alcohol can produce pancreatic disorders. It causes fatty deposits to accumulate in the liver. Cirrhosis of the liver, an often fatal illness, may be the ultimate result. Though alcohol is not a food, it does have calories and can contribute to obesity.

The effects of heavy drinking on the cardiovascular system are no less horrific. For many years doctors have observed that hypertension and excessive alcohol use go together, and according to a number of recent studies, heavy drinkers are more likely to have high blood pressure than teetotalers. Heavy alcohol consumption damages healthy heart muscle and puts extra strain on already damaged heart muscle. And it can damage other muscles besides the heart.

Some of the worst effects of alcohol are directly on the brain. The most life-threatening is an acute condition leading to psychosis, confusion, or unconsciousness. Heavy drinkers also tend to be heavy smokers and are also more likely to take and abuse other drugs, such as tranquilizers. Excessive drinking, particularly in combination with tobacco, increases the chance of cancers in the mouth, larynx, and throat. Alcohol appears to play a role in stomach, colorectal, and esophageal cancers, as well as possibly liver cancer.

Source: Lawrence Salinger (ed.), "Alcohol in Perspective," *Deviant Behavior 96/97,* annual edition. (Guilford, Conn.: Dushkin Publishing Group, 1996); and *The University of California at Berkeley Wellness Letter,* February 1993, pp. 4–6.

---

society and is only moderately disabled by his or her drinking.

The chronic, skid row alcoholic is completely debilitated by the problem. His or her involvement in crime is often equally divided between offender (public drunkenness) and victim (mugging) roles. This is not to say that the chronic alcoholic is not a serious crime problem. A study of 187 **skid row alcoholics** indicated that they had been arrested an average of 3.7 times for offenses other than public intoxication. However, by the time individuals' drinking problems have become chronic, most of their nonalcohol-related crime is behind them.[38]

Effects of Alcohol

Alcohol is a depressant; it depresses the functioning of the central nervous system. After a small amount of alcohol has been consumed, the drinker normally becomes relaxed and tranquil. Increased consumption often produces a feeling of stimulation; the drinker becomes more talkative, more active, and often more aggressive.[39] This apparent stimulation results from the depression of the inhibition control center in the brain. This loss of normal restraint may lead to criminal behavior. Alcohol does not provide a motivation for crime (as heroin addiction apparently does). Instead, it permits the drinker to act upon preexisting and previously controlled motivations. Without restraint, when inhibitions are diminished, anger may lead to violence; newfound courage may lead to the commission of property crimes.

The effects of alcohol on the drinker and the speed with which they become apparent vary from person to person and depend upon the concentration of alcohol in the blood. Several factors may influence the blood alcohol concentration, including the speed with which alcohol is consumed, the drinker's body weight, the presence of food in the stomach, the individual's drinking history and body chemistry, and the type of beverage consumed. Alcohol may affect the same individual in a different fashion on different occasions. The effects of intoxication are thus somewhat unpredictable. This unpredictability is probably the most dangerous quality of the drug.

The Alcoholic and the Problem Drinker

Definition   Distinctions between alcoholics and problem drinkers are a matter of degree. **Alcoholism** is the result of the problem drinker's loss of control and gradual deterioration. Alcoholism is more easily defined because its symptoms are more acute. Four basic elements are always present in alcoholism:

1. Compulsive, uncontrollable drinking.

2. Chronicity.

3. Intoxication.

4. Injury to function.[40]

Milt has defined alcoholism as "a chronic disorder in which the individual is unable, for psychological or physical reasons, or both, to reform from the frequent consumption of alcohol in quantities sufficient to produce intoxication and, ultimately, injury to health and effective functioning."[41]

Profile of the Alcoholic and Problem Drinker

Research on alcoholics and problem drinkers reveals a disturbing picture of the effects of alcohol abuse. **Problem drinkers** are described as "aggressive, attention-seeking, acting out, socially extroverted, lacking impulse control, resentful of authority, lacking feelings for others, power-seeking, and having self-destructive impulses."[42] In the full swing of the disease, alcoholics evidence the following traits:

[A]n extremely low frustration tolerance, inability to endure anxiety or tension, feelings of isolation, devaluated self-esteem, a tendency to act impulsively, a repetitive "acting out" of conflicts, often an extreme narcissism and exhibitionism, a tendency toward masochistic, self-punitive behavior, sometimes semantic preoccupation and hypochondriasis and often extreme mood swings.

In addition, there is usually marked hostility and rebellion (conscious or unconscious) and repressed grandiose ambitions with little ability to persevere. Most show strong (oral) dependent needs, frustrations of which will lead to depression, guilt, remorse, hostility, and rage.[43]

These characterizations of physical and psychological deterioration reflect the attributes of the alcoholic and problem drinker after the effects of alcohol consumption have been felt. No specific personality type is especially prone to alcoholism. Instead, alcoholism seems to create a new personality in the problem drinker, often different from his or her pre-alcoholic disposition.

Causes of Alcoholism

Explanations of alcoholism are much like attempts to explain narcotics addiction. They focus on such factors as biological predisposition, behavioral conditioning, psychological characteristics and conflicts, and socialization processes. Perhaps the best approach to understanding problem drinking is provided by the multifactor model developed by the Cooperative Commission on the Study of Alcoholism.

An individual who (1) responds to the beverage alcohol in a certain way, perhaps physiologically determined, by experiencing intense relief and relaxation,

Issues in Community Corrections

The Stages of Alcoholism

Stage One: The Novice. Most people never progress beyond this initial stage. Drinks are usually taken in moderation and then only at social functions. On occasion, the individual at this stage may drink to excess, experiencing a "hangover" the following morning.

Stage Two: Onset of Heavy Drinking and Blackouts. At this stage, the individual begins to drink heavily at bars or at parties and often has trouble later remembering what happened during a drinking bout.

Stage Three: Required Additional Drinking. At this stage, the person finds it increasingly difficult to "get high" and may become self-conscious about his or her drinking. Often the person drinks before going to a party or social event in order to conceal from others the amount of liquor that he or she needs to become intoxicated.

Stage Four: Early Signs of Control Loss. The individual at this stage can no longer control how much he or she will drink on a given occasion. Such a person can, however, control when the first drink will be taken.

Stage Five: Excuse Drinking. At this stage, the drinker may abstain from using alcohol for long periods of time (possibly even months) in an attempt to prove that he or she does not need to drink. However, once the drinking behavior is resumed, the individual drinks heavily, which naturally produces feelings of guilt. In order to assuage this guilt, the drinker invents excuses for drinking, claiming, for example, that he or she is celebrating some occasion or has been working too hard and needs a few drinks in order to relax.

Stage Six: Drinking Alone. At this stage, alcohol has become the individual's best friend. The drinker now drinks alone so that excuses for drinking are no longer necessary. The person at this stage gradually moves into a self-imposed dream world, which allows him or her to go on drinking without having to face what is actually happening.

Stage Seven: Hostile, Sensitive Drinker. At this stage, the drinker becomes somewhat antisocial. The drinker may provoke unnecessary fights with friends and relatives and begin abusing others—both verbally and physically—without experiencing any apparent remorse.

Stage Eight: Extended Drinking and "Benders." At this stage, the person drinks in the morning to "treat" the hangover from the previous evening's drinking bout. The drinker also begins going on "benders"—that is, extended bouts of drinking. During this period, the drinker has lost most if not all concern for personal welfare as well as that of others.

Stage Nine: "Hitting Bottom." In this final stage, the alcoholic has given up everything for drink. The drinker may remain at this point until continued drinking finally results in death—either directly or indirectly—or he or she may seek treatment. Unfortunately, because the drinker or the drinker's family failed to recognize the problem at an earlier stage, by this point, the drinker may have lost everything he or she had prior to becoming an alcoholic. Had the drinker sought treatment at an earlier stage, much human misery might have been avoided.

Source: Reprinted with permission of Macmillan Publishing Company from *Drug Abuse: A Criminal Justice Primer,* by R. J. Wicks and Jerome J. Platt, pp. 18–19. Copyright © 1977 by Benziger Bruce and Glencoe Inc.

and who (2) has certain personality characteristics, such as difficulty in dealing with and overcoming depression, frustration, and anxiety, and who (3) is a member of a culture in which there is both pressure to drink and culturally induced guilt and confusion regarding what kinds of drinking behavior are appropriate, is more likely to develop trouble than most other persons. An intermingling of certain factors may be necessary for the development of problem drinking, and the relative importance of the different causal factors no doubt varies from one individual to another.[44]

Diagnosing the Problem

When does alcohol use become alcohol abuse? One of the greatest difficulties in treating alcohol-related problems is making the judgment that, for a specific individual, alcohol consumption has become a problem; it no longer serves merely to reduce tension or facilitate social interaction but is creating more difficulties than it solves. Because no clearly defined line can be drawn between the social drinker, the problem drinker, and the alcoholic, the diagnosis of alcohol-related problems requires a comprehensive examination of the individual's drinking behavior, the social context in which it occurs, and the consequences of that behavior. The quantity of alcohol consumed, the consumption rate, the frequency of drinking episodes, the effect of drunkenness on self and others, the drinker's visibility to various law enforcing agencies, and the drinker's total social matrix must be considered in assessing the extent of the problems producing alcohol consumption.[45]

Treatment of Alcoholics and Problem Drinkers

The treatment of alcohol-related problems is not simply a correctional dilemma. Recent estimates indicate that the United States may have as many as seventeen million problem

and potential problem drinkers. More than seven million of these are estimated to meet the standard diagnostic criteria for alcohol abuse or dependence according to the National Institute of Alcohol Abuse and Alcoholism. Alcohol abuse or dependence afflicts 7.4 percent of adults.[46]

Because alcohol-related problems are so prevalent in the general community, an extensive network of programs, many of them federally funded, has developed to meet the needs of alcohol abusers. At present, more than one million persons are being treated in the community for alcohol-related problems.[47] In most communities, offenders are encouraged to participate in these existing programs if they have an alcohol-related problem. Specialized programs for drinking offenders are relatively uncommon because they would duplicate projects serving the general public, thus placing an unnecessary drain on correctional resources. Community programs can also be expected to serve reintegrative purposes better than correctional efforts. The offender receives assistance as a citizen who happens to be an alcoholic, not as a criminal with a drinking problem. In addition, rehabilitation can be continued long after correctional supervision ends.

Goals

Traditionally, the major goal of alcohol abuse treatment has been total abstinence.[48] This viewpoint is based on the belief that alcoholics are incapable of controlling their drinking and that only total abstinence can halt the progression of the disease of alcoholism. Several research studies, including a four-year RAND Corporation examination of more than 750 male alcoholics who have participated in various treatment programs, have challenged this view. The RAND study concluded that alcoholism is a chronic, unstable condition. Among persons who come to formal treatment, alcoholism appears to be a continuing condition for the great majority. Data show that remissions are frequent but are generally intermittent. Remission occurs in two forms: both long-term and nonproblem drinking. These two groups have roughly equivalent levels of social adjustment, mental health, and physical condition.[49]

Supporters of **controlled drinking** as a treatment goal propose that alcoholics can learn how to drink responsibly. They suggest that alcohol abuse is often the result of an underlying personality disorder. If the disorder can be cured, then controlled drinking is possible.[50] They consider the goal of controlled drinking to be both more realistic and more likely to encourage the reluctant alcoholic to enter treatment than the traditional goal of abstinence.

This position has been most strongly challenged by Alcoholics Anonymous (AA), a self-help group that views abstinence as the only means to recovery for the alcoholic. This organization asserts that anyone who can learn to control (instead of eliminate) his or her drinking was never an alcoholic.[51]

The proper goal of alcohol abuse treatment is still being debated. Most treatment professionals view the conflicting goals of abstinence and controlled drinking as equally appropriate, but for different types of drinkers. Some alcoholics can never safely take a drink and others can learn to control their problem. The results of many programs that emphasize total abstinence indicate that most people who complete the programs do not stop drinking but instead achieve less destructive drinking patterns.[52]

Treatment Modalities

A variety of treatment strategies are designed to help alcoholics and problem drinkers overcome their problems. The most widely utilized are prescription drugs, behavioral techniques, family therapy, and Alcoholics Anonymous.

Pharmacological Agents   Although antidepressants are sometimes used in the treatment of alcoholism, disulfiram (Antabuse) is the most widely used chemical treatment method.

Antabuse is an alcohol-sensitizing drug that alters the manner in which alcohol is metabolized so that the drinker experiences headache, nausea, vomiting, throbbing in the head and neck, breathing difficulties, and a host of other unpleasant symptoms.[53] Taking Antabuse virtually eliminates the possibility that an alcoholic will impulsively take a drink because an Antabuse user cannot consume alcohol for up to three days without experiencing unpleasant reactions. Although it has been argued that anyone so committed to abstinence that he or she takes Antabuse on a daily basis probably would not drink under any circumstances, the effectiveness of Antabuse has neither been proved nor disproved.[54] Research is currently being conducted on Antabuse implants, which slowly release the drug into the system and are effective for several weeks. In the future, the alcoholic may need to commit himself or herself to abstinence only once or twice a month to be protected from impulsive drinking.

Behavioral Methods   Behavioral approaches are receiving special attention in contemporary alcohol treatment programs. The basic strategy is simple: Reverse the sequence in which the alcoholic is rewarded for drinking so that nondrinking brings a reward or avoids a punishment.[55] The approach begins with a careful assessment of drinking behavior, focusing on cues and stimuli, attitudes and thoughts, specific drinking behavior, and the consequences of drinking.[56] Following this assessment, an individually tailored program is developed to modify the behavior. A variety of treatment techniques are employed, including:

1. Aversion therapies, designed to associate the sight, smell, taste, or thought of alcohol with unpleasant experiences such as those produced by Antabuse.

2. Assertiveness training designed to teach the drinker how to express inner rage positively.

3. Instruction in coping strategies.

4. Relaxation techniques.

5. Biofeedback and related techniques that assist the individual in recognizing and controlling body states that precipitate or result from alcohol consumption.[57]

Family Therapy   Many treatment professionals recommend treating the entire family unit, instead of just the alcoholic patient. A high correlation has been found between marital stability and treatment success.[58] There are many possible explanations for this finding. Family problems often precipitate drinking problems. In many families, alcoholism so severely damages the relationships between family members that special assistance is needed before the family can get back on its feet, even after the alcoholic has recovered. In other situations, destructive family relations impede the progression of therapy. A comprehensive evaluation of the treatment of alcoholism summarized the benefits of family therapy as follows: "Involvement of the family in treatment increases the awareness of both the alcoholic and other family members of problems other than alcoholism, such as relationship problems and the way they face reality. It reduces blaming tendencies, teaches new modes of interaction, and permits a focus on a common goal."[59]

Family therapy usually involves only the alcoholic and his or her spouse, although the children, extended family members, and even the problem drinker's friends have participated in various conjoint treatment efforts.

Many positive treatment outcomes have been identified as consequences of family treatment, including improvements in social and marital stability, employment and financial circumstances, quality of child care, and fewer difficulties with the law. Although no conclusive evidence shows that family treatment is invariably effective, evidence is sufficient to suggest that family treatment alone or in conjunction with other treatments can produce positive outcomes for both alcoholics and their families.[60]

Alcoholics Anonymous   **Alcoholics Anonymous** is probably the oldest and best-known

alcoholic treatment program. It is also one of the largest. AA currently serves more than 650,000 participants annually.[61] AA originated in Akron, Ohio, in 1935, when a stockbroker and a surgeon, both alcoholics, utilized an approach developed by Dr. Samuel Shoemaker to help each other and a third alcoholic. Together, these three persons formed Alcoholics Anonymous, a spiritually based self-help organization now operating throughout the world.

Although it is primarily a nonresidential program, AA works much like therapeutic communities for narcotics addicts. An older member takes a new member under his or her wing and fosters an interpersonal dependence that replaces the former dependence on alcohol. The personal satisfaction that the friendship brings and the ability to rely on the established AA member for assistance in self-control permits the new member to begin managing his or her drinking problem. Sobriety is achieved in large part through the Twelve Steps Program, although some AA members also seek professional help.

AA is not the answer for all alcoholics. Lower-middle-class individuals who received religious training in childhood and basically well-adjusted persons who have experienced recent reverses (for example, loss of job or drinking companions) are the best candidates for the program. Although little scientific evaluation has been done of AA's effectiveness, for some members, it seems at least as successful as alternative methods. In the 1980s, the Twelve Steps of AA became the basis for many drug and alcohol treatment programs.

Community-Based Correctional Programs for Alcoholic Offenders

As many as 50 to 75 percent of probationers and parolees have some alcohol-related problem.[62] To assist these offenders, many probation and parole offices have established specialized caseloads consisting solely of alcoholic offenders.

Program Focus

Alcoholics Anonymous: The Twelve Steps

We

1. Admitted we were powerless over alcohol—that our lives had become unmanageable.

2. Came to believe that a Power greater than ourselves could restore us to sanity.

3. Made a decision to turn our will and our lives over to the care of God as we understood Him.

4. Made a searching and fearless moral inventory of ourselves.

5. Admitted to God, to ourselves, and to another human being the exact nature of our wrongs.

6. Were entirely ready to have God remove all these defects of character.

7. Humbly asked Him to remove our shortcomings.

8. Made a list of all persons we had harmed, and became willing to make amends to them all.

9. Made direct amends to such people wherever possible, except when to do so would injure them or others.

10. Continued to take personal inventory and when we were wrong promptly admitted it.

11. Sought through prayer and meditation to improve our conscious contact with God as we understood Him, praying only for knowledge of His will for us and the power to carry that out.

12. Having had a spiritual awakening as the result of these steps, we tried to carry this message to alcoholics, and to practice these principles in all our affairs.

Source: The Twelve Steps, reprinted with permission of Alcoholics Anonymous World Services Inc. Copyright © 1939.

Officers supervising these caseloads can focus their energies on increasing their knowledge of alcoholism, enhancing their therapeutic skills, and developing and maintaining contacts with community alcoholism treatment projects (Table 9-3).

Many probation and parole offices also offer group counseling to alcoholics and problem drinkers. One of the first such programs was established in the Federal Probation office in the District of Columbia. Offenders were accepted into the program after extensive diagnosis and classification procedures or when treatment was made a condition of probation.

A former supervisor of the Alcoholic Counseling Group described its format:

1. Group discussion is encouraged in reference to alcoholism as a disease, its progressiveness, and many attendant problems, with emphasis on its being arrestable but not curable and that the only solution is complete abstinence.

2. Individuals are urged to select pertinent topics in which they are interested and concerned. These are discussed in depth.

3. Educational films are shown frequently and are selected carefully for their content and value. Usually they depict and discuss the social, psychological, and physical aspects of the problem. Case histories are presented and discussed.

Table 9-3   Levels of Prior Alcohol and Drug Use by
Adults on Probation, by Selected Characteristics, 1995

| | | Percent of Probationers | | | | | |
| | | Prior Alcohol Abuse | | Level of Prior Drug Use | | | |
Characteristic	Number of Probationers	Under the Influence of Alcohol at Time of Offense	Ever Had a Binge Drinking Experience[a]	Ever in the Past	Used Regularly[b]	In the Month Prior to Offense	At the Time of Offense
All probationers	2,065,896	39.9%	35.3%	69.4%	43.4%	31.8%	13.5%
Gender							
Male	1,636,017	43.5	40.4	69.9	44.7	33.7	14.0
Female	429,879	26.2	16.1	67.7	38.4	24.6	11.6
Race, Hispanic origin							
White, non-Hispanic	1,264,990	46.6	43.3	72.8	46.0	33.1	13.6
Black, non-Hispanic	509,919	26.2	19.2	68.1	43.8	34.7	14.7
Hispanic	228,399	32.7	27.7	56.4	32.3	23.3	10.7
Other	62,588	41.5	34.5	59.3	29.0	14.5	13.8
Age							
24 years and younger	556,760	26.1	35.0	69.9	42.3	38.3	16.4
25 to 34 years	713,204	42.8	35.1	76.9	47.3	34.9	14.5
35 to 44 years	523,583	47.4	37.6	75.4	52.8	32.5	14.0
45 to 54 years	191,382	41.6	33.1	44.1	22.4	11.6	5.3
55 years and older	80,967	55.5	30.2	21.4	6.8	3.8	1.1
Education							
Eighth grade or less	114,818	42.7	28.2	49.6	32.1	25.8	15.0
Some high school	509,091	35.1	35.7	71.5	43.2	33.8	14.6
GED	224,007	43.1	44.7	83.6	57.7	44.6	17.4
High school graduate	595,715	38.8	35.8	65.0	40.0	30.5	12.4
Some college or more	586,236	43.8	33.0	70.6	44.4	27.3	11.7

Note: From the 1995 Survey of Adults on Probation conducted by the Bureau of
Justice Statistics and the U.S. Bureau of the Census.

GED = general equivalency diploma.

[a]Binge drinking is defined as having consumed a fifth of liquor in a single day,
equivalent to twenty drinks, three bottles of wine, or three six-packs of beer.

[b]Regular use is defined as once a week or more for at least a month.

Source: U.S. Department of Justice, Bureau of Justice Statistics, *Sourcebook of
Criminal Justice Statistics, 1998* (Washington, D.C.: U.S. Department of Justice,
March 1998), p. 6.

Avenues of available help are often the climax of the films.

4. Selected AA speakers discuss their experiences and the help they received through Alcoholics Anonymous. A question-and-answer period follows. All are constantly urged to seek the help available through AA. AA literature is distributed at no cost.

5. Staff members from community resource agencies are invited to discuss their programs and the help their agencies render assistance.[63]

The program attempts to encourage insight and help offenders establish and maintain mature interpersonal relationships. Attitudes are discussed and goals are examined. One offender's success encourages the others to examine their own problems and initiate change.

A typical meeting focuses on such practical matters as the effects of alcoholism on the family, the employer, and the community as well as the importance of being aware of simple detectable symptoms, including "frequent absenteeism from work (especially on Mondays), personality changes when drinking, reporting to work or attending meetings while under the influence of alcohol, and arrests for being drunk."[64]

During the one-and-a-half- to two-hour meetings, group dynamics are observed carefully. A summary of the significant events of each meeting is recorded for later review and evaluation. Offenders are also encouraged to seek help through AA, which is available on a twenty-four-hour basis.

The Effectiveness of Alcohol Treatment

The effectiveness of alcohol treatment programs may be assessed according to several evaluation criteria. The most widely utilized measures of success are alcohol consumption, behavioral impairment, and social adjustment.[65]

Alcohol Consumption

Considerable evidence exists that alcohol treatment programs reduce program participants' alcohol consumption. A nationwide study of programs funded by the National Institute of Alcohol Abuse and Alcoholism revealed that, eighteen months after treatment, 46 percent of the male patients and 56 percent of the female patients had abstained from alcohol; one-fourth of the males and over one-third of the females had abstained for at least six months. Alcohol consumption declined to 2.5 ounces (male) and 1.3 ounces (female) per day.[66]

Behavioral Impairment and Adjustment

Patients in alcohol treatment programs generally show signs of social, vocational, and psychological adaptation "related but not parallel" to reductions in alcohol consumption.[67] Job stability seems to be particularly enhanced by alcoholism treatment. Evidence also shows that interpersonal relationships and physical condition improve and arrest rates decline among treated problem drinkers.

Patient and Treatment Characteristics

Attempts have been made to identify the most effective treatment strategies and best candidates for rehabilitation. Community-based rehabilitation programs have been found to be as successful as and less expensive than inpatient programs. The 1978 report to Congress on alcohol and health suggested that the least expensive program may be the preferred treatment option if quality treatment standards are maintained. Studies of treatment characteristics have revealed that longer, more intensive rehabilitation programs are associated with positive treatment outcome. At present, however, no optimum treatment intensity or length can be specified.[68]

After an exhaustive review of research on differential treatment effectiveness, the 1978 report to Congress concluded that the client's background and motivation to seek help may be the most important factors in the treatment process. Research indicating that many alcoholics experience spontaneous recovery without any formal treatment supports this conclusion. Intensive outpatient treatment increases the problem drinker's chance of recovery, however, perhaps by as much as 25 percent.[69] Taken together, these findings indicate that intensive community-based programs may provide the best treatment alternative available for the alcoholic offender. However, the problem of motivation remains as a principal barrier to rehabilitation.

Treatment Prerequisites and the Criminal Justice System

Only a small proportion of alcoholics and problem drinkers seek or accept treatment. This reluctance to use available assistance stems in part from the belief that alcoholism

Program Focus

The Hazelden Rehabilitation Program, Center City, Minnesota

Admissions

People come to the Hazelden Rehabilitation Program from all over the world representing all age, social, occupational, and religious backgrounds. People refer themselves, or are referred by concerned persons from the medical, legal, family, mental health, or Alcoholics Anonymous communities. Physically handicapped people capable of self-care (i.e., wheelchair capability) may also participate.

The Hazelden Admissions Office is open twenty-four hours a day, seven days a week. . . . Advance reservations are required.

For a fee, Hazelden provides daily transportation to and from the Twin Cities area, bus terminals, and the Minneapolis-St. Paul International Airport.

Medical Management

Upon arrival at Hazelden, new patients receive a complete physical examination and health assessment. If necessary, the patient undergoes a carefully controlled, individual detoxification plan. A medical evaluation is completed usually within a 48-hour period. Patients move to one of the primary treatment units usually within 24 hours.

Assessment

Because chemical dependency affects all areas of a person's life, each patient's social, emotional, intellectual, spiritual, and physical condition is carefully evaluated, with special attention to the consequences of alcohol and other drug use.

A team of chemical dependency counselors, clergy, psychologists, medical staff, and recreational therapists interviews each patient. These specialists design a highly individualized treatment plan that details specific goals in each area of the patient's life. This plan is the blueprint for the patient's treatment at Hazelden. . . .

Primary Rehabilitation

While the length of stay for patients at Hazelden varies according to individual needs, an average stay is twenty-nine days.

Treatment itself is an absorbing, intensive experience. To learn about their disease, patients attend lectures daily. Psychiatrists, psychologists, physicians, nurses, clergy, and chemical dependency counselors describe chemical dependency from their professional and personal experience.

There is also evidence that interpersonal relationships and physical condition improve and arrest rates decline among treated problem

is a symptom of weakness and that only a strong will is required to conquer the problem. Other persons fail to enter treatment because of an inability or unwillingness to recognize their problem. This denial of alcoholism may be produced by a fear of abstinence as well as a fear of treatment.

Zola has described five timing triggers that must precede a person's decision to accept help in overcoming an alcohol problem.

drinkers. However, persons who reduce their alcohol consumption do not always show signs of improved adjustment. Conversely, behavioral and social adjustment can improve even when alcohol consumption continues at an unhealthy level. Daily group therapy helps each patient better understand themselves and their disease. By sharing personal experiences, patients learn—often for the first time—to trust and seek help from friends and loved ones. Group sessions on grief, women's issues, the Steps of Alcoholics Anonymous, and other topics help patients recognize and begin to resolve personal barriers to recovery.

In individual counseling sessions counselor and patient work together to identify personal problems and set specific goals that will lead to a better life. These goals might include overcoming resentment, developing trust in others, or identifying self-defeating behaviors.

The cornerstone of our program is the Steps of Alcoholics Anonymous, with a goal of total abstinence from alcohol and other drugs. Each patient works on adopting the philosophy of Alcoholics Anonymous before leaving treatment. Upon discharge, patients are referred to Alcoholics Anonymous contacts in their home communities.

Care for the family is an important part of our rehabilitation services. Because the disease of chemical dependency directly or indirectly affects the lives of so many people, Hazelden offers a family services program. . . .

Aftercare   Aftercare-counseling that takes place after treatment eases the transition back to home life. It also prepares the patient to lead a richer, higher quality life of sobriety.

Each patient works with [his or her] counselor and the Hazelden aftercare staff to develop an aftercare plan. Typical aftercare plans include participation in Twelve Step groups such as Alcoholics Anonymous or Narcotics Anonymous. Aftercare might also include marital counseling, individual therapy, or family therapy, according to individual situations.

Because many of our patients come from outside of Minnesota, we have developed an extensive network of aftercare providers throughout the country. Through this national network, Hazelden patients living outside the metropolitan area are referred to aftercare facilities in their home communities.

Hazelden also offers special aftercare programs for people who live in the Minneapolis-St. Paul metropolitan area. . . .

Source: From the Hazelden Rehabilitation Program, Center City, Minnesota (1990 brochure). Reprinted by permission.

1. A personal crisis must emerge to cause the patient to dwell on symptoms.

2. The symptoms must begin to threaten a valued social activity.

3. Other people must begin telling him or her to seek care.

4. The consequences of not seeking help must be perceived.

5. The pain, severity, and duration of symptoms must be sufficient to produce action.[70]

The implications of Zola's research are significant. A personal crisis such as arrest may be sufficient to encourage many alcohol-abusing offenders to consider rehabilitation. If intensive therapy is available to offenders during community supervision, it may be possible to take advantage of the new willingness to accept treatment.

Correctional workers need to learn how to use these timing triggers to increase client motivation. The criminal justice system must develop effective linkages with community alcohol treatment programs and offer incentives and support to the offender who enters treatment. By providing incentives, treatment, and support, the circumstances of crime, arrest, and conviction may be used to promote meaningful behavioral change.

Summary

Narcotics addicts, problem drinkers, and alcoholics present special problems to the criminal justice system. Substance abuse is associated with both violent and property crime, alcohol abuse often produces crimes against the person, and narcotics addiction leads to economic crimes.

There are a number of similarities between alcohol and drug abuse and abusers. No single addict or alcoholic personality exists. Both alcohol and narcotics can be used on an occasional social basis as well as in a chronic fashion. Both substances offer a similar benefit to their abusers—an escape from reality.

Similar explanations are offered to describe the causes of both problems. Similar treatments are also available, including behavior modification, the use of pharmacological agents, supportive and confrontational therapies, and residential and outpatient programs. Many treatment strategies are criticized for

substituting one form of dependency for another. Neither alcohol nor drug abuse is easy to treat. Complete and permanent cures are relatively rare, and American experience with illicit drugs remains troubling. As a recent study commented,

Americans are pessimistic about the nation's drug problems. Seven in ten think drug abuse is worse today than five years ago. More than half think it will get even worse. This pessimism is understandable. The federal drug budget has grown from $1.5 billion in 1981 to $13.2 billion in 1995—a total of nearly $100 billion has been spent to date. During the same period, state and local governments spent an additional $150 billion to combat drugs. Despite this massive investment, drug addiction, drug-related crime, and drug availability have not significantly declined, and street prices for drugs have plummeted. Moreover, drug use among young people has risen substantially for the first time in more than a decade.[71]

According to surveys published by the National Drug Control Strategy office, seventy-seven million people have experimented with illicit drugs in the United States.[72] Approximately seventy million reported involvement with marijuana or hashish, and 23.5 percent reported cocaine use. Trends in drug use show that casual use of drugs is down, but drug use among young people is increasing. Trends in high school use of marijuana, LSD, inhalants, and stimulants all have increased over the last several years. National surveys have also shown that the number of hardcore users has remained unchanged over the past few years. Hardcore users are defined as individuals who use illicit drugs at least weekly and exhibit behavioral problems directly relating to their drug use. According to the federal government, hardcore drug users are the center of the problems faced by contemporary society. While representing approximately 20 percent of the drug-using population, they consume over two-thirds of the cocaine.

The societal cost of drugs is high. The illicit drug trade in the United States is a $49 billion

Program Focus

Goals of the 1995 National Drug Control Strategy

Overarching Goal

Goal 1: Reduce the number of drug users in America.

Demand Reduction Goals

Goal 2: Expand treatment capacity and services and increase treatment effectiveness so that those who need treatment can receive it. Target intensive treatment services for hardcore drug-using populations and special populations, including adults and adolescents in custody or under the supervision of the criminal justice system, pregnant women, and women with dependent children.

Goal 3: Reduce the burden on the health care system by reducing the spread of infectious disease related to drug use.

Goal 4: Assist local communities in developing effective prevention programs.

Goal 5: Create safe and healthy environments in which children and adolescents can live, grow, learn, and develop.

Goal 6: Reduce the use of alcohol and tobacco products among underage youth.

Goal 7: Increase workplace safety and productivity by reducing drug use in the workplace.

Goal 8: Strengthen linkages among the prevention, treatment, and criminal justice communities and other supportive social services, such as employment and training services.

Domestic Law Enforcement Goals

Goal 9: Reduce domestic drug-related crime and violence.

Goal 10: Reduce all domestic drug production and availability, and continue to target for investigation and prosecution those who illegally import, manufacture, and distribute dangerous drugs and who illegally divert pharmaceutical and listed chemicals.

Goal 11: Improve the efficiency of Federal drug law enforcement capabilities, including interaction and intelligence programs.

International Goals

Goal 12: Strengthen international cooperation against narcotics production, trafficking, and use.

Goal 13: Assist other nations to develop and implement comprehensive counternarcotics policies that strengthen democratic institutions, destroy narcotrafficking organizations, and interdict narcotrafficking in both the source and transit countries.

Goal 14: Support, implement, and lead more successful enforcement efforts to increase the costs and risks to narcotics producers and traffickers to reduce the supply of illicit drugs to the United States.[75]

Source: The White House, *National Drug Control Strategy* (Washington, D.C.: Office of National Drug Control Policy, April 1995).

retail industry, and American citizens are estimated to spend yearly $30.8 billion on cocaine, $9 billion on marijuana, and $7.1 billion on heroin. The impact of illicit drug use on society is significant. The estimated economic costs to society from illicit drug use is placed at $66.9 billion by the National Office of Drug Control Policy.

Although the "war on drugs" has continued for several years, the number of emergency room visits by people suffering severe reactions to drug use has continued to increase. In 1993, approximately 120,000 people were brought to emergency rooms, and more than 60,000 were brought for heroin problems. In terms of the drug epidemic's impact on the criminal justice system, there are more than one million drug arrests per year. Research conducted by the National Institute of Justice-sponsored Drug Use Forecasting found that a clear link exists between drugs and crime and that almost two-thirds of offenders arrested test positive for drug use. Prisons are rapidly filling up with substance abusers. For example, the majority of prisoners in the federal system are drug offenders, and many states are also experiencing a similar trend.

To address these problems and challenges the United States government has developed a four-point strategy consisting of the following priorities:

1. Drug education and prevention programs for America's youth. Convince children that drug use is dangerous and a potentially deadly activity that must be avoided.

2. Treatment of hardcore users. Insist that chronic hardcore drug users—individuals who consume the majority of drugs and burden the health care and criminal justice system—participate in treatment and aftercare programs or face certain punishment.

3. Community action and law enforcement. Strengthen domestic law enforcement efforts that are key to eradicating illicit drugs and drug-related crime and violence. Develop community policing programs, enhance linkages between criminal justice and treatment programs, and place more police officers on the street.

4. Supply reduction in source countries. Focus interdiction efforts within countries that are major contributors to the drug supply, and offer assistance to countries that demonstrate the political will to end drug trafficking.[73]

Key Words and Concepts

abstinence

Alcoholics Anonymous

alcoholism

Antabuse

chippers

confrontational therapy

controlled drinking

drug addiction

methadone maintenance

polydrug users

postaddiction syndrome

problem drinkers

skid row alcoholics

street life

therapeutic communities

tolerance

withdrawal

Questions for Discussion

1. How have narcotic users changed over time? How has their criminal behavior changed as a result of their drug use?

2. What new drugs have become available in recent years? What criminal behaviors are associated with these substances? What problems could these new substances pose to the enforcement of parole and probation guidelines?

3. What is postaddiction syndrome? How does it differ from withdrawal?

4. Is relapse back into drug use unusual? Would it be wise of a parole or probation officer to expect and plan for such a relapse?

5. How does methadone maintenance work? What client factors might make an addict appropriate for this type of a clinical response?

6. What factors seem to be common to failed treatment programs?

7. Compared with narcotics, how does alcohol effect the person? How do they differ in their effects on crime and the criminal justice system?

8. How do methadone and Antabuse differ in their effects on addicts and alcoholics? How are they similar?

9. How would a national drug control program work? Where would failures likely occur in such a strategy?

For Further Reading

Akers, Ronald L., *Drugs, Alcohol, and Society: Social Structure, Process, and Policy* (Belmont, Calif.: Wadsworth, 1992).

Bracer, Edward M., *Licit and Illicit Drugs* (Mount Vernon, N.Y.: Consumers Union, 1972).

Bureau of Justice and Statistics, *Drugs and Crime, Facts, 1995* (Washington, D.C.: U.S. Department of Justice, 1996).

Gropper, Bernard, *Probing the Links between Drugs and Crime* (Washington, D.C.: U.S. Department of Justice, 1985).

National Institute of Drug Abuse and Alcoholism, *Seventh Special Report to the U.S. Congress on Alcohol and Health* (Washington, D.C.: U.S. Government Printing Office, January 1990).

Ray, Oakley, *Drugs, Society, and Human Behavior* (St. Louis, Mo.: C. V. Mosby, 1983).

Chapter 10

Special Problem Offenders: Mentally Ill and Sex Offenders in Community Corrections

Mentally Ill Offenders

Prevalence of the Problem

History of the Problem

Special Problems

Mentally Ill Offenders Summary

Sex Offenders

Extent of the Problem

System Responses

Sex Offenders Summary

Releasing a special problem offender to the community is one of the most controversial and difficult decisions that a correctional system can make. When such an offender is released, the public believes it is just a matter of time before he or she re-offends. When the offender does re-offend, the public's response is outrage and anger, directed at both the offender and the mechanism that released him or her. There is little that is noncontroversial about these offenders. The focus of local media, they are viewed as undesirable, dangerous, or a combination of the two by members of the community. Often, but not always, this perception is well founded. Public disenchantment has resulted in the creation of new laws, which govern the decisions of correctional release agencies and may make the transition from prison to the community more difficult for offenders who manage to satisfy this more strict process. Furthermore, some states are changing their legal codes to allow offenders to serve their original sentence in prison and then be released to a therapeutic program where they can be held for an indeterminate amount of time, based on the suspicion that they may re-offend.

Mentally Ill Offenders

In the field of criminal justice and corrections, the link between mental illness and crime is long and time honored. This link began with the development of town centers and the emergence of a market economy—a change that represented a significant shift in the economic structure of the time. Western society made a transition from farms that produced goods that were completely consumed by the farming family to farms that had a marketable excess of goods produced with great efficiency. As a result, some farm workers were left unemployed, typically those who were the least skilled and consequently the least employable. These displaced workers existed by committing petty crimes and robberies against those who traveled to the town center to trade. Many were viewed by the justice system as having a mental illness, or being mad, and were subsequently held in **asylums.**[1]

Asylums became filled with these **vagrants,** and the conditions inside became so horrid that noblemen would take friends and family members on tours for the purposes of amusement.[2] Asylums were notorious for overcrowding, disease, and inhumanity. Furthermore, they had an impact on local crime. Offenders who had survived the brutal conditions of these asylums were motivated to commit more serious forms of crime because they were more profitable and would carry a sentence of death, which was preferable to further imprisonment in the asylum. In addition, these offenders lost what little faith they had in the justice system by their experiences. In no small way, these facilities had a serious and overall negative impact on the justice system.

In more modern times, the linkage between crime and mental impairment has become both more predictable and more clear. Mental illness and the lack of sufficient mental health care have driven offenders into the hands of the justice system for control. While criminal actions by the mentally ill present the same relative risk to the public as crimes by mentally capable offenders, their crimes should be looked at in the context of their condition. The reasons for their condition has not been addressed.

Table 10-1   Measures of Mental Illness Among State Prison Inmates, 1997

	State Prison Inmates	
Measure of Mental Fitness	Percent	Cumulative Percent
Reported a mental or emotional condition	10.1	10.1
Because of a mental or emotional problem, inmate had—		
Been admitted to a hospital overnight	10.7	16.2
Taken a prescribed medication	18.9	23.9
Received professional counseling or therapy	21.8	29.7
Received other mental health services	3.3	30.2

Source: Paula Ditton, "Mental Health and Treatment of Inmates and Probationers," *Bureau of Justice Statistics Bulletin* (Washington D.C.: Bureau of Justice Statistics, 1999).

Prevalence of the Problem

Since the 1960s, the number of persons in the justice system has been on an upswing.[3] Some have argued that the overall population of the nation has increased, which has fueled the increase in correctional populations. However, incarceration rates have increased at an alarming pace since the mid-1970s and continued to do so in recent years even with a decrease in crime (Figure 10-1).[4] A substantial portion of this growing prison population was mentally ill. A 1999 survey of inmates and probationers utilized a six-question survey to determine the mental health of respondents (Figure 10-2). This research estimated that 30 percent of the state and federal inmate population either had a current mental health problem or had been treated for one in the past (Table 10-1).[5] This rate corresponds with a total number of 179,200 mentally ill inmates in state prison systems (Table 10-2).[6]

Most inmates, however, eventually leave the prison or jail and exist on the outside with

Figure 10-1   Rate of Sentenced Prisoners in State
and Federal Institutions on December 31, 1925–1997

Number of sentenced prisoners
per 100,000 residents

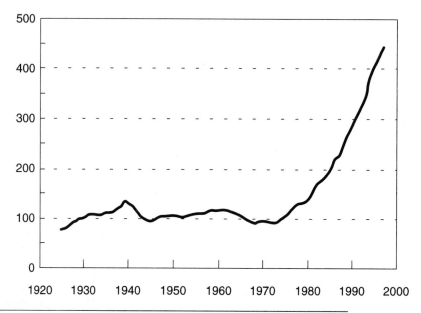

Note: Prison population data were compiled by a year-end census of prisoners held in custody
in state and federal institutions. Data for 1925 through 1939 include sentenced prisoners in
state and federal prisons and reformatories whether committed for felonies or misdemeanors.
Data for 1940 through 1970 include all adult felons serving sentences in state and federal
institutions. Since 1971, the census has included all adults or youthful offenders sentenced
to a state or federal correctional institution with maximum sentences of over one year.

Beginning on December 31, 1978, a distinction was made between prisoners "in custody" and
prisoners "under jurisdiction." As defined in a 1978 report (U.S. Department of Justice, Bureau
of Justice Statistics, *Prisoners in State and Federal Institutions on December 31, 1978,* NPS
Bulletin SD-NPS-PSF-6 (Washington, D.C.: U.S. Government Printing Office, 1980)), "in custody"
refers to the direct physical control and responsibility for the body of a confined person. "Under
jurisdiction" is defined as follows: A state or federal prison system has jurisdiction over a person
if it retains the legal power to incarcerate the person in one of its own prisons. Jurisdiction is not
determined by the inmate's physical location; jurisdiction is determined by the legal authority to
hold the inmate. Examples of prisoners under the jurisdiction of a given system, but not in its
custody, are those housed in local jails, in other states, or in hospitals (including mental health
facilities) outside the correctional system; inmates on work release, furlough, or bail; and state
prisoners held in federal prisons or vice versa.

The rates for the period before 1980 are based on the civilian population. The civilian
population represents the resident population less the armed forces stationed in the United
States. Since 1980, the rates are based on the total resident population provided by the U.S.
Bureau of the Census. Data for 1997 are preliminary and subject to revision.

Source: U.S. Department of Justice, Bureau of Justice Statistics, *Prisoners in State and Federal
Institutions on December 31, 1981,* NCJ-86485 (Washington, D.C.: U.S. Government Printing
Office, 1983), p. 3; U.S. Department of Justice, Bureau of Justice Statistics, *Prisoners in 1983,*
Bulletin NCJ-92949, p. 2; *1997,* Bulletin NCJ-170014, p. 3, Table 3 (Washington, D.C.: U.S.
Department of Justice); and U.S. Department of Justice, Bureau of Justice Statistics,
Correctional Populations in the United States, 1985, NCJ-103957, Table 5.4; *1996,* NCJ-
111611, Table 5.4; *1987,* NCJ-118762, Table 5.4; *1988,* NCJ-124280, Table 5.4; *1989,* NCJ-
130445, Table 5.4; *1990,* NCJ-135946, Table 5.4; *1991,* NCJ-142729, Table 5.4; *1992,* NCJ-
146413, Table 5.4; *1993,* NCJ-156241, Table 5.4; *1994,* NCJ-160091, Table 5.4; *1995,*
NCJ-163916, Table 5.4 (Washington, D.C.: U.S. Department of Justice). Figure constructed by
staff of *Sourcebook of Criminal Justice Statistics, 1998* (Washington, D.C.: Bureau of Justice
Statistics, 1999).

Figure 10-2   Survey Items Used to Measure Mental Illness

Do you have a mental or emotional condition?
(prison and jail inmates only)

☐ Yes
☐ No

Have you ever been told by a mental health professional
such as a psychiatrist, psychologist, social worker, or
psychiatric nurse, that you had a mental or emotional disorder?
(probationers only)

☐ Yes
☐ No

Because of an emotional or mental problem, have you ever —
   Taken a medication prescribed by a psychiatrist or other doctor?

☐ Yes
☐ No

   Been admitted to a mental hospital, unit, or treatment program
   where you stayed overnight?

☐ Yes
☐ No

   Received counseling or therapy from a trained professional?

☐ Yes
☐ No

   Received any other mental health services?

☐ Yes
☐ No

Source: Paula Ditton, "Mental Health and Treatment of Inmates and Probationers,"
Bureau of Justice Statistics Bulletin (Washington, D.C.: Bureau of Justice
Statistics, 1999).

Table 10-2   Estimated Number of
Mentally Ill Inmates and Probationers, 1998

Characteristic	Estimated Number of Offenders[a]			
	State Prison	Federal Prison	Local Jail	Probation
Identified as mentally ill	179,200	7,900	96,700	547,800
Reported a mental or emotional condition	111,300	5,200	62,100	473,000
Admitted overnight to a mental hospital	118,300	5,000	60,500	281,200

[a]Based on midyear 1998 counts from the National Prisoner Statistics and Annual
Survey of Jails and preliminary yearend 1998 counts from the Annual Probation
Survey.

Source: Paula Ditton, "Mental Health and Treatment of Inmates and Probationers,"
Bureau of Justice Statistics Bulletin (Washington, D.C.: Bureau of Justice
Statistics, 1999).

some form of correctional supervision. More than half a million probationers are believed to be identifiable as mentally ill. These offenders are slightly more likely to be female, white, and between the ages of thirty-five and fifty-five (Table 10-3).[7] Mentally ill inmates commit violent and property offenses at a greater rate than their non-mentally-ill counterparts, but they are involved in far fewer drug-related offenses, including trafficking and possession (Table 10-4).[8] These offenders are nearly three times as likely to have been homeless

Table 10-3   Inmates and Probationers Identified as
Mentally Ill, by Gender, Race/Hispanic Origin, and Age

Offender Characteristic	Percent Identified as Mentally Ill			
	State Inmates	Federal Inmates	Jail Inmates	Probationers
Gender				
Male	15.8	7.0	15.6	14.7
Female	23.6	12.5	22.7	21.7
Race/Hispanic origin				
White[a]	22.6	11.8	21.7	19.6
Black[a]	13.5	5.6	13.7	10.4
Hispanic	11.0	4.1	11.1	9.0
Age				
24 or younger	14.4	6.6	13.3	13.8
25–34	14.8	5.9	15.7	13.8
35–44	18.4	7.5	19.3	19.8
45–54	19.7	10.3	22.7	21.1
55 or older	15.6	8.9	20.4	16.0

[a] Excludes Hispanics.

Source: Paula Ditton, "Mental Health and Treatment of Inmates and Probationers,"
Bureau of Justice Statistics Bulletin (Washington, D.C.: Bureau of Justice
Statistics, 1999).

Table 10-4   Most Serious Current Offense of
Inmates and Probationers, by Mental Health Status

Most Serious Offense	State Prison		Federal Prison		Local Jail		Probation	
	Mentally Ill Inmates	Other Inmates	Mentally Ill Inmates	Other Inmates	Mentally Ill Inmates	Other Inmates	Mentally Ill Probationers	Other Probationers
Violent offenses	52.9%	46.1%	33.1%	13.3%	29.9%	25.6%	28.4%	18.4%
Murder[a]	13.2	11.4	1.9	1.4	3.5	2.7	0.5	0.9
Sexual assault	12.4	7.9	1.9	0.7	5.2	2.8	6.8	4.1
Robbery	13.0	14.4	20.8	9.1	4.7	6.9	2.0	1.4
Assault	10.9	9.0	3.8	1.1	14.4	11.0	14.0	10.5
Property offenses	24.4	21.5	8.7	6.7	31.3	26.0	30.4	28.5
Burglary	12.1	10.5	1.0	0.3	9.1	7.4	6.4	4.3
Larceny/theft	4.6	4.1	1.3	0.4	8.4	7.9	5.3	8.8
Fraud	3.1	2.6	5.0	4.9	5.2	4.4	11.7	9.2
Drug offenses	12.8	22.2	40.4	64.4	15.2	23.3	16.1	20.7
Possession	5.7	9.4	3.9	11.9	7.3	12.3	7.2	11.0
Trafficking	6.6	12.2	35.7	46.6	7.0	9.6	6.7	9.2
Public-order offenses	9.9	9.8	17.0	14.6	23.2	24.6	24.7	31.6

Note: Detail does not sum to one hundred because of excluded offense
categories.

[a]Includes non-negligent manslaughter.

during the year prior to their arrest or at the time of their arrest than non-mentally-ill inmates. In addition, the mentally ill inmates surveyed reported far greater numbers of contacts with the criminal justice system and numbers of prior incarceration and probation sentences than non-mentally-ill inmates (Table 10-5).[9]

Based upon these figures, the conclusion can easily be drawn that the mentally ill crimi-

Table 10-5   Criminal History of Inmates, by Mental Health Status

Criminal History Characteristic	State Prison		Federal Prison		Local Jail	
	Mentally Ill Inmates	Other Inmates	Mentally ill Inmates	Other Inmates	Mentally Ill Inmates	Other Inmates
Criminal history						
None	18.8%	21.2%	24.3%	38.8%	21.0%	28.4%
Priors	81.2	78.8	75.7	61.2	79.0	71.6
Violent recidivists	53.4	44.9	43.7	21.6	46.0	31.6
Other recidivists	27.8	33.8	32.0	39.6	33.0	40.0
Number of prior probation/ incarceration sentences						
0	18.8	21.2	24.3	38.8	21.0	28.4
1	15.5	19.4	14.0	18.2	14.7	17.9
2	13.8	17.0	12.9	14.7	10.1	11.5
3 to 5	26.3	25.5	23.6	18.9	23.5	19.7
6 to 10	15.6	11.6	15.4	7.3	17.6	14.6
11 or more	10.0	5.3	9.7	2.2	13.2	7.8

Source: Paula Ditton, "Mental Health and Treatment of Inmates and Probationers,"
Bureau of Justice Statistics Bulletin (Washington, D.C.: Bureau of Justice
Statistics, 1999).

nal, inmate, parolee, or probationer poses a serious threat to the safety of the public and challenges the effectiveness of the justice system. However, this should not be interpreted as a failure of the criminal justice system. Most practitioners in the corrections field acknowledge that dealing with mentally ill offenders is not what the system was designed to do. Dealing with the mentally ill is a function that has been forced upon the corrections system, not a function it has taken by choice.

History of the Problem

The causes for the mentally ill and corrections nexus have their roots in the social and economic state of the 1970s. At the time, public mental hospitals were, and to a great extent still are, supported by state-level funds. The economic recession of the early 1970s, which was fueled by rising oil prices and increased costs of production, caused the closure of many businesses and consequently harmed the financial condition of many states. Financial administrators and budget directors were anxious to find budget items that could be eliminated without any significant outcry from the state's citizenry. They targeted programs that were unpopular or had been receiving considerable criticism from special interest groups. By cutting these programs, administrators could save money for the state and eliminate a potential liability. It was a win-win situation from their perspective.

Programs that cost the most and have the least impact on voting members of the society usually deal with children and inmates (who cannot vote) and with the mentally ill. At the time of the recession of the 1970s, other factors would emerge and make the closure of mental health facilities even more attractive.

Pharmacology had been making great strides in the chemical control of aberrant behavior since the late 1950s. Compounds such as Resurpine and the new class of **antipsychotic drugs,** which were analogs of Phenothiazine, were shown to be particularly effective.[10] By the late 1960s, many drugs had been proven to have predictable effects on a wide range of behavioral disorders and were in wide use in mental hospitals. The chemical control of behavior brought relief to the violent and mentally ill, those who previously had been controlled by electroshock therapy and long-term institutionalization.[11]

Furthermore, social psychology, which emerged in 1908, had become a powerful and respected area of psychology by the 1970s. Social psychology sought to explain the individual's behavior in the context of the social order of the group and the individual's placement within that group. At the time of the recession and subsequent weakening of the economies of many states, social psychological research had indicated that residents in mental hospitals were unlikely to ever make the transition to life on the outside if they waited to be cured before they were released. The solution became to mainstream mentally ill persons back into the community through a process of increasing their time out and providing assistance to them while on the outside, in the form of outpatient treatment programs and clinical supervision. At the time this suggestion was being made, watchdog groups were chiding the state for the conditions in their hospitals and the ways these hospitals controlled their patients. Mental hospitals were often referred to as "snake pits" and the movie *One Flew Over the Cuckoo's Nest,* which was viewed by many as a documentary, helped to awaken the public to the horrors within these facilities.

The economic, medical, social, and practical elements all rolled together to create an inducement at the state level to close mental hospitals and to mainstream, with the help of new medications, the patients back into society. This solution appeared acceptable in theory, but in practice it was far from the ideal proposed by its supporters. It had serious flaws, which eventually placed the problem of the mentally ill in the hands of the justice system. Mental health clients were medically stabilized before being released into the community. Once released, the added stress of the real world and the loss of the familiar routine of the institution caused many clients to experience undermedication, which allowed their prior behaviors to again manifest themselves. In addition, compliance with the medication routine

and schedule was difficult because these individuals had never been responsible for their own medication. Some took too much, some too little; most took their drugs irregularly. Some medications (such as the lithium salts used for bipolar disorders) were toxic in the wrong dosages, and illness and death occurred. Often, while exhibiting poor behavior brought on by lack of medication and stress from the **mainstreaming** experience, clients would strike out against another person and wind up in the criminal justice system.

For many of these once-institutionalized people, life became a circuit between the jail, the street, and the secure mental institution. Offenders would arrive in jail following an arrest for a crime. The medical staff would (ideally) work to stabilize their medications and to manage their behavior. At that point, some offenders would receive probation and again hit the street. Others would be adjudicated and, if the crime was serious enough and their criminal history extensive enough, be sentenced to a secure correctional facility. If incarcerated, offenders would experience the pressures and problems of the correctional facility, which would likely overwhelm the stability created by medications, and they would again exhibit aberrant behavior. The custodial staff, recognizing that such behavior was the consequence of undermedication, would often send inmates to either a secure mental hospital or the medical unit of that facility. In either case, inmates would be stabilized within this new environment and would eventually be returned to the custodial environment once the medications had been stabilized.[12]

This process would have worked well, had it not been for the inherent instability of most correctional environments. Something would eventually destabilize the inmate. Overcrowding, violence, mismanagement of medications, or delayed med-call (the time inmates go to get medications from the pharmacy staff) would cause the inmate to become destabilized and again begin the circuit between the correctional facility and the therapeutic environment.[13]

Following this experience, assuming inmates received enough good-time credits to be released on some form of community-based corrections, offenders would be released with community supervision. This happened regularly, because the correctional facility was eager to see them leave and the court recognized that release in this way would allow someone on the outside to keep an eye on them and provide more supervision for a longer period. If offenders serve all of their sentence, they leave without any form of supervision. Early release allows the justice system to supervise them, and it relieves to some degree the overcrowding in the mental health facility.

Special Problems

Providing services and supervision to the mentally ill offender poses some unique problems, some of which are structural in their origin and some stem from the nature of the client population. Correctional staff typically receive minimal training to deal with the mentally ill offender. They are even less able to deal with the serious psychotic offender, who typically poses the greatest risk to public safety.[14] These offenders tend to be more difficult to supervise and control because of their illness and their probation or parole requirements. The mentally ill offenders' problems fall into four areas:

1. Mentally ill populations often have problems with understanding and remembering the directions given by the court.

2. The behavioral requirements placed upon mentally ill offenders by the court may be difficult or impossible for them to satisfy, given their condition and their occasional inability to control their behavior.

3. Mental health resources in the community, which are necessary to maintain the stability of offenders, are often inaccessible or over-

burdened, resulting in insufficient support and subsequent problem behavior.

4. **Service integration** necessary for all service providers and supervisors to be aware of the treatment plan for offenders and the requirements of their release program is lacking.[15]

While these problems result in revocation and new criminality for offenders, some focused strategies in use in probation and parole agencies indicate that the problem may be manageable, with the right commitment and training.

The special needs of the mentally ill offender are too often ignored. If the population were minuscule, then this would be an unimportant and insignificant issue. However, more than 500,000 probationers are believed to be suffering from some form of mental illness, and nearly 180,000 state prison inmates report having mental health issues. Thus, effective supervision of this client population is critical. In the past, effective supervision was seen as an impossible dream. Programs that worked were considered temporary at best and a mere coincidence at worst. Part of the reason for this cynicism or fatalism was that the mentally ill offender population was constantly changing. Any program that was rigid enough to control was likely to be too rigid to respond effectively and quickly to the changing needs of the mentally ill offender. What needed to be reconsidered was not the idea of specialized programming, but the structure of the programming, which required rigidity and severity to operate effectively. Some successful strategies and programming options are specialized mental health programs, specialized training for corrections professionals, and specialized supervision policies and practices.

Specialized Mental Health Programs   These may include:

- Aggressive utilization of existing mental health services.

- Locating and utilizing mental health professionals who specialize in intensive therapeutic interventions with criminal justice-based clients.

- Locating alternative sources of funding to support entry into these programs for clients who need the services but are unable to pay. [16]

Specialized Training for Corrections Professionals   Effective training should focus on the following areas:

- The characteristics of mental illness and the ways this illness changes and distorts the daily existence of those who are afflicted.

- The many mental health **treatment modalities,** and the impact these different forms of treatment can have on specific types of mental illness.

- The availability of treatment, and the various treatment providers in their area.

- The laws and legal issues surrounding the mentally ill offender, including confidentiality, the right to treatment, and legislatively mandated notification statutes.

- The reasonable goals and expected outcomes of any treatment protocol. [17]

This type of training is referred to as cross training because it helps the correctional staff member to appreciate the difficulties presented in another field. If done properly, specialized training can integrate mental health service providers and community correctional staff to achieve an enhanced understanding of the problems of both areas.

Specialized Supervision Policies and Practices   This response to mentally ill offenders focuses on modifying the practices of the specific community correctional agency. Suggested changes include:

- Specializing caseloads, making an officer or a group of officers responsible for all of the mentally ill offenders in the supervision office.

- Structuring policies and procedures to take into account the real possibility of **relapse,**

and offering specialized training to know how to deal with this relapse in the most effective manner.

- **Progressive,** increasing **sanctions.** Making policy that recognizes the differences of this population and its inclination to violate the law. [18]

Mentally Ill Offenders Summary

The mentally ill in prisons and communities present a challenge to society. Wanting to treat this population with humanity and also wanting to ensure public safety make the sentencing and supervision process difficult. A large number of mentally ill people are in the criminal justice system, and these offenders tend to be recidivists, prone toward violent acts, and difficult to manage and control. Many problems that the justice system faces today are the result of political changes and medical advances made more than thirty years ago. While the factors that closed many mental health facilities can be examined, the damage cannot be undone by instantly creating new hospitals. Without sufficient long-term space for the mentally ill, the justice system is forced to deal with them—and to deal with them in a manner that is most effective at both the therapeutic and public safety levels. While these goals are difficult and expensive to achieve, strategies exist to reach these goals for many offenders.

Sex Offenders

Sex offenders are considered by many practitioners to be the most difficult offender population to treat.[19] From a practical perspective, their release from incarceration to a community-based treatment program represents perhaps the hardest public relations task in the business of corrections. Even murderers, perpetrators of an offense considered extremely heinous by most societal standards, are accepted with less resistance than the average sex offender. These offenders are considered by clinical practitioners to be extremely complex and able to convincingly cover up the causes of their behavior as well as the potential for repeat offenses. From the outside, they often appear to present little risk, but what is being viewed may be exactly what offenders want viewed. The clinician often sees the image offenders want to portray, not the reality. One reason the public is so reluctant to accept sex offenders back into their communities is the incredible trauma their acts create within their victims.[20] The psychological effects are often long term and are especially devastating for young victims.

Because of this reality, community-based corrections has to be especially cautious about who is accepted for programming, and it must also be painfully honest about both the potential for these persons to be reformed and the threat they present to the public. Like most inmates, sex offenders will eventually be released from prison. Without some form of community correctional supervision, the public may have no hope for protection, and the offender may have little opportunity for aftercare.

Extent of the Problem

According to the Bureau of Justice Statistics, 101,900 **sex offenses** were reported in the United States in 1997, excluding forcible rape and prostitution. In the same year, 32,060 rapes were reported. In contrast, there were 132,450 reported robberies, and 18,290 reported cases of murder and non-negligent manslaughter.[21] While rape and other sexual offenses are not committed in as high a rate as motor vehicle theft, they are far more significant crimes and represent a far greater risk to the public safety. Rape statistics, which have been compiled for decades, currently indicate a declining trend that began around 1991, when rape peaked at 16 reported acts per 100,000 inhabitants. While this is, without question, good news for Americans' social and personal safety, the numbers are still high. The perpetrators of these offenses still exist in the corrections system and will likely be released to the community at the completion of their sentences. The median sentence handed down in state courts for rape or sexual assault cases was sixty months in 1997.[22] With good-time reductions, these offenders could reasonably expect to be released after serving around forty-two months. Perhaps in recognition of the reality of re-offense for this offender type, persons convicted of rape at the state level were most likely to be required to receive treatment as a condition of their sentence.[23]

That being the case, the community corrections staff in the area where the offender is released likely will be asked to provide aftercare and make certain that the conditions of release are followed. Every state and the District of Columbia offer some form of treatment for convicted sex offenders, with about half of these programs existing in the community and the remainder operating within the confines of a prison or some other residential placement (Table 10-6).[24] Over half of all probation, parole, or combined agencies offer in-house counseling for offenders deemed in need of such programming (Figure 10-3).[25]

The problems created by sex offenders are significant, but some strategies for responding to these problems have developed in the past five to ten years. Many responses have proved entirely unsuccessful, but a few show some limited statistical success.

System Responses

Notification Laws   Sex-offender notification is a relatively recent phenomenon, dating to the early 1990s. Prior to this time, the few states that required registration were unclear

Issues in Community Corrections

Sexually Violent Predators Acts

Judge Roger M. Young

The 1990s saw the first passage of what has become known as sexually violent predator laws. However, the law and the mental health sciences have long struggled with the problem of the recidivist sexual criminal. Only time will tell if this new generation of legislation will have a more lasting impact than past efforts that also enjoyed initial favorable popularity, yet ultimately lost favor with the legal and mental health professionals left with the daunting task of predicting future dangerousness.

Predicting future dangerousness lies at the heart of sexually violent predator (SVP) laws. Michigan passed the nation's first sexual psychopathy law in 1937, a result of media attention and public reaction to a series of brutal sex crimes. Almost every other state soon reacted with similar laws. There existed a notion that medical professionals could consistently and accurately identify a class of sexual psychopaths who could be separated and successfully treated. In the face of practical experience and civil libertarian concerns, these early attempts to divert sexual offenders to the mental health system until they were no longer deemed to be a threat to others began to lose favor with both the legal and psychotherapeutic communities by the 1960s. As a result, by the mid-1980s, these laws were either repealed or often left unenforced.

The pendulum began to swing back when, as a result of several heinous sex crimes in the late 1980s, Washington state passed the first of this new generation of laws. In 1994, Kansas passed an SVP law that later became the first to be challenged in the United State Supreme Court. In *Kansas v. Hendricks*, 521

U.S. 346 (1997), a five-to-four Supreme Court found that SVP laws that provided for involuntary civil commitment of a person deemed to be mentally abnormal and a future danger were constitutional "under the appropriate circumstances and when accompanied by proper procedures."

The Court held that affirmative restraint, even if for an indefinite period of time, was not punishment in fact, and that the state's use of criminal procedure in the civil commitment process did not transform a civil commitment into a criminal prosecution. The dissenters argued that determining "mental abnormality" may be too imprecise a category for justifying civil detention, and warned states against using the procedure as "a mechanism for retribution or general deterrence."

Fifteen states have now passed SVP laws: Arizona, California, Florida, Illinois, Iowa, Kansas, Massachusetts, Minnesota, Missouri, New Jersey, North Dakota, Oklahoma, South Carolina, Washington and Wisconsin. More are considering it. Typically a state approaches the problem by codifying in the health or probate section of the state's code of laws. The SVP acts usually define a "sexually violent predator" as a person who has been convicted of a "sexually violent offense" and suffers from a "mental abnormality or personality disorder" that makes the person likely to engage in acts of sexual violence if not confined in a secure facility for long-term control, care and treatment. The states usually delineate specific criminal sex acts as a "sexually violent offense," including rape, criminal sexual conduct with minors and committing lewd acts on minors. "Mental abnormality" is defined as "a mental condition affecting a person's emotional or volitional capacity that predisposes the person to commit sexually violent offenses." "Likely to engage in acts of sexual violence" means that "the person's propensity to commit acts of sexual violence is of such a degree as to pose a menace to the health and safety of others."

The commitment procedure usually begins when a person who has been convicted and incarcerated of a sexually violent offense is scheduled to be released from custody. Sometime prior to the scheduled release, usually 45–120 days, the custodial agency must notify a screening team who determines if there is enough in the person's background and character to warrant suspicion that the prisoner may commit another sexually violent crime. Early studies show this preliminary review weeds out roughly 90% of offenders who are deemed not to be any future threat. If the first level of review suggests the person meets the definition of an SVP, the committee passes on a recommendation to the prosecutorial machinery of the state, usually the state attorney general. The prosecution has its own internal committee review the file and if it agrees, the attorney general petitions a court to determine if there is probable cause to support an allegation that the person is an SVP. If the court concurs, the offender is then taken into (or remains in) custody. The court must then convene a probable cause hearing within a very short period of time to determine if the person should remain in custody. If the judge rules the state has made a showing of probable cause, the person is confined until trial. The court must then conduct a commitment trial to determine beyond a reasonable doubt whether the person is a sexually violent predator. The offender has a choice of bench or jury trial. If found to be an SVP, the person is committed to the custody of the state's public mental health facilities "for control, care, and treatment until such time as the person's mental abnormality or personality disorder has so changed that the person is safe to be at large" and a court determines that he or she is "not likely to commit acts of sexual violence" if released. The state laws typically allow the department of mental health to contract with correctional officials to house the SVP during the period of confinement.

Obviously, persons who commit a sexually violent crime are a danger to society, especially if they are likely to repeat their crimes. However, confining people for future acts raises many troubling issues, not the least of which is the ability of mental health professionals to accurately predict future dangerousness. SVP acts are also likely to face years of legal challenges as courts wrangle with issues not settled by the *Hendricks* decision, such as the breadth of constitutional rights enjoyed by the SVP at trial. Future challenges will also likely concern the scope of the usual evidentiary limitations by the state of using prior bad acts to prove the accused's misconduct at trial. Most importantly, since mental health treatment is notoriously ill-funded by states under the best of circumstances, SVP acts are likely to face serious challenges if states provide no more than *de minimus* psychiatric treatment for incapacitated offenders. Otherwise, the *Hendricks* dissenters' warning that SVP laws are mere pretexts for enhanced punishment may find favor in the courts and mental health sciences, and the cycle of events that eventually caused the early sexual psychopathy laws to lose support is likely to be repeated.

Table 10-6 Sex-Offender Programs and Treatment Providers, by State, 1996

State	Total Number of Programs	Residential Programs								Community-Based Programs						
		Total	Mental Health	Private	Court	Prison	Group Home	Half-Way House	Acute Care Hospital	Total	Mental Health	Private	Court	Prison	Group Home	Half-Way House
Total	1,391	192	55	36	7	70	18	4	2	1,199	396	745	50	4	1	3
Alabama	4	1	0	1	0	0	0	0	0	3	0	3	0	0	0	0
Alaska	4	0	0	0	0	0	0	0	0	4	0	4	0	0	0	0
Arizona	14	0	0	0	0	0	0	0	0	14	4	10	0	0	0	0
Arkansas	2	1	0	0	0	1	0	0	0	1	0	0	0	0	0	0
California	85	6	0	0	0	3	3	0	0	79	21	55	3	0	1	0
Colorado	33	7	0	4	0	3	0	0	0	26	5	21	0	0	0	0
Connecticut	27	2	1	0	0	2	1	0	1	25	6	18	0	1	0	0
Delaware	10	1	0	0	0	1	0	0	0	9	6	0	0	1	0	0
District of Columbia	6	0	0	0	0	0	0	0	0	6	0	3	0	0	0	3
Florida	56	2	0	2	0	0	0	0	0	54	8	6	0	0	0	0
Georgia	7	1	1	0	0	0	0	0	0	6	0	6	0	0	0	0
Hawaii	14	1	0	0	0	1	0	0	0	13	3	6	2	0	0	0
Idaho	13	3	0	0	0	0	3	0	0	10	3	7	0	0	0	0
Illinois	67	12	4	3	0	4	0	1	1	55	12	40	3	0	0	0
Indiana	25	8	4	2	0	2	0	0	0	17	11	6	0	0	0	0
Iowa	13	2	0	0	0	0	0	2	0	11	4	7	0	0	0	0
Kansas	33	3	0	0	0	3	0	0	0	30	26	4	0	0	0	0
Kentucky	13	4	2	0	0	2	0	0	0	9	3	5	0	1	0	0
Louisiana	9	2	0	0	0	2	0	0	0	7	0	7	0	0	0	0
Maine	17	4	0	0	2	0	0	0	0	13	0	12	1	0	0	0
Maryland	36	1	1	0	0	0	0	0	0	35	4	28	3	0	0	0
Massachusetts	51	8	4	3	0	1	0	0	0	43	9	34	0	0	0	0
Michigan	62	8	4	2	0	2	0	0	0	54	24	20	9	1	0	0
Minnesota	42	8	7	0	0	1	0	0	0	34	25	9	0	0	0	0
Mississippi	5	0	0	0	0	0	0	0	0	5	0	5	0	0	0	0
Missouri	23	5	3	0	1	1	0	0	0	18	7	9	2	0	0	0
Montana	17	2	1	0	0	1	0	0	0	15	0	15	0	0	0	0
Nebraska	11	3	0	1	0	2	0	0	0	8	3	5	0	0	0	0
Nevada	10	2	2	0	0	1	0	0	0	8	5	3	0	0	0	0
New Hampshire	18	2	0	1	0	1	0	0	0	16	9	7	0	0	0	0
New Jersey	50	5	3	0	0	2	0	0	0	45	17	23	5	0	0	0

Residential Programs | Community-Based Programs

State	Total Number of Programs	Residential: Total	Mental Health	Private	Court	Prison	Group Home	Half-Way House	Acute Care Hospital	Community: Total	Mental Health	Private	Court	Prison	Group Home	Half-Way House
New Mexico	3	2	2	0	0	0	0	0	0	1	0	1	0	0	0	0
New York	132	10	2	0	0	8	0	0	0	122	52	67	3	0	0	0
North Carolina	32	1	0	1	0	1	0	0	0	31	11	20	0	0	0	0
North Dakota	6	3	1	1	0	1	0	0	0	3	3	0	4	0	0	0
Ohio	63	5	0	1	1	1	2	0	0	58	36	18	0	0	0	0
Oklahoma	10	3	0	2	0	1	0	0	0	7	3	4	1	1	0	0
Oregon	48	2	1	0	0	0	1	0	0	46	15	30	1	0	0	0
Pennsylvania	79	21	3	6	1	11	0	0	0	58	22	35	0	0	0	0
Rhode Island	6	4	1	0	1	1	1	0	0	2	2	0	0	0	0	0
South Carolina	11	3	0	0	1	1	2	0	0	8	1	7	0	0	0	0
South Dakota	4	2	2	0	0	0	2	0	0	2	0	2	0	0	0	0
Tennessee	8	2	2	0	0	0	0	0	0	6	4	2	0	0	0	0
Texas	58	5	2	2	0	1	0	0	0	53	3	49	1	0	0	0
Utah	13	5	0	4	0	0	0	1	0	8	0	8	0	0	0	0
Vermont	21	2	1	0	0	1	0	0	0	19	6	13	0	0	0	0
Virginia	35	6	0	1	0	5	0	0	0	29	11	18	0	0	0	0
Washington	49	2	1	0	0	0	1	0	0	47	1	42	4	0	0	0
West Virginia	6	0	0	0	0	0	0	0	0	6	6	0	0	0	0	0
Wisconsin	21	8	2	0	1	5	0	0	0	13	2	11	0	0	0	0
Wyoming	9	2	0	0	0	2	0	0	0	7	3	4	0	0	0	0

Note: This information was collected by the Safer Society Foundation Inc. through a survey of 1,391 juvenile and adult sex-offender programs and service providers. These programs were identified through telephone and mail surveys; contacts with local, county, and state sex-offender treatment networks; and consultations. The 1,391 programs reflect data collected as of October 1, 1997, and represent approximately 55 percent of known treatment programs. Data collection is ongoing as programs and agencies continue to return questionnaires.

The information above does not include services provided for the incest offender when treated only within the context of the incest family, nonspecialized groups that include sex offenders, or adult sex-offender self-help programs.

The categories labeled "court" are those existing in conjunction with the court such as probation or parole offices or school districts. Categories labeled "private" refer to private nonprofit or private-for-profit agencies or professional services. "Community-based, prison" programs are those that are located in halfway houses operated by prison authorities.

Source: David Burton, Jan Levins, Joanne Smith-Darden, June A. Fiske, and Robert E. Freeman-Longo, 1996 Nationwide Survey of Treatment Programs and Models (Brandon, Vt.: The Safer Society Foundation Inc.., 2000). Table adapted by the staff of Sourcebook of Criminal Justice Statistics, 1998 (Washington, D.C.: Bureau of Justice Statistics, 2000).

Figure 10-3   Probation and Parole Agencies Offering Specific Services on January 1, 1997

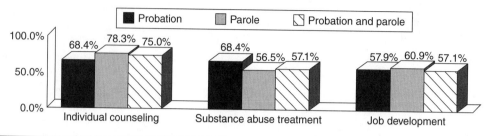

Source: George Camp and Camille Camp, *The Corrections Yearbook, 1997* (South Salem, N.Y.: Criminal Justice Institute, 1998). Reprinted with permission.

about what to do with this information once it had been reported to the proper justice agency. By 1995, all but seven states had enacted some form of mandatory **notification laws.** The goal was to create and maintain a central registry, which would serve as a community resource so sex offenders would be unable to hide from those citizens interested in knowing if their neighborhoods were at risk. Problems similar to those experienced by the older programs emerged almost immediately. These statutes, which vary from state to state, require different behaviors of the offender and allow the public differential access to the information. Some require the offender to register; others collect the information at the state level but allow local agencies to decide on public notification. One state requires the offender to do the notifying.[26] Little agreement exists as to the operations or the power of the notification procedure. States are inconsistent in the degree of proactivity they will assume with regard to community notification, how broadly they will disseminate the information, and how long the offender must continue to register after release.[27] Several states have attempted to create a set of policy guidelines and procedures to impose some consistency and structure onto this process, but as yet the process still remains individualized by state. The primary reason for this inconsistency seems to be the states' desire to strike a balance among the safety of the public, the offender's right to

privacy, and the problem with stigma and labeling of offenders.

Offender Containment Programs   The offender **containment program** represents a relatively new application of an existing approach to community corrections. The goal has less to do with offender rehabilitation than with public safety. The program builds on several beliefs about sex offenders. First, most sex-related crimes are done in secret, and the act is planned well in advance by the perpetrator. Second, most sex-offenders are high-functioning persons with well-developed social and cognitive skills. Third, sex offenders typically have serious and deep-rooted psychological problems, and they are able to create convincing facades to hide the truth about their actions. Fourth, sex offenders are likely to be repeat offenders and typically commit many and varied acts of sexual deviancy over the course of their lives.

The offender containment program places a high priority on public safety and seeks to accomplish this goal above all others. The program is structured around five key policies. First, public safety must be protected and maintained. Second, sex offenders are different from other caseloads, and officers that supervise these offenders in the community should experience more specialized training and be responsible for smaller caseloads. Third, the containment approach requires collaboration among all of the facets of the offender's life. The individual should be managed through contact with all who are in contact with the offender. If the offender has lost his or her job or his or her job duties have changed, the supervising officer has to know, especially if such a situation indicates an increased potential for a new offense. Fourth, the containment approach stresses consistent public policies, especially those that allow the offender to plead down a charge or defer sentencing until placement in a program can be arranged. If the offender has re-offended, then the program has not achieved its primary goal of public safety and the offender should not be allowed to bend the justice system to remain in the society. The system must be consistent and strict. Finally, the offender containment program supports the idea of ongoing self-examination to achieve quality in its operations. This includes monitoring the program to make certain policies are being followed and monitoring outcome variables to assure that offenders are not re-offending while on the program.[28]

Specialized Units or Caseloads   In this approach, the assumption is that the offender will likely not be receiving any supervision or treatment beyond what the probation or parole office is able to offer. Consequently, the office has to assure that the offender gets whatever is necessary in-house. To achieve some level of control or treatment, community corrections officers should work in groups and supervise a **specialized caseload** composed of sex offenders. This would allow the officers to receive specialized training; to serve a defined role within the group, a role that fits the officer's specific personal and professional strengths; and to assure that the offenders would receive competent supervision even in the absence of a primary supervisor. An enduring problem with individual probation caseloads is that the offenders often receive minimal or nonexistent supervision on the days that their officer is sick or on vacation. This should not happen

with specialized units or caseloads. Supervision would be available even in the absence of a specific member of the team.

Interagency Cooperation Programs   **Interagency cooperation programs** have been around for more than twenty years in the juvenile field. Juvenile justice was the first to recognize that the juvenile justice client often had several caseworkers dealing with different aspects of his or her case. A typical juvenile might have physical, emotional, educational, cognitive, and psychological problems. If these problems have been brought to the attention of the proper agencies, the juvenile might have had his or her case assigned to several persons, each working to repair a specific problem. Often these agents were unaware of their counterparts who were dealing with the different problems of the same client. Juvenile justice realized it could be more effective and efficient if their efforts were coordinated and did not overlap. Community corrections has learned from that experience and has attempted to achieve the same goals of increased effectiveness and enhanced efficiency.

Community Education Programs   **Community education programs** have little to do with the reform of the sex offender or the supervision of his or her actions. Instead, this approach attempts to educate the residents of the area where the offender has been located. The first goal is to make the local residents aware of the dangers, the things they should do to avoid unnecessary risks (do not let the offender babysit, for example), and who to call in the event that they suspect something potentially important is going on. The second goal is to explain to the residents what the real danger of this individual is and what they should not be afraid of. Some sex offenders are required to register with the state, which may be required to notify local residents of this person's presence. This is required, even though the offender's actions were a one-time event and may have occurred a long time ago. Educating the

Issues in Community Corrections

Principal Features of Sex Offender Registration Laws

- The registry is usually maintained by a State agency.

- Generally, local law enforcement is responsible for collecting information and forwarding it to the administrating State agency.

- Typical information obtained includes an offender's name, address, fingerprints, photo, date of birth, social security number, criminal history, place of employment, and vehicle registration. Eight States also collect blood samples for DNA identification; Michigan includes a DNA profile in the registry if available.

- The time frame for initial registration varies from "prior to release" or "immediately" to one year; the most common time frame is 30 days or less.

- In most States, the duration of the registration requirement is over 10 years, with 16 States requiring lifetime registration in all or some instances. Most States requiring lifetime registration allow the offender to petition the courts for relief from this duty.

- Most registries are updated only when the offender notifies law enforcement that he has changed residences. Seven States have annual address verification; New Jersey requires verification every 90 days.

- Twenty States specify that registry information is available only to law enforcement and related investigative authorities. The other twenty States allow broader access, ranging from criminal background checks for agencies hiring individuals to work with children, to full public access and community notification.

- Two States (California and Washington) have published compliance rates.

Source: Staci Thomas and Roxanne Lieb, *Sex Offender Registration: A Review of State Laws* (Olympia, Wash.: Washington State Institute for Public Policy, 1995), p. 1.

local residents about those facts might make them less nervous and more willing to accept the offender into their community.

Sex Offenders Summary

Notification statutes were intended to make the public more safe and to keep sex offenders from slipping unnoticed into neighborhoods. While that may have occurred in some specific cases, the inconsistency in the practice of notification, coupled with the public misuse of the information, has resulted in cases of harassment, stigmatization, and even returns to correctional environments because of the individual's inability to survive on the outside. Legal challenges to the notification statutes have been largely unsuccessful, and most states still use the statutes as they were originally written.[29] Intensive supervision programs have achieved minimal success, some claiming a 5 to 10 percent greater chance of surviving without a new offense for those in these programs. Intensive supervision pro-

Issues in Community Corrections

Containing the Sex Offender in the Supervision Triangle

Within the limits set by the supervision triangle of probation officer, therapist, and polygraph examiner, Jim was serving 4 years on probation for molesting the 7-year-old daughter of a woman he was dating. He had met the mother of the victim at church.

Although this was Jim's first conviction, he admitted he had long been attracted to young girls. Jim told his therapy group that, over the years, he attended church to "meet people." When pressed, he told the group that he had dated several women from the church and that all of them had young daughters. But he denied that this was a pattern that had preceded abuse.

The therapist called a team meeting with the probation officer and polygraph examiner to discuss Jim's pattern of accessing children.

The probation officer petitioned the court to modify probation orders to prohibit Jim from attending church unsupervised. The polygraph examiner then added the question "Have you gone to any church or religious services unsupervised since the last polygraph exam?" to the next examination.

The therapist and therapy group continued to work with Jim until he understood that going to church alone was, for him, a high-risk activity that placed him dangerously close to children.

Source: See D.C. Strate, D.C., L. Jones, S. Pullen, and K. English, "Criminal Justice Policies and Sex Offender Denial," in *Managing Adult Sex Offenders: A Containment Approach,* K. English, S. Pullen, and L. Jones (eds.) (Lexington, Ky.: American Probation and Parole Association, 1996), p. 4.9.

---

grams tend to be expensive to operate and controversial to the public, but they can achieve some limited success if they choose their participants carefully and remember that the goal of reform cannot be pursued at the expense of the goal of public safety.

Key Words and Concepts

antipsychotic drugs

asylums

community education programs

containment program

interagency cooperation programs

mainstreaming

notification laws

progressive sanctions

relapse

service integration

sex offenses

specialized caseload

treatment modalities

vagrants

Questions for Discussion

1. How would society control the mentally ill person today if antipsychotic drugs were unavailable?

2. Do vagrants exist in your area? How does society currently control this type of individual? What types of social, emotional, and practical problems exist in this population?

3. What are some of the negatives associated with mainstreaming the mentally ill back into society?

4. What different social service agencies might interact on the case of a mentally ill person? What about a sex offender?

5. Do notification laws and sexually violent predator acts serve to enhance justice or weaken personal freedom?

6. How could caseload specialization harm officer performance and job retention?

Kercher, G. A., and L. Long, *Supervision and Treatment of Sex Offenders* (Huntsville, Texas: Sam Houston State University Press, 1991).

O'Connell, M. A., E. Leberg, and C. R. Donaldson, *Working with Sex Offenders: Guidelines for Therapist Selection* (Newbury Park, Calif.: Sage, 1990).

Quinsey, V. L., G. T. Harris, M. E. Rice, and M. L. Lalumiere, "Assessing Treatment Efficacy in Outcome Studies of Sex Offenders," *Journal of Interpersonal Violence,* 8 (4), 1993, pp. 512–523.

Robins, Lee N., and Darrel A. Regier, *Psychiatric Disorders in America: The Epidemiological Catchment Area Study* (New York: Free Press, 1991).

For Further Reading

Green, R., "Comprehensive Treatment Planning for Sex Offenders," in *The Sex Offender: Corrections, Treatment, and Legal Practice,* B. K. Schwartz and H. R. Celline (eds.) (Kingston, N.J.: Civic Research Institute, 1995).

Chapter 11

Problems and Needs of Female Offenders

Special Problems of Female Offenders

Services

Community-Based Correctional Programs

Issues in the Treatment of Female Offenders

Summary

Women experience special problems when they enter the criminal justice system. About half of all female offenders have children. Many of these mothers are single or divorced women who are solely responsible for their children's physical, financial, and emotional welfare. Too often these mothers are inadequately prepared to offer the guidance and supervision effective parenting requires.

Because of the roles prescribed for women in contemporary society, the female offender often has special barriers to overcome before she can obtain employment. Jobs that provide an income sufficient to meet her family's needs and to achieve independent living are rarely available to the female offender with limited skills. Generally speaking, female offenders must meet special emotional and financial demands in an environment that offers limited economic opportunity and even less psychological support.

Incarceration in jails and prisons inevitably disrupts family ties and creates feelings of dependency. Female offenders suffer the same losses as males in this regard. Community-based programs can maintain and promote constructive relationships between family members, especially between mother and child. They can also prepare women for employment and strengthen feelings of independence and maturity. Community-based programs can treat offenders as responsible adults capable of self-direction. Because community programs provide the opportunity for successful experiences, they encourage offenders to live up to realistic expectations.

Figure 11-1   Male and Female Prisoner Populations

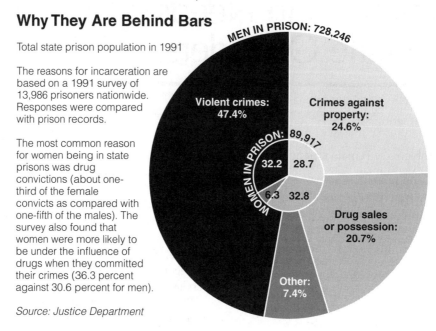

Why They Are Behind Bars

Total state prison population in 1991

The reasons for incarceration are based on a 1991 survey of 13,986 prisoners nationwide. Responses were compared with prison records.

The most common reason for women being in state prisons was drug convictions (about one-third of the female convicts as compared with one-fifth of the males). The survey also found that women were more likely to be under the influence of drugs when they committed their crimes (36.3 percent against 30.6 percent for men).

Source: Justice Department

MEN IN PRISON: 728,246

Violent crimes: 47.4%

Crimes against property: 24.6%

WOMEN IN PRISON: 89,917

32.2   28.7

6.3   32.8

Drug sales or possession: 20.7%

Other: 7.4%

Source: New York Times, July 3, 1994, p. E3. Copyright © 1994 by the New York Times Company. Reprinted by permission.

Female offenders are more likely to be placed in diversion or pretrial release programs and to be sentenced to probation if convicted than are male offenders. This is not because they receive more lenient treatment, but because the crimes women commit are generally less serious than those committed by men.

Special Problems of Female Offenders

Women and Crime

Women traditionally have contributed less to the crime problem than men. They commit fewer and less serious offenses than males, engaging in crimes of theft or victimless crimes rather than crimes of violence (Figure 11-1).

At present, however, certain types of female crime seem to be increasing at a faster pace than male crime. Between 1984 and 1997, the number of women arrested for serious violent crimes increased 86 percent, while male offenses increased only 18 percent. Female property crime increased 22.6 percent, while male serious property offenses decreased 5.6 percent (peaking in the early 1990s and declining since then).

While this growth in female crime has significant implications for corrections, which traditionally has allocated few resources for institutional or community-based programs for female offenders, little evidence is available that patterns of female criminality are changing in significant and permanent ways. In 1984, women accounted for 11 percent of serious violent crime; fourteen years later, they accounted for 16 percent. Similarly, in 1984 women were responsible for 23 percent

Issues in Community Corrections

Women Doing Crime,
Women Doing Time

Women wearing judges' robes or corporate pinstripes have become everyday images of society's changing gender roles. But what about women attired in Day-Glo prison jumpsuits?

The number of women in State and Federal prisons increased from 12,331 to 43,845 from 1980 to 1990, according to the Justice Department. That is an increase of 256 percent, compared with a 140 percent rise in the male prison population.

Arrests of women for serious felonies climbed 32.5 percent from 1988 to 1992, reaching 62,936 nationwide, according to the Justice Department canvass of more than 8,000 police agencies. The 1992 arrest figure is still small compared with the 452,453 men arrested for violent crimes that year.

The 8,000 law-enforcement agencies that responded to the canvass cover some 185 million Americans. While it does not list all people arrested in the United States, it is considered an accurate indicator of the types of crime being committed.

The fact that the rate of arrests for women under the age of 18 increased in those four years by 63 percent, compared with 45.4 percent for male youths, has attracted growing attention from law enforcement experts.

The swelling number of women being arrested and incarcerated raises questions about whether women are becoming more aggressive—in other words, more like those men who get caught up in lives of violence.

For now, a wide array of criminologists have concluded that as long as organized crime, neighborhood gangs and narcotics networks remain bastions of male domination, the answer is no, or at least not yet.

Many criminal justice scholars attribute the rise in the female crime rates more to the growing poverty among young, unattached mothers and the new ways society treats women than to the wider opportunities they have. More men are abandoning their families, leaving women with the burdens of children, and with the temptations to commit crimes to care for them.

Meanwhile, many studies find that the justice system, after decades of imposing lighter sentences, is more likely to treat wayward women harshly, be they first-time drug offenders or women who fight physically with husbands or boyfriends, even if they say the men hit them first.

"Simply put, it appears that the criminal justice system now seems more willing to incarcerate women," Meda Chesney-Lind, a University of Hawaii criminology professor, writes in a book awaiting publication.

Female criminals remain different from male wrongdoers in many respects. The percentage of women in prison for drug and property crimes is considerably higher than for male inmates. A recent study in Massachusetts, for instance, found that only 22 percent of the women imprisoned there were incarcerated for violent offenses, compared with 48 percent of the men behind bars.

Nationwide, almost two-thirds of the women in prison for violent crimes had been found guilty of assaulting or killing relatives or inmates, the Justice Department said. By contrast, violent males in prison were more than twice as likely to have assaulted or killed strangers. (But that ratio may change if the new

(continued)

Women Doing Crime,
Women Doing Time (*continued*)

attention being paid to spousal abuse results in more assault convictions for abusive husbands.)

Still, some argue that crimes committed by women, although far smaller in number, may nonetheless be more serious for society at large than the statistics reflect since rising rates of illegitimacy and divorce have made women even more responsible for future generations—thanks in no small measure to the irresponsibility of some men.

"Girls become mothers, and mothers influence the behaviors of their offspring," Joan McCord, a professor of criminology at Temple University, argued in an article published last year, "so that the net effects of antisocial behaviors may be greater for females than for males." A Justice Department study completed in March found that two-thirds of the women in prison have at least one child under the age of 18.

Early criminologists assumed that violence and criminal behavior were essentially masculine traits, and the few women who did commit acts of violence suffered some sort of biological abnormality.

Caesar Lombroso, a 19th-century Italian physician, carted home bags of women's bones from the prison of Turin to look for anatomical distinctions between criminal and noncriminal women. Lombroso's conclusion that abnormal cranium size and excessive body hair were the telltale signs of female criminal behavior were cast aside by the early 20th century.

Depicted as Deviants

But the depiction of female criminals as sexual deviants persisted through the first half of the century, until most scholars concluded that criminal behavior was mostly determined by social and economic factors.

No longer was criminality a matter of testosterone. In the widely discussed book *Sisters in Crime: The Rise of the New Female Criminal* (McGraw, 1975), the criminologist Freda Adler foresaw a "rising tide of female assertiveness" that would lead tens of thousands of women to step "across the imaginary boundary line which once separated crimes into 'masculine' and 'feminine' categories."

of all serious property arrests; that percentage had increased to only 29 percent fourteen years later.

In 1997, women were responsible for about 22 percent of all arrests. The offenses in which women were most frequently represented include larceny-theft, forgery and counterfeiting, fraud, embezzlement, and prostitution. In terms of sheer numbers of female arrests, drug abuse violations, disorderly conduct, and driving under

the influence (DUI) offenses involved the largest numbers of women, but their proportional involvement was modest in all of these offenses.

In the 1970s and 1980s, much was written about the **"new female criminal."**[1] Researchers suggested that today's female offender is more independent and aggressive than her predecessors and more likely to involve herself in white-collar crimes such as embezzlement. Some viewed the new female criminal as a

At first glance, the increase in arrest rates of women for vehicle theft, arson, robbery and aggravated assault confirm the conclusions of the first generation of female criminologists. Just as surely as women were capable of running corporate boardrooms, they said, women who commit crimes would branch out from "traditional" offenses like prostitution and shoplifting.

If examples of this growing "diversity" are isolated, they are also chilling. Last September, a 20-year-old professional thief named Patsy Jones stung the Miami tourist industry after she was accused of fatally shooting a German tourist along the Dolphin Expressway with a sawed-off hunting rifle.

In Brooklyn recently, a teen-ager shot and killed a livery cab driver in broad daylight after he resisted her and two girlfriends during a botched robbery attempt.

But the link between changing gender models and the number of women in prison remains dubious. Female criminologists increasingly reject predictions that a female crime wave is imminent. They noted that female participation in the ultimate violent crime—murder—remains extremely low.

The New York City police report that while women were accused of committing a third more felonies in 1993 than in 1975, 59 women were arrested for murder last year in the city compared with 120 women in 1975.

And while the growing number of women who work helps to explain why they are committing more forgery and embezzlement, the great majority of women in prison are poor and unemployed and not models of newly empowered, liberated women. "It's really difficult to discern whether women who commit crimes are any more liberated or have different gender-role attitudes than women who don't commit crimes," said Candace Kruttschnitt, a professor of sociology at the University of Minnesota.

"This is a murky area," she added.

Source: Clifford Krauss, "Women Doing Crime, Women Doing Time," *New York Times,* July 3, 1994, p. E3. Copyright (c) 1994 by the New York Times Co. Reprinted by permission.

product of the women's liberation movement. Because the fight for equal rights was perceived as opening up new social roles for women, both legitimate and illegitimate behavior patterns were expected to reflect the new alternatives available to women.

For better or worse, the new female criminal is largely a myth. Although women are committing more crimes of violence, it is too soon to know if this change is permanent or a simple artifact of the finding that females enter into crime as juveniles later than males and exit (age out) later. Although female crime is growing, the pattern of growth does not conclusively indicate the emergence of a new criminal behavior pattern. Instead, typical female criminal behavior appears to be a product of continuing social problems—the impact of physical and emotional abuse and extreme disadvantage, exacerbated by economic problems and drug and alcohol use. Women's violent crime is often a result of domestic abuse. Studies of female prisoners convicted of violent crimes reveal that such women generally have no criminal history and have victimized a relative, intimate, or someone they know.[2] There is little indication that female criminals engage in significant amounts of predatory violence (Table 11-1).

Women continue to demonstrate higher levels of involvement in property crime, reflecting welfare offenses, poor economic conditions, teenage pregnancies, and fathers' abandonment of their children. Women's increases in crime may also reflect the deleterious impact of drug problems such as those caused by crack, as well as physical, emotional, and sexual abuse. Such causes may lead to crimes of desperation rather than calculation. In general, most women's crime can be viewed as a response to poverty, chemical dependency, and the initial and long-term effects of current victimization and childhood abuse (Table 11-2).[3]

The Female Offender and the Criminal Justice System

Considerable debate has been waged over the nature and impact of the treatment women receive from the criminal justice system. Many observers have suggested that female offenders have benefited from special handling by chivalrous authorities. Critics of this position argue that paternalistic attempts to protect women from evil have only led to harsher treatment for the fallen woman or those women in danger of falling. Research suggests that, although there has been a slight tendency in the past to treat female criminals more leniently, the less serious nature of female crime is a more significant determinant of criminal justice processing than gender.

Criminal justice officials have traditionally viewed women as nondangerous offenders who are less in need of treatment and more easily rehabilitated than males.[4] Historically, female offenders were viewed as accessory criminals, basically good individuals who had come under the influence of a criminal male. For these offenders, the solution was to separate them from the male's influence, rather than to punish them. This attitude may have encouraged some leniency, but white middle- and upper-class women were more likely to benefit from this attitude than the majority of lower-class female offenders. Ironically, most women criminals have been victimized by the view that female offenders do not need treatment. Because of this attitude, the smaller number of female offenders, and the relative ease with which they are controlled in prison, correctional administrators have tended to minimize the female offender's special problems and needs.[5] Today, because of determinate sentences and changing socal attitudes, lenient treatment has all but disappeared from criminal justice processing, and the development of special programs for women has just begun.

The get-tough-on-crime movement has affected women as well as men, as has the "war on drugs." Mandatory sentencing has increased the number of females who receive prison sentences. Tougher sanctions for drug offenders have also increased the number of female prisoners. The number of women in state prisons increased 81 percent between 1990 and 1999—reaching almost sixty-eight thousand in 1999, with an additional 81,713 female inmates housed in federal institutions and county-level jails.[6] That represents an increase of almost ten thousand female inmates in only two years, an enormous number of offenders to absorb into the correctional system. California tops the rest of the nation with more than eleven thousand females incarcerated in its state prison system.[7]

Even with this tremendous increase in female offenders, women still account for only about 6 percent of all prison inmates, 11 percent of jail inmates, 21 percent of probationers, and 12 percent of parolees (Table 11-3).[8] Because of the larger numbers of male offenders, correctional authorities continue to focus

Table 11-1 Arrests, by Offense Charged and Gender, 1997

(9,271 agencies; 1997 estimated population 183,240,000)

Offense Charged	Persons Arrested					Percent Distribution of Offenses Charged[a]		
	Total Number	Male		Female		Total	Male	Female
		Number	Percent	Number	Percent			
Total	10,544,624	8,261,870	78.4	2,282,754	21.6	100.0	100.0	100.0
Murder and nonnegligent manslaughter	12,764	11,447	89.7	1,317	10.3	0.1	0.1	0.1
Forcible rape	22,133	21,855	98.7	278	1.3	0.2	0.3	(b)
Robbery	94,034	84,808	90.2	9,226	9.8	0.9	1.0	0.4
Aggravated assault	372,422	302,268	81.2	70,154	18.8	3.5	3.7	3.1
Burglary	245,816	216,612	88.1	29,204	11.9	2.3	2.6	1.3
Larceny-theft	1,033,901	676,219	65.4	357,682	34.6	9.8	8.2	15.7
Motor vehicle theft	116,052	98,651	85.0	17,401	15.0	1.1	1.2	0.8
Arson	13,831	11,751	85.0	2,080	15.0	0.1	0.1	0.1
Violent crime [c]	501,353	420,378	83.8	80,975	16.2	4.8	5.1	3.5
Property crime[d]	1,409,600	1,003,233	71.2	406,367	28.8	13.4	12.1	17.8
Total crime index[e]	1,910,953	1,423,611	74.5	487,342	25.5	18.1	17.2	21.3
Other assaults	965,063	759,578	78.7	205,485	21.3	9.2	9.2	9.0
Forgery and counterfeiting	83,051	51,018	61.4	32,033	38.6	0.8	0.6	1.4
Fraud	274,950	148,271	53.9	126,679	46.1	2.6	1.8	5.5
Embezzlement	12,269	6,488	52.9	5,781	47.1	0.1	0.1	0.3
Stolen property: buying, receiving, possessing	108,580	91,768	84.5	16,812	15.5	1.0	1.1	0.7
Vandalism	219,494	186,748	85.1	32,746	14.9	2.1	2.3	1.4
Weapons: carrying, possessing, etc.	152,368	139,834	91.8	12,534	8.2	1.4	1.7	0.5
Prostitution and commercialized vice	72,385	28,785	39.8	43,600	60.2	0.7	0.3	1.9
Sex offenses (except forcible rape and prostitution)	70,237	63,814	90.9	6,423	9.1	0.7	0.8	0.3
Drug abuse violations	1,102,335	911,158	82.7	191,177	17.3	10.5	11.0	8.4
Gambling	11,065	9,984	90.2	1,081	9.8	0.1	0.1	(b)
Offenses against family and children	104,997	79,884	76.1	25,113	23.9	1.0	1.0	1.1
Driving under the influence	986,339	835,326	84.7	151,013	15.3	9.4	10.1	6.6
Liquor laws	431,609	338,748	78.5	92,861	21.5	4.1	4.1	4.1
Drunkenness	509,764	446,949	87.7	62,815	12.3	4.8	5.4	2.8
Disorderly conduct	561,621	437,525	77.9	124,096	22.1	5.3	5.3	5.4
Vagrancy	20,325	15,614	76.8	4,711	23.2	0.2	0.2	0.2
All other offenses (except traffic)	2,678,140	2,137,487	79.8	540,653	20.2	25.4	25.9	23.7
Suspicion	4,409	3,503	79.5	906	20.5	(b)	(b)	(b)
Curfew and loitering law violations	128,320	88,828	69.2	39,492	30.8	1.2	1.1	1.7
Runaways	136,350	56,949	41.8	79,401	58.2	1.3	0.7	3.5

Note: Data compiled by the Federal Bureau of Investigation, through the Uniform Crime Reporting Program. Data represent only agencies that submitted complete reports for the twelve months of 1997. Estimates by the U.S. Bureau of the Census indicate that on July 1, 1997, males comprised 49.0% and females 51.0% of the total U.S. resident population. U.S. Department of Commerce, Bureau of the Census, *U.S. Population Estimates by Age, Sex, Race, and Hispanic Origin: 1990 to 1997* (Washington, D.C.: U.S. Department of Commerce, April 1998, mimeograph), Table 1.

[a]Because of rounding, percents may not add to total.

[b]Less than 0.1%

[c]Violent crimes are offenses of murder and non-negligent manslaughter, forcible rape, robbery, and aggravated assault.

[d]Property crimes are offenses of burglary, larceny-theft, motor vehicle theft, and arson.

[e]Includes arson.

Source: U.S. Department of Justice, Federal Bureau of Investigation, *Crime in the United States, 1997* (Washington, D.C.: U.S. Government Printing Office, 1998), p. 239. Table adapted by the staff of *Sourcebook of Criminal Justice Statistics, 1998* (Washington, D.C.: Bureau of Justice Statistics, 1999).

Table 11-2   Prison and Jail Inmates and Probationers Reporting Physical or Sexual Abuse Prior to Admission, by Gender of Inmate or Probationer, 1995, 1996, and 1997

| | Prison Inmates[a] | | | | Jail Inmates[b] | | Probationers[c] | |
| | State | | Federal | | | | | |
Before Admission	Male	Female	Male	Female	Male	Female	Male	Female
Ever abused	16.1%	57.2%	7.2%	39.9%	12.9%	47.6%	9.3%	40.4%
Physically[d]	13.4	46.5	6.0	32.3	10.7	37.3	7.4	33.5
Sexually[d]	5.8	39.0	2.2	22.8	5.6	37.2	4.1	25.2
Both	3.0	28.0	1.1	15.1	3.3	26.9	2.1	18.3
Age of victim at time of abuse								
17 or younger[e]	14.4	36.7	5.8	23.0	11.9	36.6	8.8	28.2
18 or older[e]	4.3	45.0	2.7	31.0	2.3	26.7	1.1	24.7
Both	2.5	24.7	1.3	14.2	1.3	15.8	0.5	12.5
Age of abuser								
Adult	15.0	55.8	6.9	39.0	12.1	46.0	8.5	39.2
Juvenile only	0.9	1.0	0.2	0.3	0.8	1.3	0.6	1.2
Experienced rape before admission	4.0	37.3	1.4	21.4	3.9	33.1	NA	NA
Completed	3.1	32.8	1.0	17.9	3.0	26.6	NA	NA
Attempted	0.8	4.3	0.3	3.2	0.7	5.6	NA	NA

Note: These data were taken from four U.S. Department of Justice, Bureau of Justice Statistics (BJS) surveys: the Surveys of Inmates in State or Federal Correctional Facilities, 1997; the Survey of Inmates in Local Jails, 1996; and the Survey of Adults on Probation, 1995. In all four surveys, nationally representative samples of inmates or probationers were interviewed about their current offense and sentence, criminal history, personal and family background, and prior drug and alcohol use and treatment.

[a]Data are from a BJS survey conducted in 1997.

[b]Data are from a BJS survey conducted in 1996.

[c]Data are from a BJS survey conducted in 1995.

[d]Includes those reporting experiences of both physical and sexual abuse.

[e]Includes those reporting experiencing abuse during both age categories

Source: U.S. Department of Justice, Bureau of Justice Statistics, *Prior Abuse Reported by Inmates and Probationers,* Selected Findings NCJ-172879 (Washington, D.C.: U.S. Department of Justice, April 1999), p. 2, Table 1.

resources and program development on prisons and programs for males.

However, signs are becoming evident that this practice is changing. Programs that originated with only men in mind, such as boot camps, are beginning to serve female offenders. With the expansion of correctional facilities for female offenders, the feasibility of programs and services designed to meet the special needs of women offenders is being examined for cost-effectiveness.

In 1995, the American Correctional Association issued a policy statement calling for equal treatment and services for male and female inmates and programs designed to meet the unique needs of female offenders. These are to include "work and programs designed to expand economic and social roles of women, with emphasis on education, career counseling, and exploration of nontraditional vocational training," as well as training in "relevant life skills, including parenting and social and economic assertiveness."[9]

Social Roles and the Needs of the Female Offender

In regard to their problems and needs, criminal offenders are more alike than different. They

Table 11-3 Number of Inmates in State
or Federal Prisons and Local Jails, by Gender,
Race, Hispanic Origin, and Age, June 30, 1999

| | Number of Inmates in State or Federal Prisons or Local Jails | | | | | | | |
| | Male | | | | Female | | | |
Age	Total[a]	White[b]	Black[b]	Hispanic	Total[a]	White[b]	Black[b]	Hispanic
Total	1,711,400	610,100	757,000	296,300	149,200	53,600	57,900	22,800
18–19	78,600	24,400	35,300	16,000	3,700	1,700	1,400	500
20–24	298,600	91,400	136,200	62,000	18,800	7,200	7,200	3,900
25–29	316,800	96,000	152,200	59,600	28,700	9,600	13,200	4,700
30–34	320,700	114,400	142,300	55,700	37,300	12,600	18,900	4,900
35–39	282,300	106,300	129,500	40,100	29,400	10,400	14,100	4,000
40–44	190,000	74,400	79,300	31,100	16,300	6,000	7,300	2,200
45–54	157,300	71,300	59,000	22,200	11,500	4,600	4,400	2,000
55 or older	48,800	27,000	12,600	7,300	2,500	1,400	800	200

Note: Based on custody counts from National Prisoners Statistics (NPS1-A), 1999
and Census of Jails, 1999, and estimates by age from Survey of Inmates in Local
Jails, 1996, and Survey of Inmates in State and Federal Correctional Facilities,
1997. Estimates were rounded to the nearest one hundred.

[a]Includes American Indians, Alaska Natives, Asians, Native Hawaiians, and other
Pacific Islanders.

[b]Excludes Hispanics.

need education, job training and placement, and counseling to be self-sufficient and to resolve various personal problems. Female offenders do have special needs, however, simply because the roles they tend to occupy in society are different from those held by males. Because women have children, they have special pressures and responsibilities. The financial demands and the all-encompassing managerial and emotional tasks of child rearing must be met. Regardless of the manner in which these obligations are performed, women with children must find the means to support themselves and their offspring.

Women, especially those in the extremely disadvantaged segments of society, are rarely encouraged to excel academically or even to complete their basic education. Like many in lower socioeconomic groups, these women view life as offering only an endless procession of menial jobs. Rising to semiskilled or skilled employment can seem to be a mysterious, arduous, and risky undertaking. For these women, achievement may undermine more important interpersonal relationships with males, so they may never learn ambition and discipline. Most

female offenders are thus poorly prepared for the world of work, especially for the positions needed to support a family.

Women today are still learning dependent behavior patterns. This learning is particularly prevalent among the more powerless and disadvantaged groups in society, where an individual's ability to change his or her economic and social status is limited. Women in these groups learn to promote a feeling of powerfulness and authority in males by assuming a subservient role. Although the dominant male and submissive female characterization is a stereotyped view of more complex social relations, this general pattern of interaction is common. An unwillingness to give up this behavioral pattern inhibits many women's efforts to assume responsibility for their own lives.

The female offender needs education and employment skills that will enable her to earn a living sufficient to support herself and her children. To obtain skills and employment and to manage her own life and raise her children, she needs confidence and the strength to be independent. Some community-based programs are designed to meet these needs. Although they are fewer in number, they demonstrate the potential of special programming for female offenders.

Services

Services for female offenders generally focus on developing economic independence, effective **parenting skills,** and the managerial or survival skills necessary to achieve independent living.

Economic Assistance

Economic assistance services attempt to break the **cycle of dependency, victimization, and crime** that is characteristic of the female offender. Four forms of assistance are possible: job readiness training, vocational training, job development and placement, and follow-up services.[10]

Job Readiness Training   Job readiness training is especially important for disadvantaged women. They normally have a stereotyped view of the types of jobs available to them and little familiarity with the world of work, the discipline it requires, or the mechanics of job seeking.

   Job readiness training can:

1. Provide vocational testing to determine the types of difficulties women may confront upon entering the employment system.

2. Offer such basic instruction as how to use public transportation, prepare a resume, or identify existing employment skills.

3. Introduce women to the types of jobs available (especially nontraditional jobs) through informational materials, visits to job sites, discussions with employed women, and exploratory training.

4. Teach job-seeking skills, such as how to locate job leads and use the want ads.

5. Prepare women for jobs and interviews through role playing and practice interviews.

6. Offer opportunities to build the confidence and self-esteem needed to make and maintain the transition to employees.[11]

Vocational Training   Women offenders have always been offered some form of vocational training, but it has not always been useful. Prison programs have been the least effective. Vocational training programs in women's prisons have tended to reflect both a traditional attitude toward women in the workforce and the proper sort of work for those with criminal records. Typically, what passes for training is in traditional female occupations, such as food preparation, garment making, and practical nursing, and low-paid or nonpaid work experience programs. The work experience programs are designed more to benefit the budget of the confining institution than they are to rehabilitate the confined individuals. Someone has to cook the food, wash the dishes, and mow the lawn. During much of the day, a major proportion of inmate energies is devoted to these in-house chores.[12]

   Today, effective vocational training for female offenders is more likely to focus on preparation for **nontraditional employment.** The reason for this shift is economic: Blue-collar jobs traditionally held by males pay higher wages than the pink-collar jobs normally filled by women. The best programs share two features: They prepare women for jobs with higher-than-average entry-level pay and focus on segments of the employment market where there is a documented demand for workers.[13]

   The need for work- or education-release programming for women was found to be particularly acute. Work-release programs serve the vital function of helping the offender make the transition to the real world of employment. Without such guidance and support, work skills alone may be insufficient to prepare the offender for successful independence.

Job Development and Placement   **Job development and placement** activities are basically the same for males and females. A particularly comprehensive program might include:

1. Screening.

2. Orientation.

3. Needs assessment.

4. Goal setting.

5. Employment-readiness counseling.

6. Employment search.

7. Placement.

8. Follow-up services.[14]

Placing women in nontraditional jobs requires special efforts to help employers as well as employees make the adjustment.[15] For example, a Washington, D.C., program prepares and distributes an employers' guide that provides information on affirmative action planning, recruitment, handling harassment, and management issues, such as employee attrition and internal mobility.[16]

Follow-up Services   **Employment follow-up services** are particularly important for female workers because of the diversity of problems they may encounter on or off the job. These services may be offered in a variety of ways. A supported work project in Los Angeles builds follow-up services into the workweek. Clients work four days a week and spend the fifth day at program headquarters, where they receive individual counseling on any topic related to job seeking or employment.[17] In other programs, staff act as intermediaries when conflicts with employers develop and provide counseling when female workers have problems with coworkers. These and similar efforts provide the female worker with continuing support after employment and facilitate her success both on and off the job.

Issues in Employment Programming   Effective employment programming has several requirements. Employment services offered to female offenders must be comprehensive. Employment readiness training must be linked to vocational training, which must in turn prepare women for existing jobs. Follow-up services must be offered to help the new employee keep her job. These services may be offered by one or a combination of community agencies, but they must all be available. A failure to offer comprehensive services can only result in women with less than enough to succeed: job readiness, but no skills; skills, but no job; or a job, but no support system to fall back on when problems develop.

If programs focus on nontraditional employment, they must recognize that this is a complex undertaking. Some evidence shows that female offenders prefer more traditional forms of employment over such jobs as truck driving and construction and do not keep jobs in nontraditional settings for long. This should not be surprising, because the independence and liberation required to prepare for and maintain these positions is missing from the lives of most female offenders.

This dilemma has no obvious solution. Nontraditional training programs could screen out all but the most enthusiastic women, but this would ignore the majority of female offenders. Reluctant offenders could be subtly coerced into nontraditional jobs, but this would result only in wasted training for many clients. A comprehensive and concerted effort to alter female offenders' perceived work options is needed, but this must be tempered with an understanding of client feelings and flexibility in providing both traditional and alternative training programs.

Finally, throughout the job preparation, training, and placement process, the availability of child care is a critical concern. Women with children need reliable day-care services if they are going to prepare for and participate in the world of work.

Programs for Parents

Raising a child is a full-time occupation. Even with a spouse or parent available to help with the task, the responsibilities can be overwhelming, and with no reliable assistance, the job can seem almost impossible. Many female offenders with children, not surprisingly, have at one time or another left their children in the care of family or friends.

The inmate mother has special problems. She may find it difficult to maintain contact with her children's caregivers. She may be unaware or ill informed about her children's growth, development, and well-being for significant periods of time.[18] Institutional visits may be few and far between. When they do occur, children may be fearful of the formidable physical structure and atmosphere of the institution. The separation of mother and child may produce emotional barriers. The child may come to see the caregiver(s) as the true parent(s) as the mother begins to assume an ambiguous status. When the mother is freed, the transfer of maternal responsibility from caregiver to biological parent may be difficult and emotionally painful.

Temporary Release Programs   Temporary release programs offer inmates an excellent opportunity to improve their parenting skills and renew ties with their children. Work-release programs have provided inmates with employment in day-care centers, where they receive the emotional rewards of child care while they learn. Furlough programs permit women to interact with their children on their home ground, where both the mothers and children are most at ease and where both can enjoy the simple pleasures of being together.

Community Programs   Community-based programs can offer comprehensive child care instruction and counseling. For example, the New York City Foundling Hospital offers a residential program for mothers who have abused their children. Women are admitted into the program under court order. They receive counseling while their children participate in a play school staffed by therapists specializing in the treatment of the abused.[19] Mothers learn to care for their children properly in a supervised

setting. The Foundling Hospital program is unique:

Because most of the mothers are quite young (on occasion no more than fourteen years old) and are guilty of neglect as well as abuse, the program emphasizes the mechanics of good parenting and orderly family life. The facility has a kitchen and dining room, and the offenders plan the menus for themselves and the children, shop for food in a nearby supermarket, and prepare and serve it in the dining room. Counselors instruct the mothers in the basics of infant and child behavior, because some have inflicted severe punishment on babies when they soiled their diapers or "talked back and wouldn't mind."[20]

Girl Scouts Beyond Bars (GSBB) is an innovative attempt to combine a traditional girls club with parenting assistance for female offenders.[21] The first program began in the Maryland Correctional Institution for Women. The girls met with mothers at the institution for two Saturdays per month. On alternate Saturdays they would meet in a local church with volunteers for traditional scouting projects. By 1995 the program had expanded to eight states and efforts are being made to develop the initiatives in ten more.

GSBB works as a result of the partnership formed between correctional organizations and the Girl Scout Association. The focus is on helping kids, but a number of programs teach parenting skills and work to facilitate the often difficult transition to the community.

Survival Training

Women offenders need both the skills and attitudes necessary for independent living. The female offender must learn how to manage money, rent an apartment, locate and use community resources, maintain her own and her children's health, and administer the many legal and contractual requirements that occur in everyday life.[22]

Survival skills programs are currently being offered in a number of women's correctional institutions and community programs.

The most frequently offered courses of instruction include banking, money management and budgeting, housing, and using credit and community resources.[23] Community-based courses have the advantage of being able to draw upon a large pool of outside speakers. Community program instruction can encourage clients to assume active roles in the learning process because the women are often able to use the skills they develop immediately. Clients can prepare budgets, open a bank account, or search for housing with the direct aid of project staff, who provide guidance and encourage their efforts (Figure 11-2).

One of the most important aspects of survival training is the teaching of problem-solving skills. Learning how to determine objectives, analyze a problem, and identify and select from alternative courses of action permits the offender to meet and resolve new demands as they present themselves. Of even greater significance is the feeling of self-confidence and personal reliability such education can provide. Knowing that she can work out solutions to her own problems may encourage the offender to take greater responsibility for her life and to be less vulnerable to victimization.

Community-Based Correctional Programs

As with male offenders, the vast majority of female offenders are in community-based programs. But an understanding of the variety of programs available to serve women and what works best for female offenders has only begun. In response to the unique needs of female offenders and the general lack of information on women under community supervision, the National Institute of Corrections (NIC) sponsored a conference of researchers and practitioners to identify the issues and concerns affecting community supervision strategies for female offenders.[24]

Major Issues in Programming

The following were identified as major issues that inhibit the justice system from meeting the needs of women under community supervision:

- Lack of data, which impedes program and service design for women. Without statistics for crime pattern and sentencing trends, it is difficult to target programs effectively.

- Lack of policy development or systematic planning for the female offender in the criminal justice system at either the state or local level. Community placements and services are usually determined as a result of crisis management rather than as part of a rational planning process.

- Concern that sentencing guidelines will serve to increase the number and rate of sentenced women, given the assumption that the guidelines are gender neutral.

- Tension between a criminal justice system that fosters dependence and a female population that needs to become more independent.

- Gender, race, and cultural biases in the criminal justice system that have a negative impact on women of color.

- Potential value conflict between the needs of the criminal justice system and the needs of offenders; that is, treatment versus sanction.

- Need to design classification systems to accurately assess women's level of risk to the community.

- Imposition of male paradigms on women that fail to address their unique needs; for example, parenting and independent living skills.

- Models of probation and parole that set women up to fail in the community by their lack of attention to basic survival issues; for example, homelessness and child care needs.

- Failure to institutionalize programs as they mature and prove their effectiveness.[25]

Figure 11-2   Life Skills Education: Outlines for
Classes Offered by the Women's Out-Services Program

Self-awareness

Objective: To inform clients of their history as
females and to enhance their understanding of their
feelings and emotions that are uniquely female.

Course Content: What does it mean to be female?

A. Different physically
    1. Anatomy, physiology, hormones
    2. Illness, infections, good health
    3. Sexually
B. Society has treated us differently
    1. Jesus's view of women/religious views
    2. Laws
    3. Legal rights
    4. Society's view
C. Understanding feelings/mental health
    1. Tensions of life
    2. Responses to life—physical/mental
    3. Good/bad feelings
    4. Exercise/Yoga/activities/dancing
D. Develop own self-concept/awareness
    1. Journal/dreams
    2. Ten commandments for self-awareness
    3. Wishes
    4. Living book—reflect on life
    5. Sexual/assertiveness in general

Parent Effectiveness Training

Objective: To improve parents' ability to relate
to children to achieve desired and appropriate
behavior. To teach parents how to stop reacting
to provocations, but to act deliberately instead.

Problem Solving and Communications Skills

Objective: To educate the client to the process of
problem solving so that she will be better equipped
to identify and work through existing problems or
future problems that may arise in her life. To help
clients become aware of their communicating styles
and to show them other ways of communicating.

Course Content:

A. Introduction to problem-solving process
    1. Five steps to problem solving
B. Group process of problem solving
    1. "Quaker meeting," group exercise
C. Communication skills
    1. Verbal
    2. Nonverbal
D. Four kinds of people
    1. Your personality/communicating styles
E. Responses to frustrations and tensions
    1. Group exercise to help clients become aware
      of their responses

Consumer Education

Objective: To provide the clients with knowledge
of how, where, and why to purchase goods and
services.

Course Content:

A. Shopping/needs vs. wants
    1. Purchasing for the kitchen
      a. Handouts
        (1) How to eat better for less
        (2) Stretching your food dollar
        (3) Good food shopping makes "cents"
        (4) Utilizing leftovers
        (5) Vegetables
      b. Discussion
        (1) Purchasing in a grocery store
        (2) Planning before shopping

Source: Diane Wilson, *Women's Out-Services Program, Life Coping Skills Training
Manual* (Atlanta, Ga.: Department of Offender Rehabilitation, 1981).

Out of that session emerged a description of
information and resources needed in this area.
One of the major needs identified was information on "current practices and innovative responses of community corrections agencies to
the special supervision and intervention needs
of female offenders."[26]

National Council on Crime and Delinquency Survey

NIC subsequently funded a project to gather
this information. Support was provided to the
National Council on Crime and Delinquency
(NCCD) to survey approximately three hun-

Figure 11-2 (continued)

(3) Fewer trips mean less cash
(4) Nutrition and food storage
2. Advertising and buying
B. Money management and budget
  1. Meeting your housing needs
    a. Public housing vs. private housing
    b. Location—schools, shopping, employment
    c. Size
  2. Planning your household budget
  3. Banking services/credit cards (use and abuse)
  4. Your local utilities
    a. Ways to cut costs
  5. Public services provided by the government

Values Clarification

Objective: To help clients in clarifying, under-standing, and developing their own personal values. To assist in facilitating the implementation of these values into their lives.

Course Content:

A. Value clarification process
  1. Seven criteria
  2. Value indicators
B. Relationship of values of society
  1. How do you relate your lives to your surroundings?
  2. Clarity of relationship
C. Group exercises
  1. Thirteen (13) questions (form)
  2. What do I value in life? (forms) Complete in order the forms to be used in this exercise.

Job Readiness/Career Development

Objective: To inform clients of the skills needed to obtain and maintain skillful employment. To expose clients to nontraditional jobs. To help clients set career goals.

Course Content:

A. Planning to get a job
  1. Class objectives and their importance
  2. Hand out forms
    a. Abilities checklist
    b. Preemployment consideration
    c. Personal views about work
  3. Job readiness pretest
B. Job information
  1. Discussion on job readiness pretest
  2. How to get a job and keep it
    a. Finding job information
    b. Knowing the job market
  3. Avenues to job skills
  4. The job hunt
  5. Job sources
C. How to fill out necessary paperwork
  1. Job application handouts
    a. Summary of work experience
    b. Quiz—following directions
    c. Words used on application forms
    d. Sample applications
D. Interviewing
  1. Interviewing techniques
    a. Making the job interview
    b. The art of interviewing
    c. Tips
    d. Points to ponder
    e. Negative factors list
    f. Expectations of employers and employees
    g. Common interview questions asked
  2. Selling yourself to an employer
  3. After the interview
E. Self-directed search
F. Needle sort

dred individuals and organizations in an at-tempt to identify programs for female offend-ers on probation or parole or in diversion or pretrial release programs, or ex-offenders. Pro-grams identified had to either serve women ex-clusively, serve a population that was at least 50 percent female, or provide services to women that were not available to men and track out-comes of that service delivery.

The NCCD survey identified a total of 342 programs in thirty-eight states and the District of Columbia. Verification of information and elimination of duplicate programs reduced this number to 111. Structured interviews were then conducted with the directors of one hun-dred of these programs, and site visits were conducted on twenty-three programs. This in-formation was utilized to determine the most

Program Focus

Girl Scouts Beyond Bars: Florida's Programs

Within a few months of hearing about GSBB [Girl Scouts Beyond Bars], the Girl Scouts of the Apalachee Bend (GAB) and officials from the Florida Department of Corrections had their own program. The Florida groups learned of NIJ's [National Institute of Justice's] pilot program in October 1993. By late January 1994 they had developed a more intensive program at Jefferson Correctional Institution (JCI).

The Florida Governor's Office is impressed with what the Girl Scouts, the Florida Department of Corrections, and their collaborating partners have accomplished at JCI. In April 1995 the program was recognized by the governor with his annual "Peace at home: Preventing domestic violence" award.

Focus on training in parenting. Pat Chivers, GAB's executive director, said, "We were really anxious to implement the visitation program here. I knew that the community would get behind this project. But I also knew we would need to put together a comprehensive program if we hoped to make a difference." The Florida mother-daughter meeting schedule is similar to the Maryland program. Two Saturdays each month the girls work with their Girl Scout troop leaders in the community. On alternate Saturdays, the mothers and their daughters meet for troop meetings at JCI. Kerry Flack, assistant to Florida's secretary of corrections, pointed out how the program aimed, however, to expand on the Maryland pilot: "We wanted to do all that we could to support this program. Dr. Shayn Lloyd, JCI's staff psychologist, has been assigned to work with the mothers for at least an hour after each mother-daughter meeting."

Not only do the mothers at JCI meet for a longer time than they do in Maryland, they also meet more frequently. Mothers meet four times per month for almost 2 hours each session. Airie Sailor, a certified parenting instructor who works with the mothers, explained, "Our sessions are a hybrid of formal parenting instruction utilizing a text developed specifically for incarcerated parents and the Girl Scout contemporary issues material. Mothers also have adequate time to plan for upcoming Girl Scout troop meetings."

effective strategies for working with female offenders. Assessment criteria included elements of design and operation: structure, supervision, role modeling, coordination of community resources, aftercare, mission or objective statements, screening procedures, ongoing needs assessment, evaluation, and funding sources.[27]

Program Characteristics   The majority of community-based programs for female offenders are small, private, nonprofit entities with an average daily population of twenty-four (Table 11-4). Most programs last for about seven to eight months and cost a little more than $50 per day. Most of the programs are designed to provide reentry services; about one-third serve as alternatives to incarceration. As would be expected given the reentry focus, two-thirds of the offenders in these programs are referred by prisons. Most of the remaining offenders are referred by courts, jails, probation, or parole.

The perceived lack of information on female offenders, which provided the basis for the

Partnerships. "Our program is small, 7 mothers and 12 girls, but growing monthly," said Donna Schestopol, GAB's health promotion director. She pointed out, "We have coordinated our effort with other local agencies. We work with the school system to monitor the girls' school performance. We are also collaborating with Community Intervention Program, Inc., and the Glenn Terrell Foundation, an organization that provides services to inmates and their families, to provide social services for the girls, their guardians, and the mothers after they are released. These services are provided at no cost to us. We are just taking advantage of existing community resources."

"Thus far three families in the program have been referred to us," said Deborah Lloyd, director of Community Intervention Program, Inc. "We have an ability to take our services to the home. Crisis intervention, behavioral counseling, resolving school concerns, and working with the care giver on various parenting issues are some of the services we have provided."

Release from prison. "We are also targeting the mothers participating in the Girl Scout program for our services," said Manuel Godfrey, program director for the Glenn Terrell Foundation. While the mother in the Girl Scout program is in JCI, staff from the Glenn Terrell foundation meet with her to determine her transition needs. A postrelease plan that includes job placement counseling and links to other needed social services is tailored to suit her specific needs. Once she is released, the staff continue to meet with her to carry out the plan. The staff also perform a family assessment and collaborate with other agencies and organizations in an effort to meet the entire family's needs. At least once each week, staff members continue meeting with the entire family until the social services are no longer needed.

Source: Marilyn C. Moses, *Keeping Incarcerated Mothers and Their Daughters Together: Girl Scouts Beyond Bars,* Program Focus (Washington, D.C.: National Institute of Justice, October 1995).

NCCD study, was verified in the review of program management characteristics. Most of the programs simply collect no data. They operate without management information systems and have limited capacity to compile and review client information. None of the organizations had conducted a rigorous cost-effectiveness evaluation. Almost half of the programs had conducted no formal evaluation of any kind.

Client Selection and Characteristics

Virtually all of the programs serve felons. One out of five admit probation or parole violators. About one-third of the programs exclude participants convicted of crimes that pose a potential risk to the program or community, but most do not have screening criteria to measure risk levels. The majority of clients are African American women, 37 percent are white, and 16 percent are Hispanic. Less than one out of five participants were married at the time of program involvement. More than two-thirds had children under the age of six. Twelve percent of the offenders were pregnant, and 18

Table 11-4   Characteristics of
One Hundred Community Programs for Women

Program Attribute	Number of Programs
Type of agency	
Federal	0
State	12
Local	4
Private nonprofit	83
Private for-profit	2
Funding sources	
Federal	20
State	76
Local	35
Foundations/corporations	51
Client fees	20
Aid to Families with Dependent Children	8
Targeted offenses	
Felony	97
Misdemeanor	37
Probation/parole violators	21
Offense restrictions on program admission	33
(Average client population)	(24)
(Average program duration)	(227 days)
(Average per diem costs)[a]	($53)
(Average 1990–1991 budget)[b]	($388,173)
(Average number of staff)	(11)
(Average annual salary)	($21,000)
Sources of referrals	
Prosecutor	5
Courts	44
Jails	32
Prisons	66
Probation	35
Parole	43
Other	16
Primary program objective or goals	
Alternative to incarceration	29
Service provider	33
Reentry	49
Family services	18
Management information system	29
Evaluation	48
Program location	
Urban	86
Suburban	9
Rural	3
Length of program's existence	
0–3 years	26
4–6 years	14
7–10 years	16
More than 10 years	30

[a] Only forty programs reported.

[b] Only sixty-three programs reported.

Source: James Austin, Barbara Bloom, and Trish Donahue, *Female Offenders in the Community: An Analysis of Innovative Strategies and Programs* (San Francisco, Calif.: National Council on Crime and Delinquency, 1992), p. 11.

percent gave birth within six months of entering the program. The vast majority of participants needed drug and alcohol treatment, employment, education, and housing services.

Program Services The primary service (62 percent of the programs) provided to clients was residential care, including some services for women and children. The number of available beds in these programs was 1,733, plus 114 spaces for children. More than half of the programs provided case management or day treatment services to clients. Virtually all of the programs provided or brokered at least three types of services.

The treatment services most often provided were counseling, followed by living skills, alcohol and drug treatment, parenting skills, and job-seeking skills (Table 11-5). Counseling services typically consisted of individual and group sessions on general life issues, as well as domestic violence and sexual abuse. In living skills training, women learned and practiced money management, meal planning and preparation, job and housing search skills, household management, health and hygiene, use of community resources, and other tasks of daily living.

Supervision and Security Strict supervision and residential security were significant elements of three-quarters of the programs. Probation and parole officers provided supervision in the remaining programs. Urine tests and breathalyzers were frequently used to detect alcohol and drug use. Fifty-eight of the programs, including both residential and nonresidential programs, monitored women's activities in the community through personal visits and telephone checks.

NCCD Program Illustrations

The NCCD study identified programs serving women at different points in the criminal justice system—prior to trial, as an alternative

Table 11-5 Community-Based Program Services

Service	Number of Programs
Type of program services offered	
Residential treatment	62
Day treatment	18
Case management	42
Infant care	14
Work release	28
Treatment services offered	
Alcohol/drug treatment	68
Codependence	41
Health care	26
Counseling	82
Parenting	66
Job-seeking skills	63
Job training	43
Living skills	76
Recreation activities	50
Education	33
Housing	28
Religious activities	29
Primary service provided	
Alcohol/drug treatment	30
Job training	9
Parenting	8
Housing	7
Living skills	6
Counseling	5
Employment seeking	5
Transition from prostitution	3

Source: James Austin, Barbara Bloom, and Trish Donahue, *Female Offenders in the Community: An Analysis of Innovative Strategies and Programs* (San Francisco, Calif.: National Council on Crime and Delinquency, 1992), p. 15.

to incarceration, and at reentry from prison or jail.[28]

Pretrial Diversion Programs Eleven programs, serving drug offenders, prostitutes, and women convicted of theft, were identified as deferred prosecution programs. Two of the programs were developed specifically for diversion services; the other nine included women at a variety of stages of the criminal justice system. Five of the nine programs that served women from across the criminal justice system were residential programs focusing on alcoholism and addiction treatment. The other nonresidential programs focused on comprehensive services delivery or specifically targeted female prostitutes, attempting to assist them in the transition out of prostitution. All of the programs monitor clients' conduct and report failures to the prosecutor's office.

Women convicted of economic crimes are selected for Hennepin County's Personal Growth Group in Minneapolis, Minnesota. The group meets weekly for one year and focuses on the psychological aspects of theft, as well as basic survival skills. The ARC Community Services Treatment Alternative Program in Madison, Wisconsin, provides additional treatment services to women arrested for drug crimes. Treatment lasts for approximately six months, during which time offenders are required to report regularly and submit to urine tests.

Pretrial Release Programs   Twenty-two of the programs served women awaiting trial. Program participation often was a condition of release from jail. Most were larger programs that also served women from throughout the criminal justice system, but four focused on pretrial services for women. Community Services for Women, a project of Social Justice for Women in Boston, Massachusetts, and Alternative Directions Inc. in Baltimore, Maryland, work with women before arraignment to design sentencing alternatives. Individualized plans generally include substance abuse treatment, employment services, parenting support, and urine monitoring. Comprehensive Services for Women in Wilmington, Delaware, and Genesis House in Chicago, Illinois, serve women awaiting trial or sentencing. The former program provides case management and mentoring services; the latter operates a transition-from-prostitution program that includes Prostitutes Anonymous groups and human immunodeficiency virus (HIV) testing and counseling.

Court-Sentenced Programs   Forty-four of the programs accepted women sentenced directly from the courts, either as an alternative to incarceration or as part of a split sentence to jail or prison. Programs in this category were categorized as residential, residential for women and children, day treatment, and special focus.

Residential programs are generally small, with populations of less than twenty, and provide services from four months to a year. Most of these programs, such as Project Greenhope in New York, include women from across the criminal justice system. This women's recovery program emphasizes sobriety through a focus on the factors that contribute to women's addiction: sexual abuse, domestic violence, and relationship issues. Services include six months of treatment and six months of aftercare and are culturally focused to meet the needs of the project's predominantly African American and Hispanic clients.

Residential programs for women and children, which are relatively new, nonprofit organizations, house between twenty and forty women and children generally under the age of six. Residents are typically a mix of offenders from across the criminal justice system, although Summit House in Greensboro, North Carolina, serves only sentenced offenders convicted of felonies and their children. The program's structured, in-house services emphasize family preservation and basic life skills. The Bringing It All Back Home Family Teaching Model stresses behavior change through rewards and consequences. Participants are required to have affordable housing, stable employment, and a reasonable budget before graduation. Aftercare services are available to provide both practical and emotional support.

Day treatment programs provide individualized treatment plans for each participant and then provide or broker needed services for women who live at home. Most day treatment services focus on substance abuse treatment and life skills training, enhancing them with ancillary counseling, child care, employment, and other services. Most programs provide between four and ten hours of services daily, and they monitor offenders through home visits, regular reporting requirements, telephone checks, and urine monitoring.

Genesis II for women in Minneapolis is believed to be the country's first day treatment program for women. It provides both individual and group counseling, life skills training, parenting education, general equivalency diploma (GED) preparation, and career development services. Its Children's Center operates a child development program for newborns through twelve-year-olds. Parenting strategies are monitored by professional staff, who are prepared to intervene in potentially abusive situations.

Special focus programs tend to be newer, honing in on the special needs of pregnant women, prostitutes, victims of domestic violence convicted of assault on their abusers, and sexual abuse survivors. Programs for pregnant women stress health care and parenting education, while other programs emphasize group strategies to achieve emotional and practical support. The Council for Prostitution Alternatives, in Portland, Oregon, was created to empower women to make the transition out of prostitution. A four-phase program provides intensive counseling, recovery groups, advocacy, and practical support, including financial assistance, clothing, food, and so on. Clients progress from stabilization to reorientation, rebuilding, and mentoring. Case management focuses on prostitutes as victims and survivors of long-term abuse.

Reentry from prison or jail programs accounted for the largest number of programs for female offenders. Fifty-six provided services for offenders released from jail and prison, including forty-nine facilities that served women in prerelease status. Nine programs also served parole violators.

These programs fell into the same general categories as those serving women sentenced directly from the courts: residential programs for women, with and without their children; day treatment; and special focus. The only major distinction is that state government-funded projects are most likely to serve this population. The Duval County Community Correctional Center in Jacksonville, Florida, a residential program for women released from prison, provides addiction recovery and relapse prevention services. Women live at the center and work in the community for ten weeks prior to release. The California Department of Corrections contracts with nonprofit organizations, such as the Elizabeth Fry Center, for the operation of seven mother and infant care programs. The programs provide a variety of services to women and their children, in a homelike and secure residential setting.

New Jersey's Camden Urban Women's Center provides parolees with training and assistance in starting their own small businesses. The Community Connection Resource Center in San Diego, California, provides vocational assessment; training for job seeking and job placement; life skills education; family services; support groups; and referrals for food, clothing, and child care assistance. The program's Jobs Plus support group works with county jail inmates, who are placed in jobs upon release. Special focus programs for offenders reentering the community include services for offenders who have assaulted or murdered a spouse or partner, wilderness training, and advocacy and mentoring services for parolees with children.

Program Effectiveness

The NCCD study concluded that the best programs combined supervision and services to address women's special needs in a highly structured, safe environment, where accountability was stressed.[29] Women were held responsible for their actions and learned the skills necessary for economic and emotional independence. The best programs worked with offenders not to cure them but to broaden their range of responses to various types of behavior and needs, enhancing their coping and decision-making skills. The best programs used the concept of empowerment, linking emotional support with practical assistance, and provided a comprehensive range of services. For example, the Program for Female Offenders links therapeutic and skill-building services with employment in the program's telemarketing business. Women A.R.I.S.E., a day treatment program, combines transportation and child care with life skills training and counseling. ARC Community Services includes residential services for women and their children, an outpatient diversion program for prostitutes, and a day treatment program for substance abuse, along with children's programming.

Although no solid evaluation data are available upon which to build these assessments, several elements of program design seemed to influence treatment outcome. These elements included:

- Structure: The most promising programs were designed with a high degree of organization and accountability. Regular schedules of organized activities, including structured leisure time, appeared to be most effective.

- Supervision: Consistent, reliable, and coordinated supervision was necessary to maintain women in the least restrictive setting consistent with public safety. House rules and sequential stages of programming were useful, as were structured rewards and sanctions, explicit reporting requirements, and prompt responses to violations.

- Role modeling: Staff and volunteers who served as role models were especially effective when they included ex-offenders and recovering addicts, and when they reflected the racial and ethnic composition of the programs' clients.

- Case management: Individualized treatment plans, combined with referrals to community resources and systematic tracking of activities, assisted programs in more effectively meeting offender needs.

- Aftercare: Many women were unable to sustain the gains they made even in the best programs without continued emotional support and practical assistance.

- Program operations: Programs with clear goals and consistent admissions criteria, which were responsive to changing client needs and which integrated client outcome assessments into program planning and evaluation tended to have the most positive impact on offenders. A diverse and stable funding base was also an important element of program operations.

The study concluded with recommendations for increasing the number and type of community-based programs for women; conducting meaningful evaluations, including systematic data collections and making better use of management information systems; and providing more gender-specific services, such as those that emphasize family preservation and the needs of children of female offenders.

Drug Treatment Programs

The tremendous increase in the number of women arrested for drug offenses over the last decade has prompted special interest in the needs of female abusers and the programs available to serve them. The results of a national survey of programs for female drug abusers were reported in 1994.[30] Programs were identified from literature reviews, the recommendations of colleagues, lists of Treatment Alternative to Street Crime (TASC) program directors, and directors of state departments of corrections and departments of alcohol and drug programs. This exhaustive approach identified 165 community-based programs, of which about one-third were for women only.

Most of the programs (61 percent) were outpatient drug-free programs. The nonresidential programs were the largest, averaging 141 persons, of which about one-third were female. The residential programs averaged about fifty-one participants, of whom twenty-one were female. A little more than half of the women in residential programs had been referred by the criminal justice system, usually from probation or directly from the courts.

Most of the programs provided treatment for both drug and alcohol offenders. The average program lasted about six to seven months, but some provided up to two years of treatment. Services provided included case management, relapse prevention, HIV/AIDS (acquired immune deficiency syndrome) education, counseling, and twelve-step meetings. Women-only programs were found to provide significantly more programming for women's special needs.

Two-thirds of the residential programs and half of the others had gynecological, prenatal, and obstetrical services. Family planning was available in more than two-thirds, as was parenting education. Personal empowerment was offered in 70 percent of the programs, and in virtually all of those for women only. Both educational and vocational training were offered more frequently in residential than nonresidential programs. Residential programs routinely offered transportation, as well as assistance with postdischarge housing. In almost all areas, women-only programs provided significantly more programming for women's special needs.

Most of the programs urged participants to continue treatment and attendance at meetings following release, but great disparity was evident in the range of additional services provided. Residential programs provided the most aftercare assistance. Some of the programs permitted immediate reentry upon relapse, and others required a waiting period (as a disincentive to relapse as well as a means of distributing scarce program resources).

Although the study concluded that the range of services identified appeared significant and the number of community-based programs was growing, most of the treatment was found to be of such limited intensity and duration that its impact was likely to be minimal. Relatively few programs accommodated infants and children, and few prepared for the repeat admissions often required to teach the abuser how to sustain the initial achievements of treatment.

One problem of particular note was the absence of standardized methods of client assessment. Most programs relied on intake interviews, supplemented by observation and client records. Overreliance on the clinical interview was considered to be an impediment to program planning as well as individualized needs assessment. The informality of this approach also makes data gathering and program evaluation difficult to achieve. Programs subsequently are hard pressed to be responsive to changing client profiles and needs.[31]

Intermediate Sanctions

A national survey of the use of intermediate sanctions for female offenders found that of the 110 programs studied, half were available to both males and females. Most of these provided intensive supervision; ten provided house arrest or electronic monitoring to women; and four boot camps had female participants. About 15 percent of the total population of intensive supervision clients were female.[32]

Many of the programs were poorly designed for women. While the emphasis of most was on surveillance, the female offenders were in greater need of services—programs to promote economic self-sufficiency, including safe and reliable child care, skills training, and education. The vast majority of women had longstanding drug and alcohol problems, for which they were receiving little assistance.

House arrest was considered a potential threat to women in situations of domestic violence and in providing opportunities to exacerbate drug and alcohol problems. Boot camps were described as especially inappropriate for women who have experienced the negative side of abusive control. These programs may prolong the female offender's sense of powerlessness and capitulation, making it harder for her to achieve self-esteem and self-direction.[33]

Issues in the Treatment of Female Offenders

A major concern of treatment programs is that attention must be paid to female offenders' problem of dependence and their lack of self-trust and personal responsibility. These programs often place persons in passive, dependent, patient roles. Such practices are contrary to treatment goals and can easily subvert the helping process. Programs for women may unconsciously encourage the acceptance of traditional social roles by assigning female offenders to women's work in coed programs, by emphasizing femininity and a gentle demeanor over responsibility and assertiveness, and by failing to focus on the effects of societal role definition and expectations of the female self-image and behavior. These practices are contrary to treatment objectives and can only reinforce the negative self-perceptions that invariably result from the cycle of dependency, victimization, and crime. Fallen women do not need to be put back on a pedestal; they need to learn to stand on their own two feet.

A second major concern in programs for female offenders is the issue of comprehensiveness. Single-focus programs for female offenders are unlikely to provide much benefit. Effective programs for women need to address issues of **self-esteem** and self-image, education, and economic assistance, and they must provide assistance for women with children. Substance abuse treatment also must be provided when alcohol or drug problems are present, and they generally are. Failure to address any one of these issues will leave the female offender ill equipped for success.

Significant evidence shows that programs that serve both male and female offenders are less able to address women's needs. The volume of male offenders and the generally more serious nature of their crimes tend to overwhelm the focus of coed programs. Single-sex projects, however, do a better job of providing the same services to women that all offenders need—education, employment assistance, and substance abuse treatment—and they more frequently offer assistance in areas that coed programs do not.

Single-sex programs also tend to monitor and track the progress of their clients more effectively. Such tracking is necessary to gain a better understanding of what strategies work most effectively with different female offender subpopulations. At present, the only guides are observations of programs that seem to be working. There is no coherent body of data on offender changes resulting from treatment or assistance, and no reliable long-term data on female offender recidivism.

Summary

In the past, female offenders have been ignored by correctional administrators because they were relatively few in number and often seen as less in need of treatment than male offenders. Today, women criminals receive more attention but not necessarily better treatment.

A number of innovative programs have been developed to prepare female offenders for the tasks of employment and parenting, as well as to provide them with the skills necessary for independence. Such preparation and training is a difficult and complex process. Most female offenders must overcome the disadvantages of social class and minority status as well as gender in their attempt to achieve self-sufficiency. Often the offender's own negative self-image and limited view of her abilities is the greatest barrier to achievement. Still, some programs have persevered and are successful in treating and training female offenders for life on the outside. Some of these programs have recognized that female offenders are unique in that they often suffer less prisonization and are more motivated to survive on the outside. Sometimes this motivation comes from the simple desire to never again experience incarceration, but often the motivation comes from the desire to gain custody of their children and to create for these children the family life that they have been denied. Whatever the reason, the desire to remain free and law abiding is often strong in female offenders, and some programs have learned how best to harness that energy and turn it into something that helps to maintain the female offender in the community.

Key Words and Concepts

cycle of dependency, victimization, and crime

employment follow-up services

job development and placement

job readiness training

"new female criminal"

nontraditional employment

parenting skills

self-esteem

survival skills

Questions for Discussion

1. Why has the criminal justice system traditionally viewed female offenders as being different from male offenders? What types of crime did they traditionally commit? What was the usual criminal justice system response to their crime?

2. What special family issues does the typical female offender face?

3. How has female criminality changed in recent years? What explanations are offered for this change?

4. How do programs designed to enhance personal and vocational skills differ between male and female offenders?

5. What is the typical female offender's response when she is offered placement in a nontraditional employment program?

6. What are some of the characteristics that make women's programs effective?

For Further Reading

Adler, Frieda, *Sisters in Crime* (New York: McGraw-Hill, 1975).

Chapman, Jane R., *Economic Realities and the Female Offender* (Lexington, Mass.: Lexington Books, 1980).

McCarthy, Belinda R., *Easy Time: Female Inmates on Home Furloughs* (Lexington, Mass.: Lexington Books, 1979).

Miller, Eleanor M., *Street Woman* (Philadelphia, Pa.: Temple University Press, 1986).

Morash, Merry (ed.), *Teaching About Women in Criminal Justice and Criminology Courses: A Resource Guide* (Columbus, Ohio: Women and Crime Division, American Society of Criminology, 1988).

Chapter 12

Programs for Juveniles

Criminal Justice and Juvenile Justice

Overview of the Juvenile Justice System

A Closer Look at Intake

Community-Based Programs for Juveniles

Programs for Runaways

Juvenile Diversion Programs

Community Alternatives to Secure Detention

Juvenile Probation Programs

Community-Based Residential Programs for Juveniles

Juvenile Aftercare

Research and Program Models for Serious Chronic Delinquents

Problems and Issues in Community-Based Correctional Programs for Youths

The Future of Community-Based Corrections Programs for Juveniles

Summary

The juvenile justice system uses community-based correctional programs to a significantly greater degree than the adult criminal justice system because juveniles, more often than adults, have family and community ties that re-integration programs can enhance and reinforce. The widely held belief that most juveniles deserve a second or third chance to remain in the community also facilitates the use of community programs for juveniles. A community's willingness to provide community-based programs for adults often depends upon its experience and success or failure with programs for juveniles. Programs that appear to benefit youthful offenders are often subsequently established to serve the needs of adult first offenders or others who have committed only minor crimes. Many community-based correctional programs for juveniles are similar to those for adults; others reflect the special problems of the adolescent and preadolescent offender.

Criminal Justice and Juvenile Justice

The similarities between the juvenile justice and the criminal justice systems are greater than the differences. Both attempt to respond to the problems posed by individuals who violate the law. The methods of handling offenders differ somewhat, but both systems carry out similar tasks: Suspected offenders are identified and apprehended, evidence is examined to determine what laws have been broken, and judgments regarding appropriate dispositions

Table 12-1   Juvenile Justice System Goals

Philosophical Goals Stated in Juvenile Code Purpose Clauses		
Prevention, Diversion, Treatment	Punishment	Both
Florida	Arkansas	Alabama
Idaho	Georgia	California
Kentucky	Hawaii	Colorado
New Hampshire	Illinois	Delaware
New Mexico	Iowa	Indiana
North Carolina	Kansas	Maryland
North Dakota	Louisiana	Massachusetts
Ohio	Minnesota	Nevada
Pennsylvania	Mississippi	Oklahoma
South Carolina	Missouri	Utah
Tennessee	New Jersey	Washington
Vermont	Oregon	
West Virginia	Rhode Island	
Wisconsin	Texas	

Note: Juvenile codes in states not listed did not contain a purpose clause. Most juvenile codes contain a purpose clause that outlines the philosophy underlying the code. Most states seek to protect the interests of the child, the family, the community, or some combination of the three. Nearly all states also indicate that the code includes protections of the child's constitutional and statutory rights.

Source: Howard N. Snyder and Melissa Sickmund, *Juvenile Offenders and Victims: A National Report* (Washington, D.C.: Office of Juvenile Justice and Delinquency Prevention, 1995), p. 71.

are made and executed. During some periods in history, these justice systems were not just similar, they were identical. In the late 1890s, the American criminal justice system decided that juveniles deserved separate courts and correctional systems. The Illinois Juvenile Court Act of 1899 created the first official juvenile court in the United States. Prior to that time, a few states were sending juveniles to correctional processes that were different in scope and operations from adult corrections, but the juveniles were getting to these programs via the adult court system. With the creation of the juvenile courts, the U.S. justice system made a symbolic recognition of the differences of juvenile offenders and of the hope that these offenders could be viewed as less responsible for their actions and would prove more amenable to treatment programs.

Overview of the Juvenile Justice System

The most significant difference between the criminal and juvenile justice systems is philosophical. The principal objectives of the criminal justice system are to control crime and punish offenders. The juvenile justice system is also expected to control crime, but it emphasizes helping offenders as well as punishing them (Table 12-1).

This philosophy of helping or treating juveniles rather than punishing them has a long history in the United States and springs from two sources. First, there is the belief that the juvenile is too immature to be held fully responsible for his or her behavior under the law. Thus, punishment cannot be justified. Second, there

Figure 12-1   Major Due Process
Decision Affecting Juvenile Justice

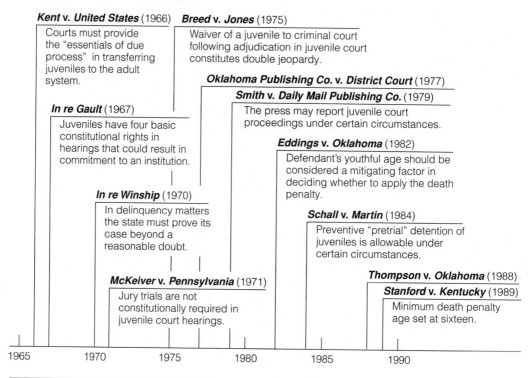

Source: Howard N. Snyder and Melissa Sickmund, *Juvenile Offenders and Victims: A National Report* (Washington, D.C.: Office of Juvenile Justice and Delinquency Prevention, 1995), p. 81.

is an equally strong belief that young offenders are more amenable to treatment than their older counterparts. The philosophy is that "if we can help the boy, we won't have to punish the man." Because juveniles are not held legally responsible for their behavior in the same way that adults are and because the emphasis is on helping the offender receive needed assistance rather than providing punishment, the juvenile justice system originally adopted a somewhat informal approach to evaluating an offender's problems and behavior and seeking an appropriate remedy.

During the 1960s and 1970s, critics argued that the juvenile justice system's objectives were less than benevolent. They suggested that the juvenile justice system was a societal mechanism for encouraging conformity to middle-class norms and otherwise controlling youthful behavior, especially that of lower-class youths. Similarly, they argued that the sanctions that juveniles received for their offenses more frequently resembled punishment than treatment. Viewed from this perspective, the informality of the juvenile court was considered to rob juveniles of the legal protections provided in criminal proceedings, rather than facilitating their rehabilitation.

These charges were answered by efforts to incorporate greater due process guarantees into the juvenile justice system (Figure 12-1). Observers concerned about rehabilitation feared that such steps would make it harder to help children, but few signs indicated that this has occurred.

In recent years, new criticisms of the juvenile justice system have been raised. Instead of questioning its benevolent intentions, some of today's critics argue that the system should be more punitive and that juveniles who commit serious crimes should be held legally responsible for their actions, just as adults are. In most states, efforts have been made to modify the juvenile justice system so that it more closely resembles criminal proceedings. Increasingly, juveniles charged with serious crimes are transferred to the criminal justice system.[1] In many states, this transfer is automatic for serious offenses committed by juveniles as young as fourteen years of age. While this transfer process is not without its critics, it does better guarantee a balanced trial and more aggressive legal protections than exist in the juvenile and family courts. Today the juvenile justice system, both in objectives and practice, lies somewhere between the extremes of rehabilitation and punishment, of due process guarantees and informality (Table 12-2).

The Offenders

Status Offenders   One important distinction between the criminal justice and juvenile justice systems lies in the types of persons who fall under the jurisdiction of the criminal and juvenile courts. The criminal court has jurisdiction over adults charged with violations of the penal law. The juvenile court, or family court, has jurisdiction over status offenders and dependent and neglected children as well as **delinquents,** who are defined as juveniles (generally persons under the age of eighteen) who have violated the criminal law. **Status offenders** are juveniles who commit acts that are prohibited solely because of the youth's status as a minor. Typical status offenses include truancy, running away, and ungovernability. **Dependent and neglected children** are juveniles who have violated no laws whatsoever. Dependent children are those whose parents are unable to care for them; neglected children have been abandoned or physically, emotionally, or financially neglected by their parents.

Serious Chronic Juvenile Offenders   Over the past two decades, a considerable volume of research has been conducted to determine the incidence and prevalence of juvenile delinquency within the general population. This research has consistently revealed that a small number of juvenile offenders commit the majority of serious juvenile acts. The earlier research in Philadelphia reported that 6 percent of the boys had more than five police contacts before their eighteenth birthday.[2] These boys accounted for one-half of all delinquencies and 82 percent of all delinquent acts involving robbery, 73 percent of forcible rape, 71 percent of homicide, and 69 percent of aggravated assault. Eighty percent of these **serious chronic juvenile offenders** went on to commit serious crimes as adults. More recent research has substantiated these findings, indicating that nationally as many as 83 percent of serious juvenile crimes were committed by 5 percent of the youth.[3]

Violent Juvenile Offenders   Considerable concern has arisen about **juvenile violence,** particularly the increase in juvenile homicide. Indications are that the rate of such offenses is increasing much more rapidly for juveniles than for adults. While crime as a whole is on the decline across major American cities, rates of juvenile violence are increasing by double-digits. A number of explanations have been posed for these trends, the most popular focusing on the availability of handguns and the role of violence in illegal drug markets.[4]

The Whole Picture   Despite the focus on serious chronic offenders and violent offenders, the majority of juveniles do not commit violent crimes. When the patterns of juvenile involvement in criminal activity are examined, juveniles are most likely to be involved in crimes such as arson, vandalism, and motor vehicle theft (Figure 12-2). Juveniles account for only 29 percent of all serious crime, one-third of property crime, and 18 percent of serious violent crime.

Table 12-2 Similarities and Differences Between Criminal and Juvenile Justice

Juvenile Justice System	Common Ground	Criminal Justice System
	Operating Assumptions	
■ Youth behavior is malleable. ■ Rehabilitation is usually a viable goal. ■ Youth are in families and not independent.	■ Community protection is a primary goal. ■ Law violators must be held accountable. ■ Constitutional rights apply.	■ Sanctions proportional to the offense. ■ General deterrence works. ■ Rehabilitation is not a primary goal.
	Prevention	
■ Many specific delinquency prevention activities (e.g., school, church, recreation). ■ Prevention intended to change individual behavior—often family focused.	■ Educational approaches to specific behaviors (drunk driving, drug use).	■ Generalized prevention activities aimed at deterrence (e.g., Crime Watch).
	Law Enforcement	
■ Specialized "juvenile" units. ■ Some additional behaviors prohibited (truancy, running away, curfew violations). ■ Limitations on public access to information.	■ Jurisdiction involves full range of criminal behavior. ■ Constitutional and procedural safeguards exist. ■ Both reactive and proactive (targeted at offense types, neighborhoods, etc.).	■ Open public access to all information.
↓		↓
Diversion—A significant number of youth are diverted away from the juvenile justice system—often into alternative programs.		Discretion—Law enforcement exercises discretion to divert offenders out of the criminal justice system.
	Intake—Prosecution	
■ In many instances, juvenile court intake, not the prosecutor, decides what cases to file. ■ Decision to file a petition for court action is based on both social and legal factors. ■ A significant portion of cases are diverted from formal case processing.	■ Probable cause must be established. ■ Prosecutor acts on behalf of the state.	■ Plea bargaining is common. ■ Prosecution decision based largely on legal facts. ■ Prosecution is valuable in building history for subsequent offenses.
↓		↓
Diversion—Intake diverts cases from formal processing to services operated by the juvenile court or outside agencies.		Discretion—Prosecution exercises discretion to withhold charges or divert offenders out of the criminal justice system.

The most recent report on status offenses indicates that almost 100,000 status offenses are petitioned in juvenile court annually. Of that number, most involve liquor violations or truancy (31 and 27 percent). Almost one out of five involve running away, and about one in ten involve ungovernable behavior. Miscellaneous cases account for the rest.[5]

The juvenile justice system handles an extraordinary diversity of offenders, ranging from those whose actions are troublesome to themselves and others but not criminal, to those who engage in serious chronic and violent delinquencies. Many of these latter offenders continue to engage in crime as adults, especially when the onset of delinquency occurred at an early age. Although interest exists in dealing with offender problems as early in the career sequence as possible, most offenders do not go on to become adult offend-

Table 12-2   *(continued)*

Juvenile Justice System	Common Ground	Criminal Justice System
	Detention—Jail/lockup	
■ Juveniles may be detained for their own or the community's protection. ■ Juveniles may not be confined with adults without "sight and sound separation."	■ Accused offenders may be held in custody to ensure their appearance in court.	■ Right to apply for bond.
	Adjudication—Conviction	
■ Juvenile court proceedings are "quasi-civil"—not criminal—may be confidential. ■ If guilt is established, the youth is adjudicated delinquent regardless of offense. ■ Right to jury trial not afforded in all states.	■ Standard of "proof beyond a reasonable doubt" is required. ■ Rights to a defense attorney, confrontation of witnesses, remain silent are afforded. ■ Appeals to a higher court are allowed.	■ Constitutional right to a jury trial is afforded. ■ Guilt must be established on individual offenses charged for conviction. ■ All proceedings are open.
	Disposition—Sentencing	
■ Disposition decisions are based on individual and social factors, offense severity, and the youths' offense history. ■ Dispositional philosophy includes a significant rehabilitation component. ■ Many dispositional alternatives are operated by the juvenile court. ■ Dispositions cover a wide range of community-based and residential services. ■ Disposition orders may be directed to people other than the offender (e.g., parents). ■ Disposition may be indeterminate—based on progress.	■ Decision is influenced by current offense, offending history, and social factors. ■ Decision made to hold offender accountable. ■ Victim considered for restitution and "no contact" orders. ■ Decision may not be cruel or unusual.	■ Sentencing decision is primarily bound by the severity of the current offense and offender's criminal history. ■ Sentencing philosophy is based largely on proportionality and punishment. ■ Sentence is often determinate based on offense.
	Aftercare—Parole	
■ A function that combines surveillance and reintegration activities (e.g., family, school, work).	■ A system of monitoring behavior upon release from a correctional setting. ■ Violation of conditions can result in reincarceration.	■ Primarily a surveillance and reporting function to monitor illicit behavior.

Source: Howard N. Snyder and Melissa Sickmund, *Juvenile Offenders and Victims: A National Report* (Washington, D.C.: Office of Juvenile Justice and Delinquency Prevention, 1995), p. 74.

ers, or even serious juvenile offenders. The task of the juvenile justice system is to try to find the right disposition for every offender. It is an enormous task.

Processing Juvenile Offenders

Further differences between the criminal and juvenile justice systems can be identified by considering the processing of a delinquent or status offender through the juvenile justice system (Figure 12-3). Offenders may come to the attention of the family court in a number of ways. Victims, parents, school officials, or other concerned parties, such as social service agencies, refer offenders directly to the juvenile court. In most cases, however, complaints are first made to the police. Once the police have identified the juveniles suspected of committing the offense, they may reprimand and release them or release them after counseling, contacting their parents, or referring them to a community agency for assistance. Alternately, they may choose to take the offenders into **custody.**

Figure 12-2   Juvenile Involvement
in Crime as a Percentage of Arrests

Juveniles accounted for a much larger proportion of all property crime arrests (33%) than violent crime (18%) or drug arrests (8%) in 1992

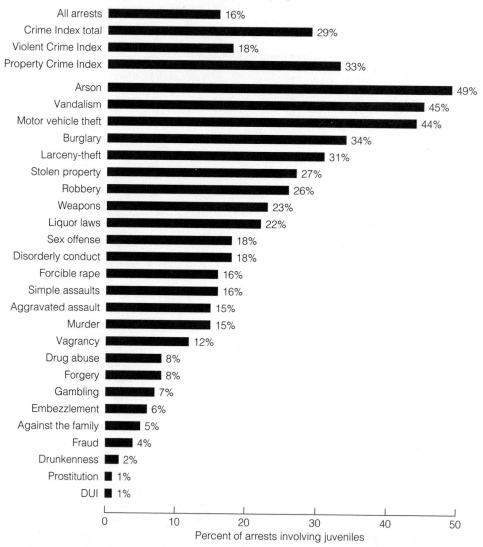

Percent of arrests involving juveniles

- More than one-fourth of all persons arrested in 1992 for robbery were below age eighteen, well above the juvenile proportion of arrests for murder (15%), aggravated assault (15%), and forcible rape (16%).

- Juveniles were involved in 1% of all arrests for driving under the influence (DUI) and prostitution, but more than 40% of all arrests for arson, vandalism, and motor vehicle theft.

Note: Running away and curfew violations are not presented in this figure because, by definition, only juveniles can be arrested for these offenses.

Source: Howard N. Snyder and Melissa Sickmund, *Juvenile Offenders and Victims: A National Report* (Washington, D.C.: Office of Juvenile Justice and Delinquency Prevention, 1995), p. 101.

Figure 12-3 Delinquency Case
Processing in the Juvenile Justice System

What are the stages of delinquency case processing in the juvenile justice system?

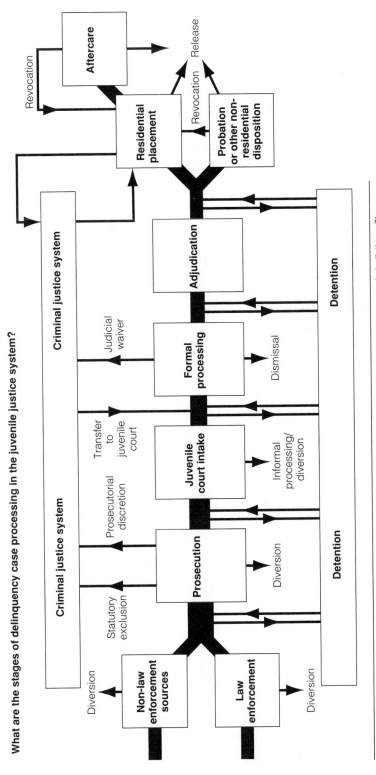

Note: This chart gives a simplified view of caseflow through the juvenile justice system. Procedures vary among jurisdictions. The weights of the lines are not intended to show the actual size of caseloads.
Source: Howard N. Snyder and Melissa Sickmund, *Juvenile Offenders and Victims: A National Report* (Washington, D.C.: Office of Juvenile Justice and Delinquency Prevention, 1995). pp. 76, 77.

Intake   Once in custody, juveniles are taken directly to family court or to an office that functions in a similar capacity. If this court office is unavailable, the juvenile may be taken to detention until a judge or juvenile probation officer is contacted. All youths referred to the juvenile court undergo a screening process known as **intake.** During this process, a juvenile court official, usually a juvenile probation officer, interviews the juvenile, his or her family, the complainant, and other concerned parties to determine the best course of action in dealing with the youth. A variety of alternatives is usually available, but there are basically four options: dismissal of the complaint, informal supervision by juvenile court staff, referral to a community-based program, or formal action initiated by filing a **petition** that will serve as the formal charge brought before the juvenile court. In some courts, intake officers have an additional option: They may file a waiver petition to transfer the case to adult court; in other jurisdictions prosecutors initiate the transfer. The initial decision regarding whether to detain a juvenile is also normally made at intake.

Detention   Most juveniles are released to their families after being taken to family court. Those who are likely to abscond, who are considered a danger to themselves or others, or who have no place to go are taken to a detention facility. Federal law prohibits the detention of juveniles in adult jails.

Instead of jail, many communities have established separate secure facilities solely for the temporary care of youthful offenders. Secure **detention facilities** are physically restrictive, locked environments designed to ensure that the youth will be available to appear in court. Juveniles may be held in detention until the disposition of their offense. The juvenile court judge normally reviews the youth's need for continued detention on a regular basis. Larger jurisdictions may utilize two separate facilities for this function. One facility may be constructed and operated to deal specifically with

status offenders who are given a place to stay but are free to leave if they desire. The other facility may be operated more like an adult-level jail, with locked doors and secure cells, for the protection of both the juvenile and the public.

Adjudication   If a petition is filed, the next stage is **adjudication,** the fact-finding process comparable to an adult offender's trial. Although there are a few notable exceptions, such as the lack of a right to bail, juvenile defendants are protected by most of the same constitutional rights traditionally guaranteed adults charged with violations of the law. However, the process of adjudication frequently differs from the trial model. Both prosecutors and defense attorneys often view their task as assisting the judge in determining what action is in the child's best interests.

Disposition   Following adjudication, an attempt is made to select the **disposition** that best meets the juvenile's needs and serves community interests. The dispositional alternatives available to the court normally include dismissal, probation, residential and nonresidential community-based programs, and commitment to a secure residential facility, often referred to as a training school. Juveniles released from training schools are generally supervised by juvenile court counselors or juvenile parole officers; this supervision is commonly known as **aftercare.**

A Closer Look at Intake

Intake refers to the pretrial investigation and screening of cases referred to juvenile court.[6] Complaints are assessed in terms of the alleged offense, the circumstances surrounding its commission, prior behavior of the youth, and the needs of the youth, his or her family, and the community.[7] Intake decision making is critical because it determines all future actions by the juvenile court, whether the court will dismiss the accusations against the offender or handle them informally or formally.

After a complaint has been received, intake staff have three initial decisions to make: (1) whether legal grounds exist for a formal petition of delinquency, (2) whether to dismiss or handle the case formally or informally if legal grounds exist for a petition, and (3) whether to detain alleged offenders if a petition is to be filed.[8] The intake interview with the juvenile and his or her parents begins with a reading and explanation of the complaint. The youth is questioned about the allegations and given an opportunity to respond. If the juvenile denies the offense, the complaint must be dismissed or formally handled. If the youth admits to the substance of the complaint, additional questions will be asked to determine the circumstances surrounding the offense and to assess the complaint's accuracy. Additional persons, such as teachers, family and friends, and social service workers, may subsequently be interviewed. After deliberation, a decision regarding informal or formal processing is made.

If a petition has been filed or if grounds for a petition exist but the final decision on handling has not been made, the intake worker must determine whether the juvenile requires detention. Normally, the worker should consider detention whenever the youth's behavior presents a danger to himself or herself or others or whenever the juvenile's behavior indicates that he or she may abscond prior to the juvenile court hearing.

If a petition is to be filed, the intake worker must next determine how the case should be handled. The best rule of thumb in this area is "the intervention by the court should be proportionate to the severity of the case, that is, the degree of imminent danger the youth poses to self or others."[9] Intake units have sometimes been criticized for placing too much emphasis on the nature of the offender's problems and not enough emphasis on the nature of the juvenile's conduct. Juveniles who have engaged in minor misconduct have received more restrictive dispositions than youth who have engaged in serious delinquency, because staff were hopeful that the youth's personal problems could be solved.

About half of the cases referred to the juvenile court are handled informally, and most informally processed cases are dismissed.[10] For those cases not dismissed, a consent decree specifies those conditions the offender agrees to follow, such as drug or family counseling, school attendance, restitution, or community service. If the conditions are met, the case is dismissed; if they are not met, the decision may be made to proceed formally with a petition.

About 10 percent of status offenders are placed in detention at some point during the adjudication process. Almost two-thirds of adjudicated status offenders are placed on formal probation; one in six receives residential placement. Most status offenders who require out-of-home placements do so because their family situation has significantly broken down, and as a result they have been charged with ungovernable behavior or running away.[11]

About 20 percent of the juveniles charged with delinquency are detained at some point during the processing of their cases. For adjudicated delinquents, the sanctioning options include probation, a variety of community-based programs, and residential facilities, which range from secure, prisonlike facilities to community-based residences. Generally speaking, about 60 percent of adjudicated delinquents receive probation and three out of ten receive a residential placement.[12] Little relationship can be found between the type of offense and nature of placement (Table 12-3). Youths are more likely to receive an out-of-home placement for public order offenses than person or property crime.[13]

Community-Based Programs for Juveniles

When evaluating community-based programs for juveniles, the type of offender and the behavior problems that are appropriate for

Table 12-3 Juvenile Court Case Outcomes, by Characteristics of Juvenile Offenders and Type of Offense, 1996

Characteristic	Delinquency Cases		Petitioned Cases		Cases Adjudicated Delinquent				Nonadjudicated Cases[a]			
	Detained Prior to Juvenile Court Disposition	Petitioned	Adjudicated Delinquent	Transferred or Waived to Adult Court	Placed Out of Home	Placed on Probation	Dismissed	Other[b]	Placed Out of Home	Placed on Probation	Dismissed	Other[b]
Total	18.3%	55.9%	57.7%	1.0%	28.1%	54.1%	4.4%	13.4%	1.4%	27.5%	49.3%	21.0%
Sex												
Male	19.5	58.8	58.8	1.2	29.4	53.1	4.4	13.0	1.6	26.8	50.5	20.0
Female	13.9	46.0	52.6	B	21.6	59.0	4.3	15.0	0.8	29.5	45.8	23.7
Race												
White	14.2	53.5	58.7	0.8	26.0	55.5	3.6	15.0	1.3	29.6	46.7	21.7
Black	27.2	61.6	55.0	1.4	31.9	52.1	6.7	9.4	1.7	22.7	54.8	19.5
Other[c]	18.0	52.8	65.6	B	31.9	48.2	B	18.8	B	27.3	52.6	19.1
Age at referral to court												
12 years and younger	10.1	39.0	50.7	B	18.5	63.0	3.9	14.6	B	32.6	47.0	19.9
13 years	16.2	49.9	58.6	B	26.4	58.6	3.4	11.5	1.0	31.6	46.8	20.5
14 years	18.4	54.9	60.2	B	29.0	56.1	3.6	11.3	1.4	29.6	48.5	20.3
15 years	20.2	59.1	60.1	0.5	29.8	54.6	4.2	11.5	1.6	27.3	50.3	20.3
16 years	20.2	58.8	58.4	1.4	29.6	52.0	4.8	13.6	1.6	26.1	49.6	21.3
17 years and older	19.1	62.5	54.0	2.6	27.1	49.3	5.7	17.8	1.6	21.2	51.7	22.9
Type of offense												
Person	22.8	58.6	54.5	1.9	30.9	53.5	5.0	10.7	1.3	26.3	54.6	16.1
Property	14.4	52.1	59.0	0.8	26.1	56.4	3.8	13.8	1.1	29.9	44.3	24.0
Drug	22.5	62.1	58.2	1.2	24.5	54.1	6.9	14.5	1.5	29.8	48.8	18.7
Public-order	21.0	59.7	58.1	B	32.0	49.4	4.0	14.6	2.1	20.7	57.5	19.4

Note: Care should be exercised when interpreting age, sex, or race differences because reported statistics do not control for variations in the seriousness of the offense or the prior criminal history of the juvenile.

[a] Includes petitioned cases that were not adjudicated delinquent and nonpetitioned cases.

[b] Includes dispositions such as fines, restitution, community service, and referrals outside the court for services with minimal or no further court involvement anticipated.

[c] Includes persons having origin in any of the original peoples of North America, the Far East, Southeast Asia, the Indian Subcontinent, or the Pacific Islands. Nearly all Hispanics were included in the "white" racial category.

Source: Howard Snyder et al., "Easy Access to Juvenile Court Statistics: 1987–1996" (Online). Washington, D.C.: U.S. Department of Justice, Office of Juvenile Justice and Delinquency Prevention, 1998. Available: http://ojjdp.ncjrs.org/facts/ezaccess.html (June 28, 1999).

each program must be considered. The issue is whether status offenders, property offenders, and violent offenders should be treated alike because of the similar personal problems these youths may share or whether the type of violation should limit the degree of intervention.

Another issue involves minorities in the juvenile justice system and the matter of disparity. Research has consistently revealed that the potential for bias exists at every stage of the juvenile justice system. The problem is greatest at the early stages of processing, but evidence shows that bias accumulates at the various decision-making stages of the system. These findings are distinct from research on the adult criminal justice system, which has produced much less evidence of discrimination.[14]

The introduction of bias occurs principally through two channels. First, police may be more likely to pick up minority youths, and second, intake staff may be influenced in their judgments about detention and the filing of a petition by a view of the juvenile's family situation, which is highly correlated with race. The informality of the juvenile justice system, and the ability to respond to noncriminal behavior and youth problems rather than just crime, may contribute to the introduction of racial discrimination. Efforts to intervene, and intervene early, however well intentioned, thus have a potential flip side of targeting minority youth whose conduct may be not dissimilar to their majority peers.

Not all community-based juvenile programs are available in every jurisdiction. In many communities, juvenile probation is the only community-based dispositional alternative available on a regular basis. In such areas, probation staff must work with community agencies to serve the needs of all offenders who do not require institutionalization. Other communities can offer one or two group facilities and perhaps a diversion or other community supervision program for children with family, school, alcohol, or drug problems. The full range of programs is generally seen only in large metropolitan areas where the numbers

of youths permit increased programming and greater specialization. Even in such environments, however, significant gaps in services may be found.

Programs for Runaways

Emergency shelters for runaways developed to provide food, shelter, and often clothing, counseling, and medical care to juveniles who have committed no crime other than being AWOL (absent without leave) from home. Many times the youth's family has encouraged him or her to leave or forcibly ejected him or her. Emergency shelters offer these youthful throwaways a way station while efforts can be made to find them a suitable long-term placement. Whenever possible, however, the goal of counseling efforts is a reconciliation with the family.

Juveniles generally enter emergency shelters through self-referrals or through police referrals. In addition to providing the basic necessities and attempting to work with the youth and his or her family, the programs may provide drug or employment counseling and offer a referral service to community agencies. Because the average length of stay in an emergency shelter is no more than two weeks, the program must focus its primary efforts on meeting the youth's most immediate needs.

Special Approaches in Juvenile Assistance Inc. (SAJA), in Washington, D.C., is fairly typical of programs for runaways. Emergency shelter and crisis intervention are provided for up to fourteen youths between the ages of eleven and seventeen.[15] A staff of four full-time counselors, ten volunteers, and several consultants offer casework, family counseling, court advocacy, and referral services. The average length of stay in SAJA is one week.

Amicus House in Pittsburgh, Pennsylvania, is a program for local runaways.[16] Youths are referred to the shelter by the court or social service agencies as well as through self-referrals. Upon entering the program, youths are restricted to the house for forty-eight hours. They are informed, "You're here to think." Counseling is available, but the youth is otherwise forbidden outside contacts. If the youth appears to be trying to resolve his or her difficulties, the parents may be contacted and a meeting arranged. If the family members are unwilling to work with Amicus House staff to iron out their problems, attempts are made to find an alternative placement for the youth. This measure is normally unnecessary, as most juveniles return to their families after two or three weeks.

Juvenile Diversion Programs

Many strategies are available for diverting offenders from the juvenile justice process. Some juvenile diversion projects are almost identical to those established for criminal offenders. For example, the Community Arbitration Project (CAP) in Anne Arundel County, Maryland, is a dispute-settlement mechanism that mediates juvenile offenses.[17] Police issue citations to juveniles who commit CAP-eligible offenses ranging from vandalism to assault. Offenses are then mediated at a hearing that involves the juvenile, his or her parents, and often the victim. Community service is routinely utilized as an informal disposition. Other juvenile diversion programs focus on problems that are more specific to juveniles, such as getting along with parents or staying in and completing school.

Outreach Programs

Much of the focus today is on identifying high-risk youth before they come into contact with the juvenile justice system. These prevention and diversion programs can take a variety of forms, often blurring the lines between formally accused and adjudicated delinquents and those youths who appear to be moving toward delinquent behavior patterns. A number of these **outreach programs** specifically target minority youths, in an effort to tailor the intervention to the particular types of challenges these juveniles confront.

Boys and Girls Clubs of America   Boys and Girls (B&G) Clubs of America were established in 1865 and incorporated in 1906.[18] They are primarily located in communities where youths are the most disadvantaged, helping to motivate at-risk youths with the opportunity to lead productive and meaningful lives. In 1987, recognizing the special problems of youths in public housing—high risk of alcohol and drug use, health problems, school failure, pregnancy, crime, and violence—a major initiative was launched to establish new programs in public housing communities. A three-year research study concluded that these programs effectively reduced juvenile crime (13 percent) and drug activity (22 percent) and improved the quality of life for the families and children in public housing.

Wishing to expand B&G efforts, the Bureau of Justice Assistance provided funding of more than $7 million to support the establishment of new clubs and strengthen existing ones. During the early 1990s, thirty-one additional clubs were established. Furthermore, training and technical assistance were provided to many existing locations in an effort to develop and implement violence prevention strategies and to improve youth health and education.

The basic resources to club members include:

- A safe haven away from the negative influences of the street;

- Guidance, discipline, and values modeling from caring adult leaders;

- Constructive youth development activities and programs in supervised supportive environments;

- Access to comprehensive, coordinated services that meet the complex needs of youths at risk;

- Educational support, increased awareness of career options, and goal-setting skills;

- A comprehensive violence-prevention initiative; and

- A future vision of life beyond public housing.[19]

B&G clubs vary in terms of the programs they offer, based on the resources available and community needs. All programs include a physical facility—a club open five to six days per week, four to five hours per day. They are staffed by both full- and part-time workers and volunteers. School-age children from all races, religions, and ethnic backgrounds are welcome, with no personal recommendations or proof of character required for membership. The juveniles join their local club by completing an application and paying an annual membership fee that is low enough for any youngster to afford to join—often $1 to $5.

In 1994, B&G clubs reached 2.2 million youths in 1,672 clubs, about 270 of which are in public housing areas. Programs are now available on Indian reservations and to military families, with services in a wide variety of facilities, including shopping malls. The national organization provides numerous services to local clubs, including more than twenty-five model programs, alcohol, drug, and pregnancy prevention, career exploration, citizenship and leadership, cultural enrichment, delinquency and gang prevention, environmental education, and health, sports, and fitness.[20]

Programs Targeting Minority Youth

Concerns about the overinvolvement of minority youth in the juvenile justice system have led to the development of many programs that specifically target these juveniles for outreach and prevention and diversion activities. Recognizing the importance of culture in the establishment of program strategies and activities, these projects hope to encourage young people to accept intervention and assistance. Such programs offer personal counseling and services that can help juveniles overcome stereotyped behavior and expand their sometimes limited visions of the options available to them in the future.

Men of Distinction   The Men of Distinction (MOD) program in Nashville, Tennessee, attempts to boost self-esteem and correct the false notions of manhood associated with crime and drug abuse among young African American males. MOD provides positive educational and recreational training and programs for boys nine to seventeen in some of Nashville's toughest housing projects.[21] Originally funded by the Governor's Black Health Care Task Force of Tennessee, the Office of Juvenile Justice and Delinquency Prevention (OJJDP) recommends it as a model worthy of replication across the nation.

The program's components include mentoring, peer counseling, professional counseling, academic activities, field trips, manhood development, and responsibility training. One of the most important elements of the program is mentoring, provided by individuals recruited and matched with the juveniles based on similarity of interests. The mentors agree to telephone the youth at least once a week and take him out at least once a month. The program offers youths positive relationships with males that are often lacking in the single-parent households in which most program participants live. Manhood development training includes lessons in African American history, culture, and contemporary issues. Basic skills instruction focuses on the obligations and responsibilities of manhood. Completion of this part of the program is recognized with a rite of passage ceremony.

Peer counselors are often individuals who have previously participated in MOD and have continued involvement with the program to offer their insights and experiences to others. These part-time employees also lead informal rap sessions. A professional psychologist runs traditional counseling programs, plus conflict-resolution training and parent support groups, and works with teachers and guidance counselors when intervention is required.

Program Focus

Mentoring Men of Distinction

"We are trying to give these children direction and guidance," says MOD [Men of Distinction] program coordinator Ron King. "We do this by providing mentoring and conflict resolution sessions and by working directly with the kids and their parents. We demand discipline and high standards. . . ."

Reflecting on MOD mentor John Coleman's impact on her son's life, Sharon Rhodes said, "I can't believe the change in his attitude. Jason behaves better in school and shows me more respect. I am really thankful for the time Mr. Coleman spends with Jason because he's needed a male figure in his life."

"There are cases where MOD youths have witnessed parents involved in abusing drugs and alcohol, experienced or witnessed sex at an early age, or have endured physical and mental abuse," King said. "The mentor for these youths may very well be someone who grew up in the same environment and has had some involvement with correctional institutions but has decided not to live the same type of life as an adult."

Source: Rita Grant and Juanita Buford, "Tennessee Program Prevents Violence in Young African American Males," *Corrections Today,* August 1994, p. 152.

Activities for MOD participants are extensive: team sports, martial arts, drama, dance, arts and crafts, and academic quiz games. Field trips have included visits to the zoo, prisons, and private businesses to learn about the responsibilities of various professions. Out-of-state trips have been arranged to Georgia, South Carolina, and Washington, D.C., both for educational purposes and to give the participants (who may never have eaten in a restaurant or stayed in a hotel) a sense of hope about the future.

Existing data on the program indicate that participants have lower rates of behavioral problems than noninvolved youths.[22]

Mentoring Programs

Mentoring can be an extremely valuable approach to working with juveniles. The one-to-one relationship with a mentor can replace otherwise missing relationships and provide the juvenile with an important resource for guidance as well as friendship. Mentoring programs tend to be relatively unstructured and work on the quality of the chemistry that develops between the mentor and the youth. Often other family members benefit as well, because the mentor provides a new perspective on family dynamics and can serve as a buffer in family relationships. For juveniles who need personal attention to find and stay on the right path, a mentoring program can be extremely valuable.

Mentoring programs for juvenile offenders are expanding rapidly, and the concept of mentoring is now found in many community-based programs for juveniles. In April 1995, forty-one projects were selected for federal funding to establish juvenile mentoring programs (JUMP).[23] JUMP matches adults with children having trouble in school and showing signs of dropping out or getting into further difficulty. The goals of the programs are threefold: preventing delinquent behavior, reducing school dropout rates, and improving academic performance.

The new programs will take a variety of forms. A number will rely on sworn law enforcement officers or firefighters as mentors; others will recruit college students, senior citizens, and businesspeople. Several programs emphasize tutoring and academics, while others focus on vocational counseling and job skills. Several programs will accept youth referred by juvenile courts, and two will work exclusively with youth incarcerated or on probation.

Youth Service Bureaus

Youth service bureaus (YSBs) are publicly or privately administered agencies developed to address a broad range of youth problems. Their most immediate objective, however, often is diverting delinquents and predelinquents from the juvenile justice system, especially when the bureau is administered by a police or juvenile probation department. The basic functions of YSBs include:

1. Identifying community problems affecting juveniles;

2. Developing, monitoring, and strengthening community responses to youths;

3. Improving the attitudes and practices of social service and juvenile justice agencies through youth advocacy (system modification);

4. Referring youths to appropriate community resources and monitoring those referrals (service brokerage);

5. Providing direct services; and

6. Gathering and distributing information.

Youth service bureaus accept referrals from any source, including schools, social service agencies, police, and self-referrals. They often operate twenty-four hours a day, seven days a week, and thus can offer immediate assistance without appointment or delay.

The youth service bureaus originated in urban centers in the midwestern United States in the 1950s. The programs generated considerable support. After receiving an enthusias-

tic endorsement from the 1967 President's Commission on Law Enforcement and Administration of Justice, the bureaus expanded throughout the nation. Although the discontinuation of federal funds in the late 1970s and early 1980s led to the closing of many programs, YSBs still operate across the United States. Their names vary—some are known as youth assistance centers, others as youth resource bureaus—but they all share a single aim: meeting the needs of troubled youths.

The list of possible youth service bureau activities is almost endless: twenty-four-hour-a-day counseling, drop-in clinics, family counseling, outpatient medical treatment, crisis intervention, employment assistance, advocacy for youths appearing in juvenile court, **temporary shelters** and group homes, sponsorship of police-youth dialogues, parent education, self-improvement classes, recreational activities, craft and hobby classes, alternative schools and other education programs, and group discussions with prison inmates.[24] Within the community, a YSB works with various agencies to promote the development of new community resources and to ensure that youths receive the assistance they need from existing programs.

Figure 12-4 illustrates the linkages that a YSB might establish in a typical community. While no youth service bureau offers all these services, each program is designed to meet some of the special problems of youths within a particular community. Some programs emphasize direct services; others focus on developing new programs or coordinating existing community resources. Programs administered by police or juvenile justice agencies normally emphasize direct services to youths who might otherwise require juvenile court intervention.

Youth Courts

An increasingly popular method of diverting juveniles from the justice system involves the use of a youth court. The program originated in Ithaca, New York, in 1962 and spread quickly across the nation. In 1995, more than 190 teen

Figure 12-4   Typical Community-Youth Service Bureau (YSB) Linkages

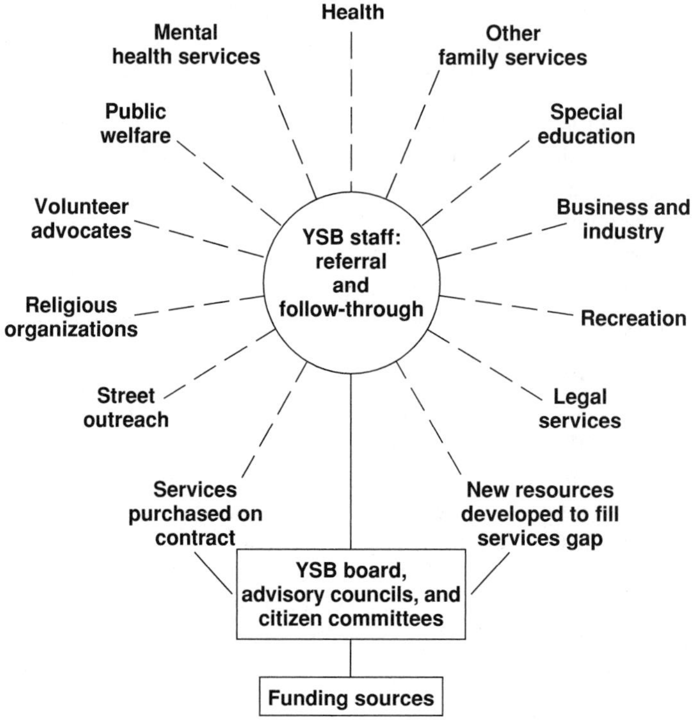

Source: Sherwood Norman, *The Youth Service Bureau: The Key to Delinquency Prevention* (Hackensack, N.J.: National Council on Crime and Delinquency, 1972). p. 15. Reprinted by permission.

courts were operating in twenty-five states.[25] They are run by juvenile courts, probation departments, law enforcement agencies, schools, and nonprofit agencies. Most require defendants to plead not guilty, although a few will require the determination of guilt or innocence. There are two models: trial and peer juries. Trial models generally have an adult as judge, although a few permit juveniles. A few operate with no jury. In the peer jury model, there is no trial—the peer jurors question the youth directly. Most teen court programs target first offenders, but 58 percent will accept repeaters, 20 percent will handle felonies, and 29 percent accept status offenders. Table 12-4 lists the types of offenders most frequently handled by youth courts.

Orange County's Teen Court in Orlando, Florida, is typical.[26] The purpose of Teen Court is to divert less serious cases away from the juvenile court. The Teen Court process provides a forum for defendants to explain their involvement in the offense; a structured environment in which the words and actions of defendants who admit their wrongful acts are evaluated and judged by a jury of peers; and the opportunity for defendants to accept responsibility for their actions by fulfilling the jury's sentence of community service hours and future jury duty assignments, both of which are designed to be constructive and rehabilitative.

The jury may also decide that the teen has to make restitution or abide by a curfew. He or she may have to write a report or make an apology. The defendant has five weeks to complete the sanction; if it is not completed the case is referred to juvenile court. If the youth is successful, all charges are dropped.

Teen Court is staffed by volunteer jurors, who must be in grades nine to twelve, be in satisfactory academic standing, agree to serve six months or one year, respect the oath of confidentiality, demonstrate maturity and sensitivity, and meet the requirements of the Teen Court Agreement.

Offenses considered by the court might include shoplifting, vandalism, possession of alcohol, disorderly conduct, trespassing, interference in a school function, or petty theft. First-time assault, battery, and possession of a controlled substance may also be considered. All cases follow an arrest; defendants must admit guilt to participate. The defendant has a teen defense attorney assigned to his or her case who will try to bring out all mitigating circumstances and attempt to sway the jury to reduce the penalty. A teen prosecuting attorney attempts to bring forward the reason that a stiffer penalty is in order. Definitions of terms are provided to assist all parties in understanding the legal system, and role requirements are spelled out.

Specialized Programs

Some diversion programs focus on particular types of juvenile problems, such as school attendance or family difficulties. Others focus on particular types of offenses. Shoplifters Alternatives, for example, is a national program that offers Youth Education Shoplifting as a diversion program for young property offenders. The program's focus is on those youths who steal because "they want to see if they can get away with it, or don't have the money to buy all the things they want, are mad at the world, or simply feel depressed and confused"—not for those who steal to buy drugs or resale.[27] The program is based on a home study model, which can be implemented by the national office with results sent to the local court, or local staff can be trained to implement the program.

The home study package includes a workbook and two audiocassette tapes and takes five to six hours to complete. The youth com-

Table 12-4 Types of Offenders Most Frequently Handled by Youth Courts

Offense	Percent
Theft	97
Alcohol and drug offenses	95
Vandalism	92
Disorderly conduct	90
Assault	83
Traffic	59
Truancy	48
Violence	20
Other	27

Source: Tracy Godwin, "Teen Courts: Empowering Youth in Community Prevention and Intervention Efforts," *APPA Perspectives,* Winter 1996, p. 23.

pletes an answer sheet, which is then scored for program completion, with feedback given to the youth and the agency. This is followed by a one-day class or workshop session for those youth with moderate to high risk.

The workbook includes a series of exercises designed to help the youth to learn the facts about shoplifting and reasons that he or she shoplifts, as well as to recognize the danger signals that lead up to an act of theft, to examine his or her own experiences, to recognize the risks in shoplifting, and to develop a personal plan to stop. The classroom experience builds on this foundation, with further personal exploration and planning exercises in a group setting designed to help the youth take responsibility for his or her action. This program is widely used in many states. Florida alone is employing it in more than twenty counties.[28]

Diversion and the Juvenile Justice System

The manner in which a community-based program for juveniles is used—that is, as a diversion alternative or a disposition for adjudicated offenders—depends upon the particular treatment or rehabilitative philosophy present within a given community. Programs used only

Program Focus

Teens Face Jury of Their Peers

SANFORD—The shoplifter sat silently as her punishment was announced: 12 hours of community service, a written explanation of her crime—and an apology to her mom.

The 14-year-old girl, who makes good grades and belongs to the math club at her school, stood timidly in the courtroom and told her mother she was sorry for stealing a pair of shorts and a skirt from Burdines.

The sentence was handed down by a jury of her peers—six teens. If she fulfills it, she will have no juvenile record.

Teen Court is a program recently launched by the Prosecution Alternatives for Youth [PAY] program in Seminole County [Florida] and headed by PAY counselor Dick Harbaugh. The lawyers, jury, bailiffs and clerks are youths, mostly volunteers from local high schools. Some are prior Teen Court defendants sentenced to jury duty.

"That's the great thing about this program," PAY director Nancy DeLong said. "It lets them

do what they need to do: Get it over with and move on."

The only adult court worker is the judge, played by local attorneys who volunteer their time. But the sentence, within reasonable guidelines, is up to the jury.

The idea is that disapproval will be more meaningful coming from other youths. To go through Teen Court, teens must admit their guilt and abide by their sentences—which include at least two nights as a juror.

The program works, according to a boy who served on a jury last week to fulfill his Teen Court sentence for retail theft. He liked the service so much, he asked to be a lawyer next time.

"It's easy to say all the adults are against you, but when it's your own friends up there, you really feel bad," he said. "It makes you feel more responsible."

Similar programs in Orange and Osceola counties have had good results. Karen Kerr,

for divertable first offenders in one setting may be used for more serious delinquents in others. A single program will often be made to serve both adjudicated and nonadjudicated offenders because it is considered desirable to consolidate resources.

For example, in late 1995, the Justice Department announced that six local communities would receive a total of nearly $8 million in grants to develop programs that would divert at-risk youth and impose graduated sanctions upon youth who commit crimes.[29] The goal is to attack the problem of youth crime from all directions. Law enforcement and juvenile corrections organizations will work with

private programs that offer youths prevention opportunities such as after-school activities and mentoring programs, and they will intervene when youths commit offenses. Communities were selected on the basis of their existing efforts to combat delinquency and their plans to further reach out to problem youths.

Community Alternatives to Secure Detention

The vast majority of offenders do not require detention; they await adjudication in their own

who runs Osceola's Teen Court, said fewer than 6 percent of teens who went through the program since it started in 1991 returned to the system by the end of 1993.

PAY counselor Jean Jeffcoat said Seminole's program has drawn great interest from students, about 250 of whom have volunteered to serve. Some are interested in careers in law; others receive high school credit for their service.

"The kids are so enthusiastic, we have kids waiting in line," she said. "It turns peer pressure into something positive."

The teens take their court jobs seriously. Aaryn Fuller, a volunteer prosecutor for the shoplifting trial, implored the jury to throw the book at the girl because thieves drive up prices for everyone. Bill Mitchell, a volunteer public defender, was just as passionate, noting that the items were recovered, and the girl had only been in the country for a short time.

Fuller asked for 24 hours of community services; Mitchell sought the minimum, eight

hours. The jury settled on 12, plus the public apology and two nights of jury service. In addition, the girl must complete a retail theft workbook, which makes teens sit down and think about what they did and the consequences.

Fuller praised the idea of Teen Court.

"Teen-agers care more about what their peers think about them than adults," she said. "We're tougher on them because we're the ones that have to carry the stigma of being thought to be stealing every time we walk through a store. Also, we know an excuse when we hear one, because we've given them."

Source: Beth Taylor, "Teens Face Jury of Their Peers," *Orlando Sentinel,* November 26, 1995, p. B3. Reprinted by permission.

homes. Those who do require detention do not necessarily need placement in a secure, locked facility. Alternative detention programs may be residential or nonresidential.

Home Detention Programs

The nonresidential programs, often referred to as home detention, are similar to supervised pretrial release programs for adults. Youths are permitted to live at home while they are supervised by juvenile court counselors, who attempt to keep them out of trouble and available to the juvenile court. The juvenile, his or her parents, teachers, and employers may be

contacted on a daily basis. Frequently, the juvenile is required to attend school or work, obey a curfew, keep his or her parents or supervisor informed of his or her whereabouts, and avoid drugs and unsavory persons and places during supervision. Additional rules may be written into a home detention contract. Counseling and referral services are usually provided to the youth under supervision.

A survey of **home detention programs** revealed that the average program serves between two hundred and three hundred youths per year.[30] Between 2 and 13 percent of the juveniles run away or are rearrested during supervision. Failures were found to result from excessive delays in adjudication and attempts to use home detention to test the youth's potential as a probationer.

The San Diego County Home Supervision Program illustrates home detention.[31] Counselors check on the minors in their caseload every morning, afternoon, and evening, seven days a week. Personal, unannounced contacts are made every day on a varying schedule. Youths thought to be violators may be contacted as many as four times a day. Minors who violate supervision may be taken into custody. During the first two years of the program's operation, almost twenty-five hundred boys were supervised; about 20 percent were violators, but only thirty-three committed new offenses while in the community. The Home Supervision Program costs less than one-third the amount required to place a youth in secure detention.

Today, some of the most notable home detention programs are in St. Louis, Missouri (which established the first home detention program in the early 1970s); Louisville, Kentucky; and Cleveland, Ohio. These programs are intensive. They utilize small caseloads—as few as ten youths per supervisor—and expect staff to have at least daily contact with the juveniles. The workers are on call twenty-four hours a day for crisis intervention and have frequent contacts with parents, schools, and other agencies. These programs have all established failure-to-appear rates averaging about 5 or 10 percent, with approximately twice that number of youths acquiring additional charges.[32]

Detention Aftercare

A new approach to the detention issue developed in New York City, where efforts have been made to provide aftercare to youths leaving secure detention.[33] An audit of the program revealed that it has been effective in reducing further crime and incarceration, and it has subsequently reduced costs to both the city and the juvenile justice system of New York. In addition, this program has enhanced public safety by reducing subsequent crime.

Juvenile Probation Programs

The majority of youths adjudicated by the juvenile court are placed on **probation.** Many nonadjudicated youths are placed on **informal probation,** a diversion strategy initiated at intake in which probation staff defer the filing of a petition while the juvenile receives probation counseling and supervision. If the juvenile successfully adjusts to and completes supervision, a petition against the child will not be filed. If the child fails to adjust, a petition is filed. Juvenile probation is clearly the most far-reaching community-based correctional program for juveniles. The nature and scope of its services often determine the types of alternative community programs that will be established within a particular jurisdiction.

Like adult probation, juvenile probation services may be administered locally or centralized within a state agency. Although either the executive or judicial branch may administer juvenile probation, the executive branch usually directs state-administered services and the juvenile court usually organizes locally administered agencies (Table 12-5). Within the probation department, activities are normally divided into intake and supervision duties.

The National Assessment of Juvenile Corrections found that the median caseload size of juvenile probation officers was fifty-five youths.[34] They contact most probationers once a month; they see half of the juveniles for less than thirty minutes per visit. Most of the probation officer's time is not spent in counseling clients; in fact, less than one-third of his or her time involves providing direct services to probationers. Officers responsible only for probation supervision (and not intake) spend over half their working hours conducting investigations, attending meetings, appearing in court, and reading and preparing reports.

The counseling that juvenile probationers receive focuses on personal, school, employment, and drug-related problems and pro-

Program Focus

Detention Aftercare in New York

A New York City program that aims to improve delinquent youths' school attendance also helps to keep them out of trouble, according to a study by the city comptroller's office. Youths who participated in the city's "Aftercare" program had significantly lower re-arrest rates than youths who did not participate, the comptroller found.

Youths are told about the Aftercare program while they are being detained in the city's Spofford Juvenile Center or other detention facilities. The program, which is voluntary, consists of meetings between case workers and youths and their families, to discuss the youths' needs.

"The central focus is on education," the comptroller's office said. "Aftercare aims to improve children's school attendance and performance, connect them with community resources and provide the children and their families with the support that is needed for the children to remain in school." On average, case workers spend seven months working with a youth and his family.

To evaluate the effectiveness of Aftercare, the comptroller reviewed the arrest histories of 100 youths who participated in Aftercare and another 100 youths who did not participate. Of the 100 Aftercare participants, 51 were re-arrested a total of 76 times. Of the 100 non-participants, 66 were re-arrested a total of 157 times.

The Aftercare participants spent a total of 10,550 days in detention or jail, compared to 17,970 days for the non-participants.

"We also found that the results of participating in the Aftercare program last over time," the comptroller said. Three years after completing the program, 36 percent of a group of Aftercare participants did not have any subsequent arrests, compared to 19 percent of a group who did not participate in Aftercare.

Because incarceration of juveniles in New York is expensive—$238 per child per day in secure detention, $183 per day for non-secure detention, $176 per day in a state juvenile corrections facility, and $162 per day in a state prison—Aftercare saves New York City and New York State money, the auditor said. The average cost of Aftercare per child, $1,445, was dwarfed by the costs of subsequent arrest and reincarceration, which were more likely for youths who did not participate in Aftercare, the study showed. The net savings per Aftercare participant were nearly $12,000, according to the comptroller's report.

Source: "Detention Aftercare in New York Said to Cut Recidivism Rates," *Criminal Justice Newsletter,* September 15, 1995, p. 5.

---

bation rules and regulations. Individual and group counseling is the most widely utilized form of treatment, although about one-third of the probation agencies provide employment services, vocational training, or academic education. Although most juveniles on probation receive little counseling, some jurisdictions have developed special programs to meet the needs of serious delinquents or youths for whom assistance might make a difference.

Juveniles are normally placed on probation for an indefinite period. The length of time a youth spends on probation is influenced by such factors as his or her age and the end of the school year. The average youth spends 11.5 months on probation.

Table 12-5   The Administration of Juvenile Probation Services

State Administration		Local Administration	
Judicial Branch	Executive Branch	Judicial Branch	Executive Branch
Connecticut	Alaska	Alabama	California
Hawaii	Arkansas	Arizona	Oregon
Iowa	Delaware	Arkansas	Idaho
Kentucky	District of Columbia	California	Kentucky
Nebraska	Florida	Colorado	Minnesota
North Carolina	Georgia	Georgia	Mississippi
North Dakota	Idaho	Illinois	New York
South Dakota	Kentucky	Indiana	Washington
Utah	Louisiana	Kansas	Wisconsin
West Virginia	Maine	Kentucky	
	Maryland	Louisiana	
	Minnesota	Massachusetts	
	Mississippi	Michigan	
	New Hampshire	Minnesota	
	New Mexico	Missouri	
	North Dakota	Montana	
	Oklahoma	Nevada	
	Rhode Island	New Jersey	
	South Carolina	Ohio	
	Tennessee	Oklahoma	
	Vermont	Pennsylvania	
	Virginia	Tennessee	
	West Virginia	Texas	
	Wyoming	Virginia	
		Washington	
		Wisconsin	
		Wyoming	

Source: Howard N. Snyder and Melissa Sickmund, *Juvenile Offenders and Victims: A National Report* (Washington, D.C.: Office of Juvenile Justice and Delinquency Prevention, 1995), p. 90.

Programs for Youths with School-Related Problems

Alternative Schools   Alternative schools provide special education and intensive counseling to juveniles with behavior problems. The juvenile court or the public school in which the student has had difficulty refers youths to these schools. The model for most **alternative schools** is the Providence Education Center (PEC), established in St. Louis.[35]

PEC offers remedial education and counseling services to juveniles who have had difficulty adjusting to public school. PEC students often have delinquent histories and are minority youths from large, poor families. They usually enter the program at about age twelve and are academically several years behind their peers. PEC has five service components:

1. An Assessment Center that provides extensive diagnostic testing and orientation to referred juveniles.

2. The Education Center, responsible for the academic program.

3. The Student Work Assistance Program, which provides work-study opportunities for students.

4. An aftercare component to help with counseling, alternative placements, and readjustment.

5. Two group homes, one for girls and one for boys.[36]

PEC relies on small classes, averaging fourteen students, to provide individualized attention to the juveniles enrolled in the program. The academic work emphasizes the traditional subjects, such as math and reading, but no conventional grading is done in the school. An attempt is made to take the learning experience out of the classroom and bring it into the students' world. For example, a math class might be taken to a used-car lot and a bank in an effort to learn about the financial side of owning a car.[37]

The Providence Educational Center has achieved considerable success in reducing both truancy and delinquent behavior in its students. A study of three hundred PEC students revealed that, although the youths averaged five adjudicated offenses each when they entered the program, only 20 percent had been rearrested following participation.[38] Not surprisingly, the program has earned the confidence and support of local criminal justice officials. As one probation officer noted: "I think the public school system is failing a lot of kids. It is not developing a curriculum that meets the needs of inner city youth. It takes a different breed of teacher, with patience and understanding, to do that. And I think that is what we have in Providence."[39]

Programs for Juveniles in Traditional Schools

Some programs for youths attempt to work with juveniles who are still able to function within the public school system. For example, the Teacher Probation Officer Program provides a reduced teaching load to selected teachers so they may provide probation-like supervision to students attending the school.[40] **In-school suspension programs,** which currently operate throughout the United States, provide an alternative method for dealing with disruptive and truant children who commit minor offenses. The students attend school but are physically and socially isolated from their peers during the school day. The juveniles spend their time entirely in one room, where they concentrate on remedial work or regular school assignments. The average length of in-school suspension is three days. The youth's parents are frequently asked to attend a parent-teacher conference before the student is returned to the regular classroom.[41]

Other programs in public education use behavior contracts to reduce disruptive behavior. School or community service activities are often assigned to misbehaving youths, and those who demonstrate responsible behavior earn special privileges. Special remedial or compensatory educational programs and intensive tutoring are often provided to disruptive students in conjunction with efforts to improve their in-school behavior.

The School-Based Probation Services Program in Allentown, Pennsylvania, places regular probation officers in public schools as a means of reaching high-risk youth on probation.[42] The program resulted from a recognition that Allentown was experiencing an increase in the number of dropouts, as well as behavior, family, and drug use and abuse problems among its students. The Student Assistance Program (SAP) managed by the school district recognized that students who present one high-risk behavior are often involved with another. Sometimes the SAP teams realized too late that they were working with juveniles also being served by juvenile probation officers. Efforts were disjointed and uncoordinated.

A grant from the state was awarded to initiate the School-Based Probation Services Program, designed to:

1. Strengthen cooperation and communication between the school district and the probation department;

2. Enable juvenile justice staff to educate school personnel about the duties, functions, and limitations of the system;

3. Provide to the schools an alternative for dealing with students with behavioral problems and those who have been suspended;

4. Act as a liaison among the family, probation department, school district, and police department to meet the best educational interests and needs of the students; and

5. Attack drug use and abuse by having probation officers trained to work with students as contributing members in the district's SAP.[43]

The program is staffed by two juvenile probation officers who work in Allentown's middle schools. The officers report jointly to the chief juvenile probation officer and, while in the school, to the school principals. The objectives of the program are to decrease disciplinary referrals and periods of detention, suspension, and absenteeism and to increase positive school reports as measured by teacher quarterly comments, completed homework assignments, and grades. The school-based probation officer is responsible for keeping school officials informed of the students on probation, while maintaining confidentiality and being available to deal with targeted students involved with school violations. Normal school disciplinary procedures are followed first, then a referral is made to the probation officer. The probation officer also deals with alcohol or drug policy violations, out-of-school suspensions, and absenteeism.

The school-based probation officers become members of the school's SAP team. They attend group facilitator training and facilitate in school support groups with team members. They also coordinate reentry conferences for students following an out-of-home placement, in an effort to increase the chances of a positive reintegration. They visit the students at home, working with targeted students to improve decision-making skills, social coping, self-esteem, refusal, and home-school bonding. When students receive an out-of-school suspension, the school probation officer becomes immediately involved. Most of these students are required to work at one of the county's community worksites or are placed on a supervised work crew.

Statistics on the program appear promising, showing decreases in detention, absenteeism, suspensions, and dropouts.[44] In addition, the presence of the probation officer serves to counter the perception that wrongdoing has no consequences. Previously, students on probation were known to boast about their trouble with the legal system and how they "got away with it." The active presence of the probation officer counters this misplaced perception and appears to serve as a deterrent to those who might have been encouraged to try their luck with the juvenile justice system.

Drug Treatment Programs

Drug treatment programs for juveniles encounter the same basic problems of those that serve adults with substance abuse problems. Most program participants have multiple problems, may be returning to environments where drugs are readily available, and thus may need to develop a variety of skills and abilities if they are to overcome their drug problems for the long term. As with adult substance abusers, group strategies and counseling provided by former drug users are typically utilized to address the problems of adolescents. The therapeutic community is the strategy most often employed in residential programs. One element that differentiates drug treatment programs for youth is the aspect of education.

These juveniles are required, like all juveniles under the age of sixteen, to participate in educational programs. This simple difference creates a risk for those youth who have been known to use drugs with persons they met at school. While this does pose a significant risk, it also allows the youth to practice the skills and strategies they have learned in the program in a real-life setting. All drug treatment programs provide skills and counseling, and all programs will eventually have to release their charges back to the environment that has helped to create the problem. Programs for youth are no different, and the school is often the place where these youth receive the first difficult challenge to their sobriety.

Restitution and Community Service Programs

Restitution and community service programs for juveniles are much like those for adults; the major distinction reflects the fact that more juveniles are unemployed. Restitution programs invariably offer assistance in locating part-time employment so juveniles can make financial restitution. Community service activities are similar to those for adults, although sometimes a greater effort is made to include direct service to the victim or the disadvantaged as part of the youth's service to the community. Like those in the criminal justice system, restitution and community service projects for juveniles have become increasingly popular in recent years. The Law Enforcement Assistance Administration greatly facilitated program expansion in the late 1970s when forty-one juvenile restitution programs were established with federal funds. Additional support was provided by research conducted in the mid-1980s that indicated restitution programs may be more effective for juveniles than other means of reducing recidivism.[45]

In that study, juvenile offenders were randomly assigned to restitution or one of three other alternatives. In each comparison, restitution participants did as well or better than youths in other programs. The study concluded that restitution was effective because it provided a positive experience in a real-job situation that contributed to the development of self-confidence. Restitution also is less stigmatizing than other sanctions because it offers a chance to pay the debt and be redeemed. As a result of being held accountable, the youths may have a more realistic understanding of the consequences of their actions.[46]

This growing focus on juvenile offender accountability makes restitution and community service especially attractive. These programs fit the balanced approach to community corrections that emphasizes community safety, accountability, and competency in every dispositional order. Proper screening of program participants, the designation of appropriate restrictions, and consistent offender monitoring achieve the element of safety, while the introduction of both punitive elements and opportunities to learn vital skills provides offender accountability and opportunities to develop competencies. Both restitution and community service appear ideally designed for these purposes.[47]

Community Service   Achieving the objectives of community safety, offender accountability, and skills development means selecting work projects with a purpose and structuring the projects for maximum advantage:

Worthwhile Work The benefits of meaningful service work should be apparent to the youths. For example, before beginning a brush-clearing project, the project leader should discuss the fire hazards caused by brush and highlight the fire prevention benefits of the cleanup.

Youths as Resources When community service operates on its highest plane, the work is the focus of attention, and workers are treated as essential resources needed to complete the job. Many delinquents have been on everybody's most wanted list since early childhood. When community service programs focus on tackling tough local problems, staff should convince the youths that they are genuinely

Program Focus

Making a Difference

When a tornado ravaged a small town in southern Minnesota, the state's Sentenced to Service Program was summoned in the middle of the night and told to assemble a cleanup team. Early the next day, court-ordered community service workers reported to the hardest hit area where they raised shelters, removed fallen trees and helped families search through the rubble for belongings.

In Quincy, Mass., young offenders ordered to complete community service work listened intently as the neighborhood theater producer discussed the importance of authenticity in set designs. Following a brief demonstration, the young people worked enthusiastically to construct the props.

By 11 P.M. Friday, the work was done and the entire cast presented the young workers with free tickets for Saturday's opening performance. When the curtain went up, no one in the audience knew they shared the room with a group of probationers.

In Bend, Ore., more than 30 court-ordered youths braved ten-degree weather to report to the Mt. Bachelor ski area where they loaded donated canned goods and clothing into trucks. The event, known as "Sharelift," culminated a week-long effort to gather food and clothing and raise money for construction of a 26-unit homeless shelter.

During the week, the young workers stuffed envelopes for a special mailing, distributed posters to downtown stores and hung promotional banners throughout town. With the help of these youths, the project raised $600,000 and thousands of pounds of food and clothing for the poor.

Source: Dennis Maloney and Gordon Bazemore, "Community Service Helps Heal Troubled Youths," *Corrections Today,* December 1994, p. 74.

---

needed to solve problems. As one long-time community service team leader describes it:

Most of these folks don't need someone getting into their heads to find out about their bed-wetting habits as kids. They need somebody who has high expectations of their capabilities and pushes them to make a contribution. I've never understood why we spend so much time probing about what they can't do. When I'm on work detail I try to bring out their strengths. Everybody is good at something. We've got a firewood program in our county. If one of my workers slacks off, I jump on him and say something like, "Hey, fella, if we don't get this wood in, some widow is going to be cold tonight." You'd be surprised how much firewood we get to the folks with our approach.[48]

Attention to Transferable Competencies The ideal is to impart skills that can be used be-

yond the community service experience—basic work skills, social competencies, and, when possible, specific technical skills.

Sense of Accomplishment, Closure, and Community Recognition Projects should have a beginning and an end, allowing participants to see the products of their accomplishment and allowing staff to formally recognize youth for their contributions.

Focus on Helping the Disadvantaged The opportunity to help those less fortunate than themselves can add to the benefits of all other program elements, conveying the true meaning of community service.[49]

The best community service programs do even more than carefully structure their work experiences. Mentoring is increasingly considered a valuable strategy in achieving positive bondings between youths with problems and positive role models, but many mentoring programs lack structure. Service projects where youths and adults work together to improve their communities provide an important vehicle for placing participants in productive roles that increase bonding and solidify the mentoring relationship.

Programs that advance economic development are likely to achieve greater public support and financial backing. This can be achieved even through such simple strategies as making commercial areas more hospitable to business through landscaping projects or removing graffiti. Service projects that engage youth in responding to community problems can create a sense of shared responsibility, thus enhancing citizenship. By working on projects that repair some of the damage caused by crime, participants are directly exposed to the reality that crime threatens the safety and quality of life for all citizens. Finally, programs that require offenders to give something back, to assist others with problems similar to their own, may reinforce their own efforts to overcome their difficulties while providing a sense of accomplishment and enhanced feelings of self-worth.[50]

Restitution   The concept of restitution recognizes two distinct levels of impact of crime. First, crime has an impact at the social level. Crime makes everyone feel a little less safe and a little more at risk of victimization. Second, crime has an impact at the individual level. Someone was harmed and the punishment should include the restoration of the person. Restitution has traditionally been an individualized disposition, with each offender finding his or her own means to complete restitution payments. Because so many youths require assistance in obtaining employment, it was perhaps a natural outgrowth that both employment opportunities and supervised work projects would be established to assist youths in meeting their restitution conditions. The supervised work projects have the additional advantage of pro-

viding more monitoring of the youths than could be otherwise achieved, which may also provide opportunities for mentoring, counseling, and instructing youths in ways designed to increase offender competencies. Typically, youths are given the choice of obtaining their own employment or working in projects funded by the community. They are paid a minimum wage, which is then given to the victim in the form of restitution.[51] These programs tend to be moderately to highly structured.[52] The goal is to incapacitate the offender in a highly structured program of restrictions, monitoring, and graduated sanctions to achieve compliance with the court order and to gain restoration of the victim, the community, or both. Programs require a minimum number of hours of service and often utilize drug testing to make certain the youth is following all elements of the court order. Some programs require the offender to meet with the victim (if the victim consents) and see the impact of his or her actions at the personal level. This forces the offender to break down offender rationalizations and impresses upon the juvenile the full impact of his or her conduct. A probation staff member who is trained in mediation may conduct this conference, set the ground rules, and facilitate dialogue. These meetings also allow the victim an opportunity to ask how and why the crime was committed and inform the offender of the victim's choice for sentencing (usually incarceration for a long period). This perhaps impresses upon the offender the seriousness of the act and the potential seriousness of the punishment. These meetings also may provide the victim with a better understanding of the offender and have resulted in the victim's effort to find work for the offender to fulfill restitution. These meetings have been found in this and other programs to enhance the repayment of restitution.[53]

Day Treatment Programs

Day treatment programs provide a means of offering multiple services to youths with a variety of problems, while limiting their unstructured free time.

The Kids in Need of Development Project (KIND) in Louisiana illustrates day treatment programming for juveniles.[54] The project serves youths committed to the state juvenile corrections agency for mid-range offenses such as burglary and vandalism, and it is operated by a nonprofit group that contracts with the state. KIND awards high school credits for course work. Five days a week, the juveniles report to the center for schooling, counseling, and recreation. The program lasts an average of six months, at which point graduates are given a certificate of completion by a judge. Youths may stay for up to a year. The lack of a termination date is used to shock the kids into taking the program seriously.

The program begins with a three-week assessment period, during which staff note the youth's problems. The juvenile is then presented with a list of about ten target behaviors—areas that could use improvement. The youth and counselor each select one of the behaviors to target for change. The idea is that youths will not work to change behaviors they do not believe are in need of change. Youths who do well are praised, while those who fail to respond can be returned to the office of youth development for transfer to a secure setting. Follow-up is an important part of the program. Youths are tracked for a year after they receive their certificates, through face-to-face visits, telephone calls, and contacts with the schools.

At present the program is small—only thirty youths are served at any one time, and another thirty are in follow-up status. The program appears effective: Of the eighty-four youths referred to the project, only five have failed to complete the program.

Wilderness Experience Programs

Wilderness experience programs provide youths with the opportunity for a successful experience through environmental education and wilderness training. Youths who are able to complete their education and training are expected to feel better about themselves. Because delinquency is viewed as self-destructive behavior engaged in by children with poor self-images, delinquent acts should decline after program participation.

Wilderness training programs did not originate with the aim of reducing youthful recidivism. Instead, they were developed during World War II after observers noted that young British seamen quickly gave up their lives when forced to abandon ship in the North Atlantic. Older, more experienced seamen managed to survive, although they were in poorer physical condition. The first Outward Bound program was established to build muscles and physical stamina in young seamen. More important, it attempted to develop feelings of group pride, personal self-worth, and trust in others among the sailors.[55]

The success of the Outward Bound school led to its replication throughout the world as a program for troubled youths. The first U.S. school was established in the Rocky Mountains of Colorado in 1962. Its curriculum included instruction in mountain walking, backpacking, high-altitude camping, solo survival, rappelling, and rock climbing. Similar programs were established in Maine, Massachusetts, North Carolina, Oregon, and Texas. More than one thousand youths have now participated in the 150 to 200 wilderness programs in the United States.

The original Outward Bound program lasted three weeks and consisted of four basic phases: (1) training in the basic skills, (2) a long expedition, (3) a solo, and (4) a final testing period. This format has been modified in a variety of ways in recent years, to focus on and expand selected program elements. Associated Marine Institutes, for example, has translated the wilderness experience to the sea.

Many of the newer programs incorporate extensive environmental education into their efforts, while continuing to take advantage of the therapeutic qualities of the great outdoors. A number of these programs focus less on

Figure 12-5 Specialized Gang Suppression Program

Goal statement

A. Ensure compliance with conditions of probation through intensive supervision, close surveillance of probationers, and the prompt detection and reporting of all violations to court for appropriate action: and,

B. Participate in community-based activities that enhance the gang members' readjustment to society.

Objectives

A. Initiate attempts to contact probationer within five days of receipt of case by the District Probation Office (DPO) or release from camp.
  • Instruct adults in custody to report immediately upon release from jail.
  • Make a minimum of three contacts each month on behalf of each probationer. These may be a combination of two contacts with the probationer plus one collateral contact or one face-to-face contact with the probationer plus two collateral contacts.
  • Spend a minimum of 35 percent of available work time in the field.
  • Report all potential violations to the court within fifteen days of knowledge by the DPO.
  • Make extensive efforts to obtain information from a variety of sources including family, law enforcement, schools, community agencies, gang neighborhood, and interested parties.

B. Be cognizant of resources in the community which provide services that can be of assistance to probationers in developing a crime-free life.
  • Refer probationers, as appropriate, to agencies that can assist in an adjustment to a productive crime-free life and track their progress.
  • Participate in community events that promote the objectives of the Specialized Gang Suppression Program and Probation Department.

Suggestions for what should be measured

A. Violations reported to court within fifteen days of knowledge by the DPO.
  • Number of home calls made.
  • Number of collateral contacts.
  • Number of special activities, i.e. sweeps, searches, conducted.

B. Number of contacts with community organizations.
  • Referrals to community agencies including schools and training programs.
  • Number of probationers enrolled in school or trade school or employed.

Source: Specialized Gang Suppression Program, undated materials.

physical challenge and more on recreation, team building, and interpersonal development.

Specialized Programs

Communities often develop specialized programs to meet the problems and needs of particular offender groups. Programs focused on gang members have been established where gang membership has become an impediment to rehabilitation and community protection. The Specialized Gang Suppression Program (SGSP), for example, of the Los Angeles County Probation Department illustrates a program designed to meet a special community need.[56] The program was established to increase surveillance and control of gang-identified probationers and reduce gang-related activity and violence. Both adult and juvenile probationers are supervised by the unit. The program is organized in six units, one of which focuses on Asian gangs.

The goals and objectives of the unit are clearly specified, focusing on crime control and efforts to aid community adjustment of the offender (Figure 12-5). Individuals may be referred to the unit if they have been participants in a homicide, shooting, or other violence-related gang activity; been identified as gang members who are actively associating with a gang known to be involved with violence, drug offenses, or other crime; or are

Program Focus

Marine Institute Graduates Celebrate Love, Life Skills

The program in New Port Richey [Florida] teaches juvenile offenders a mix of academics and personal responsibility. It also gives them hope.

Sixteen-year-old Dasha knows she has come a long way.

The diploma she held and the blue cap and gown she wore at Friday's graduation ceremony from the New Port Richey Marine Institute provided visible evidence of her recent success. But she holds the real story close in her heart and in her head.

"I really love these guys—I'm really going to miss them," Dasha said of those who have taught and advised her at the Marine Institute. "We've gotten very close. I've learned that they're not here just to get paid, they're here because they want to be. They really care."

Their love and support helped Dasha find a future that seems hopeful. A felony charge for strong-arm robbery and a probation violation preceded her six-month stint at the Marine Institute.

"I ended up in jail for two weeks," she said. "It was a really bad experience."

Dasha is thankful to have ended up at the Marine Institute. "I've learned a lot more here in this program than I ever could have learned just sitting around in jail." She now plans to enter her junior year at Clearwater High and eventually go on to college to study radiology. "I've definitely changed a lot," she said. "I've gained more self-esteem, more confidence."

Dasha was one of six students to graduate Friday at a ceremony held at Leverock's Restaurant in New Port Richey. Marine Institute is a non-profit organization that assists juvenile offenders through a program that includes academic and physical education, life skills, seamanship, diving, aquatics, oceanography and earth sciences. It is one of 40 such institutes located in eight states and in the Cayman Islands.

"Academic and job skills are an important part of the curriculum, and so is learning that positive behavior pays off," said Bob Milla, a student adviser at the Marine Institute. Students earn points for academic accomplishments and completion, attendance, participation, enthusiasm and leadership. Those points are tallied daily and can be used to bid on special trips and activities.

As a New York City police detective, Milla once worked the other side of the fence, putting

siblings of a probationer who is under SGSP supervision and whose case acceptance would enhance efforts to meet SGSP goals.

Probationers in the SGSP unit submit to a number of standard probation conditions, which include requirements for curfew, reporting, notification of change of address, attending school or seeking and maintaining employment, not associating with gang members, not possessing weapons, and not utilizing alcohol or drugs. Probationers enter the program after a ninety-day period of detention.

Probation officers on this unit work with law enforcement, maintaining extensive contact for the purpose of sharing information and developing teamwork. Mutual goals include the identification and investigation of gang members and their activities and prosecution of all

away those offenders he now tries to help. "This is really a fun job," he said. "These are the greatest kids—and I'm not giving you a snow job when I say that. It's rewarding to see the changes in their lives. When they come here, they are so bitter. Many of these kids have missed their youth. They haven't ever heard someone say I love you, or 'You can do it.' When you take a personal interest in these kids, and they realize that you're sincere, they really grab hold of it, and you see them take off."

Fred Mack, another former New York City detective, acts as an adviser for students in the Student and Family Enhancement program at the Marine Institute. "It's an after-care program. I get the kids that come out of boot camp. They stay (at the Institute) till nine at night," he said.

Sherry is one of Mack's students, a graduate who spent seven months in the Life Enhancement for Adolescent Females program before coming to the Marine Institute. Sherry said she had a problem dealing with her anger. A charge of aggravated assault and battery with a deadly weapon landed her in the program.

"I used to just go out and fight before," Sherry said, adding that one of the most use-

ful lessons she has learned is anger management. "They taught me how to talk about my problems before jumping into action and to think about consequences before."

The Marine Institute also helped Sherry land a job as a waitress. Her plans include passing the General Educational Development test and heading to vocational school where she hopes to go into cosmetology. "Or maybe I'll become a marine biologist."

It is rewarding to watch kids like Sherry make their way out of the program, Mack said. "You know you've accomplished something when you see the parents when they first come in here. They don't know what to do; they're lost and helpless. Then you see the looks on their faces today, when their kids are graduating.

"This is a happy day because you know these kids have changed their lives, but it's a sad day, too, because these kids have found a place in my heart, and I'm sorry to see them go."

Source: Michele Miller, "Marine Institute Graduates Celebrate Love, Life Skills," *St. Petersburg Times,* July 29, 1995, pp. 1, 10, copyright 1995. Reprinted by permission of Michele Miller.

---

violations of probation. Probation officers visit schools, consulting with all personnel, and work with community agencies to further develop informal information sources regarding the probationer and his or her activity. All violations are reported, and detention is utilized as a sanction. Emergency calendaring of any new offense is done when necessary to ensure prompt action.

Community-Based Residential Programs for Juveniles

Foster Care

Foster care refers to the placement of a youth in an alternative home in which the adult or adults maintaining the home serve as surrogate or substitute parents. The parental surrogate(s) may care for the child for a finite period—as short as a few days or as long as several years. The length of stay depends upon the youth's need, as determined by his or her legal status, family circumstances, and the success of the child-foster parent(s) arrangement. Foster care may be used for any youth who requires an out-of-home placement. The principal concern in selecting foster care as a placement is that the child has dependency needs and requires parental protection and supervision. Children who demonstrate a strong desire to break free of parental authority and achieve independence are generally poor candidates for foster care. In most cases, youths placed in foster homes require individual attention and are capable of responding to affection. They are normally not serious delinquents and do not have extensive prior records.

The first systematic use of foster care for delinquent children occurred in Massachusetts in 1866. In return for taking youths into their homes, these New England foster parents were paid for the child's board.[57] The use of foster care grew with the juvenile court movement. The placement of a child in an improved family environment seemed to most reformers to be an ideal solution to the problem of a troubled child in a troubled family. That view remains today, although it is tempered by a desire to maintain the juvenile in his or her own home if at all possible. Juvenile probation and aftercare agencies use foster care for juveniles with severe family problems. Some jurisdictions are also experimenting with using it as a diversion and temporary detention alternative for such youths. Specialized foster care programs that focus on juveniles with behavior problems are part of this new correctional effort. The low cost of foster care relative to other out-of-home placements, as well as its intrinsic benefits, make it an appealing correctional alternative.

Unfortunately, there is a shortage of good foster homes. The increased willingness of correctional authorities to place juveniles in foster homes and the growing numbers of throwaway children who are pushed out of their own homes have created an usually high demand for foster parents. Even under normal circumstances, however, good foster homes are in limited supply because foster care is a difficult and demanding undertaking. Children generally enter foster homes after a history of poor relationships with their biological parents and prior parental surrogates. The youths have often been repeatedly moved from one home to another and have learned to anticipate problems that will quickly lead to yet another move. The children develop few behavioral controls. Having received little or no affection, they are virtually incapable of giving or accepting it from others. They test each new foster parent by observing his or her response to disruptive or otherwise inappropriate behavior. Even the most sincere and dedicated foster parent may fail these tests. Because the time and emotional investment of foster care is high and the financial compensation is low, securing and keeping good foster parents is extremely difficult. Successful programs often train the foster parents; provide financial compensation that is both fair and sufficient for the work required; require the biological family members of the foster child to participate in counseling when applicable; screen foster children carefully to avoid dangerous or difficult placements; and require the foster parent to parent the children, not just warehouse them.[58]

Group Homes

Group homes may be known as group centers, group residences, or group foster homes. Like halfway houses for adults, group homes provide supervision and support for persons who can function in a community living situation and do not require institutionalization.

The National Assessment of Juvenile Corrections (NAJC) developed the only available profile of group homes and the youths who live in them.[59] The average group home was found to house eleven children; slightly more than half of the youths in the program were white. Three-fourths of the youths are between sixteen and eighteen years old. Surprisingly, almost two-thirds of the residents could be categorized as middle or upper class, based on their parents' occupation. This finding may be at least partially explained by examining the types of offenses the youths committed: 57 percent were status offenses; 20 percent were property crimes; and only 7 percent were crimes against a person. Many of the status offenses indicated the existence of family problems (such as ungovernability); so the need for an out-of-home placement may have led to assigning the youth to a group home. In addition, most group home residents had prior experiences with the juvenile court. The average youth had been arrested more than six times and had been previously institutionalized.

The NAJC surveyed group home staff members to determine the most popular treatment objectives within the programs. The three objectives most frequently reported were to develop interpersonal relationships, to develop an environment conducive to positive change, and to enhance the youth's self-concept.[60] To accomplish these objectives, eight out of ten programs used individual or group counseling or both. At least half the programs used reality therapy, behavior modification, and family therapy. Educational services normally were obtained from community resources.

One of the most popular group home models is the teaching-family model, developed in 1962. First implemented in the Achievement Place group home in Lawrence, Kansas, this approach is now used in more than forty homes in more than a dozen states. A training and evaluation program has been developed to ensure a consistent level of quality in all programs.

Youth Homes Inc.   Youth Homes Inc., in Charlotte, North Carolina, utilizes the teaching-family model.[61] The program serves youths experiencing emotional and behavior problems, delinquents, predelinquents, status offenders, and juveniles referred by human service agencies. The program is staffed by a professionally trained married couple who provide around-the-clock care, supervision, and instruction to assist youths in correcting their behavior problems. The couple also works with the residents' parents or parental surrogates, teachers, and other social service agency staff assigned to work with the youth.

The program attempts to teach social, self-help, and problem-solving skills to residents and to help them accept responsibility for their behavior. Formal and informal individual and group counseling are offered. In addition, the home employs a system of self-government and a token economy to help teach the youths that life's consequences are a direct result of their actions. As the juveniles near the end of their stay in the program, they gradually spend more time in their natural or foster homes. After leaving the program, visits with and support from the teaching parents are still available.

Evaluation is an important program component. Community professionals, parents, and group home residents periodically evaluate Group Homes Inc. The teaching parents are professionally evaluated on an annual basis. Program effectiveness is assessed through the routine gathering and assessing of information regarding the resident's post-group home adjustment.

Independent Living Programs

One of the most persistent problems in juvenile corrections is the situation of the older adolescent who requires neither institutionalization nor a group home placement, but who is too independent to accept the parental confines of a foster home. These emancipated minors are often mature enough to live on their own, but they are unable to manage financially or require some guidance and support. **Independent living** is designed to meet the needs of these youths.

Youths placed on independent living status may live in an apartment, Young Men's Christian Association (YMCA) or Young Women's

Christian Association (YWCA), or another group residence. The supervising agency provides part or all of the juvenile's room, board, and miscellaneous expenses while the youth attends school, receives vocational training, or works at a part-time job. Independent living programs are highly individualized and flexible offerings. Supervision is provided only to assist the youths in meeting their personal objectives as they progress toward self-sufficiency.

Twelve Inc. is an independent living program in Ohio, serving eleven male youths.[62] The program serves older, more mature juveniles who cannot return home. The program begins with a two-week orientation phase in which the youths reside in an apartment near the program office. Staff provide participants with assistance in basic living skills (maintaining a schedule, buying groceries, laundry) as well as assistance in obtaining employment, completing school, or enrolling in vocational training. Following orientation, staff contacts are reduced to three per week and the youths live alone in an apartment in another location.

Juvenile Aftercare

Virtually all juveniles who are committed to correctional institutions are released under some type of supervision, which is commonly referred to as juvenile aftercare or juvenile parole. In thirty-eight states and Washington, D.C., the state executive branch that administers institutions also provides aftercare services. In two states aftercare is a local judicial function and in two others it is a state judicial function. In eight states a combination of agencies, state and local, provides aftercare services in various counties.[63]

Although juvenile aftercare is in many ways comparable to adult parole, there are some important differences. Most juveniles receive indeterminate commitments to training school. Because they may be released at any time prior to the age of majority, the release decision is

of special importance. In most jurisdictions, the total responsibility for release decision making rests with the institutional staff. Although administratively imposed minimum terms and the requirement that the committing judge approve the release decision may influence the decision-making process in some jurisdictions, institutional staff invariably play the most significant role in determining the length of time a youth will be institutionalized.

Providing institutional staff with the authority to make release decisions has advantages and disadvantages. Ideally, this practice allows both community safety and rehabilitative objectives to be related to the individual characteristics of each juvenile. Offenders are released when they are no longer a threat to the community and when they are ready to assume productive roles in the community. However, permitting institutional staff to have almost complete control over the period of confinement presents a number of problems. Although the staff may be more familiar than anyone else with the youths' problems and their progress during institutionalization, their ability to function in the community may be difficult to predict from institutional observations. Correctional staff normally have little contact with the youths' family and friends in the community and are generally unfamiliar with the community resources available to assist the youths on their return. The release decision is therefore made with little knowledge of the youths prior to confinement and less information regarding the nature of the free-world environment awaiting them. Remedying this problem—the lack of information from the family and community— would go a long way toward improving release decision making for the majority of offenders.

Other problems still remain, however. Correctional staff may consciously or unconsciously use release as a reward for conformity and the denial of release as a punishment for disobedience. Under such conditions, decision making about release ensures the maintenance of institutional order instead of the natural progression of rehabilitated youth into the community. Mandatory minimum sentences and fixed sentences pose other difficulties. Such sentences cannot be individualized at all, presenting difficulties both in terms of institutional control and the ability to respond to the differential needs and problems posed by particular offenders. Trying to achieve the appropriate balance of sanction severity and accountability (minimum and fixed sentences) and community protection and rehabilitation (individualized judgments) is a matter of continuing concern and, in many ways, makes the job of rehabilitation more difficult.

Few statistics are available on programs for youthful parolees. Although this lack of information is partially the result of variations in the organization and administration of aftercare services, the absence of programs designed specifically for juvenile parolees is a more significant factor. The explanation for this absence is fairly simple: Community resources tend to be distributed to programs for juveniles with a greater potential for rehabilitation (that is, probationers); youths who have repeatedly failed in therapeutic programs and are subsequently institutionalized generally return to a community that has given up on or forgotten them. At best, they receive limited supervision from counselors, who are too overworked to attempt seriously the task of facilitating the youths' reentry into the community.

Juvenile parolees can enter nonspecialized, community-based programs for youthful offenders, such as group homes, but relatively few such youths are provided with these services.[64] Juveniles on aftercare receive little general or specialized assistance when they return to the community. The absence of reentry programs for youths is a critical problem in the juvenile justice system. Considering the difficulties faced by the returning adult parolee and adding to them the special problems of adolescence, it is apparent that returning a child to the community after institutionalization requires special attention and assistance. Far too often, the needed attention and assistance are not forthcoming.

There are some bright spots on the horizon in juvenile aftercare. Government initiatives to increase programming for serious and chronic offenders have prompted research and the development of program models for both juvenile probationers and youths leaving secure custody.

Delaware County Intensive Supervision Aftercare Program

The Delaware County, Ohio, program illustrates what can be done to serve serious offenders released from confinement to the community. The program also illustrates the extensive involvement of family services in juvenile corrections. The Delaware County Juvenile Court is located in a small city-rural area within the Columbus region. The county initiated its intensive aftercare services in 1985, with a program designed to serve all youth. The program utilizes

- In-home family work performed by paraprofessionally trained family advocates,
- Strictly enforced limit setting accompanied by community monitoring,
- Four phases of progressively increased freedom and flexibility,
- Immediate and graduated consequences for infractions, and
- Heavy reliance on community agencies.[65]

When the program was initiated, it was staffed by a case manager, two family advocates, and three supervision monitors. The program served only fourteen youths in its initial year, indicating a high degree of intensity of services. The two family advocates each make a minimum of two in-home visits per week. They are trained in a behavioral systems approach (functional family therapy) that is directed toward family dynamics and behavioral contracting. Advocates are selected for their experience in working with youths and families and their interpersonal skills.

Planning for aftercare begins thirty days prior to the youth's release. The local program already has much data on the youth and his or her family at the time that planning begins, because the juvenile court processed the offender's case when sentencing to custody was accomplished. Upon release, the youth signs a contract, which is also signed by the judge, intensive supervision counselor, and the youth's parent or guardian. Depending on the youth's progress, the juvenile can complete the program within four to six months.

Research and Program Models for Serious Chronic Delinquents

Research identifying a small group of juvenile offenders as the source of much serious juvenile delinquency and evidence of increasing juvenile violence have prompted the Office of Juvenile Justice and Delinquency Prevention to develop a comprehensive strategy to deal with serious, violent, and chronic juvenile offenders.[66]

Research on Urban Delinquency and Substance Abuse

Longitudinal studies in three major American cities (Denver, Colorado; Rochester, Minnesota; and Pittsburgh, Pennsylvania) were conducted to examine the patterns of delinquency development and associated causal factors. High-risk youths were targeted by the research, although a representative sampling of other youth groups was also achieved. The results indicated that high levels of delinquency, drug activity, and sexual activity were interrelated phenomena. Males seemed to enter patterns of serious delinquency from three distinct behavioral pathways: (1) an early authority conflict pathway prior to age twelve, starting with stubborn behavior, followed by defiance, and subsequently followed by authority avoidance; (2) a covert pathway, starting with minor covert behaviors, followed by property damage, and subsequently followed by moderate to serious forms of delinquency; and

(3) an overt pathway, starting with minor aggression, followed by fighting, and subsequently followed by violence (Figure 12-6).[67]

Serious chronic and violent delinquency was explained by reference to a series of factors involving family, education, neighborhoods, and peers. Individuals lacking a strong emotional bond to their parents and youths with parents with limited or poor child-rearing skills (poor communication and supervision, inconsistent punishment, and the avoidance of discipline) were more likely to engage in serious delinquency, as were youths with limited commitment to school and low reading achievement. Youths in underclass neighborhoods had a greater likelihood of serious delinquency, even when other causal factors were not present. Not surprisingly, association with delinquent peers, gang membership, and gun ownership were correlates of juvenile crime. Serious delinquents often had parents who had tried to find assistance for them but made too little effort or were unsuccessful in achieving aid. Employment was found to be no barrier to delinquency.

The research produced a variety of recommendations for prevention and treatment programs focusing on family, schools, communities, and peer groups. Areas of emphasis included early intervention, programs that target youths in specific pathways to delinquency, programs that focus on the interrelationship of multiple problem behaviors (for example, precocious sexual activity, school failure, and gang involvement), and the development of long-term, even multiyear, programs for offenders.[68]

The OJJDP Plan

OJJDP reviewed numerous studies of programs for juvenile offenders, including prevention programs, intensive supervision strategies, and a variety of innovative programs. In addition, it reviewed the effective and cost-saving efforts of several states to close juvenile training schools and establish secure and nonsecure community-based residential and nonresidential programs. The integration of research on the causes of

Figure 12-6 Developmental Pathways to Delinquency

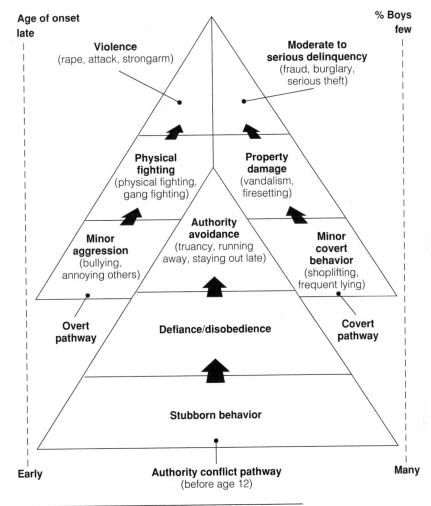

Source: David Huizinga, Rolf Loeber, and Terence Thornberry, *Urban Delinquency and Substance Abuse* (Washington, D.C.: Office of Juvenile Justice and Delinquency Prevention, 1994), p. 12.

delinquency with the program review of the experiences in Denver, Rochester, and Pittsburgh led to the formulation of OJJDP's plan for serious chronic and violent juvenile offenders.

The plan is organized around five general principles:

1. Strengthen the family in its primary responsibility to instill moral values and provide guidance and support to children.

2. Support core social institutions—schools, religious institutions, and community organizations—in their roles of developing capable, mature, and responsible youth.

3. Promote delinquency prevention as the most cost-effective approach to dealing with juvenile delinquency.

4. Intervene immediately and effectively when delinquent behavior occurs.

5. Identify and control the small group of serious, violent, and chronic juvenile offenders.[69]

The goal is to prevent and interrupt the progression of delinquency, using community planning teams to develop programs and strategies to reduce risk and develop protective factors. Examples are individual characteristics of resilience and positive social orientation; bonding with prosocial family members, teachers, and friends; and healthy beliefs and clear standards for behavior.[70] Of special importance is a highly structured system of graduated sanctions, with special programs for female offenders and special populations, including sex offenders and mentally retarded, emotionally disturbed, and learning disabled youths.

Immediate intervention with first offenders, followed by intermediate sanctions for more serious delinquents and secure confinement for the most serious of juveniles are required. In many ways, this approach mirrors the approach recommended for adult offenders, but it is a new step for a juvenile justice system in which the original emphasis stressed treatment more than accountability. This is clearly no longer the case for serious juvenile offenders. The focus on graduated sanctions combines accountability and sanctions with increasingly intensive treatment and rehabilitation services.[71] The emphasis includes three gradations of interventions: immediate sanctions, intermediate sanctions, and secure corrections, including community confinement as well as incarceration, followed by aftercare. Programs are expected to use risk and needs assessments to determine the appropriate placement for the offender.

Immediate Interventions   Interventions are expected to reflect a balanced approach that integrates accountability, competency development, and community protection. First-time delinquents involving misdemeanors and nonviolent felonies and nonserious repeat offenders should be targeted for immediate intervention based on the likelihood of future delinquency. Nonresidential programs, including those that serve at-risk youths, may be appropriate for this group. Such programs maintain the youth in his or her home and surroundings, and they can rely on community police officers to help monitor the juvenile's progress. Other youths may require programming more tailored to their needs, including:

- Neighborhood resource teams,
- Diversion,
- Informal probation,
- School counselors serving as probation officers,
- Home on probation,
- Mediation (victims),
- Community service,
- Restitution,
- Day treatment programs,
- Alcohol and drug abuse treatment (outpatient), and
- Peer juries (teen courts).[72]

Violent offenders or those who commit their first serious offense or who fail to respond successfully to immediate intervention (such as repeat offenders and drug-involved juveniles) are appropriate for intermediate sanctions. Many of these offenders would be appropriate for an intensive supervision program as an alternative to secure confinement.

Intermediate Sanctions: Intensive Supervision Probation   The OJJDP intensive supervision probation (ISP) model represents a highly structured, continuously monitored individualized plan that consists of five phases with decreasing levels of restrictiveness: (1) short-term placement in community confinement, (2) day treatment, (3) outreach and tracking, (4) routine supervision, and (5) discharge and follow-up (Table 12-6).[73]

Phase One: Residential Placement Residential placement should last for fifteen to forty-five

Table 12-6 Supervision-Control Components by Phase

Component	Phase 1: Residential	Phase 2: Day Treatment	Phase 3: Outreach and Tracking	Phase 4: Transition	Phase 5: Discharge and Follow-up
Secure care	Up to 45 days	Short-term detention or return to intensive supervision probation facility as required for program violations			N/A
Day structuring	N/A	Duration of phase 4–6 months	Duration of phase 3–4 months	As needed	N/A
Surveillance	N/A	3–4 times daily, months 1 and 2; 1–2 times daily, months 3 to end.	2–3 times daily, month 1; 1–2 times daily, month 2; 1–2 times weekly, months 3 to end.	1 time weekly, month 1; as needed, months 2 to end.	N/A
House arrest	N/A	Total, month 1; partial, month 2; as needed, months 3 to end.	As needed for program violations		N/A
Prior permission	N/A	Required, month 2; as needed, months 3 to end.	As needed for program violations		N/A
Curfew	N/A	Months 2–6 with decreasing restrictiveness.	Required, months 1 and 2; as needed, months 3 to end.	As needed	N/A
Daily sanctioning	By program staff	By program staff	By program staff and parents	By parents	By parents
Case manager contacts	3–5 times weekly	3–5 times weekly, months 1–2; 2 + times weekly, months 3 to end (includes weekend coverage).	1–2 times weekly, months 1–2; 1 time weekly, months 3 to end.	2 times monthly	Sporadic or as requested by youth
Urinalysis	N/A	Random 2 times per week	Random 1 time per week	Random	N/A
Electronic surveillance	N/A		As needed— selected cases		N/A

N/A = Not applicable.
Source: Barry Krisberg, Deborah Neuenfeldt, Richard Wiebush, and Orlando Rodriguez, *Juvenile Intensive Supervision: Planning Guide* (Washington, D.C.: Office of Juvenile Justice and Delinquency Prevention, 1994).

days. The primary objectives are to stabilize the youth's behavior, orient him or her to program rules and expectations, conduct an assessment of the youth's need for control and services, and develop a comprehensive service plan. There is limited programming during this pe-

riod. The focus is on education activities, facility work projects and chores, and individual and group counseling. This restrictive phase of programming could also be seen as holding the youth accountable for the offense. Release from residential placement is contingent upon the

Figure 12-7   Prior Permission Rules

After earning their way off house arrest, youth will be required to enter the prior permission phase. Under prior permission, a youth must call the designated ISP [intensive supervision probation] counselor for permission to go from one place to another, except school, work, and program appointments. A youth cannot go to his or her next destination without the verbal permission of ISP staff. The youth will call the ISP and either speak directly with the staff, leave a message with a secretary, or leave a message on the answering machines (if after 5 P.M.). After placing the call, the youth must stay off the phone and wait until an ISP staff member returns the call. When calling for prior permission, the youth must provide the following information: time of call, name, phone number, where the youth wants to go, what time he or she wants to go, when he or she wants to return, and with whom he or she will be staying. During evening and weekend hours, on-duty staff will retrieve messages at half-hour intervals. The staff person's decision to grant or disapprove permission for the movement is final.

Source: Delaware Intensive Supervision Program as cited in David Altschuler and Troy Armstrong, *Intensive Aftercare for High Risk Juveniles* (Washington, D.C.: Office of Juvenile Justice and Delinquency Prevention, 1994), p. 138.

completion of case planning, meeting the program's behavioral expectations, and demonstrated understanding by the youth and parents or guardians of phase two requirements.

Phase Two: Day Treatment In this day treatment model, the youth is enrolled full time (six hours) in center programming during the day. The goal is to allow the youth to function in a highly controlled environment prior to fuller community integration. Programming is intensive and focuses on:

- Educational, vocational, and social skill development;

- Linking the youth with nonprogram persons and organizations in the community;

- Referrals for special needs, such as substance abuse or mental health counseling;

- Working with parents to strengthen their influence and control over the youth;

- Making preparations for phase three involvement in traditional school or work settings;

- Involvement in community service or restitution programming;

- Participation in evening and weekend recreational and cultural activities; and

- Full implementation of the system of rewards and sanctions.[74]

House arrest, strict curfews, and a prior permission system are used to structure evening and weekend hours (Figure 12-7).

During this period, the juvenile might live at home, in foster care, or in a group home. The phase normally lasts four to six months and is completed when the youth has made sufficient academic or prevocational progress to warrant placement in the public schools or full-time employment, has established regular involvement with one or more role models or traditional community organizations, and has compiled a sufficient number of points or good days to reflect a positive adjustment.

Phase Three: Outreach and Tracking The goal is to assure that the youth can function productively and responsibly in the community. The phase includes frequent client and ancillary contacts, assistance to youth and the community social units with which he or she is involved, maintenance of treatment for special needs, and a gradual transition of the balance of control from the program to community institutions to the youth. The youth lives at home or in an appropriate alternative placement and goes to school or works full time.

During phase three the youth is intensively monitored by a tracker with a caseload of fifteen to twenty youths. Tracking coverage is seven days a week, including evening hours. It includes unannounced and random contacts made at school, work, home, or other locations. The number of contacts may be as high as two to three times per day during the first month, followed by a decreasing number of contacts if compliance is demonstrated.

Phase Four: Regular Supervision (Transition) The purpose is to prepare the youth for discharge, for functioning in the community without benefit of extensive controls. Control elements are minimal, but services to the youth are continued as necessary. Mentors are often recruited and utilized to provide ongoing support and encouragement.

Phase Five: Discharge and Follow-up Discharge occurs when regular supervision has been completed. The relationship with the mentor should be continued for a minimum of two months. Termination is noted with a small ceremony that recognizes the hard work of the youths and their families.[75]

Other programs might include:

- Drug testing,
- Weekend detention,
- Alcohol and drug abuse treatment (inpatient),
- Challenging outdoor programs,
- Community-based residential programs,
- Electronic monitoring, and
- Boot camp facilities and programs.[76]

Secure Corrections and Aftercare   Secure programs neither have to be institutions nor have to have large facilities. Small community-based programs are recommended in an effort to provide intensive treatment and monitoring of behavior. Services in community-based programs might include individual and group counseling, educational programs, medical services, and intensive staff supervision. Proximity to the community facilitates family involvement as well as phased reentry that draws upon community resources.[77] Those youths who must be removed from the community may be placed in training schools, camps, and ranches, facilities that should offer comprehensive programs focusing on education, skill development, and vocational or employment training and experience.

OJJDP has developed an Intensive Aftercare Model for High Risk Juvenile Parolees that incorporates five programmatic principles:

1. Preparing the youth for progressive responsibility and freedom in the community.

2. Facilitating youth-community interactions and involvement.

3. Working with both the offender and targeted community support systems (for example, families, peers, schools, and employers) to facilitate constructive interaction and gradual community adjustment.

4. Developing needed resources and community support.

5. Monitoring and ensuring the youth's successful reintegration into the community.[78]

The model is derived from an integration of several theories of delinquency. It relies on a strong overarching case management strategy to achieve coordinated planning and continuous, consistent service provision, referral, and monitoring of juvenile offenders (Figure 12-8).

The aims of all these OJJDP efforts are to increase juvenile justice system responsibility and juvenile accountability, decrease the cost of juvenile corrections, increase the responsibility of the juvenile justice system, increase program effectiveness, and ultimately to reduce crime.[79] The OJJDP plan is expected to guide agency efforts and funding priorities for years to come. In 1994, OJJDP received a 39 percent budget increase (to $107 million) to pursue its mission.[80]

Problems and Issues in Community-Based Correctional Programs for Youths

Treatment Versus Control

The most significant issue in community-based correctional programs for youths is neither new nor limited to the juvenile justice system. Since the development of the juvenile court, observers have been debating whether juvenile

Figure 12-8   Intervention Model for Juvenile Aftercare

An Integration of Strain, Social Learning, and Social Control Theories

Underlying Principles	**Program Elements**	**Service Areas**
Progressively increased responsibility and freedom	Assessment and classification	Special needs and special populations
Facilitating client-community interaction and involvement	Individual case planning	Education and school
Working with both offenders and targeted community support systems	Surveillance service mix	Vocational training, job readiness, and placement
Developing new resources, supports, and opportunities	Incentives and consequences	Living arrangements
Monitoring and testing	Brokerage and linkages	Social Skills
Case management		Leisure and recreation
		Client-centered counseling (individual & group)
		Family work and intervention
		Health
		Special technology
		Management information and program evaluation

Source: David Altschuler and Troy Armstrong, *Intensive Aftercare for High Risk Juveniles: A Community Care Model: Program Summary* (Washington, D.C.: Office of Juvenile Justice and Delinquency Prevention, 1994), p. 10.

court intervention should serve treatment or control objectives.

The juvenile court was supposedly established to protect youths from neglectful parents and harmful environments and to offer each child the opportunity required to mature into a physically and emotionally healthy adult. Some observers and workers in the juvenile justice system believe that the juvenile court does work, or attempts to work, in the best interests of the child. System critics feel that the nature of juvenile crime has evolved so that community protection needs to be better integrated into the handling of serious offenders. Some individuals would have this matter addressed through substantive modification of the juvenile court; others would increase the use of waiver of juveniles to the adult court.

The greatest challenge to resolution of this debate is the great diversity of youths who ap-

pear in juvenile court, ranging from the ungovernable truant to the chronic serious offender. These offenders require different degrees of treatment and control. Even the most hardened critic of the courts' original therapeutic mission will generally agree that some sanctions, such as those that require institutionalization, are too severe for status offenders. However, most persons who question the true aim of the juvenile court will also accept the necessity of controlling chronic property or violent offenders.

Discussion of the treatment versus control issue depends not only on the debaters' ideological positions but also on the nature of the programs they have in mind and the types of youths they are considering. Much of the confusion on this issue results from a failure to specify the types of problems and the general goals that are seen as appropriate for juvenile justice system intervention.

Deinstitutionalization of Juvenile Corrections

Although a lack of consensus exists regarding the appropriate role of the juvenile justice system, reform-minded activity has been abundant in juvenile corrections. The most significant reform of the 1970s was the advent of the deinstitutionalization movement. Proponents of **deinstitutionalization** promote establishing community-based programs for all but the most serious offenders and using closed institutions only as a last resort. The movement originated in Massachusetts during the early 1970s. At that time, Jerome Miller, then director of the state's Department of Youth Services, found it impossible to reform the existing training schools by establishing therapeutic programs for youths or training staff. As a last resort, he closed the existing institutions and gradually assigned the residents to newly developed community programs or simply sent them home.

Movement to a community-based system was not easy to achieve. During the first years of the Massachusetts reform, significant problems arose with youths who proved too difficult to manage in community-based programs. Many of these juveniles were inappropriately sent to secure detention facilities designed principally for the short-term nonadjudicated offenders. The need for graduated sanctions and alternative punishments (other than confinement) for offenders who fail in community programs has proven as problematic for juvenile offenders as adults.

A different type of problem can arise when deinstitutionalization is accomplished through private agencies contracted to provide services to youthful offenders. Ideally, these private agencies provide more creative, grassroots responses to the problems of juvenile offenders than a state bureaucracy could offer. Avoiding civil service requirements and restrictive red tape, new programs can be developed as needed and maintained only if they prove their effectiveness; otherwise an alternative program will be selected to receive state funds. The preceding ideal is not always realized, however. Over a period of years, private agencies that continue to receive state funds may expand their efforts into many communities and centralize their organizations. These minibureaucracies may develop their own red tape and lose their sensitivity to local problems. Monitoring numerous small programs operated by private agencies throughout a state is a difficult task. Most state youth agencies do not yet have the staff or expertise to oversee and evaluate these many small projects. Without effective monitoring, quality control is impossible to achieve.

Another general problem is that each state desiring to release its incarcerated population must determine the appropriate level of deinstitutionalization; develop a strategy to sell the idea to the community, legislators, police, and juvenile justice personnel; establish procedures for removing children from training schools or restricting their future commitment to institutions; and identify and develop appropriate alternatives to incarceration. Defining these goals, processes, and alternative programs is difficult enough; implementing them is a long and arduous task. Unfortunately, many states give up or give in to the public's plea for more crime control and community protection and continue their high rates of incarceration.

The irony is that deinstitutionalization efforts are often a community's best strategy to reserve precious confinement space for the serious offenders who truly need it. Too many states continue to confine large numbers of youths who represent no threat to the community and who could safely be managed in community programs. Chronic offenders are frequently the beneficiaries of the confinement shortages created by collective incarceration.

Research on Deinstitutionalization   Little comprehensive research has been done on community-based corrections for juveniles since the advent of the deinstitutionalization movement, when the objective was to compare the effectiveness of community-based programs with that of incarceration. At that time, the National Evaluation Program (NEP) found that community-based correctional programs for juveniles were as effective as institutional programs, which were more costly.[81] At the same time, community correctional programs needed to be closely monitored. Too often they were used to supplement rather than replace institutional efforts. Finally, NEP emphasized the partnerships necessary for community-based programs to be effective. The study pointed out that *community-based* means more than unlocked doors or a city or suburban location. Community-based programs must develop meaningful ties to community resources if they are to warrant their community-based designation.

The Future of Community-Based Correctional Programs for Juveniles

Two major trends will continue to influence the development of community-based correctional programs for juveniles. These are efforts to enhance the severity of punishments for juvenile offenders and strategies to create more community-based sanctions, especially for serious offenders. The greater use of incarceration for serious offenders, coupled with the increased severity of juvenile crime, makes the establishment of community alternatives a necessity. Unlike earlier efforts to create community-based alternatives, the newer strategies focus on developing programs that can provide community protection as well as treatment, accountability as well as reintegration.

Crime Control Moderated by a Continuing Concern for Rehabilitation

Many states are struggling with the issue of juvenile crime and juvenile justice. A survey conducted by the National League of Cities found that local government officials indicated that juvenile crime was the top concern and most important issue confronting their communities. Youth crime led the list of local problems that had deteriorated over the last five years.[82]

State legislators are responding to these concerns in a variety of ways, but most are undertaking efforts to increase the punitiveness of their juvenile court system. Texas, for example, implemented an overhaul of its juvenile justice code designed to make the system stricter from beginning to end. Greater numbers of juveniles will be incarcerated under the legislation, for fixed terms of up to forty years. The age of majority is lowered to fourteen for youths charged with capital murder, first-degree felonies, and aggravated drug crimes, and legislation widens the list of felonies for which youths can received fixed terms of ten, twenty, and forty years. The appropriation accompanying the legislation will add 2,360 beds to Texas boot camps for youthful offenders.[83]

Virginia also has recently attempted to adopt tough new legislation, but a number of the original proposals were later modified to include treatment-oriented measures. Current proposals call for increased transfer of juveniles to criminal court—juveniles age fourteen or older charged with the most serious crimes would be automatically transferred. The plan also calls for expanding sentencing options between probation and incarceration, including boot camps and wilderness programs. Virginia plans to spend $27 million to develop additional correctional facilities for youths.[84]

Connecticut, too, has attempted to balance treatment and crime control objectives. While new legislation provides for automatic transfer of youths fourteen and above charged with serious felonies and enhanced sanctions for repeat offenders, the law calls for a network of community services for juveniles, such as peer tutoring and mentoring, and special programs for youth expelled from school. The new Office of Alternative Sanctions will be charged with developing a continuum of sanctions for juvenile offenders, including probation treatment plans; drug and alcohol addiction programs; and treatment of emotional, physical, and educational problems.[85]

Continued Efforts to Develop Alternatives to Confinement

A number of jurisdictions are also attempting to find ways to limit the use of confinement, an increasingly scarce resource in juvenile as well as adult corrections. In most cases this involves efforts to reduce institutionalization and develop community-based sanctions for serious offenders. In late 1995, the Justice Department awarded $4.1 million to nine jurisdictions to develop intermediate sanctions for nonviolent juvenile offenders who would otherwise be institutionalized. Hartford intends to use the money to establish a bilingual day incarceration center for young Latino felony drug offenders who would otherwise be sent to jail. The center will provide classroom instruction, family counseling, and gang intervention, as well as cultural and recreational opportunities. Louisiana's program will utilize education and family therapy for fifteen- and sixteen-year-olds who have arrest histories of three to five years in length.[86]

Private foundations are active in efforts to encourage the use of alternatives to incarceration. The Robert Wood Johnson Foundation and Robert F. Kennedy (RFK) Memorial established the National Juvenile Justice Project to encourage jurisdictions to reduce reliance on incarceration.[87] The project's goal is to help jurisdictions create a balanced system of care, which includes secure facilities for serious offenders, group homes and community-based alternatives for less serious delinquents, and day treatment and outreach and tracking programs for youths reintegrating into the community. First-time and nonviolent offenders are managed through home detention and electronic monitoring.

In each of the jurisdictions (including Detroit, Los Angeles, San Francisco, Washington, D.C., and the states of Connecticut, Maryland, and Nebraska) in which the RFK project will be implemented, efforts will be made to incorporate the following elements:

1. A classification process, whereby serious offenders are separated from less serious offenders and whereby all adjudicated youths are evaluated as to the degree of their dangerousness, the seriousness of their crime, and the most appropriate placement setting.

2. A treatment plan for each youth, based on a caseworker's assessment of that youth after gathering in-depth information pertaining to the youth and his or her family, social, and medical history.

3. A case management plan, to ensure that the treatment plan is adhered to and is adjusted according to the changing needs of the youth or any new and relevant information. Ideally, the caseworker responsible for developing the treatment plan would remain the supervisor of the youth's case for the duration of his or her commitment.

4. The establishment of a decentralized system whereby geographic regional offices are set up to house caseworkers and regional administrators with designated budgets to buy specific services for the youth from their region. This ensures that systems live within their budget and encourages that money be spent more wisely. The operation of regional offices fosters enhanced community relations and allows for increased access to community resources. It also provides for an overall better relationship between the justice system and those living near programs.

5. Privatization, whereby systems contract for services through private providers offering specific services and programs, which creates healthy competition and ensures the best services available at the most competitive price. This also enables systems to seek out services that best match the specific needs of the youth in custody, instead of providing the same

rehabilitative service to all youths, regardless of the special needs they present.

6. A continuum of care approach, which has as its goal the gradual reintegration of the youth back into the community and schools. This approach takes into consideration that not every youth needs to start his or her placement in a secure facility and that the degree of risk posed by many would allow them to begin in a community-based program or even a day treatment or outreach and tracking program, thus bringing the overall costs down.

7. A treatment component that has at its core an education curriculum that is superior to what youths were receiving in public school. This includes special education classes, enhanced teacher-to-youth ratios, and a course design that will facilitate the eventual return of the youth to his or her public school. Caseworkers must work closely with school systems in preparing a youth to reenter the public school system. The treatment component must also contain drug treatment and prevention, individual and group counseling, job training, peer mediation, and violence prevention.

8. Job training for all committed youths. This will require systems to work closely with community organizations such as YouthBuild and Job Corps to enroll youths in their programs, which are designed specifically for underskilled urban youths. The success of a youth often depends upon the ability of the system to return the youth to school or to assist him or her in securing a job.

9. A revocation policy, which provides for the ability of a system to return a youth to a program when he or she is failing in the community, without having to go through the court system. An internal hearing can be held through an appointed hearing officer. This policy creates the kind of flexibility that is critical in following through in the reintegration phase of a youth's commitment.

10. An intensive, preservice training program, for all those who work directly with youths, and a modified version for those in nondirect care positions. Specific training must take place in the areas of sex offender treatment, suicide prevention, crisis management, mental health, acquired immune deficiency syndrome (AIDS) and its prevention, drug treatment, and teenage pregnancy prevention. Additional training on how to deal effectively with the media and to use them as a resource should also be included.[88]

Ohio juvenile court judges will have the opportunity to develop local treatment options under a new statewide program. RECLAIM (Reasoned and Equitable Community and Local Alternatives to Incarceration of Minors) provides juvenile court judges a specified amount of money to buy treatment programs for delinquent youth.[89] The program also charges approximately $100 a day per youth if the court chooses to utilize state-run institutions as a sanction (counties are not charged for the incarceration of youths who commit murder or rape).

The program, which functions like a Community Corrections Act, is encouraging the establishment of a variety of alternatives to incarceration, including intensive supervision probation and the African American Alternative Center in Erie County, Pennsylvania, which provides tutoring and other services to black males found to have committed felonies. The pilot program resulted in a 43 percent reduction in commitments to a state institution in the nine counties that participated before the program went statewide. The involved counties were able to keep nearly $3 million of RECLAIM funds and provide local treatment to nearly one thousand adjudicated offenders.

Summary

The juvenile justice system makes greater use of community corrections programs than the adult criminal justice system because the philosophy and structure of the juvenile justice system encourage diversion, informal processing, and community supervision of offenders, rather than incarceration. Like adult community-based programs, community corrections programs for juveniles serve offenders who have committed crimes. Juveniles who commit crimes are referred to as delinquents. In addition, status offenders, or juveniles who commit such acts as truancy, running away, or ungovernability—acts that are prohibited solely because of the youth's status as a minor—are also commonly placed in community-based programs.

Some community-based programs for juveniles, such as probation, aftercare (parole), and group homes (halfway houses), are similar to those for adults. Others, such as youth courts, alternative schools, programs for runaways, wilderness experience programs, and foster care, are designed to meet the specific problems and needs of adolescent offenders.

Considerable debate has been waged regarding the proper function of the juvenile justice system and the appropriate role of community-based programs in juvenile justice. Some critics feel the system is too lenient with serious juvenile offenders and that such serious offenders should be managed by the criminal justice system. Others feel that the juvenile justice system should become more punitive so that all juveniles experience a greater sense of accountability. These perspectives have prompted many states to take steps to make it easier for juveniles to be transferred to the criminal justice system and to provide greater punishment for delinquents within the juvenile justice system.

These changes have led to the evolution of the community-based sanctions for juveniles into a complex network of programs for a diverse group of offenders. Many youths are served by programs whose fundamental values, and emphasis on family, school, and constructive peer groups, have changed little over the years. More serious offenders, however, now participate in programs that look much like the more rigorous intermediate sanctions meted out to adults.

The extensive range of community-based correctional programs for youths should make it possible to appropriately meet the needs of all juveniles, but most communities have established only a few programs. A lack of resources, as well as a lack of agreement regarding program objectives, often results in the misuse of community corrections programs. Much planning and conscientious program implementation are required if the juvenile justice system is to help prevent youthful offenders from becoming adult criminals.

Key Words and Concepts

adjudication

aftercare

alternative schools

custody

deinstitutionalization

delinquents

dependent and neglected children

detention facilities

disposition

emergency shelters

foster care

group homes

home detention programs

independent living

informal probation

in-school suspension programs

intake

juvenile violence

outreach programs

petition

probation

restitution and community service programs

serious chronic juvenile offenders

status offenders

temporary shelters

wilderness experience programs

youth service bureaus (YSBs)

Questions for Discussion

1. What are some of the similarities and differences between the adult and juvenile justice systems?

2. Why does the juvenile justice system prefer treatment over punishment for its offenders? What does this preference say about the juvenile offender as compared with the adult offender?

3. How does status offending differ from delinquency?

4. What are some of the methods the juvenile and family courts use to divert juvenile offenders out of the justice system?

5. What are some of the changes juvenile programs make to address the specific needs of the juveniles in their areas?

6. What is a mentoring program? What does it intend to accomplish? In general, do these programs appear successful?

7. Does a youth court administered and operated by other youths seem like a successful idea? Why do programs such as these have a dramatic impact on the juveniles they process?

8. Would being a juvenile probation officer be more or less difficult than doing the same job with adults? What factors would make the job easier? What factors would make it more difficult?

9. Does the concept of restorative justice seem to apply well to justice offenders? Why or why not?

10. How does delinquency, and the community-based approaches designed to address this delinquency, differ from urban to rural settings?

11. Is deinstitutionalization of juvenile offenders a good idea? Which offender types would seem most appropriate for such a program?

For Further Reading

Altschuler, David, and Troy Armstrong, *Intensive Community Based Aftercare Programs: An Assessment* (Washington, D.C.: Office of Juvenile Justice and Delinquency Prevention, 1990).

Barton, William, and Ira Schwartz, *Juvenile Detention: No More Hidden Closets* (Columbus: Ohio State University Press, 1994), p. 6.

Gottfredson, D. C., and W. H. Barton, *Deinstitutionalization of Juvenile Status Offenders* (College Park: University of Maryland, 1992).

Howell, James C., *Guide for Implementing the Comprehensive Strategy for Serious, Violent, and Chronic Juvenile Offenders* (Washington, D.C.: Office of Juvenile Justice and Delinquency Prevention, 1995).

Mathias, Robert (ed.), *Violent Juvenile Offenders: An Anthology* (San Francisco, Calif.: National Council on Crime and Delinquency, 1984).

Notes

Chapter 1

[1]President's Commission on Law Enforcement and Administration of Justice, *Task Force Report: Corrections* (Washington, D.C.: U.S. Government Printing Office, 1967), p. 7.

[2]Ibid.

[3]R. Martinson, "What Works—Questions and Answers About Prison Reform," *The Public Interest*, pp. 22–54.

[4]"Time Served in Prison," *Balanced & Restorative Justice*, program summary (Washington, D.C.: Office of Juvenile Justice and Delinquency Prevention).

[5]Sharon Levant, Francis T. Cullen, Betsy Fulton, and John F. Wozniak, "Reconsidering Restorative Justice: The Corruption of Benevolence Revisited," *Crime & Delinquency*, 45 (l), January 1995, pp. 3–27.

[6]*Interview with Visiting Fellow Thomas Quinn* (Washington, D.C.: U.S. Department of Justice, National Institute of Justice, March 1998), pp. 10–16/17.

[7]Todd R. Clear, *Toward a Correction of 'Place': The Challenge of Community in Corrections* (Washington, D.C.: U.S. Department of Justice, National Institute of Justice, August, 1996), pp. 52–56/7.

[8]Ibid.

[9]H. G. Moeller, "Community-Based Correctional Services," in *Handbook of Criminology*, Daniel Glaser (ed.) (Chicago: Rand McNally, 1974).

[10]Allen Beck and Darrell Gilliard, *Prisoners in 1995* (Washington, D.C.: Bureau of Justice Statistics, August 1995).

[11]P. Reuter, John Haaga, Patrick Murphy, and Amy Praskac, *Drug Use and Drug Programs in the Washington Metropolitan Area* (Santa Monica, Calif.: RAND Corporation, 1988).

[12]P. Griset, "Increasing Correctional Control Over Time Served: A Case Study of the Politics of Prison Policy in New York" (unpublished manuscript).

[13]"Crime Bill Contains Billions for State and Local Agencies," *Criminal Justice Newsletter*, August 15, 1994, pp. 1–6.

[14]Lawrence Greenfield, *Prison Sentences and Time Served* (Washington, D.C.: Bureau of Justice Statistics, 1995).

[15]"New York Governor Aims to Save Prison Space for Violent Crimes," *Criminal Justice Newsletter*, 26 (4), February 15, 1995, pp. 4–5.

[16]"Under New Law, Illinois Inmates Will Serve 85% of Sentences," *Criminal Justice Newsletter*, 26 (16), August 15, 1994, pp. 1–2.

[17]Randall Wright, "North Carolina Avoids Early Trouble with Guidelines," *Overcrowded Times*, 6 (1), February 1995.

[18]Paula M. Ditton and Doris James Wilson, *Truth in Sentencing in State Prisons*, special report (Washington D.C.: Bureau of Justice Statistics, January 1999).

[19]Jodie M. Brown, Patrick Langan, and David Levin, "Felony Sentences in State Courts, 1996," *Bureau of Justice Statistics Bulletin*, May 1999.

[20]Peter Greenwood, C. Peter Rydell, et al., "Three Strikes and You're Out: Estimated Benefits and Costs of California's New Mandatory-Sentencing Law" (Santa Monica, Calif.: RAND Corporation, 1994).

[21]Walter J. Dickey, *'Three Strikes' Five Years Later: Campaign for an Effective Crime Policy*, Public Policy Report, November 1998.

[22]Ibid.

[23]Callie Marie Rennison, *Criminal Victimization, 1998: Changes 1997–98 with Trends 1993–98* (Washington, D.C.: Bureau of Justice Statistics, July 1999).

[24]Allen J. Beck and Christopher J. Mumala, *Prisoners in 1998* (Washington, D.C.: Bureau of Justice Statistics, August 1999).

[25]Ibid.

[26]Alfred Blumstein, "U.S. Criminal Justice Conundrum: Rising Prison Populations and Stable Criminals," *Crime and Delinquency*, 44 (l), January 1998, pp. 127–135.

[27]Ibid.

[28]Michael Tonry, "Parochialism in U.S. Sentencing Policy," *Crime and Delinquency*, 45 (l), January 1999, pp. 48–65.

[29]Ronald Weight, *Managing Prison Growth in North Carolina through Structured Sentencing*, Program Focus (Washington, D.C.: U.S. Department of Justice, National Institute of Justice).

[30]Ibid.

[31]W. Spelman, *Criminal Incapacitation* (New York: Plenum Press, 1994).

Chapter 2

[1]National Center for State Courts, *An Evaluation of Policy-Related Research on the Effectiveness of Pretrial Release Programs* (Denver, Colo.: National Center for State Courts, 1975), p. 5.

[2]Ibid., p. 6.

[3]Roscoe Pound and Felix Frankfurter (eds.), *Criminal Justice in Cleveland* (Cleveland, Ohio: Cleveland Foundation, 1922); Arthur L. Beeley, *The Bail System in Chicago* (Chicago: University of Chicago Press, 1927); Missouri Association for Criminal Justice, *The Missouri Crime Survey* (New York: Macmillan, 1926); and Wayne L. Morse and Ronald H. Beatties, "Survey of the Administration of Criminal Justice in Oregon, Report No. 1: Final Report in 1971 Felony Cases in Multnomah County," *Oregon Law Review I* (June 1932): supplement.

[4]President's Commission on Law Enforcement and Administration of Justice, *The Challenge of Crime in a Free Society* (Washington, D.C.: U.S. Government Printing Office, 1967), p. 134.

[5]Don Oberdorfer, "The Bail-Bond Scandal," *Saturday Evening Post,* June 20, 1964, p. 66.

[6]Charles Ares, Anne Rankin, and Herbert Sturz, "The Manhattan Bail Project: An Interim Report on the Use of Pretrial Parole," *New York University Law Review,* 38, 1963, p. 67.

[7]Bureau of Justice Statistics, *Pretrial Release and Detention: The Bail Reform Act of 1984* (Washington, D.C.: U.S. Government Printing Office, 1988).

[8]Bureau of Justice Statistics, *Correctional Populations in the United States, 1996* (Washington, D.C.: U.S. Department of Justice, April 1999), p. 23.

[9]Bureau of Justice Assistance, *Treatment Alternatives to Street Crime: TASC Programs Program Brief* (Washington, D.C.: U.S. Department of Justice, 1992).

[10]System Sciences Inc., *Evaluation of the Treatment Alternatives to Street Crime Program, Phase II—Final Report* (Bethesda, Md.: System Sciences Inc., 1978), p. vii.

[11]Bureau of Justice Assistance, *Treatment Alternatives to Street Crime.*

[12]James Swartz, "TASC—The Next 20 Years: Extending, Refining, and Assessing the Model," in *Drug Treatment and Criminal Justice,* James Inciardi (ed.) (Newbury Park, Calif.: Sage, 1993).

[13]Bureau of Justice Assistance, *Treatment Alternatives to Street Crime.*

[14]M. Douglas Anglin, Douglas Longshore, and Susan Turner, "Treatment Alternatives to Street Crime: An Evaluation of Five Programs," *Criminal Justice and Behavior,* 26 (2), June 1999, pp. 168–195.

[15]Ibid.

[16]Bureau of Justice Assistance, *Special Drug Courts* (Washington, D.C.: U.S. Department of Justice, 1993).

[17]U.S. Department of Justice, "President Clinton Announces $27 Million for More Drug Courts," Office of Justice Programs News, http://www.ojp.usdoj.gov/dcpopr710.htr.

[18]Office of Justice Programs, Drug Courts Program Office website, www.ojp.usdoj.gov/dcpo, pp. 4–5

[19]Bureau of Justice Assistance, *Special Drug Courts.*

[20]Drug Court Resource Center, "Preliminary Assessment of the Drug Court Program Experience," National Association of Drug Court Professionals Congressional Kit, 1995.

[21]U.S. General Accounting Office, *Drug Courts: Overview of Growth, Characteristics, and Results* (Washington, D.C.: U.S. Government Printing Office, July 1997).

[22]Ibid.

[23]Steven Belenko, "Research on Drug Courts: A Critical Review," *National Drug Court Institute Review,* 1 (1), 1998, p.1.

[24]Adele Harrell, Foster Cook, and John Carver, "Breaking the Cycle of Drug Abuse in Birmingham," *National Institute of Justice Journal,* 236, July 1998, pp. 9–13.

[25]Daniel McGillis, *Community Dispute-Resolution Programs and Public Policy: Issues and Practices* (Washington, D.C.: U.S. Department of Justice, National Institute of Justice, December 1986), p. ix.

[26]Roger Cook, Janice Roehl, and David Shephard, *Neighborhood Justice Centers Field Test* (Washington, D.C.: National Institute of Justice, 1980), p. 8.

[27]Ibid.

[28]Daniel McGillis, *Issues and Practices: Community Mediation Programs: Developments and Challenges* (Washington, D.C.: U.S. Department of Justice, Office of Justice Programs, July 1997) pp. 14–15

[29]Ibid.

[30]Ibid.

[31]Stevens Clarke et al., *Mediation of Interpersonal Disputes: An Evaluation of North Carolina's Programs* (Chapel Hill: University of North Carolina, Institute of Government, 1992).

[32]Ibid.

[33]Daniel McGillis, *Resolving Community Conflict: The Dispute Settlement Center of Durham, North Carolina* (Washington, D.C.: U.S. Department of Justice, September 1998).

[34]Mark S. Umbreit, "Victim Empowerment Through Mediation: The Impact of Victim Offender Mediation in Four Cities," *APPA Perspectives,* 18 (3), pp. 25–30.

[35]Mark S. Umbreit and Robert Coates, "Cross Site Analysis of Victim-Offender Mediation in Four States," *Crime and Delinquency,* 39 (4), 1993, pp. 565–585.

[36]Enhanced Pretrial Services Project, 1991.

[37]Michael McCann and Douglass Weber, "Pretrial Services: A Prosecutor's View," *Federal Probation,* March 1993, pp. 18–22.

[38]Enhanced Pretrial Services Project, 1991, pp. 126–128.

[39]Keith Cooprider, "Pretrial Bond Supervision: An Empirical Analysis with Policy Implications," *Federal Probation,* September 1992, pp. 41–49.

[40]D. Alan Henry and John Clark, *Pretrial Drug Testing: An Overview of Issues and Practices* (Washington, D.C.: U.S. Department of Justice, Bureau of Justice Assistance, July 1999).

[41]Ibid.

[42]Christy Visher, *NIJ Research in Brief: Pretrial Drug Testing* (Washington, D.C.: U.S. Department of Justice, 1992).

[43]Henry and Clark, *Pretrial Drug Testing.*

[44]Bureau of Justice Assistance, *Special Drug Courts: Program Brief* (Washington, D.C.: U.S. Department of Justice, 1993).

[45]David Rottman and Pamela Casey, "Therapeutic Jurisprudence and the Emergence of Problem-Solving Courts," *National Institute of Justice Journal,* July 1999, pp. 12–19.

[46]David Anderson, *In New York City, a 'Community Court' and a New Legal Culture,* Program Focus (Washington, D.C.: U.S. Department of Justice, National Institute of Justice, February 1996), p. 2.

[47]Jane Nady Sigmon, M. Elaine Nugent, John Goerdt, and Scott Wallace, *Key Elements of Successful Adjudication Partnerships* (Washington, D.C.: U.S. Department of Justice, Bureau of Justice Assistance, May 1999).

[48]Rottman and Casey, "Therapeutic Jurisprudence."

[49]Ibid., p. 6.

[50]Ibid., p. 8.

Chapter 3

[1]American Bar Association, "Model Adult Community Corrections Act," in *Community Corrections Report on Law and Corrections Practice,* February 1994.

[2]Harry Boone, Betsy Fulton, et al., *Results-Driven Management Implementing Performance-Based Measures in Community Corrections* (Lexington, Ky.: American Probation and Parole Association, 1995), p. 39.

[3]Robert Carter and Leslie Wilkins (eds.), *Probation, Parole, and Community Corrections* (New York: Wiley, 1976), p. 82.

[4]George Killenger, Hazel Kerper, and Paul Cromwell, *Probation and Parole in the Criminal Justice System* (St. Paul, Minn.: West Publishing, 1976), p. 29.

[5]United Nations Department of Social Affairs, *Probation and Related Measures, 1951,* as cited in *Probation, Parole, and Community Corrections,* Robert Carter and Leslie Wilkins (eds.) (New York: Wiley, 1976), pp. 81–88.

[6]Killenger, Kerper, and Cromwell, *Probation and Parole in the Criminal Justice System,* p. 3.

[7]Ibid., p. 23.

[8]David Rothman, *Conscience and Convenience: The Asylum and Its Alternatives in Progressive America* (Boston: Little, Brown, 1980), p. 44.

[9]Ibid., p. 6.

[10]Ibid., p. 44.

[11]*Sourcebook of Criminal Justice Statistics, 1994* (Washington, D.C.: U.S. Department of Justice, 1995).

[12]*State and Local Probation Systems in the United States: A Survey of Current Practice* (Washington, D.C.: U.S. Department of Justice, National Institute of Corrections, 1993), p. 23.

[13]National Advisory Commission on Criminal Justice Standards and Goals, *Corrections* (Washington, D.C.: U.S. Government Printing Office, 1973), p. 316.

[14]*State and Local Probation Systems in the United States,* p. 23.

[15]Ibid., p. 7.

[16]National Advisory Commission on Criminal Justice Standards and Goals, *Corrections,* p. 313.

[17]Thomas Ellsworth, "The Goal Orientation of Adult Probation Professionals: A Study of Probation Systems," *Journal of Crime and Justice,* 13 (2), 1990, pp. 55–76.

[18]*State and Local Probation Systems in the United States,* p. 14.

[19]Joan Petersilia et al., *Granting Felons Probation* (Santa Monica, Calif.: RAND Corporation, 1985).

[20]*Recidivism of Felons on Probation, 1986–89* (Washington, D.C.: Bureau of Justice Statistics, 1987).

[21]*Sourcebook of Criminal Justice Statistics, 1994.*

[22]Harry Allen, Eric Carlson, and Evalyn Parks, *Critical Issues in Adult Probation: Summary* (Washington, D.C.: National Institute of Law Enforcement and Criminal Justice, 1979), p. 62.

[23]Ibid., pp. 34–36.

[24]Ibid., p. 36.

[25]Ibid., pp. 144–159.

[26]Vincent P. Dole and Herman Joseph, "Methadone Patients on Probation and Parole," *Federal Probation,* 34, June 1970, pp. 42–58.

[27]Seymour Rosenthal, *Report on the Evaluation of Philadelphia County Probation Department Adult Probation Drug Unit* (Philadelphia, Pa.: Temple University, 1974).

[28]Robert L. Polakow and Ronald M. Doctor, "A Behavior Modification Program for Adult Drug Offenders," *Journal of Research in Crime and Delinquency,* 11, January 1974, pp. 63–69.

[29]Petersilia et al., *Granting Felons Probation.*

[30]Ibid., p. v.

[2]Ben Crouch, "Is Incarceration Really Worse? An Analysis of Offender's Preferences for Prison over Probation," *Justice Quarterly,* 10 (1), March 1993, p. 69.

[3]American Bar Association Project on Minimum Standards for Criminal Justice, *Standards Relating to Probation* (New York: American Bar Association, 1970).

[4]Ibid.

[5]Robert Carter and Leslie Wilkins, "Some Factors in Sentencing Policy," pp. 211–235 in *Probation, Parole, and Community Corrections,* Robert Carter and Leslie Wilkins (eds.) (New York: Wiley, 1976).

[6]Ibid.

[7]Pamala Griset, *Determinate Sentencing: The Promise and the Reality of Retributive Justice* (Albany: State University of New York Press, 1991).

[8]*State and Local Probation Systems in the United States.*

[9]Ibid.

[10]William Clements, "Judicial Use of Private Presentence Reports: The Case of Client Specific Planning," presented at the annual meeting of the Academy of Criminal Justice Sciences, Orlando, Florida, 1986.

[11]Michael Tonry and Kate Hamilton (eds.), *Intermediate Sanctions in Overcrowded Times* (Boston: Northeastern University Press, 1995), p. 169.

[12]Marc Maurer, "Defense-Based Sentencing," pp. 170–172 in *Intermediate Sanctions in Overcrowded Times,* Michael Tonry and Kate Hamilton (eds.) (Boston: Northeastern University Press, 1995).

[13]Ibid., p. 171.

[14]Ibid.

[15]Harry Allen, Eric Carlson, and Evalyn Parks, *Critical Issues in Adult Probation: Summary* (Washington, D.C.: National Institute of Law Enforcement and Criminal Justice, 1979), p. 62.

[16]John Rosecrance, "A Typology of Presentence Probation Investigators," *International Journal of Offender Therapy and Comparative Criminology,* 31 (2), 1987.

[17]James J. Dahl and Michael Chapman, *Improved Probation Strategies: Trainers Handbook* (Washington, D.C.: U.S. Government Printing Office, 1980).

[18]Toch Hans, "Case Managing Multiproblem Offenders," *Federal Probation,* 59 (4), 1995.

[19]National Advisory Commission on Criminal Justice Standards and Goals, *Correction* (Washington, D.C.: U.S. Government Printing Office, 1973), pp. 159–161.

[20]United States Sentencing Commission, *Guidelines Manual,* 1995, p. 276.

[21]Ibid.

[22]*State and Local Probation Systems in the United States,* p. 32.

[23]Harry Boone, Betsy Fulton, et al., *Results Driven Management,* 1995, p. 64.

[24]Nancy Martin, *National Bulletin on Domestic Violence Prevention* (Boston, Mass.: Northeast Publishing Group, March 1996), pp. 1–4.

[25]Ibid., p.4.

[26]Joan Petersilia, "Conditions That Permit Intensive Supervision Programs to Survive," *Crime and Delinquency,* 36 (1), 1990, pp. 126–145.

[27]Crouch, "Is Incarceration Really Worse?" p. 69.

Chapter 4

[1]*State and Local Probation Systems in the United States: A Survey of Current Practice* (Washington, D.C.: U.S. Department of Justice, National Institute of Corrections, 1993), p. 16.

Chapter 5

[1]Citizen's Inquiry on Parole and Criminal Justice, Inc., *Prison Without Walls, Report on New York Parole* (New York: Praeger, 1975).

[2]National Institute of Corrections, Status Report on Parole, 1995: Results of an NIC Survey, U.S. Department of Justice, November 1995, p. 1.

[3]George Killinger, Hazel Kerper, and Paul Cromwell, *Probation and Parole in the Criminal Justice System* (St. Paul, Minn.: West Publishing, 1976), pp. 201–209.

[4]William Parker, *Parole: Origins, Development, Current Practices and Statutes* (College Park, Md.: American Correctional Association, 1975), p. 14.

[5]Ibid., p. 15.

[6]Ibid., p. 16.

[7]Ibid., p. 17.

[8]Ibid.

[9]Killinger, Kerper, and Cromwell, *Probation and Parole,* p. 209.

[10]Harry E. Allen and Clifford E. Simonsen, *Corrections in America: An Introduction* (New York: Macmillan, 1981), p. 191.

[11]National Institute of Corrections, Status Report on Parole, 1995: Results of an NIC Survey, U.S. Department of Justice, November 1995, p. xxi.

[12]American Correctional Association, *Manual of Correctional Standards* (Washington, D.C.: American Correctional Association, 1969), pp. 115–116.

[13]National Advisory Commission on Criminal Justice Standards and Goals, *Corrections* (Washington, D.C.: U.S. Government Printing Office, 1973), p. 392.

[14]American Correctional Association, *Manual of Correctional Standards,* pp. 29–30.

[15]National Institute of Corrections, Status Report on Parole, 1995: Results of an NIC Survey, U.S. Department of Justice, November 1995, pp. 6–10.

[16]Ibid.

[17]Ibid., p. xxii.

[18]American Correctional Association, *Manual of Correctional Standards,* pp. 29–30.

[19]National Advisory Commission on Criminal Justice Standards and Goals, *Corrections,* pp. 420–421.

[20]Parker, *Parole,* pp. 29–30.

[21]American Correctional Association, *Manual of Correctional Standards,* p. 124.

[22]American Law Institute, "Model Penal Code: 1962" pp. 111–156 in *American Law Institute Compendium of Model Correctional Legislation and Standards,* Vol. 3 (Washington, D.C.: U.S. Department of Justice, 1972). Copyright 1972 by the American Law Institute. Reprinted with the permission of the American Law Institute.

[23]National Institute of Corrections, Status Report on Parole, 1995: Results of an NIC Survey, U.S. Department of Justice, November 1995, p. x.

[24]Ibid., p. 9.

[25]D. M. Gottfredson, L. T. Wilkins, and Peter Hoffman, *Guidelines for Parole and Sentencing* (Lexington, Mass.: Heath, 1978), p. 37.

[26]U.S. Department of Justice, *U.S. Parole Commission Rules and Procedures Manual,* January 1, 1995.

[27]Parolee Corrections Project, *The Mutual Agreement Program: A Planned Change in Correctional Service Delivery* (College Park, Md.: American Correctional Association, 1973), p. 6.

[28]E. K. Nelson, H. Ohmart, and N. Harlow, *Promising Strategies in Probation and Parole* (Washington, D.C.: U.S. Department of Justice, 1978), pp. 2–3.

[29]Ibid., pp. 20–21.

[30]Oscar D. Shade, "The Demise of Wisconsin's Contract Parole Program," *Federal Probation,* 45, 1981, 34–43.

[31]S. Christopher Baird, "Probation and Parole Classification: The Wisconsin Model," *Corrections Today,* 11, May/June 1981, 36–41. Reprinted with permission from the American Correctional Association.

[32]Ibid., p. 41.

Chapter 6

[1]Joan Petersilia, "How California Could Divert Nonviolent Prisoners to Intermediate Sanctions," *Overcrowded Times,* 6 (3), June 1995.

[2]Joan Petersilia and Susan Turner, *Evaluating Intensive Supervision Probation/Parole: Results of a Nationwide Experiment,* Research in Brief (Washington, D.C.: National Institute of Justice, May 1993).

[3]Betsy A. Fulton, Susan Stone, and Paul Gendreau, *Restructuring Intensive Supervision Programs: Applying What Works,* American Probation and Parole Association, 1994.

[4]James M. Byrne and April Pattavina, "The Effectiveness Issue: Assessing What Works in the Adult Community Corrections System," pp. 281–303 in *Smart Sentencing: The Emergence of Intermediate Sanctions,* James M. Byrne, Arthur J. Lurigio, and Joan Petersilia (eds.) (Newbury Park, Calif.: Sage, 1992).

[5]Jody Klein-Saffran, "The Development of Intermediate Punishments at the Federal Level," pp. 261–280 in *Smart Sentencing: The Emergence of Intermediate Sanctions,* James M. Byrne, Arthur J. Lurigio, and Joan Petersilia (eds.) (Newbury Park, Calif.: Sage, 1992).

[6]Fulton, Stone, and Gendreau, *Restructuring Intensive Supervision Programs.*

[7]Byrne and Pattavina, "The Effectiveness Issue."

[8]Ibid.

[9]Petersilia and Turner, *Evaluating Intensive Supervision Probation/Parole.*

[10]Dennis Wagner and Christopher Baird, *Evaluation of the Florida Community Control Program,* Research in Brief (Washington, D.C.: National Institute of Justice, January 1993).

[11]Petersilia and Turner, *Evaluating Intensive Supervision Probation/Parole,* p. 8.

[12]Roberta C. Cronin, *Boot Camps for Adult and Juvenile Offenders: Overview and Update* (Washington, D.C.: U.S. Government Printing Office, October 1994).

[13]Ibid.

[14]Ibid., pp. 15–21.

[15]Donald J. Hengesh, "Think of Boot Camps as a Foundation for Change, Not an Instant Cure," *Corrections Today,* October 1991.

[16]Cronin, *Boot Camps for Adult and Juvenile Offenders,* p. 30.

[17]Ibid., p. 33.

[18]Ibid., pp. 40–47.

[19]Doris Layton Mackenzie and Claire Souryal, *Multisite Evaluation of Shock Incarceration,* Final Summary Report submitted to the National Institute of Justice, November 1994.

[20]Ibid.

[21]Ibid., p. 12.

[22]Norval Morris and Michael Tonry, *Between Prison and Probation: Intermediate Punishment in a Rational Sentencing System* (New York: Oxford University Press, 1990).

[23]Marc Renzema, "Home Confinement Programs: Development, Implementation and Impact," pp. 41–53 in *Smart Sentencing: The Emergence of Intermediate Sanctions,* James M. Byrne,

Arthur J. Lurigio, and Joan Petersilia (eds.) (Newbury Park, Calif.: Sage, 1992).

[24]Ibid., pp. 43–44.

[25]Ibid., pp. 44–45.

[26]Ibid., p. 41.

[27]J. Robert Lilly, "Electronic Monitoring in the U.S.," pp. 112–116 in *Intermediate Sanctions in Overcrowded Times*, Michael Tonry and Kate Hamilton (eds.) (Boston: Northeastern University Press, 1995).

[28]Ibid.

[29]Joseph E. Papy, "Electronic Monitoring Poses Myriad Challenges for Correctional Agencies," *Corrections Today*, July 1994, pp. 132–135.

[30]J. Robert Lilly, Richard A. Ball, G. David Curry, and John McMullen, "Electronic Monitoring of the Drunk Driver: A Seven Year Study of the Home Confinement Alternative," *Crime and Delinquency*, 39 (4), 1993, pp. 462–484.

[31]Papy, "Electronic Monitoring," 1994.

[32]Terry L. Baumer and Robert I. Mendelsohn, "Electronically Monitored Home Confinement: Does It Work?" pp. 54–67 in *Smart Sentencing: The Emergence of Intermediate Sanctions*, James M. Byrne, Arthur J. Lurigio, and Joan Petersilia (eds.) (Newbury Park, Calif.: Sage, 1992).

[33]Ibid., pp. 58–59.

[34]Ibid., p. 59.

[35]Ibid., p. 60.

[36]Ibid., p. 61.

[37]Ibid., p. 62.

[38]Scott Christianson, "Defective Electronic Monitoring Equipment May Lead to Further Crime and Civil Liability," *Community Corrections Report*, July/August 1995, p. 5.

[39]Dale Parent, Jim Byrne, Vered Tsarfaty, Laura Valade, and Julie Esselman, *Day Reporting Centers* (Washington, D.C.: National Institute of Justice, 1995).

[40]Ibid., p. 3.

[41]Ibid.

[42]Ibid.

[43]Ibid., pp. 28–32.

[44]Ibid., pp. 28–29.

[45]Ibid., pp. 30–31.

[46]Ibid., pp. 32–36.

[47]Ibid., p. 43.

Chapter 7

[1]Sally T. Hillsman, Barry Mahoney, George Cole, and Bernard Auchter, *Fines as Criminal Sanctions* (Washington, D.C.: U.S. Department of Justice, National Institute of Justice, 1987).

[2]Ibid.

[3]Ibid.

[4]Ibid.

[5]Douglas C. McDonald, Judith Greene, and Charles Worzella, *Day Fines in American Courts: The Staten Island and Milwaukee Experiments* (Washington, D.C.: U.S. Department of Justice, National Institute of Justice, 1992).

[6]Ibid.

[7]Ibid.

[8]Ibid.

[9]Ibid.

[10]Joan Petersilia and Susan Turner, *Structured Fines Research: An Impact Evaluation Project Summary* (Santa Monica, Calif.: RAND Corporation, 1992).

[11]Hillsman, Mahoney, Cole, and Auchter, *Fines as Criminal Sanctions*, p. 3.

[12]Su Perk Davis, "Parolees, Probationers Help Pay Costs," *Corrections Compendium*, 16 (10), 1991.

[13]Hillsman, Mahoney, Cole, and Auchter, *Fines as Criminal Sanctions*, p. 3.

[14]Davis, "Parolees," p. 6.

[15]Dale Parent, *Recovering Correctional Costs Through Offender Fees*, National Institute of Justice Issues and Practices (Washington, D.C.: U.S. Department of Justice, 1990), p. 10.

[16]Ibid., pp. 8–9.

[17]Ibid., p. 8.

[18]Ibid., p. 24.

[19]George Cole, "Monetary Sanctions: The Problem of Compliance," in *Smart Sentencing: The Emergence of Intermediate Sanctions*, James Byrne, Arthur Lurigio, and Joan Petersilia (eds.) (Newbury Park, Calif.: Sage, 1992).

[20]National Institute of Corrections, *Topics in Corrections*, Summer 1992, pp. 11–14.

[21]Norval Morris and Michael Tonry, *Between Prison and Probation: Intermediate Punishments in a Rational Sentencing System* (New York: Oxford University Press, 1990), pp. 137–140.

[22]*Merriam-Webster Dictionary* (New York: Simon & Schuster, 1974), p. 597.

[23]Burt Galaway, "The Use of Restitution," *Crime and Delinquency*, 23 (1), 1977, 57.

[24]Ibid., p. 63.

[25]Ibid., p. 60.

[26]Harry E. Allen et al., *Halfway Houses* (Washington, D.C.: U.S. Government Printing Office, 1978), pp. 98–107.

[27]Douglas C. McDonald, *Restitution and Community Service* (Washington, D.C.: U.S. Government Printing Office, 1988).

[28]Joe Hudson and Burt Galaway, *Considering the Victim* (Springfield, Ill.: Thomas, 1975), p. xix.

[29]Ibid., p. xx.

[30]Margaret Fry, *Arms of the Law* (London: Victor Gollancz, 1951), p. 126.

[31]Ibid., p. xxiii.

[32]American Bar Association Commission on Correctional Facilities and Services and Council of State Governments, *Compendium of Model Correction Legislation and Standards*, 2nd ed. (Washington, D.C.: American Bar Association, 1975), pp. 111–148.

[33]Ibid., pp. 11–19.

[34]Ibid., pp. 11–57.

[35]Ibid., pp. 57–58.

[36]John T. Gandy, "Community Attitudes Toward Creative Restitution and Punishment" (unpublished doctoral dissertation, University of Denver, 1975).

[37]Robin S. Bluestein et al., "Attitudes of the Legal Community Toward Creating Restitution, Victim Compensation, and Related Social Work Involvement" (unpublished master's thesis, University of South Carolina, 1977).

[38]James Beha et al., *Sentencing to Community Service* (Washington, D.C.: U.S. Government Printing Office, 1977), p. 14.

[39]Joe Hudson and Steven Chesney, "Research on Restitution," in *Offender Restitution in Theory and Action*, Burt Galaway and Joe Hudson (eds.) (Lexington, Mass.: Lexington Books, 1978), p. 136.

[40]Ibid., p. 137.

[41]Ibid.

[42]Joseph Singleton, "CASES: The Community Service Sentencing Project," *IARCA Journal on Community Corrections,* April 1993, pp. 6–8, 17.

[43]National Institute of Corrections, *Topics in Corrections,* pp. 10–11.

[44]Anne Newton, "Aid to the Victim," *Crime and Delinquency Literature,* 8 (3), 1976, pp. 374–375.

[45]Ibid., pp. 376–377.

[46]Steve Novack, *National Assessment of Adult Restitution Programs: Preliminary Report III* (Duluth: University of Minnesota Press, 1980).

[47]Alan T. Harland, "Court-Ordered Community Service in Criminal Law: The Continuing Tyranny of Benevolence?" *Buffalo Law Review,* 29 (3), 1980, pp. 425–486, as cited in *Criminal Justice Abstracts,* December 1980, p. 78.

Chapter 8

[1]Edward Latessa and Harry E. Allen, "Halfway Houses and Parole: A National Assessment," *Journal of Criminal Justice,* 10 (2), 1982, pp. 153–163.

[2]George Camp and Camille Camp, *The Corrections Yearbook* (South Salem, N.Y.: Criminal Justice Institute, 1997), p. 64.

[3]Ibid., p. 39.

[4]Ibid., p. 47.

[5]Wayne Huggins, *Residential Community Corrections: Developing an Integrated Correctional Policy* (Washington, D.C.: U.S. Department of Justice, National Institute of Corrections, 1990), p. 1.

[6]Harry E. Allen et al., *Halfway Houses* (Washington, D.C.: U.S. Government Printing Office, 1978), pp. 2, 6.

[7]J. T. L. James, "The Halfway House Movement," p. 148 in *Alternatives to Prison,* Gary R. Perlstein and Thomas R. Phelps (eds.) (Pacific Palisades, Calif.: Goodyear, 1975).

[8]Edwin Powers, "Halfway Houses: A Historical Perspective," *American Journal of Correction,* 21, July/August 1959, p. 35. Reprinted with permission from the American Correctional Association.

[9]Ibid., p. 238.

[10]Oliver J. Keller and Benedict S. Alper, *Halfway Houses: Community-Centered Correction and Treatment* (Lexington, Mass.: Lexington Books, 1970), p. 8.

[11]Robert F. Kennedy, "Halfway Houses Pay Off," *Crime and Delinquency,* 21 (1), 1964, p. 3.

[12]Edward M. Koslin et al., "Classification, Evaluation, and Treatment Models in Community Ex-Offender Residency Programs," *Proceedings of the 103rd Annual Congress of Correction of the American Correctional Association* (College Park, Md.: American Correctional Association, 1974), pp. 134–136.

[13]Ibid., p. 135.

[14]Richard P. Seiter et al., *National Evaluation Program Phase I Summary Report—Halfway Houses* (Washington, D.C.: U.S. Government Printing Office, 1977), pp. 9–13.

[15]Ibid., p. 9.

[16]Ibid., p. 10.

[17]Ibid.

[18]Ibid.

[19]Ibid., p. 12.

[20]Michael S. Serrill, "Profile: Massachusetts Adult Correctional System," *Corrections Magazine,* 2 (2), 1975, p. 48.

[21]Kenneth Schoen, "PORT: A New Concept of Community-Based Correction," *Federal Probation,* 36, September 1972, pp. 35–40.

[22]Ibid., p. 36.

[23]Ibid., pp. 36–37. Reprinted with permission from *Federal Probation,* 1972.

[24]Ibid., p. 37. Reprinted with permission from *Federal Probation,* 1972.

[25]U.S. Department of Justice website, www. usdoj.gov/bop/ facilnot.html.

[26]Allen et al., *Halfway Houses,* pp. 5–22.

[27]Ann Parker et al., *So You Want to Start a Community Corrections Project* (Hackensack, N.J.: National Council on Crime and Delinquency, 1974), pp. 3–4.

[28]U.S. Bureau of Prisons, *The Residential Center—Corrections in the Community* (Washington, D.C.: U.S. Government Printing Office, 1973), p. 14.

[29]Ibid.

[30]Ibid.

[31]American Correctional Association, *Manual of Correctional Standards* (College Park, Md.: American Correctional Association, 1966), p. 137.

[32]Keller and Alper, *Halfway Houses,* p. 107.

[33]Richard L. Rachin, "So You Want to Open a Halfway House," *Federal Probation,* 36 (1), 1972, pp. 34–36.

[34]Richard P. Seiter et al., *Residential Inmate Aftercare: The State of the Art,* Supplement A: *Survey of Residential Inmate Aftercare Facilities* (Columbus: Ohio State University, 1976).

[35]Ibid.

[36]Allen et al., *Halfway Houses,* p. 16.

[37]Seiter et al., *Residential Inmate Aftercare.*

[38]Ibid.

[39]Allen et al., *Halfway Houses,* p. 17.

[40]Seiter et al., *Residential Inmate Aftercare.*

[41]Allen et al., *Halfway Houses,* pp. 7–8.

[42]U.S. Bureau of Prisons, *The Residential Center,* p. 20.

[43]Joan Potter, "The Dilemma of Being Half In and Half Out," *Corrections Magazine,* 5 (2), 1979, p. 69.

[44]Ibid., p. 68.

[45]Ibid., p. 69.

[46]Ibid., p. 69.

[47]Rachin, "So You Want to Open a Halfway House," p. 171.

[48]Margo C. Lindsay, *A Matter of Partnership: Public Involvement in Residential Community Corrections* (Washington, D.C.: U.S. Department of Justice, National Institute of Corrections, 1990), p. 5.

[49]Seiter et al., *National Evaluation Program Phase I Summary Report,* pp. 25–33.

[50]Ibid., p. 19.

[51]Allen et al., *Halfway Houses,* p. 74.

[52]General Accounting Office, *Federal Guidance Needed If Halfway Houses Are to Be a Viable Alternative to Prison,* Microfiche Collection (Rockville, Md.: National Criminal Justice Reference Service, 1975), p. i.

[53]Governor's Commission on Crime Prevention and Control, *Residential Community Corrections Programs in Minnesota: An Evaluation Report,* Microfiche Collection (Rockville, Md.: National Criminal Justice Reference Service, 1976).

[54]Ibid., pp. 288–296.

[55]Allen et al., *Halfway Houses,* p. 80.

[56]Ibid.

[57]Ibid.

[58]Ibid., p. 85.

[59]Ibid., p. 98.

[60]Ibid., p. 99.

Chapter 9

[1]Jared R. Tinklenberg, "Drugs and Crime," pp. 242–299 in *Drug Use in America: Problem in Perspective,* vol. 1, appendix, National Commission on Marijuana and Drug Abuse (Washington, D.C.: U.S. Government Printing Office, 1973).

[2]C. D. Chambers, "A Review of Recent Sociological and Epidemiological Studies in Substance Abuse" (paper presented at the Neurobiology Seminar, Vanderbilt University, Nashville, Tennessee, May 6, 1977).

[3]Robert Gandossy et al., *Drugs and Crime: A Survey and Analysis of the Literature* (Washington, D.C.: U.S. Government Printing Office, 1980), p. xiv.

[4]Richard Stevens and Rosalind Ellis, "Narcotic Addicts and Crime: Analysis of Recent Trends," *Criminology,* 12, 1975, pp. 474–488.

[5]James Inciardi, "The Vilification of Euphoria: Some Perspectives on an Elusive Issue," *Addictive Diseases,* 1, 1974, pp. 241–267.

[6]Edwin M. Schur, *Crimes Without Victims* (Englewood Cliffs, N.J.: Prentice-Hall, 1965), p. 122.

[7]Gandossy et al., *Drugs and Crime,* p. 36.

[8]Ibid.

[9]Oakley Ray, *Drugs, Society, and Human Behavior* (St. Louis, Mo.: C. V. Mosby, 1978), p. 323.

[10]Gandossy et al., *Drugs and Crime,* p. 75.

[11]Ibid., p. 76.

[12]Ibid., p. xii.

[13]Jerome J. Platt and Christine Labate, *Heroin Addiction—Theory, Research, and Treatment* (New York: Wiley, 1976), p. 319.

[14]Isidor Chein et al., *The Road to H: Narcotics, Delinquency, and Social Policy* (New York: Basic Books, 1964), pp. 273–274.

[15]Gandossy et al., *Drugs and Crime,* p. xii.

[16]Robert J. Wicks and Jerome Platt, *Drug Abuse: A Criminal Justice Primer* (Beverly Hills, Calif.: Glencoe Press, 1977), p. 44.

[17]Edward A. Preble and John J. Casey Jr., "Taking Care of Business—The Heroin User's Life in the Street," *International Journal of the Addictions,* 4, 1969, pp. 2–3. Reprinted with permission of Marcel Dekker Inc.

[18]Ibid., pp. 21–22.

[19]Platt and Labate, *Heroin Addiction,* p. 318.

[20]Quoted by permission from *Licit and Illicit Drugs* by Edward M. Bracer, and the editors of *Consumer Reports.* Copyright 1972 by Consumers Union of United States Inc.

[21]National Drug Abuse Treatment Utilization Survey (NDATUS), *National Drug Abuse Treatment: Insights and Perspectives* (Washington, D.C.: U.S. Government Printing Office, 1977), p. 18.

[22]Gandossy et al., *Drugs and Crime,* p. 114.

[23]Platt and Labate, *Heroin Addiction.*

[24]Edward Preble and Thomas Miller, "Methadone, Wine, and Welfare," pp. 229–248 in *Street Ethnography,* Robert S. Weppner (ed.) (Newbury Park, Calif.: Sage, 1977).

[25]Ibid.

[26]D. M. Alpern, E. Sciolino, and S. Agrest, "The Methadone Jones," *Newsweek,* February 7, 1977, p. 29.

[27]NDATUS, *National Drug Abuse Treatment,* p. 17.

[28]Platt and Labate, *Heroin Addiction,* p. 218.

[29]Ibid., p. 220.

[30]Mildred K. Klein, "Maintaining Drug Abusers in the Community: A New Treatment Concept," *Federal Probation,* 36 (2), 1972, pp. 18–26.

[31]Michael L. Peck and David Klugman, "Rehabilitation of Drug Dependent Offenders: An Alternative Approach," *Federal Probation,* 37 (3), 1973, pp. 13–23. Reprinted with permission from *Federal Probation* (1973).

[32]Ibid., pp. 22, 23.

[33]Gilbert Geis, "A Halfway House Is Not a Home: Notes on the Failure of a Narcotic Rehabilitation Project," *Drug Forum,* 4 (1), 1974, pp. 7–13.

[34]Lawrence T. Williams, *An Analysis of Recidivism Among Residents Released from Drug Contract Houses* (Boston: Massachusetts Department of Correction, 1980).

[35]U.S. Department of Health, Education, and Welfare (HEW), *Third Special Report to the U.S. Congress on Alcohol and Health* (Washington, D.C.: U.S. Government Printing Office, 1978), p. 243.

[36]Ibid., p. 242.

[37]Ibid., p. 245.

[38]David J. Pittman and C. Wayne Gordon, "Criminal Careers of Chronic Drunkenness Offenders," in *Society, Culture, and Drinking Patterns,* David Pittman and Charles R. Snyder (eds.) (New York: Wiley, 1962), p. 540.

[39]National Institute of Mental Health (NIMH), *Alcohol and Alcoholism: Problems, Programs, and Progress* (Washington, D.C.: U.S. Government Printing Office, 1972), p. 3.

[40]Alexander B. Smith and Louis Berlin, *Treating the Criminal Offender* (Dobbs Ferry, N.Y.: Oceana Publications, 1974), pp. 254–265.

[41]Harry Milt, *Basic Handbook on Alcoholism* (Fair Haven, N.J.: Scientific Aids Publications, 1967), p. 7.

[42]Smith and Berlin, *Treating the Criminal Offender,* p. 255.

[43]Ruth Fox, "Alcoholism and Depression," *American Journal of Psychotherapy,* as quoted in Milt, *Basic Handbook on Alcoholism,* p. 40.

[44]NIMH, *Alcohol and Alcoholism,* p. 13.

[45]Ibid., p. 18.

[46]"Substance Abuse Letter," National Institute of Drug Abuse, April 3, 1995.

[47]Ibid., p. 273.

[48]HEW, *Third Special Report to the U.S. Congress on Alcohol and Health,* p. xii.

[49]J. M. Polich, D. J. Armor, and H. B. Baker, "Patterns of Alcoholism," *Journal of Studies on Alcohol,* 41 (5), 1980, p. 414.

[50]HEW, *Third Special Report to the U.S. Congress on Alcohol and Health,* pp. 255–256.

[51]Ray, *Drugs, Society, and Human Behavior,* p. 156.

[52]Ibid.

[53]Ibid., p. 157.

[54]Ibid., p. 158.

[55]HEW, *Third Special Report to the U.S. Congress on Alcohol and Health,* p. 259.

[56]Ibid.

[57]Ibid.

[58]Curtis Janzen, "Families in the Treatment of Alcoholism," *Journal of Studies on Alcohol,* 38 (1), 1977, p. 120.

[59]Ibid., p. 122.

[60]Ibid., p. 124.

[61]U.S. Department of Health and Human Services, *Fourth Special Report to the U.S. Congress on Alcohol and Health* (Washington, D.C.: U.S. Government Printing Office, 1981), p. 137.

[62]Edward W. Soden, "Constructive Coercion and Group Counseling in the Rehabilitation of Alcoholics," *Federal Probation,* 30 (3), 1966, p. 56.

[63]Ibid., p. 59.

[64]Ibid.

[65]HEW, *Third Special Report to the U.S. Congress on Alcohol and Health,* p. 264.

[66]Ibid., p. 266.

[67]Ibid., p. 269.

[68]Ibid., p. 270.

[69]D. J. Armor, J. M. Polich, and H. B. Stambull, *Alcoholism and Treatment* (Santa Monica, Calif.: RAND Corporation, 1976).

[70]I. K. Zola, "Illness Behavior of the Working Class," pp. 350–361 in *Blue Collar World: Studies of the American Worker,* A. B. Shostak and W. Gomberg (eds.) (Englewood Cliffs, N.J.: Prentice-Hall, 1964).

[71]"Keeping Score: What We Are Getting for Our Drug Control Dollars 1995," *Drug Strategies,* 1996.

[72]Office of National Drug Control Policy, *Reducing the Impact of Drugs on American Society* (Washington, D.C., March 1995).

[73]The White House, *National Drug Control Strategy* (Washington, D.C.: Office of National Drug Control Policy, April 1995).

Chapter 10

[1]Michael Foucault, *Madness and Civilization* (Vintage Books, 1973).

[2]Ibid.

[3]*Sourcebook of Criminal Justice Statistics, 1998* (Washington, D.C.: Bureau of Justice Statistics, 1999).

[4]"Survey of Inmates in State or Federal Correctional Facilities," *Bureau of Justice Statistics Bulletin* (Washington D.C.: Bureau of Justice Statistics, 1998).

[5]Paula Ditton, "Mental Health and Treatment of Inmates and Probationers," *Bureau of Justice Statistics Bulletin* (Washington, D.C.: Bureau of Justice Statistics, 1999).

[6]Ibid.

[7]Ibid.

[8]Ibid.

[9]Ibid.

[10]Charles L. Zirkle, "From Tranquilizers to Antidepressants, From Antimalarials to Antihistimines," in *How Modern Medicines Are Discovered,* Frank Clark (ed.) (Mount Kisco, N.Y.: Futura Publishing, 1973).

[11]Ibid.

[12]Hans Toch, "The Disturbed, Disruptive Inmate, Where Does the Bus Stop?" *Journal of Psychiatry and Law,* 1982.

[13]Ibid.

[14]Bonita Vesey, "Mentally Ill Offenders in the Community, Challenges for the Future," in *Mentally Ill Offenders in the Community* (Longmont, Colo.: National Institute of Corrections, 1995).

[15]Ibid., p. 6.

[16]Ibid., p. 7.

[17]Ibid., p. 7.

[18]Rudolph Alexander Jr., *Counseling Treatment and Intervention Methods with Juvenile and Adult Offenders* (Belmont, Calif.: Wadsworth, 2000).

[19]G. E. Wyatt and G. J. Powell, *The Lasting Effects of Child Sexual Abuse* (Newbury Park, Calif.: Sage, 1998).

[20]Ibid.

[21]*Sourcebook of Criminal Justice Statistics.*

[22]Ibid., p. 443.

[23]Ibid., p. 435.

[24]Ibid., p. 89.

[25]George Camp and Camille Camp, *The Corrections Yearbook, 1997* (South Salem, N.Y.: Criminal Justice Institute, 1998).

[26]Peter Finn, *Sexual Offender Community Notification,* NIJ Research in Action (Washington D.C.: National Institute of Justice, 1997).

[27]Ibid., p. 4.

[28]Kim English, Suzanne Pullen, and Linda Jones, *Managing Adult Sex Offenders in the Community, A Containment Approach,* National Institute of Justice Research in Brief (Washington D.C. National Institute of Justice), 1997.

[29]Finn, Sexual Offender Community Notification, p. 14.

Chapter 11

[1]Freda Adler, *Sisters in Crime* (New York: McGraw-Hill, 1975).

[2]Tracy Snell, *Women in Prison: Survey of State Prison Inmates, 1991* (Washington, D.C.: Bureau of Justice Assistance, March 1994).

[3]Robin A. Robinson, "Intermediate Sanctions and the Female Offender," pp. 245–260 in *Smart Sentencing,* James M. Byrne, Arthur J. Lurigio, and Joan Petersilia (eds.) (Newbury Park, Calif.: Sage, 1992).

[4]Darrell J. Steffensmeier, "Assessing the Impact of the Women's Movement on Sex-Based Differences in the Handling of Adult Criminal Defendants," *Crime and Delinquency,* 26 (3), 1980, pp. 344–357.

[5]Nic Howell, "Special Problems of Female Offenders," *Corrections Compendium,* 17 (9), pp. 1, 5–6.

[6]Allen J. Beck, "Prison and Jail Inmates at Mid-Year 1999," *Bureau of Justice Statistics Bulletin,* April 2000, p. 6.

[7]Ibid., p. 6.

[8]Thomas P. Bonczar and Lauren E. Glaze, "Probation and Parole in the United States, 1998," *Bureau of Justice Statistics Bulletin,* August 1999, p. 7.

[9]"ACA Calls for Equal Treatment of Male and Female Offenders," *Criminal Justice Newsletter,* 26 (22), November 15, 1995, p. 4.

[10]Jane Roberts Chapman, *Economic Realities and the Female Offender* (Lexington, Mass.: Lexington Books, D.C. Heath, 1980). Copyright 1980, D.C. Heath and Company. This and all quotations from this source are reprinted with permission.

[11]Ibid., pp. 104–109.

[12]David North, "Women Offenders: Breaking the Training Mold," *Manpower,* February 1975.

[13]Chapman, *Economic Realities and the Female Offender,* p. 112.

[14]Ibid., p. 117.

[15]Ibid., p. 116.

[16]Ibid., p. 118.

[17]Ibid., p. 119.

[18]Belinda R. McCarthy, "Inmate Mothers: The Problems of Separation and Reintegration," *Journal of Offender Counseling, Services, and Rehabilitation,* 4 (3), 1980, p. 200.

[19]Chapman, *Economic Realities and the Female Offender,* p. 119.

[20]Ibid., p. 133.

[21]Marilyn C. Moses, *Keeping Incarcerated Mothers and Their Daughters Together: Girl Scouts Beyond Bars,* Program Focus (Washington, D.C.: National Institute of Justice, October 1995).

[22]Chapman, *Economic Realities and the Female Offender,* pp. 133–134.

[23]Ibid., p. 134.

[24]James Austin, Barbara Bloom, and Trish Donahue, *Female Offenders in the Community: An Analysis of Innovative Strategies and Programs* (San Francisco, Calif.: National Council on Crime and Delinquency, 1992).

[25]Ibid., p. 6.

[26]Ibid., p. 7.

[27]Ibid., pp. 10–15.

[28]Ibid., pp. 16–20.

[29]Ibid., pp. 21–29.

[30]Jean Wellisch, Michael L. Prendergast, and M. Douglas Anglin, *Drug Abusing Women Offenders: Results of a National Survey,* Research in Brief (Washington, D.C.: National Institute of Justice, October 1994).

[31]Ibid., pp. 5–6.

[32]Robinson, "Intermediate Sanctions and the Female Offender," p. 248.

[33]Ibid., pp. 250–255.

Chapter 12

[1]Howard Snyder and Melissa Sickmund, *Juvenile Offenders and Victims: A National Report* (Washington, D.C.: Office of Juvenile Justice and Delinquency Prevention, 1995), p. 154.

[2]Marvin Wolfgang, Robert Figlio, and Thorsten Sellin, *Delinquency in a Birth Cohort* (Chicago: University of Chicago Press, 1972).

[3]Snyder and Sickmund, *Juvenile Offenders and Victims,* p. 50.

[4]Alfred Blumstein, "Violence by Young People: Why the Deadly Nexus?" *National Institute of Justice Journal,* 229, August 1995, pp. 2–9.

[5]National Center for Juvenile Justice, *Juvenile Court Statistics, 1992* (Washington, D.C.: Office of Juvenile Justice and Delinquency Prevention, 1994).

[6]Mark Creekmore, "Case Processing: Intake, Adjudication, and Disposition," p. 120 in *Brought to Justice? Juveniles, the Courts, and the Law,* Rosemary Sarri and Yeheskel Hasenfeld (eds.) (Ann Arbor, Mich.: National Assessment of Juvenile Corrections, 1976).

[7]Ibid.

[8]Ibid., p. 125.

[9]Ibid., p. 136.

[10]Snyder and Sickmund, *Juvenile Offenders and Victims,* p. 77.

[11]National Center for Juvenile Justice, *Juvenile Court Statistics.*

[12]Snyder and Sickmund, *Juvenile Offenders and Victims,* p. 79.

[13]Ibid., p. 133.

[14]Carol Pope and William Feyerherm, *Minorities in the Juvenile Justice System: Research Summary* (Washington, D.C.: Office of Juvenile Justice and Delinquency Prevention, 1993).

[15]Arthur D. Little Inc., *Community Alternatives* (Washington, D.C.: Office of Juvenile Justice and Delinquency Prevention, 1978), pp. 13, 14.

[16]Thomas M. Young and Donnell M. Pappenfort, *NEP Phase I Summary Report: Secure Detention of Juveniles and Alternatives to Its Use* (Washington, D.C.: U.S. Government Printing Office, 1977), pp. 21, 22.

[17]Carol H. Blew and Robert Rosenblum, *The Community Arbitration Project: Anne Arundel County, Maryland, An Exemplary Project* (Washington, D.C.: U.S. Government Printing Office, 1979).

[18]Bureau of Justice Statistics, *BJA Fact Sheet: Boys and Girls Clubs of America* (Washington, D.C: Bureau of Justice Statistics, October 1995).

[19]Ibid., pp. 1, 2.

[20]Ibid., p. 2.

[21]Rita Grant and Juanita Buford, "Tennessee Program Prevents Violence in Young African American Males," *Corrections Today,* August 1994, pp. 152, 153.

[22]Ibid.

[23]"JUMP," *Criminal Justice Newsletter,* January 17, 1995, p. 7.

[24]National Advisory Commission on Criminal Justice Standards and Goals, *Report on Community Crime Prevention* (Washington, D.C.: U.S. Government Printing Office, 1973), pp. 51–69.

[25]Tracy Godwin, "Teen Courts: Empowering Youth in Community Prevention and Intervention Efforts," *APPA Perspectives,* Winter 1996, pp. 20–24.

[26]Orange County (Florida) Corrections, *Teen Court Volunteer Procedural Manual,* undated.

[27]Shoplifters Alternatives, Youth Educational Shoplifting Program, undated materials,

[28]Correspondence of Peter Berlin, February 1995.

[29]"Justice Department Announces 'Safe Futures' Grant Program," *Criminal Justice Newsletter,* November 15, 1995, p. 6.

[30]Young and Pappenfort, *NEP Phase I Summary Report,* p. 15.

[31]William G. Swank, "Home Supervision: Probation Really Works," *Federal Probation,* 43 (4), 1979, pp. 50–52.

[32]William Barton and Ira Schwartz, *Juvenile Detention: No More Hidden Closets* (Columbus: Ohio State University Press, 1994), p. 6.

[33]"Detention Aftercare in New York Said to Cut Recidivism Rates," *Criminal Justice Newsletter,* September 15, 1995, p. 5.

[34]Rosemary Sarri, "Service Technologies: Diversion, Probation, and Detention," p. 158 in *Brought to Justice? Juveniles, the Courts, and the Law,* Rosemary Sarri and Yeheskel Hasenfeld (eds.) (Ann Arbor, Mich.: National Assessment of Juvenile Corrections, 1976).

[35]Rob Wilson, "Corrections on the Local Level," *Corrections Magazine,* 2 (6), 1976, p. 30.

[36]Dale Mann, *Intervening with Serious Convicted Juvenile Offenders* (Washington, D.C.: U.S. Government Printing Office, 1976), p. 53.

[37]Wilson, "Corrections on the Local Level," p. 30.

[38]Ibid.

[39]Ibid.

[40]Vernon Fox, *Community-Based Corrections* (Englewood Cliffs, N.J.: Prentice-Hall, 1977), p. 221.

[41]Arthur D. Little Inc., *Alternative Education Options* (Washington, D.C.: U.S. Department of Justice, 1979), p. 6.

[42]Gretchen Saul and Paul Werrell, "Working Together Through School-Based Probation," *Student Assistance Journal*, May/June 1993, pp. 26–27.

[43]Ibid., p. 26.

[44]Ibid.

[45]Susan Jacobs and David Moore, "Successful Restitution as a Predictor of Juvenile Recidivism," *Juvenile and Family Court Journal*, 1994, pp. 3–14.

[46]Ibid., p. 6.

[47]Dennis Maloney and Gordon Bazemore, "Community Service Helps Heal Troubled Youths," *Corrections Today*, December 1994, pp. 74, 76, 78, 79, 82–84, 149.

[48]Ibid., p. 84.

[49]Ibid., pp. 83–84, 149.

[50]Ibid., p. 76.

[51]Susan Jacobs and David Moore, "Successful Restitution," pp. 3–14.

[52]Andrew Klein, "Restitution and Community Work Service: Promising Core Ingredients for Effective Intensive Supervision Programming," in *Violent Juvenile Offenders: An Anthology*, Robert Mathias (ed.) (San Francisco, Calif.: National Council on Crime and Delinquency, 1984).

[53]Ibid.

[54]"Kids in Need of Development," *Criminal Justice Newsletter*, March 1, 1995, pp. 6, 7.

[55]Ibid.

[56]Los Angeles County Probation Department, Specialized Gang Suppression Program, undated materials, provided by Paul Muntz, program director, correspondence, February 1996.

[57]Clifford E. Simonsen and Marshall S. Gordon III, *Juvenile Justice in America* (Encino, Calif.: Glencoe, 1979), p. 230.

[58]Chinita Heard, "Strategies for Establishing Mentor Home Placement for Juvenile Offenders: A Community Based Model," *Journal of Juvenile Justice and Detention Services*, 7 (2), Fall 1992, pp. 1–6.

[59]Robert D. Vinter et al., *Time Out: A National Study of Juvenile Correctional Programs* (Ann Arbor, Mich.: National Assessment of Juvenile Corrections, 1976), pp. 1–53.

[60]Ibid., p. 128.

[61]Youth Homes Inc., *Group Homes* (Charlotte, N.C.: Youth Homes Inc., n.d.).

[62]David Altschuler and Troy Armstrong, *Intensive Aftercare for High Risk Juveniles* (Washington, D.C.: Office of Juvenile Justice and Delinquency Prevention, 1994), pp. 135–136.

[63]Snyder and Sickmund, *Juvenile Offenders and Victims*, p. 90.

[64]Vinter et al., *Time Out*, p. 204.

[65]Altschuler and Armstrong, *Intensive Aftercare for High Risk Juveniles*, pp. 137–138.

[66]Office of Juvenile Justice and Delinquency Prevention, *Comprehensive Strategy for Serious, Violent, and Chronic Juvenile Offenders* (Washington, D.C.: Office of Juvenile Justice and Delinquency Prevention, 1993).

[67]David Huizinga, Rolf Loeber, and Terence Thornberry, *Urban Delinquency and Substance Abuse* (Washington, D.C.: Office of Juvenile Justice and Delinquency Prevention, 1994).

[68]Ibid., p. 23.

[69]Office of Juvenile Justice and Delinquency Prevention, *Comprehensive Strategy for Serious, Violent, and Chronic Juvenile Offenders*, p. 9.

[70]Ibid., p. 13.

[71]Ibid., p. 18.

[72]Ibid., pp. 20–21.

[73]Barry Krisberg, Deborah Neuenfeldt, Richard Wiebush, and Orlando Rodriguez, *Juvenile Intensive Supervision: Planning Guide* (Washington, D.C.: Office of Juvenile Justice and Delinquency Prevention, 1994).

[74]Krisberg, Neuenfeldt, Wiebush, and Rodriguez, *Juvenile Intensive Supervision*, p. 26.

[75]Ibid., pp. 24–30.

[76]Office of Juvenile Justice and Delinquency Prevention, *Comprehensive Strategy for Serious, Violent, and Chronic Juvenile Offenders*, p. 21.

[77]Ibid., p. 22.

[78]Ibid., p. 22.

[79]Ibid., pp. 23–24.

[80]"Detention Aftercare in New York Said to Cut Recidivism Rates," *Criminal Justice Newsletter*, pp. 5–6.

[81]Andrew Rutherford and Osman Benger, *NEP Phase I Summary Report: Community-Based Alternatives to Juvenile Incarceration* (Washington, D.C.: U.S. Government Printing Office, 1976), pp. 27–31.

[82]"Survey Finds Youth Crime Is Top Concern of Local Officials," *Criminal Justice Newsletter*, February 15, 1996, pp. 3, 4.

[83]"Texas Governor Signs Bill to Make Juvenile Code Stricter," *Criminal Justice Newsletter*, June 1, 1995, pp. 6, 7.

[84]"Virginia Governor and Lawmakers Agree on Juvenile Justice Plan," *Criminal Justice Newsletter*, February 1, 1996, pp. 6, 7.

[85]"Connecticut Takes Middle Road in Juvenile Justice Overhaul," *Criminal Justice Newsletter*, July 17, 1995, pp. 1–3.

[86]"$4.1 Million Targeted to Widen Alternatives to Incarceration," *Criminal Justice Newsletter*, November 1, 1995, pp. 6, 7.

[87]Robert F. Kennedy Memorial, National Juvenile Justice Project, undated materials.

[88]Ibid.

[89]"Ohio Program Gives Judges Money to Create Treatment Options," *Criminal Justice Newsletter*, August 1, 1995, pp. 1, 2.

Index

AA (Alcoholics Anonymous), 285*box*, 299, 300, 301*box*, 302, 305*box*
absconders: probationer, 89; temporary release, 154
abstinence: alcohol, 298, 299, 304; drug, 282, 285–86
accountability: community court, 76; diversion programs, 47, 70; ISPs enhancing, 166; juvenile offender, 379; probationer, 107; restorative justice, 5, 7*fig*
addiction. *See* drug addiction
addict personality, 278
adjudication: drug court compared with traditional, 50–51*box*; of juvenile offenders, 362, 363, 372–73. *See also* courts
adjudication partnerships, 40, 76–77
Adler, Freda, 332*box*
administration: halfway house, 267–69; parole, 130, 135, 146, 148; probation, 85–87, 86*table*, 374, 376*table*. *See also* local administration; states; United States
African American Alternative Center, Pennsylvania, 400
African Americans: alternatives to incarceration, 400; incarceration rates, 46; jail preferred over ISPs, 181*box*; Men of Distinction (MOD), 367–68; probationers, 89; three-strikes law harsh on, 23
aftercare: for alcohol abuse treatment program, 305*box*; detention, 374, 375*box*; for female offenders, 348, 350, 351; for juvenile offenders, 362, 374, 375*box*, 386, 388–90, 395, 396*fig*; for sex offenders, 319. *See also* postrelease services
Alabama, Break the Cycle (BTC), 53–54
Alaska: fees rejected, 221; victim compensation programs, 235
alcohol abuse treatment, 273, 298–300; community-based correctional programs, 300–303; effectiveness, 303–6; for female offenders, 350–51; goals, 298–99; modalities, 299–300; participant population, 298, 300; patient and treatment characteristics, 303; prerequisites/willingness to accept, 303–6. *See also* alcohol counseling
alcohol consumption: after alcohol abuse treatment programs, 303; becoming abuse, 298; controlled drinking, 299; crime linked with, 293–95; effects, 295–96; long-term effects of heavy, 295*box*; problem drinkers, 293–95, 296, 298–300, 301; social drinkers, 293–95; special problems of abusers, 293–300
alcohol counseling, 301–2, 305*box*; boot camp, 183; halfway house, 256

alcoholic offenders: CIU and, 65; community-based corrections for, 300–303; halfway houses for, 253
Alcoholics Anonymous (AA), 285*box*, 299, 300, 301*box*, 302, 305*box*
alcoholism: causes, 296–98; crime linked with, 293–95; defined, 296; diagnosing, 298; in families, 278, 300; population, 298; vs. problem drinking, 296; skid row, 295; stages, 297*box*. *See also* alcohol abuse treatment
alternative schools, 376–77
American Arbitration Association, 54
American Bar Association (ABA): and diversion programs, 44, 54; Model Adult Community Corrections Act (1984), 80; probation sentencing guidelines, 103; and restitution, 228
American Correctional Association (ACA): diversion programs, 44; and female offenders, 336; on halfway house neighborhoods, 254; on parole elements, 130, 131, 134, 146
American Law Institute, Model Penal Code, 138–40, 228
American Probation and Parole Association, 114–15, 146–47
Amicus House, 365–66
Amity Righturn Program, 284*box*
amphetamines, 173
Antabuse (disulfiram), 299
antipsychotic drugs, 315–16
ARC Community Services Treatment Alternative Program, Wisconsin, 348, 350
Arizona: Maricopa County DRC, 202–4, 202–3*figs*; parole abolished, 132; SVP laws, 320*box*
Arkansas, parole abolished, 132
arrest: drug offenses, 15–16, 17*table*; for failure to appear in court, 64, 65–66; gender linkages, 330–34; house, 4; juvenile, 360*fig*; rearrest recidivism, 93–95, 96–97, 99. *See also* house arrest
asylums, 311
Atlanta, NJCs, 55
Augustus, John, 83, 84*box*, 109
Australia, parole history, 126
autonomous model, parole administration, 130

back-end approaches, 170
bail: avoidance of, 43; deposit, 62; evaluation unit, 64; excessive, 42; reform, 45–46; release on, 42. *See also* bond
Balanced and Restorative Justice Project, OJJDP, 5–6

barbiturates, 273
basic necessities, halfway house provision of, 240, 243
behavioral management: temporary release programs and, 153. *See also* behavior modification; mental health treatment
behavior modification: alcohol abuse treatment, 299–300, 303; drug treatment, 99; home confinement and, 190
benefits: of clergy, 82; community-based corrections, 4; halfway house, 243–44; restitution/community service, 228–30, 235–37; victim compensation, 235–36. *See also* economic costs/benefits
Bentham, Jeremy, 227
blacks. *See* African Americans
Bleeding-Heart Liberals, 108, 109
bond: commercial, 40, 42, 43; unsecured appearance/personal recognizance, 59. *See also* bail
bondsmen, commercial, 42, 43
boot camps, 165, 179–88; attitude changes from, 185; community protection and, 182; defined, 179; DRCs and, 198; eligibility, 179, 182, 186–87*boxes*; federal, 183; females in, 182, 336; future of, 188; Georgia, 179, 184, 186–87*boxes*; graduates, 183, 198; New York State, 183, 184, 185, 186–87*box*; perceived objectives, 182; physical training, 186*box*, 201*box*; population, 182; program characteristics, 182–83; program development, 182; program objectives, 179; research, 183–88; Texas, 184, 200–201*box*, 398; today, 182–83
Booth, Maud, 245
Boys and Girls Clubs of America (B&G), 366–67
Break the Cycle (BTC), 53–54
Breed v. Jones, 356*fig*
Brewer, Coy E., Jr., 107
Bringing It All Back Home Family Teaching Model, 348
Brockway, Zebulon, 126–27
budget cuts, correctional, 14, 315
budgeting, by work-release inmates, 150
budget procedure, parole, 145
Bureau of Justice Assistance (BJA): boot camp funding, 183–84; Boys and Girls Clubs of America funding by, 366; DRC funding, 202; and drug treatment, 47, 286–87*box*; ISP funding, 115, 176, 177*box*; Key Elements of Successful Adjudication Partnerships, 76; structured fines research funding, 220

Bureau of Justice Statistics, 19, 21, 96–97, 114
Bureau of Prisons. *See* Federal Bureau of Prisons
burnout, halfway house personnel, 255
Bush administration, 14–15, 17, 155*box*
Busher, Walter H., 149

California: costs of collective incapacitation, 22–23; diversion vs. confinement costs, 163–65, 164*table*; mother and infant care programs, 349; NJCs, 55, 57; parole abolished, 133*box*; probationers, 87; probation study, 99–100; San Francisco Project, 103–4, 167; SVP laws, 320*box*; three strikes law, 133; tough-on-crime approach, 163. *See also* Los Angeles; San Diego
California Policy Seminar, 163
Carter administration, 14
caseload management, 110–11; generalized, 111; specialized, 111, 325
caseload size: ISP, 176; juvenile home detention, 374; juvenile ISP, 394; juvenile probation, 374; probation and parole supervision, 167–68
case management, 31, 33–34, 159–270; for female offenders, 350; for juvenile delinquents, 395, 399; parole, 145; Willamette Criminal Justice Council, 77. *See also* caseload management; caseload size; case processing; sanctions; supervision
case management classification, parole, 145
case processing: delinquency, 359–62, 361*fig*; differentiated, 70–74
casework, 98, 109, 110
castration, for sex offenders, 122*box*
checks, worthless, 58
children: dependent and neglected, 357; of female offenders, 52*box*, 329, 337, 339–40, 348, 349, 351. *See also* juvenile offenders; parenting skills
chippers, 278
citizenship rights, parolees' loss of, 123
CIU (Court Intervention Unit), Milwaukee, 64–65
civil disabilities, 123
client specific plans (CSPs), 107
Clinton administration, 69
collateral consequences of conviction, 123
collection procedures: fees, 222–25, 224*table*; fines, 213, 216–18, 219, 223–25. *See also* debt collection
collection rates: fees, 221–22, 223–25; fines, 211–12, 215, 216–18, 223–25
collective incapacitation: costs of, 22–23, 26, 29; current emphasis, 26; defined, 15; as intermediate sanction, 162. *See also* prisons
co-location of services, 194
Colorado, Outward Bound program, 382
commercial bonding, 40, 42, 43
community: boot camp graduates' adjustment to, 185–88; Great Society meaning, 13; halfway house benefits for, 244; halfway house relations with, 262–63; parole-related attitudes, 123, 124–25, 129–30, 131, 140, 145–47; restitution/community service affecting attitudes of, 230; restitution/community service benefits for, 228, 230; restorative justice roles, 7*fig*; and special problem offender, 310; temporary release acceptance, 154. *See also* community-based corrections; community protection; therapeutic communities
Community Arbitration Project (CAP), 366
community-based corrections: conflicts among goals of, 9; contemporary, 17–23; defined, 1, 11–12; development of, 9–31; distinction from other correctional

programs, 4; effectiveness research, 14; eligibility, 1–2, 33; eras in, 161; future of, 23–31, 398–400; history, 11–17; objectives, 1–9, 229–30; perspectives on study of, 31–34; as program alternatives, 32–33; reexamination of, 14–17; selection process, 2
community courts, 74–76, 74–75*box*. *See also* drug courts
community education programs, on sex offenders, 325–26
community justice, 5–9
community policing, 6, 57
community protection, 1–2, 3; boot camps and, 182; EM and, 189; halfway houses and, 242–43, 256–57; home confinement and, 189; intermediate sanctions and, 30, 161–62, 163; ISPs and, 166, 168, 169, 175–76; juvenile aftercare and, 389; parole and, 120, 123, 124; postrelease community supervision for, 147; probation objective, 80, 81, 102; restorative justice and, 5, 6–8, 7*fig*; sex offender containment programs for, 324. *See also* dangerousness
community residential centers, 240–69; defined, 242; objectives, 242–44. *See also* community restitution centers; halfway houses; residential programs
Community Resource Management Team model, 91–92
community restitution centers, 227, 234
community service, 165, 211, 225–37; amount of, 231–32; benefits, 228–30, 236–37; community court and, 76; contemporary support for growth in, 228–29; correctional objectives served by, 229–30; DRC, 197, 199–202; eligibility, 230–31, 233; enforcement of, 232–34; ISPs and, 166; juvenile offenders, 379–81, 380*box*; offense categories for, 226, 230; process, 230–33; in stages of criminal justice system, 226–27; as symbolic restitution, 226; universal appeal of, 228; victim-offender relations and, 229, 232, 236
community services: halfway house help with, 244, 249–50. *See also* services; social services
Community Service Sentencing Project (CSSP), 233–34
community supervision: adults under (1990–1998), 26*fig*; drug treatment, 287–88; parole, 121, 123; after parole abolition, 147. *See also* community restitution centers; day reporting centers (DRCs); intensive supervision programs (ISPs)
community supervision officer (CSO), 34
compensation programs. *See* victim compensation programs
competency development, in restorative justice, 7*fig*
conditional parole, 125
conditional pretrial release, 59–60, 62, 65*table*
conditional release, 121
conditions of parole, 139–40
conditions of probation, 111–13, 226
conditions of release, 111–13, 166
confrontational therapy, 283, 292
Connecticut: Hartford DRC, 196; juvenile crime legislation, 398–99
consolidated model, parole administration, 130
Constitution, U.S.: on bail, 42; and imprisonment for debt, 237
containment programs, sex offender, 324–25, 327*box*
continuous contact EM, 188, 190
continuum of care, for juvenile offenders, 400

continuum of programs, 3
continuum of sanctions, 2–3, 30–31, 202, 210. *See also* correctional continuum
continuum of sentencing, Maricopa, 202*fig*
Contract with America, crime bill, 19–20
contracts, juvenile: aftercare, 389–90; for behavior in public education, 377
controlled drinking, 299
control level, 2; halfway houses, 256–57; intermediate sanctions, 163, 168; ISP, 175, 176, 178
Cooperative Commission on the Study of Alcoholism, 296–98
coordination, restorative justice, 8
correctional continuum, 3, 32–33; intermediate sanctions and, 161–63, 165–66, 210; Maricopa, 202, 202*fig*. *See also* continuum of care; continuum of programs; continuum of sanctions
correctional costs. *See* costs
correctional officers (COs): interviews on boot camps, 184–85, 186–87*boxes*. *See also* parole officers; probation officers
Corrections Compendium, on fees, 220–21
cost-effectiveness: of community-based corrections, 3, 8–9, 163–64, 176; selective incapacitation, 29–31. *See also* cost reductions, correctional
cost reductions, correctional: boot camps and, 184, 188; community-based vs. confinement, 9, 163–65, 164*table*; EM and, 189, 190; home confinement and, 189, 191; ISPs and, 169–71, 174, 178; for probation uses, 163. *See also* savings
costs: boot camp, 183; of collective incapacitation, 22–23, 26; court, 220; DRC, 197, 204; drug testing, 71*table*; external, 9; federal justice system, 14–15; fees and surcharges covering, 211, 220–21; government services, 26; halfway house per diem, 264, 265*fig*; incarceration, 115, 163, 375*box*; intermediate sanctions, 9, 163, 165*table*; juvenile detention aftercare vs. incarceration, 375*box*; juvenile home detention, 374; mental health, 315; NJC, 55; prison, 15, 27, 163, 242; restitution, 235–37; spending for corrections in Reagan-Bush era, 15, 15*table*; state correctional, 15, 18, 19, 27–29, 163; victim compensation, 235–36. *See also* cost-effectiveness; cost reductions, correctional; funding
counseling: alcohol, 183, 256, 301–2, 305*box*; boot camp, 183; crisis, 289; halfway house, 255, 256; of juveniles, 365, 366, 367–68, 375–76, 387; mental health, 62; peer, 367–68; probation, 91–92, 95*box*, 98–99, 108; sex offender, 319. *See also* drug counseling; therapy
court costs, 220
Court Intervention Unit (CIU), Milwaukee, 64–65
court notification, 64
courts: community, 74–76, 74–75*box*; debt collection role, 223; failure to appear, 63–64, 65–66, 66*table*, 67, 70; mediation referred to, 56*box*; on parole goal, 124; and probation, 81–82, 85–86, 91, 102–4, 107, 226; revocation process, 113–14; sentencing guidelines, 102–4, 111; suspending sentences, 83; teen, 370–71, 372–73*box*; youth, 369–71, 372–73*box*. *See also* adjudication; defendants; drug courts; judicial system; juvenile courts
court-sentenced programs, for female offenders, 348–49
crack cocaine, 15, 24, 274, 282, 284
crime: alcohol linked with, 293–95, 294*table*; decreasing rates, 23–24; drug abuse linked with, 67, 273–75, 274*table*,

293, 294*table*; gender linkages, 330–34; mental illness linked with, 310–11, 313–15, 315*table*; during temporary release, 154, 155*box*; war on, 15–16. *See also* offenses

crime prevention: juvenile, 366; restorative justice and, 8

crime severity level: economic sanctions based on, 213–15, 216, 217*table*; intermediate sanctions and, 162–63; for parole guidelines grid. *See also* dangerousness; violent crime

criminal contamination, 245

criminal history score, in standardized sentencing instruments, 104, 105*table*

criminal justice system: academic studies, 13; alcohol abuse treatment linkages, 306; community attitudes toward, 230; dissatisfaction with, 13, 26; female offender and, 334–36, 341–42; halfway houses benefits for, 244; interdependence of agencies, 31–32; international, 25–26; ISPs enhancing credibility of, 171–74; juvenile justice system and, 354–57, 358–59*table*, 359–62; mentally ill in hands of, 316; reform, 13; restitution/community service stages in, 226–27; restorative justice, 5; stigmatization from, 12; vagrants' experiences with, 311. *See also* federal justice system; juvenile justice system

crisis counseling, for drug abusers, 289

crisis intervention, for juveniles, 365, 374

Crofton, Sir Walter, 126, 245

crowding: jail, 40, 64, 202, 316, 317; probation, 103, 107. *See also* prison overcrowding

Crystal Meth, 275*box*

curfews, 166, 169, 189, 198, 394

custody: of children of offenders, 52*box*; of juvenile offenders, 359–62. *See also* incarceration; minimum custody

cycle of dependency, victimization, and crime, of female offenders, 338

dangerousness: intermediate sanctions and, 162–63; juvenile, 363; sex offender, 320–21*box*. *See also* crime severity level; violent crime

Davis, Richard Allen, 133*box*

day fines, 3, 210, 213–20; calculation of, 216; means-based, 165; Milwaukee Municipal Court, 215, 215*table*, 219–20; offenses appropriate for, 216, 217–18*tables*, 218–19; program effectiveness, 219; research, 215, 216–20; Staten Island Experiment, 216–19, 217*table*

day reporting centers (DRCs), 162, 194–205, 207*box*; composite, 195*box*; development, 194–96; eligibility, 197–98; future of, 204–5; Harris County, 198–202; Maricopa County, 202–4, 202–3*figs*; objectives, 194; participant success, 197–98, 204; program characteristics, 196–98; research needs, 204–5; services, 196–97, 197*table*; staffing, 197. *See also* day treatment programs

Daytop Village, 283–84

day treatment programs: for female offenders, 348–49, 350; for juvenile offenders, 381–82, 394. *See also* day reporting centers (DRCs); residential programs

DCPSA (District of Columbia Pretrial Services Agency), 67, 70

debt collection, 223–25, 237; New Jersey model, 223–25; privatization of, 225; probation agency, 81, 112, 223–25, 237; problems of, 223

decentralized system, for juvenile offenders, 399

defendants: automatic conditions on, 65*table*; failure to appear in court,

63–64, 65–66, 66*table*, 67, 70; felony (in seventy-five largest counties), 61*table*

defense attorneys, differentiated case processing, 71

deinstitutionalization: of juvenile corrections, 397–98. *See also* institutionalization

Delancey Street Foundation, 283–84, 285*box*

Delaware: Comprehensive Services for Women, 348; parole abolished, 132

Delaware County Intensive Supervision Aftercare Program, Ohio, 389–90

delinquents: case processing, 359–62, 361*fig*; defined, 357; developmental pathways, 391*fig*; intermediate sanctions, 392–95, 399; plan for serious chronic, 390–95, 393*table*, 394*fig*; sanctions, 363; serious chronic, 357, 390–95, 396. *See also* juvenile offenders

demand reduction goals, drug control, 307*box*

Department of Health, Education and Welfare, funding for community-based corrections, 14

Department of Justice, 43–44; dispute resolution programs encouraged by, 54; Drug Courts Program, 49; and juvenile programs, 372, 399; PSI study, 106

Department of Labor funding: for community-based corrections, 14; for pretrial intervention programs, 43

dependent and neglected children, defined, 357

dependent behavior patterns, female, 337, 338, 351–52

deposit bail, 62

detention: alternatives to juvenile, 372–84, 399–400; facilities for juveniles, 362, 363, 397; pretrial, 13, 40, 42–43, 59; pretrial alternatives to, 40, 42–43, 59–60, 60*fig*. *See also* incarceration; institutionalization

determinate sentencing, 15, 115, 132*box*, 154–55

deterrence: boot camps and, 179, 182, 185; economic sanctions and, 210; EM providing, 189, 193–94; incarceration level and, 24; probation sanction, 79

detoxification, heroin, 282

Detroit, handgun intervention program, 76–77

differentiated case processing, 70–74

discretion, 40; freedom from influence, 135; parole board, 20–21, 131–33, 135, 141; in sentencing, 15, 103

discretionary release, 20–21, 127–28, 131–33

discrimination: against juvenile minorities, 365; against poor and disadvantaged, 13

Dismas House, 246

disposition, for juvenile offenders, 362, 365

dispute resolution programs, 5, 43–44, 54–59, 226; for juvenile offenders, 366. *See also* mediation programs

District of Columbia: alcohol abuse treatment programs, 301; job development and placement program, 339; life without parole statutes, 133; Special Approaches for Juvenile Assistance Inc. (SAJA), 365

District of Columbia Pretrial Services Agency (DCPSA), 67, 70

disulfiram (Antabuse), 299

diversion, 39–59; alternatives to, 70–76; candidates for, 164*fig*; concept of, 40–41; contemporary, 46–59; costs compared with confinement, 163–65, 164*table*; development of contemporary, 43–44; for drug-abusing offenders, 46–54; eligibility, 2; for female offenders, 330, 347–48; ISPs and, 177*box*, 178; juvenile, 366–72, 374; objectives, 46; policebased, 41, 43; postconviction, 82;

traditional, 41. *See also* dispute resolution programs

diversion centers, 227. *See also* community restitution centers

domestic violence: and EM, 192; house arrest for females and, 351; probation guidelines, 114–15; women's violent crime linked to, 334

DRCs. *See* day reporting centers

drug abusers: casual/heavy, 67; crime linked to, 67, 273–75, 274*table*, 293, 294*table*; diversion programs for, 46–54; female, 52*box*, 334, 350–51; halfway houses for, 253, 289, 291–92; methadone maintenance, 282–83; polydrug, 274; pretrial releasees, 67; on probation, 98–99, 288*box*, 289, 302*table*; special problems of, 273–82; temporary release and, 154; therapeutic communities for, 283–86, 292. *See also* drug addiction; drug offenders; drug treatment; narcotics users

drug addiction: causes/purposes of, 278–79; community-based correctional programs for, 286–92; crime linked with, 274, 293; defined, 276–77; post-addiction syndrome, 280–82; stopping, 280–81*box*; therapeutic communities and, 284. *See also* drug abusers

drug counseling, 282, 289; boot camp, 183; Delancey Street, 285*box*; emergency shelter, 365; halfway house, 256

Drug Court Resource Center, American University, 52

drug courts, 49–50, 52*box*, 75–76; differentiated case processing, 70–74; first (1989), 44; funding for, 18; process, 50–51*box*; research, 51–53; traditional adjudication compared with, 50–51*box*

drug offenders: arrests, 15–16, 17*table*; boot camps for, 182; diversion programs, 46–54; on EM, 192; fees charged to, 224; female, 52*box*, 334, 348, 350–51; National Drug Control Strategy, 307*box*; after prison, 24; prisons flooded with, 17; removal from prisons, 18, 19. *See also* alcoholic offenders; drug abusers; drug courts

drugs: alcohol abuse treatment with, 299; amphetamines, 173; antipsychotic, 315–16; barbiturates, 273; crack cocaine, 15, 24, 274, 282, 284; emerging, 276–77*box*; mental health treatment with, 315–16; methamphetamine, 275–76*boxes*; war on, 15–17, 280–81*box*, 334. *See also* drug offenders; heroin; substance abuse

drug testing: cost comparison, 71*table*; methods, 70; pretrial release, 62, 65, 67–70; of probationers, 288*box*, 289; program and policies by site, 72–73*table*; research, 67–70. *See also* urine monitoring

drug treatment, 273, 282–92; DRCs and, 198; for female offenders, 350–51; for juvenile offenders, 378–79; methadone maintenance, 282–83; population in, 282; for probationers, 98–99; staff, 289. *See also* drug counseling

Drug Use Forecasting (DUF), 275*box*

due process: for juveniles, 356, 356*fig*, 357; for parole revocation, 140; for probation revocation, 113–14

Dukakis, Michael, 155*box*

East Los Angeles Halfway House, 292

economic costs/benefits: of economic sanctions, 210; of restitution/community service, 228–29. *See also* cost-effectiveness; costs; economic sanctions; financial aid; funding; income; revenue generation; savings

economic objectives: of intermediate sanctions, 163–65. *See also* economic costs/benefits

economic offenses. *See* property crime

economic sanctions, 210–38. *See also* community service; debt collection; fees; fines; restitution

Eddings v. Oklahoma, 356*fig*

education: boot camp, 183, 187*box*; DRC, 199; of females, 337, 338–39; halfway house goals, 256; within institutional walls, 151; ISPs and, 166; juvenile programs, 376–79, 400; preparole, 135–36; study-release programs, 149, 150–51, 259*box*. *See also* community education programs; training

electronic monitoring (EM), 9, 162, 165, 166, 188–94; continuous contact, 188, 190; effectiveness, 193; fees for, 220; future of, 193–94; implementation issues, 191–92; objectives, 189–90; offender selection, 191–92; organizational issues, 192; population on, 190; pretrial release, 62, 66–67, 191–92; program development, 190–91; programmed contact, 188, 190; research needs, 194; technology, 190–91, 192–93

eligibility: boot camp, 179, 182, 186–87*boxes*; community-based corrections, 1–2, 33; DRC, 197–98; ISP, 170–74*boxes*; parole, 132–33; pretrial release, 2, 60, 62, 63*table*; restitution/community service, 230–31, 233

Elizabeth Fry Center, 349

EM. *See* electronic monitoring

emergency shelters, for runaways, 365

emotional support, halfway house, 244

employment: federal inmate, 252; for female offenders, 329, 337, 338–39, 349; follow-up services, 339; gender-nontraditional, 338, 339; halfway house residents, 256, 258*box*, 259, 259*box*; halfway house staff, 254–55; ISPs and, 166, 176; for juveniles, 365, 379–81; parolee, 243; programming issues, 339; restitution/community service emphasis on, 228, 379–81; work-release, 149–50, 151. *See also* community service; job development and placement; vocational training; work

enforcement: of community service, 232–34; drug-related, 307*box*; fine and fee collection, 211–25, 224*table*; in probation supervision, 107, 108; of restitution, 232–33, 237; rule, 2

England: Bill of Rights, 42; DRCs, 196; fines, 211; parole history, 125–26; pretrial release history, 41; probation history, 82–83

English Penal Servitude Act (1853), 126

Enhanced Pretrial Services Project, 60

enhancement programs, 170–71, 176

equity: in punishment, 115; restitution as, 229; in sentencing, 168. *See also* proportionality of punishment

executive branch of government: aftercare services, 388; probation services, 86–87, 374

failure to appear: in court, 63–64, 65–66, 66*table*, 67, 70; in home detention, 374

fairness, parole and, 120–21, 123, 124, 141

families: of alcohol abusers, 300, 305*box*; EM/home confinement reactions, 193; foster care, 385–86; of heroin addicts, 278; restitution/community service benefits for, 228; of runaways, 366; of serious chronic delinquents, 390, 391; victim compensation to, 235. *See also* children; parenting skills

family courts. *See* juvenile courts

family services, in juvenile corrections, 389

family therapy, for alcohol abuse, 300

Federal Anti-Drug Abuse Initiative, 47

Federal Bail Reform Act (1984), 45–46, 67

Federal Bureau of Prisons: boot camps, 183; on halfway houses, 252, 256–57; Reagan administration and, 14–15

federal funding: alcohol abuse treatment, 298; boot camp, 182, 183–84; community-based corrections (general), 14; drug testing, 69; drug treatment, 286*box*; Great Society, 13; halfway house, 246; ISP, 115, 176; juvenile diversion programs, 366, 368, 363; juvenile intermediate sanction programs, 399; juvenile restitution programs, 379; new prisons, 182; pretrial intervention, 43–44, 47, 49, 54, 67, 69; restitution, 228; structured fines research, 220; tough-on-crime movement and, 17, 18–19

federal justice system, 14–16, 83; drug treatment, 291; fines and restitution, 211; inmate employment, 252; ISPs, 168; on juvenile detention, 362; mentally ill inmates, 311; parole, 90; prison population (1925–1997), 16*fig*; probation, 90–92, 94–95*box*, 97, 114, 168. *See also* Federal Bureau of Prisons

Federal Prisoner Rehabilitation Act (1965), 246

Federal Prison Industries Inc., 252

Federal Probation Service, 91–92

Federal Sentencing Commission, 104, 111

fees, 211, 220–23; collection, 221–25, 224*table*; nonpayment penalties, 223, 224*table*; probation, 112, 220, 222*table*; revenue generation and, 221, 222*table*; schedules, 221–23; transportation, 125; victim compensation from, 226, 235–36

female offenders, 329–53; boot camp, 182, 336; client selection/characteristics in programs for, 345–47; community programs for, 340, 341–51, 346*table*; crimes, 330–34; criminal justice system and, 334–36, 341–42; drug abusers/offenders, 52*box*, 334, 348, 350–51; furloughs for, 152, 340; intermediate sanctions, 351; NCCD survey, 342–49; "new female criminal," 332–34; number of, 334; pregnant, 349; prison population, 330*fig*, 334; program characteristics, 344–45, 346*table*; program effectiveness, 349–50; services for, 338–41, 347–51, 347*table*; as sexual deviants, 332*box*; social roles, 337, 338, 351–52; special problems and needs, 330–38, 341–42, 349–50, 351; supervision/security in programs for, 347; Temporary Asylum for Discharged Female Prisoners, 245; treatment issues, 351–52

finance. *See* bail; debt collection; economic costs/benefits; financial aid; funding

financial aid: gate money, 243; halfway house, 256; study-release programs, 151; victim assistance, 229, 235

fines, 165, 210, 211–20; collection, 211–19, 223–25; impediments to use of, 211–13; Model Adult Community Corrections Act and, 80; offenses appropriate for, 211, 212*table*, 214*table*, 216, 217–18*tables*, 218–19; restitution and, 228; traditional, 165, 215, 215*table*. *See also* day fines

fixed sentences, 388–89

flight risk, 43

Florida: boot camps, 184, 185; Duval County Community Correctional Center, 349; Girl Scouts program, 344–45*box*; halfway houses, 259*box*, 266; ISPs, 168, 176–78, 190; Mariana Community Center, 259*box*; New Port Richey Marine Institute, 384–85*box*; parole abolished in, 131; SVP laws, 320*box*; Tallahassee

Community Correctional Center, 258*box*; Teen Court, 370–71, 372–73*box*

Florida Community Control Program (FCCP), 176–78, 190

follow-up services: for female offenders, 339; halfway house, 250; for juveniles, 395; pretrial release, 60, 62–64, 65

foster care, 385–86

front-end approaches, 170

Fry, Margaret, 227

full restitution, 231

funding: BTC, 53; DRC, 202; mental health treatment, 315; prison population increases and, 17, 18–19, 26; RECLAIM, 400; spending for corrections in Reagan-Bush era, 15, 15*table*; for study-release programs, 151. *See also* costs; federal funding; financial aid

furloughs, 151–53, 154; as alternatives to conjugal visiting, 149; for female offenders, 152, 340; from halfway houses, 258–59; Horton, 155*box*

Gagnon v. Scarpelli, 113–14

gangs, juvenile programs focused on, 382–84, 383*fig*

GAO. *See* General Accounting Office

gate money, prison, 243

gender: and criminality, 330–34, 336–37; delinquency development, 390; job development and placement and, 338–39; prison population, 330*fig*, 334; probationer, 89, 334; single-sex vs. coed programs, 352. *See also* female offenders

General Accounting Office (GAO), U.S.: boot camp study, 183–84, 188; drug court surveys, 52–53; halfway house survey, 266; ISP survey, 175–76

geography, restorative justice, 8

Georgia: boot camps, 179, 184, 186*box*, 187*box*; community restitution centers, 227; ISPs, 115, 170–71*box*, 174; NJCs, 55; parole staff qualifications, 135

Georgia Peace Officers Standards and Training Act, 135

Girl Scouts of Apalachee Bend (GAB), 344–45*box*

Girl Scouts Beyond Bars (GSSB), 340, 344*box*

good-time credits, 121, 122*box*, 123, 126, 127, 317

good-time statutes, 121, 127

graduated release, 4, 155

graduated sanctions, 53, 392, 397

Great Britain: DRCs, 196. *See also* England

Great Society, 13, 14

Greenholtz v. Inmates of the Nebraska Penal and Correctional Complex, 125

group homes, for juvenile offenders, 386–87, 389

group therapy: for alcohol abuse, 301–3; Delancey Street, 285*box*; DRC, 199; East Los Angeles Halfway House, 292. *See also* family therapy

half-in and half-out, 246, 257–62

halfway houses, 240–69; administrative strategies, 267–69; agency-operated/funded, 242*box*; boot camp graduates, 183; capacity, 241; community relations, 262–63; coordination with other correctional services, 266, 267; for drug abusers, 253, 289, 291–92; efficiency, 264; employment of residents, 256, 258–59*boxes*, 259; evaluations of, 263–67, 264*table*; facilities, 259–62; furloughs, 258–59; future of, 267–69; history, 244–52; inmate code, 260–61*box*, 262; intake process, 247; kick pad, 289; length of stay, 241, 253; location/site selection, 253–54, 266; Massachusetts prerelease centers, 245, 250–51; Minne-

sota PORT programs, 251–52, 266–67; objectives, 242–44; for parolees, 141, 240–41; per diem costs, 264, 265fig; population (1995), 241; problems of, 257–63; program illustrations, 250–52; programming, 149, 247–50; program models, 246–50; program planning and operations, 252–57; recommendations for, 265–66; referrals to, 247; release or transfer from prison to, 240–41, 241fig; security, 244, 256–58, 265; services, 244, 249–50, 255–56, 257table, 264–65; staff, 254–55; target population, 252–53; temporary release in, 149; today, 242; U.S. numbers of, 241. See also community residential centers
hallucinogens, 276–77box
Hardliners, 108, 109
Hazelden Rehabilitation Program, Center City, Minnesota, 304–5box
hearings: parole-related, 90, 138–39; probation revocation, 113–14
heroin, 276box; chippers using, 278; methadone maintenance and, 282–83; postaddiction syndrome, 280–82; therapeutic communities and, 284
Hispanics: jail preferred over ISPs, 181box; probationers, 89
home confinement, 162, 165, 188–94; boot camp graduates, 183; effectiveness, 193; future of, 193–94; implementation issues, 191–92; objectives, 189–90; offender selection, 191–92; research needs, 194. See also house arrest
home detention programs, juvenile, 373–74
homelessness, mentally ill offenders, 313–14
homes. See residential programs
homicide, juvenile, 357
Hope Hall, 245
Horton, Willie, 155box
house arrest, 4, 162, 166, 188; for female offenders, 351; for juvenile delinquents, 394. See also home confinement
humanitarianism: restitution/community service, 229; temporary release programs, 153

Ice (form of methamphetamine), 274, 275box
Illinois: boot camps, 184, 185; Cook County domestic violence probation program, 114–15; Genesis House, 348; Juvenile Court Act (1899), 355; Lake County EM, 67; parole abolished in, 131; SVP laws, 320box; truth-in-sentencing law, 19
immediate interventions, for serious chronic delinquents, 392
incapacitation. See collective incapacitation; incarceration; selective incapacitation
incarceration: alternatives to, 372–84, 399–400; costs, 115, 163, 375box; inmates preferring vs. ISPs, 180–81box; juvenile, 375box, 398; myth of benefits of massive, 24; probation revocation to, 114; probation term with, 89; problems caused by prolonged, 148; rates, 23–24, 46, 311, 312fig; reincarceration recidivism, 96; shock incarceration (boot camp), 179, 186–87boxes; truth-in-sentencing law and, 15. See also detention; jail; prisons
incentive grants, for prisons or boot camp construction, 18–19, 20
incentives, drug court, 53
income: day fines based on, 213–15, 216; federal inmates, 252; fees and, 221, 222; foster care parent, 386; prison inmates, 243; restitution and, 231–32, 233, 237, 381; work-release, 150, 258box. See also economic sanctions
indentured servants, 126

independent living programs, for juvenile offenders, 387–88
indeterminate sentencing, 121, 126, 131, 132box, 138
Indiana, parole abolished in, 131
informal probation, 374
Inmate Financial Responsibility Program, 252
inmates: absconding on temporary release, 154; alcohol/drugs linked with crime, 293–95, 294table; furlough, 152; gate money, 243; gender of populations, 330fig, 334; halfway house code, 260–61box, 262; interviews on boot camps, 184–85; mentally ill, 311–15, 311table, 313–15tables, 317; parole release of, 121, 123, 125, 126–27, 147; preferring incarceration vs. ISPs, 180–81box; study-release, 151, 259box; work in prison, 126, 243; work-release, 149–50. See also parolees; prisons; probationers; state prison inmates
inputs, systems analysis and, 31
In re Gault, 356fig
In re Winship, 356fig
in-school suspension programs, 377–78
Institute for Mediation and Conflict Resolution, 54
institutionalization: effects of, 148; juvenile, 388; mental health, 315–16. See also deinstitutionalization; detention; incarceration
institutional model, parole administration, 130
insurance, 41–42
intake process: halfway house, 247; juvenile justice system, 362–63, 365
integrated approach: to corrections, 18; to mentally ill offenders, 317
intensive supervision programs (ISPs), 3, 162, 165, 166–206; CIU, 64–65; drug court, 50box; federal drug treatment, 291; federal funding, 115; Florida, 168, 176–78, 190; future of, 178–79; Georgia, 115, 170–71box, 174; goals, 168–74; home confinement costs compared with, 191; inmates preferring incarceration vs., 180–81box; Massachusetts, 174box; New Jersey, 172–73box; OJJDP model for delinquents, 392–95, 393table, 394fig; percentage of offenders in, 168; probation alternative of, 103; program development, 167–68; research, 115, 168, 174–78; staffing, 170box, 172box, 174box; statements of purpose, 170box, 172box, 174box
interagency cooperation programs, 325
interdependence: debt collection, 223; in systems analysis, 31–32
intermediate sanctions, 3, 161–206; collective incapacitation as, 162; community corrections era of, 161; correctional continuum and, 161–63, 165–66, 210; costs, 9, 163, 165table; defined, 165; European, 25; for female offenders, 351; inmates preferring incarceration vs., 180–81box; ISPs providing, 171–74, 176; for juvenile delinquents, 392–95, 399; objectives, 161–66; selective incapacitation with, 29–31; summary listing, 166–67table. See also boot camps; day reporting centers (DRCs); economic sanctions; electronic monitoring (EM); home confinement; intensive supervision programs (ISPs)
international goals, drug control, 307box
International Halfway House Association (IHHA), 246
International Penal Association Congress, 227
international perspective, correctional, 25–26

intervention programs: halfway house, 247; pretrial, 43; in probation supervision, 107
interviewing, for pretrial release, 60–62
interviews, on boot camps, 184–85, 186–87boxes
investigation. See presentence investigation (PSI) reports; research
Iowa: parole board, 136–37box; SVP laws, 320box
Irish convict system, 126, 245
Isaac T. Hopper Home, New York City, 245
ISPs. See intensive supervision programs

jail: adult population, 26fig, 46; for community service violators, 234; construction, 46; female population, 334; juveniles prohibited in, 362; overcrowding reduction, 40, 64, 202, 316, 317. See also detention; prisons
Jefferson Correctional Institution (JCI), Girl Scout program, 344–45box
job development and placement: in drug treatment programs, 289; for female and male offenders, 338–39. See also employment; job readiness training
job readiness training: for female offenders, 338, 339; for juvenile offenders, 400. See also vocational training
job stability, after alcoholism treatment, 303
judicial reprieve, 82, 83
judicial system: bail reform, 45–46; probation administration, 374. See also adjudication; courts
JUMP (juvenile mentoring programs), 368–69
justice systems. See criminal justice system; federal justice system; judicial system; juvenile justice system; police
Juvenile Court Act (1899), Illinois, 355
juvenile courts: case outcomes, 364table; creation (1890s), 84, 355; increase of punitiveness, 398; informality, 356; intake process, 362, 363; jurisdiction, 357; parens patriae and, 124; teen courts run by, 370; treatment vs. control objectives, 395–96
Juvenile Justice and Delinquency Prevention Act, extension (1992), 182
juvenile justice system, 354–402; criminal justice system and, 354–55, 358–59table, 359–62; deinstitutionalization, 397–98; diversion and, 371–72; goals, 355table; intake process, 362–63, 365; interagency cooperation programs, 325; overview, 355–62; processing of offenders, 359–62, 361fig; restorative justice, 5–6, 7fig; runaways, 365–66. See also juvenile courts
juvenile mentoring programs, 368–69, 380
juvenile offenders, 357–59; aftercare, 362, 374, 375box, 386, 388–90, 395, 396fig; alternatives to confinement, 372–84, 399–400; boot camps, 182, 183; classification of, 399; community-based programs for, 354, 363–401; day treatment programs, 381–82, 394; diversion programs, 366–72, 374; diversity of, 358–59; DRCs, 196; female, 333; mediation programs, 56box, 58–59; probation programs, 84, 87, 363, 365, 374–84, 376table, 386; problems/issues in programs for, 395–98; processing, 359–62, 361fig; release on recognizance, 83; research related to, 365, 379, 390–95; residential programs, 363, 385–88, 392–94; as resources, 379–80; restitution and community service programs, 379–81, 380box; restorative justice roles, 7fig; school-related programs, 376–78; serious chronic, 357, 390–95,

396; specialized programs for, 371, 382–84, 383*fig*; status, 357, 358, 363, 396; treatment vs. control of, 355–56, 395–96; violent, 357, 390, 391*fig*, 392. *See also* delinquents

Kansas: Achievement Place group home, 387; fees rejected, 221; parole abolished, 132; SVP laws, 320*box*
Kansas City, Missouri, NJCs, 55
Kansas v. Hendricks, 320–21*box*
Kennedy, Robert F., 246
Kentucky: home detention programs, 374; offenders on probation, 87–88
Kent v. United States, 356*fig*
Ketamine, 276*box*, 277*box*
kick pad, halfway house, 289
Kids in Need of Development Project (KIND), 381–82
Klaas, Polly, 133*box*

labeling, offender, 12–13, 162–63, 230
Lake County EM, 67
law enforcement. *See* enforcement
Law Enforcement Assistance Administration (LEAA) funding: for correctional programs, 14; for diversion programs, 44, 47; for juvenile restitution programs, 379; for restitution programs, 228
legal violations, parole, 140
life sentences, mandatory, 18–19, 133
life skills training: boot camp, 201*box*; Delancey Street, 285*box*; DRC, 199; for female offenders, 340–41, 342–43*fig*. *See also* survival skills; vocational training
lifestyle: crime-free, 166; drug abuser, 289–90
local administration: boot camp, 182, 183; probation, 85, 86*table*, 374
Los Angeles: East Los Angeles Halfway House, 292; LA Fast, 77; Narcotics and Drug Abuse Rehabilitation Program, 289; Narcotic Treatment and Control Unit, 289; NJCs, 55; Specialized Gang Suppression Program (SGSP), 383–84, 383*fig*
Louisiana: boot camps, 184, 185; Kids in Need of Development Project (KIND), 381–82
LSD, 276–77*box*

Machonochie, Alexander, 126
MacKenzie, Doris L., 183–84
Maine: parole abolished in, 131; wilderness program, 382
mainstreaming, mental health, 316
maintenance of justice system, parole objective of, 124
males. *See* gender
management by objectives (MBO), 267–68
management information system (MIS), 148, 268
mandatory release, 121, 122*box*, 127, 133*box*; supervised, 121, 127, 147
mandatory sentencing, 162, 334; life, 18–19, 133; minimum, 132*box*, 163, 388
Manhattan: Bail Project, 44–45, 62; Court Employment Project, 43, 44; Hope Hall, 245; Midtown Community Court, 76
Manhattan Institute, "Broken Windows" probation, 10–11*box*
MAP (mutual agreement programming), 141–45, 268–69
Maricopa County DRC, Arizona, 202–4, 202–3*figs*
marijuana, 276*box*
Marine Institute, New Port Richey, Florida, 384–85*box*
Martin, Nancy, 115
Martinson, Robert, 147, 168
Maryland: Alternative Directions Inc., 348; Community Arbitration Project

(CAP), 366; Girl Scouts Beyond Bars, 340, 344*box*; ISPs, 168; Montgomery County Work-Release/Pre-Release Center, 248–49*box*
Massachusetts: Community Services for Women, 348; deinstitutionalization movement, 397; DRCs, 196; drug contract houses, 292; EM studies, 190; foster care program, 386; Horton case, 155*box*; ISP, 174*box*; juvenile community service, 380*box*; prerelease centers, 245, 250–51; probation practices, 83–84; release on recognizance, 83; SVP laws, 320*box*; Temporary Asylum for Discharged Female Prisoners, 245; wilderness program, 382
Mavericks, 108–9
maximum expiration of sentence, 121–23
McKeiver v. Pennsylvania, 356*fig*
McQuay, Larry Don, 122*box*
MDMA, 276*box*
media: parole attacked by, 146; and special offenders, 310, 320*box*
mediation, voluntary, 54–55
mediation programs, 5; court-referred involving juveniles, 56*box*; North Carolina, 57–58; restitution in, 226; victim-offender, 58–59. *See also* dispute resolution programs
medical care, mental health, 12, 315–16
Men of Distinction (MOD), Tennessee, 367–68, 368*box*
mental health treatment: asylums, 311; DRCs and, 196, 198, 199; funding, 315; pretrial release, 62, 65; reintegration after hospitalization, 12, 315–16; for sex offenders, 321*box*; specialized, 317–18
mentally ill offenders, 310–18; history, 315–17; measures of illness, 311*table*, 313*fig*; population, 311, 313*table*, 317; prevalence of problem with, 311–15; problems with services and supervision for, 317–18; sexually violent predators, 320–21*box*
mentally retarded offenders, DRCs and, 198
mentoring programs, juvenile, 368–69, 380, 395
meritorious good time, 121
methadone maintenance, 282–83
methamphetamine, 275*box*, 276*box*
Michigan: handgun intervention program, 76–77; MAP evaluations, 145
Miller, Jerome, 397
Milwaukee: Court Intervention Unit (CIU), 64–65; day fines, 215, 215*table*, 219–20; ISP, 177*box*
minimum custody, halfway house for, 241–42
minimum sentencing, 15, 132*box*, 162, 163, 388–89
Minnesota: Genesis II, 349; halfway house evaluation, 266–67; Hazelden Rehabilitation Program, 304–5*box*; Hennepin County's Personal Growth Group, 348; parole abolished in, 132; PORT programs, 251–52, 266–67; Sentenced to Service Program, 380*box*; SVP laws, 320*box*
minorities. *See* female offenders; race
Mississippi: early release laws, 133; parole abolished, 132
Missouri: halfway houses, 266; home detention programs, 374; NJCs, 55; Providence Education Center (PEC), 376–77; SVP laws, 320*box*
Model Adult Community Corrections Act (1984), 80
Model Penal Code, 138–40, 228
Montana, early release laws, 133
Morales, Dan, 122*box*
More, Sir Thomas, 227
Morrissey v. Brewer, 113–14

Mossbacks, 108
mutual agreement programming (MAP), 141–45, 268–69

Narcotics and Drug Abuse Rehabilitation Program, Los Angeles, 289
narcotics users: causes/purposes of addiction, 278–79; characteristics, 278; community-based correctional programs for, 286–92; crime linked to, 273–74; diversity, 276–78; methadone maintenance, 282–83; on parole, 290–91*box*; unmotivated, 292. *See also* heroin
Narcotic Treatment and Control Unit, Los Angeles, 289
National Advisory Commission on Criminal Justice Standards and Goals: on diversion, 44; on parole board, 134; on probation, 85, 111; on restitution, 228; on sentencing models, 130–31
National Assessment of Juvenile Corrections (NAJC), 374–75, 386–87
National Association of Pretrial Service Agencies, 60
National Center on Addiction and Substance Abuse, 53
National Center on Institutions and Alternatives (NCIA), 107
National Consortium of TASC programs, 47
National Council on Crime and Delinquency (NCCD): female offender studies, 342–50; on halfway house target population, 252–53; and restitution, 228
National Drug Control Strategy, 307*box*
National Drug Court Institute, 49, 53
National Evaluation Program (NEP), on halfway houses, 255, 263–66
National Institute of Alcohol Abuse and Alcoholism, 298, 303
National Institute of Corrections (NIC): budget cuts, 14; on community residential centers, 242; and female offenders, 341–42; mandatory release survey, 127; probation surveys, 85, 87, 106
National Institute of Drug Abuse, 282
National Institute of Justice (NIJ): boot camp study, 183, 184–88; community court evaluation, 76; DCPSA funded by, 67; DRC survey, 196–98; Drug Use Forecasting (DUF), 275*box*; felony probation study, 99–100; Girl Scouts pilot program, 344*box*; and ISPs, 176, 177*box*, 178
National Institute of Law Enforcement and Criminal Justice (NILECJ): halfway house report, 252; probation study, 97–98
National Institute of Mental Health, 292
National Juvenile Justice Project, 399
NCCD. *See* National Council on Crime and Delinquency
Nebraska, early release laws, 133
Neighborhood Justice Centers (NJCs), 43–44, 55–57
"new female criminal," 332–34
New Jersey: Camden Urban Women's Center, 349; debt collection model, 223–25; ISP, 172–73*box*; SVP laws, 320*box*
New Mexico, parole abolished in, 132
New York City: community court, 74–75*box*, 76; community service program, 233–34; diversion programs, 43, 44–45; drug courts, 71; Foundling Hospital, 340; Isaac T. Hopper Home, 245; juvenile detention aftercare, 374, 375*box*. *See also* Manhattan
New York State: boot camps, 183, 184, 185, 186–87*box*; Elmira Reformatory, 126–27; good-time statute, 127; indeterminate sentencing law, 126; mediation programs, 57; Monroe County Jail Utilization Systems Team, 77; prison

capacity, 19; Project Greenhope, 348; Staten Island Experiment, 216–19, 217table; victim compensation programs, 235; work-release inmates, 149. See also New York City
NIJ. See National Institute of Justice
NJCs (Neighborhood Justice Centers), 43–44, 55–57
nontraditional employment, for female offenders, 338, 339
normative sanctions and programs, 8–9
North Carolina: mediation programs, 57–58; parole abolished, 132, 147; PRAC program, 147; restitution policies, 227; structured sentencing, 27–29; Summit House, 348; wilderness program, 382; Youth Homes Inc., 387
North Dakota, SVP laws, 320box
"nothing works" perspective, 147, 168
notification, court, 64
notification laws, about sex-offenders, 319–24, 326box

Odyssey House, 283–84
offenders: boot camp candidates, 179, 182; community-based corrections benefits for, 4; diversity of, 2; DRC, 197–98, 202; on EM and home confinement, 190, 191–93; fee schedules for, 222–23; geography, 8; habitual, 15; halfway house benefits for, 243–44; halfway house inmate code, 260–61box, 262; ISP release percentage, 168; labeling, 12–13, 162–63, 230; mentally ill, 310–18, 320–21box; parole conditions, 139–40; probation conditions, 111–13; probation decision related to characteristics of, 103–4; probation importance to, 102; probation as legal status of, 80; "reform-through-isolation," 10–11; restitution/community service benefits for, 229–30; restrictions on, 2; types served by probation, 87–88; unnecessary jailing, 42–43; victim relations with, 229, 232, 236; willingness to accept probation, 103. See also case management; control level; defendants; diversion; drug offenders; eligibility; female offenders; inmates; parolees; pretrial release; probationers; rehabilitation; reintegration; selection; sentencing; special problem offenders; supervision; violent crime offenses: bailable, 42; community service appropriate for, 226, 230; felony punishment chart, 28fig; by females, 330–34; fines appropriate for, 211, 212table, 214table, 216, 217–18tables, 218–19; by juveniles, 357–58, 360fig; prohibited from probation, 102–3; punishment proportional to, 2–3, 168, 215, 216; range of, 2; restitution categories, 226, 230; serious, 357; sex, 319, 320–21box; status, 357, 358; youth court, 370, 371, 371table. See also crime; crime severity level; offenders; property crime; violent crime
Office of Justice Assistance, Research, and Statistics, budget cuts, 14
Office of Juvenile Justice and Delinquency Prevention (OJJDP): Balanced and Restorative Justice Project, 5–6; boot camp funding, 182; community-based corrections funding, 14; Men of Distinction (MOD) recommendation, 367; plan for serious chronic violent delinquents, 390–95, 393table, 394fig; restitution program funding, 228
Office of National Drug Control Policy, 49
Ohio: AA originating in, 300; Delaware County Intensive Supervision Aftercare Program, 389–90; dispute settlement, 43; home detention programs, 374; ISPs, 168; parole abolished, 132; RECLAIM,

400; Twelve Inc. independent living program, 388
OJJDP. See Office of Juvenile Justice and Delinquency Prevention
Oklahoma: boot camps, 184; SVP laws, 320box; truth-in-sentencing law, 20–21box
Oregon: Council for Prostitution Alternatives, 349; ISPs, 176, 177box; Marion County diversion program, 177box; parole abolished in, 132; "Sharelift," 380box; wilderness program, 382; Willamette Criminal Justice Council, 77
outcome measures, on probation, 93, 96
outputs, systems analysis and, 31
outreach programs, for juveniles, 366, 394
Outward Bound program, 382

pardons: parole history, 125, 126. See also reprieve
parens patriae, 124–25
parental surrogate, foster care, 385–86
parenting skills: for female offenders, 338, 339–41, 344box, 349. See also children
parole, 120–48; abolished, 131–32, 133box, 147, 155; administration, 130, 135, 146, 148; conditions of, 139–40; contemporary, 127–47; coordination with other correctional services, 148; defined, 121–23; elements of, 130–47; failure rate, 128; federal system, 90; fees, 222table; future of, 147; guidelines, 121, 139–40, 141; history, 125–27; innovations in, 140–47; juvenile, 388–90; narcotics addicts on, 290–91box; objectives, 123–25; probation confused with, 123; procedures, 135–40; promising strategies, 140–47; public attitudes toward, 123, 124–25, 129–30, 131, 140, 145–47; revocation of, 3, 23, 121, 140, 142–43table, 237; shock parole (boot camp), 179; violations, 140, 142–43table. See also aftercare; parolees; parole staff; parole supervision
parole board, 123, 124, 135; and attacks on parole, 146; and castration of sex offender, 122box; decision making, 20–21, 121, 124, 131–35, 141–45, 146; hearings, 138–39; Iowa, 136–37box; and parole conditions, 139–40; probation review, 90–91; PSI used by, 104–6; qualifications, 134
Parole Commission, U.S.: budget cuts, 14; parole abolished, 132; Salient Factor Score, 141, 144fig
parole d'honneur, 125
parolees: adjustment problems, 123; alcoholic, 300–303; characteristics, 127table, 138–39; DRCs and, 198; due process for, 140; female, 334, 349; halfway house, 141, 240–41; population, 127–30, 128–29table, 140–41; vs. probationers, 123; restitution centers, 227; work by, 243
parole officers: boot camp postrelease supervision, 183; interviews on boot camps, 185, 187box
parole review, 120
parole staff: boot camp, 187box; debt collection, 237; and parole population increases, 141; qualifications, 134–35; specific services, 324fig. See also parole board; parole officers
parole supervision, 120, 123, 124, 139–40; caseload size, 167–68; classification system, 145; population released to, 128–30; supervised mandatory release, 121, 127, 147
partial restitution, 236
partnerships: adjudication, 40, 76–77; in Girl Scout program, 345box
PCP (phencyclidine), 277box

peer counselors, for juveniles, 367–68
peer juries courts, youth, 370, 371, 372–73box
penal servitude, 126
penalties: for nonpayment of fees, 223, 224table. See also fines; punishment; sanctions
Pennsylvania: African American Alternative Center, 400; Amicus House, 365–66; halfway houses, 266; Philadelphia House of Industry, 245; School-Based Probation Services Program, 377–78
per diem costs, halfway house, 264, 265fig
personal recognizance, 59
personal victimization, decreased rates of, 23
Petersilia, Joan, 96, 115, 163
petition, against juvenile offenders, 362, 363, 374
pharmacological agents: alcohol abuse treatment with, 299; mental health treatment with, 315–16
Philadelphia House of Industry, 245
Phoenix House, 283–84
physical training, boot camp, 186box, 201box
plan development, in halfway house programming, 248–49
planning: for juvenile aftercare, 389–89; preparole, 135–36
police: community policing, 6, 57; diversion programs based with, 41, 43; and drugs, 277box; and failure to appear in court, 63–64; and juveniles, 365, 366; restitution permitted by, 226
policy of transportation, 125–26
polydrug users, 274
PORT programs (Probational Offenders Rehabilitation and Training programs), 251–52, 266–67
Posey, Mike, 280–81box
postaddiction syndrome, 280–82
postbooking interviews, for release, 60
postrelease services, 139–40, 147; for boot camp graduates, 183; Girl Scout, 345box. See also aftercare
PRAC (Pre-release and After Care), 147
prebooking interviews, for release, 60
preparation, preparole, 135–38
preparole activities, 135–38
Pre-release and After Care (PRAC), 147
prerelease centers, 242
prereleasees, at halfway houses, 240
prescriptive restrictions, 2
presentence investigation (PSI) reports, 104–7; content, 106–7; objectives, 104–6; options, 110fig; preparation, 106, 107; probation and, 80, 81, 103, 104–7; purpose, 106–7; typology of investigators, 108–9, 109table. See also probation supervision
President's Commission on Law Enforcement and Administration of Justice, 4, 44, 369
President's Task Force on Prisoner Rehabilitation, 44
President's Task Force Reports on Law Enforcement and Administration of Justice, 13
presumptive sentencing guidelines, 132box
pretrial detention, 13, 42–43, 59; alternatives to, 40, 42–43, 59–60, 60fig. See also diversion; pretrial release
pretrial release, 39–40, 41–46, 59–70; alternatives to, 70–76; basic services, 60–64; concept of, 41–46; conditional, 59–60, 62, 65table; contemporary, 59–65; development of contemporary, 44–46; drug testing, 62, 65, 66–70; eligibility, 2, 60, 62, 63table; EM supervision, 62, 66–67, 191–92; for female offenders, 330, 348; financial, 42, 62,

64*table*; follow-up, 60, 62–64, 65; history, 41; interviewing for, 60–62; non-financial, 62; objectives, 46; options proposed, 68–69*box*; on recognizance (ROR), 44–45, 59–60, 62; recommendations for, 60, 62; research, 65–70; supervised (SPTR), 45, 59–60, 62, 64–65; verification, 60, 62; work, 59–60

Pride Inc., 190

prior permission rules, in OJJDP plan for delinquents, 394, 394*fig*

prison overcrowding: boot camp and, 179, 184, 188; halfway houses and, 244; parole revocation and, 140; parole use affected by, 127, 128, 129–30; work release and, 149, 156. *See also* jail

prison population: adults (1990–1998), 26*fig*; decrease in crime and, 23–24; federal (1925–1997), 16*fig*; gender, 330*fig*, 334; increasing, 15–26; state, 16*fig*, 17, 18*table*, 25*fig*, 27–29; truth-in-sentencing law and, 15, 17–18, 19–22. *See also* prison overcrowding

prisons: actual time served, 19; costs, 15, 27, 163, 242; double bunking in maximum security, 19; drug offenders flooding, 17; drug offenders removed from, 18, 19; federal funding for new, 182; female offenders in, 330*fig*, 331–33*box*, 334; gate money, 243; to halfway houses from, 240–41, 241*fig*, 243; "hotel," 13; inadequate facilities, 13; incentive grants for construction of, 18–19, 20; and MAP, 141–44; parole from, 121, 123, 126–27; parole revocation to, 121, 140, 142–43*table*; rehabilitation not occurring in, 13; sentencing guidelines, 103–4. *See also* inmates; jail; postrelease services; prison population; state prison inmates

privately prepared presentence reports, 107

privatization: debt collection, 225; juvenile corrections, 397, 399–400; prison construction and operation, 19

probation, 79–101; administration, 85–87, 86*table*, 374, 376*table*; alternatives to, 3, 118; after boot camp, 186; classification systems, 114; community corrections era, 161; conditions of, 111–13, 226; crowding problem, 103, 107; defined, 79–80; federal, 90–92, 94–95*box*, 97, 114, 168; fees, 112, 220, 222*table*; future of, 115–18; granting, 102–7; guidelines for sentencing to, 102–4; history, 82–84; informal, 374; innovations in, 114–15; juvenile programs, 84, 87, 363, 365, 374–84, 376*table*, 386; Manhattan Institute's "Broken Windows," 10–11*box*; objectives, 80–81; offenses prohibited from, 102–3; as organizational structure, 79–80; parole confused with, 123; as process, 79, 80; research, 93–100; restitution/community service in, 81, 226, 227, 228, 237; revocation of, 3, 112, 113–14, 237; as sanction, 79, 80; sentencing to, 79, 80, 81–82, 89, 99, 102–4; shock probation (boot camp), 179; as social reform, 84; success rates, 90, 114; today, 88–90; as trap, 180–81*box*. *See also* probation agencies; probationers; probation supervision

probation agencies: administration by, 85–87; debt collection, 81, 112, 223–25, 237; PSI prepared by, 106; specific services, 324*fig*; supervision function, 107; and toughened sanctions, 114. *See also* probation officers

Probational Offenders Rehabilitation and Training programs (PORT programs), 251–52, 266–67

probationers: absconders, 89; adjustment problems of, 123; alcoholic, 300–303,

302*table*; characteristics, 92*table*; cost reductions utilized for, 163; DRCs and, 198; drug abusers, 98–99, 288*box*, 289, 302*table*; due process for, 113–14; female, 330, 334; halfway house, 240–41; male, 89; mentally ill, 313, 313–14*tables*, 317; misdemeanants and low-level felons, 79; offender types, 87–88; vs. parolees, 123; population, 79, 87–89, 88–89*table*, 92, 115; race, 89–90; recidivism, 93–99; Texas boot camp, 200–201*box*. *See also* probation

probation officers: availability of, 103; and drug abuse, 289; federal, 91–92, 94–95*box*; interviews on boot camps, 185, 186*box*; juvenile, 374–75, 377–78, 384; probation sentencing guidelines, 104; PSI reports prepared by, 106, 107; responsibilities for probation conditions, 112; and revocation process, 113; teams, 110. *See also* probation agencies; probation supervision

probation supervision, 79, 80, 81, 107–14; availability of, 103; caseload size, 167–68; fees for, 220; juvenile, 374–75; population, 87, 88–89; research, 97–98, 108; service delivery strategies, 109–10, 112–13*figs*; styles, 107–9, 109*table*. *See also* probation officers

problem drinkers, 293–95, 296, 298–300, 301. *See also* alcoholism

problem-solving skills, in survival training, 341

Program for Female Offenders, 349–50

programmed contact EM, 188, 190

programming: employment, 339; for female offenders, 339, 341–42; halfway house, 149, 247–50; juvenile delinquent day treatment, 394; MAP, 141–45, 268–69; parole, 147

Progressives, 84

progressive sanctions, 318

promise to appear (PTA), 59

property crime: decreased, 23; and EM, 192; by females, 334; fines for, 211; by juveniles, 357, 371; by mentally ill offenders, 313, 314*table*; restitution for, 226

"property in service," 125–26

proportionality of punishment, 2–3, 168, 215, 216

propriety, parole ensuring, 123, 124

proscriptive restrictions, 2

prosecutions, avoidance of unnecessary, 41

prosecutors: diversion by, 41; restitution permitted by, 226

prostitution, help with transition from, 348, 349

protection. *See* community protection

Providence Education Center (PEC), St. Louis, 376–77

PSI. *See* presentence investigation (PSI) reports

public safety. *See* community protection

punishment: boot camps and, 182, 201*box*; equal, 115; intermediate sanctions and, 162–63, 165, 168, 176, 189–90, 210, 215; for juvenile offenders, 357, 398; proportionality of (punishment fitting crime), 2–3, 168, 215, 216; "reform-through-isolation," 10–11; restitution/community service and, 236; summary, 183. *See also* incarceration; sanctions; tough-on-crime approach

race: incarceration rates, 46; and jail preferred over ISPs, 181*box*; and juvenile diversion programs, 366–68; juvenile justice system discrimination, 365; probationer, 89–90. *See also* African Americans

RAND Corporation studies: alcoholism, 298–99; drug arrests, 15–16; probation, 99–100; structured fines, 220; three-strikes law, 22–23

rape statistics, 319

Reagan administration, 14–15

rearrest, recidivism as, 93–95, 96–97, 99

recidivism: boot camps and, 182, 185–88; defined, 93–96; drug courts reducing, 51–52; of halfway house residents, 244, 264; intermediate sanctions and, 165; ISPs and, 174, 175–76, 178, 179; juvenile, 379, 382; MAP effectiveness in reducing, 145; of probationers, 93–99; sex offender, 320*box*; simple, 93; specific, 93; studies on, 96–98

RECLAIM (Reasoned and Equitable Community and Local Alternatives to Incarceration of Minors), 400

recognizance, release on (ROR), 44–45, 59–60, 62, 82–83

reconviction, recidivism as, 95–96, 99

reentry programs: for female offenders, 349, 351; for juvenile offenders, 389

referrals: to emergency shelters, 365; to halfway house, 247; mediation, 56*box*; to youth service bureaus, 369

"reform-through-isolation," 10–11

rehabilitation, 3–5, 13; boot camps and, 179, 182, 185, 186–87*boxes*; DRC orientation, 194–96; intermediate sanctions and, 163, 166–68; of juvenile offenders, 356, 357, 389, 398–99; parole and, 120, 125, 140; Progressives supporting, 84; restitution/community service and, 227, 229–30, 236–37; for substance abusers, 273, 287–88, 289, 292, 298, 303–6, 304–5*box*

reincarceration, recidivism as, 96

reintegration, 3–5, 9; alcohol abuse treatment and, 298; halfway houses and, 243, 253–54, 262; intermediate sanctions and, 163, 168; juvenile, 399, 400; after mental health hospitalization, 12, 315–16; postrelease community supervision for, 147; probation objective, 81; temporary release programs and, 151, 152, 155; of veterans, 12

relapse: mental health, 318; substance abuse, 351

Relative Adjustment Scale, 265–66

release: conditions of, 111–13, 166; discretionary, 20–21, 127–28, 131–33; graduated, 4, 155; to halfway house, 241*fig*; of juvenile offenders, 388–89; postconviction, 82; on recognizance (ROR), 44–45, 59–60, 62, 82–83; third-party, 41, 59; unconditional, 121–23, 128. *See also* mandatory release; parole; pretrial release; temporary release programs

release decision and process, in halfway house programming, 250

reprieve: judicial, 82, 83; in parole history, 125–26

research: alcoholics/problem drinkers, 296, 303; alcohol-related crime, 293; boot camp, 183–88; community-based corrections effectiveness, 14; day fines, 215, 216–20; debt collection, 224; deinstitutionalization, 397–98; DRC, 204–5; drug courts, 51–53; drug testing, 67–70; home confinement and EM, 194; ISP, 115, 168, 174–78; juvenile justice and delinquency, 365, 379, 390–95; pretrial release, 65–70; probation, 93–100; revenue generation through fees, 221, 222*table*; social psychological, 316; structured fines, 220; TASC, 47–49; therapeutic communities, 285–86; urine monitoring, 67–70; victimization, 229. *See also* RAND Corporation studies

residential community corrections, 242.
See also community residential centers;
residential programs
residential programs, 162, 205–6, 240–69;
for female offenders, 340, 347, 348, 349,
350–51; for juvenile offenders, 363,
385–88, 392–94; objectives, 205–6; program characteristics, 205–6. See also
community residential centers; halfway
houses; home confinement
resident participation, in halfway house
programming, 249–50
resource brokerage, 109–10, 112–13figs
restitution, 165, 210, 211, 225–37; amount
of, 231–32; benefits, 228–30, 235–36;
centers, 227, 234; contemporary applications, 226–27; contemporary support
for growth in, 228–29; correctional
objectives served by, 229–30; defined,
225; eligibility, 230–31; enforcement of,
232–33, 237; extent of use, 227; full,
231; history, 227–28; ISPs and, 166, 176;
by juvenile offenders, 379–81; nonpayment, 237; offenses appropriate for,
214table; partial, 236; probation agency
and, 81; process, 230–33; in stages of
criminal justice system, 226–27; symbolic,
226; universal appeal of, 228; victim
compensation and, 226, 227, 234; victim-
offender relations and, 229, 232, 236
restorative justice, 5–9, 6table, 7fig
restrictions, 2; ISP, 169; purpose of, 166.
See also control level; detention; rules;
sanctions
Resurpine, 315–16
retributive justice: economic sanctions
and, 210; increased acceptance of, 115;
restitution/community service and, 229;
vs. restorative justice, 6table
revenue generation, by economic sanctions,
210, 221, 222table
review of program participation and progress, in halfway house programming, 250
revocation: alternatives to, 3, 251; for juvenile offenders, 400; parole, 3, 23, 121,
140, 142–43table, 237; probation, 3,
112, 113–14, 237
"revolving door of justice," 130
rights: parolee and, 123, 125; women's,
333
risk: flight, 43. See also recidivism; risk
assessment
risk assessment: defined, 2; pretrial, 62;
risk and needs assessment, 33–34, 114,
116–17fig, 145, 174box
risk management, defined, 2
Robert F. Kennedy (RFK) Memorial,
National Juvenile Justice Project, 399
Robert Wood Johnson Foundation, 399
Rohypnol, 276–77boxes
role modeling, for female offenders, 350
rules, 2; prior permission, 394, 394fig
runaways, programs for, 365–66

safety, public. See community protection
St. Leonard, 244–45, 246
Salient Factor Score, 141, 144fig
Salvation Army, 246, 254
sanctions: continuum of, 2–3, 30–31, 202,
210; graduated, 53, 392, 397; for juvenile offenders, 363, 397; normative,
8–9; parole and, 123–24; probation as,
79, 80; progressive, 318; scaling of,
165–66; for technical violations, 67;
toughening, 114, 170–71, 334. See also
economic sanctions; incarceration;
intermediate sanctions
San Diego: Amity Righturn Program,
284box; Community Connection Resource Center, 349; County Home
Supervision Program, 374
San Francisco Project, 103–4, 167

savings: boot camp, 183, 184; DRC, 204;
EM, 190; external, 9; home confinement, 189; restitution program, 235.
See also cost reductions, correctional
Schall v. Martin, 356fig
School-Based Probation Services Program,
Allentown, Pennsylvania, 377–78
schools for juveniles: alternative, 376–77;
traditional, 377–78; training, 388. See
also education; training
Schweitzer, Louis, 44
Schwitzgebel, Ralph, 190
screening, for pretrial release eligibility,
60, 62
security: female residential programs, 347;
halfway house, 244, 256–58, 265. See
also community protection; control level
selection: community-based corrections,
2; EM and home confinement, 191–92;
female offender programs, 345–47; halfway house location/site, 253–54, 266;
halfway house resident, 253; ISP,
170–73boxes
selective incapacitation, 18–19; advantages
of, 29–31; defined, 15
self-esteem: female, 352. See also self-worth
self-worth: offenders' feelings of, 229; therapeutic communities and, 283; victims'
feelings of, 229. See also self-esteem
sentences: fixed, 388–89; maximum expiration of, 121–23; split, 123; suspending, 83
sentencing: changes affecting parole eligibility, 132–33; community court, 74–75;
continuum of, 202fig; determinate, 15,
115, 132box, 154–55; equity in, 168;
flexibility in, 130–31; guidelines, 27–29,
29fig, 102–4, 105table; 111, 132box,
176–78; impact statements, 27–29;
indeterminate, 121, 126, 131, 132box,
138; minimum, 15, 132box, 162, 163,
388–89; models, 130–31, 132box; to
probation, 79, 80, 81–82, 89, 99, 102–4;
in Reagan-Bush era, 14–15; sex offender, 319; standardized instruments
for, 104; structured, 27–29; toughening,
14–22; work-release, 148–49. See also
community service; mandatory sentencing; truth-in-sentencing law
Sentencing Reform Act (1984), 14–15, 17
service delivery: DRC, 194; probation,
109–10, 112–13figs
service integration, for mentally ill offenders, 317
services: co-location of, 194; DRC, 196–97,
197table, 204; for female offenders,
338–41, 347–51, 347table; halfway
house, 244, 249–50, 255–56, 257table,
264–65; postrelease, 139–40, 147, 183;
pretrial release basic, 60–64. See also
community service; community services; counseling; follow-up services;
medical care; mental health treatment;
service delivery; social services
sex offenders, 318–27: castration for,
122box; containment programs, 324–25,
327box; DRCs and, 198; on EM, 67,
192; extent of problem, 319; notifica-
tion/registration laws, 319–24, 326box;
system responses, 319–26; treatment
programs, 319, 322–23table
sex offenses, 319, 320–21box
sexual deviants, female offenders depicted
as, 332box
sexually violent predator (SVP) laws,
320–21box
shelters: for juveniles, 365, 369. See also
residential programs
shock incarceration/shock parole/shock
probation, 179, 186–87box. See also
boot camps
Shoplifters Alternatives (SA), 371

single-sex programs, vs. coed programs, 352
Sisters in Crime (Adler), 332box
skid row alcoholics, 295
Smith v. Daily Mail Publishing Co., 356fig
social drinkers, 293–95
social psychology, 316
social roles, female offenders and, 337,
338, 351–52
social services: for furlough inmates, 152;
in parole supervision, 124; in probation
supervision, 98, 108
South Carolina: boot camps, 184; restitution centers, 227, 234; study-release
programs, 151; SVP laws, 320box
Special Approaches for Juvenile Assistance
Inc. (SAJA), 365
specialized caseload, 111, 325
Specialized Gang Suppression Program
(SGSP), 383–84, 383fig
special problem offenders, 310–28. See
also mentally ill offenders; sex offenders
speedy processing, through justice system,
70–76
Spencer, Herbert, 227
spending, correctional: in Reagan-Bush
era, 15, 15table. See also costs; funding
split sentences, 123
stalkers, DRCs and, 198
Stanford v. Kentucky, 356fig
Staten Island Experiment, 216–19, 217table
state prison inmates: mentally ill, 311,
311table; rate of (1925–1997), 312fig
states: boot camp population, 182; boot
camp program characteristics, 183,
186–87box; budget cuts, 315; correctional costs, 15, 18, 19, 27–29, 163; and
deinstitutionalization, 397; diversion
programs, 43; EM programs, 190; federal funding requirements, 18; fees
charged by, 220–21, 222; ISPs, 115,
168, 170–74boxes, 174, 175–78, 190;
juvenile aftercare services, 388; juvenile
crime and justice struggles, 398; and
MAP, 143–44; mental hospitals, 315–16;
new court commitments (1990 and
1996), 22fig; parole abolished by, 131–32,
133box, 155; parole responsibilities,
146; paroling process modified by, 140;
prison population, 16fig, 17, 18table,
25fig; probation programs, 83–84, 85,
86table, 374; restitution programs, 228;
sentencing guidelines, 27–29, 29fig,
102–4, 105table; sex offender notifica-
tions, 319–24, 326box; sex offender
treatment programs, 319, 322–23table;
spending on corrections (1980–1988),
15table; truth-in-sentencing laws, 15,
17–22, 20–21box; victim compensation
programs, 234–35. See also state prison
inmates; individual states
status offenders, juvenile, 357, 358, 363, 396
statutory good time, 121
stigma, labeling offenders, 12–13, 162, 230
street life, drug addict and, 279
structured fines research, 220. See also
day fines
structured sentencing, 27–29
Student Assistance Program (SAP), 377–78
study release, 149, 150–51, 154; for female offenders, 338, 340; Mariana
Community Center, 259box
substance abuse: problems and needs,
273–309; research on urban delinquency
and, 390. See also alcohol consumption;
drug abusers; substance abuse treatment
substance abuse monitoring: DRC, 199;
pretrial release, 62
substance abuse treatment: boot camp,
187box. See also alcohol abuse treatment; drug treatment; substance abuse
monitoring
summary punishment, 183

supervised pretrial release (SPTR), 45, 59–60, 62, 64–65

supervision, 159–270; control and public safety issues, 161–209; female offender, 347, 349–50; juvenile aftercare, 388, 389; juvenile restitution work projects, 381; mental health specialized, 318; OJJDP plan for delinquents, 394–95; postrelease, 147, 183; of special populations, 271–402; styles, 107–9, 109table. *See also* aftercare; community supervision; electronic monitoring (EM); incarceration; parole supervision; probation supervision; supervised pretrial release (SPTR)

support groups, DRC, 199

supportive programs: drug treatment, 282, 291–92; halfway house, 246–47

surcharges, 211, 220–23

surety: pretrial release, 41; recognizance with and without, 82–83

surveillance: DRC, 194, 196; ISPs and, 166, 167, 176; in parole supervision, 124; in probation supervision, 107; purpose of, 166. *See also* electronic monitoring (EM)

survival skills: for female offenders, 340–41. *See also* life skills training

SVP (sexually violent predator) laws, 320–21box

symbolic restitution, 226. *See also* community service

systems analysis, 31–32; closed, 31; open, 31; probation, 80

target population, halfway house, 252–53

TASC. *See* Treatment Accountability for Safer Communities; Treatment Alternatives to Street Crime

teaching-family model, group home, 386

Team Players, 108

technical violations: EM for, 67, 193–94; ISPs and, 176, 178–79; parole, 140

Teen Court, Florida, 370–71, 372–73box

teen courts, 370–71, 372–73box

Temporary Asylum for Discharged Female Prisoners, Massachusetts, 245

temporary release programs, 148–56; absconding from, 154; evaluation purposes of, 153; for female offenders, 152, 338, 340; new directions, 154–56; objectives, 152–53; problems and issues of, 153–54; types of contemporary programs, 149–52; violations, 153–54. *See also* furloughs; study release; work release

temporary shelters, juvenile, 369

Tennessee, Men of Distinction (MOD), 367–68, 368box

Texas: boot camps, 184, 200–201box, 398; and castration of sex offender, 122box; early release laws, 133; fees, 221; halfway houses, 266; Harris County Community Supervision and Corrections Department (HCCSCD), 198–202; Harris County CRIPP facility, 200–201box; juvenile justice code, 398; offenders on probation, 87; wilderness program, 382; Wilkes case, 141

therapeutic communities: boot camps structured as, 187box; dependence on, 284–85; for drug abusers, 283–86, 292; evaluation of, 285–86

therapy: behavior modification, 99; confrontational, 283, 292; DRC, 199; family, 300; for juveniles, 387; probation service, 91–92. *See also* counseling; group therapy

third-party release, 41, 59

Thompson v. Oklahoma, 356*fig*

three-strikes laws, 17–19, 27, 129, 133; costs of, 22–23

ticket of leave, 125, 126

tolerance, drug, 277–78

tough-on-crime approach, 15–19, 41; California, 163; and female offenders, 334; in fine enforcement, 212–13; and juvenile offenders, 398; parole abolition and, 131, 133box. *See also* punishment

tracking, for juvenile delinquents, 394

traffic offenders, EM for, 191, 192

training: boot camp, 186box, 201box; halfway house personnel, 254–55; job readiness, 338, 339, 400; for juveniles, 379–81, 382, 388, 400; mental health specialized, 318; wilderness, 382. *See also* education; life skills training; vocational training

transportation: policy of, 125–26; for temporary release programs, 149–50, 152; traffic offenders, 191, 192

Treatment Accountability for Safer Communities (TASC), 286–87box

Treatment Alternatives to Street Crime (TASC), 43, 46–49; Break the Cycle (BTC), 53; drug treatment programs, 287; evolving focus, 47, 48fig; for female offenders, 350; research, 47–49

treatment modalities: alcohol abuse, 299–300; mental health, 318

treatment plans: halfway house, 255. *See also* services

trial courts, youth, 370

truth-in-sentencing law, 15, 17–22; Oklahoma struggling with, 20–21box

Twelve Inc. independent living program, Ohio, 388

Twelve Steps, AA, 301box

unconditional release, 121–23, 128

United States: Constitution, 42; DRC origins, 194–96; drug treatment programs, 282; early probation practices, 83–84; fines, 210, 212, 214table, 215; halfway house history, 245–46; halfway house numbers, 241; parole history, 125–26; restitution programs, 226, 227. *See also* federal funding; federal justice system; states; *individual federal agencies and administrations*

United States v. Killets, 83, 84

United States v. Salerno, 46

Urban Institute, 54

urine monitoring, 4, 288box; DRC, 199; in methadone maintenance programs, 283; research, 67–70

vagrants, 311

Vera Institute of Justice, 44–45; Community Service Sentencing Project (CSSP), 233; Staten Island Experiment, 216; Vera Foundation, 44

verification, pretrial release, 60, 62

veterans, adjustment to civilian life, 12

victim assistance: financial aid, 229, 235; restitution/community service for, 229, 381

victim compensation programs, 226, 227, 234–36. *See also* victim assistance

victim impact statement, 81

victimization: decreased rates of personal, 23; in female cycle of dependency, victimization, and crime, 338

Victim-Offender Mediation Programs (VOMPs), 58–59

victim-offender relations, restitution/community service and, 229, 232, 236

victim's rights movement, 5, 122box

violations: community service, 234; legal, 140; parole, 140, 142–43table; temporary release, 153–54. *See also* technical violations

violent crime: alcohol linked with, 293–95, 294table; collective incapacitation and, 162; decreased, 23; drugs linked with, 273–74, 293, 294table; and EM, 192; by females, 330, 333box, 334; four measures of, 24fig; by juveniles, 357, 390, 391fig, 392; by mentally ill, 313, 314table, 320–21box; sexual, 320–21box; toughening sentences for, 18–19; victim compensation programs, 235. *See also* domestic violence

Violent Crime Control and Law Enforcement Act (1994), 18–19, 49, 133

Virginia: juvenile crime legislation, 398; parole abolished, 132

vocational training: DRC, 199; for female offenders, 338, 339, 351. *See also* job readiness training

voluntary/advisory sentencing guidelines, 132box

voluntary mediation, 54–55

voluntary participation, offender: furlough, 152; halfway house, 248–49box, 251; restitution/community service, 229, 236

volunteers, community: in halfway house staffs, 254; in probation, 83–84. *See also* community service

Volunteers of America, 246

Wales, DRCs, 196

war on drugs, 15–17, 280–81box, 334

warrants, for community service, 234

Washington, D.C. *See* District of Columbia

Washington State: offenders on probation, 87; parole abolished in, 132; SVP laws, 320box

West Germany, fines, 211

White House Special Action Office for Drug Abuse Prevention, 43

whites: incarceration rates, 46; probationers, 89

wilderness experience programs, for juveniles, 382

Wilkes, John, 141

Wisconsin: ARC Community Services Treatment Alternative Program, 348, 350; ISPs, 176, 177box; MAP evaluations, 145; parole case management and classification system, 145; SVP laws, 320box. *See also* Milwaukee

Wisconsin Risk Assessment Scale, 145

withdrawal, drug, 278, 280, 289

women. *See* female offenders

Women A.R.I.S.E., 350

work: boot camp, 186box; parolee, 243; prison, 126, 243; restitution/community service skills for, 230. *See also* employment; work release

workload deployment and budget procedure, parole, 145

work release, 148–50, 151, 154, 156; for female offenders, 338, 340; pretrial, 59–60

work-release centers: for parolees, 141; Tallahassee, 258box

Young Men's Christian Associations (YMCAs), 254, 387

Young Women's Christian Associations (YWCAs), 387

youth courts, 369–71, 372–73box

Youth Education Shoplifting, 371

Youth Homes Inc., Charlotte, North Carolina, 387

youth service bureaus (YSBs), 369, 370fig